CRIMINAL INVESTIGATION

FOURTH EDITION

CRIMINAL INVESTIGATION

Charles R. Swanson
University of Georgia, Athens

Neil C. Chamelin
Florida Division of Motor Vehicles

Leonard Territo
University of South Florida, Tampa

Random House   New York

Fourth Edition

98765

Copyright © 1988 by Newbery Award Records, Inc.

Library of Congress Cataloging-in-Publication Data

Swanson, Charles R., 1942–
  Criminal investigation.

  Includes bibliographies and index.
  1. Criminal investigation. 2. Criminal investigation—
United States. I. Chamelin, Neil C., 1942–
II. Territo, Leonard. III. Title.
HV8073.S84 1988   363.2'5   87–4827
ISBN 0–394–36321–3

Manufactured in the United States of America

Designed by Dorothy Bungert

PREFACE

When the preface to the first edition was written we were concerned about how the book would be received because it broke with traditional investigation texts in a number of ways. It was unclear, if not unsettling, to contemplate what would happen. What did happen is that the book was accepted. While it is tempting to conclude that we "built a better mousetrap," it is clear that people had to be openminded enough to try something a little different. We are keenly appreciative of their reaction and have tried to keep the best features of prior editions while again trying to improve, to forge ahead with this edition.

This book continues to differ from traditional investigation texts; it is important to understand these differences as they are again reflected throughout this edition. The distinction made in the first edition between this and other investigative texts remains; first, investigation generally has been conceived of, and touted as, an art. This approach depreciates the precision required to conduct inquiries; it denies the existence of, and adherence to, rigorous methods; and it associates investigation with unneeded mysticism. Investigation is in large part a science. The fact that criminals are not always apprehended does not make it less so. The rational scientific method will, of necessity, be supplemented by initiative and occasional fortuitous circumstances, but it is the application of the method rather than shrewd hunches which most frequently produce results. This book unfolds along the same logical continuum as does an investigation. A

second major difference is our judgment that writing about techniques takes on more substance if one understands something of the nature of the event being investigated. Thus, we have discussed typologies—including offenses, offenders, and victims. The treatment of these has not been equal in the crime specific chapters because of the literature available. Collateral approaches have been the extensive use of illustrations, primary citations, and the judicious use of case studies. Third, the advent of a crime prevention technology has been a significant milestone for both the police and the public, and so the insertion of short sections on prevention in the crime specific chapters. The complexity of crime prevention dictates it as a specialization within police departments. Yet, at the scene of a crime the investigator may be in a unique position to make a few helpful, if only rudimentary, suggestions to a victim on how to avoid further loss. Finally, most investigative books in the past have blurred the distinction between the roles of the uniformed officer and the detective. While everyone may not agree with our dichotomizing, it is essential that the importance of the uniformed officer's role be properly recognized for the contribution it makes to the ultimate success of an investigation.

While the basic plan of the book remains unchanged, there is much that is new. Based on the recommendation of those who use the book, we have added a chapter on the evolution of criminal investigation and criminalistics. There are many new photographs and case histories, as well as new material on such topics as designer drugs, rock cocaine, super glue fuming, the importance of listening during interviews, conducting line ups, genetic markers, bite mark evidence, serial murders, suicide insurance schemes, headlight examination in hit-and-run accidents, the National Center of the Analysis of Violent Crime, the Violent Criminal Apprehension Program, high technology responses to automobile theft, wildlife crimes and determination of death by means of carrion insects. Other changes include updated tables, citations, and figures, along with the deletion or expansion of certain material due to changes in its investigative significance.

It is our intention that the changes made in this edition reflect the dynamic nature of criminal investigation. Many investigative techniques are fundamental and basically unchanging over time. However, new concepts, scientific advancements, and social priorities simultaneously create new thrusts in criminal investigation. The field of criminal investigation, thus, is always in the process of evolving.

Charles R. Swanson
Neil C. Chamelin
Leonard Territo

ACKNOWLEDGMENTS

We again recognize our dependence on others, the willingness with which they gave their suggestions, and our thankfulness for their friendship and contributions. Our acknowledgments include many of those recognized in earlier editions as well as some new individuals and organizations. Some of the people identified have retired or taken on new responsibilities since making their contributions. Unless otherwise requested, we show their organizational affiliation as of the time of their original contributions, feeling that the agencies then employing them are also deserving of some continuing recognition. To all persons mentioned we owe our deepest appreciation.

Photographs in the book are credited as requested by the agency that contributed them. Some individuals and agencies supplied numerous or unique photographs and illustrations. In this regard, we note that photographs were supplied by R. Keppel, New Scotland Yard, London, England; Jim Besonen, Michigan State Police; John Stewart, Austin, Texas, Police Department; Jim Arena, New Jersey State Police; Robert Edmons, Los Angeles Country Sheriff's Office; W. W. Pope, Atlanta Police Department; Ruben Ortega, Tim Black and Ken Johnson, Phoenix, Arizona, Police Department; George O'Neil, Pinkerton, New York; James Todd and David Easthon, Geauga County, Ohio, Sheriff's Department; Fred Taylor, Metro-Dade Police Department, Miami, Florida; Mike Cox, Texas Department of Public Safety; Dick Hand, DeKalb County, Georgia, Department of Public Safety; Raymond Davis, Santa Ana, California, Police Department; John Donaldson and Robert Lane, Oregon Department of Public Safety; Robert Dempsey and Dale Heidman, Florida Department of Law Enforcement; Tom Evans, Pinellas County, Florida, Sheriff's Office; Tom Carbone, Maine Department of Inland Fisheries and Wildlife; Barbara Carlsen, Wyoming Game and Fish Department; Barry Glover and Sandy Stevens, Clearwater, Florida, Police Department; Craig Carnevale, Gemprint, Ltd., Chicago, Illinois; Steve Munday, Texas and Southwestern Cattle Raisers Association, Fort Worth, Texas; Johnny Perkins, Nelson Horne, Mario Alberti, Frank Jensen, and Charles Otero, retired, Tampa Police Department; William Barker and Jay Cochran, FBI; Antonia Cutillas, Argentine Embassy, Washington, D.C.; Joe Terlizzese and Henry Marchman, Palm Beach, Florida, Police Department; Joseph McNamara and Lester Harris, Kansas City Police Department; Truett Ricks, formerly with the Kentucky State Police; Dick Mellard, retired, Wichita Police Department; and Frank Flanagan, Marsh Considine and Art Paholke, presently or formerly with the Chicago Police Department. Art and Marsh also made themselves available to answer questions and added immeasurably to the book with their patience and thoroughness. All uncredited photographs in the book appear by courtesy of the Chicago Police Department. Over the years Thomas Deakin, editor, *F.B.I. Law Enforce-*

ment Bulletin, has graciously provided photographs and other types of assistance that have been invaluable.

Richard Souviron, Dade County Medical Examiner's Office, was the principal author of the material dealing with bite marks and dental evidence. In addition, he also provided us with most of the photographs for that section. Dr. Wally Graves, Medical Examiner for Lee, Henry and Glade Counties, Florida, and John Valor, forensic artist and photographer gave information on forensic odontology and associated photographs and illustrations. Former Sheriff Ken Katsaris, Leon County, Florida, was helpful with the coverage of death investigation. Dr. William C. Rodriguez, Forensic Anthropologist and Director of Laboratories, Caddo Parrish Coroner's Office, Shreveport, Louisiana, and William M. Bass allowed us to use portions of their research findings in our discussion of the determination of death by means of carrion insects.

Tom Costigan, Mike Rendina, Jim Wilder and Richard Frank, presently or formerly of the Drug Enforcement Administration, provided photographs and authorization to reproduce printed material. Tom Matthews, Temple Terrace, Florida, Police Department, reviewed the narcotics chapter, as did Mike Sciales, formerly of the Hillsborough County, Florida, Sheriff's Office; Mike Rendina also contributed the sections dealing with freebasing and speedballing. Robert J. Roberton, Chief, Department of Alcohol and Drug Programs, Division of Drug Programs, California, provided us with most of the material on designer drugs.

Lt. Gill Kerlikowske, St. Petersburg, Florida, Police Department, provided information on lineup identification. Charles Steinmetz and Roger F. Depue, Federal Bureau of Investigation, provided us with material dealing with the National Center for the Analysis of Violent Crime (NCAVC) and the Violent Criminal Apprehension Program (VI-CAP)

and John E. Eck, Police Executive Research Forum, Washington, D.C., allowed us to draw freely from his *The Investigation of Burglary and Robbery.*

Dr. William Mooney and Frank Sass, formerly with the Federal Bureau of Investigation's Academy, provided information on sex offenses, and the latter authorized the use of portions of two of his articles. Mickey Kelley Tagliarini assisted in researching materials on sex offenses and was helpful in identifying trends in that area. Robert R. Hazelwood, Behavioral Science Unit, FBI Academy, Quantico, Virginia, allowed us to draw extensively on his findings on auto-erotic death and the behavior-oriented interviews of rape victims.

Wayne Hopkins of the United States Chamber of Commerce permitted the use of certain materials in the chapter on larceny. James Dunn and John Reynolds of the Federal Bureau of Investigation granted permission to reproduce materials from their agency. Bob Smith, Director of Public Safety, Tampa, a colleague of long standing, unstintingly made a variety of information available. Dick Arther, National Training Center of Lie Detection, sent material on the polygraph and made criticisms that were helpful in improving that section. Steve Mraz, formerly with the Pinellas County, Florida, Fire Academy, contributed to and reviewed the arson chapter; Bruce Bogart, American Insurance Association, provided photographs and materials also used in that chapter. Sergeant Bill Bacon, of the Los Angeles County Sheriff's Office, supplied some figures and content in Chapter 15.

We also wish to thank our long-time friend and colleague, Dr. Harold Vetter, Department of Criminology, University of South Florida, and Guy Andrichuk for their writing and research contributions in Chapter 7, "Latent Investigation," and Chapter 21, "Behavioral Science in Criminal Investigation."

Jim Halligan, formerly with the Florida

Department of Law Enforcement and Zug Standing Bear, Valdosta State College, reviewed portions of the third edition as a personal favor and suggested changes that have found their way into this edition.

Marilyn Bruce, Mike Copeland, Maggie Deutsch, Gregg Gronlund, Lynn Humphrey, Robin Kester, Chris Pfleger, Marian Pittman, Cecile Pulin, and Linda Steed typed various portions of the manuscript expertly and with good cheer despite our last minute changes and the pressures of deadlines.

Finally, Bert Lummus, our editor at Random House has been a constant source of support. Beena Kamlani, our text editor at Random House, has invested a considerable amount of personal attention and effort in the book and handled it skillfully and sensitively.

C. R. S.
N. C. C.
L. T.

CONTENTS

4 / PHYSICAL EVIDENCE   56

5 / INTERVIEWS   123

6 / FIELD NOTES AND REPORTING   141

7 / LATENT INVESTIGATION   156

8 / INTERROGATION   197

11 / SEX-RELATED OFFENSES   306

12 / ROBBERY   342

13 / BURGLARY INVESTIGATION   364

14 / LARCENY OFFENSES   407

15 / AGRICULTURE AND WILDLIFE CRIMES   456

18 / THE DECISION TO INITIATE THE CRIMINAL PROCESS   563

19 / THE RULES OF EVIDENCE   573

20 / THE INVESTIGATOR AS A WITNESS   588

21 / BEHAVIORAL SCIENCE IN CRIMINAL INVESTIGATION   599

INDEX   613

1

THE EVOLUTION OF CRIMINAL INVESTIGATION AND CRIMINALISTICS

INTRODUCTION

The writing of two separate but entwined fields—criminal investigation and criminalistics—is a difficult task. Many volumes have been written on each of these two fields, but the space which can be devoted to them here is limited. However, sufficient broad perspectives and supporting details are provided in this chapter to allow those intrigued by these subjects to independently pursue their interest with a basic working knowledge.

THE EVOLUTION OF CRIMINAL INVESTIGATION

Criminal investigation has evolved within certain social, economic, political, and legal contexts. For present purposes, the evolution of criminal investigation begins in eighteenth century England, as massive changes were being unleashed. To fully appreciate the development of criminal investigation, it is important to understand the social, economic,

political, and legal contexts in which it evolved. Thus, the balance of this section provides this content under the major headings of: 1) the impact of the agricultural and industrial revolutions, 2) the Fieldings: Crime Information and the Bow Street Runners, 3) the Metropolitan Police Act of 1829, and 4) American initiatives.

THE IMPACT OF THE AGRICULTURAL AND INDUSTRIAL REVOLUTIONS

During the eighteenth century two series of events—an agricultural and an industrial revolution—began a process of change that profoundly affected how police services were delivered and investigations conducted. Improved agricultural methods, such as the introduction in 1730 of Charles Townshend's crop rotation system and Jethro Tull's four-bladed plow, gave England increased agricultural productivity in the first half of the eighteenth century.[1] Improvements in agriculture were essential preconditions to the Industrial Revolution, in the second half of the eighteenth century, because they freed people from farm work for city jobs. As the population of England's cities grew, slums also grew, crime increased, and disorders became more frequent. Consequently, public demands for government to control crime grew louder.

THE FIELDINGS: CRIME INFORMATION AND THE ══ BOW STREET RUNNERS ══

In 1748, Henry Fielding became chief magistrate of Bow Street and set out to improve the administration of justice. In 1750, he established a small group of volunteer, nonuniformed homeowners to "take thieves." Known as the "Bow Street Runners," these London homeowners hurried to the scenes of reported crimes and began investigations, thus becoming the first modern detective force. By 1752, Fielding began publishing *The Covent Garden Journal* as a means of circulating the descriptions of wanted persons. Upon his death in 1754, Henry Fielding was succeeded by his blind half-brother, John Fielding, who carried on his brother's ideas for another 25 years.[2] Under John Fielding, Bow Street became a clearinghouse for information on crime, and by 1785 at least four of the Bow Street Runners were no longer volunteers, but paid government detectives.[3]

THE METROPOLITAN POLICE ══ ACT OF 1829 ══

In 1816, 1818, and again in 1822, England's Parliament rejected proposals for a centralized professional police force for London. Strong opposing political philosophies were at odds. One group argued that such a force was a direct threat to personal liberty. The other group—composed of reformers such as Jeremy Bentham and Patrick Colquhoun—argued that the absence, rather than the presence, of social control was the greater danger to personal liberty. Finally, in 1829, due in large measure to the efforts of Sir Robert Peel, Parliament created a metropolitan police force for London. Police headquarters became known as Scotland Yard, because the building formerly had housed Scottish royalty. Police constables were referred to as "Bobbies," a play on Peel's first name, Robert. Peel selected Charles Rowan and Richard Mayne as police commissioners, responsible for the development of this new force, and important new principles governing police work were stated:

1. The police must be stable, efficient, and organized along military lines.
2. The police must be under government control.
3. The absence of crime best proves the efficiency of police.
4. The distribution of crime news is essential.
5. The development of police strength both over time and by area is essential.
6. No quality is more indispensable to a police officer than a perfect command of temper; a quiet, determined manner has more effect than violent action.
7. Good appearance commands respect.
8. The securing and training of the proper people is at the root of efficiency.
9. Public security demands that every police officer be given a number.
10. Police headquarters should be centrally located and easily accessible to the people.
11. Police should be hired on a probationary basis.
12. Police records are necessary to the correct distribution of police strength.[4]

FIGURE 1-1   **New Scotland Yard**

In 1890, the Metropolitan police left their original quarters and were housed in New Scotland Yard, which is pictured above circa 1895. Subsequently in 1967, the Metropolitan Police moved again to their present facilities, which are also referred to as New Scotland Yard.

Courtesy of the London Metropolitan Police

Because French citizens had experienced oppression under centralized police, the British public was suspicious and at times even hostile to the new force. In response to the high standards set for the police force, during the first three years of operations, there were 5,000 dismissals and 6,000 forced resignations from the force.[5] This record was a clear indication to the public that police administrators were requiring officers to maintain high standards of conduct. Within a few years, the London Metropolitan Police had won a reputation for fairness, and it became the international model of professional policing. Despite the growing popularity of the uniformed bobbies, there was fear that the use of "police spies"—detectives in plain clothes—would reduce civil liberties.

In the years immediately following 1829, some Metropolitan Police Constables were temporarily relieved from patrolling in uniform to investigate crimes on their beats.[6] However, as the distinction between the use of uniformed constables to prevent crime and the use of plainclothes detectives for investigation and surveillance became clear, the public became uneasy. Illustratively, in 1833, a Sergeant Popay was dismissed following a Parliamentary investigation which revealed that he had infiltrated a radical group, acquired a leadership position, and argued for the use of violence. Until 1842, Metropolitan Constables assigned to investigate crimes competed with the Bow Street Runners; in that year, a regular detective branch was opened at Scotland Yard, superseding the Bow Street forces.[7] Under Commissioner Mayne, the detective force was limited to no more than 16 investigators, and its operations were restricted because of his distrust of "clandestine methods."[8]

Following a scandal in which three of four Chief Inspectors of detectives were convicted of taking bribes,[9] a separate, centralized Criminal Investigation Department (CID) was established in 1878 at Scotland Yard. It was headed by an attorney, Howard Vincent.[10] Uniformed constables who had shown an aptitude for investigation were recruited to become CID detectives.[11] Interestingly, at least since Vincent's time, the use of strong central control has been a recurrent theme in the reform of police organizations to correct for abuses.

AMERICAN INITIATIVES

The success of Peel's reform in England did not go unnoticed in this country. Stephen Girard bequeathed $33,190 to Philadelphia to develop a competent police force. In 1833, Philadelphia passed an ordinance creating America's first paid, daylight policing. Although repealed just three years later, this concept of a paid police force would reappear as American cities staggered under the burdens of tremendous population growth, poverty, and massive crime. In 1836, New York City rejected the notion of a police force organized along the lines of those advocated by Peel. The committee studying the idea concluded that:

> Though it might be necessary, at some future period, to adopt a system of police

similar to that of London . . . the nature of our institution is such that more reliance may be placed upon the people for aid, in case of any emergency, than in despotic governments[12]

Thus before mid-century, few American cities had police service, and what existed was inadequate. Many cities had only paid police service at night or treated day and night police services as entirely separate organizations. Finally, in 1844, the New York state legislature created the first unified police force in this country, although New York City did not actually implement the measure until a year later. Other cities rapidly followed New York's lead: Chicago in 1851, New Orleans and Cincinnati in 1852, and Baltimore and Newark in 1857. By 1880, virtually every major American city had a police force based on England's Peelian reforms of 1829 and pioneered in this country by New York City.

If one of the problems of the Metropolitan London Police had been getting the public to accept some constables working out of uniform as detectives, in this country the problem was getting the police to wear uniforms in the first place. American officers felt that a uniform made them easy targets for public harassment and made them look like servants. Only after the Civil War did the wearing of a uniform—invariably blue—become widely accepted by American police officers.

PINKERTON'S NATIONAL DETECTIVE AGENCY

American cities needed reliable detectives for several reasons. First, graft and corruption were common among America's big city police officers. Second, police jurisdiction was limited. Third, there was little communication of information among departments in different cities. Thus, offenders often fled from one jurisdiction to another with impunity.

FIGURE 1-2

Allan Pinkerton, President Lincoln, and General McClellan at Antietam, Maryland, about October 3, 1862.

Courtesy of Pinkerton's Archives

In 1846, seeing the need for reliable investigators, two former St. Louis police officers formed the first recorded private detective agency.[13] But the major private detective agency of the nineteenth century was formed by Allan Pinkerton (1819–1884). In 1849, Chicago's Mayor Boone appointed Pinkerton as Chicago's first detective. Pinkerton enjoyed great success, but he resigned due to political interference and took a job as a Special United States Mail Agent to solve a series of post office thefts and robberies in the Chicago area.[14] In 1850, after succeeding in this job, Pinkerton, by then a well known public figure, formed a private detective agency with a Chicago attorney, Edward Rucker.[15] Pinkerton's trademark was an open eye above the slogan, "We never sleep."[16] The trademark gave rise to the term "private eye" to designate any private investigator.[17] The Pinkertons enjoyed such enormous importance in this country and throughout the world that some people thought "Pinkerton" was a nickname for any American government detective.[18]

The list of achievements by Pinkerton and his operatives is impressive. Pinkerton reportedly discovered and foiled an assassination attempt on President elect Lincoln in Baltimore as Lincoln traveled to his inauguration in Washington, D.C.[19] At the outbreak of the Civil War in 1861, Pinkerton organized a Secret Service Division within the army (not to be confused with the U.S. Secret Service, which was organized after that war) and worked closely with Union General George McClellan until 1862, when McClellan was dismissed.[20] Although Pinkerton infiltrated Confederate lines in disguise on several occasions, he usually functioned as a military analyst.[21]

Following the Civil War, the Pinkertons were primarily engaged in two broad areas: 1) controlling a discontented working class, which was pushing for better wages and working conditions and 2) pursuing bank and railroad robbers.[22] Unrestricted by jurisdictional limits, Pinkerton agents roamed far and wide pursuing law breakers. In a violent time, they sometimes used harsh and unwise methods. For instance, suspecting that they had found the hideout of Jesse James's gang, Pinkerton agents lobbed in a 32-pound bomb, killing a boy and injuring a mother.[23]

Pinkerton understood the importance of information, records, and publicity and made good use of all of them. For example, in 1868, Pinkerton agent Dick Winscott was assigned responsibility for smashing a group of bandits known as the Reno gang. Taking a camera with him, Winscott located Fred and John Reno, and after a drinking bout persuaded them to let him photograph them.[24] He sent these photographs to Pinkerton files, and within a year the Reno gang was smashed.[25] Pinkerton also collected photographs of jewel thieves and other types of criminals and photographed horses to prevent illegal substitutions before races.[26] The Pinkertons also pushed Butch Cassidy (Robert Parker) and the Sun Dance Kid (Harry Longabaugh) into leaving America for South America, where they were reportedly killed by Bolivian soldiers at San Vincente in 1909.

The Pinkertons investigated other major types of crimes as well. They caught two safecrackers who stole $1,250,000 from a Massachusetts bank and a state treasurer of South Dakota who had embezzled $300,000.[27] Because of their better known anti-labor activities, the Pinkertons' other work often is overlooked. But they were the only consistently competent detectives available in this country for over 50 years[28] and provided a good model for government detectives.

THE EMERGENCE
OF MUNICIPAL DETECTIVES

As early as 1845, New York City had 800 plainclothes officers,[29] although not until 1857 were the police authorized to designate

FIGURE 1-3

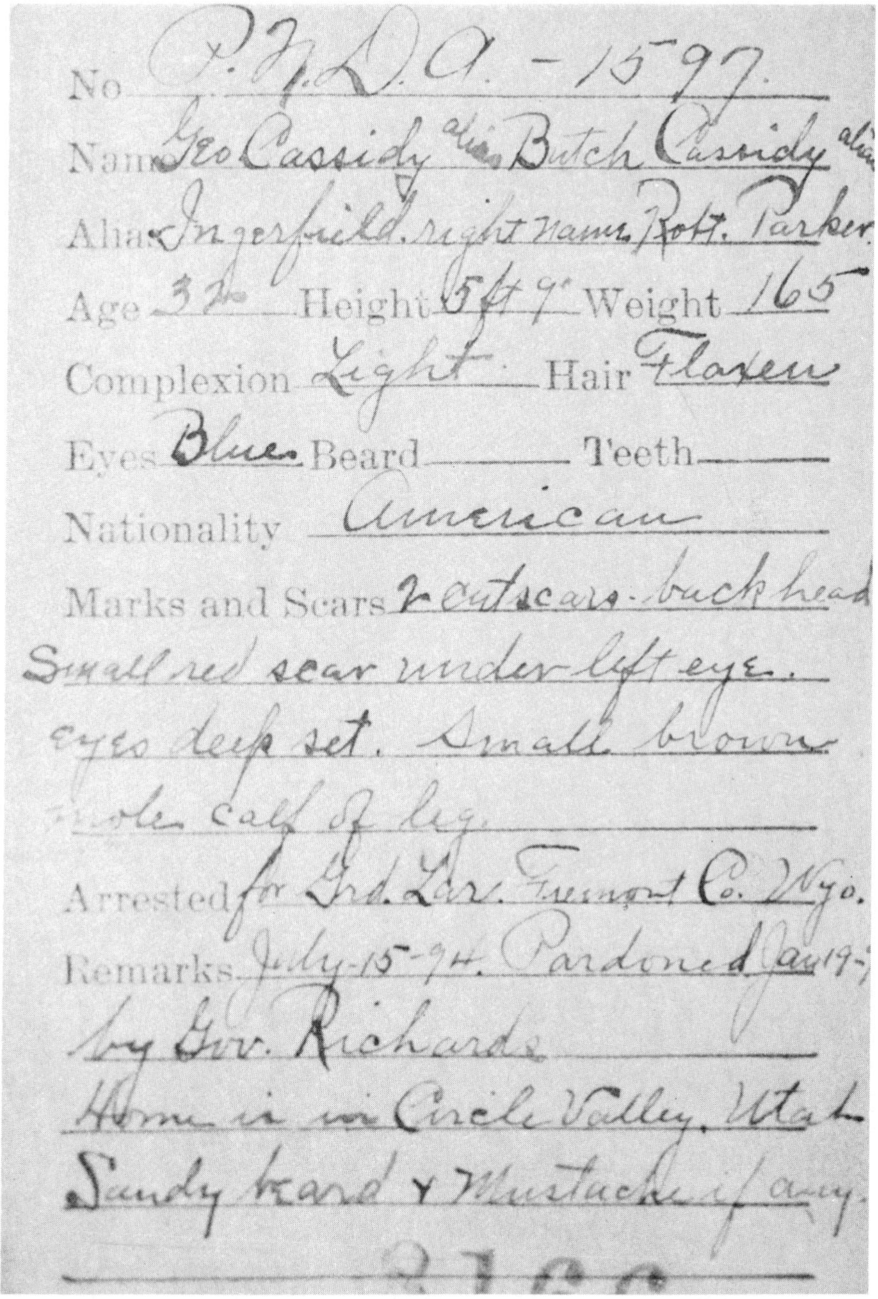
No. P.N.D.A. - 1597.
Name Geo Cassidy alias Butch Cassidy alias
Alias Ingerfield, right name Robt. Parker
Age 32 Height 5 ft 9" Weight 165
Complexion Light Hair Flaxen
Eyes Blue Beard ___ Teeth ___
Nationality American
Marks and Scars 2 cut scars back head
Small red scar under left eye.
eyes deep set. Small brown
mole calf of leg.
Arrested for Grd. Lar. Fremont Co. Wyo.
Remarks July-15-94. Pardoned Jan 19-
by Gov. Richards
Home is in Circle Valley, Utah
Sandy beard & Mustache if any.

Butch Cassidy's Pinkerton record; note the "P.N.D.A." initials on the first line, which stand for Pinkerton National Detective Agency.

Courtesy of Wyoming State Archives and Historical Department

FIGURE 1-4

Uniformed officers of the New York City Police Department maintaining a rogues' gallery in the detective bureau, circa 1896.

Courtesy of the Library of Congress

20 patrol officers as detectives.[30] In November 1857, the New York City Police Department set up a rogues' gallery—photographs of known offenders arranged by criminal specialty and height—and by June 1858, it had over 700 photographs for detectives to study so that they might recognize criminals on the street.[31] Photographs from rogues' galleries of that era reveal that some offenders grimaced, puffed their cheeks, rolled their eyes, and otherwise tried to distort their appearance to lessen the chance of later recognition.

To assist detectives, in 1884 Chicago established this country's first municipal Criminal Identification Bureau.[32] The Atlanta Police Department's Detective Bureau was organized in 1885 with a staff of one Captain, one Sergeant, and 8 detectives.[33] In 1886, Thomas Byrnes, the dynamic chief detective of New York City, published *Professional Criminals in America,* which included pictures, descriptions, and the methods of all criminals known to him.[34] Byrnes thereby contributed to information sharing among police departments. To supplement the rogues' gallery, Byrnes instituted the "Mulberry Street Morning Parade." At 9 every morning, all criminals arrested in the past 24 hours were marched before his detectives, who were expected to make notes and to recognize the criminals later.[35] Despite such innovations Byrnes was tragically flawed; in 1894 he was forced to leave the department when

he admitted having grown wealthy by having tolerated gambling dens and brothels.[36] In spite of such setbacks, by the turn of the century many municipal police departments used detectives.

STATE AND FEDERAL DEVELOPMENTS

From its earliest days, the federal government employed investigators to detect revenue violations, but their responsibilities were narrow and their numbers few.[37] In 1865, Congress created the U.S. Secret Service to combat counterfeiting. In 1903—two years after President McKinley was assassinated by Leon Czolgosz in Buffalo—the previously informal arrangement of guarding the President was made a permanent Secret Service responsibility.[38]

In 1905, the California Bureau of Crimi-

FIGURE 1-5

Troop D, Pennsylvania State Police, Punxsutawney, Pennsylvania, 1906. Note that both plainclothes and uniformed personnel are represented.

Courtesy of the Pennsylvania State Police

nal Identification was set up to share information about criminal activity, and Pennsylvania Governor Samuel Pennypacker signed legislation creating a state police force. Widely regarded then by labor as "strikebusters on management's side," the Pennsylvania State Police nevertheless were the prototype for modern state police organizations. New York and Michigan in 1917 and Delaware in 1919 adopted the state police concept. One function that state police forces since have

assumed is to provide local police with help in investigations.

After Prohibition was adopted nationally in 1920, the Bureau of Internal Revenue was responsible for its enforcement. Eventually the ranks of prohibition agents swelled to a massive 4,000.[39] Because the Bureau of Internal Revenue was lodged in the Department of Treasury, these federal agents were referred to as "T-men."

In 1908, U.S. Attorney General Charles

FIGURE 1-6

J. Edgar Hoover (foreground wearing a dark suit and light colored hat) with Alvin "Old Creepy" Karpis (in handcuffs) in New Orleans on May 1, 1936. Nicknamed "Old Creepy" because of his cold stare and his precision in carrying out crimes, Karpis was personally arrested by Director Hoover. Karpis was a key member of Ma Barker's gang, which included her four sons, and he participated in a number of bank robberies and kidnappings. By the late 1930s, all the members of the notorious Barker-Karpis gang had been killed in gunbattles or imprisoned, marking the end of the "gangster era."

Courtesy of the Federal Bureau of Investigation

Bonaparte created the embryo of what was later to become the Federal Bureau of Investigation (FBI) when he ordered that investigations were to be handled by a special group. In 1924, J. Edgar Hoover (1895–1972) assumed leadership of the Bureau of Investigation; eleven years later Congress passed a measure giving the FBI its present designation. When Prohibition was repealed by the Eighteenth Amendment to the U.S. Constitution in 1933, many former bootleggers and other criminals turned to bank robbery and kidnapping.[40] During the Depression, some people saw John Dillinger, "Pretty Boy" Floyd, Bonnie and Clyde, and Ma Barker and her boys as "plain folks" and did not grieve over a bank robbery or the "snatching" of a millionaire.[41] Given the restricted roles of other federal investigative agencies, it became the FBI's role to deal with these criminals.

Under Hoover, who understood the importance and uses of information, records, and publicity as well as Allan Pinkerton had, the FBI became known for investigative efficiency.

In 1932, the FBI established a crime laboratory and made its services available free to state and local police. In 1935, it opened the National Academy, a training course for state and local police. In 1967, the National Crime Information Center (NCIC) was made operational by the FBI, providing data on wanted persons and property stolen from all 50 states. Altogether, these developments gave the FBI considerable influence over law enforcement throughout the country. Although some people argue that such federal influence is undesirable, others point out that Hoover and the FBI improved police practices in this country, from keeping crime statistics to improving investigation.

The Hague Conference in 1914 called for international action against illicit drugs. Subsequently, Congress passed the Harrison Act, making the distribution of nonmedical drugs a federal crime. Enforcement responsibility was initially given to the Internal Revenue Service, although by 1930 a separate Narcotics Bureau was established in the Treasury Department. In 1949, a federal commission noted that federal narcotics enforcement was fragmented among several agencies, resulting in duplication of effort and other ills. In 1968, some consolidation of effort was achieved with the creation of the Bureau of Narcotics and Dangerous Drugs in the Department of Justice, and in 1973, with the creation of its successor, the Drug Enforcement Administration (DEA). Today the DEA devotes many of its resources to fighting international drug traffic. Like the FBI, DEA trains state and local police in investigative work. The training focuses on recognition of illegal drugs, control of drug purchases, surveillance methods, and handling informants.

THE POLICE AND THE SUPREME COURT: THE DUE PROCESS REVOLUTION

From 1961 to 1966—a period frequently referred to as the "due process revolution"— the United States Supreme Court took an activist role, becoming quite literally givers of the law rather than interpreters of it.[42] Under Chief Justice Earl Warren (1891–1974), the Court used the due process clause of the Fourteenth Amendment to extend the provisions of the Bill of Rights to criminal proceedings in the various states.[43]

The Supreme Court could scarcely have picked a worse time to police the police. A burgeoning crime rate far outstripped population increases. Many politicians campaigned on "law and order" platforms. The problem of crime increasingly came to public notice through the mass media. In effect, the court extended procedural safeguards to defendants in criminal cases just when public fear of crime and social pressure to combat crime were intense. The reaction of the country was swift; "Impeach Warren" billboards dotted the landscape.

Why did the Supreme Court undertake its activist role? What decisions so aroused public ire? How did the decisions affect police work, and how did police react? Fundamentally the Supreme Court's role in the due process revolution was a response to a vacuum created when the police themselves failed to provide necessary leadership. The era of strong social activism by special-interest groups was not yet at hand, and neither state courts nor legislatures had displayed any broad interest in reforming the criminal law. What institution was better positioned to undertake this responsibility? The Court may even have felt obligated by the inaction of others. The high court did not move into this arena until after it had issued warnings which, to responsive and responsible leaders, would have been a mandate for reform. It thus became the Warren Court's lot to provide the reforms so genuinely needed but so unpopularly received.

Among the key decisions in the due process revolution were *Mapp*. v. *Ohio* (1961), *Gideon* v. *Wainwright* (1963), *Escobedo* v. *Illinois* (1964), and *Miranda* v. *Arizona* (1966). For present purposes, the facts of these and related cases are less important than their focus and effect. Their focus was upon the two vital areas of search and seizure and the right to counsel; their effect was to markedly extend the rights of defendants. Their effect on police work was staggering: they greatly reduced the use of questionable and improper tactics, thereby creating the need for new procedures in interrogations, line-ups, and seizure of physical evidence. In general police reacted to this whirlwind of due process with wariness tinged with outcries that they were being "handcuffed" and could not adequately perform their jobs. Many people felt that the decisions went beyond seeking a fair trial in quest of a perfect one.

By the early 1970s, many police executives had recognized that, although these Supreme Court decisions had placed new demands on policing, the decisions also had subtly hastened the development of professional policing, because the police had been forced to abandon improper tactics and to engage in virtually continuous, sophisticated training in order to conduct interrogations and searches legal under Supreme Court guidelines. Another important side-effect of the due process revolution was to reinforce the importance of the police gathering and using physical evidence and obtaining criminalistical analysis of such evidence.

HISTORICAL MILESTONES OF CRIMINALISTICS

The origins of criminalistics are largely European. Criminalistics draws from diverse disciplines, such as geology, physics, chemistry, biology, and mathematics, to study physical evidence related to crime. The first major book describing the application of scientific disciplines to criminal investigation was written in 1893 by Hans Gross, a public prosecutor and later a judge from Graz, Austria.[44] Translated into English in 1906 under the title of *Criminal Investigation,* it remains highly respected today as the seminal work in the field.

Criminalistics, like other scientific disciplines, enjoys periods of stability, but on the whole it is dynamic and in constant progress. To illustrate this principle of dynamic change, the histories of two commonly used services—personal identification and firearms identification—are traced in the following sections.

PERSONAL IDENTIFICATION

Historically, there have been two major scientific systems for personal identification of criminals: anthropometry and dactylography. The first was relatively short lived. The second, dactylography or fingerprint identification, remains in use today throughout the world.

ANTHROPOMETRY

Anthropometry was developed by Alphonse Bertillon (1853–1914), who is rightly regarded as the father of criminal identification. The first method of criminal identification that was thought to be reliable, anthropometry, "was based on the fact that every human being differs from every other one in the exact measurements of their body, and that the sum of these measurements yields a characteristic formula for each individual."[45] Figure 1-7 depicts a New York City police detective taking one type of measurement used in the "Bertillon system."

There was little in Alphonse Bertillon's early life to suggest that he would later make significant contributions. The grandson of a well known naturalist and mathematician and the son of a distinguished French physician and statistician, who was also the vice president of the Anthropological Society of Paris,[46] Bertillon came from a family with a strong scientific tradition.[47] Moreover, in the late nineteenth century, there was a basic belief that all of life's problems could be solved by scientific knowledge, precise thinking and scholarly deductions.[48] Yet Bertillon's early life reflected several failures and suggested little ability. He was expelled from several schools for poor grades, dismissed from an apprenticeship in a bank after only a few weeks, performed poorly as a tutor in England, and while in the army had difficulty telling the difference between the bugle signals for reveille and roll call.[49] He was, therefore, able to obtain only a minor position in 1879, filing cards on criminals for the Paris police, because of his father's good connections.[50] The cards described criminals so

vaguely that they might have fit almost anyone: "stature: average . . . face: ordinary."[51]

With growing resentment over the dreariness and senselessness of his work, Bertillon asked himself why so much time, money, and human energy were wasted on a useless system of identifying criminals.[52] Bertillon became a source of jokes and popular amusement as he began comparing photographs of criminals and taking measurements of those who had been arrested.[53] Bertillon concluded that if eleven physical measurements of a person were taken, the chances of finding another person with the same eleven measurements were 4,191,304 to 1.[54] His report outlining his criminal identification system was not warmly received. After reading it, the chief said:

> Bertillon? If I am not mistaken, you are a clerk of the twentieth grade and have been with us for only eight months, right? And already you are getting ideas? . . . Your report sounds like a joke.[55]

Yet in 1883, the "joke" received worldwide attention, because when it was implemented on an experimental basis, within 90 days Bertillon would correctly make his first criminal identification. Soon almost all European countries adopted Bertillon's system of anthropometry. In 1888, Bertillon's fertile mind produced yet another innovation, the "portrait parlé" or "speaking picture," which combines full face and profile photographs of each criminal with his or her exact body measurements and other descriptive data onto a single card.

Around the turn of the century, many countries abandoned anthropometry and adopted the simpler and more reliable system of fingerprints instead. Bertillon himself was not insensitive to the potential of fingerprints. In 1902, he solved the murder of Joseph Riebel when he discovered the prints of Henri Scheffer on the pane of a glass cupboard.[56] Yet Bertillon's rigid personality

FIGURE 1-7

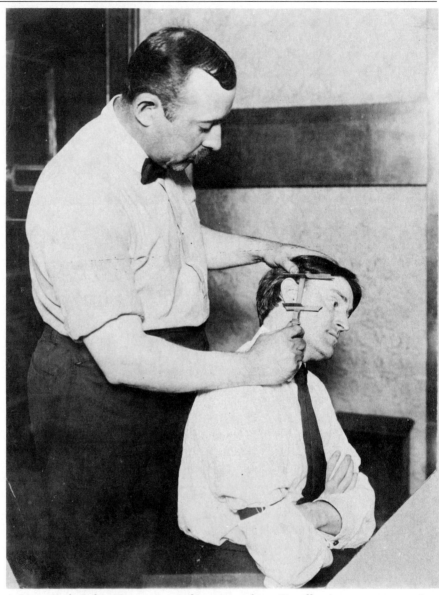

A New York Police Department detective taking Bertillon measurements circa 1896.

Courtesy of the Library of Congress

would not allow him to acknowledge the clear superiority of dactylography to anthropometry. In 1906, Bertillon testified as an expert in handwriting—although he was unqualified—and his testimony helped to convict Captain Dreyfus of spying for Germany. Although the French government later admitted that the Dreyfus conviction had been an injustice, Bertillon refused to admit his error.[57] The Dreyfus incident tarnished Bertillon's reputation on two counts: 1) acting as an expert out of one's field and 2) refusing to admit error; it also illustrates from another perspective his rigid character.

Even so, Bertillon's place in history is secure as the father of criminal identification. His portrait parlé—an ancestor of the "mug shot"—was a significant innovation, to which Bertillon reluctantly added fingerprints, at first only four from the left hand but later all ten fingerprints from both hands.[58] Bertillon was also a pioneer in police photography beyond its application in the portrait parlé; when Bertillon found the fingerprint in the 1902 Riebel murder, his primary interest was in how to best photograph it. Ironically, his success in photographing this fingerprint found at the crime scene not only underscored the practical use of photography in criminal investigation, but it also illustrated the value of dactylography, which even then was quickly gaining favor over Bertillon's anthropometry. Upon Bertillon's death in 1914, France became the last major country to replace anthropometry with dactylography as its system of criminal identification.

DACTYLOGRAPHY

Early Discoveries Although in 1900 England became the first country to use dactylography as a system of criminal identification, fingerprints have a long legal and scientific history. In a legal context, in the first century, the Roman lawyer Quintilianus introduced a bloody fingerprint in a murder trial, successfully defending a child against the charge of murdering his father.[59] Fingerprints also were used on contracts during China's T'ang Dynasty in the eighth century as well as on official papers in fourteenth century Persia and seventeenth century England.[60]

In a scientific context, in 1684 in England, Dr. Nehemiah Grew first called attention to the system of pores and ridges in the hands and feet.[61] Just two years later, Mercello Malpigni made similar observations.[62] In 1823, John Perkinje, a professor at the University of Breslau, named nine standard types of fingerprint patterns and outlined a broad method of classification.[63] Despite these early stirrings, dactylography as a system of criminal identification took nearly another 75 years to emerge.

The Herschel-Faulds Controversy Beginning in 1858, William Herschel, a British official in India, requested the palm and fingerprints of those with whom he did business, thinking that it might awe people into keeping agreements.[64] Over the next 20 years, Herschel noted from his records that the patterns of the lines on the fingerprints never changed for an individual; a person might grow and undergo other physical changes, and yet the fingerprints remained the same. Excited by the prospects of applying this knowledge to the identification of criminals, Herschel wrote in 1877 to the Inspector General of the Prisons of Bengal. The reply was kindly in tone, but it was clear that the Inspector General thought that Herschel's letter was the product of delirium. Herschel was so dispirited by the reply that he made no further efforts to pursue his discovery. Meanwhile, Henry Faulds, a Scottish physician teaching physiology in Tsukiji Hospital in Tokyo, had been interested in fingerprints for several years before 1880. When a thief left a sooty print on a white-washed wall, Faulds was able to tell that the person in police custody was not the thief[65] and to match another suspect's fingerprints with those on the wall.[66] Faulds reported his findings in the journal *Nature* in 1880. Herschel read the account and published a reply, claiming credit for the discovery over 20 years before. A controversy broke out which was never resolved to anyone's satisfaction. Because there was also no official interest in using fingerprints, both Herschel and Faulds were even further frustrated.

Galton's and Vucetich's Systems In 1888, Sir Francis Galton (1822–1911), a cousin of Charles Darwin, turned his attention to criminal identification.[67] When the thorough Galton contacted the editor of *Nature* for both Herschel's and Faulds's addresses, he was by chance sent only Herschel's. Contacted by Galton, Herschel unselfishly turned over all of his files in the hopes that this revived interest would lead to practical uses of fingerprints.[68] In 1892, Galton published the first definitive book on dactylog-

FIGURE 1-9   Edward Henry

Courtesy of the London Metropolitan Police; original copyright Hargrave L. Adam, The Police Encyclopedia, London: The Waverly Book Company, 1910, 1919

raphy, *Finger Prints.* It presented statistical proof of the uniqueness of fingerprints and outlined many principles of identification by fingerprints.[69] In Argentina, in 1894, Juan Vucetich (1858–1925) published *Dactiloscopia Comparada,* outlining his method of fingerprint classification. A disciple of Vucetich's, an Inspector Alvarez, obtained South America's first criminal conviction based on fingerprints in 1892, by using Vucetich's system to convict a woman of beating her two children to death.[70]

The Henry System The final breakthrough for the fingerprint method of personal identification was made by Edward Henry (1850–1931). At the age of 23 he went to India and by 1891 had become the Inspector General of Police of Nepal, the same province in which Herschel had worked some 15 years previously.[71] Subject to many of the same influences as Herschel, but apparently working independently, Henry developed an interest in fingerprints[72] and instituted Bertillon's system, with the addition of fingerprints to the cards. In 1893, Henry obtained a copy

FIGURE 1-8   Juan Vucetich

Courtesy of the Argentine Embassy, Washington, D.C.

of Galton's book and began working on a simple, reliable method of classification. The Governor General of India received a report from Henry in 1897 recommending that anthropometry be dropped in favor of Henry's fingerprint classification system. It was adopted throughout British India just six months later.[73] In 1900, Henry's system was adopted in England. The next year, Henry enjoyed two personal triumphs, the publication of his *Classification and Use of Finger Prints* and his appointment as Assistant Police Commissioner of London,[74] rising to the post of Commissioner two years later.

Faurot and "James Jones" In 1904 New York City Detective Sergeant Joseph Faurot was sent to England to study fingerprints, becoming the first foreigner trained in the use of the Henry classification system. Upon Faurot's return, the new police commissioner told him to forget about such "scientific notions" and transferred him to walking a beat.[75] In 1906, Faurot arrested a man dressed in formal evening wear, but not wearing shoes, as the man crept out of a suite in the Waldorf-Astoria Hotel.[76] Claiming to be a respectable citizen named "James Jones," the man demanded to see the British Consul and threatened Faurot with nasty consequences.[77] Faurot sent the man's fingerprints to Scotland Yard[78] and got back a reply that "James Jones" was actually Daniel Nolan, who had 12 prior convictions of hotel thefts and who was wanted for burglarizing a home in England. Confronted with this evidence, Nolan confessed to several thefts in the Waldorf-Astoria and received a sentence of seven years.[79] Newspaper stories about the case brought Faurot appropriate credit and advanced the use of fingerprints in this country.

The West Case Despite the fame achieved by Faurot, the most important incident to advance the use of fingerprints in this country was the West case. In 1903, Will West

arrived at the U.S. penitentiary at Leavenworth, Kansas. While West was being processed in through identification, a staff member said that there was already a photograph and Bertillon measurements for him on file. But a comparison of fingerprints showed that despite identical appearances and nearly identical Bertillon measurements, the identification card on file belonged to a William West, who had been in Leavenworth since 1901. The incident accelerated the recognition that fingerprints were superior to anthropometry as a system of identification.

Rivalry of Vucetich's and Henry's Systems
Vucetich's book on fingerprint classification was published in 1894, seven years before Henry's, but Henry's system has become much more widely used. But to this day some experts prefer Vucetich's system.[80] The rivalry between partisans of the two classification systems deserves attention.

In 1911, the provincial government of Buenos Aires passed a law requiring fingerprint registration for all adults subject to military service and eligible to vote.[81] By 1913 Vucetich had completed the task and decided to travel. In his travels, he was showered with decorations for his classification system. But when he visited Bertillon to pay his respects to the father of criminal identification,[82] Bertillon kept Vucetich waiting and finally opened the door just long enough to yell, "Sir, you have done me great harm," before slamming it shut again.[83] They were never to meet again. Upon his return to Argentina, Vucetich was to face further humiliation. When Buenos Aires planned an expansion of fingerprint registration, there were strong protests. In 1917 the Argentine government canceled registrations, seized Vucetich's records, and forbade him to continue his work.[84] In 1925, much as Bertillon had in 1914, Vucetich died a disappointed man. Although Vucetich's system is in use in South America today, Vucetich did not live

FIGURE 1-10

Photographs and Bertillon Measurements of William West versus Will West.

	William West	Will West
Bertillon Measurements (in centimeters)		
Height	177.5	178.5
Outstretched arms	188.0	187.0
Trunk	91.3	91.2
Head length	19.8	19.7
Head width	15.9	15.8
Cheek width	14.8	14.8
Right ear	6.5	6.6
Left foot	27.5	28.2
Left middle finger	12.2	12.3
Left little finger	9.6	9.7
Left forearm	50.3	50.2

Source: Compiled from Federal Bureau of Investigation Records

long enough to see the vindication of his life's work.

In contrast, Henry became the head of what was then the world's most prestigious police organization and enjoyed the support of his government. These advantages, coupled with Vucetich's loss of support in his own country, meant that the Henry classification would become adopted virtually throughout the world.

FIREARMS IDENTIFICATION

Personal identification grew as several rival systems, with one of them finally predominating. In contrast, firearms identification moved forward in a series of successive steps. In this country, the frequency of shootings has made firearms identification extremely important.[85] As a specialty within criminalistics, firearms identification extends far beyond the comparison of two fired bullets. It also includes identification of types of ammunition, the design and functioning of firearms, the restoration of obliterated serial numbers on weapons, and estimation of the distance between a gun's muzzle and a victim[86] when the weapon was fired.

In 1835 Henry Goddard, one of the last of the Bow Street Runners, made the first successful attempt to identify a murderer from a bullet recovered from the body of a victim.[87] Goddard noticed that the bullet had a distinctive blemish on it, a slight gouge. At the home of one suspect, Goddard seized a bullet mold with a defect whose location corresponded exactly to the gouge on the bullet.

The owner of the mold confessed to the crime when confronted with this evidence.[88]

Professor Lacassagne removed a bullet in 1889 from a corpse in France; upon examining it closely, he found seven grooves made as the bullet passed through the barrel of a gun.[89] Shown the guns of a number of suspects, Lacassagne identified the one that could have left seven grooves. On the basis of this evidence, a man was convicted of the murder.[90] However, any number of guns manufactured at that time could have produced seven grooves. There is no way of knowing whether the right person was found guilty.[91]

In 1898, a German chemist named Paul Jeserich was given a bullet taken from the body of a man murdered near Berlin. After firing a test bullet from the defendant's revolver, Jeserich took microphotographs of the fatal and test bullets and on the basis of the agreement between both their respective normalities and abnormalities, testified that the defendant's revolver fired the fatal bullet, contributing materially to the conviction obtained.[92] Unknowingly at the doorstep of scientific greatness, Jeserich did not pursue this discovery any further, choosing instead to return to his other interests.

Gradually, attention began to shift from just bullets to other aspects of firearms. In 1913, Professor Balthazard published perhaps the single most important article on firearms identification. In it, he noted that the firing pin, breechblock, extractor, and ejector all leave marks on cartridges and that these vary among different types of weapons. With World War I looming, Balthazard's article was not widely recognized for some years.

Calvin Goddard (1858–1946), a U.S. physician who had served in the army during World War I, is the person considered most responsible for raising firearms identification to a science and for perfecting the bullet comparison microscope. To no small degree, Goddard's accomplishments were contrib-uted to heavily by three other Americans—Charles Waite, John Fisher, and Phillip Gravelle—working as a team on firearms identification. In 1925, Goddard joined Waite's team and upon his death a year later, Goddard became the undisputed driving force and leader of it.[93] Like many pioneers, Waite's contributions are often overlooked. He had been interested in firearms since 1917, and from 1920 on visited firearms manufacturers to get data on those manufactured since 1850. Because of Waite, the first significant catalogued firearms collection was assembled in this country. Nonetheless, ultimately it was Goddard who raised firearms identification to the status of a science.

A PARTING VIEW

There are many other contributors to the evolution of investigation and criminalistics. For example, in 1910 Albert Osborn (1858–1946) wrote *Questioned Documents*, still regarded as a definitive work. From at least 1911 onward, Edmond Locard (1877–1966) maintained a central interest in locating microscope evidence; all crime scenes processed today are based on the presumed validity of Locard's principle: there is something to be found. Leone Lattes (1887–1954) developed a procedure in 1915 which permitted blood typing from a dried bloodstain, a key event in forensic serology. Although more an administrator and innovator than a criminalist, August Vollmer's (1876–1955) support helped John Larson produce the first workable polygraph in 1921, and Vollmer established America's first full forensic laboratory in Los Angeles in 1923. In 1935, Harry Soderman and John O'Connell coauthored *Modern Criminal Investigation*, the standard work for the field for decades, until the publication of Paul Kirk's *Crime Investigation* in 1953. A biochemist, educator, and criminalist, Kirk helped develop the careers of many criminalists.

QUESTIONS

1. Who were the Bow Street Runners, and of what historical importance are they?
2. Why did the British public object to the use of detectives following the Metropolitan Police Act of 1829?
3. Why did the office of detective in this country basically evolve in the private sector?
4. What assessment can be made of the work of Pinkerton and his National Detective Agency?
5. What is a rogues' gallery?
6. What parallels can be drawn between Allan Pinkerton and J. Edgar Hoover?
7. With reference to publications specifically named in this chapter on investigation and criminalistics, how many can you identify and of what significance are they?
8. What is anthropometry, and why was it abandoned in favor of dactylography?
9. What are the milestones in the development of dactylography?
10. Why does the Henry classification system enjoy greater use than Vucetich's system?
11. What are the milestones in the development of firearm identification?

NOTES

1. Material on the evolution of criminal investigation is drawn, in part, from Thomas R. Phelps, Charles R. Swanson, Jr., and Kenneth Evans, *Introduction to Criminal Justice* (New York: Random House, 1979), pp. 42-55.
2. T.A. Critchley, *A History of Police in England and Wales,* 2nd ed. (Montclair, N.J.: Patterson Smith, 1972), p. 34.
3. Ibid., p. 34.
4. A.C. Germann, Frank D. Day, and Robert J. Gallati, *Introduction to Law Enforcement and Criminal Justice* (Springfield, Illinois: Charles C. Thomas, 1970), pp. 54-55.
5. Melville Lee, *A History of Police in England* (Montclair, N.J.: Patterson Smith reprint, 1971), p. 240.
6. Thomas A. Reppetto, *The Blue Parade* (New York: The Free Press, 1978), p. 26.
7. Ibid., pp. 26-28.
8. Ibid., p. 29.
9. Ibid., p. 29 states three of four; John Coatman, *Police* (New York: Oxford, 1959), pp. 98-99 notes only one such conviction. Vincent's CID was based on his study of the Paris centralized detective system.
10. Coatman, *Police,* pp. 98-99.
11. Ibid., p. 99.
12. James F. Richardson, *The New York Police* (New York: Oxford, 1970), p. 37.
13. James D. Horan, *The Pinkertons* (New York: Bonanza Books, 1967), p. 25.
14. Ibid., p. 23.
15. Ibid., p. 25.
16. Jurgen Thorwald, *The Marks of Cain* (London: Thames and Hudson, 1965), p. 129.
17. Reppetto, *The Blue Parade,* p. 258.
18. Thorwald, *The Marks of Cain,* p. 129.
19. Reppetto, *The Blue Parade,* p. 257; there seems to be some dispute over whether there was ever any real threat and, if so, whether Pinkerton or New York City Police actually discovered it.
20. Ibid., pp. 257-258.
21. Ibid., p. 258; Reppetto asserts that as a military analyst Pinkerton was a failure and that his overestimates of enemy strength made General McClellan too cautious, contributing to McClellan's dismissal as head of the Union army.
22. Ibid., p. 258.
23. William J. Bopp and Donald Shultz, *Prin-*

ciples of American Law Enforcement and Criminal Justice (Springfield, Illinois: Charles C. Thomas, 1972), pp. 70-71.

24. Thorwald, *The Marks of Cain,* p. 131.
25. Reppetto, *The Blue Parade,* p. 259 notes that in two separate instances a total of 8 Reno gang members arrested by the Pinkertons were subsequently lynched. In the first instance, three gang members reportedly were taken from Pinkerton custody.
26. Thorwald, *The Marks of Cain,* p. 131.
27. Reppetto, *The Blue Parade,* p. 261.
28. Ibid., p. 263.
29. Clive Emsley, *Policing and Its Context 1750–1870* (New York: Schocken Books, 1983), p. 106.
30. Augustine E. Costello, *Our Police Protectors* (Montclair, N.J.: A Patterson Smith 1972 reprint of an 1885 Edition), p. 402.
31. Richardson, *The New York Police,* p. 122.
32. Bopp and Shultz, *Principles of American Law Enforcement and Criminal Justice,* p. 66.
33. William J. Mathias and Stuart Anderson, *Horse to Helicopter* (Atlanta: Community Life Publications, Georgia State University, 1973), p. 22.
34. Thorwald, *The Marks of Cain,* p. 136.
35. Ibid., p. 136.
36. Ibid., p. 137.
37. Reppetto, *The Blue Parade,* p. 263.
38. Ibid., p. 267.
39. Ibid., p. 278.
40. Ibid., p. 282.
41. Ibid., p. 283.
42. Material in this section is drawn from Phelps, Swanson, and Evans, *Introduction to Criminal Justice,* pp. 128-131.
43. The Supreme Court opted for piecemeal application when it rejected the "shorthand doctrine," that is, rejected making a blanket application of the Bill of Rights binding on the states, in its consideration of *Hurtado* v. *California* (110 U.S. 516 [1884]).
44. Richard Saferstein, *Criminalistics* (Englewood Cliffs, New Jersey, 1977), p. 5.

45. Jurgen Thorwald, *Crime and Science* (New York: Harcourt, Brace & World, 1967), p. 4.
46. Jurgen Thorwald, *The Century of the Detective* p. 6.
47. Thorwald, *Crime and Science* p. 233.
48. Ibid., p. 233.
49. Thorwald, *The Century of the Detective,* p. 6.
50. Ibid., p. 6.
51. Ibid., p. 7.
52. Ibid., p. 9.
53. Ibid., p. 9.
54. Ibid., p. 10.
55. Ibid., p. 12.
56. Ibid., pp. 83-84.
57. Ibid., p. 89.
58. Raymond D. Fosdick, *European Police Systems* (Montclair, N.J.: A 1969 Patterson Smith reprint of the 1915 original), p. 323.
59. Anthony L. Califana and Jerome S. Levkov, *Criminalistics for the Law Enforcement Officer* (New York: McGraw-Hill, 1978), p. 20.
60. Ibid., p. 20, also see Frederick R. Cherrill, *The Finger Print System of Scotland Yard* (London: Her Majesty's Stationery Office, 1954), p. 3.
61. Cherrill, *The Finger Print System at Scotland Yard,* p. 2.
62. Califana and Levkov, *Criminalistics for the Law Enforcement Officer,* p. 20.
63. Cherrill, *The Finger Print System at Scotland Yard,* p. 4.
64. Thorwald, *The Century of the Detective,* pp. 14-16.
65. Ibid., p. 18.
66. Ibid., p. 18.
67. Ibid., p. 32.
68. Ibid., p. 33.
69. Saferstein, *Criminalistics,* p. 4.
70. Thorwald, *The Marks of Cain,* p. 81.
71. Thorwald, *The Century of the Detective,* p. 58.
72. Ibid., p. 58.
73. Ibid., p. 60.
74. Ibid., p. 62.

75. Thorwald, *The Marks of Cain*, p. 138.
76. Ibid., p. 138.
77. Ibid., p. 138.
78. Ibid., p. 139.
79. Ibid., p. 139.
80. Saferstein, *Criminalistics*, p. 281.
81. Thorwald, *The Century of the Detective*, p. 88.
82. Ibid., p. 88.
83. Ibid., p. 87.
84. Ibid., p. 88.
85. Saferstein, *Criminalistics*, p. 300.
86. Ibid., p. 30.
87. Thorwald, *The Marks of Cain*, p. 161.
88. Ibid., p. 161.
89. Thorwald, *The Century of the Detective*, pp. 418-419.
90. Ibid., p. 419.
91. Thorwald, *The Marks of Cain*, p. 164.
92. Ibid., p. 164.
93. Thorwald, *The Century of the Detective*, p. 434.

2

CRIME AND ITS INVESTIGATION

THE IMPACT OF CRIME

Although crime is a national problem, its control is primarily the responsibility of local government. When officials fail to prevent or cannot deal effectively with crime, there are a number of negative consequences. First, when individuals commit crimes and escape prosecution, future illegal acts are encouraged. Second, an escalating crime rate requires that resources which could be devoted to other social problems be diverted to the crime-control effort, resulting in the further entrenchment of such ills as poverty, substandard housing, and inadequate medical care. Third, as the crime rate increases, our system of government faces the real possibility of a crisis of confidence in its ability to maintain public welfare. Finally, crime tears the fabric of social relations and living patterns. People become fearful of strangers and of being on the streets after dark, homes become fortresses, and families move to new locations in search of a secure life. A terrible reality is that until significant inroads are made in controlling crime, the overall quality of life is lower than it could be.

CRIME AND ITS INVESTIGATION

A crime is the commission of an act prohibited or the omission of an act required by the penal code of an organized political state. There can be no crime unless there is advance notice of the behavior prohibited or required. Legislatures enact criminal codes which distinguish between felonies and misdemeanors. A felony is an act often punishable by incarceration for a term of one or more years in a penitentiary, or by death. The test to determine whether a person was convicted of a felony is not whether imprisonment actually took place for such a period of time, but rather whether the sentence was possible. All violations of the criminal code not deemed to be felonies are misdemeanors, lesser offenses often punishable by a fine not to exceed $500 and/or imprisonment of not more than one year.

An investigator is an individual who gathers, documents, and evaluates facts about a crime; investigation is the process through which these are accomplished. The purposes of the investigator's actions are several:

1. To establish that, in fact, a crime was committed
2. To identify and apprehend the suspect
3. To recover stolen property
4. To assist the state in prosecuting the party charged with the offense

The achievement of these objectives requires that the investigator have certain knowledge concepts and techniques and have particular skills. Among the most important skills is the ability to converse equally well with a wide range of people. This is particularly critical because investigation essentially is working with people. Thus, investigators must be as adroit in talking to bartenders, elevator operators, and prostitutes as they are with art gallery owners, corporate heads, and attorneys. Other knowledge and skills needed by the investigator include the recognition, collection, marking, and preservation of evidence; crime scene sketching and photography; note taking and report preparation; appreciation of the potential contributions to be made to an investigation by psychologists, crime laboratory personnel, and medical examiners; interrogation; the elements needed to prove specific crimes were committed; the rules under which evidence will be admitted into court; and how to testify effectively.

Knowledge and skills will not in and of themselves make a successful investigator. A hallmark of the competent investigator is the clarity with which he or she sees the relationship between knowing and doing; they are very different, yet they are inexorably bound together. Investigation is fraught with challenges and complexities. These will be most successfully met when investigators consistently translate their knowledge into actual behaviors.

THE IMPORTANCE OF INVESTIGATION

The investigation of any crime imposes heavy responsibilities on the individual assigned that function. This burden is greater in the investigation of felonies because of the latitude of police discretionary judgment involved and the possible consequences. In order to make a legal arrest an officer, unless in possession of a warrant, generally must personally witness a misdemeanor. In felony cases an arrest may be executed on the basis of probable cause, which, however, often requires a subjective evaluation of both the event and the intent of the suspect. While deadly force cannot be invoked as a last resort in effecting a misdemeanor arrest, its application in a felony apprehension is a possibility necessitating the exercise of sound discretionary judgment within a critically limited time frame. The consequences in felony investigations are of the utmost seriousness. An individual arrested, let alone convicted of a felony, is often socially stigmatized to a significant degree. If convicted, such a person stands to lose his or her freedom for a period of years or perhaps even to forfeit his or her life.

If an individual is to meet the responsibilities associated with the criminal investigation function successfully, certain personal qualities are essential.

ESSENTIAL QUALITIES OF THE INVESTIGATOR

The investigator who consistently solves the most difficult and bizarre cases is often said to be lucky. While good fortune occasionally plays a key role in successful investigations, no one is constantly lucky. The investigator referred to as being lucky is, instead, an individual who possesses—in addition to adequate professional preparation—an abundance of certain qualities.

Successful investigators will invariably possess a high degree of self-discipline; it is not the presence or absence of others which regulates their behavior, but rather internalized control. Such individuals have knowledge of, and practice, methods which are legally acceptable. Patience and thoroughness are indispensable; successful investigators approach each case with alert, fastidious attention to detail, leaving nothing to chance. In so doing they forfeit no opportunities to develop evidence, while creating many. The fact that a particular step or steps of an investigation are only rarely productive does not mean they should be omitted; the opposite is true. Investigation is a systematic method of inquiry that is more science than art. The logic of the scientific method must, however, be supplemented by the investigator's initiative and resourcefulness. Investigations cannot always be performed successfully by rote application of procedures outlined in texts. Rather, the sequences of investigation should be regarded as a scientific, operating framework which, when applied to a particular case, may require improvisation on the investigator's part.

The successful investigator is also characterized by objectivity and freedom from preconceived notions or predispositions. An officer makes an arrest with the belief that the actual perpetrator has been identified; while personally certain of that individual's guilt, he or she recognizes that the legal condition of guilt arises only out of a judicial proceeding. Investigators, therefore, never disregard or fail to document anything which might tend to weaken the state's case. However unsavory the character of a suspect, the investigator must be steadfast in the role of fact-finder. This action is inescapable if we are to be a nation of laws and the investigator is to be ethical.

Criminal investigation may be likened to a series of gates at each of which certain evaluations and judgments must be made before advancing to the next. The investigator must possess keen decision-making capabilities, drawing on deductive or inductive reasoning when a course of action is not immediately apparent. The use of inductive reasoning involves examination of the evidence and particulars of a case and the use of this information as a basis for formulating a unifying and internally consistent explanation of the event. Deductive reasoning begins with the formulation of an explanation of the crime, which is then tested against the available information. The use of either process requires considerable ability as both are fraught with the dangers of untenable inferences, logical fallacies, the failure to consider all alternatives, persuasive but false analogies, and the distortion of personal bias. Despite these dangers, however, deductive and inductive reasoning are an important part of the repertoire of the complete investigator.

In dealing both with suspects and complainants, a high degree of sensitivity and compassion is important. For example, desiring to solve a rape case, the investigator must conduct the interview of the victim in such a fashion as to elicit available information without causing unnecessary anguish. Due to constant association with the criminal element and its fringe, the investigator will find abundant opportunity to become calloused and cynical. Foremost in mind must be the understanding that while investigators will frequently come into contact with unsavory characters in the performance of their duties, they do not represent the population as a whole. The failure to maintain this distinction results in a cynicism which may be the precursor of unethical behavior.

As a final note, successful investigators lose no opportunity to learn something from every person with whom they have contact, for they recognize that the wider their understanding of occupations, life styles, vocabularies, and related topics, the more effective they will be.

ORGANIZATION OF THE INVESTIGATIVE FUNCTION

The major events in the investigation of crime are depicted in Figure 2-1; a discussion

FIGURE 2-1   **Major Events in the Investigation of a Crime**

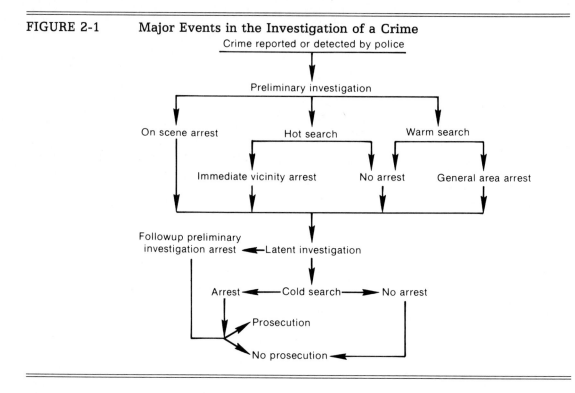

of these and their subelements will serve to provide an overview of the investigative process and introduce concepts covered in greater detail in subsequent chapters.

Once a criminal offense has been committed three immediate outcomes are possible. It may be undetected, as in the case of a carefully planned and conducted murder by organized crime figures, in which the body is disposed of so that it will remain undiscovered. If a violation is detected, it may not be reported, such as when a proprietor finds his or her business premises have been burglarized, but does not contact the police because the loss is minor or because the insurance coverage would be adversely affected. Finally, the crime may come to the attention of the police through their observation or a complaint by the victim or witnesses.

Regardless of the outcome, a crime has occurred in each of the three preceding in-

stances; however, only in the last case, when it is detected or reported, is the offense of concern to the investigator because only at that time does it become subject to formal processing.

THE PRELIMINARY INVESTIGATION

The actions taken at the scene of a crime immediately following its detection and reporting constitute what is termed the *preliminary investigation*. It is desirable to vest the uniformed officer with the responsibility for the preliminary investigation. This should be the case even when departmental size permits some degree of specialization, which ordinarily occurs where personnel with the power of arrest total approximately twenty or more. The following list outlines the key elements of this preliminary phase of investigation.

1. There should be an immediate request for medical services in those instances where the victim or suspect has sustained a serious injury.
2. A determination must be made as to whether a crime was committed, and if so, what the specific type of offense was. Occasionally this can be a difficult problem, as the following case histories suggest:

For four years, a 47-year-old woman was terrorized in a series of incidents by a mysterious individual identified as the "Poet" due to the verse form used in threatening letters sent to her. She reported receiving a butcher knife at Christmas, having her telephone line cut, having chunks of concrete thrown at her home, and being kidnapped and stabbed in the lower back. When the woman was discovered mailing letters from the "Poet" along with her bills and normal correspondence, she admitted that there was no "Poet" and that she had even stabbed herself to lend credence to her stories. A psychologist working on the case speculated that an assault on the woman when she was 16 years old had been the motivating force behind the "Poet" episode. In that assault, an unknown assailant had drugged her and branded her on both thighs.[1]

The police found an adult male, approximately 30 years old, wandering in the woods. The man presented himself as a 4-year-old who had been abandoned. The police couldn't find any identification, there were no matching fingerprints on file, and the person didn't correspond to any of the descriptions on missing persons reports. A psychologist became convinced that he was working with someone with multiple personalities when the subject suddenly started snarling, growling, and sounding diabolical. Medical personnel later discovered that the man had up to 27 different personalities, none of which was aware of the other. His IQ ranged from 88 to 128, depending on which personality took the test. Among the personalities identified were a punk rocker who went to concerts with his hair dyed purple and

got into fights; blind Jeffrey; Robert, the intellectual; the sinister T. K.; Mark, the angry enforcer; and three women, including Tina, the prostitute, Maria, the 48-year-old housekeeper, and a lesbian named Rachel. The psychologist said that it made the hair on the back of his head stand up because it was almost like a scene from The Exorcist, *a story of demonic possession. The break came when the sinister T. K. committed suicide in the man's mind, setting the other characters free. Thus, the real character of who the person was awoke one morning with no memory of what had happened to him during the nine months that T. K. had dominated his life.[2]*

Clearly these are unusual cases. The first case is unusual in the duration of the deception and the lengths to which the "victim" went to maintain it. The second case is an excellent example of the complexity of the human mind and how specialists trained in fields other than law enforcement are an absolutely essential adjunct to the investigative effort from time to time. There are, however, examples of deception by "victims" which are not quite as unusual. First, an individual may become intoxicated, be involved as a driver in a hit-and-run accident, abandon the car, walk to another location, and report the car stolen in an attempt to escape culpability for the violation. A variation on this is that the individual, after abandoning the car, goes home and "falls asleep." The police find the abandoned vehicle and trace it to the person's residence. "Awakened from sleep" by the police, the person admits to having been drinking, but claims to have made it home and parked the car in the driveway, from which it "has been stolen." A second example is the man who cashes his paycheck and stops by a bar to have a few drinks. An attractive woman finds him "fascinating," and they agree to go to her place. In the process the man is, by prior plans, robbed by the female's accomplice. The victim, knowing that this explanation will cause conflict with his wife, decides the only way out is to fabricate a story of being robbed.

Although the majority of complaints are made honestly, the investigator must remain alert for indications of a false complaint. Included in these indications are possible motivations for the crime or the concealment of the crime on the victim's part, inconsistencies in accounts about the incident, illogical relationships between the account of the incident as given by the victim as compared with the available physical evidence, and sufficient time, opportunity, and motive to have been involved with the incident in ways other than that which the victim reports. It is sometimes difficult to distinguish between a frightened victim and a person attempting to file a false crime report. Many times, through skillful and apparently innocuous questioning, the reality of the situation will finally emerge. In other situations the suspicions of the investigator cannot be resolved through questioning alone and other means will prove useful:

A cashier at a loan company reported a robbery of $400 cash and $1,600 in checks. An investigator responded to the crime scene and spoke with the victim. The victim's statement was very vague and at times inconsistent. She stated that two males approached her, pulled a gun, and demanded all the money. There were no witnesses to the crime, and the victim said she was too shaken to notice any of the physical features of the perpetrators.

The investigator interviewed the victim further and was suspicious about the circumstances of the robbery. He asked the woman to take a polygraph test, which she submitted to and failed. The "victim" subsequently confessed that the robber was not real, and that she had conspired with the two men she was living with to falsify the report.[3]

A doctor in a small town created a stir when he announced that he had diagnosed an unusually high number of cancer cases. He speculated that a river apparently polluted by a local plant was among the possible explanations for the cancer rate. Subsequently, the doctor's home was set on fire as he and his family slept in it, and the doctor was attacked while fishing. He was stabbed four times and wounded in the abdomen by a 5-inch knife, which miraculously missed all vital parts. The doctor expressed the belief that his announcement might have led to the attacks. Investigators became suspicious when the laboratory found traces of pain-killing medication on the blade of the knife that had inflicted the wounds. After failing a lie detector test, the doctor admitted that he had set fire to his own home and stabbed himself.[4]

The receipt of a radio message to proceed to a particular location to handle a specific type of call does not ensure that any particular type of offense has occurred. While every effort is made to properly screen and classify calls for service, errors will be made. Sometimes the results are harmless and at other times tragic:

A marked unit was dispatched to the Red and Black Grocery Store on a call designated as a robbery with two juvenile white males as perpetrators. Legally, robbery is a felony defined as the taking of something of value from the control, custody, or person of another by threatening, putting in fear, or by the use of force. Upon arrival at the scene it was found that the proprietor had reported a robbery, but had used the term in a loose sense, meaning that property had been taken. An interview of the complainant revealed that she had discovered the two youths removing cartons of empty bottles from the rear of the store in order to present them for a deposit refund elsewhere. Thus, the specific offense was petty larceny, a misdemeanor.

A thirteen-year-old girl called the emergency dispatcher and stated, "There is someone trying to break into my house right now." The radio dispatcher classified the call as a "34"—a routine disturbance in which no one's life is in imminent danger. The girl, either before or after calling the police, also called her mother at work who rushed home to find her daughter raped and stabbed to death. Only then were the police dispatched to the scene, some forty minutes after the girl's original call to the police.[5]

3. To the maximum extent possible, and simultaneous with executing the two preceding steps, the investigator must also preserve the integrity of the crime scene to ensure that evidence is not lost, destroyed, or altered in such a manner as to eliminate its value in court.

4. In those instances where witnesses to the offense exist and the perpetrator has escaped arrest at the scene, certain immediate actions are necessary. The witnesses should be separated to avoid a discussion of their perceptions of the event being investigated. Each must then be individually interviewed to gain sufficient details and descriptions in order to place a preliminary pickup order with the radio dispatcher who, in turn, will transmit it to all units. To maximize the likelihood of apprehension, this first order must be placed as rapidly as possible following confirmation of the offense and the gathering of sufficient descriptive data. While the officer assigned to the call conducts the preliminary investigation, other units should be available to assist, where the suspect had fled the scene, by conducting hot and warm searches. A hot search is an examination of the immediate vicinity of the crime scene when the perpetrator is known or believed to be there. A warm search is a check of the general area beyond the immediate vicinity of the crime scene when it is believed the perpetrator may still be there. A swift issuance of the preliminary pickup order is also necessary to minimize the chance that an unsuspecting officer may stop what appears to be an ordinary traffic violator when in reality he has unknowingly stopped the perpetrator of a major offense and is suddenly assailed. The temporary pickup order should minimally include the following points: the number of suspects; their age, race, sex, height, weight, build, coloration; clothing, scars, marks, tattoos, jewelry

worn, names and nicknames applicable to each suspect, which may have been overheard; whether the suspects were unarmed or armed and, where used, the numbers, types, and descriptions of weapons; and the method and direction of flight, including a full description of any vehicle involved. The description of the vehicle should include not only the year, make, model, and color but other distinguishing factors such as damage to the vehicle, stickers, articles and markings on and within the vehicle, and unusual conditions, such as the existence of loud motor noise. A case history illustrates the importance of complete descriptions:

An armed robbery of a convenience store was committed. At the scene it was determined that a toy pistol may have been employed and the suspect's vehicle had a construction worker's hard hat on its rear shelf. A vehicle matching the description broadcast was found parked behind a tavern with a box for a toy gun on the rear floorboard, and a hard hat on the rear seat. Interviews with personnel operating the tavern established that a person of the suspect's description entered hurriedly, made a phone call, had a drink, and left. A check with a cab company revealed that a pickup near that location was taken to the airport. A check of the airline counters revealed that the suspect had been ticketed and departed from Tampa to Miami, Florida, where an apprehension was made as he left the plane.

5. The case must be documented and evidence gathered. This requires in-depth interviews of witnesses and the complainant along with the collection, marking, and preservation of evidence. Additional tasks include photographing the scene and, where warranted, preparing a crime scene sketch. The investigator must be particularly alert to search for evidence not only at the immediate scene of the crime, but also, where discernible, along the perpetrator's lines of approach and flight from the scene. Ordinarily, the suspect will approach the scene with care, but in haste to

flee the scene, he or she may drop something which will be of significant evidenciary value.

6. An offense report must be prepared which includes the facts known to the investigator, all actions taken, and the listing of all items of evidence seized.

7. Ordinarily in the detailed interviews which follow the placement of the preliminary pickup order, the investigator will obtain additional information from witnesses concerning the description of the suspect and any vehicle involved. Thus, a second pickup order, termed the *permanent pickup,* must be placed. This is accomplished by calling a central point, often called the pickup desk, where the information is recorded and then relayed to the radio dispatcher for rebroadcast to all units. A copy of this second order is also posted for the information of officers coming on duty, who will record it in their notebooks and refer to it as may be required during their tour of duty. After a permanent pickup order is placed, it continues to be in effect until it is cancelled by an arrest, by a determination that the offense was "unfounded" (i.e., without a factual basis), or for other reasons. A cancellation of the permanent pickup order is formally placed and processed in the same manner as the permanent pickup order.

8. All evidence seized must be transmitted to the police station, where it will be stored in the central depository to which access is limited in order to ensure the integrity of materials. Upon receipt of the evidence, the evidence custodian will issue a receipt, a copy of which should be appended to the offense report. At this point the supervisor of the officer conducting the preliminary investigation will review the report for completeness, accuracy, and conformity to reporting standards and regulations. Ordinarily in major case investigations the report is immediately referred to the unit of the

police department responsible for the latent or follow-up investigation, which most frequently is conducted by a plainclothes officer.

THE LATENT INVESTIGATION

Latent investigation is the effort expended by the police in gathering information subsequent to the initiation of the original report until the case is ready for prosecution.

Upon receipt of a major case offense report, a supervisor in the investigative unit will assign it to a particular individual who will be responsible for the latent or follow-up work, which often involves a cold search for the perpetrator. When the suspect is not already in custody as a result of an on-scene arrest or the hot or warm searches, the latent investigator must:

1. Read and become thoroughly conversant with the offense report in order to follow up leads and begin to consider what activities might produce additional leads.

2. View all evidence seized and arrange to have it submitted to a crime laboratory for analysis.

3. Effect a liaison with the officer initiating the report, reinterviewing witnesses and the complainant as necessary in an attempt to develop further information and to clarify aspects of the case. In many instances the officer originating the report may not have been able to locate any witnesses, requiring an effort in this phase to determine whether they exist and, if so, to locate them.

4. Evaluate the legal significance of statements, evidence, and laboratory findings.

5. Employ, where appropriate, specialized techniques such as physical or electronic surveillance and polygraph examinations.

6. Identify, locate, and arrest the suspect.

7. Conduct an in-custody interrogation in conformity with legal requirements.

8. Recover stolen property.

TABLE 2-1
National Clearance Rates by Percentage for Selected Major Cases[a]

Offense	Cleared	Not Cleared
Criminal homicide	72	28
Rape	54	46
Aggravated assault	62	38
Robbery	25	75
Burglary	14	86
Larceny	20	80
Auto theft	15	85
Arson	17	83

[a]These data include cases cleared by arrest and exceptionally cleared.

Source: Federal Bureau of Investigation, *Crime in the United States.* Washington, D.C., Government Printing Office, 1986, pp. 12-39.

9. Arrange to meet with the prosecuting attorney.

A final note is required with respect to various perceptions of what constitutes a successful investigation. In the public's mind that status is attained when the perpetrator is arrested, property is recovered, and the person charged subsequently enters a guilty plea or is convicted. In administrative terms success is achieved when the offense is accorded one of two classifications: it may be "exceptionally cleared," in that a factor external to the investigation, such as a complainant's refusal to testify, results in no charge being filed against a suspect; or "cleared by arrest," when the perpetrator has been arrested and there is sufficient evidence to file a formal charge. Here it must be ob-

served that every arrest will not result in prosecution; the police can and do make mistakes, or the evidence may be found to be legally insufficient.

An examination of the data in Table 2-1 leads to the conclusion that in many types of major case offenses the investigator will not experience success as defined by the public or administrative classifications. What, then, should be the investigator's attitude? How can feelings of frustration be avoided? The investigator knows that many crimes are highly resistant to clearance and some crimes are simply insoluble because of insufficient evidence or legal restrictions. Therefore, success for the investigator must rest in the knowledge that the case was vigorously pursued and all avenues leading to clearance examined.

QUESTIONS

1. What is the definition of a crime?
2. How are felonies and misdemeanors distinguished?
3. What are the four major aims of an investigator's action?
4. The investigator must have certain essential

qualities. What are they?
5. Contrast inductive and deductive reasoning.
6. What are the major steps in preliminary and latent investigations?
7. Identify the varying definitions of what constitutes a successful investigation.

NOTES

1. "Mysterious 'Poet' Assailant Proves to Be Victim Herself," *The Atlanta Journal Weekend, Atlanta Constitution,* October 3, 1981, 3–A. For a similar case, see B. Kava, "Police Arrest Woman who Reported Family Was Being Harassed," The Kansas City *Times,* April 10, 1985, pp. A1 and A10.

2. "Man Troubled by Having Up to 27 Personalities," *Miami* (Florida) *Herald,* October 4, 1982, 1–B and 2–B.

3. Peter W. Greenwood et al., *The Criminal Investigation Process, Vol. 111: Observations and Analysis* (Santa Monica, Calif.: Rand Corporation, 1975), p. 138.

4. "Doctor Confesses to Self-Stabbing, Setting Fire," *The Atlanta Journal Weekend, Atlanta Constitution,* October 2, 1982, p. 2–A; Hal Clarendon, "Altha Doctor's Confession Is Talk of Town," *Florida Times-Union* (Jacksonville), October 4, 1982, 2–A.

5. "Girl Slain as Help Call Handled as Routine," *The Atlanta Journal,* December 2, 1980, 16–A.

3

CRIME SCENE AND ITS ASSOCIATED PROCEDURES

INTRODUCTION

During the 1960s the United States Supreme Court handed down decisions restricting the circumstances under which the police could interrogate persons suspected of having committed a crime. A subtle and often overlooked collateral effect was the new premium placed on the use of physical evidence. The value of such evidence lies in the fact that it is inanimate and therefore factual. Unlike eyewitness testimony or the innocent individual who confesses to a crime because of some personality disorder, physical evidence can never be intrinsically wrong.[1] The contributions of physical evidence to an investigation are diminished primarily by the inability, unwillingness, or failure to locate, properly collect, mark, and preserve it, and the drawing of improper conclusions from its analysis. Also, because evidence cannot speak for itself, its proper value can be altered by incomplete or inaccurate testimony.[2]

A crime scene may be defined as the location at which the offense was committed; the search of the crime scene for physical evidence must, however, involve a wider area, including the lines of approach and flight by the perpetrator. Thus, a crime scene search must include the specific setting of the crime and its general environs. Crimes vary by type with respect to their propensity to yield physical evidence. For example, examination of the counter of a business at which a worthless check was passed is highly unlikely to produce any physical evidence. On the other hand, the scene of a criminal homicide may be expected to produce an abundance of items of considerable importance to the investigation.[3] Regardless of the type of offense involved, the fundamental assumption which underlies the crime scene search is that there is something to be found.

ORGANIZATION OF THE CRIME SCENE INVESTIGATION

There are three major functions to be executed at the scene of an offense: coordination, technical services, and investigative services. The first function is vested in the crime scene coordinator who has overall responsibility for the investigation at that time, including technical and investigative services. This individual will make or approve all major decisions as they relate to the case. Technical services are concerned with processing the scene; they encompass the identification, collection, marking, and preservation of evidence, along with scene documentation, including sketching and photography. Technical services are also responsible for transmitting the evidence to the central depository or to the laboratory, according to departmental procedure. Those providing technical services will be specially trained technicians whose sole function is the processing of crime scenes. The investigative service function includes interviewing witnesses and the complainant; if the suspect is in custody, the field interrogation; and the conducting of a neighborhood canvass to identify additional witnesses. While investigative services at the scene are usually performed by uniformed officers, they will occasionally be complemented by plainclothes personnel. In smaller departments where there is no specialization, these three functions will generally be accomplished by a patrol officer. The larger the department, the more certain it is that one or more persons will be working in each of the technical and investigative service areas under the scene

FIGURE 3-1

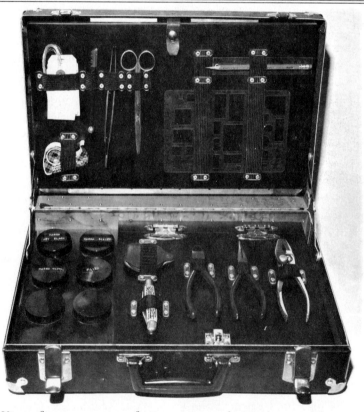

View of center portion of crime scene technician's case. The containers at the bottom left are various colored powders used for dusting latent prints.

coordinator. In such situations the scene co-ordinator will often be a supervisor with at least the rank of sergeant.

TYPICAL CRIME SCENE
PROBLEMS

Although the procedures to be followed at a crime scene investigation may be neatly delineated, any number of conditions may render their accomplishment a good bit less or-derly than the ideal. The resources of a police department are finite, and there are considerable demands made upon them. Ideally, every crime scene should be fastidiously processed. In reality, the scenes of misde-meanor offenses receive at best a cursory examination, and even the thoroughness with which felony crime scenes are processed will frequently be affected by the severity of the offense. To the person victimized, the situation is of considerable importance, pos-sibly even traumatically so, and may have

FIGURE 3-2

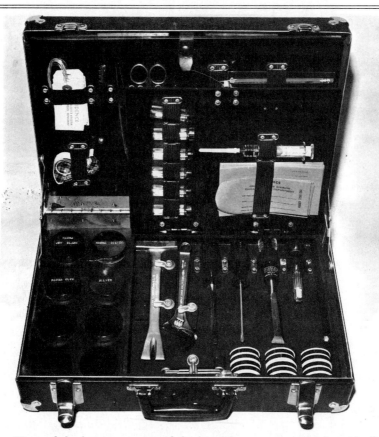

View of the bottom section of the kit. The containers in the right foreground are for smaller pieces of evidence such as bullets. The syringe is used for picking up blood samples. The tools are employed in a variety of ways, such as removing doors from crime scene to laboratory.

FIGURE 3-3

The top portion of the kit contains report forms, brushes for dusting for latent prints, and other items.

brought him or her into direct contact with the police for the first time. From the police standpoint, the offense committed may be a nonpriority crime, the investigation of which—due to limitations of personnel and time—does not warrant employing the full range of technical and investigative services. For example, in one of our nation's largest cities it is reportedly a practice not to conduct any investigation beyond the preliminary stage where the property loss in a burglary is less than $2,000, unless there are promising leads. However, even when investigating a nonpriority case, officers must display a genuine interest in their work.

At the scenes of violent crimes, especially when they are interracial, emotions may run high. Even a small crowd may add considerable confusion to the process of ascertaining what has happened and along what lines the investigation should proceed. In such situations it is not unusual for witnesses to be lost, their versions and perceptions of what occurred altered by contamination through contact with the crowd, or even to find so-called witnesses added. In this last circumstance, an individual standing in the crowd may have been at, or very near to, the scene when the crime occurred, without actually viewing the offense. However, in the emotionally charged atmosphere, hearing the comments and descriptions of people standing nearby, the person suddenly and earnestly believes that he or she has something of value to share with the investigative team.

Limitations on the availability of equipment may force an investigator to use less desirable procedures or to eliminate a particular step. Police officers and supervisors occasionally make investigations more difficult, when they "drop by" to see if they can be of help when in reality they are simply curious. Too many people at the scene may lead to confusion of assignments or accidental alteration or destruction of evidence. Finally, at the scenes of major crimes, such as bank robberies and criminal homicides, members of the press typically arrive shortly after the investigation and immediately attempt to obtain information from any police officer or witness, creating no small amount of confusion and sometimes producing erroneous reports.

RULES FOR THE CRIME SCENE INVESTIGATOR

Regardless of the type of crime involved, certain fundamentals must be observed.

MAINTENANCE OF CONTROL

Without control a life might be lost, evidence destroyed, assignments overlooked, or the investigation conducted in a generally slovenly manner. Control begins with the arrival of the first officer on the scene, whose immediate responsibility is to rope off or otherwise secure the area, positioning personnel to prevent unauthorized access to the scene and covering areas or individual pieces of evidence which might be adversely affected by inclement weather. The values of life and investigative proprieties may occasionally be at odds. The inadvertent or deliberate destruction of evidence by an officer seeking to render first aid to a victim or checking for the presence of life is, under all circumstances, to be regarded as a necessary cost of fulfilling a higher duty.

The person in charge of the crime scene investigation should never allow a superior officer anxious for information, the presence of the press, or other factors to distract him or her from doing a deliberate and thorough job. In addition to the importance of control, this is necessary because the investigator is personally responsible for the operation.[4] Additional aspects of maintaining control include ensuring that: there is no unnecessary walking about the crime scene; items or surfaces likely to yield latent fingerprints are not indiscriminately picked up; and evidence to be removed from the scene is properly inventoried and taken with the knowledge and permission of the crime scene coordinator.[5]

CONCEPTUALIZATION

In processing the crime scene, it is necessary to keep both known facts and inferences in mind. This facilitates the reconstruction of the offense and identification of the perpetrator's method of operation, suggests the possible existence of certain types of physical evidence, and assists in establishing appropriate lines of inquiry. Assumptions which are made must be checked for accuracy as quickly as possible. The failure to do so may result in an offender escaping prosecution and embarrassment for the investigator and the department. It may also produce confusion in, or misdirect, the investigation. For example, a woman in a large city was murdered in her apartment. The investigators assumed that the woman's husband had thoroughly searched the apartment for their missing infant child when he first arrived and found his wife's body. Thus, they further assumed that the baby had been kidnapped. Some four days later the baby's body was found by the grandmother in the apartment under a sofa cushion.[6]

Human behavior is rich in its variety; in reconstructing the crime, investigators must be alert to the danger of imparting their own probable motives or actions to the perpetrator unless there are solid grounds for so doing. Alternately stated, this proposition dictates that simply because, under the same or a similar set of circumstances, we would not have acted in a particular fashion does not preclude the possibility that the perpetrator may have acted in that way. Two cases illustrate the importance of this point. In Woodbridge, New Jersey, a series of burglaries was cleared when it was established that two inmates had been breaking out of a correctional facility to commit the offenses, returning nightly to the facility.[7] In Palm Beach, Florida, a guard at a bank was surprised one night by an intruder who took $50,000 in gold coins. Unable to find a point of entry, investigators were puzzled until they received an anonymous tip that the intruder had shipped himself into the bank in a crate and broken out of it after the regular employees had gone home.[8]

Gross physical evidence, such as a hand gun used in a criminal homicide, is often easily found at the crime scene and requires little in the way of conceptualization; however, more minute pieces of evidence, termed trace evidence, require a very thoughtful and conceptual approach if they are to be recovered.

CAUTION

Many crime scenes provide an immediate focus and, to use the example of criminal homicide, there is a tendency to move directly to the body. Such action, where the person is obviously deceased, has a number of disadvantages. In approaching the point of focus, minute but extremely important evidence may be altered or destroyed; the area to be searched may be too rapidly defined; and other areas which might be fruitfully explored are overlooked or given only a cursory examination.

INCLUSIVENESS

The rule of inclusiveness dictates that every available piece of evidence be obtained and, where there is question as to whether a particular item constitutes evidence, to define it as such. The rationale is that mistakes made in excluding potential evidence often cannot be rectified. One cannot always return to the crime scene and recover evidence. The rule of inclusiveness also requires that standard samples and elimination prints are always obtained whenever appropriate. If, for example, a burglary has been committed and a safe inside the building successfully attacked, exposing the insulation of the safe, then standard samples of the insulation should be obtained. This will ensure that if at some future time a suspect is identified, comparisons can be made between the standard sample of safe insulation and any which might be recovered from the soles of the suspect's shoes or car floormat. Elimination prints are useful in determining whether a latent fingerprint found at a crime scene belongs to the suspect. To use the hypothetical case of a residential burglary, if a latent print were developed inside the house on the window ledge where the perpetrator entered, the residents of the household should be fingerprinted and a comparison made between the latent fingerprint and those of the residents. If the latent fingerprint does not belong to any of the residents, there is a good possibility that it belongs to the perpetrator. In some instances, the fingerprint might belong to someone having authorized access to the dwelling. In cases where this is found to be true, however, the possibility cannot be overlooked that the person with authorized access may be the perpetrator. An example of this possibility is the case of a licensed real estate dealer operating in the Washington, D.C., area who may have entered more than 100 homes that were being offered for sale, stealing furs, tape recorders, silverware, and other valuables worth between $200,000 and $300,000.[9]

DOCUMENTATION

Note taking should be a constant activity throughout the process of the investigation; everything learned during its course should be written down. The inexperienced investigator will have a tendency simply to record the basic facts of the case and indicate those steps which yielded positive results. However, even those elements of the investigation which were examined but failed to yield useful information should be recorded. The purpose of this is to establish the completeness of the investigation which, in turn, may reveal that additional investigation in a particular area may not be profitable.

Many, but not all, crime scenes must also be graphically documented using sketches and photography, so that the offense report draws upon all the sources of documentation. Like the adage "Many a good game was left on the practice field," it is also true that many excellent investigations are reduced to virtually meaningless exercises because of inadequate documentation.

TYPES OF EVIDENCE AND THEIR UTILITY

The search of the crime scene forms the main focus of the preliminary investigation. Its importance lies in the fact that ordinarily its fruits, or the lack thereof, will shape much of what occurs in the latent investigation. It can uncover several types of evidence.

CORPUS DELICTI EVIDENCE

Each criminal offense contains a distinct set of elements whose commission or omission must be demonstrated to have occurred in order to prove a case; corpus delicti evidence serves to substantiate these elements. Thus, at each crime scene the investigator must keep in mind the unique requirements of proof required and attempt to locate related evidence.

ASSOCIATIVE EVIDENCE

This type of evidence is bidirectional in that it connects the perpetrator to the scene or victim, or connects the scene or victim with the suspect; a case history illustrates this:

> A silent burglary alarm was triggered at a bar in a high-crime area. Officers responding to the scene found a point of forced entry at a rear window of the building. An individual was detected hiding in a small shed attached to the building. His statement was that when walking up the alley he suddenly saw police cars, panicked, and hid in the shed. The search of this person following his arrest revealed the presence of valuables and materials taken from the burglarized premises, connecting the suspect with the scene.

TRACING EVIDENCE

The identification or locating of the suspect are the goals of tracing evidence; corpus delicti and associative evidence may also serve these purposes:

> A 20-year-old female was at a laundromat washing her clothes. A male loitered nearby, observing her. When the woman was alone, he walked rapidly to the laundromat and entered the men's room. A few minutes later, with his pants and un-

derwear around his ankles, he approached the woman, shook his genitals at her, pulled up his clothing, and ran off. The officer who responded to the call found a man's wallet on the floor of the men's restroom. A records check on the identification contained in it revealed that the owner of the wallet had a history of sex offenses and lived in the neighborhood of the laundromat. When the victim identified the suspect from a series of photographs, a warrant for the suspect's arrest was obtained.

=== THE CRIME SCENE SEARCH ===

The purpose of the crime scene search is to obtain physical evidence useful in: establishing that, in fact, an offense has been committed; identifying the method of operation employed by the perpetrator; reducing the number of suspects; and identifying the perpetrator. Five major considerations dominate the crime scene search:

BOUNDARY DETERMINATION

The crime scene coordinator must make a decision concerning what the perimeters of the search shall be. In buildings the boundary determination is defined by the structure and is, therefore, easily established. In addition, the perpetrator must have approached the crime scene and fled from it, and these avenues must be established and searched. Here the most vexing decision is how far along the lines of approach and flight might the search profitably extend. Crimes committed in the open may require a considerable amount of attention and thought as to what the boundaries of the search pattern should be. For example, if an individual is taken into a field and murdered, it is a far different situation than if the same crime were committed in a house. As a rule, when examining an out-of-doors scene it is better to define the limits of the search in very broad terms. While this might result in some possible waste of effort due to searching a larger area than perhaps is absolutely nec-

FIGURE 3-4   The Spiral Search Pattern

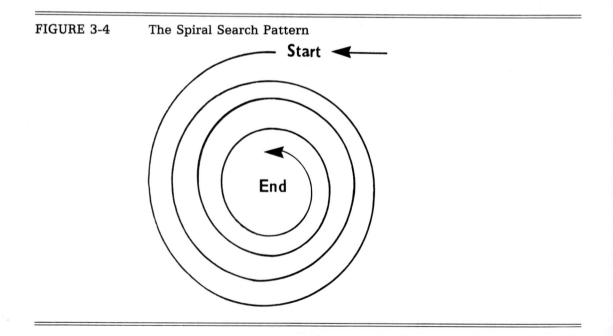

essary, it is an acceptable trade-off as more than occasionally evidence is unexpectedly encountered.

CHOICE OF SEARCH PATTERN

There are five fundamental search patterns from which the crime scene coordinator may select. The spiral, depicted in Figure 3-4, is usually employed in outdoor scenes and is normally executed by a single person. It involves the searcher's walking in slightly ever decreasing, less than concentric circles from the outermost boundary determination toward a central point. This pattern should not be operated in the reverse, i.e., beginning at some central point and working towards the perimeter of the crime scene in ever increasing less than concentric circles, as there is a real danger that some evidence may be inadvertently destroyed while walking to the central point to initiate the search. Use of the strip search, shown in Figure 3-5, involves the demarcation of a series of lanes down which one or more persons proceed. Upon reaching the starting point, the searchers proceed down their respective lanes, reverse their direction, and continue in this

fashion until the area has been thoroughly examined. If multiple searchers are being used in this method, then whenever physical evidence is encountered, all searchers should stop until it is properly handled and they have received information with respect to its nature. The search is then resumed in the fashion previously described. A variation of the strip search is the grid, depicted in Figure 3-6. After having completed the strip pattern, the searchers are doubled back perpendicularly across the area being examined. While more time-consuming than the strip search, the grid offers the advantage of being more methodical and thorough; examined from two different viewpoints, an area is more likely to yield evidence which might otherwise have been overlooked.

Figure 3-7 shows the zone search pattern, which requires an area to be divided into four large quadrants, each of which is then examined using any of the methods previously described. Where the area to be searched is particularly large, a variation of the zone would be to subdivide the larger quadrants into four smaller quadrants. The pie search pattern, also referred to as the wheel, is shown in Figure 3-8. It entails dividing the

FIGURE 3-5   The Strip Search Pattern

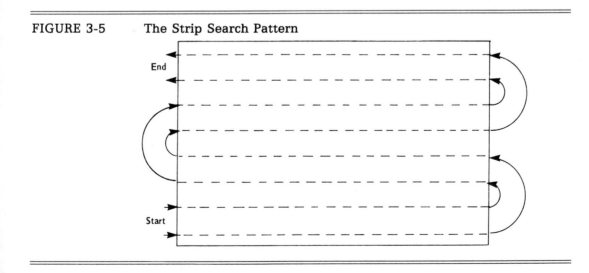

FIGURE 3-6   The Grid Search Pattern

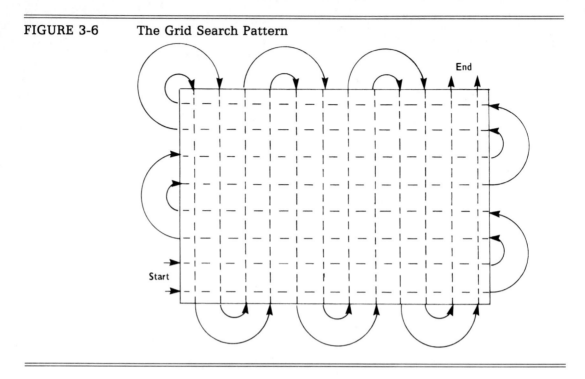

FIGURE 3-7   The Zone Search Pattern

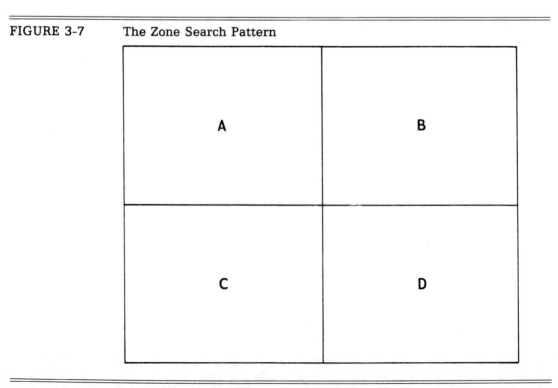

FIGURE 3-8   **The Pie or Wheel Search Pattern**

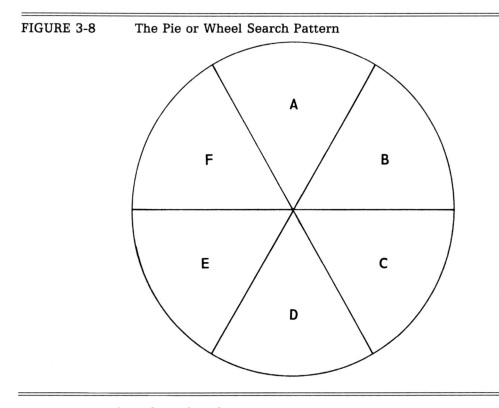

area into a number of pie-shaped sections, usually six, which are then searched, usually by a variation of the strip method.

In actual practice, both the spiral and pie or wheel search patterns are rarely employed; however, under certain unique circumstances they might profitably be employed. Where the area to be searched is not excessively large, the strip or grid patterns are normally utilized. When the crime scene is of significant size, the zone search pattern normally is used.

INSTRUCTION OF PERSONNEL

Even when the same type of criminal offense has been committed, the variation between crime scenes may be enormous. These variations are due to such factors as the physical setting, the manner and means which the perpetrators used to execute the offense, and the lengths to which they may have gone to

eliminate or destroy evidence. Thus, it is of paramount importance that the crime scene coordinator call together all those individuals who will be, in various capacities, processing the scene and share with them all of the available information concerning the case. This serves to minimize the possibility of excluding any available evidence. Upon receipt of this information, the members of the crime scene processing team may then begin their work.

COORDINATION

One of the most important responsibilities of the person in charge of the crime scene is to integrate the efforts of those assigned to the technical and investigative service functions, along with ensuring the timely flow of pertinent information. For example, if a suspect is in custody and the interrogation yields information concerning the weapon or tool which may have been used, or where it may be located, then the crime scene coordinator should rapidly relay this information to those involved in technical services at the scene so that they will be alert to specific possibilities for the recovery of physical evidence. Conversely, as significant physical evidence is recovered, the information should be conveyed to the crime scene coordinator who can then transmit it to the investigators so that they can move toward apprehending a suspect or be assisted in the interrogation of a possible perpetrator already in custody.

TERMINATION OF CRIME SCENE SEARCH

The amount of time required to process a crime scene varies considerably depending upon such variables as the amount and nature of the area to be examined, the complexity of a case, the abundance or scarcity of physical evidence, and available personnel. Once it has been established that a crime has been committed, under no circumstances should the search be terminated until all possible fruitful avenues for developing physical evidence have been thoroughly explored. Occasionally it may be necessary to suspend an operation temporarily; one of the most common situations would be that of a priority crime with evidence subject to decay requiring temporary diversion of personnel from a scene where delayed processing would not result in any loss of physical evidence. If it becomes necessary to cease the examination of one scene for a time, it should be secured in such a fashion that there is no possibility of contamination, alteration, or accidental destruction of any evidence which may exist.

THE COLLECTION AND CARE OF EVIDENCE

The location of physical evidence during the crime scene search merely marks the first step in its long odyssey toward presentation in court. To satisfy legal requirements related to its introduction in a judicial proceeding, the investigator must be able to:

1. Identify each piece of evidence, even years after it was collected
2. Describe the location and condition of the item at the time it was collected
3. Assist in establishing that, from the time of its collection until presentation in court, the evidence was continuously in proper custody
4. Assist in describing any changes which may have occurred in the evidence between the time of collection and the subsequent introduction as evidence in court.[10]

Where photography is employed, shots should be taken of each piece of evidence prior to its examination. After the photograph has been taken, or when this service is not used, the investigator may then handle and examine the article. At this time the evidence is marked; the standard practice is to place the officer's initials, shield number, and date on the article. When the article is too small to permit this, or of such a character as to prohibit it—such as narcotics evidence—or when to do so would alter its evidentiary value, for example, dislodging blood from a murder weapon, the material should be placed in a container and tape sealed, with the necessary information written across the tape in such a fashion that any opening of the container would be immediately apparent.

Very small pieces of evidence are normally placed in test tubes or pill boxes, while evidence envelopes are used for larger articles.[11] The most common evidence envelope presently in use, shown in Figure 3-9, measures nine inches by twelve inches and is manufactured from heavy kraft or manila paper. The envelope may be fastened in one or more different ways. The flap, in addition to being adhesive or gummed, may also be equipped

FIGURE 3-9   A Typical Gum-Sealed Evidence Envelope

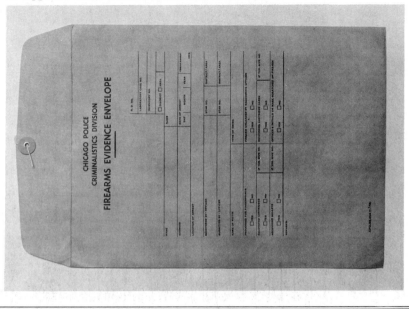

with a clamp or lock; because of their high tamper-resistant quality, envelopes equipped with lock-type seals, depicted in Figure 3-10, are used by many police agencies. The seals are pronged metallic fasteners affixed to the envelope flap, which, when the flap is folded, can be inserted into a metal receptacle at the bottom of the envelope. Once inserted, the metal prongs automatically lock into place and cannot be removed without damaging or destroying the entire device, thus making any tampering readily apparent. The locking-type envelope ordinarily has two flaps, one to which the locking seal is attached and, underneath the first flap, another which can be sealed adhesively. Figure 3-11 shows another type of evidence container, the clear polyester or plastic pouch. A container of this type is sealed by applying heat near the open end of the pouch in a manner which will cause one side of the container to adhere to the other; one important advantage is that the evidence may be viewed and handled without removing it from the container. The identifying information can be entered on a label attached to, or placed inside, the bag. As in the case of a metallic lock-type envelope, evidence cannot be removed without the action being detected. Although perhaps prohibitively costly for many agencies, an interior envelope of plastic used in conjunction with an exterior heavy envelope of a locking type represents the ultimate in evidence packaging.

Administratively, the chain of custody is the witnessed, written record of all individuals who have maintained unbroken control over the evidence since its acquisition by a police agency. It begins when an item of evidence is collected and is maintained until its final disposition. Continuous accountability is secured by maintaining this chain of custody. Each individual in the chain of custody has personal responsibility for an item of evidence, including its care and safekeeping.

Record-keeping systems and the attendant

FIGURE 3-10   Front and Reverse Side Views of a Lock Seal Evidence Envelope

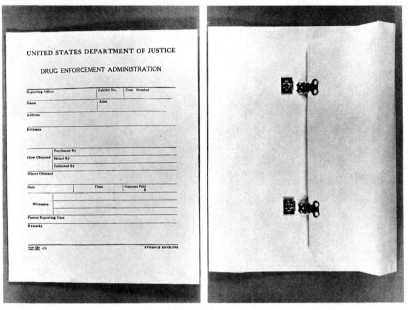

Courtesy Drug Enforcement Administration

FIGURE 3-11   Hermetically Sealed Plastic Evidence Container

Courtesy Drug Enforcement Administration

forms vary from one police agency to another. A good evidence control system will, however, embody the following characteristics:

1. Prevent loss or unauthorized release of evidence
2. Establish and maintain a continuous chain of custody
3. Establish custodial responsibility for evidence
4. List, identify, and indicate the location of items held in custody
5. Require a supervisor's approval before evidence is released
6. Identify the individual to whom evidence is released
7. Indicate the reasons for any release of evidence
8. Provide documented proof that the evidence release is authorized, and indicate its final disposition[12]

Investigators should not regard such requirements as administrative decisions beyond the purview of their concern; being in an excellent position to observe the inner workings of the system, they can help identify actual or potential deficiencies and recommend improvements. In the absence of a workable records system supported by uncomplicated forms, the security of evidence is considerably weakened, the chain of custody is in danger of being severed, and the opportunity is created for mishandling, tampering, stealing, or accidental loss of physical evidence.

SUBMISSION OF EVIDENCE TO THE LABORATORY

Evidence submitted to the crime laboratory for examination is most often transmitted by courier, air express, registered mail, or railway express. Ideally, a member of the investigative team intimately familiar with the details of the case personally conveys the evidence to the laboratory. As a practical matter, the method of transmittal is determined by two factors: the nature of the evidence and the urgency with which results must be obtained. Certain types of materials cannot be transmitted through the mail. For example, Interstate Commerce Commission regulations and various state and local provisions shape the conditions under which explosive or flammable materials may be transported. Where chemicals, blasting caps, or similar materials are to be sent to the laboratory, it is sound procedure to advise the laboratory and to get instructions from the laboratory before the actual transmittal.

The laboratory must be provided with certain information if it is to make an intelligent and complete examination. Ordinarily this includes:

Administrative Data

1. The identity of the subject under investigation
2. The name of the victim or complainant
3. The nature of the offense and its date of commission
4. The location at which the offense occurred
5. The case number assigned by the agency submitting the material for examination

Summary of Facts

- This information includes a synopsis of the case; often a copy of the crime report is included.

A List of Articles Submitted and Examinations Requested

- So that the laboratory examiners can perform their work rapidly and return the results to the requesting agency, a list of requested examinations should be included. For example, the agency may ask whether the bullet contained in the submission as Exhibit A was fired from the revolver labeled Exhibit B.

Miscellaneous Information

- Such matters as the identity of the officer to whom the laboratory report should be directed, to whom the evidence should be returned, the inclusion of pertinent photographs, and, where applicable, the degree of urgency for rapid processing, as in the case of a suspect's being held in custody pending findings in the report, all are miscellaneous information.

The proper packaging of evidence is depicted in Figure 3-12. Great care must be exercised in the packaging of evidence in order to prevent breakage or other accidental destruction while in transit and to avoid the contamination of one piece of evidence by another. Also, it should be noted that evidence pertaining to several different cases should not be included in the same package; each case should always be submitted separately.

SKETCHING THE CRIME SCENE

Sketches are useful during questioning, in preparing the offense report, and in presenting information in court.[13] The sketch complements the photographs and notes made during the crime scene search. It has the communication value of any illustration with the additional advantage that unnecessary detail can be eliminated to portray the essential elements of the scene and their relationships. Several techniques may be used to establish the location of evidence and other important items on a sketch. It is important to remember that the purpose of the sketch is to portray the information accurately, but not necessarily artistically; the investigator need not have any artistic ability to draft an adequate sketch.

BASIC EQUIPMENT

Although any type of paper may be used in preparing a crime scene sketch, plain, unlined paper is adequate, and graph paper is best. The following basic equipment should be available for producing the sketch:

1. One 50-foot steel tape
2. Several thumbtacks to hold one end of the tape when an investigator is working alone
3. One straightedge, preferably 18 inches long
4. One 8- or 12-foot steel tape for ancillary measurements

Additional equipment which is useful, but not essential, includes a T-square, several templates for easy drawing of curves, special symbols and related figures, two plastic triangles of different angles, and a compass for making circles. An infrequently used but occasionally helpful item is a magnetic compass.

INFORMATION TO BE INCLUDED IN THE SKETCH

The items of information which are essential in a crime scene sketch are listed below. The list is not comprehensive in the sense that it restricts the investigating officer's judgment as to what might be included. The major constraint on detail in sketching is that the result must be easily intelligible to the viewer without detailed study. If too much detail is included, a major advantage of the sketch over the photograph is lost. The sketch should include at least the following information:

1. The investigator's full name, rank, and shield number
2. The date, time, crime classification, and case number
3. The full name of any person assisting in taking measurements
4. The address of the crime scene, its lo-

FIGURE 3-12   **Proper Sealing of Evidence**

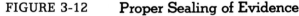

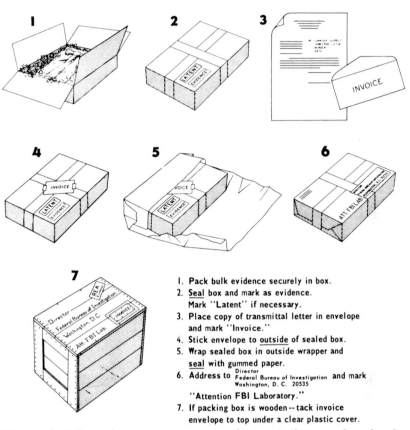

1. **Pack** bulk evidence securely in box.
2. **Seal** box and mark as evidence.
   Mark "Latent" if necessary.
3. **Place** copy of transmittal letter in envelope
   and mark "Invoice."
4. **Stick** envelope to <u>outside</u> of sealed box.
5. **Wrap** sealed box in outside wrapper and
   <u>seal</u> with gummed paper.
6. **Address** to Director Federal Bureau of Investigation and mark Washington, D. C. 20535
   "Attention FBI Laboratory."
7. **If** packing box is wooden -- tack invoice
   envelope to top under a clear plastic cover.

The method shown here permits access to the invoice letter without breaking the inner seal. This allows the person entitled to receive the evidence to receive it in a sealed condition just as it was packed by the sender.

Courtesy Federal Bureau of Investigation

cation within a building, landmarks, and compass direction

5. The scale of the drawing, if a scale drawing has been made. When a scale drawing has not been made, the sketch should include a notation: "Not to scale, dimensions and distances tape measured."

6. The major items of physical evidence and the critical features of the crime scene along with the location of such items, indicated by accurate measurements from at least two fixed points, or by other methods discussed later in this chapter

7. A legend of the symbols used to identify objects or points of interest on the sketch. Color may be used to distinguish objects or features; however, the use of large numbers of colors may be confusing

and eliminates the ability to reproduce the sketch rapidly.

SOME GENERAL CONSIDERATIONS INVOLVED IN CRIME SCENE SKETCHING

It is critical that measurements shown on the sketch be as accurate as possible and that they be made and recorded uniformly; if one aspect is inaccurate, such as the dimensions of a field in which a body was found, the distortion introduced renders the sketch relatively useless. The coordinate distances of an item in the sketch must be measured in the same manner; one coordinate leg should not be paced and the other measured. It is also a poor practice to pace off a distance and then show it on the sketch expressed in feet and inches. Such an indication connotes a greater degree of accuracy than actually exists. If the point arose in court, such an inconsistency would significantly detract from the value of the sketch. An erroneous measurement in a drawing, once discovered, is difficult to explain, and can frequently introduce doubt as to the competency of the entire investigation.

===== SKETCHING METHODS =====

This section deals with various techniques which can be employed to prepare sketches, particularly the methods which can be used to establish the location of evidence and other important items.

COORDINATE METHOD

This technique involves measuring the distance of an object from two fixed points. One form of the coordinate method uses a baseline which is drawn between two known points. The baseline may also be a wall or be drawn as the mathematical center of a room, the exact dimensions of which are known. The measurements of a given object are then taken from left to right along the baseline to a point at right angles to the object which is to be plotted. This distance is indicated on the sketch by a number, and the object is indicated by a corresponding number in the legend. Figure 3-13 illustrates this method, which is the simplest form of a sketch, namely the two-dimensional presentation of the scene as if viewed directly from above, using numbers keyed to descriptions of the items located in it. Figure 3-13 incorporates the full range of information essential to a proper sketch; however, this is omitted from subsequent diagrams to avoid needless repetition.

TRIANGULATION METHOD

This method, illustrated by Figure 3-14, is particularly useful in an outdoor situation where there are no easily identifiable edges of fields or roads for use as baselines. Two or more widely separated reference points are located, and the item of interest is located by measuring along a straight line from each of the reference points.

CROSS-PROJECTION METHOD

Depicted in Figure 3-15, the cross-projection method is useful when the items or locations of interest are on or in the walls as well as elsewhere in an enclosed space. The walls, windows, and doors in a cross-projection sketch are drawn as though the walls had been folded flat on the floor. The measurements from a given point on the floor to the wall then are indicated.

"ROUGH" AND "SMOOTH" SKETCHES

A rough sketch is one drawn by the investigator at the scene of the crime. Changes should not be made after the investigator

FIGURE 3-13   Baseline or Coordinate Method of Sketching

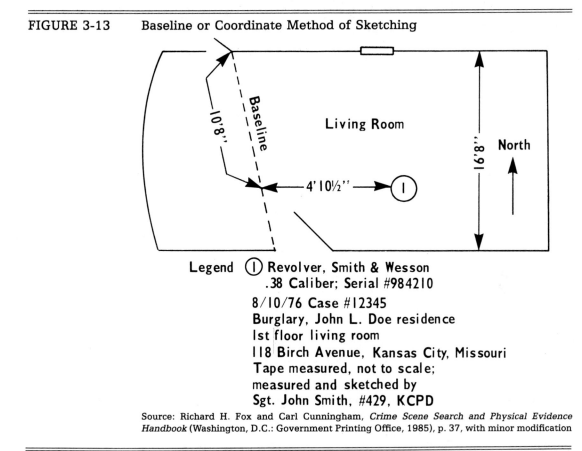

Legend (I) Revolver, Smith & Wesson
.38 Caliber; Serial #984210
8/10/76 Case #12345
Burglary, John L. Doe residence
1st floor living room
118 Birch Avenue, Kansas City, Missouri
Tape measured, not to scale;
measured and sketched by
Sgt. John Smith, #429, KCPD

Source: Richard H. Fox and Carl Cunningham, *Crime Scene Search and Physical Evidence Handbook* (Washington, D.C.: Government Printing Office, 1985), p. 37, with minor modification

leaves the scene. The rough is not drawn to scale but indicates accurate distances and dimensions. To eliminate excessive detail, it may be necessary to prepare more than one sketch. For example, one sketch may be devoted to the position of the victim's body and a limited number of critical evidence items. Additional sketches might depict the location of other evidence with respect to the point of entry or other critical areas.

The smooth sketch is simply one that is finished, frequently being drawn to scale using information contained in the rough sketch. In a scaled diagram, the numbers concerning distances can be eliminated; if the smooth sketch is not drawn to scale, these distances must be shown. The person preparing the rough sketch must verify the accuracy of the final product whenever the smooth sketch is drafted by someone else.

PHOTOGRAPHING THE CRIME SCENE

The statement "One picture is worth a thousand words" may or may not be true; it is certain, however, that good photography is an invaluable asset in documenting crime scenes. Investigative photographs are those which are made to record an object or event, or to clarify a point which is related to a particular investigation. A number of pictures are taken in crime laboratories and constitute investigative photographs; for the purposes at hand, treatment shall be limited to

FIGURE 3-14   The Triangulation Location Method

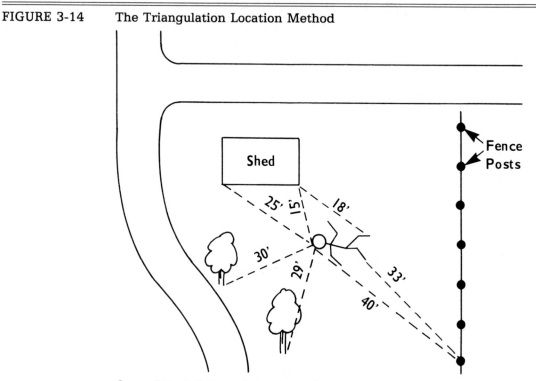

Shed

Fence
Posts

Source: Richard H. Fox and Carl Cunningham, *Crime Scene Search and Physical Evidence Handbook* (Washington, D.C.: Government Printing Office, 1985), p. 39, with minor modification

those taken at the crime scene. Comprehensive photographic coverage of a crime scene is possible without great expertise; the handling and use of cameras and associated equipment is not a topic of this section. Instead, the purpose is to provide an overview of those matters relating to photographic coverage of a crime scene and the use of photographs.

GENERAL CONSIDERATIONS

Time is an essential factor and photography may preempt other aspects of the investigation. Objects must not be moved until they have been photographed from all necessary angles. As there are situations in which the object of interest undergoes significant change with the passage of time, photo-

graphic equipment must be in a constant state of readiness.

The camera position for all exposures may be recorded on the crime scene sketches or in the offense report from notes made at the scene. Photographs of interior scenes, intended to depict the area as a whole, should be taken as overlapping segments moving in one direction around the room or area. In making such photographs, it is best to have the camera at about eye level unless a tripod is used.

The most important element in crime scene photography is maintaining perspective. Proper photographic perspective produces the same impression of relative position and size of objects as when they are viewed with the naked eye. Any significant distortion in the perspective will reduce, or

FIGURE 3-15   **The Cross-Projection Sketch Method**

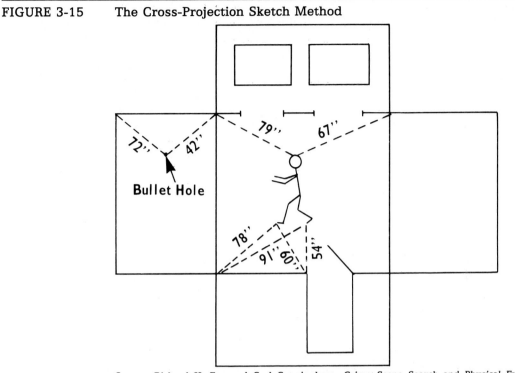

Bullet Hole

Source: Richard H. Fox and Carl Cunningham, *Crime Scene Search and Physical Evidence Handbook* (Washington, D.C.: Government Printing Office, 1985), p. 40, with minor modification

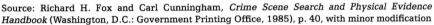

destroy altogether, the evidentiary value of a photograph.

CRITICAL PHOTOGRAPHIC REQUIREMENTS

Using a criminal homicide committed in a house as an example, the following represent the essential photographs which must be taken:

1. The line of approach to, and flight from, the scene
2. Significant adjacent areas, such as the yard of the house in which the homicide occurred
3. Close-up photographs of the entrance and exit to the house used by the suspect or those most likely to have been used if these are not obvious
4. A general scenario photograph showing the location of the body and its position in relation to the room in which it was found
5. At least two photographs of the body, at 90-degree angles to each other, with the camera positioned as high as possible, pointing downward toward the body
6. As many close-ups of the body as needed to show wounds or injuries, weapons lying near the body, and the immediate surroundings
7. The area underneath the body and under each item of evidence immediately after its removal, if there is any mark, stain, or other apparent alteration produced by the presence of the body or evidence
8. All blood stains, preferably in color film
9. All latent fingerprints before they are lifted and the weapons on which the

prints were found, showing its relationship to the general surroundings. Latent fingerprints likely to be destroyed by lifting always must be photographed, even when it is not standard practice to shoot all fingerprints before handling.

ADMISSIBILITY OF PHOTOGRAPHS AS EVIDENCE

Photographs are admissible in court if testimony can establish that they accurately depict the scene. The accuracy of the photograph always relates to the degree to which it represents the appearance of the subject matter as to form, tone, color, and scale. The use of a lens that will record objects and areas in focus may not always portray correct distances between objects or reproduce them with the proper perspective. In such situations, the crime scene sketch and field notes take on added importance.

Usually the negative is considered suffi-

cient proof to refute any allegation that a photograph has been altered. However, if enlarged photographs are made for presentation in court, a contact print without borders should also be made. Because of the importance of scale, distances, and perspective in interpreting the photographs taken at crime scenes, it is good procedure to include a ruler or other scale measurement in the photograph, when this is practical. However, because some courts have not allowed even this minor modification of the scene, an identical photograph without the scale indicator should also be taken.

If the photograph is to have the highest quality as evidence, it must depict the scene, persons, or objects precisely as they were found. Therefore, the photograph must depict the crime scene exclusively. No people should be working within the scene at the time, nor should extraneous objects, such as police equipment, be included.

QUESTIONS

1. What is a crime scene?
2. What are the major crime scene functions?
3. At the scene of a crime, what are some typical problems which may be encountered?
4. Of what importance is crime scene control?
5. What does the rule of inclusiveness dictate?
6. Identify and give examples of the three types of evidence.
7. What are the purposes of a crime scene search?
8. What five considerations dominate a crime scene search?

9. Identify the five crime scene search patterns.
10. What are the characteristics of a good evidence control system?
11. By what means may evidence be submitted to a crime laboratory, and which two factors shape the choice of which method to use?
12. What information should accompany evidence submitted for laboratory examination?
13. Distinguish between rough and smooth sketches.

NOTES

1. A number of texts contain similar statements; for example, see Paul L. Kirk, *Crime Investigation* (New York: Interscience, 1960), p. 4.

2. In this regard see Joseph L. Peterson et al., *Crime Laboratory Proficiency Testing Research Program* (Washington, D.C.: Government Printing Office, 1978).

3. For information on how the frequency with which physical evidence is found varies by type of crime, see Brian Parker and Joseph Peterson, *Physical Evidence Utilization in the Administration of Justice* (Washington, D.C.: Government Printing Office, 1972).

4. Arne Svensson and Otto Wendel, *Techniques of Crime Scene Investigation* (New York: American Elsevier, 1965), p. 15.

5. Richard H. Fox and Carl L. Cunningham, *Crime Scene Search and Physical Evidence Handbook* (Washington, D.C.: Government Printing Office, 1985), pp. 12–13.

6. Bill Berkeley, "Wrong Assumptions Ruined Probe," *The Atlanta Journal*, February 17, 1982, pp. 1-A and 13-A.

7. "But Some Have Ins and Outs," *St. Petersburg* (Florida) *Times*, February 24, 1979, p. 1A.

8. "Man Accused of Shipping Self to Bank," *The Atlanta Journal*, May 10, 1979, p. 18A.

9. "Real Estate Agent Pleads Guilty to 5 'Lock Box' Thefts," *The Washington Post*, September 12, 1978, p. B5.

10. Fox and Cunningham, *Crime Scene Search and Physical Evidence Handbook*, p. 14.

11. The description of the various evidence envelopes is taken from Drug Enforcement Administration and International Association of Chiefs of Police, *Guidelines for Narcotic and Dangerous Drug Evidence Handling and Security Procedures* (1975), p. 4.

12. Ibid., pp. 57–58.

13. The material on sketching and photography is taken, with modification, from *Crime Scene Search and Physical Evidence Handbook*, pp. 35–43, by permission.

4

PHYSICAL EVIDENCE

CLASS VERSUS INDIVIDUAL CHARACTERISTICS

To fully appreciate the potential value of physical evidence, the investigator must understand the difference between class and individual characteristics. When the characteristics of physical evidence are common to a group of objects or persons, they may be termed *class*. Regardless of how thoroughly examined, such evidence can be placed only into a broad category; an individual identification cannot be made because there is a possibility of more than one source for the evidence.[1] Examples of this type of evidence include hair, soil, glass fragments too small to be matched to broken edges, and tool marks or shoeprints in instances where microscopic or accidental markings are insufficient for positive individual identification.[2] Evidence with *individual characteristics* can be identified as originating with a particular person or source. The ability to establish individuality distinguishes this type of physical evidence from that possessing only class characteristics. Among the best illustrations of evidence with individual characteristics are finger, palm, and footprints.

Conceptually, the distinction between class and individual characteristics is clear. But as a practical matter, the crime scene technician or investigator often may not be able to make this differentiation and must rely on the results yielded by crime laboratory examination. For example, a shoeprint collected at one scene may yield only class characteristics: left by a man's shoe of a particular brand from the left foot and of such newness as to yield no individual markings. However, Figure 4-1 illustrates a situation in which a heelprint yielded not only class characteristics but also individual ones. Thus, while the investigator must recognize that physical evidence which allows for individualization is of more value, for no reason should he or she disdain evidence which appear to offer only class characteristics, as these may yield individual characteristics through laboratory examination. Furthermore, a preponderance of class characteristic evidence tying a suspect or tools in the suspect's possession to the scene strengthens the case for prosecution; it should also be noted that occasionally class characteristic evidence may be of such an unusual nature that it has value much greater than that ordinarily associated with evidence of this type. In an Alaska case a suspect was apprehended in the general area

FIGURE 4-1

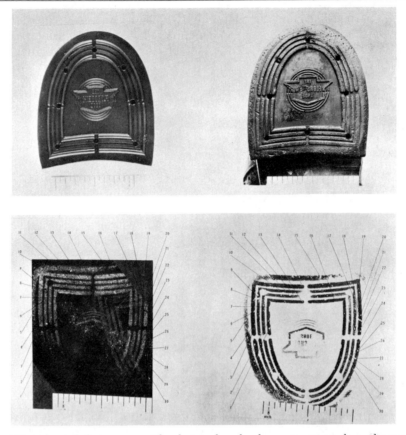

The upper left is a new Florsheim shoe heel representing class characteristics while the upper right is a shoe heel of a suspect, incorporating both class and individual characteristics. The lower left is a shoe heel print left on a piece of carbon paper at the scene of a burglary while the lower right is an inked print of the suspect's shoe heel, indicating positive identification as the donor of the print on the carbon paper.

where a burglary had been committed; the pry bar found in his possession contained white stucco which was of considerable importance, as the building burglarized was the only white stucco building in that town.[3]

SOIL

Combinations of particles of earth materials—soils, rocks, minerals, and fossils—occurring by themselves or in conjunction with contamination by other types of minute debris may serve a variety of critical functions.[4] For example, while soil is class characteristic evidence, it may be useful in establishing the presence of a suspect at the scene and sustaining or destroying an alibi.[5]

A man was arrested and charged with the beating death of a young girl. The scene of the crime was a construction site adjacent to a newly poured concrete wall. The soil was sand, which had been transported to the scene for construction purposes. As such, it had received additional mixing during the moving and construction process and was quite distinctive. The glove of the suspect contained sand that was similar to that found at the scene and significantly different in composition and particle size from the area of the suspect's home. This was important because the suspect claimed the soil on the gloves came from his garden.[6]

An elderly woman was robbed and murdered in a Washington, D.C., park and her body was found under a park bench. Within a short time, a suspect was apprehended as a result of a description given by a witness who had seen the person leaving the park on the night of the murder. It was obvious that the suspect had been involved in a struggle and had soil adhering to his clothing and inside his trouser cuffs. He claimed to have been in a fight in another part of the city and gave the location of the fight. Study of the soil near the park bench and of that collected from the scene of the alleged fight revealed that the soil from the suspect's clothing was similar to soil near the park bench but did not compare favorably with samples from the area of the described fight. These comparisons strongly suggested that the suspect had been in contact with the ground in that area and cast strong doubt on his statement that he had not been in the park for years.

Furthermore, the lack of similarity between the clothing soil samples and those from the area in which he claimed to have been fighting questioned the validity of his alibi.[7]

Thus although soil is class characteristic evidence, its specificity can approach the level of individual characterization:

In a rape case, the knees of the suspect's trousers contained encrusted soil samples; the sample from the right knee was different from that collected from the left. In examining the crime scene, two impressions were found in the soil corresponding to a right and left knee; samples taken from these two impressions were different. The soil sample from the left knee impression compared with that removed from the left trouser knee of the suspect as did the right knee impression and the right trouser knee soils. The significant difference in soil type between the two knee impressions and their consistency with samples obtained from the suspect's trousers strongly indicated his presence at the scene.[8]

LOCATING AND HANDLING SOIL EVIDENCE

"Soil and rock evidence is most likely to be obtained when the crime is committed out of doors or when the suspect was required to drive or to walk on unpaved areas."[9] Offenders may pick up soil or rock particles from crime scenes and retain them in the cracks or heels of their shoes or cuffs. Suspects also may deposit on floors or paved areas soil particles which were picked up outside of the area of the crime.

It is important to collect soil samples that may have been dislodged from the undercarriage of a vehicle at the scene of a crime. Such evidence may be particularly valuable when the clothing of a victim of a hit and run accident retains particles from the striking vehicle. In an unusual case, a solid soil crust approximately the shape of a triangle, about three inches on each side, was recovered at the scene. Subsequently, when the suspect and the vehicle were identified, it was found the triangular piece fitted exactly into an area on the underside of the vehicle.

Once shoe or tire impressions have been photographed and a cast made, samples of the soil should be collected from the impression.[10] Then additional samples should be systematically obtained from the area around the first sample; the areas chosen for these additional samples should be measured with respect to their relationship to the impression and the information documented in a sketch (see Figure 4-2).[11] Ordinarily soil samples are gathered from the first one-quarter inch of soil in an amount of about three table-

spoons.[12] The spoon or other similar item used to collect the samples must be carefully cleaned between each gathering to eliminate the likelihood of contamination. If there is to be any delay in transmitting moist soil samples to the crime laboratory, they should be spread on separate pieces of nonabsorbent paper and allowed to air dry to avoid the formation of mold. Subsequently, they should be placed in separate pill boxes or Mason-type jars and sealed.

Where soil samples have been gathered at the scene of the crime and a suspect subsequently identified, the suspect's shoes and garments should be seized and forwarded to the laboratory for examination, ensuring in the packaging that there is no possibility of cross-contamination. Additionally, it is desirable to process the floor of the interior of the suspect's vehicle, if any, in an attempt to

---

FIGURE 4-2   **Method of Collecting Soil Samples from Foot and Tire Impressions and from the Surrounding Area**

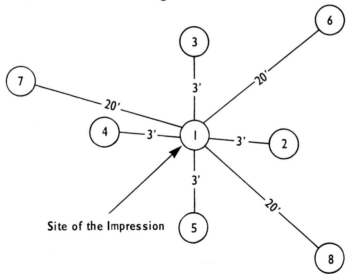

The numbers in the figure suggest the sampling sequence.

Source: Richard H. Fox and Carl Cunningham, *Crime Scene Search and Physical Evidence Handbook* (Washington, D.C.: Government Printing Office, 1985), p. 82, with minor modification

locate samples. If, however, the floor board of the vehicle has not been cleaned in some time and represents an accumulation of material, then the results are not likely to be conclusive. The comparison of soil materials obtained at the scene of a crime with material collected from a dirty floor board is roughly analogous to the attempted comparison of the fibers of a jacket found at the scene of a crime with the floor sweepings from a clothing store.[13] Despite limitations such as this, the investigator must never fail to realize the potential import of soil as evidence.

COLLECTING SHOEPRINT AND IMPRESSION EVIDENCE

Shoeprints are formed on a hard base when the sole, contaminated by foreign matter such as dust or blood, is placed on a hard, smooth surface.[14] Shoe or tireprints should first be photographed before any attempt is made to recover them. If the print is on a movable surface, such as a piece of paper, it should be collected and preserved in such a manner that there is no danger of its rubbing off. If, however, the print is on a surface which cannot be removed, it will be necessary to lift it. Several techniques are employed.[15] One method is to lay individual strips of fingerprint lifting tape, which overlap by about one-quarter inch, starting at one edge and rolling them forward over the shoe or tireprint, keeping out air bubbles, which would cause distortions. It is not necessary to dust or otherwise treat the print when it is obtained in this manner. Photographic film may also be used to lift prints. Clear film, for lifting dark prints, is made by fixing and washing; dark film, for lifting light-colored

FIGURE 4-3   Tireprint left on the trousers of the victim struck by an automobile in a hit-and-run offense.

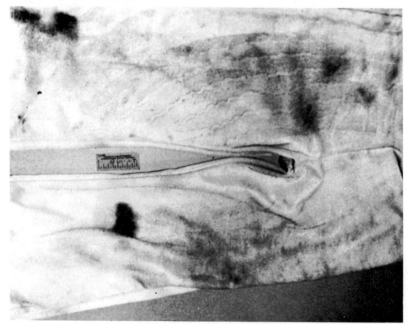

prints, is made by exposing, developing, fixing, and washing. In both cases the film is subsequently placed in water, wiped off, and allowed to dry until tacky. The tacky film is them applied to the print; the moistened gelatin on the film forms an excellent lifting surface. When applying the tacky film to the print, a roller should be used starting at one edge and moving along the print, using care to avoid the formation of air bubbles. Prints lifted in this fashion should be handled and packaged carefully to ensure that they are not subjected to accidental erasure.

In contrast to prints, shoe or tire impressions occur when the subject treads in some moldable material, such as earth or clay (see Figure 4-4).[16] As in the case of prints, impressions should first be photographed from directly overhead, the camera lens held parallel to the surface being photographed.

Traditionally police departments have used a good grade of plaster of paris to cast shoe or tire impressions in earth. While it is inexpensive and readily available, in recent years other products have been found to be more suitable for such casts and there has been some movement away from using plaster of paris.[17] However, because of its continued widespread popularity and use, the proper employment of plaster of paris is described here.

The first step is the removal of all foreign materials such as grass, leaves, or twigs; however, this should be done only in those cases where they are not actually embedded in the impression. Regardless of whether the impression is in a firm surface such as clay or in loose soil, it is necessary to spray it with shellac, colorless acrylic lacquer, or even hair spray from an aerosol can. In the case of impressions in fairly solid materials, this will allow for the preservation of the finer details, and in sand or loose soil it is required to prevent shifting when the plaster of paris is applied. The surface being cast should receive two coats of spray with sufficient time

for drying allowed in between applications; when applying the spray, the can should be held far enough away from the surface to avoid disturbing any of the minute details by the force of the aerosol. After the second coat of spray has dried, a light coat of talcum powder should be laid on the impression; this facilitates removing the shell formed by the spray without danger of damaging the cast. At this juncture a frame is constructed around the impression to be cast; it should rise approximately three inches above the surface of the impression being cast and extend at least two inches beyond its outer edges. While any of a number of materials, such as cardboard, may be used, strips of aluminum, ordinarily used for gardening purposes around plants and shrubbery, are most easily employed.

Generally, approximately one quart of plaster and a similar amount of water are sufficient to cast a foot impression. The plaster must be dry and free from lumps and granules.[18] The type of container in which to mix the plaster of paris should be considered; if the container is to be used again, then a rubber bowl is best suited as it will clean easily; however, if this is not a factor, any container free of contaminations—such as a coffee can—is acceptable. The plaster of paris should be slowly added to the water by sprinkling it onto the surface and stirring it in until the mixture of plaster of paris and water achieves a consistency of pancake batter. While the stirring must go on continuously and evenly to get it to mix, care must be taken to avoid stirring so energetically that air bubbles form which, when poured on the impression, would fail to incorporate details.

The plaster of paris mixture must be placed rapidly onto the surface being cast; otherwise one portion may begin to dry before the plaster of paris evenly covers the impression, forming lap marks which could eliminate individual identifying marks. The plaster of paris should either be spooned out,

FIGURE 4-4   Shoe impressions left in the safe insulation at the scene of a burglary

Courtesy Tampa, Florida, Police Department

using a large cooking type utensil, or poured slowly from the container onto some instrument such as a spoon which is held just above the surface, gently breaking the fall of the plaster of paris from the container onto the surface. At the time the impression is covered with plaster of paris to a depth of about one-half inch, it is necessary to reinforce it; the best means is by laying down a wire mesh. In no case should dry sticks be used, as they have a capacity to absorb the water in the plaster of paris, thereby creating the danger of cracking the cast. Once reinforced, an additional one to one and one-half inches of plaster should be added to complete the process. Ordinarily, in a shoe impression, where the plaster of paris has been applied to the depth indicated, the time for drying will not exceed thirty to forty minutes. While the plaster is damp, identifying data should be scratched into it. After the cast has dried, the frame may be removed and the cast recovered by digging the earth material away from its sides. Even considering the fact that the crime scene technician or investigator has reinforced the cast, it is a relatively fragile item and should be handled with caution. The removal of debris from the bottom portion of the cast should wait until the next day, when it may be gently washed away. In packing the cast, care should be taken to minimize the danger of breakage in transit to the crime laboratory.

PAINT

Ordinarily, paint is class characteristic evidence, although circumstances may combine to make it individual. It will be encountered in one of three different states: chips from dried paint, smears from fresh or "chalking" paint, or in either of the two previous states intact on objects of evidence.[19] Examination of paint evidence is conducted chemically, spectrographically, and microscopically with the important variables in identification being shades of color, chemical composition, and the number of coats. Paints such as synthetic lacquers, which contain no metallic constituents, are difficult to identify, but chemical examination under favorable conditions may yield meaningful results.[20]

While paint evidence may be found in a variety of crimes, it is commonly encountered in breaking and entering and hit-and-run offenses (see Figure 4-5). Of particular evidentiary value are samples which have received several different coats of paint and those recovered in chip form, allowing for the possibility of a fracture match. The Federal Bureau of Investigation maintains the National Automotive Paint File, consisting of paint panels from automobile manufacturers which are representative of the original finishes on cars at the time of manufacture. Thus, paint recovered from the victim or at the scene of a hit-and-run may be particularly useful in the investigative process as the year and make of the car involved may be determinable.[21] Samples of paint at the point of forced entry in a breaking and entering should be recovered as there is the possibility that matching layered paint or fracture matches may be obtained from samples recovered from a suspect's trouser cuffs, shoes, or tools.

In no case should paint chips or particles be collected with scotch tape or mounted on a card using this material, as it makes separation in the laboratory difficult without damage. Similarly, small particles should not be placed in cotton as it is difficult to separate them. Paint evidence should be placed in an envelope protected by some type of soft wrapping. Samples of paint should be obtained from a vehicle or at the point of entry of breaking and entering by chipping down to the bare wood or metal surface. "Scraped off samples of paint are almost useless for comparison purposes."[22] Where it is particularly difficult to gather paint samples, a small por-

FIGURE 4-5

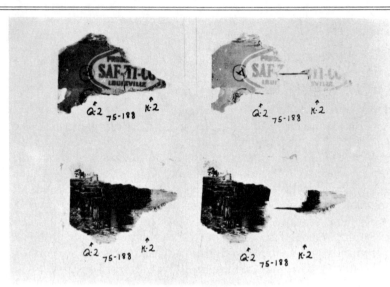

Case 75-188 represents paneling recovered from the crime scene of a hit and run accident. Specimen Q-2 was a painted plywood chip found at the scene of the hit and run. It gave a positive physical match with specimen K-2. Specimen K-2 was removed from the suspect's vehicle. The bottom two photographs represent the reverse slides of the top two photographs.

Courtesy Kentucky State Police

tion of the surface to which the paint has adhered should be cut or chipped off.

GLASS

"One of the most important types of physical evidence, which is frequently overlooked by the investigator, is glass; its evidentiary value lies in the fact that there are thousands of different formulae used in the manufacturing of glass."[23] While ordinarily class characteristic evidence, glass has high evidentiary value because of the variations in density, refractive index, and light dispersion characteristics.[24] Additionally, where the fragments are sufficiently large to allow for a fracture match, glass may assume individuality. Most commonly this will occur in hit-

and-run cases where a piece of the headlight lens found at the scene or embedded in the victim's body or clothing matches a missing portion of lens from a suspect's vehicle (see Figure 4-6). Before the accident, cleaning or other actions may create surface striations on the headlight lens. Along with a fracture match, these further strengthen the condition of individuality.

Glass, too, is a common form of evidence, particularly at the scenes of burglaries where a window has been the point of entry. When a suspect is apprehended soon after the commission of an offense, his or her clothing should be carefully examined for minute traces of glass evidence. Although they may be so small as to permit only the conclusion that they are consistent with samples obtained at the scene, this conclusion can strengthen the case for prosecution. A per-

FIGURE 4-6   Glass Fracture Match of Headlight Lens

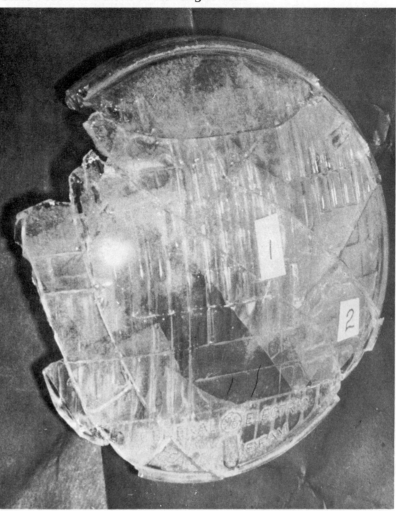

Pieces 1 and 2 were recovered at the scene of a hit and run automobile accident. The remaining pieces were obtained from the grille and light housing of the suspect's vehicle.

Courtesy Regional Criminalistics Laboratory, Metropolitan Kansas City, Missouri

petrator also may have committed a burglary and still have pieces of glass large enough to provide for fracture matches. A case history illustrates this possibility:

Walking a beat in a downtown business section in the late evening hours, a uni-

formed officer heard an alarm go off and saw an individual round the corner and run toward him at full speed. Upon seeing the officer, the individual started to double back the other way, then stopped. As the officer approached, the man started to flee, but stopped upon

FIGURE 4-7   **Bullet Holes Found in Window**

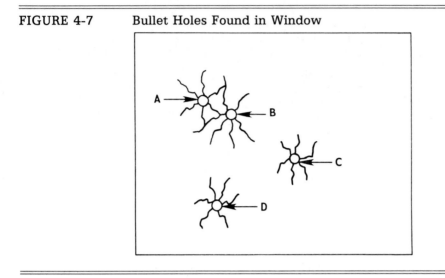

being commanded to do so. The man then told the officer that he had observed two people standing in front of a jewelry store window take a brick from a shopping bag and throw it through the window. Upon seeing this, the person related that he became frightened and ran. Subsequent investigation revealed that the person who had rounded the corner was in fact the perpetrator of the offense and that he had fled before obtaining any material from the display window because a lookout had seen a police car responding to a call in an adjacent block and had given warning. Processing of the perpetrator's clothing revealed pieces of glass in the cuff of his pants sufficiently large to make fracture matches with glass at the scene.

Glass evidence should be packed in a rigid container to prevent breakage. Glass evidence found in separate areas should be packaged separately. For example, in a burglary where a window has been the point of attack, the glass found on the floor inside the broken window should be packaged separately from that found on the ground outside and that, in turn, should be kept separate from any remaining in the frame of the broken window.[25]

It is essential that the crime scene technician and investigator understand the ways in which glass reacts to force.[26] Often this knowledge is critical in determining whether a crime has been committed and in establishing the credibility of statements given by parties at the scene. A case history illustrates this:

Police were called to a residence where the occupant alleged that while standing in his living room he was suddenly fired upon by someone standing outside the window. The occupant further related that he immediately fell to the floor and crawled to a desk in which a handgun was kept and after a short period of time stood up, when second and third shots were fired from outside the building. The complainant stated he could clearly see the person and, in turn, fired one shot. The perpetrator identified by the complainant lived a short distance away and was at home when contacted by the police. The alleged suspect maintained that he was walking by the home of the complainant, with whom there had been a history of ill feelings, and was suddenly fired upon three times, but admitted firing one shot in return.

Figure 4-7 illustrates the bullet holes found in the window by the police. An examination of this figure reveals that shot B preceded shot A, as the radial fractures created by the former stop those created by the latter. However, we know nothing of the relationship from examination of Figure 4-7 of holes C and D. However, as suggested in Figure 4-8, it is possible to determine the direction from which a bullet penetrated glass: on the side opposite the surface of initial impact, there will be a characteristic cone-shaped area. In the case being illustrated, shots A, B, and D all contained a cone-shaped characteristic on the inside of the window, indicating that these three shots had been fired from the outside. Shot C had the cone-shaped area on the outside, revealing that it had been fired from inside the house. Thus the physical evidence substantiated the complainant's statement.

Before any glass or window pane is moved at all, it should be photographed in detail to reflect the exact nature of the existent glass fractures. Moving the evidence may cause fracture extensions that could confuse or reverse the findings of the investigator and laboratory examiner. This same principle applies to fractures of automobile glass when a vehicle is pulled to the side of the road by a wrecker operator. Such illustrations under-score the importance of the investigator's paying particular attention to what has occurred between the time of the crime and the time that he or she arrives at the scene. In this light, a key question that the investigator must attempt to answer with all types of evidence is whether the characteristics could have been caused by someone other than the suspect, such as a witness, the victim, emergency medical personnel, or another officer.[27]

FIBERS, CLOTH FRAGMENTS, AND IMPRESSIONS

Fibers are of greater value as evidence than is hair because they incorporate such variables as number of fibers per strand, number of strands, the thickness of fibers and strands, the amount and direction of twists, dye content, type of weave, and the possible presence of foreign matter which may be embedded in them (see Figures 4-9 and 4-10).[28] When something composed of fibers, such as clothing, comes into contact with other clothing or objects, there is the opportunity for the exchange or transfer of fibers. Fibers may also be located on the body of the victim or the suspect, serving to connect one to the other. While the value of fiber evi-

FIGURE 4-8   Determining Direction of Bullet's Penetration of Glass

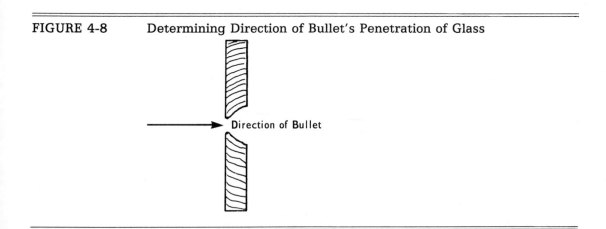

Direction of Bullet

FIGURE 4-9   Comparison of Questioned and Known Cotton Fiber Samples

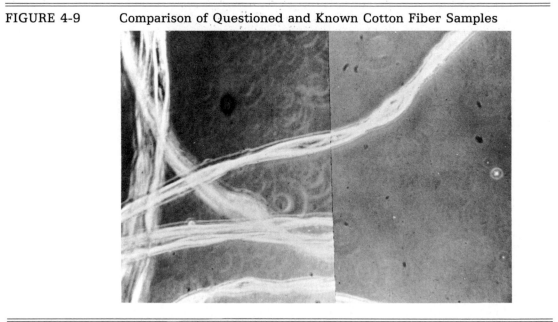

FIGURE 4-10   Comparison of Questioned and Known Wool Fibers

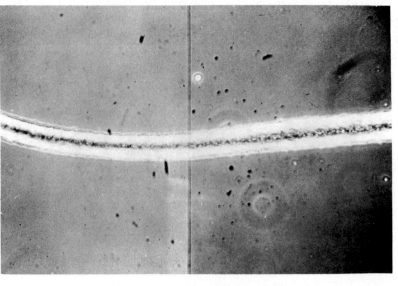

TABLE 4-1
The Prosecution's Fiber Links

Possible Fiber Sources	Victims											
	1	2	3	4	5	6	7	8	9	10	11	12
Violet & green bedspread	X	X	X	X	X	X	X	X	X	X	X	X
Green bedroom carpet	X	X	X	X	X		X	X	X	X		X
Pale green carpet squares in office/workroom area	X							X		X		
Yellow blanket found under bed	X	X	X	X	X		X					
Trunk liner from 1979 Ford LTD										X	X	
Red carpet from 1979 Ford LTD											X	
Dark carpet from 1970 Chevy station wagon		X	X	X			X					
Yellow toilet cover						X				X	X	
Gray glove found in station wagon		X					X					
Brown waist and collar from leather jacket							X					
Yellow kitchen rug									X			
Blue acrylic throw rug			X									
Trunk liner from 1973 Plymouth Fury												X
Fibers found in debris from station wagon (several colors)	X	X	X	X	X	X	X			X		
White polyester fibers found in debris from rug in station wagon cargo area								X	X	X		
Animal hairs consistent with suspect's dog	X	X	X	X	X		X	X	X	X	X	X
Bedspread hanging in carport area				X	X							

Source: Hyde Post and David B. Hilder, "Fibers Found on Victims Form Links in Williams Case," *The Atlanta Journal,* February 2, 1982, p. 1A, with modification.

dence is well recognized, perhaps in no other major case was its collection and analysis as critical to a successful prosecution as it was in a 1982 conviction for murder. Although the prosecution introduced other types of evidence, the preponderance of fiber evidence played a key role in this case. Table 4-1 summarizes the fiber evidence used in this case; although the suspect was charged only with the murders of victims designated one and three on Table 4-1, the trial judge allowed prosecutors to introduce evidence related to the slayings of ten others to see if they were part of a pattern of murders dating back to 1979.[29] The fibers identified in Table 4-1 were found on or associated with the various victims and were consistent with fiber sources from the suspect's environment,

such as his home and vehicles to which he had access (see Figure 4-11). The verdict in this case has been appealed, and the results of that process may affect future use of fiber evidence.

Cloth fragments may be found at the scene of violent crimes or along the perpetrator's point of approach or exit from a crime scene. They may be found on such diverse points as a chain fence, the splintered edge of a wooden building, or protruding nails. In hit and run offenses, cloth fragments may be found in the grille or undercarriage of the striking vehicle (see Figure 4-12). Cloth impressions are found infrequently in investigations, usually on wet paint or some surface of a vehicle involved in striking a pedestrian (see Figure 4-13).

FIGURE 4-11

Scanning electron micrograph (570×) of a nylon fiber removed from a sheet used to transport the body of a murder victim. The fiber, associated with a carpet in the offender's residence, was only manufactured in small quantities about a decade before it was recovered as part of the investigation.

Courtesy of the Federal Bureau of Investigation

Both fibers and cloth fragments should be packaged in the manner described for handling hair later in this chapter. Only rarely will it be possible to obtain a cast of a cloth impression; this effort, however, should invariably be preceded by the taking of several photographs, at least one of which shows a ruler to allow for comparisons at a future date.

STRING, CORD, AND ROPE

String, cord, and rope evidence is usually found in robbery, criminal homicide, rape, and abduction cases. Less frequently it is found in accidental hangings by children and accidental sexual asphyxiations.

String can be identified by its fibers and the method of its manufacture. The follow-

FIGURE 4-12

The inserted fragment was found in the grille of the suspect's vehicle, which had been involved in a hit and run case. The fragment fitted the victim's shirt.

ing synopsis of a case processed by the Kansas City Police Department illustrates the potential evidentiary value of such evidence:

At the scenes of three different arsons, the remains of a cotton wick used to delay the ignition of gasoline were recovered in the debris. The string used for the wicks was examined and found to be of the category 23-strand white cotton. A check with manufacturers of this type of string revealed that it was never intentionally manufactured with 23 strings, but only with 20 or 24. Thus, this particular sample had added value due to its rarity. The string wick gave strong indication that the three wicks were from the same spool of string and suggested that the fires were

set by the same individual. This, along with other evidence, led to a successful clearance of the case.[30]

Cord and rope evidence have essentially the same characteristics as string, and all have some characteristics of fibers. "To decide whether two cords or ropes come from one and the same piece is possible only in exceptional cases and then only if characteristic and incontestable agreement is found."[31] When rope evidence is removed from the victim or other place, knots should never be severed. Instead, a place away from the knot should be cut and a piece of twine used to loop the two ends together. A tag should be attached to indicate that the investigator has

FIGURE 4-13

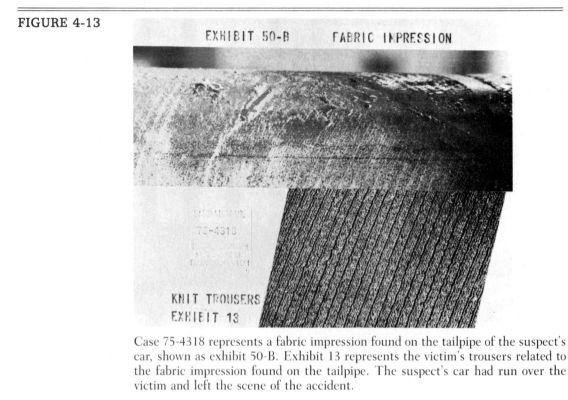

EXHIBIT 50-B   FABRIC IMPRESSION

KNIT TROUSERS
EXHIBIT 13

Case 75-4318 represents a fabric impression found on the tailpipe of the suspect's car, shown as exhibit 50-B. Exhibit 13 represents the victim's trousers related to the fabric impression found on the tailpipe. The suspect's car had run over the victim and left the scene of the accident.

Courtesy Kentucky State Police

cut the rope. Ordinarily, because of its resilient nature, the packaging of this type of evidence poses no particular problem when standard procedures are followed. (See Figures 4-14 and 4-15.)

=== **FINGERPRINTS** ===

Fingerprints, a not uncommon form of physical evidence, are one of the most valuable types of evidence.[32]

Fingerprints of the offender are found on a wide variety of surfaces and in various states. In all cases, however, the prints are fragile and susceptible to destruction by any careless act. They are also in many instances difficult to locate.

With but a few exceptions, that is, the physically impaired, everyone has fingerprints. This universal character is a prime factor in establishing a standard of identification. Since a print of one finger has never been known to duplicate exactly another fingerprint—even of the same person or an identical twin[33]—it is possible to identify an individual with just one impression. The relative ease with which a set of inked fingerprints can be taken as a means of identification is a further basis for using this standard. Despite such factors as aging and environmental influences, a person's fingerprints do not change. This unaltering pattern is a permanent record of the individual throughout life.

FIGURE 4-14   Photomicrograph of Electrical Cord Edge Match

The piece on the left was seized in the suspect's custody and matched with the end on the right, which was part of the length used to tie up a homicide victim.

Courtesy Regional Criminalistics Laboratory, Metropolitan Kansas City, Missouri

Although there are several different filing systems for fingerprints, each is based on classification of common characteristics. The classification system works to categorize a set of fingerprints readily as well as to provide quick access to a set of prints with a given characteristic.

A direct or inked print is an impression of the ridge detail of the underside of the fingers, palms, toes, or the soles of the feet. This is contrasted with a latent print, which is an impression caused by the perspiration through the sweat pores on the ridges of the skin being transferred to some surface. Fingerprints also occur as residues when the finger ridges have been contaminated with such materials as oil, dirt, blood, or grease.

BASIS OF IDENTIFICATION OF FINGERPRINTS

The ridge detail of fingerprints—including ends of ridges, their separations, and their relationship to each other—constitutes the

FIGURE 4-15

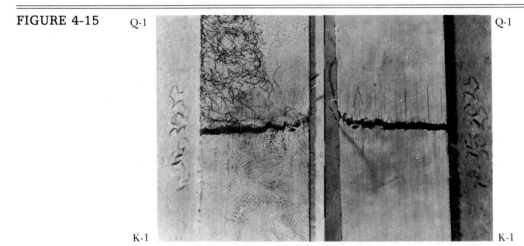

Q-1   Q-1

K-1   K-1

Case 75-3025 represents ends of adhesive tape used to tie up the victim of an armed robbery. Specimen Q-1 represents the torn end of tape removed from the victim's arms and legs. Specimen K-1 represents the end of a roll of tape found in the suspect's pocket when he was arrested. The torn ends of Q-1 and K-1 gave a positive physical match. In addition, identifiable fingerprints were present on Q-1 and K-1.

Courtesy Kentucky State Police

basis for identification of fingerprints. The major fingerprint patterns are shown in Figure 4-16. To establish individual identity, some courts require from ten to 12 points, although no specific number is universally demanded. *Points* are identical characteristics found in fingerprints from known and questioned sources. Positive identification cannot be made when an unexplained difference appears, regardless of the points of similarity.

There is no standard requirement of print size for positive identification. It is only necessary that the partial print be large enough to contain the necessary points of individuality. This number may be found in an area as small as the flat end of a pencil. Thus, the rule whenever an investigator develops a partial latent print which appears to have only several ridges is that it should be submitted to the laboratory.

Some persons, including experienced of-

ficers, erroneously believe the points used for identification of the fingerprint occur only in the pattern area of the finger. In fact, all the different types occur outside of the pattern area on the finger as well as on the first and second joints of the finger and the entire palm of the hand. They are also present on the toes and the entire sole of the foot; they may be found in any area where friction ridges occur.

LIMITATIONS OF LATENT PRINTS

Even though latent prints are invaluable in the course of investigative work, there are certain limitations as to what information these prints can be expected to provide. It is impossible, for example, to determine the age of the latent print because there are a number of factors other than time which change its appearance. However, it is occasionally possible to estimate the age of the print in

FIGURE 4-16   Major Fingerprint Patterns

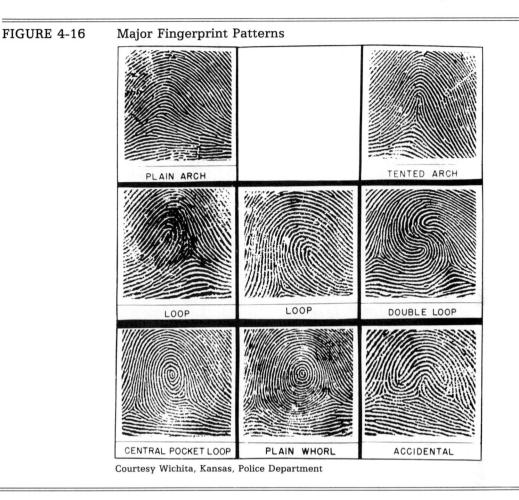

Courtesy Wichita, Kansas, Police Department

relation to events. For example, prints appearing on an object recently thoroughly cleaned can be dated as occurring after that event.

Likewise it is not possible to determine from the examination of the print alone the age or sex of the person leaving the print. Even though a rough correlation does exist between age and sex and such characteristics as size of the ridge or pattern, individual variations limit the reliability of such judgments.

Prints cannot be used to identify the race of a suspect,[34] nor can occupational groups be determined with a high degree of accuracy. It is true that many occupations, such as bricklaying, cause characteristic damage to the skin of the fingers and hands, but any conjecture as to a suspect's occupation should be considered an investigative lead and not substantive evidence.

There are two types of prints that the investigator will encounter which do not need developing. The first of these is the visible type created after the suspect's hand has come in contact with blood, ink, paint, grease, or dirt, and the print transferred to some surface area. Prints under these conditions are usually immediately distinct. The procedure used in collecting such prints is first to photograph and then to cover them with protective tape. In such instances the surface on which the print rests must be transported to the crime laboratory. Common sense must guide the decision as to just how much damage is justifiable in collecting items or surface areas where this type of print is found. The second type of print which requires no further developing is an impression in a soft substance such as putty, clay, or fresh paint. Again, the procedure is to photograph the impression first, then transport the entire object or the section containing it to the crime laboratory. If a physical transfer of the impression is not possible, a cast should be prepared using silicone rubber.[35] The cast is then sent to the laboratory in place of the actual imprint.

DEVELOPING LATENT FINGERPRINTS: GENERAL CONSIDERATIONS

The types of surfaces from which latent prints can be lifted fall into two broad categories: those which are hard, smooth, and nonabsorbent, and those which are smooth and absorbent. The investigator must be able to distinguish between these two types of surfaces, because each requires different procedures for developing latent prints. To determine in which category a given surface belongs, it is useful to think of what would happen to a drop of water if it were placed on it. If the water would bead up—as in the case of formica—the surface is hard, smooth, and nonabsorbent. However, if the water would soak in, as in cardboard, the surface is absorbent. Before attempting to develop any print, the brush used for dusting prints should be cleaned and the bristles separated. This is best done by rolling the handle rapidly between the palms of the hands and letting the bristles spread out naturally. Fingerprint powder tends to compact and be-

comes difficult to handle. Before opening the container it should be shaken vigorously to loosen the powder.

CONDITIONS WHICH AFFECT LATENT PRINTS

The quality of latent fingerprints is affected by such conditions as the type of surface, the manner in which the print was transferred, the nature and quantity of the substance, for example, perspiration, that covered the ridge surfaces,[36] and to some extent the physical or occupational defects of the person transferring the print.

The nature and condition of the surface on which the latent print is deposited are critical factors in defining quality. For optimum quality, the surface must be fairly clean and smooth. Conversely, such surfaces as coarse cloth, unfinished wood, and grained leather are not likely sources of good latent prints.

Another important consideration is the manner in which the object was handled by the person depositing the latent print. For example, the ridges on fingers are very close together; should the finger move merely the distance between two ridges when touching or releasing an object, most of the ridge detail will be lost. This is why most latents which are developed are smeared in the pattern area and only their ridges outside the pattern area have enough detail for identification.

Additionally, the friction surfaces may become completely covered with perspiration or other substances. When this occurs, both the ridge surfaces and their valleys are filled and no ridge detail will be yielded. Latent prints in this category generally develop very dark and have the same appearance as a print developed with too much powder.

Weather affects the latent print in several ways. The print may be dried out or washed away. Humidity will cause latent prints on paper to become smudged or even to disappear. Due to the sponge nature of paper, moisture enters it from all directions causing the ridge detail to diffuse to such an extent that it is not recognizable.

The greater the amount of oil deposited with perspiration, the longer the print will last; perspiration is mostly water, and oil deposited with it will float on the surface reducing the rate of evaporation. After all water evaporates, the oil remains in tacky condition permitting better development of the ridge detail with the use of fingerprint powder. Body oil is brought to the friction ridges of the fingers as contamination from the hairy parts of the body; if these parts have not been touched, oil may not occur in the latent print at all. When no oils are present, the water content of the deposited material is subject to the same evaporation rate as any like amount of water under the same conditions and the print will be less tacky.

COLLECTION BY THE INVESTIGATOR

Latent prints are such valuable evidence that extraordinary efforts should be made to recover them. The investigator must adopt a positive attitude about this, regardless of apparent problems or past failures.

It is imperative that the investigator thoroughly search all surface areas in and around the crime scene that might retain prints. The fact that an individual may have worn gloves in no way lessens the need for a complete search. On occasion, gloves themselves leave impressions as individualized as fingerprints. Moreover, although it is rare, it may be possible to develop a latent fingerprint on the inside of a glove recovered at a crime scene.[37] Particular attention should be paid to less than obvious places, such as the undersides of toilet seats, toilet handles, table tops and dresser drawers; the surfaces of dinner plates and filing cabinets; the backs of chairs, rear view mirrors; and the trunk lids of automo-

biles. Often handled objects, such as doorknobs and telephones, ordinarily do not yield good prints. But because they are likely to have been touched, they should always be processed.

It is never safe to assume that the offender took precautions against leaving prints or destroyed those left. The commission of a criminal offense involves stress, and the offender may commit some oversight. If gloves were worn, for example, the suspect may have removed them for some operation.

It helps to attempt to view the scene as the criminal did. Such conditions as time of day, weather, and physical layout may suggest that certain surfaces should be more closely examined. In conducting the examination for latent prints in a burglary case, for example, the search should begin at the point of entry. For other crimes, such as the issuance of worthless checks, the point of entry often takes on less importance. Ordinarily, however, whatever the crime and its attending circumstances, reconstruction by the investigator gives direction to the search.

A person who is familiar with the environment, such as the owner of the building or the occupant of an apartment, may give valuable aid in obtaining latent prints. The person should be allowed to observe the scene, so that he or she might indicate items out of place or brought to the scene by the suspect.

DEVELOPING PRINTS ON NONABSORBENT, HARD, SMOOTH SURFACES

Prints made on nonabsorbent, hard, smooth materials remain entirely on the surface of the object as a delicate liquid or semi-solid deposit. The print, consisting mainly of oil and water, extends upward from the surface, making an ideal adhesive base for the fingerprint powder.

Development is begun with the application of a small amount of powder to the area to

FIGURE 4-17

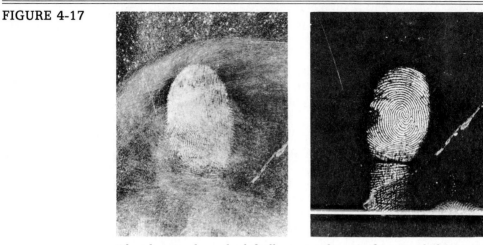

The photograph on the left illustrates the use of too much fingerprint powder in developing a latent print, resulting in the needless destruction of detail. The photograph on the right portrays a latent fingerprint developed by the use of the correct amount of powder.

Courtesy Wichita, Kansas, Police Department

be examined. Great caution must be exercised, because too much powder makes a dark print in which points are difficult to identify (see Figure 4-17). The brush should never be submerged in the powder; it should merely touch it lightly. The entire area to be processed should be covered with powder in gentle, even strokes until ridge detail begins to show. As the ridges become visible, the brush strokes should follow their contours. After all of the details of the print are developed, the excess powder is removed by gentle brushing or blowing. The powder should be allowed to adhere to the latent print but not to the surface on which the print is deposited. As a general rule, all latent prints should be photographed with a 1:1 camera before they are lifted. The photographs provide a record, should the lifting fail or accidentally destroy the prints. The print is lifted after one end of a length of clear tape—usually 5 to 6 inches—is placed just before one end of the print; pressure is

applied at this point, and the tape forced progressively and gently over the print. If the print is wider than the tape, it may be lifted if extra tape strips are placed to overlap by ¼ inch until the area is covered. If air bubbles are created accidentally, the tape should be smoothed over them carefully to avoid damage to the print.

Once the tape is in place, one of two procedures may be followed. The tape may be left on and the entire object submitted to the laboratory. If this is not practical, the print may be removed by pulling up on the tape. Once the tape is free of the surface, it is placed on a fingerprint card in the same manner as when placed over the latent print.

Occasionally items such as beer cans or glasses which have condensation on their outsides must be processed for prints. These items should first be allowed to dry under natural conditions in a sheltered area. Under no circumstances should heat lamps or artificial heat of any kind be used to dry an object. Objects exposed to freezing temperatures should be allowed to warm up and dry out naturally before any attempt is made to develop latent prints. The investigator may encounter a surface, such as glass or polished metal, on which a print can readily be seen, but efforts to develop it with fingerprint powder prove useless. On such occasions, a photograph should be taken before any further attempts at processing are made. If a camera is not available, it may be possible to rejuvenate the print by blowing on it several times and allowing the condensation on the surface to evaporate naturally. The print is then repowdered and the lift made.

If in dusting an area only one print appears to have ridge detail and the others around it are smeared so that no ridge detail remains, the smeared ones should also be included in the same lift. Even though the smeared prints cannot be identified, they may be of value to the lab specialist in later examinations to determine the relationship of an identifiable latent to the whole hand.

DEVELOPING PRINTS ON ABSORBENT, POROUS, AND SMOOTH SURFACES

No attempt should be made at the scene by an investigator to develop latent prints on absorbent surfaces. Such efforts usually result in failure and may create insurmountable problems for the fingerprint specialist at the laboratory. Additionally, high humidity will cause the destruction of prints on absorbent surfaces by causing them to diffuse. The investigator must take great pains, therefore, to avoid adding moisture by accidentally dropping perspiration on the print or carelessly handling the item with wet hands. The item, e.g., paper or cardboard, should be placed into a container, using tweezers or by careful handling at its edges. After the item is collected, the container should be sealed and marked with all re-

quired data plus the notation "To be processed for latent prints."

DEVELOPING LATENT PRINTS ON BODIES AND OTHER TRADITIONALLY RESISTANT SURFACES

Internationally, there have been a number of experiments and developments in the area of developing prints left on human bodies and other surfaces which ordinarily do not yield them; these are discussed in this section.

Lasers The application of laser beam technology to the detection of latent prints is a product of work by the Ontario Provincial Police Department and the XEROX Research Center in Toronto dating from 1976.[38] Certain compounds in perspiration, such as vitamins, have a natural fluorescence which is not revealed under normal illumination conditions. Laser illumination causes these compounds in latent prints to luminesce a vivid yellow-orange color when viewed through special lenses. Prints detected in this fashion can be viewed directly and photographed. The laser beam is also nondestructive in that conventional detection techniques can be used following its employment (see Figure 4-18).

Lasers have helped investigators to locate prints on a variety of surfaces resistant to traditional detection methods, including styrofoam (see Figure 4-19) and cloth. In laboratory tests, fingerprints of varying qualities have been found: on paper baked for two weeks at 75 degrees and then soaked in running water for five minutes; on the pages of a book that had not been opened for nine years; and on human skin. In one actual case, a drug dealer was convicted after a laser beam located a print on the sticky side of a piece of black electrical tape. The print had not been found through conventional processing.

Another basis for establishing individual-

FIGURE 4-18   Laser in Use

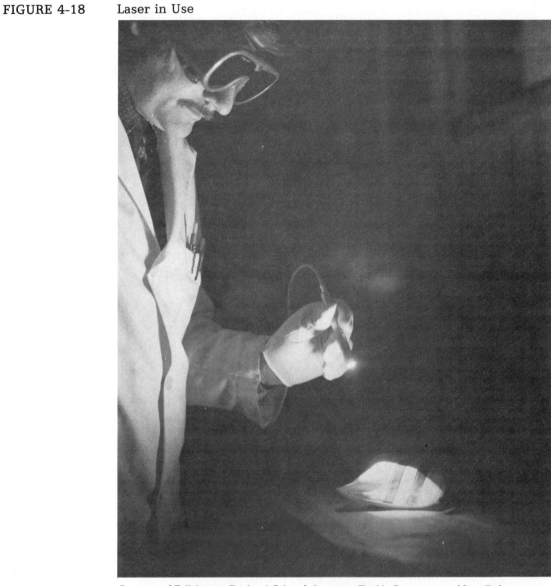

Courtesy of Tallahassee Regional Crime Laboratory, Florida Department of Law Enforcement

ity may also be provided through the use of laser beams. A fluorescent fingerprint also displays a structure of pores which are not seen following the use of standard detection methods. The analysis of pore patterns shows potential for becoming a new method for identifying prints. There have also been other successful applications of laser beams to criminal investigation. Through its use we are now able to positively identify an individ-

FIGURE 4-19

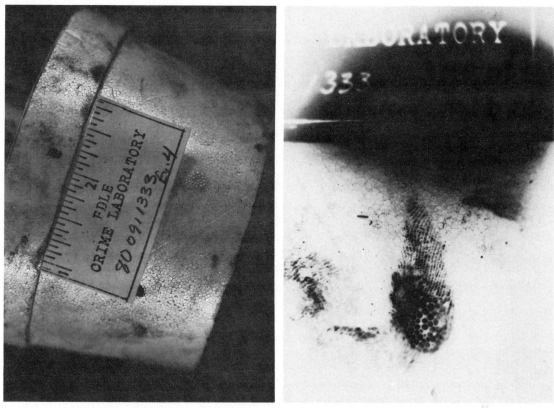

Following unsuccessful conventional processing of a styrofoam cup for prints (left), the laser was used and produced identifiable latent prints on the cup (right).

Courtesy of Tallahassee Regional Crime Laboratory, Florida Department of Law Enforcement

ual stolen diamond if a laser beam illuminated photograph is taken of it prior to the theft and no alterations have been made of the diamond prior to its recovery.[39] In 1986, there were at least 15 crime laboratories in this country with operational lasers, and the numbers of laboratories with this capability is expected to increase in the near future.

Super Glue Fuming As early as 1978, scientists in Japan and the United States were independently exploring the use of adhesive agents to develop latent fingerprints. In this country, the process is usually referred to as Super Glue or crazy glue fuming. The first criminal conviction in this country using crazy glue fuming was in Florida in 1982, when tape which had been collected as evidence some four and one-half months before yielded latent prints when processed using this technique. Initially, the use of crazy glue fuming took from several hours to several

FIGURE 4-20

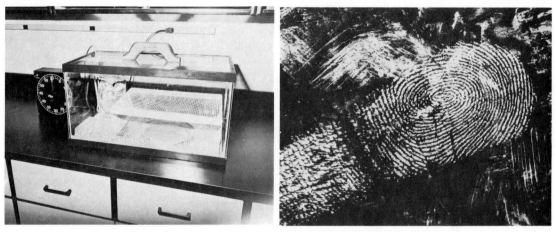

A typical "crazy glue" fuming tank and a latent print obtained from fuming a clear plastic zip-lock type bag; the photograph of the fingerprint is enhanced by using a dark background.

Courtesy of the Michigan State Police

days to develop latent prints. The technique has undergone a number of changes designed to reliably speed up the process and is practiced somewhat differently in various parts of the country.[40] Presently, under laboratory conditions a 10 gallon fish tank is used as a fuming chamber. The top to the tank is closed by covering it with glass or plexiglass. A flat container such as a pie plate is kept in the tank and filled with water at all times because high humidity is a factor in obtaining good results. A light bulb in one corner of the tank is covered with a coffee-can like object which has holes at the highest point of its sides. These holes allow the heat generated by the light bulb to escape, which accelerates the time necessary to develop prints. The objects to be fumed are either hung or placed on platforms. Then, approximately one-third of a small tube of glue (which must specifically contain cyanoacrylate ester) is emptied onto a small piece of aluminum foil (which is curved to prevent the glue from running) which is located on top of the coffee-can like container. The tank is quickly sealed and within 5 to 15 minutes latent prints will appear, typically with a white ridge detail. If there are little or no signs of a latent print, the item should be examined in a cross light and latent prints may appear as a dark stain. In either case, the latent print can be photographed and, if needed, lifted using conventional techniques.

The use of crazy glue fuming has proved to be very effective upon surfaces traditionally resistant to attempts to develop prints, such as plastic bags which contain narcotics. Because crazy glue fuming can be successful regularly on many surfaces which only occasionally responded to conventional processing, it is rapidly becoming a workhorse for many jurisdictions in terms of locating latent prints. Moreover, if crazy glue fuming attempts are not successful, then they can be followed by laser examination and the prior fuming process may enhance the laser's effectiveness in locating latent prints.

Other Methods The absence of some sophisticated technology does not mean that efforts to obtain a latent print from a body using conventional methods should not be made. Presently, the likelihood that such efforts will be productive may be a "longshot," given that so few cases have appeared in the literature in which a claim was made that a latent print obtained from the body of a victim played a role in convicting a suspect of criminal homicide.[41] Even in an early case, which occurred in Florida during 1978 and involved three murder victims, some unusual factors were in operation, namely, the victim on whom the print was located was found in a spa, which offered a controlled environment; the victim had just shaved her legs and the smooth leg skin on which the print was detected was a good surface with which to work; and the victim had not placed any lotions on her legs which would have hampered recovery efforts (see Figure 4-21). However, to some extent the lack of finding latent prints on bodies may be a product of our not looking because we "know" you can't get them. Although efforts to obtain prints from other areas of the body may also be successful, the areas which ordinarily will provide the best surfaces are the undersides of the biceps, the sides of the neck and torso, and the tops of feet. Success is also affected by the skin not being damp or noticeably clammy, the amount of surface hair, the oiliness of the skin, and the amount of elasticity in the skin.[42]

In 1982 a new and relatively simple way to develop latent fingerprints on live human skin was reported.[43] The suspected area is fumed with iodine and a specially treated 35mm clear plastic strip is placed over the fumed area. A few seconds later a dark purple ridge pattern develops; it is a stable, direct positive which can be mounted on a 35mm slide for direct viewing. As many as two to three lifts from the same latent print may be obtained using this method. One precaution which must be taken before fuming is checking to make sure that the person is not allergic to iodine.

MARKING AND IDENTIFYING PRINT LIFTS

When a latent print has been developed, lifted, and placed on a card, it is necessary that the card be properly identified. Information recorded on the card should include the date, title of the case or number, address of the crime scene, name of the officer who made the lift, the exact place of the lift, and the type of object. Regardless of how well the latent was developed and lifted, if the card is not properly marked with all the data required or if the fingerprint specialist is not furnished with the information required, the entire process may be wasted effort. In describing the exact place the lift was made, it is sometimes helpful to draw a simple sketch of the object. This sketch should be made on the fingerprint card which is sent to the laboratory. The inclusion of corresponding numbers on both the lift and the sketch establishes the placement of the latent print.

COLLECTION OF ELIMINATION PRINTS

Before submitting lifted latent prints to a print technician for examination, elimination prints of all persons who may have had access to the area should be made. With elimination prints, it is usually possible to exclude as donors all persons who had legal access to the crime scene.

AUTOMATED EXAMINATION OF LATENT PRINTS

Until recently, practical limitations of fingerprint classification and searching have minimized the investigative value of latent prints which were developed while processing the crime scene.[44] In the past, the development of a single latent print at the crime scene

FIGURE 4-21

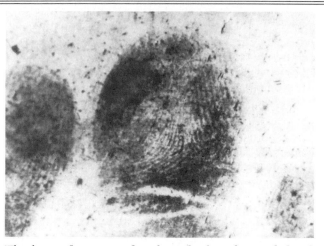

The latent fingerprint found on the leg of one of the three victims in the spa murders; when compared with the suspect's fingerprints, a positive identification was made.

had little utility unless there was a specific suspect or small number of suspects, as fingerprints were classified and filed based on entire sets rather than on single prints. In California, for example, that state's department of justice files have over 6 million fingerprint cards; a manual search to try to match a single developed latent fingerprint with one of the file cards was an impossible task. Now, however, California and other jurisdictions have the growing capability to make such matches by use of computer technology. In California this system is termed the *Automated Latent Print System* (ALPS) and in its first year of operation, without all capabilities in place, the system provided matches that contributed to the solution of over seventy felony cases.

DENTAL EVIDENCE

Forensic dentistry is a specialty that relates dental evidence to investigation. The dental apparatus, including teeth, prosthetic appliances, and morphological peculiarities, are of primary importance in the identification of mutilated, decomposed, or otherwise visually unrecognizable human remains. Teeth themselves also leave patterns in the skin, and bite mark analysis has played a major role in many criminal cases. The analysis of a bite mark in and of itself can be of great value in assisting investigators in eliminating suspects as well as aiding in the identification of a suspect.

HISTORY

The teeth and facial bones are major means of identification of skeletal remains and have been used by anthropologists for many years. It is interesting to speculate that the first forensic dentist in the United States may have been Paul Revere. In 1775 he constructed a silver bridge for his friend Dr. Joseph Warren. Warren was later killed by the British during the battle of Bunker Hill.

He was buried in a mass grave and his remains were later identified by Paul Revere by the bridgework he had constructed for Warren—the earliest known dental identification in the United States.

Nearly 100 years after Revere's identification, it is interesting to note that the body of President Lincoln's assassin, John Wilkes Booth, was identified by a gold "plug tooth" on the right side of his jaw. Probably the most publicized bite mark case involved a man who allegedly had committed homicides in Washington, California, Utah, and Colorado. He was suspected of murdering several women in a sorority house in late 1978. At trial, the positive relationship between bite mark evidence obtained from one of the victims and the teeth of the suspect contributed to his successful prosecution.

Modern-day forensic dentistry dates to the mid-1960s, when texts written by Gustafson and Furuhata and Yamamoto titled *Forensic Odontology* were published.[46] A formal course in forensic dentistry was started at the Armed Forces Institute of Pathology, Washington, D.C., in 1964. Until the early 1970s, the forensic dentist was used almost exclusively for identification of skeletal, burned, or otherwise unrecognizable remains. It was not until the early 1970s that forensic dentists in this country generally became involved in bite mark identification. In 1970, a group of eight dentists formed the odontology section of the American Academy of Forensic Sciences. Theirs was the first effort by dentists to participate formally with other forensic scientists. In 1973, a grant funded an organization for forensic dentists. This board is now known as The American Board of Forensic Odontology. Its primary purpose is to establish criteria for the specialty of forensic dentistry. Since its founding in 1973, the board has certified seventy-five dentists in the United States and Canada as specialists in the field of Forensic Odontology.

DENTAL IDENTIFICATION

Skeletal, burned, or mutilated remains can best be identified with dental records. The forensic dentist compares antemortem (before death) records with postmortem (after death) findings to determine if there is a positive match. No set number of points are required for a positive match. Sometimes one unique remain is enough for positive identification.

Like human fingerprints, human dentition (teeth) is unique. The average adult has thirty-two teeth. A combination of tooth form and arrangement, missing teeth, and mechanical alterations from dental fillings or accidents produce hundreds of thousands of possible combinations. It is important that the crime scene search not overlook dental evidence which appears to be useless. A single tooth with unusual anatomy may provide a basis for individual identification. Through skull and jaw formations, a forensic dentist may be able to give investigators valuable opinions and information as to the victim's age, race, sex, and possible unusual habits. A forensic dentist can state with reasonable certainty the approximate age within six months of an individual through age 13. From age 14 through 25, a one year plus or minus estimate is possible. After age 25, certain sophisticated tests can be performed to approximate age. The skull and jaws vary with race, age, and sex.

Certain groups—Orientals and Indians—have deep grooves in the inner aspect of the upper front teeth. These are referred to as shovel-shaped incisors. The functioning of the third molars is common within the black race, but is found in less than 20 percent of the white race. Crowding of the teeth is common with whites but not in blacks or Indians. The absence of certain teeth may help identify age and race. For example, the first premolars are usually extracted for orthodontic reasons (crowding) in the white race. A large percentage of the white population have had their third molars (wisdom teeth) extracted to prevent crowding of their remaining teeth. Anterior wear will suggest habits such as pipe smoking or nail biting. Fractured upper incisors are very useful not only in visual identification and photographic comparisons but also in bite mark analysis. The jaws will also show evidence of previous injuries as well as past or present disease. In discussing these and other aspects of the case with a forensic dentist, investigators must be sure that they understand any distinctions made between scientific fact and investigative opinion.

Sometimes the victim has not been to a dentist and no antemortem (before death) dental records exist. Comparisons and positive identifications still may be made from photographs; Figure 4-22 illustrates an example of this type of identification.

BITE MARK ANALYSIS AND COMPARISON

Bite mark evidence is the most recently developed and perhaps the most significant contribution the forensic dentist can make to an investigation. The bites left by the attacker (aggressive bites) or the bites left by the victim (defense bites) into human flesh take place in a significant number of cases of violent crimes, such as child abuse, homicide, and rape. As with fingerprints, bites have always been there, but other than observing them, little was done with them as evidence until recently. Bite mark identification, even in its present developmental stages, can be very valuable as a means of identification.

The earliest use of bite marks at a crime scene were bites into objects, such as food, chewing gum, and pencils. The evidentiary examination of bites in human flesh only appeared in the literature in the United States in the early 1970s. During this time, the successful introduction of bite mark evidence

into the courts has also helped solidify its use.[47]

Collection of Bite Mark Evidence Biting frequently takes place in rape, child abuse, and homicide cases and may be inflicted on the victim or by the victim on the attacker as an act of self-defense.[48] Investigators must be alert for the possibility that what appears to be abrasions or bruises may actually be evidence of a bite mark, especially when the victim is unconscious or deceased and therefore unable to tell how the marks were made. Any suspected bite area should not be touched, cleaned or disturbed until after certain steps which are described later in this section are taken.

Appearance Bite marks take a variety of forms; in Figure 4-23 note that the bite marks on the victim's lower left side could be mistaken for injuries caused by being beaten with some blunt object. Also note in Figure 4-23 that immediately to the right of the area just discussed is a bite mark shaped like a donut. In Figure 4-24, yet another pattern is seen, the double horseshoe. The double horseshoe in Figure 4-24 is somewhat lacking in detail because it was made through the victim's clothing.

It is important to note that not all marks left by teeth are bite marks; in Figure 4-25 the "teeth marks" are actually an abrasion caused when the assailant struck the victim in the mouth. In another case, what initially appeared to be bite marks on a victim's neck later were determined to have been caused by a pearl necklace found at the scene and which had inflicted the marks during the murder victim's struggle with her assailant.

If there is a question as to whether an injury is a bite mark, the injury pattern should be protected from contamination until a forensic dental expert and laboratory technician have an opportunity to examine the evidence.

FIGURE 4-22

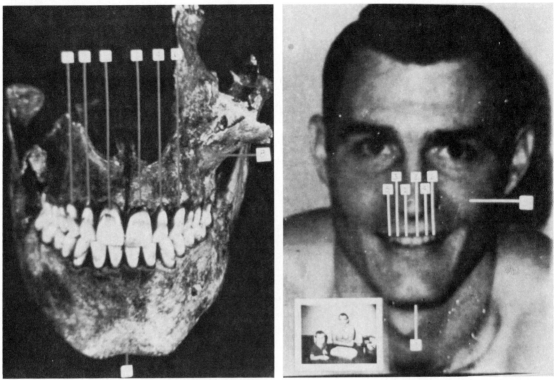

Left photo shows upper and lower jaws of unknown white male. Some bone loss (pyorrhea) and tobacco staining is evident. There were no fillings, decay, or missing teeth and no evidence of any dental treatment. Right photo is enhancement and enlargement of victim pictured at his son's birthday party. His kidnappers/killers were sentenced to life terms.

Courtesy of Dr. Richard R. Souviron, D.D.S., A.B.F.O., Chief Forensic Dentist, Dade County Medical Examiners Office, Miami, Florida

PHOTOGRAPHS

As a general practice, bite mark evidence should be collected from the victim at the crime scene whenever feasible to eliminate the possibility of disturbing the area during transit. However, if the bite area is well protected, then the evidence can be gathered at the morgue or hospital. Bite marks should be photographed as rapidly as possible. Ideally, both black and white and color photographs should be taken; the first or preliminary sets of photographs are taken before cleaning or wiping the affected area. In both the black and white and color photographs, a ruler or scale should appear. This allows an exact one to one print to be made. In color photographs, a color scale must be included; it will be of value in determining from the bruise color the approximate time the bite was inflicted. Flexible tapes should never be sub-

FIGURE 4-23   Two Forms of Bite Marks on the Same Victim

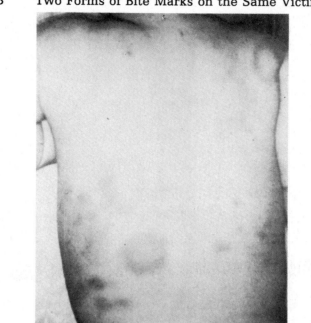

Courtesy Norman D. Sperber, D.D.S., San Diego County Coroner's Office

stituted for rigid rulers or scales, even when the bite mark is on a rounded portion of the body, such as the breast or buttocks, because such tapes may introduce distortion. These preliminary photographs should include orienting exposures, which serve to demonstrate the relationship of the bite mark to the body. Close-up photographs should be taken at a 90 degree angle to the bite mark. These practices must be followed very carefully. Photographic evidence is extremely valuable, and the failure to adhere to sound practices makes it very difficult for the forensic dentist to be helpful.

SWABBING

After taking the preliminary photographs, qualified personnel, wearing sterile gloves to avoid contamination of the bite mark area, should swab the area, using distilled water or saline solution.[49] This swabbing process begins at the periphery of the bite mark and proceeds toward the center; swabs are changed each time a new area is touched. Each individual swab should be allowed to air dry for several minutes and should then be placed into a separate test tube. In many instances this type of evidence, which is intended to gather some of the suspect's saliva, can be subjected to laboratory analysis to determine the major blood group of the suspect. Blood and saliva specimens should be collected from the victim. Following the swabbing process, the bite mark should be cleaned and a second set of orienting and close-up photographs taken.

When possible, serial photographs of the bite wound should be taken at 12- to 24-hour intervals for the next two to three days. On

FIGURE 4-24

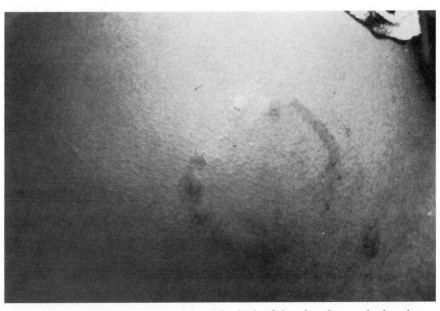

Bite mark on shoulder of rape victim. The lack of detail is due to the bite being made through clothing.

Courtesy of Dr. Richard Souviron, D.D.S., A.B.F.O., Dade County Medical Examiners Office, Miami, Florida

deceased victims they should be kept refrigerated during this photographing process. On a live victim or suspect, serial photographs may be difficult. However, because a bite mark is a wound pattern and the bleeding into the tissue becomes less diffused over a period of time, later photographs can be more helpful in obtaining the outlines than those originally taken. Deceased victims should be kept in the morgue during the photographing process and not embalmed. Embalming tends to wash out bite mark coloration.

LIFTING AND CASTING THE BITE MARK

Preserving the bite mark by means other than photography may prove invaluable in the prosecution of a case. The lifting and casting of the bite mark are two methods for preserving the details of the injury.

The lifting of the bite mark is accomplished by the use of fingerprint powder and clear fingerprint lifting tape. The lifting of a bite mark and converting it into a bite print should be attempted only after all photographic evidence has been obtained. In lifting a bite mark the technician uses standard fingerprint black powder and a hair brush. The procedure is very similar to what an investigator trained in lifting prints is accustomed to doing. A small amount of the fingerprint powder is picked up by the brush and the bite mark area is lightly dusted. Excess powder is brushed away. The indentations of the bite will show up quite clearly. If the evidence area is hairy it is recommended that shaving be done prior to this

FIGURE 4-25

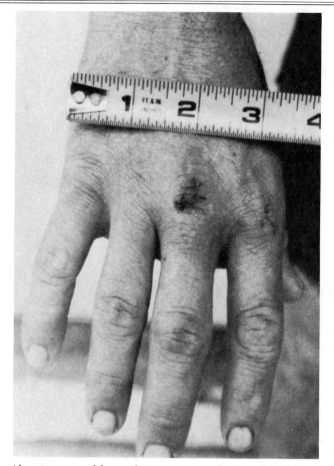

Abrasion caused by striking victim in the mouth.

Courtesy of Dr. Richard Souviron, D.D.S., A.B.F.O., Dade County Medical Examiners Office, Miami, Florida

procedure. Once the entire bite mark has been dusted with the fingerprint powder a section of four inch wide clear fingerprint lifting tape is used to "lift" the bite mark. This procedure should be performed carefully so as not to trap skin or to put excess pressure which would cause distortion of the bite pattern. Once the tape is in position, light pressure is used over the tape in order to pick up maximum amount of recording. The tape is then removed from the skin and placed on a glossy fingerprint card. It is recommended that at least three different bite prints be lifted in order to get the maximum amount of detail.[50]

A cast of the bite mark should be made by a forensic dentist or qualified laboratory technician. If experienced personnel are not available, the following procedures are recommended: (1) use standard, accurate casting materials such as silicone or rubber paste impression; (2) position the bite mark area

FIGURE 4–26   The Application of Orthopedic Tape over the Casting Material

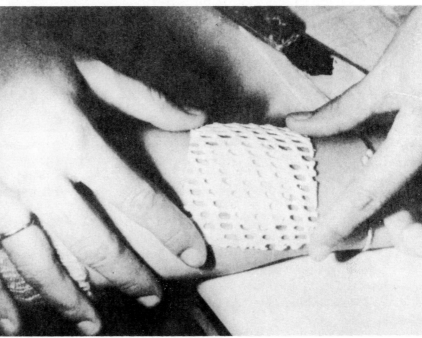

Courtesy Norman D. Sperber, D.D.S., San Diego County Coroner's Office

horizontally so the casting material does not flow away; (3) place the casting material gently onto the area and allow to set; (4) warm orthopedic tape in hot water and place it over the casting material as shown in Figure 4-26 to provide support; (5) place a layer of casting material over the orthopedic tape to lock it in place; and (6) after the second layer of casting material has set, lift the cast from the area. Later, under laboratory conditions, a model of the bite mark can be made.

RECORDS FROM THE SUSPECT

The records needed from the suspect for comparison are photographs and impressions of the teeth, wax bite records, X-rays, and saliva and blood samples. All may be obtained quickly and with little or no discomfort to the suspect. Duplicates of everything should be taken to safeguard against loss or breakage. It is best that the forensic dentist making the comparisons get the evidence from the victim and the records from the suspect. Teeth can be altered, broken off, or removed by a suspect. If a suspect does this before dental impressions are taken, the bite mark comparison becomes more difficult or even impossible to make. Therefore, bite mark evidence should not be publicized.

If the suspect does not give informed consent, the courts provide two methods of obtaining these records from the suspect—a court order or a search warrant. A court order is often used, but it has the disadvantage of informing the suspect and in some cases his attorney, of the pending examination and permits sufficient time for the teeth to be altered. Thus, the search warrant is a safer method if the alteration of teeth is a distinct possibility. In this way the suspect is prevented from knowing of the examination until the exact designated time. It is important that the dentist taking these records have a signed copy of the court order or search warrant before he or she examines the suspect; proceeding on any other basis will jeopardize the admissibility of any evidence obtained. The presence of the prosecutor or his or her representative is desirable, but not a requirement.

HAIR

Hair evidence is most frequently found in violent crimes; its value in an investigation does not lie in its capacity to identify a suspect positively, but rather in its utility in reducing the number of suspects and as a supplement to other evidence.[51] The first step in the examination of hair evidence by laboratory personnel is to make the determination of whether or not it is human. As human hair is quite characteristic in appearance, this is always determinable unless subject to some gross destruction. Where the hair is nonhuman in origin, it is possible to establish the species involved, such as dog, cat, or horse.

If the hair is human in origin, the following conclusions may be reached:[52] the race of the donor—subject to biological overlap and variation; the part of the body from which it originated, within certain limitations; whether the hair was forcibly removed; the manner in which cut—for example, with a dull or sharp instrument; whether it has been treated with chemical dyes or bleach; and whether it has been the recipient of some force, such as crushing or burning. Occasionally hair evidence will also contain significant evidence such as blood, fibers, or paint.

The sex of the donor of hair evidence cannot be established conclusively; however, laboratory technicians may render a tentative judgment which the investigator must regard as just that.[53] Age, too, is a possible determination but will generally only fall within broad categories, such as "very young" or "elderly." Laboratory examination may yield information about habits of consumption or ingestion; for example, it can be determined if certain drugs such as opiates or phencyclidine (PCP) have been taken. Moreover, hair grows at the rate of approximately 1mm per day; thus, analysis of different sections of a single hair from a donor may allow statements about the last time of drug use.[54]

Upon completing the examination of human hair, the laboratory will normally advance one of three findings: that the known and questioned hair samples match in terms of microscopic characteristics and that they originated from either the same individual or another individual whose hair exhibits the same qualities; that the known and questioned hair samples are not similar and did not originate from the same individual; or that no conclusion can be reached.[55] Figure 4-27 shows a comparison of two hair specimens.

Hair recovered at the scene of the crime should be carefully gathered, using a pair of tweezers.[56] Samples recovered at different points, as in the case of other types of evidence, should be individually packaged. Hair evidence may be placed in envelopes or in pill boxes. Because most examinations of hair are comparative in nature, a collection of standards from both the victim and the suspect, where the latter is known, is critical. The collection of hair standards is a function for medical personnel. When hair standards are collected from a deceased victim, representative samples should be obtained from throughout the body areas which are pertinent to the investigation; ordinarily, the collection of approximately thirty to forty hairs from each area is sufficient, taking care to

FIGURE 4-27   Comparison of Questioned and Known Hair Specimens

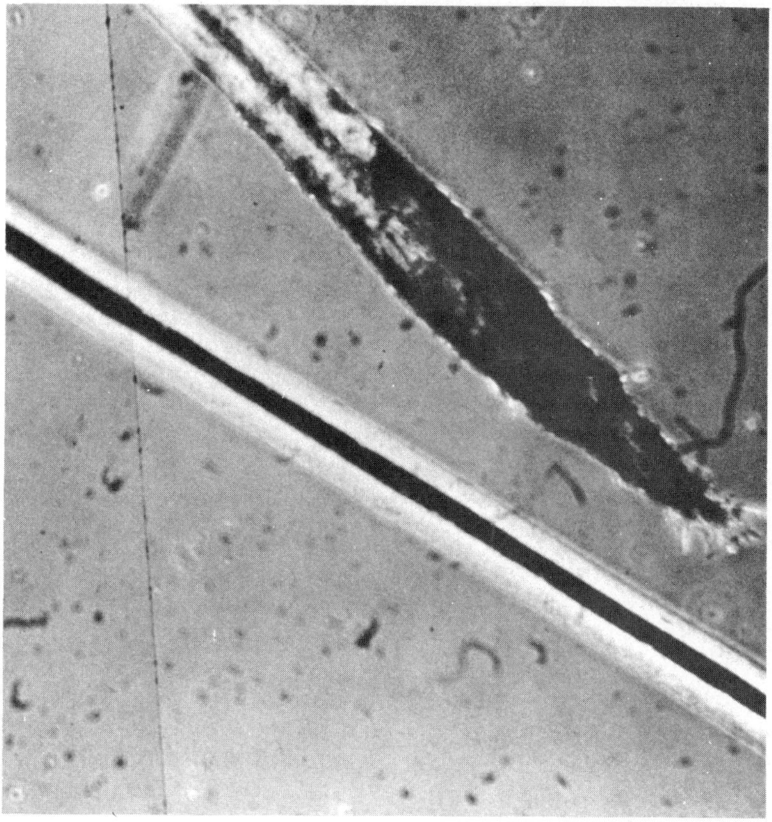

package the samples from each body area separately. Where hair surrounds wounds on the body of a victim, special notation should be made of this point on the container in which the hair is placed. Where there is a living victim or a suspect, medical personnel should first attempt to comb the quantity of samples required. Ordinarily, with a living victim or suspect, approximately twenty hairs from each area are sufficient. Where combing fails to yield a sufficient number of samples, the hair should be cut from the body as close to the skin as possible. It is desirable that the investigator be present at the time the hair samples are obtained by medical personnel: if the latter are unfamiliar with in-

vestigative procedures, they might fail to clean the tweezers, comb, or scissors after each area is sampled, thereby introducing contamination.

BLOOD

Blood is one of the most common types of physical evidence found at the scene of serious crimes. Blood is found as trace amounts, drops, smears, or small pools. "In the living body, blood consists mainly of blood plasma together with red and white blood corpuscles. In a healthy person, the blood makes up about one thirteenth part of the body weight, which means that a full-grown person has more than nine pints of blood."[57] A 1971 report stated that given our present technology, blood is class characteristic evidence and that it was our present lack of knowledge rather than the nature of blood itself which limits our ability to use it as a means of personal identification.[58] This study speculated that technological advances would one day prove that blood is as individualized as fingerprints. By 1983, work on genetic markers was advancing and the prediction of the 1971 study was quickly becoming a reality. Genetic markers are special properties in the blood—there are about 70 of these substances—that can be identified by a process like blood typing, although the technology is more complex. At present, the probability that two individuals would match exactly is 1 in 200 for the most common combinations and from 1 in 10 million to 1 in 200 million for the least common.[59] A 1984 Iowa case illustrates the potential investigative usefulness of genetic markers:

> An unidentified woman's torso was pulled from the Mississippi River by commercial fishermen. A chain saw had been used to cut up the body, and only the section from the navel to the mid-thighs was found. The woman had been reported as having disappeared by her husband, who alleged that she had run away from marital problems. A search of the man's home resulted in the seizure of a chain saw. Additionally, the police obtained a recording of a conversation with her husband that the victim had secretly made in which being "cut . . . in tiny pieces" was discussed. Analysis of the genetic markers in the remains of the victim revealed that it was the "runaway wife" with a probability of 90 to 98 percent. The trial in this case is pending and will be watched by criminalists with great interest.[60]

In 1985, British scientists announced the development of DNA fingerprints. DNA is the basic genetic material in body cells which allows the identification of individual suspects from blood, semen stains, and hair roots. Still regarded as being in the developmental stage despite its virtually total accuracy, DNA fingerprints probably will be used first in a criminal case in England. Success there would speed the transfer of this capability to other criminalistics laboratories.

Particularly in light of some of the new developments just discussed, the value of blood as evidence cannot be overemphasized. In those instances where the perpetrator has left his or her own blood (the sex of the donor of a blood sample cannot presently be determined, although the results of certain tests may suggest a certain sex and race, they are not conclusive) at the scene of an offense, samples of which are subsequently recovered at the time of the crime scene search, the processing of such evidence can produce a considerable savings in interrogation and other investigatory techniques by eliminating all those who do not have the same blood type. It should be noted here that as a portion of the criminal history file, a notation should routinely be made of each arrestee's blood type, in the event that he is implicated in some future investigation where blood samples may be recovered. By excluding those who could not have shed the blood, the innocence of certain people may be established and the direction of the investigation more properly focused.[61]

There are a number of determinations which can be made with respect to the examination of blood, in response to the types of questions which the investigator ordinarily would have.[62]

Is this stain blood? On the surface this would appear to be a relatively easy question to answer. However, dried blood stains have a variety of appearances, including gray, blue, or greenish hues, and apparent blood samples may be a variety of other things, such as rust combined with some liquid or paint. Moreover, blood mixed with another liquid, such as grease or earth, may take on a very nonbloodstain appearance; where there is any suspicion that blood might be present, the investigator should take a sample and submit it to the laboratory for a determination rather than attempting to arrive at this decision on the basis of nonscientific judgment. Ordinarily, whether the stain is in a solid or liquid state, the laboratory will be able to make a determination as to whether it is blood or not.

What is the origin of the blood? Regardless of whether the stain is in a liquid or dried state, if it has not been subject to gross deterioration, whether it is of human or animal origin can be determined. Furthermore, if the blood is nonhuman, it is frequently possible to determine the species of animal from which it originated. After the disappearance of labor leader James Hoffa, it was thought that an individual close to the victim may have been involved because blood stains were found in his car; laboratory examination corroborated the statement of the person in question that the stains had originated from a fish. If the blood is human, under certain circumstances it may be possible to determine what part of the body it came from. If the blood was recovered in a liquid state, it may be possible to determine whether it was venous, fetal, or menstrual in origin.[63] Additionally, there may be rare instances in which the blood contains impurities—secretions and hairs—which might make it possible to identify it as having come from the nose.[64]

How old are these blood stains? The determination of the age of blood stains is a difficult proposition. A variety of factors affect the rapidity with which blood dries; among these are presence or absence of wind or a draft, temperature, and humidity. Wind and higher temperatures accelerate the drying process; increased humidity retards it. "Blood begins to clot within three to five minutes after it is exposed to air; as it dries, the clot darkens in color, becoming reddish brown or dark brown when completely dry . . . an old dried blood clot may appear black."[65] On a smooth surface at room temperature a drop of blood, depending upon the size and thickness of the stain, will take about an hour to dry fully; the process begins at the edges, working toward the center. Under the same conditions, small pools will take some two to three hours to reach a dry state. If the blood is between the fluid and dry state, due to the formation of fibrin, it may be termed gelatinous. "On further drying, the stain will contract and finally pucker and crack around the edges."[66]

What was the condition of the donor of this sample of blood? If the blood sample is recovered in liquid form, it may be possible to determine, where there is a sufficiently large quantity, whether the person leaving the stain was under the influence of alcohol or drugs. Additionally, it may be possible to detect such conditions as the presence of carbon monoxide or the existence of venereal disease. In attempting to make these determinations, it is essential not only that the blood not be dried out, but that it not have undergone any degree of decomposition or contamination by foreign materials.

What contributions might blood stains contribute to the reconstruction of the crime? The study of blood drops or splashes, along with their direction and placement, occasionally makes it possible to determine where an assault occurred, the position of the injured portion of the body at the time of the assault, where the perpetrator was positioned at that particular time, whether the victim was attempting to evade blows, the number of blows struck, and related factors.[67] The shape of the blood stain provides an indication as to the height from which it has fallen.[68] Where the stain is uniformly round, a height of up to twenty inches is indicated; if the spines radiating outward from the blood stain are thick and relatively few, a drop height of twenty to forty inches is suggested. In cases where the spines radiating outward from the blood stain are numerous and fairly fine, a height of forty to sixty inches is implied. Moreover, if the person or the object releasing the blood is in motion, it will fall downward obliquely in the direction in which the person or object was moving. Examination of the blood stain will reveal by its shape the direction of this movement.[69] In general, the shape of the blood stain under such circumstances will be similar to an exclamation mark with the period indicating the direction of flight.

LOCATING BLOOD EVIDENCE

The places at which the investigator will find blood stains are virtually unlimited. For example, if a criminal homicide occurred indoors, blood might be found not only on the floor, but perhaps on the walls or even the ceiling. Ordinarily when perpetrators of violent crime get blood on their person or clothing, they will attempt to rid themselves of it immediately. In some instances, they may be so repelled by the sight of blood on their hand, they will impulsively wipe it on a piece of furniture such as a stuffed chair; if the fabric is multicolored or sufficiently dark, the stain may escape detection by the unobservant investigator. They may also attempt to clean bloodied hands prior to leaving the scene by using such places as the reverse side of a small throw rug or on the undersides of cushions on a couch. Occasionally, a criminal homicide will occur indoors, and the perpetrator will remove the body to an outdoor area to avoid discovery, return to the scene, and attempt to eliminate all traces of the crime. Typically, this would indicate the washing of hands and scrubbing or mopping the floor on which the body had lain. A case illustrates these types of behaviors and the actions required by the investigator:

An aggravated assault occurred between two friends who mutually agreed to misrepresent the crime and claim the cutting was an accident. When the victim appeared at the local hospital for treatment, the police were summoned due to the nature of the several wounds and their locations which suggested to the doctor that they were not accidentally inflicted. Subsequent examination of the scene revealed blood traces under the faucet handles in the kitchen where the perpetrator had turned on the water to wash his hands, blood was found in the trap of the sink, and although the perpetrator had washed portions of his shirt on which the victim's blood had fallen, he had done so in hot water, which merely set the stain, making it fairly readily observable to the naked eye. Additionally, although the floor at the scene had been mopped, traces of the same type blood as the victim's were also recovered. The location of the blood evidence was particularly pertinent because the people involved alleged that the incident had happened outside the house while they were barbecuing and that they had gone directly to the hospital.

The investigator must also be alert to the fact that although there are no apparent blood stains, laboratory examinations may be able to detect their existence. For example, if the perpetrator has blood stains from the victim on his clothing and attempts to use a wash cloth or some other means to rub it out, this may dilute the stain so that it is not visible, but laboratory examination may still be able to detect it. Furthermore, if the perpetrator has walked through blood stains at the scene and collected samples on the soles of the shoes, even though these may have been scrubbed or rubbed by walking some distance, minute traces may still be available up inside the nail holes, cracks in the soles, or other such crevices.[70] Very often, it will be possible to detect smaller drops of blood under daylight conditions if the investigator crouches close to the floor, viewing the surface at an angle. From the same position under conditions of darkness, the use of a flashlight held at an oblique angle to the floor will often allow otherwise unobservable stains to be seen.

HANDLING BLOOD EVIDENCE

Prior to the actual handling of blood evidence, the investigator should make notes concerning such aspects as the physical state of the stain, the amount present, the shape, the exact location of the stain in relationship to fixed objects, the pattern of the stain, temperature, humidity, and other pertinent details.[71] Naturally, as part of processing the crime scene, photographs should be taken. In criminal homicide cases the recording of the amount of blood found at the crime scene may be particularly important; the existence of severe wounds or numerous wounds coupled with the absence of any significant amount of blood at the scene may suggest the actual killing took place elsewhere and the body was removed to its present location.

If blood is collected in a liquid state, five cubic centimeters should be placed in a clean glass vial. A syringe, medicine dropper, spoon, or similar instrument—which is clean and will not contaminate the blood—is useful in the recovery process. When there may be a delay in transporting the sample to a place where it can be refrigerated, the container should be packed in ice or dry ice; under no circumstances should it be frozen. No anticoagulant, such as EDTA or heparin, should be added.[72] On immovable objects, blood stains which are dried and in crust form may be gathered using one of several methods. A clean razor blade will free the crust, which is then placed into a container, or a piece of clean paper can be slid under the crust,

freeing it. The paper is then folded, sealed, and placed into an evidence envelope. Whether the blood is recovered in liquid or solid state, it is a good practice to obtain an unstained sample of the surface from which it was gathered in order to allow the laboratory to demonstrate that the result of the tests performed was not affected by the surface on which the blood stain was deposited.[73] When fresh blood stains appear on a weapon, they should be allowed to air-dry and then be packaged with the dry crust still on the weapon for transmittal to the laboratory. When dried blood crusts appear on a movable object or weapon, they are not to be removed, but should be carefully packaged with these stains intact. In violent crimes it will not be unusual that the investigator recovers, either at the scene of the crime or at the hospital, articles of clothing which contain wet blood stains. Such garments should be hung and allowed to air-dry. In no case should they be subject to accelerated drying by hanging them close to a heat source as this may produce decomposition, thereby reducing the evidentiary value of the blood stain. Once bloodstained garments have dried, they should be folded so that none of the creases are in the same areas as the encrusted blood stains, as this may have a tendency to dislodge them. Moreover, when packaging such garments, tissue paper should be used to separate the various portions of the garment in order to lessen the possibility of dislodging blood crusts. Blood stains on soil are best gathered using a trowel or similar instrument, and the samples placed in a wide-mouthed Mason jar. It is essential that the sample be at least as deep as the depth the blood may have seeped into the soil; in gathering such samples, it is better to collect samples too deep than too shallow. The advantage of using a Mason-type jar is that it enables the crime scene technician or investigator to examine the sample to ensure that there are no earthworms or insects which could destroy the blood by consuming it.

HUMAN EXCRETIONS AND SECRETIONS

Evidence falling into this category includes saliva, urine, semen, perspiration, vaginal secretions, feces, and vomitus.[74] With the exception of semen and vaginal secretions, this type of evidence will only rarely be encountered. However, the investigator must be prepared to take advantage of the opportunities presented. The principal value of this category of evidence lies in the fact that approximately 80 percent of all humans are secretors, meaning that their body materials contain a substance, which makes it possible to establish their blood group.

Saliva may be found on cigarette butts, gags, cups, toothpicks, and related items. In addition to the possibility of determining the blood type of the donor, if sufficient quantity is available, it may be possible to determine any alcohol content.

Urine is ordinarily associated with sex offenses and breaking and enterings. It may be possible with urine evidence to determine the alcohol content in the donor's blood; however, unless there is a fairly large sample, it may be difficult to distinguish between animal and human samples. Semen is found as evidence in sexual offenses, auto-erotic deaths (sexual asphyxiations), occasionally in burglaries, and on rare occasions in criminal homicides. Semen is grayish-white in color, and in liquid form it has a chlorinelike odor. When dried, it is stiff and starchlike in consistency. Semen is subject to contamination by foreign agents, such as blood; it may be virtually invisible to the eye, but can be detected by laboratory examination. Semen evidence should be left intact on the item on which it is observed, or suspected to be, or alternatively—if the object is immovable—

dissolved with clear water and gathered using a clean eyedropper. Perspiration will only rarely be encountered due to the rapidity with which it evaporates. It will ordinarily be found in handkerchiefs, gloves or other similar items left at the crime scene.

Feces are occasionally encountered at the scenes of burglaries, particularly those involving attacks on money chests or safes. Opinion varies as to whether this is done as a sign of nervousness, as a matter of convenience, or as an indication of contempt toward the police or owners of the property. If the person is a secretor, this type of evidence might help to establish the blood type of the donor, and the paper or other material used by the person for cleaning himself may yield useful information, including fingerprints.

Vomitus is highly unusual evidence and is often associated with violent personal crimes or burglaries; it is possible from examination of this type of evidence to make some determination about the content and time of the last meal, along with an occasional indication as to the medical condition of the suspect.

LIPSTICK

One forensic analysis of lipstick underscores its potential value.[75] As depicted in Table 4-2, a total of 117 different lipsticks were collected from 15 manufacturers. No extreme colors were included in the sample; all were pink, red, red-brown, and red-violet. When subject to three different types of analysis, all 117 different lipsticks were correctly identified.

Lipstick is a type of evidence which is occasionally encountered in a variety of offenses, but is often not appreciated for the contributions it can make to an investigation, particularly its potential to connect the offender with the scene and/or victim and to help evaluate a suspect's alibi. For example, lipstick may be transferred from the victim

TABLE 4-2
Manufacturers of Lipsticks Examined

Manufacturer	No. of Lipstick Samples
Revlon	21
Max Factor	19
Helena Rubinstein	18
Ellen Betrix	16
Pierre Robert	10
Cutex	9
Jane Hellen	8
Laponie	5
Clinique	4
Mary Quant	2
Avon	1
Charlie	1
Marbert	1
Estee Lauder	1
Harriet Hubbard	1
Total:	117 samples

Source: Jan Andrasko, "Forensic Analysis of Lipsticks," *Forensic Science International,* Vol. 17, No. 3, May/ June 1981, p. 236.

to her assailant's clothing during a rape. If the suspect is stopped in the general area shortly thereafter with lipstick on the collar or shoulder of his shirt, he may claim that it was that of his girl friend. Comparisons of the victim's lipstick, the lipstick on the suspect's clothing, and that of the girl friend could reveal that only the victim's lipstick and that on the suspect's clothing are consistent. Other types of crimes in which lipstick may be encountered as evidence include ritualistic slayings, strong-armed robberies, and other crimes of violence. Even in property offenses, where there has been no victim-suspect contact, obscene messages may be left, with lipstick used to write on mirrors, walls, or other places. Lipstick evidence should be photographed before disturbing it. When on clothing, the entire garment should be submitted to the laboratory, and care should be taken to pack it in such a fashion

that the affected area is well protected. Where there are sufficient quantities on other surfaces, a sample should be collected with a clean razor blade or similar instrument and placed in a clean pillbox. Lipstick evidence encountered at several different locations of a crime scene should be collected and packaged separately. Dry cotton should not be used to protect lipstick evidence because it creates problems in handling the evidence in the laboratory. Nor should lipstick evidence be allowed to sit in the sun or to remain in the trunks of cars where it may be subject to extreme heat. In all cases a generous sample of the victim's or other donor's lipstick should also be obtained.

FIREARMS EVIDENCE

Firearms evidence is one of the most common types to be encountered, consisting of such items as revolvers, pistols, rifles, shotguns, loaded cartridges, misfired cartridges, bullets, shell cases, powder residues, magazines, clips, shot pellets, and the wads used in older shotgun ammunition.

The investigator must develop a familiarity with firearms in order to answer such important questions as: Is the weapon a pistol or a revolver? Is it a rifle or a shotgun? Of what shot construction is the weapon—that is, single shot, tubular fed, semiautomatic, automatic, or rotating cylinder? How many shots does the weapon hold? How are expended cartridges ejected? Does the weapon chamber load or is it fed by a magazine or clip? Is the weapon intended for rimfire or centerfire ammunition? What caliber is the weapon? What are lands and grooves? Is the barrel of the weapon rifled and, if so, does it have left- or right-handed twist?[76]

As in the case of blood and other types of evidence, there are certain determinations which can be made from the examination of firearms evidence; these are presented in re-

FIGURE 4-28   Important Features of a Rifled Firearm's Barrel

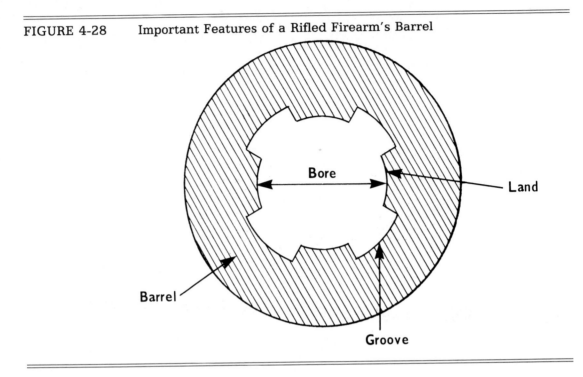

sponse to typical questions facing the investigator.

Was this bullet fired from this particular weapon? Figure 4-28 depicts one view of the interior of the rifled barrel of a firearm and Figure 4-29 the comparison of two bullets. In contrast, the barrel of a shotgun is smooth. *Bore* is the correct term to apply to the diameter of the interior of a weapon's barrel; in a rifled barrel, this is measured between two opposing lands, or ridges. Technically, caliber refers to the diameter of the bullet intended for use in the weapon. Generally, a bullet is somewhat larger than the diameter of the bore, so that as it passes through the barrel, the lands grip it, causing it to rotate, usually in a right-hand direction.[77] It is this process of movement which creates the highly individualized striations on the bullet. Additionally, in defective revolvers, where the barrel and the chamber containing the loaded cartridge do not align properly, there will be a sheering effect which is

observable on the recovered bullet. In order to determine whether a particular firearm fired a particular bullet, it is necessary to compare the bullet recovered at the scene with a test bullet fired through the gun which is suspected of having fired the bullet in question. Whether or not it is possible to make a positive identification is affected by the condition of the recovered bullet and the condition of the gun at the time it is finally located.

What findings are possible by examination of a bullet? A fired bullet yields evidence of the class characteristics of the weapon which fired it with respect to the number of lands and grooves and their height, depth, and width. The class characteristics of a firearm are those design specifications to which it was manufactured; weapons of a given make and model will have the same class characteristics.[78] The individual characteristics of the bore are found in the striae along the fired bullet. Examination of a fired bullet will

FIGURE 4-29

On the left, a photomicrograph of a bullet recovered at autopsy; on the right, a test bullet fired from a .38 caliber revolver.

Courtesy Regional Criminalistics Laboratory, Metropolitan Kansas City, Missouri

suggest the type of weapon from which it was fired, whether the bullet is a hard-nose or soft-nose projectile, and the pitch and direction of twist within the barrel. Additionally, if the fired bullet is recovered in sufficient size, it may be possible, through weighing and measurement, to determine its caliber. Since bullets are often recovered as fragments, the caliber may only be implied by the weight's ruling out smaller calibers. While it is possible to determine the caliber of the bullet, some caution must be taken with respect to determining the bore of the weapon from which it was fired, as it is possible to fire a smaller caliber bullet through a larger bored weapon.

Fired bullets ordinarily will have experienced some damage as a result of their impacting. In some cases it will be possible to see fabric impressions on the bullet's nose,

the impression being made as it passed through the victim's outer garment. Additionally, there may be minute traces of blood, tissue, bone, or other such materials. Great care must be taken by the investigator not to destroy or in any way alter such evidence. Where the fired bullet is recovered from the person or body of the victim, the investigator should, if there is any doubt about their familiarity with proper handling procedure, alert the attending medical personnel as to the irreparable damage which can be wrought by the careless application of forceps or other such instruments in removing the bullet.

It should be noted at this juncture that it is ordinarily not possible to make a positive identification as to whether pellets were fired from a particular shotgun. However, in extraordinarily rare circumstances involving

FIGURE 4-30

Photomicrograph showing comparison of questioned and known firing-pin impressions on a .22 caliber rimfire cartridge case.

Courtesy Regional Criminalistics Laboratory, Metropolitan Kansas City, Missouri

smoothbore firearms, it may be possible to make an individual identification due to gross defects in the barrel.[79]

What findings can be made by examining fired cartridge cases? While the fired bullet is marked by the barrel only, the fired cartridge case is marked by several parts of the weapon in the actions of loading, firing, and extracting.[80] When the firing pin strikes the weapon, its impression is recorded; this is true in both centerfire and rimfire ammunition.[81] Subsequent to the firing pin's striking the primer, the burning gases inside the casing begin to expand, forcing the cartridge outward against the walls of the chamber and

back against the breach face of the weapon. Any striations present on the breach face and any damage in the chamber will thereby be recorded on the cartridge case. In semiautomatic and automatic weapons, extractor and ejector markings are left on the rim of the casing, even if the cartridge is merely run through the action of the weapon and not actually fired. Additionally, in the case of semiautomatic pistols, the cartridge case may be marked by the magazine. Other markings may appear on the cartridge casing due to a particular type of action by a firearm. (See Figures 4-30, 4-31, and 4-32.)

What miscellaneous determinations can

FIGURE 4-31

Photomicrograph of the breach face markings on questioned and known .38 caliber automatic cartridge case. The cartridge on the left was recovered at the scene of an aggravated assault and compared with the cartridge on the right, which was recovered at the scene of a criminal homicide. No firearm was recovered.

Courtesy Regional Criminalistics Laboratory, Metropolitan Kansas City, Missouri

be made by examination of firearms evidence? If a firearm is received at a crime laboratory, its general mechanical condition can be assessed, which will lend credence to or discredit statements that the shooting was accidental. For example, if the trigger pull on a weapon is of the "hair" nature, requiring only the slightest pressure to pull it, this would indicate that an accidental shooting was possible. Laboratory examination might reveal that a firearm is constructed—or malfunctioning—so that it could discharge by being dropped on its hammer, thereby giving more credibility to a claim that a shooting was accidental.[82] Furthermore, even though invisible to the naked eye, obliterated serial numbers can sometimes be restored by the laboratory, thus providing an additional investigative lead. Proximity of the gun to the victim at the time of discharge may be established by an examination of powder residues on the victim's clothing. These usually are only produced when the firearm is within approximately twenty-four inches of the

FIGURE 4-32

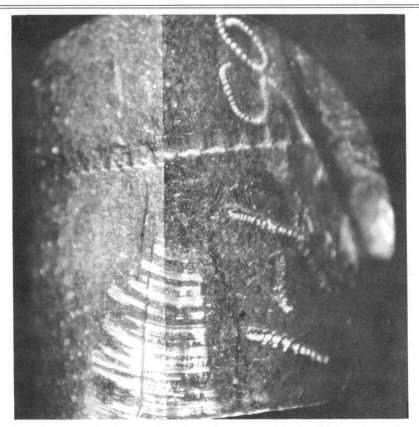

Photomicrograph of striated marks made on questioned and known cartridge cases. The marks were made as a slide acted on the mouths of cartridge cases in a Colt .45 caliber semiautomatic pistol.

Courtesy Regional Criminalistics Laboratory, Metropolitan Kansas City, Missouri

clothing; their presence or absence might be an important factor in assessing whether or not a shooting was a criminal homicide or a suicide.[83] Additionally, even though there is no apparent presence of powder residues, the victim's clothing should be processed by the laboratory. Finally, by assessing the amount of dust or other debris inside the barrel of a seized weapon, the expert can come to a conclusion with respect to the recency with which the weapon was fired. Ordinarily, this will range from "very recently" to "some time ago," which may mean from several weeks to a number of years.[84]

COLLECTING FIREARMS EVIDENCE

A cardinal rule in handling weapons at the scene of a crime is that they should never be picked up or moved until they have been photographed and measurements made for the crime scene sketch. As in the case of many rules for criminal investigations, there are several exceptions to this. First, when the weapon is found out of doors, if there is any likelihood that inclement weather may destroy the possibility of obtaining latent fingerprints, it should be immediately removed to a protected area. Second, at the scenes of aggravated assaults and murders, feelings run high and there is a danger that an emotion-charged person may suddenly attempt to pick up the weapon and shoot another party. Third, there may be some compelling safety need, such as uncocking the weapon. Ordinarily, however, the first handling of a weapon should be to process it for fingerprints. The investigator must pick up a firearm with great care, despite familiarity with weapons, as many weapons have individual peculiarities which may produce an accidental discharge through careless or indiscriminate handling.

In no case should a pencil or similar object be placed into the barrel of the gun to pick it up; this can dislodge evidence which may be in the barrel, such as tissue, blood, hair, or other trace evidence; and it can contaminate the barrel, thereby confusing the laboratory examiner. The proper method of packaging a hand gun—once unloaded—is to suspend it in a small box by a ring which passes through the trigger guard. As bullets, cartridge cases, and related firearms evidence are gathered, they should be packaged separately. The practice of putting a handgun in a coat or pants pocket until transferred to an evidence envelope at some later time is to be strictly avoided.

MARKING FIREARMS EVIDENCE

While certain sources recommend marking a bullet on its nose, the practice is to be condemned; this will destroy fabric impressions or dislodge trace evidence such as blood, hair, fiber, tissue, paint, or similar materials which may be of considerable importance. The proper place to mark a bullet seized as evidence is on its base. If the bullet is frag-

mented or of small caliber, it should be placed in cotton in a small box and sealed with tape, with the appropriate identifying information placed on the tape. It is desirable that a cartridge case be marked inside the mouth of the cartridge. If the necessary equipment is lacking or if the cartridge is of very small caliber, such as .22 or .25, it should be marked in the same fashion as a small-caliber bullet or fragment. Guns themselves should be marked in a place that is a permanent part of the weapon, for example, on the frame, when the weapon is an automatic or semiautomatic; the clip or magazine should also be marked. Care should be taken in marking firearms to avoid unnecessary defacement. There are certain permanent places which can be marked unobtrusively: inside the frame of a revolver which has been broken open; on the magazine of a pump-action gun, after moving the slide to the rear; and inside the handle of semiautomatic pistols. The proper method of recording the positions of cartridges recovered in a revolver is depicted in Figure 4-33.

TOOL MARKS

Crimes against property frequently involve forcible entry or the application of some type of tool; as these types of crimes are among the most difficult to clear, the associated physical evidence takes on considerable importance.[85] Tool marks may be created when an instrument is pressed into some physical object, such as a doorjamb, creating a negative impression; by being scraped across a surface, cutting tiny furrows termed *striae;* or in some combination of marks, such as both an impression and striae. In the broad context, the examination of tool marks includes the identification of objects which have forcibly contacted each other, were joined together under pressure for a period of time and then removed from contact, or

FIGURE 4-33   Marking Positions of Cartridges Recovered in Revolvers
FACING REAR OF CYLINDER

Appearance of cylinder
as recovered.

Diagram to be made by officer
recovering firearm.

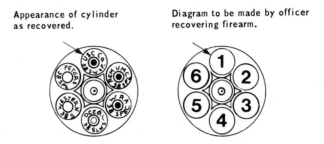

Scratch arrow on rear of cylinder to indicate the chamber position under
hammer (in line with barrel) when recovered. Then prepare diagram numbering
in clockwise direction the remaining chambers, i.e.,2,3,4,5,6, etc.

Chamber Position	Condition	Maker
#1	Fired	U.S. Cartridge Co.
#2	Fired	Remington Arms Co.
#3	Fired	Winchester Repeating Arms Co.
#4	Misfire	Dominion Cartridge Co.
#5	Loaded	Western Cartridge Co.
#6	Loaded	Peters Cartridge Co.

Source: Crime Laboratory Division, *Criminal Investigation and Physical Evidence Handbook.*
Madison: State of Wisconsin, 1969, p. 127.

were originally a single item before being broken or cut apart.[86]

The examination of a tool mark may yield a great deal of useful information, such as the type, size, and action employed when the instrument was operated. For example, a clear impression may suggest the use of a hammer or punch; scrape marks may indicate the employment of some flat-bladed tool such as a crowbar or screwdriver; a shearing instrument—where the blades pass one another as in the case of scissors and tin snips—may be suggested; or a pinching-type tool—where the blades butt against each other, as in wire cutters—may seem to have been used.

Additionally, by examining the manner in which the tool was employed, it is often pos-

sible to make a determination with some degree of reliability with respect to the skill of the perpetrator. Perhaps most important in the examination of a tool mark is whether it offers sufficient characteristics to allow for individual identification should a tool be located in a suspect's possession.

In those instances where a tool is found in a suspect's possession, the examination of it may yield foreign deposits, such as paint or metal, which may have either class or individual characteristics. The comparison of the tool with the tool mark may establish whether they have consistent class characteristics and, when sufficient microscopic marks are present, whether there are sufficient individual characteristics to say with certainty that this particular tool made this

FIGURE 4-34

Photomicrograph on left depicts microscopic striae left by a burglar on the head of a woodscrew when attacking a door. The right side is a known or test impression made by the laboratory examiner using the screwdriver seized in the suspect's custody.

particular mark (see Figures 4-34 and 4-35).[87]

When collecting evidence of tool marks, every effort should be made to obtain and submit the actual area for direct comparison. Where this is not possible, a cast should be made. In no case should materials which have a tendency to shrink or expand—such as plaster of paris—be employed. Dental compounds ordinarily are the most satisfactory for this purpose and are available at most dental supply outlets.[88] While photographs are useful in establishing the overall location of the mark, they are ordinarily of no value for identification purposes.[89] In no event should the investigator place a tool against a tool mark for size evaluation, as it may lead to accidental cross contamination or result in the accidental destruction of evidence. When submitting a tool to the crime laboratory for examination, the actual tool should be submitted; the making of test impressions or cuts are functions of qualified technicians in the laboratory. The importance of this last point is illustrated by the fact that under test conditions in the laboratory it was found that when there was more than 15 degrees difference between the vertical angle at which

FIGURE 4-35

Photomicrograph on left reveals striae left by a burglar using pliers to attack a doorknob. At right is a test impression made with the suspect's pliers in the laboratory.

a screwdriver was actually used and the comparison mark made in the laboratory, an improper finding of no identity from the same tool could result.[90]

THE EXAMINATION OF QUESTIONED DOCUMENTS

A document is loosely defined as anything on which a mark is made for the purpose of conveying a message. Many seemingly insignificant documents involved in investigations subsequently offer conclusive proof of certain facts if examined properly. For example, frequently it can be proved that a handwritten notation was the work of a certain person, that a typewritten message was produced by a particular machine, or that a copy of a document was made on one specific duplicating machine. Beyond these often recognized contributions, the document examiner may be able to detect erasures, alterations, or obliterations of key portions of documents; cause decisive information to be yielded from apparently useless charred paper fragments; or link the torn edges of documents together conclusively. The possibility that a document

FIGURE 4-36

Fracture mark of claws of hammer, found at the scene of a burglary, with remainder of tool.

may bear evidence of importance must never be overlooked.[91]

CARE, HANDLING, AND SUBMISSION OF DOCUMENTS

All documentary evidence should be packed so that it is preserved in the same condition as when obtained by the investigator. The general rule is to place documents in protective folders and handle them only when necessary. Documents should never be folded or creased. If torn or mutilated, such evidence is to be submitted in that condition with precautions taken to prevent further damage. Due to its fragile nature, charred paper should be packed in cotton or similar material and transported personally to the laboratory.

While preliminary opinions are possible from the examination of copies, in the vast majority of cases, it is imperative that the original documents be submitted for examination. Information which might prejudice the examiner should not be forwarded. However, any information of assistance to the examiner—such as abnormal physical or mental condition of the person executing a certain writing, unusual conditions associated with its production, or the fact that a typewriter related to the case was recently repaired—should be submitted.

STANDARDS OF COMPARISON

Standards of comparison are defined as any handwriting, printing, typewriting, or like material from a known source that is used as a standard for comparison with a questioned document. Such standards must be proved to the satisfaction of the court to be from a particular source. It is the responsibility of the investigator to establish that such documents are from a particular known source. The collection of suitable and adequate standards is one aspect of the investigation that should be given the most careful attention.

TYPES OF EXAMINATIONS

It is not possible within the limitations of this section to describe thoroughly every type of examination to which a document may be subjected; however, the most common are as follows:

Handwriting Examinations Through the development of personal habits, an individual's handwriting becomes individualistic. In the vast majority of cases, it is possible to identify a certain writing as having been produced by a particular individual, provided a sufficient quantity of questioned writing and known standards are available for examination. The field of handwriting identification has no connection with "graphology" or "graphoanalysis"—the so-called art or science of reading character and personality traits from handwriting.

Before a positive opinion of identity can be stated, there must be present in both the questioned and known writing a sufficient number of individualistic writing characteristics which, when considered in combination with one another, are sufficient to establish beyond all doubt that both writings are the work of one individual. Additionally, there must be no basic differences in the two writings. In some instances, the amount of evidence necessary to support a positive opinion will be lacking for a number of reasons: The questioned writing may be too limited, too highly disguised, written under some unusual circumstances, or for some similar reason fail to exhibit a sufficient number of individualistic habits to isolate it as the work of one person. In such cases, it is necessary to express a "qualified" or inconclusive opinion. Ordinarily, however, when qualified opinions are expressed, the fault most often lies in a failure to obtain sufficient proper known standards for comparison with the writing in question.

In tracing or copying another person's signature, people attempt to exclude their own writing habits and adopt those of the person from whom they are copying; in effect, they are drawing rather than writing. In such cases, it is usually possible to state that the signature in question is a forgery, but it is practically impossible to identify the author by comparing it with normal writing specimens of the suspect.

Standards of Comparison: Handwriting The writing of every person contains a certain range of variation, some having little variation, others having a great deal. The conditions under which the writing was executed, the type of writing instrument and surface, the position of a letter in a word, the purpose for which the writing was prepared—e.g., signature on a delivery slip versus that on a legal document—the mental and physical condition of the writer, and other factors will cause additional variation with most people. One of the most common causes of variation in dealing with specimen writing, written on request, is intentional disguise.

In view of the fact that a person's writing will vary under different writing conditions, it is imperative that the following basic rules be adhered to when obtaining specimen writing: duplicate the conditions as closely as possible; duplicate the text of the questioned writing as closely as possible; and secure an adequate quantity of known standards.

Handwriting standards fall into two basic groups: collected and requested. Collected writings are those which were executed during the normal course of business or social activities at a time when the author had no knowledge that they would later be used for comparison purposes. They should include writings made as close in time as possible to the date of the writing in question and should be in the same style as the questioned writing, i.e., signatures for comparison with signatures and extended writing for comparison with extended writing.[92] Among the sources from which collected writings may be obtained are diaries, personal letters, notebooks, cancelled checks, statements, receipts, and applications for employment. It is advisable to obtain some collected writings in each case, even though it may also be possible to obtain specimens written on request. The admission of a certain standard as the known writing of a particular person is at the discretion of the trial judge. However, the source of a standard can usually be proved to the satisfaction of the court by: an admission from the author; the testimony of a person who saw the writing executed; or testimony that the writing is undenied writing that would normally be considered that of the particular person, such as that in notebooks, ledgers personally kept, cancelled checks not claimed to be forgeries, and letters to friends.

Requested writings are those executed at the request of the investigator for the purpose of comparing them with writing in question. The type of paper, the writing instrument, and other variables should be duplicated as closely as possible. The suspect should be comfortably seated at a desk or table, put at ease, and the text dictated at various speeds with no suggestions as to arrangement, spelling, or punctuation. The donor should never be allowed to see the writing in question before providing standards. Each specimen should be removed from view as soon as it is written, and initialed and dated. Specimens obtained during the early stages of an interview, before lengthy interrogation, are more likely to reflect normal writing habits—and more likely to be given willingly—than those obtained later in the interview.

The suspect is asked to write his or her name and address, date of birth, occupation, and other miscellaneous material. It is also preferable to dictate a lengthy text prior to securing the actual comparable standards, i.e., the same name, address, etc., as that in question. The following text contains all numerals and letters of the alphabet and is therefore good material to dictate:

> Our London business is good, but Vienna and Berlin are quiet. Mr. D. Lloyd has gone to Switzerland and I hope for good news. He will be there for a week at 1496 Zermont St. and then goes to Turin and Rome and will join Col. Parry and arrive at Athens, Greece, on Nov. 27th or Dec. 2nd. Letters there should be addressed: King James Blvd., 3580. We expect Chas. E. Fuller on Tuesday. Dr. L. McQuaid and Robert Unger, Esq., left on the "YX" Express tonight.

After securing these initial specimens, the suspect should then be asked to provide "comparable standards," which are samples that can be examined in comparison with the

TABLE 4-3
Guidelines for Obtaining Comparable Standards for Commonly Encountered Questioned Documents

Questioned	Standards
Writing on face of check	Ten to fifteen blank checks of the same size completed by the suspect, using the same test.
Endorsement on check	Same signature on the back of ten to fifteen blank checks or separate slips of paper of comparable width. Draw in the base line if one appears on the questioned document.
Extended writing, e.g., obscene letter, holdup note, etc.	Same test written approximately five times on separate sheets of paper of approximately the same size.[a]

[a] If disclosing contents of extended writing is undesirable, another text should be dictated that contains similar words, misspelled words, addresses, etc.

questioned document. Table 4-3 provides guidelines for obtaining comparable standards for commonly encountered questioned documents.

Hand Printing and Numerals The hand printing and numerals of an individual can usually be identified as that person's work. The fundamental rules and principles discussed in relation to handwriting hold true for the examination of hand printing and numerals.

Typewriting Generally typewriters and printers in a word-processing system can be equipped with conventional typebars (Figure 4-37), a single-element ball (Figure 4-38), or a print wheel (Figure 4-39).[93] Although the technology is in the process of transition, a typewriter is a machine with no or very limited memory capabilities. Since the introduction of the first commercially successful typewriter by Remington in 1873, there have been steady, if not dramatic, changes and improvements in the technology involved.

The printed text on a document can now be the result of a typewriter, a word-processing system, or a high-speed printer. Looming beyond high-speed ink jet and laser printers are such developments as voice-activated printing devices, for which a prototype already has been built.[94] These factors require continuing research to ensure that technological advances do not diminish the ability of document examiners to make important discriminations. The two most common determinations which document examiners are asked to make in this regard are: (1) the make and model machine used to prepare the document, and (2) whether a specific machine was employed to prepare the document in question.

In collecting evidence from a suspect typewriter or printer, the investigator should adhere to the following guidelines:

1. Remove the ribbon and submit it to the laboratory as the text of the material in question may be discernible on it.
2. Prepare all samples of printing with a fresh ribbon.

FIGURE 4-37   A Conventional Typebar

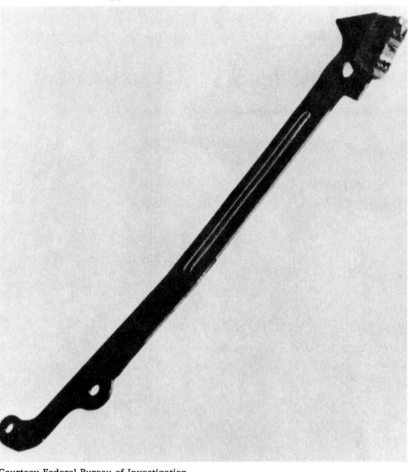

Courtesy Federal Bureau of Investigation

3. The entire text of the questioned document should be reproduced unless it is unusually long, in which case a representative sample will be sufficient.

4. After either removing the ribbon or placing the machine in the stencil position, obtain samples of each character by typing through carbon paper onto a piece of white bond paper.

5. It is usually not necessary to submit the machine to the laboratory, although the document examiner may subsequently request it when comparisons of the questioned and known documents reveal questions about such matters as alignment which can only be satisfactorily determined by examining the machine itself.

6. It must be determined when the machine was last cleaned, maintained, and repaired, as all of these could affect the examiner's conclusion. Whenever possi-

FIGURE 4-38   A Single-Ball Element

Courtesy Federal Bureau of Investigation

ble, the machine should be maintained in its current condition until the document examiner submits his or her findings in the event that the machine may have to be sent to the laboratory.

7. All specimens obtained by the investigator should include the machine's make, model, and serial number in addition to the investigator's usual identifying marks.

Checkwriters If at all possible, the suspected machine should be submitted. Failing this, specimen impressions should be obtained on similar paper, each questioned combination of figures being duplicated approximately five times. It is often possible to determine the make of a checkwriter used to prepare certain checks and whether or not a particular checkwriter was used.

Age of Documents The exact age of a certain writing or document is usually very difficult to determine. However, it is occasionally possible to establish age within broad limits through an examination of the writing paper, typewriting, ink, writing instrument,

and other features. In one case, thirty-three original letters bearing the letterhead stationery and handwriting of a physician were dated between January 1978 and June 1979.[95] If those letters, which dealt with Medicaid patients, were not actually prepared when dated, they would form part of the evidence of Medicaid fraud. The laboratory examination revealed that they had been recently prepared, steamed, and then baked to give them the appearance of being older than they actually were.

Inks Some problems connected with inks can be answered; others cannot. Sometimes it is demonstrable that different inks were used to complete different portions of a document, but it is rarely possible to determine that ink from a certain pen or bottle was used. In the latter case, it may be shown that the ink is similar in all respects, but this will not eliminate the possibility of other sources.

Table 4-4 covers proper handling of some other forms of documentary evidence.

TABLE 4-4
The Handling of Miscellaneous Documentary Evidence

Material	Handling	Determinations Possible[a]
Rubber and steel stamps	Pack carefully to avoid accidental damage to imprinting surface.	Whether a certain stamp made a certain impression.
Paper	Avoid folding or creasing.	Within broad limits, the source of a paper specimen and whether two pieces are from the same source. Whether a certain paper once was joined with a particular piece or stub.
Charred/water-soaked documents	Charred documents are extremely fragile and should be packed carefully with cotton or some other delicate nonabrasive material and hand-carried to the laboratory.	If not reduced to ash, may be possible to decipher writing.
Mechanical printing	Avoid folding or creasing.	Process used to print or duplicate. Whether a particular machine produced a particular writing. Whether two or more specimens are from a common and particular source.
Indented writing	Avoid folding or creasing.	The text of the indented message. Whether the sample containing the indented writing was in contact with a particular pad or other supportive surface.

[a] Although these determinations are possible, not even the most diligent examination always yields them.

FIGURE 4-39   A Print Wheel

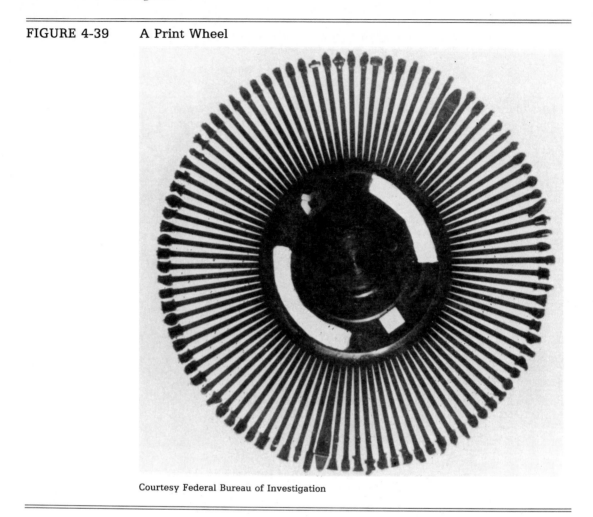

Courtesy Federal Bureau of Investigation

QUESTIONS

1. Define and give two examples of class and individual characteristic evidence.
2. What is the proper method of collecting soil evidence?
3. How do shoe residues and shoe impressions differ?
4. Describe the steps in preparing a plaster of paris cast of a shoe impression.
5. What are the important considerations in collecting and packaging glass evidence?
6. Why are fibers of greater evidential potential than hairs?
7. What are the major fingerprint patterns?
8. Describe the conventional procedure for developing and lifting latent fingerprints.
9. What conclusions may the laboratory reach from the analysis of blood evidence?
10. How are liquid and dried blood evidence collected?
11. What is a "secretor"?

12. What are lands and grooves?
13. What is the cardinal rule in handling firearms at the scene of a crime?
14. Where should firearms evidence be marked?
15. What is a fracture match?

16. What is a document?
17. What guidelines should investigators follow when gathering evidence from a typewriter suspected of being used in a criminal offense?

NOTES

1. Federal Bureau of Investigation, *Handbook of Forensic Science* (Washington, D.C.: Government Printing Office, October 1984), p. 2.
2. Ibid., p. 2.
3. Federal Bureau of Investigation, *Handbook of Forensic Science* (Washington, D.C.: Government Printing Office, 1978), p. 2.
4. Raymond C. Murray and John C. F. Tedrow, *Forensic Geology* (New Brunswick, New Jersey: Rutgers University Press, 1975), p. 22.
5. For additional information see S. Kijewski and U. Von Mulmann, "The Influence of Soil Differences in Quantification of and Recognizability of Serological Properties of Blood Traces in Soil," *Journal of Legal Medicine,* 1975, Vol. 75, no. 4, pp. 253–263.
6. Murray and Tedrow, *Forensic Geology,* pp. 17–19.
7. Ibid., p. 23.
8. Ibid., p. 25.
9. United States Department of Justice, Law Enforcement Assistance Administration, National Institute of Law Enforcement and Criminal Justice, *Crime Scene Search and Physical Evidence Handbook,* prepared by Richard H. Fox and Carl L. Cunningham (Washington, D.C.: Government Printing Office, 1985), p. 80.
10. Ibid., p. 81.
11. Ibid., p. 81.
12. Crime Laboratory Division, *Criminal Investigation and Physical Evidence Handbook* (Madison: State of Wisconsin, 1969), p. 105.
13. Murray and Tedrow, *Forensic Geology,* p. 26.
14. Arne Svensson and Otto Wendel, *Techniques of Crime Scene Investigation* (New York: American Elsevier, 1965), p. 75.
15. FBI, *Handbook of Forensic Science,* 1984, pp. 86–89.
16. Svensson and Wendel, *Techniques of Crime Scene Investigation,* p. 75.
17. For information on the comparative performances of various products see J. V. Vandiver and J. H. Wolcott, "Identification of Suitable Plaster For Crime Scene Casting," *Journal of Forensic Sciences,* 1978, Vol. 23, pp. 607–614.
18. Svensson and Wendel, *Techniques of Crime Scene Investigation,* p. 79.
19. Paul L. Kirk, *Crime Investigation* (New York: Interscience, 1960), p. 257.
20. Svensson and Wendel, *Techniques of Crime Scene Investigation,* p. 153.
21. In this regard see S. G. Ryland and R. J. Kopec, "The Evidential Value of Automobile Paint Chips," *Journal of Forensic Sciences,* 1979, Vol. 24, pp. 40–47; R. F. E. Percy and R. J. Audette, "Automobile Repaints: Just a New Look?" *Journal of Forensic Sciences,* 1980, Vol. 25, No. 1, pp. 189–239; and S. G. Ryland, R. J. Kopec, and P. N. Somerville, "The Evidential Value of Automobile Paint, Part II: Frequency of Occurrence of Topcoat

Colors," *Journal of Forensic Sciences,* 1981, Vol. 26, No. 1, pp. 64–74.

22. Svensson and Wendel, *Techniques of Crime Scene Investigation,* p. 154.

23. State of Wisconsin, *Criminal Investigation and Physical Evidence Handbook,* p. 110. Also see W. C. McCrone, "Collaborative Study of the Microscopical Characterization of Glass Fragments," *Journal of the Association of Official Analytical Chemists,* 1973, Vol. 56, No. 5, pp. 1223–1226.

24. See, for example, Law Enforcement Standards Laboratory, *The Characterization of Auto Headlight Glass By Refractive Index and Density* (Washington, D.C.: Department of Commerce, October 1981); D. P. Slater and W. Fong, "Density, Refractive Index, and Dispersion in the Examination of Glass: Their Relative Worth as Proof," *Journal of Forensic Sciences,* 1982, Vol. 27, No. 3, pp. 474–483; and David A. Stoney and John I. Thornton, "The Forensic Significance of the Correlation of Density and Refractive Index in Glass Evidence," *Forensic Science International,* 1985, Vol. 29, pp. 147–157.

25. State of Wisconsin, *Criminal Investigation and Physical Evidence Handbook,* p. 111.

26. For further reading see S. P. McJungkins and J. I. Thornton, "Glass Fracture Analysis: A Review," *Forensic Science,* 1973, Vol. 2, No. 1, pp. 1–27; H. Kijewski, "Problems in the Interpretation of Gunshots through Glass," *Journal of Legal Medicine,* 1974, Vol. 74, No. 3, pp. 167–175; and C. J. Stahl et al., "The Effect of Glass as an Intermediate Target on Bullets," *Journal of Forensic Sciences,* 1979, Vol. 24, pp. 6–17.

27. Zug Standing Bear, "Glass Examinations in Old and New Reflections," a paper presented at the 1983 meeting of the American Academy of Forensic Sciences.

28. See E. P. Martin, "Wool Fibers as Evidence: Their Probative Value in Criminal Procedure," *International Criminal Police Review,* 1975, Vol. 30, No. 288, pp. 126–137; Nicholas Petraco, P. R. Deforest, and Howard Harris, "A New Approach to the Microscopical Examination and Comparison of Synthetic Fibers Encountered in Forensic Science Cases," *Journal of Forensic Sciences,* 1980, Vol. 25, No. 3, pp. 571–582; and Ronald Resua, "A Semi–Micro Technique for the Extraction and Comparison of Dyes in Textile Fibers," *Journal of Forensic Sciences,* 1980, Vol. 25, No. 1, pp. 168–173.

29. Hyde Post and David B. Hilder, "Fibers Found on Victims Form Links in Williams Case," *The Atlanta Journal,* February 2, 1982, 1–A and 6–A.

30. Fox and Cunningham, *Crime Scene Search and Physical Evidence Handbook,* p. 79.

31. Svensson and Wendel, *Techniques of Crime Scene Investigation,* p. 165.

32. The material in this section is taken, with permission and some alterations which are the responsibility of the authors, from Fox and Cunningham, *Crime Scene Search and Physical Evidence Handbook,* pp. 47–59; footnotes in this section were the addition of the present authors. For further information see Federal Bureau of Investigation, *The Science of Fingerprints* (Washington, D.C.: Government Printing Office, 1979); W. Micik, "Latent Print Techniques," *Fingerprint and Identification Magazine,* 1974, Vol. 56, No. 4, pp. 3–9; J. H. Grant et al., "The Fingerprinting of Cadavers," *Forensic Photography,* 1974, Vol. 3, No. 9, pp. 2–3; and W. Konopka, "Fingerprinting Mummified Tissue," *Fingerprint and Identification Magazine,* 1974, Vol. 55, No. 2, pp. 3–5. A contribution to this section by the present authors is the material dealing with the detection of prints on bodies.

33. Although the fingerprints of twins may have a high degree of similarity, variations still occur which permit their differentiation; see C. H. Lin, J. H. Liu, J. W.

Osterburg, and J. D. Nicol, "Fingerprint Comparison I: Similarity of Fingerprints," *Journal of Forensic Sciences,* 1982, Vol. 27, No. 2, pp. 290–304.

34. Others indicate, however, that it may be possible to distinguish among races but not among various subdivisions of a race. See O. L. Glasow, "Finger Pattern Differences among the Races," *Fingerprint and Identification Magazine,* 1974, Vol. 55, No. 9, pp. 3–5.

35. For information on the use of silicone for casting latent plastic fingerprints, see R. D. Olsen, "Lifting Plastic Fingerprints," *Journal of Police Administration,* 1975, Vol. 3, No. 1, pp. 29–32.

36. Blood represents a special case; see J. R. Harrell, "Recovering the Bloody Fingerprint," *Criminologist,* 1973, Vol. 8, No. 29, pp. 49–58.

37. A. J. Brooks, "The Search for Latent Prints When an Offender Wears Gloves," *Fingerprint and Identification Magazine,* 1972, Vol. 53, No. 12, pp. 3–7 and 15–16.

38. See B. E. Dalrymple, J. M. Duff, and E. R. Menzel, "Inherent Fingerprint Luminescence—Detection by Laser," *Journal of Forensic Sciences,* 1977, Vol. 22, pp. 106–115. This article was subsequently modified into less technical form, appearing as "Luminescence of Fingerprints—by Laser," *Royal Canadian Mounted Police Gazette,* 1977, Vol. 39, pp. 1–6. Also see Jim A. Burt and E. Roland Menzel, "Laser Detection of Latent Fingerprints: Difficult Surfaces," *Journal of Forensic Sciences,* 1985, Vol. 30, No. 2, pp. 364–370.

39. "Positive Gem Identification," *FBI Law Enforcement Bulletin,* 1977, Vol. 46, p. 26.

40. The authors appreciate the contributions made by James A. Besonen, Michigan State Police, in conversations on March 18 and 19, 1986 regarding the super glue fuming process. Also see Joseph Almòng and Amnon Gabay, "A Modified Super Glue® Technique," *Journal of Forensic Sciences,* 1986, Vol. 31, No. 1, pp. 250–253.

41. For example, see Richard Hall, "Latent Skin Print Identification Solves Homicide," *FBI Law Enforcement Bulletin,* 1979, Vol. 48, pp. 9–11. It is also to be noted in the Hall article that a technique reported by G. J. Reichard, T. C. Carr, and E. G. Stone in "A Conventional Method of Lifting Latent Fingerprints from Human Skin," *Journal of Forensic Sciences,* 1978, Vol. 23, pp. 135–141, was tried initially without success. In the Reichard approach, a Kromekote card, which is a high-gloss cast-coated surface similar to photographic paper, is pressed against the body and then dusted. Any image thereby obtained is a mirror copy, a notation of which must be made when submitting the print to the laboratory to avoid confusion. When the victim's body at the spa did not yield prints, the powder was then applied directly to the body and the print detected, photographed, and lifted. If initial applications of the Kromekote card directly to the body are not positive, subsequent attempts to use it may still be successful because the prior attempts may soak up excess oils.

42. Reichard, Carr, and Stone, "A Conventional Method of Lifting Latent Fingerprints from Human Skin," pp. 139–140.

43. M. A. Feldman, C. E. Meloan, and J. L. Lambert, "A New Method for Recovering Latent Fingerprints from Skin," *Journal of Forensic Sciences,* 1982, Vol. 27, No. 4, pp. 806–811.

44. Kirby Vickery, "California's Automated Latent Print System," *FBI Law Enforcement Bulletin,* 1981, Vol. 50, No. 7, pp. 2–6; for information on a program written in FORTRAN to match single latent prints with file prints, see J. H. Liu, C. H. Lin, J. W. Osterburg, and J. D. Nicol, "Fingerprint Comparison II: On the Development of a Single Print Filing and

Searching System," *Journal of Forensic Sciences,* 1982, Vol. 27, No. 2, pp. 305–317.

45. Dr. Richard R. Souviron, a nationally recognized authority in the field, who lives in Coral Gables, Florida, wrote portions of this section for the 3rd and 4th editions of this text. Space limitations have meant that Dr. Souviron's contributions were more extensive than appear here. The content therefore may not fully reflect his views.

46. See G. Gustafson, *Forensic Odontology.* New York: American Elsevier, 1966 and T. Furuhata and K. Yamamoto, *Forensic Odontology,* Springfield, Ill.: Charles C. Thomas, 1967.

47. Among these cases are *People v. Johnson,* 289 N.E. 2nd 772; *Patterson v. State of Texas* 509 S.W. 2d 857; *People v. Milone,* 356 N.E. 2d 1350; and *People v. Marx,* 54 Cal. App. 3d 100. For an early case, see one arising in Texas in 1954 in which a burglary suspect was convicted on the basis of a comparison of a bite mark found in cheese at the scene with one he subsequently donated; *Doyle v. State* 263 S.W. 2d 779. In *Bruce Allen Bradford v. Florida,* Second District Case No. 83–837, November 30, 1984, expert opinion that victim's teeth had caused abrasion on defendant's hand was upheld. Also see *Bundy v. State Supreme Court of Florida,* Case No. 57,772, June 21, 1984, Appeal from Circuit Court, Leon County Case No. 78–670.

48. Some of the material in this section is drawn, with modifications, from Norman D. Sperber, "Bite Mark Evidence in Crimes against Persons," *FBI Law Enforcement Bulletin,* 1981, Vol. 50, No. 7, pp. 16–19.

49. Roger Mittleman, W. Stuver, and R. Souviron, "Obtaining Saliva Samples from Bite Mark Evidence," *FBI Law Enforcement Bulletin,* Vol. 49, No. 11, 1980, pp. 16–19.

50. Valerie Rao and Richard Souviron, "Dusting and Lifting the Bite Print: A New Technique" *Journal of Forensic Sciences,* Vol. 29, No. 1, January 1984, pp. 326–330.

51. Fox and Cunningham, *Crime Scene Search and Physical Evidence Handbook,* pp. 74–75. On using hair to establish individual identity, see B. D. Gaudette, "Some Further Thoughts on Probabilities and Human Hair Comparisons," *Journal of Forensic Sciences,* 1978, Vol. 23, pp. 758–763. The citations in this article are a rich source of information on hair as evidence.

52. Fox and Cunningham, *Crime Scene Search and Physical Evidence Handbook,* p. 75.

53. This may change. See J. L. Mudd, "The Determination of Sex from Forcibly Removed Hairs," *Journal of Forensic Sciences,* 1984, Vol. 29, pp. 1072–1080. On p. 1076 he notes that determinations of sex could be made with only 2.28 percent inconclusive findings.

54. A. M. Baumgartner, P. R. Jones, and C. T. Black, "Detection of Phencyclidine in Hair," *Journal of Forensic Sciences,* 1981, Vol. 26, No. 3, pp. 576–581.

55. Fox and Cunningham, *Crime Scene Search and Physical Evidence Handbook,* pp. 75–76.

56. The procedures for gathering hair were taken from Fox and Cunningham, *Crime Scene Search and Physical Evidence Handbook,* p. 77.

57. Svensson and Wendel, *Techniques of Crime Scene Investigation,* p. 117.

58. Bryan J. Culliford, *Examination and Typing of Bloodstains in the Crime Laboratory.* (Washington, D.C.: Government Printing Office, 1971), p. 15. This book contains an extensive treatment of blood evidence.

59. Mary Gibbons Graham and Joseph Kochanski, "Forensic Science: beyond the Microscope," *NIJ Reports,* November 1983, pp. 4–8.

60. "Chiropractor Is Charged in Chain Saw

Death of Wife," *The State Journal* (Frankfort, Kentucky) April 26, 1984, p. 13.

61. Culliford, *Examination and Typing of Bloodstains in the Crime Laboratory,* p. 19.

62. In addition to the specific citations, a number of sources were generally useful in preparing this section. See R. O. Arthur, *The Scientific Investigator.* Springfield, Ill.: Charles C. Thomas, 1970, pp. 40–49; *Techniques of Crime Scene Investigation,* pp. 118–120; and *Crime Scene Search and Physical Evidence Handbook,* p. 62.

63. Fox and Cunningham, *Crime Scene Search and Physical Evidence Handbook,* p. 62.

64. Svensson and Wendel, *Techniques of Crime Scene Investigation,* p. 119. Also see E. G. Adams and B. G. Wraxall, "Phosphatases in Body Fluids: The Differentiation of Semen and Vaginal Secretion," *Forensic Science,* 1974, Vol. 3, No. 1, pp. 57–62.

65. Fox and Cunningham, *Crime Scene Search and Physical Evidence Handbook,* p. 63.

66. Svensson and Wendel, *Techniques of Crime Scene Investigation,* p. 120.

67. Ibid., pp. 127–129.

68. Ibid., p. 127.

69. Arthur, *The Scientific Investigator,* p. 47.

70. Ibid., pp. 50–51.

71. State of Wisconsin, *Criminal Investigation and Physical Evidence Handbook,* p. 16.

72. FBI, *Handbook of Forensic Science,* 1984, p. 32.

73. Fox and Cunningham, *Crime Scene Search and Physical Evidence Handbook,* p. 65.

74. See Fred E. Inbau et al., *Scientific Police Investigation.* (New York: Chilton Books, 1972), p. 125; *Techniques of Crime Scene Investigation,* pp. 134–140; and William W. Turner, editor, *Criminalistics* (San Francisco: Bancroft–Whitney, 1965), pp. 319–348.

75. J. Andrasko, "Forensic Analysis of Lipsticks," *Forensic Science International,* 1981, Vol. 17, No. 3, pp. 235–251.

76. Svensson and Wendel, *Techniques of Crime Scene Investigation,* p. 210. Also see V. "Jack" Krema, *The Identification and Registration of Firearms* (Springfield, Ill.: Charles C. Thomas, 1971).

77. Svensson and Wendel, *Techniques of Crime Scene Investigation,* pp. 212–213. See also Frederick C. Kerr and Walter F. Rowe, "Effects of Range, Caliber, Barrel Length, and Rifling on Pellet Patterns," *Journal of Forensic Sciences,* 1985, Vol. 30, No. 2, pp. 405–419. Kerr and Rowe note that shotgun ammunition for .22 caliber handguns and rifles, .38 caliber and .44 caliber magnum handguns is also available. What appear to be wounds inflicted by a long shotgun may have been inflicted by a handgun, although experienced homicide investigators could tell the difference by visual inspection of the wounds.

78. John E. Davis, *An Introduction to Toolmarks, Firearms and the Striagraph* (Springfield, Ill.: Charles C. Thomas, 1958), p. 108.

79. This was reported in a 1972 case. See R. Thomas. "Contribution to the Identification of Smooth Bore Firearms," *International Criminal Police Review,* 1974, Vol. 28, No. 280, pp. 190–193.

80. The material in this section is drawn from Fox and Cunningham, *Crime Scene Search and Physical Evidence Handbook,* p. 91.

81. The firing pin impression may be found at different places due to secondary impacts. See Basalo J. Martiney, "Study of Spent Cartridge Cases," *International Criminal Police Review,* 1973, Vol. 28, No. 270, pp. 220–222.

82. Accidental gunshots remain rare, even though from 1960 to 1973 alone, 33,000,000 firearms were bought in the United States; see V. J. DiMaio, "The Frequency of Accidental Gunshot Wounds," *Forensic Science Gazette,* 1973, Vol. 4, No. 3, pp. 2–3.

83. There are some unique exceptions to determining proximity by gunpowder residues. At one time a compressed air ex-

plosive propellant .22 caliber was commercially available which used caseless ammunition; as no nitrates were present in the discharge residues, this method was voided. See H. L. MacDonell and V. J. Fusco, "An Unusual Firearm Suicide Case," *Canadian Society of Forensic Science Journal*, 1975, Vol. 8, No. 2, pp. 53–55. For information on the collection of gunpowder residues, see J. J. Fay, "Collection of Gunpowder Residue," *Military Police Journal*, 1973, Vol. 22, No. 8, pp. 20–23; C. Maitip, "Powder Patterns around Bullet Holes in Bloodstained Articles," *Journal of the Forensic Science Society*, 1973, Vol. 13, No. 3, p. 127; K. Pillay and J. Sagans, "Gunshot Residue Collection Using Film-Lift Techniques for Neutron Activation Analysis," *Journal of Police Administration*, 1974, Vol. 2, No. 4, pp. 388–394; N. K. Nag and M. Mazumdar, "Detection of Firearm Discharge Residues in Bloodstained Articles by Fluorescence," *Forensic Science*, 1975, Vol. 5, No. 1, pp. 69–71; E. Rudzitis, "Analysis of The Results of Gunshot Residue Detection in Case Work," *Journal of Forensic Sciences*, 1980, Vol. 25, No. 4, pp. 839–846; J. W. Newton, "Rapid Determination of Antimony, Barium and Lead in Gunshot Residue via Automated Atomic Absorption Spectrophotometry," *Journal of Forensic Sciences*, 1981, Vol. 26. No. 2, pp. 302–312; and R. S. Maloney and J. I. Thornton, "Color Tests for Diphenylamine Stabilizer and Related Compounds in Smokeless Gunpowder,'" *Journal of Forensic Sciences*, 1982, Vol. 27, No. 2, April 1982, pp. 318–329.

84. Arthur, *The Scientific Investigator*, p. 78.

85. Fox and Cunningham, *Crime Scene Search and Physical Evidence Handbook*, p. 99.

86. FBI, *Handbook of Forensic Science*, 1984, p. 60.

87. Ibid., p. 60.

88. State of Wisconsin, *Criminal Investigation and Physical Evidence Handbook*, p. 100.

89. FBI, *Handbook of Forensic Science*, 1984, p. 61.

90. H. S. Maheshwari, "Influence of Vertical Angle of a Tool on Its Tool Mark," *Forensic Science International*, 1981, Vol. 18, No. 1, pp. 5–12.

91. Florida Institute for Law Enforcement, *The Examination of Questioned Documents* (St. Petersburg, Fla.: St. Petersburg Community College, 1972), pp. 1–8; also see Ordway Hilton, *Scientific Examination of Questioned Documents* (New York: Elsevier, 1982).

92. On the subject of dating a signature, see D. J. Purtell, "Dating a Signature," *Forensic Science International*, 1980, Vol. 15, No. 3, pp. 243–248.

93. D. W. Arrenberger, "Examination of a Typewritten Document," *FBI Law Enforcement Bulletin*, 1981, Vol. 50, No. 6, pp. 22–25, from which this discussion was drawn with modification.

94. See J. M. Winchester, "Computer-Printed Documents as Part of a Computer Crime Investigation," *Journal of Forensic Sciences*, 1981, Vol. 26, No. 4, pp. 730–738, A. G. Leslie and T. A. Stimpson, "Identification of Printout Devices," *Forensic Science International*, 1982, Vol. 19, No. 1, pp. 11–38, and Ordway Hilton, "Problems in Identifying Work from Print Wheel Typewriters," *Forensic Science International*, 1986, Vol. 30, pp. 53-63.

95. L. F. Stewart, "Artificial Aging of Documents," *Journal of Forensic Sciences*, 1982, Vol. 27, No. 2, pp. 450–453.

5

INTERVIEWS

INTRODUCTION

The business of the police is people. Every facet of police work is concerned with the problems of people. The job of the criminal investigator is no exception. People and the information they supply help accomplish investigative tasks; collecting information is the key investigative task of police work. Roughly 90 percent of an investigator's activity involves gathering, sorting, compiling, and evaluating information. The investigator cannot function without information, and information cannot be obtained without help from people.

Interviewing is both an art and a skill that must be cultivated and practiced. Not all people who possess information needed by the investigator are willing to share it. The successful interviewer must fully understand the techniques of interviewing and have the ability to evaluate the psychological reasons why people are willing or reluctant to impart information. The interviewer-investigator's own capabilities and limitations must be recognized. Personality and the manner in which interpersonal communications are handled can greatly influence the quality and quantity of information obtained.

Interviewing in criminal investigation is face to face conversation for the purpose of getting information from individuals who possess knowledge of a crime or its circumstances.[1]

Interviewing is the process by which an officer seeks, obtains, and evaluates information given by persons having personal knowledge of events or circumstances of a crime.[2]

It is the questioning of persons believed to possess knowledge that is of official interest to the investigator.[3]

A witness is defined as, "in general, one who, being present, personally sees or perceives a thing; a beholder, spectator, or eyewitness."[4] The job of the investigator-interviewer is to extract from the witness information actually perceived through one or more of the witness's five senses—sight, hearing, smell, taste, and touch. In any given case, any or all of a witness's senses may be involved. For example, in a case involving a drug related killing, a witness may see the perpetrator pull the trigger, hear the victim scream, smell the pungent odor of marijuana burning, taste the white powdery substance later identified as heroin, and touch the victim to feel for a pulse.

Because witnesses report perceptions based on their own interests, priorities, and biases, extracting information from witnesses is not as easy as it may first appear. Investigators must always be sensitive to any and all psychological influences and motivations affecting witness perceptions, the specifics of which are discussed in the next section.

At the outset of the interview, the person to be interviewed must satisfy three requirements of being a witness: presence, consciousness, and attentiveness to what was happening.[5] Presence and consciousness are relatively easy to establish in the interview process; attentiveness is more difficult. Yet all three elements are important to establishing the accuracy of a witness's perception.

WITNESSES: MOTIVATIONS AND PERCEPTIONS

There are many types of witnesses, and each has different motivations and perceptions that influence his or her responses during an interview. The interviewer must learn to recognize, overcome, and compensate for these factors. Because the witness's information also must be evaluated in light of its potential value in court, the interviewer must evaluate the witness's competency and credibility. (These concepts are treated in more detail in Chapter 19.)

COMPETENCY OF A WITNESS

Competency describes a witness's personal qualifications to testify in court. It must be determined before he or she is permitted to give any testimony. The witness's personal qualifications depend on circumstances that affect his or her legal ability to function as a sworn witness in court. Competency has nothing to do with the believability of a witness's information.

Among the factors an investigator must evaluate in determining the competency of a witness are age, level of intelligence, mental state, relationship to individuals involved in the case, and background characteristics that might preclude the testimony of the witness from being heard in court. For example, in many jurisdictions, a young child cannot be a witness unless it can be shown that the child knows the difference between truth and imagination and understands the importance of telling the truth. Chronological age is not the determining factor. Similarly, any person whose intelligence or mental state prevents him or her from understanding the obligation of telling the truth is not permitted to testify, regardless of the information he or she may possess.

Relationships among individuals involved in a case may also affect a witness's competency. Husbands and wives need not testify against each other, nor may attorneys testify against clients, doctors against patients, nor ministers against penitents. Privileges vary by state (see Chapter 19). Background characteristics also may preclude a witness's testimony from being accepted in court. For example, some state laws forbid a convicted perjurer from testifying in court.

Possibilities as those described in the preceding paragraphs necessitate that the investigator learn as much as possible about the witness before and during the interview.

CREDIBILITY

Credibility is distinguished from competency in that the latter is based on the assumption that a witness is qualified and will be permitted to testify. Credibility relates to that quality of a witness which renders his or her testimony worthy of belief.[6] Credibility in this sense is the same as weight or believability. The credibility of a witness is established in terms of presence, consciousness, and attentiveness during the interviewing process. An investigator must examine each of these requirements carefully and in detail. Among the questions to which the interviewer must receive satisfactory answers in evaluating the credibility of a witness are:

- Was the witness conscious at the time of the event?
- Was the witness under the influence of alcohol or drugs?
- How did the witness happen to be in a position of seeing, hearing, or otherwise perceiving the crime?
- Where was the witness coming from or going to?
- What was the witness doing at the exact moment of occurrence?
- What else was going on at the time that might have distracted the witness's attention?

The rules of evidence, which guide the admissibility and use of witnesses and their testimony in court, also guide the impeachment or attack by the opposing side on cross-examination of a witness's testimony (see Chapter 20). The investigator-interviewer must be aware of these factors to prevent the witnesses who appear for the state from being impeached. To do this, the investigator must ascertain the truth of the following:

- Does the witness have any particular bias, prejudice, or personal interest in the case?
- Does the witness have any physical or mental impairments which may affect his or her ability to observe, recollect, or recount the events? (Does the witness normally wear glasses? Was the witness wearing them at the time? Does the witness have a hearing problem?)
- What physical conditions, such as weather, lighting, and visibility, existed at the crime scene?
- What is the witness's reputation for being a truthful person?

The effective interviewer cannot accept any witness's account at face value. The interviewer must question and requestion,

check and recheck. The investigator must recognize and gauge the effects which physical and emotional characteristics, external influences, and attitudinal and behavioral factors have on the witness's perception and on the reliability of the information possessed.

RELIABILITY OF EYEWITNESS IDENTIFICATION

Information provided by eyewitnesses to a criminal event is relied on heavily by both the police and courts in the investigative and adjudication stages of our system of justice, yet research indicates that eyewitness testimony may be unreliable:

> Eyewitness identification and description is regarded as the most unreliable form of evidence and causes more miscarriages of justice than any other method of proof.[7]

> Research and courtroom experience provide ample evidence that an eyewitness to a crime is being asked to be something and do something that a normal human being was not created to be or do. Human perception is sloppy and uneven.[8]

Human perception and memory are selective and constructive functions, not exact copiers of the event perceived:

> Perception and memory are decision-making processes affected by the totality of a person's abilities, background, attitudes, motives and beliefs, by the environment and the way his recollection is eventually tested. The observer is an active rather than a passive perceiver and recorder; he reaches conclusions on what he has seen by evaluating fragments of information and reconstructing them. He is motivated by a desire to be accurate as he imposes meaning on the overabundance of information that impinges on his senses, but

also by a desire to live up to the expectations of other people and to stay in their good graces. The eye, the ear, and other sense organs are, therefore, social organs as well as physical ones.[9]

Loftus also agrees with this theory of eyewitness perception. She notes:

> Studies of memory for sentences and pictures indicate that when we experience an event, we do not simply file a memory, and then on some later occasion retrieve it and read off what we've stored. Rather, at the time of recall or recognition we reconstruct the event, using information from many sources. These include both the original perception of the event and inferences drawn later, after the fact. Over a period of time, information from these sources may integrate, so that a witness becomes unable to say how he knows a specific detail. He has only a single, unified memory.[10]

Experts distinguish a number of factors that limit a person's ability to give a complete account of events or to identify people accurately. The following are among those factors:

- The significance or insignificance of the event. When an insignificant event occurs in the presence of an individual, it does not generally motivate the individual to bring fully into play the selective process of attention.
- The length of the period of observation. If ample opportunity is not provided for observation, the capability of the memory to record that which is perceived is decreased.
- Lack of ideal conditions. As previously noted in this chapter, where ideal conditions for observation are absent, the ability of the witness to perceive details is significantly decreased. Distance, poor lighting, fast movement or the presence of a crowd

may significantly interfere with the efficient working of the attention process.
- Psychological factors internal to the witness. A witness under stress at the time of observation may find this to be a major source of unreliability in his or her observations.
- The physical condition of the witness.
- Expectancy. Research has shown that memory recall and judgment are often based on what psychologists term *expectancy*. This means that an individual perceives things in a manner in which he or she expects them to appear. For example, a right-handed eyewitness to a homicide might, in answer to a question and without positive knowledge, state that the assailant held the gun in his right hand, while a left-handed person might say the opposite. Biases or prejudices also are illustrated by this expectancy theory, as is the classic problem associated with stereotyping.[11]

Hence, the human memory is fallible. Perfect recall of information is basically unnecessary in our daily lives and is rarely, if ever, displayed. One of the keys to this imperfection is the tendency for people to improve their recollection by making it seem more logical:

> The process of filling in is an efficient way to remember but it can lead to unreliable recognition testing: the witness may adjust his memory to fit the available suspects or pictures. The witness need not be lying; he may be unaware that he is distorting or reconstructing his memory. In his very effort to be conscientious he may fabricate parts of his recall to make a chaotic memory seem more plausible to the people asking questions.[12]

Research shows significant error connected with similar descriptions by two or more eyewitnesses:

One might expect that two eyewitnesses—or ten or one hundred—who agree are better than one. Similarity of judgment is a two-edged sword, however; people can agree in error as easily as in truth. A large body of research results demonstrates that an observer can be persuaded to conform to the majority opinion even when the majority is completely wrong.[13]

In one test, people were asked to describe a mock crime they had viewed earlier. They first gave individual responses, then met as a group. The group descriptions were more complete and in greater detail than those reported by individual subjects, but group descriptions also gave rise to significantly more errors as well as an assortment of incorrect and stereotyped details.[14]

Just as the memory tends to change to reconstruct events for the sake of logic, it may also conform to a theory concerning the events:

> In criminal investigations, as in scientific investigations, a theory can be a powerful tool for clarifying confusion, but it can also lead to distortion and unreliability if people attempt, perhaps unconsciously, to make fact fit theory and close their minds to the real meanings of facts. The eyewitness who feels pressed to say something may shape his memory to fit a theory, particularly a highly publicized and seemingly reasonable one.[15]

In summary, the problems associated with eyewitness identification can result in errors. Mistaken identifications of people, things, places, times, events, and other facts can result in miscarriages of justice. In some instances, these errors can be corrected. Figure 5-1 is a case in point.

Hypnosis is one means to insure the accuracy of witnesses' and victims' information and to aid in the recall of repressed information.

HYPNOSIS AS AN INVESTIGATIVE TOOL

The increasing use of hypnosis as a means of aiding witnesses in recalling facts buried in the subconscious is often thought to overcome many of the difficulties experienced by Loftus and others in seeking accuracy of the human memory. Although hypnosis does have the unique capability to elicit many repressed and forgotten memories from witnesses to and victims of crimes, its use is not without problems. Theories which purport that the human brain is like a videotape recorder which stores all experiences accurately and, with sufficient prodding, can be made to recall an "exact copy" of a prior event, are seriously questioned through research. For example, Putnam conducted an experiment the results of which indicated a good possibility that people under hypnosis will remember items inaccurately where there is even the slightest suggestion by the hypnotist to lead or mislead them.[16]

LEGAL CONSIDERATIONS

The forensic use of hypnosis gained popularity in the 1960s, yet courts addressing the issue of its admissibility during the 1960s and 1970s were inconsistent in their decisions and did not offer specific standards or guidelines.[17] For example, some courts excluded evidence obtained through hypnosis if the evidence was being introduced to exculpate the defendant[18] but admitted such evidence presented by the prosecution if it were for refreshing memory.[19] (The same principle that allows a law enforcement officer to refer to notes while testifying; see Chapter 20). Other courts allowed such evidence on the theory that its use presented a question of credibility of witnesses rather than admissibility of evidence.[20]

In 1980, the Minnesota Supreme Court

FIGURE 5-1

Mistaken identifications led to the arrests of two innocent men: Lawrence Berson (left) for several rapes and George Morales (right) for a robbery. Both men were picked out of police lineups by victims of the crimes. Berson was cleared when Richard Carbone (center) was arrested and implicated in the rapes. Carbone was convicted. Later he confessed to the robbery, clearing Morales.

Reprinted by permission of *Scientific American,* 1974, Vol. 231, No. 6

articulated a decision which has caused many states to reevaluate their positions on the admissibility of hypnotically enhanced testimony. In *State* v. *Mack,*[21] the victim-witness was hypnotized by a self-taught lay hypnotist in an effort to recall the events leading to her hospitalization for a vaginal wound. Initially, she had told attending physicians that she had been involved in a motorcycle accident and afterward had been sexually involved with the defendant, Mack. She claimed not to know what had caused the injury, but after being told at the hospital that her injury was unlikely to have been caused by a motorcycle accident, she filed a complaint charging the defendant with sexual assault. Under hypnosis she said that the defendant had used a switchblade knife in her vagina during the sexual encounter. This testimony was admitted at trial. After conviction, the defendant appealed.

The Minnesota court, after careful study of the issues, including the absence of precedents and the lack of agreement by the "experts" in the field, including those who tes-

tified at the trial, concluded that the evidence should not have been admitted at trial. In its ruling, the court relied on a standard established in a 1923 federal case, *Frye* v. *United States.*[22] In *Frye,* the federal court ruled inadmissible the results of a "deception test," an early version of the polygraph, and established a standard which provided that, for the results of a scientific technique to be admissible, the technique must be sufficiently established to have gained general acceptance in its particular field. Because of the controversy over the admissibility of hypnotically enhanced testimony, this standard was not met and cannot be achieved.

Many states now follow the reasoning in *Mack* and *Frye* to exclude the results of hypnosis including the highest courts of Arizona,[23] California,[24] Indiana,[25] Maryland,[26] Massachusetts,[27] Michigan,[28] Nebraska,[29] New York,[30] North Carolina,[31] Pennsylvania,[32] and Washington.[33] Wyoming still follows the pre-Mack analysis.[34] New Jersey,[35] New Mexico,[36] and Wisconsin[37] provide for the admissibility of hypnotically enhanced evidence only where certain stringent procedures are followed.

The greatest concern about the admissibility of hypnosis evidence is the potential for the hypnotist to suggest or mislead the subject into giving false information, whether by design or not. There is virtual agreement among hypnosis experts that this can occur unless extreme caution is exercised. Subjects may come to believe such false information after hypnosis, potentially affecting the truthfulness and reliability of subsequent testimony in court. Thus, a constitutional issue involving the Sixth Amendment right of cross-examination has also been raised. It is the basis on which many other states refuse to admit testimony developed under hypnosis, the theory being that even the witness may not know the truth after being subjected to suggestive influences while hypnotized.

The technique most often used in hypnotized subjects is to suggest they are reliving the event in issue but are doing so in a detached manner, as if they were watching it on a mental TV screen. This is done to avoid a first-hand reinvolvement in a potentially traumatic experience. In addition to Putnam's experiments noted above, other "suggestive" cases involved encouraging a subject to picture a license plate and describe its numbers when, in fact, the witness never saw the car;[38] describing a suspect's facial features which, in actuality, were not seen;[39] or confessing to a crime which the subject did not commit.[40]

Such experiments do not indicate that hypnosis is absolutely useless as an investigative tool. On the contrary, law enforcement officials can cite numerous cases in which hypnosis contributed to the identification of suspects. Hypnosis is proving to be such a useful tool that many law enforcement agencies are establishing hypnosis-investigative units and training officers in the use of hypnosis.[41]

THE CALL FOR PROCEDURAL SAFEGUARDS

The results of hypnosis, whether used solely as an investigative aid or as admissible evidence, must be cloaked in procedural safeguards to insure truthfulness. Among the criteria suggested are that:

1. The hypnotist be a mental health person, preferably a psychiatrist or psychologist, with special training in the use of hypnosis
2. The hypnotist be informed about the case only in writing subject to scrutiny
3. All contact between hypnotist and subject be videotaped
4. The hypnotist be independent and not responsible to the parties
5. Nobody representing either party be with the hypnotist and the subject during the session
6. Before the session the hypnotist examine the subject to exclude the possibility of physical or mental illness and to establish that the subject has sufficient intelligence, judgment, and comprehension of what is happening
7. The hypnotist elicit all facts from the subject prior to the hypnosis
8. During the session the hypnotist strive to avoid adding any new elements to the subject's description, including any explicit or implicit cues, before, during, or after the session
9. Corroboration be sought for any information elicited during the session[42]

The last criterion is of extreme importance if there is to be any hope of using the results in court. Although there is general agreement on most of these criteria, the propriety of the first and third criteria have been questioned by at least one respected teacher and practitioner of hypnotherapy who writes that physicians and psychologists are not qualified by their training to conduct investigative interviews and, in fact, have little if any training in hypnosis—which makes them no better qualified than a trained police hypnotist-investigator.[43]

Hypnosis is often erroneously believed to be a form of sleep. In fact, it is the opposite. It is best described as a state of heightened awareness where the subconscious is somewhat surfaced and the conscious is somewhat repressed.

Although research is continuing, much more is needed. Meanwhile, hypnosis continues to grow as a viable investigative tool for the criminal investigator.[44]

TYPES OF WITNESSES

Motivation, perception, attitude, past experience, and a host of other variables affect the types of witnesses to be interviewed, the manner in which they should be interviewed, and the nature of the reactions which the interviewer can anticipate. There is no way to categorize personalities, attitudes, and other character traits. The variables are too numerous and individualized; the combinations are as complex as the human mind. Nevertheless, some basic patterns can be described.

THE HONEST AND COOPERATIVE WITNESS

Witnesses of this type who possess information useful to the investigator are indeed a valuable find, but the substance of their information must not be accepted unquestioned. Despite these admirable qualities, the information is still affected by those factors which influence all witnesses—such as age, physical characteristics, and emotions. The readily identified honest and cooperative witness should be interviewed first. In this manner the interviewer can obtain basic information with which to compare later stories.

THE SILENT, KNOW-NOTHING, OR UNINTERESTED WITNESS

Although these labels may in fact represent three different types of witnesses, they all have one thing in common: they are the most difficult to interview. They want to give no information, good or bad, right or wrong, accurate or not to the investigator. Their reasons and motives may differ, but the effects are the same—no information. Some witnesses refuse to talk because they don't want to get involved. Others fear any contact with the law. A third group may be of limited intelligence or so unobservant as to render their information useless. Still a fourth group may have no desire to do anything to aid the police. The investigator must skillfully use techniques of interviewing discussed later in this chapter to get witnesses to open up.

THE RELUCTANT OR SUSPICIOUS WITNESS

Reluctant and suspicious witnesses are only slightly easier to interview than the silent or know-nothing types. They can be convinced to impart information only if the police officer can establish the importance of the contribution to be made. Like the know-nothing type, the reluctant witness may want to avoid getting involved for fear of reprisal, dislike of police officers, or other reasons. The interviewer must gain cooperation from such witnesses if the interview is to be productive.

THE HOSTILE AND DECEITFUL WITNESS

Witnesses who deliberately attempt to impede an investigation by misleading or lying about information are often the most frustrating, though not necessarily the most difficult, witnesses to interview. The interviewer must examine the motives behind such behavior. A relationship may exist between the witness and other persons involved in the investigation, such as a suspect. The witness may have a criminal record or other background which has created a distrust or dislike for police officers. The witness may be a pathological liar. Pathological lying is both a disease and a habit. The pathological liar is somewhere between the person who desires to tell the truth and the one who does not. The exact position depends on the extent to which the individual confuses falsehoods with reality. "Pathological lying, *pseudologia phantastica,* is false recollection or fabrication of memory. A witness who can relate with conviction and circumstantiality events that never took place or can give a false picture by adding untrue details and meanings to a true recollection may be a pathological liar."[45]

Falsehoods are commonly detected by the skillful interviewer. Inconsistencies in information can be turned to advantage if they are pointed out to the witness. The idea is to give the witness enough rope to hang him or herself with.

THE TIMID OR BASHFUL WITNESS

People are timid or bashful for a number of reasons: lack of education, language barrier, fear of police, and lack of understanding of the investigation process. Recent immigrants to this country are especially susceptible to this last reaction. Female victims of criminal acts, particularly sex-related offenses, are prone to be bashful about revealing the intimate details. A great deal of time and care must be spent communicating with these witnesses about the investigator's role, interest, sincerity, and desire to help.

THE TALKATIVE OR BOASTFUL WITNESS

This kind of witness can be both valuable and dangerous. The person's willingness to impart information can be of substantial benefit to the interviewer, but the substance of the witness's remarks must be carefully evaluated to ensure its relevance. Some garrulous people like to boast. In so doing, they offer imaginative observations and give improper emphasis to portions of their stories.

THE "UNDER THE INFLUENCE" WITNESS

It is not uncommon for an investigator to interview a witness who is drunk or under the influence of narcotics or other drugs. The legality of the state of intoxication is immaterial to the interviewer's mission. The degree to which the intoxicant has freed the inhibitions of the witness can serve the interviewer well, but caution must be employed in relying on the information.

QUALIFICATIONS OF THE INTERVIEWER

The effective interviewer must be knowledgeable in the art and science of criminal investigation and know how to use psychology, salesmanship, and dramatics. Persuasiveness and perseverance are essential to success. The interviewer must be emphatic, sympathetic, objective, and must establish rapport with witnesses. A positive, firm approach, an ability to inspire confidence, and knowledge of a broad range of topics of general interest all are necessary as well.

A critical element in the interviewer's success is preparation before an interview. Acquiring as much information about the person to be interviewed as possible should be the investigator's first step. The interviewer also must become familiar with the facts of the case under investigation, to test the information given by witnesses and to establish a base line along which to direct the interview.

FIGURE 5-2   Field Interview of a Witness at a Crime Scene

Courtesy of Los Angeles Sheriff's Department

TIME, PLACE, AND SETTING OF THE INTERVIEW

Police officers conduct interviews in a number of situations. The most common is the on-the-scene interview. Whether it is a routine traffic accident investigation or a major felony case, officers who respond to the scene should, at the earliest possible moment, seek out and identify those individuals who may have knowledge of the event and whose information may contribute to the investigation (see Figure 5-2). This, of course, includes victims and other participants as well as uninvolved witnesses. Once witnesses have been identified, they should be separated from each other and, as much as possible, isolated from other people who may be loi-

tering in the area. This prevents the witnesses from seeing or hearing irrelevant matters which may taint their actual knowledge. All witnesses should be interviewed as soon as practical, while their memory is still fresh, but this rule must be flexible in its application to take into account all circumstances.

The physical circumstances under which the interview takes place can be critical to the value of the information obtained. Immediacy may have to be sacrificed in some instances due to lack of privacy, inconvenience, or physical discomfort of the witness. Conditions which tend to distract the ability or desire of the witness to give full attention to the interview should be avoided. If such conditions exist, investigators may wisely choose to seek only basic preliminary information at the scene, followed by a more detailed interview at a more convenient time and place.

Although convenience of the witness is important to a successful interview, the interviewer need not relinquish the psychological advantage in selecting the time and place of the interview. It is not a good practice, for example, to rouse a witness from bed in the middle of the night. However, there are certain psychological advantages to questioning a witness at police headquarters rather than in the witness's own home or office. A witness may feel in a better position to control the interview in familiar surroundings. The investigator cannot let this happen; he or she must be fair but always in command of the situation.

After taking into account the factors of immediacy, privacy, convenience, and control, and weighing the importance of each in context of the total circumstances, it may be best to interview witnesses at their homes or places of business (see Figure 5-3). As a matter of courtesy, the investigator should attempt to make an appointment to ensure convenience, particularly for professional and business people. Others, such as salespersons, office workers, and laborers may be interviewed during working hours with approval of their supervisors.

Privacy is of the utmost importance in conducting interviews. Distractions, whether in the home, office, or police station, tend to have an adverse effect on the interview and its results. The interviewer should insist on as much privacy as possible, but the circumstances of on-the-scene interviews often have to be recognized as a fact of life for the investigator, who can only be expected to perform to the best of his or her ability in the given case. Similarly, investigators are often called on to canvass neighborhoods and interview residents. In these instances, investigators often are in no position to influence the conditions under which the interview takes place. Noisy children, blaring television sets, nosy neighbors, and similar factors must be accepted.

The physical and emotional states of the witness are important in conducting or in determining whether to conduct an interview. "Cold, sleepy, hungry, or physically uncomfortable people generally prove to be unsatisfactory witnesses."[46] Similarly, persons suffering noticeable emotional problems can give, at the most, highly questionable information. Most investigators can recognize this state and wisely prefer to wait until the witness becomes lucid before conducting the interview.

Particular caution must be exercised in interviewing juveniles. Parents should be notified of the purpose of the interview and the nature of the information sought from the juvenile. In some instances the presence of a parent during the interview is required or desirable. If so, the parent should not be allowed to distract or in any way influence the juvenile's responses.

Reinterviewing witnesses should be avoided if the reinterview is likely to produce nothing beyond the information given in the initial statement. Reinterviewing tends to become less and less convenient for witnesses, even though they may be friendly and cooperative. There may also be a tendency for reinterviewed witnesses to feel that the investigator does not know his or her job or was not prepared during the initial interview. To avoid this problem, the investigator should first tell the witness that the purpose of the interview is not to rehash old information and then to explain what new information is being sought. The investigator should ask for the information in a manner that does not elicit a repetition of the previous interview. But, investigators should not hesitate to conduct follow-up interviews when necessary, whether there was lack of skill in obtaining an initial statement, new information has developed, or because the time or setting of the initial interview did not get the full attention of the witnesses.

FIGURE 5-3   **Interviewing Witnesses at Home and in Their Place of Business**

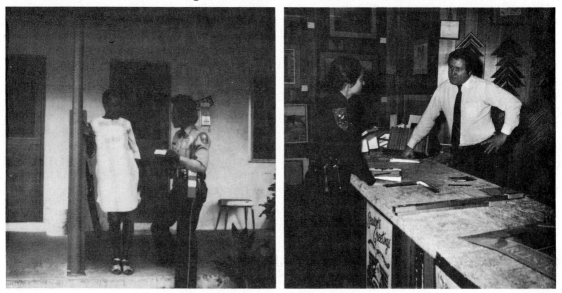

Courtesy of Metro-Dade Police Department, Miami, Florida, and the DeKalb County, Georgia, Police Department

INTERVIEWING: PROCESSES AND TECHNIQUES

"An interview . . . has a beginning, a middle—its main segment—and an end."[47] The beginning is the warm-up period, the time when the interviewer must establish rapport. The main segment is devoted to acquiring the desired information, and the end is when the investigator has accomplished certain goals and shows appreciation to the witness.

The investigator must remember that the mission is to gather all relevant information possessed by the witness about a particular occurrence. Regardless of the attitude of a particular witness, the interviewer must establish rapport. The warm-up period allows the interviewer to provide identification, state the purpose of the interview, and to put the witness at ease with small talk. Matters of common interest may be discussed, such

as children, sports, military service, or membership in civic organizations. Friendly conversation can convey interest in the witness, get the witness talking, and provide the interviewer with an opportunity to evaluate the witness. Now the investigator can determine the type of witness being interviewed, the appropriate techniques and approaches to use, and, in general, the tone to be taken in the interview. The length of the warm-up period depends on a number of variables, including the attitude of the witness, the level of cooperation, and the degree to which the witness can be motivated to provide useful information. The warm-up is time well spent if it helps to accomplish a successful interview.

When leading into the main body of the interview, the investigator should remember that his or her role is to direct the flow of the interview and to do so in a nonsuggestive manner. That is, care should be taken not to lead the witness by asking questions that imply the answer.

Questions should always be phrased positively so that the response is also positive. Questions such as, "You don't really believe that, do you?" imply that anything other than a negative answer will be unacceptable. "Do you believe that?" allows the witness more freedom to respond.

Studies made by Elizabeth Loftus and others in the mid-1970s also substantiate that the exact manner in which interview questions are asked is critical to the response. The choice of a single word and its use in a sentence can dramatically affect the nature of a response. Loftus cites laboratory studies in which subjects were shown a film of a traffic accident. Portions of the study group were later asked if they had seen *the* broken headlight; others were asked if they had seen *a* broken headlight. The group presented with the question using *the* said yes significantly more often than did the group presented with the question containing *a*. These results were consistent whether witnesses had or had not seen a broken headlight. The significance of this illustration is that use of *the* by the questioner implies the existence of a broken headlight, causing the witness to assume its existence and potentially influencing the answer given by the witness.[48]

In further studies, Loftus attempted to determine if word substitutions could also affect quantitative judgments as well as a simple yes or no answer. Seven films of traffic accidents were shown to a group of subjects. Later, they were all asked *substantially* the same question, "About how fast were the cars going when they hit each other?" The only difference was in the verb used in the question. When various subjects were asked the question, the words *smashed, collided, bumped,* or *contacted* were substituted for *hit*. Although any of the words could be used properly in the question, each tends to imply a difference in speed and force of impact. Results showed that estimates of the speed of vehicles involved tended to increase as a more forceful verb was used in the question.[49]

To avoid such problems, interviewers should begin by asking witnesses to relate in their own words the events of which they have knowledge. Witnesses should be allowed to continue this narrative uninterrupted, unless the amount of superfluous or irrelevant material becomes excessive. Interviewers must remain attentive to what is and is not said and to prepare questions that separate facts from inferences and implications.

When beginning the questioning process, investigators should recall that their objective is to gather information so that they may picture the occurrence with the same clarity and in the same order as the witness. Questions should be asked in systematic and chronological order. They should be stated simply and clearly so that the witness understands them. Concise questions should be asked one at a time. Long, complex questions must be avoided, because they tend to produce disorganized and confused answers. For example, take the question, "Was the man you saw with the scar on his face walking south from where you saw the other man lying near the curb, or did he have the gun in his hand, and was he going the other way, toward the hill, and about how old would you say he was?" This question certainly looks ridiculous on paper. But many people utter questions like these—run-on, complicated, and disorganized.

In developing the chronology of events through questioning, the interviewer should first establish where the witness was positioned and related facts. The interviewer must keep the witness talking and discourage digressions as much as possible. Perhaps the most successful technique for keeping the witness talking is the use of open-ended, nondirectional questions, such as, "What happened next?" They are designed to compel the witness to elaborate on the issue rather than merely respond in a yes or no fashion.

The interviewer should always permit witnesses to save face if errors in their statements become apparent. Provided the interviewer is satisfied that the mistake is an honest one and not the result of deliberate misrepresentations, the investigator should attempt to assist the witness in clarifying the statement without seeming judgmental.

The complexity of the case and the amount of information possessed by the witness are critical variables in the amount of time required for the interview. When satisfied that all relevant information has been obtained, the interviewer has reached the primary goal and may terminate the interview, preferably with a thank-you and a short discourse of appreciation for the witness's time and efforts to cooperate with the police in the investigation.

THE IMPORTANCE OF LISTENING

Regardless of the amount of their preparation and experience, an interview is fully successful only when interviewers are good listeners. There never was and never will be a completely successful interview if the interviewer *hears* but does not *listen*. Hearing without listening, without concentrating, without comprehending that which is being communicated by the other party, provides little useful information.

Listening is as valuable in interviewing as questioning. Interviewers first should listen to witnesses' full stories and then ask specific questions triggered by that careful listening. The resulting information is likely to be complete and accurate.

Being a good listener is not easy. To be effective, one must be an active listener, too. It has been estimated that 65 percent of communication is nonverbal.[50] Active listening requires listeners to be conscious of their own body movements, eye contact, hand ges-

tures, facial expressions, head nodding, and tones of voice. All of these nonverbal forms of communication must convey interest in a witness and what the witness is saying. Even a slight movement, such as leaning toward a witness while listening, conveys interest and enthusiasm. Discouraging nonverbal messages may adversely affect the interview and cause an otherwise cooperative witness to become evasive or defensive. In such an instance, a witness might wonder, "Why should I try to help if this investigator isn't interested enough to care what I'm saying?"

Another tactic in good listening is for interviewers to repeat or paraphrase witnesses' stories. This tactic provides the opportunity to check the stories and insure the quality of communication in the interview.

Every communication has two components—the verbal, consisting of the content, and the nonverbal, emotional, or attitudinal component. Both are critical to listening and, hence, effective communication.

Notes or other methods of documenting the interview should, when possible, reflect the emotional as well as factual content of the interview.[51]

DOCUMENTING THE INTERVIEW

In the majority of routine cases involving interviews, handwritten notes made by the investigator during and immediately following the interview generally serve as sufficient documentation. Investigators should not rely on memory for the storage of investigative information. The human mind can absorb and recount only a limited amount of information at one time, and most of the information is soon lost if notes are not taken.

Note taking during the interview raises two primary concerns for the interviewer. First, it may occasionally be distracting or suspicious to a witness; witnesses may be reluctant to give information knowing that it

TABLE 5-1
Comparison of Interview Documentation Methods

Method	Advantages	Disadvantages
Memory	Quick and easy	Limited absorption and recall Most information lost shortly afterward
Note taking by interviewer	Sufficient in most cases Captures salient details Prevents need for reinterviewing	May distract or offend witness May preoccupy interviewer, creating appearance of inattentiveness May cause interviewer to miss nonverbal messages
Handwritten or signed statement by witness	Useful if witness cannot testify Can be used to impeach if witness changes story in court	Request may be offensive to witness Not necessary in routine cases
Sound or sound and visual recordings	Relatively inexpensive Some equipment portable All information recorded in witnesses' own words Does not rely on inaccuracies of memory or another's notes Does not distract Prevents unnecessary reinterviews	Not necessary except in the most important cases Generally not practical

is being documented. Consequently, the investigator should tell witnesses that notes will prevent the need for subsequent interviews due to lapses of the investigator's memory. This will usually ease the reluctance of the witness. Second, the interviewer should avoid becoming preoccupied with taking notes, for it creates the appearance of inattentiveness. As important as notes may be, the interviewer should treat them as less important than conversation with the witness. Note taking during the interview should be kept to a minimum, recording only salient details. As soon as possible after the interview, the investigator should complete the notes, before memory wanes.

In some instances, it is desirable for witnesses to write or sign statements concerning the events of which they have knowledge. Statements generally are not necessary in routine cases. However, in important cases, when there is a likelihood that the witness may change statements in the courtroom or may not be available to testify, a signed statement, in the witness's handwriting, can be extremely valuable.

The best form of documentation is a sound recording or a sound and visual recording of the interview. Visual recordings are generally not practical when the interview is held anywhere other than a police station, where equipment can be permanently situated. Cassette tape recorders, however, are inexpensive, portable, and helpful in the majority of cases. The recorded interview has many significant advantages: All information is recorded in the witness's own words, details are not left to be recalled by the human memory, concerns about detracting from the interview by note taking are absent, interviewers may listen to the verbatim conversations over and over at a later time to be

TABLE 5-2
Post-Interview Self-Evaluation Checklist

	With this witness, did I:
1	Conduct the interview as quickly, privately, yet conveniently as possible?
2	Establish good rapport with the witness?
3	Listen?
4	Ask good questions?
5	Control the interview?
6	Establish the witness's presence, consciousness, and attentiveness?
7	Determine any factors which now would affect the witness's competency in court?
8	Evaluate the witness's potential credibility in court?
9	Use the right approach in seeking information?
10	Get complete and accurate information?
11	Document the interview well?

sure that they have understood completely and accurately, and the taped interview might avoid unnecessary reinterviews. The advantages and disadvantages of each method of documentation are shown in Table 5-1.

At the conclusion of an interview, it is wise for investigators to review and evaluate their performance. The checklist in Table 5-2 may serve as a good review and basis for self-evaluation.

QUESTIONS

1. What is the importance of information to the criminal investigator? How is information obtained?
2. What criteria will affect the competency of a witness?
3. In evaluating the credibility of a witness, with what factors must the investigator be concerned?
4. Despite the amount of reliance placed on information supplied by eyewitnesses, how reliable are they? Why?
5. What criteria motivate witnesses to give or withhold information?
6. What are the qualifications for an effective interviewer?
7. Assuming the setting for an interview is not ideal, what conditions should be established for conducting the interview?
8. Describe the interview process.
9. How can the investigator best document an interview?
10. Why is listening important to a successful interview?

NOTES

1. Paul B. Weston and Kenneth M. Wells, *Criminal Investigation: Basic Perspectives* (Englewood Cliffs, N.J.: Prentice-Hall, 1970), p. 151.
2. Charles C. Vanderbosch, *Criminal Investigation* (Washington, D.C.: International Association of Chiefs of Police, 1968), p. 196.
3. Charles E. O'Hara with Gregory L. O'-Hara, *Fundamentals of Criminal Investigation,* 5th ed. (Springfield, Ill.: Charles C. Thomas, 1980), p. 88.
4. Henry Campbell Black, *Black's Law Dictionary,* 4th ed. (St. Paul: West, 1951), p. 1778.
5. Marshall Houts, *From Evidence to Proof* (Springfield, Ill.: Charles C. Thomas, 1956), pp. 10–11.
6. Vanderbosch, *Criminal Investigation,* p. 188.
7. Robert L. Donigan, Edward C. Fisher, et al., *The Evidence Handbook,* 4th ed. (Evanston, Ill.: The Traffic Institute, Northwestern University, 1980), p. 205.
8. Robert Buckhout, "Eyewitness Testimony," *Scientific American,* December 1974, Vol. 231, No. 6, p. 23; also see Graham Davies, Haydn Ellis, and Donald Christie, "Exploring New Strategies for Facial Recall," *Medicine, Science and the Law,* 1981, Vol. 21, No. 2, pp. 137–145; and D. M. Thompson, "The Realities of Eye Witness Identification," *Australian Journal of Forensic Sciences,* 1982, Vol. 14, No. 4, pp. 150–157.
9. Buckhout, "Eyewitness Testimony," p. 24.
10. Elizabeth Loftus, "Incredible Eyewitness," *Psychology Today,* December 1974, Vol. 8, No. 7, p. 118.
11. Buckhout, "Eyewitness Testimony," pp. 24–26.
12. Ibid., pp. 26–27.
13. Ibid., p. 28.
14. Ibid.
15. Ibid.
16. Bill Putnam, "Some Precautions Regarding the Use of Hypnosis in Criminal Investigations," *The Police Chief,* May 1979, p. 62. Also see G. D. Burrows, "Forensic Aspects of Hypnosis," *Australian Journal of Forensic Sciences,* 1981, Vol. 13, No. 4, pp. 120–125.
17. Ephraim Margolin and S. Coliver, "Forensic Use of Hypnosis," *Trial,* Vol. 19, No. 10, October 1983, p. 45. Also see H. W. Timm, "Suggested Guidelines for the Use of Forensic Hypnosis Techniques in Police Investigations," *Journal of Forensic Sciences,* 1984, Vol. 29, pp. 865–873.
18. Ibid.
19. Re refreshing memory: *Harding* v. *State,* 5 Md. App. 230, 246 A. 2d 302 (1968).
20. Re witness credibility: Martin T. Orne, David F. Dinger, and E. Carota Orne, "The Forensic use of Hypnosis," *National Institute of Justice, Research in Brief,* December 1984, p. 3. Also see *United States* v. *Narcisco,* 446F. Supp.252 (E.D.Mich.1977), and *State* v. *McQueen,* 295N.C.96, 244S.E.2d414(1978).
21. 292N.W.2d764(1980).
22. 293F.1013(D.C.Cir.1923).
23. Arizona: *State* v. *Mena,* 128Ariz.226, 624P.2d1274(1981); *Arizona ex rel. Collins,* 132Ariz.180, 644P.2d1266(1982).
24. California: *People* v. *Shirley,* 31Cal.3d18, 641p.2d775(1982); See also *People* v. *Guerra,* 690 P2d 635(1984).
25. Indiana: *Strong* v. *State,* 435 N.E.2d 969(Ind.1982); *Peterson* v. *State,* 448 N.E.2d673(1983).
26. Maryland: *Polk* v. *State,* 48Md. App.382, 427A.2d1041(1981); *State* v. *Collins,* 296Md.670(1983).
27. Massachusetts: *Commonwealth* v. *Kater,* 338Mass.519, 447N.E.2d1190(1983).
28. Michigan: *State* v. *Gonzales,* 415 Mich.615, 329N.W.2d 743(1982).

29. Nebraska: *State v. Palmer,* 210Neb.206, 313N.W.2d 648(1981); *State v. Patterson,* 213Neb.686,331N.W.2d 500(1983).

30. New York: *People v. Hughes,* 453 N.E.2d484(N.Y.1984).

31. North Carolina: *State v. Peoples,* 319 S.E.2d 177 (N.C.1984).

32. Pennsylvania: *Commonwealth v. Nazarovich,* 496 Pa. 97, 436 A.2d 170(1981).

33. Washington: *State v. Martin,* 684 P.2d651 (Wash.1984).

34. Wyoming follows pre-*Mack* analysis: *Chapman v. State,* 638 P.2d1280 (Wyo.1982).

35. New Jersey: *State v. Hurd,* 86 N.J.525, 432 A.2d 86 (1981).

36. New Mexico: *State v. Beachum,* 97 N.M.682, 643 P.2d 246 (Ct.App.1981).

37. Wisconsin: *State v. Armstrong,* 329 N.W.2d 386 (Wisc.1983).

38. Fred Graham, "Should Our Courts Reject Hypnosis?," *Parade Magazine,* October 25, 1981, p. 10.

39. Ibid.

40. Ephram Margolin, "Hypnosis Enhanced Testimony: Valid Evidence or Prosecutor's Tool?," *Trial,* 1981, Vol. 17, No. 110, p. 43.

41. J. Larry Hogan and Harry G. Roberts, "Training Officers in Investigative Hypnosis," *The Florida Police Chief,* Summer 1979, p. 11.

42. Margolin, "Hypnosis Enhanced Testimony," p. 45.

43. Frank J. Monaghan, "Warning: Doctors May Be Dangerous to the Health of Your Investigation," *The Police Chief,* August 1981, pp. 73–76.

44. For other interesting and informative articles on hypnosis in criminal investigation, see: Martin Reiser, "Hypnosis As a Tool in Criminal Investigation," *The Police Chief,* May 1979, p. 36; Richard Gordon Douce, "Hypnosis: A Scientific Aid in Crime Detection," *The Police Chief,* May 1979, p. 60; Steven C. Millwee, "The Hypnosis Unit in Today's Law Enforcement," *The Police Chief,* May 1979, p. 65; Rob Wilson, "Hypnosis: Investigating the Subconscious," *Police Magazine,* January 1979, p. 14. For an authoritative text on the theory and practice of investigative hypnosis, see Martin Reiser, *Handbook of Investigative Hypnosis* (Los Angeles: Lehi Publishing, 1980).

45. Weston and Wells, *Criminal Investigation,* p. 155.

46. Vanderbosch, *Criminal Investigation,* p. 197.

47. Weston and Wells, *Criminal Investigation,* p. 157.

48. Loftus, "Incredible Eyewitness," p. 118.

49. Ibid., p. 119.

50. Lawrence B. Rosenfeld and Jean M. Cirkly, *With Words Unspoken,* (New York: Holt, Rinehart, and Winston, 1976), p. 5.

51. Edgar M. Miner, "The Importance of Listening in the Interview and Interrogation Process," *FBI Law Enforcement Bulletin,* June 1984, pp. 12–16.

6

FIELD NOTES AND REPORTING

FIELD NOTES

From the time of arrival at the scene of an offense, the police officer is constantly engaged in obtaining, assessing, and correlating information. The crime scene is observed, witnesses interviewed, evidence collected, and other functions performed. It is impossible—except for those rare individuals blessed with extraordinary memories—to remember all of the details necessary to prepare a report immediately following an investigation, let alone months or years later when the case comes to trial. Therefore, a continuous written record must be made as the inquiry progresses; the product of this process is termed *field notes*.

There are two main reasons why field notes are of importance: They represent the basic source of information which will be drawn upon in writing the offense report, and they are often of assistance when the officer testifies in court.

A small loose-leaf notebook lends itself best to field note-taking. The identity of its owner and related pertinent information should be entered on the inside cover; this is best accomplished by the use of the business card which many police departments supply their officers. In no case should an officer's home address and telephone number be entered; this merely provides easy opportunity for harassment should the notebook ever be lost. Entries should be made on a chronological basis; when the notebook is nearly full, its contents should be removed and placed in an envelope in a secure place.

The field notes should include the answers to the following questions, subject to the availability of the information and its relevance to the type of offense involved:

Who?

Who was the victim?

Who made the report?

Who discovered the offense?

Who saw or heard something of importance?

Who had a motive for committing the offense?

Who committed the offense?

Who helped the offender?

Who was interviewed?

Who worked on the case?

Who marked the evidence?

Who received the evidence?

What?

What type of offense was committed?

What actions were taken by the suspect and using what methods?

What happened?

What do the witnesses know about it?

What evidence was obtained?

What was done with the evidence?

What tools or weapons were used?

What actions did you take?

What further action is needed?

What knowledge, skill, or strength was needed to commit the crime?

What other agencies were notified?

What witnesses were not contacted?

What time was the offense committed?

What time was the offense reported?

What was the time of your arrival?

What time did you contact witnesses?

Where?

Where was the offense discovered?

Where was the offense committed?

Where were the tools or weapons found?

Where was the victim?

Where was the suspect seen?

Where were the witnesses?

Where does the perpetrator live or frequently go?

Where is the perpetrator?

Where would he be most likely to go?

Where was he apprehended?

Where was the evidence marked?

Where was the evidence stored?

When?

When was the perpetrator arrested?

When was the victim last seen?

When did help arrive?

How?

How was the offense committed?

How did the perpetrator get to and from the scene?

How did the perpetrator obtain information needed to commit the offense?

How were the tools or weapons obtained?

How did you get your information regarding the offense?

How did you effect the arrest?

With What?

With what trade or profession are the tools associated?

With what other offense is this one associated?

Why?

Why was the offense committed?

Why were particular tools or weapons used?

Why was the offense reported?

Why were witnesses reluctant to talk?

Why was the witness anxious to point out the perpetrator?

Why was there a delay in reporting the offense?

With Whom?

With whom does the perpetrator associate?

With whom was the victim last seen?

With whom are the witnesses connected?

With whom do you expect to locate the suspect?

How Much?

How much damage was done?

How much property was taken?

How much money was taken?

How much did the victim claim was stolen?

How much knowledge was necessary to commit the offense?

How much trouble was it to carry the property away?

How much information are the witnesses not giving out?

How much is the victim withholding?

How much additional information do you need to help clear the offense?[1]

THE IMPORTANCE AND USE OF REPORTS

Among the least popular duties of police officers, reporting is also one of the most important. More than a few excellent investigations have been undone by an officer's failure to document fully in writing the results obtained. By preparing proper reports, investigators also protect themselves from allegations that their investigations were not competent, complete, and professionally correct. A case history illustrates this point:

A burglary in progress was reported at a doctor's office. As two officers moved to cover the building, a suspect was seen leaping from an office window carrying a small flight bag. The suspect ran from the scene, followed by one of the officers. He attempted to scale a fence. In the ensuing struggle, the suspect fell on the far side of the fence, breaking his arm. During treatment at a hospital, the suspect told the officer, in front of medical personnel, that he was going to claim his arm had been broken during questioning. He further indicated this would be an attempt to discredit the police as he had only recently been released from the state prison and feared that such an immediate second violation would cause the court to invoke a stringent sentence upon conviction. Because many arrested persons stated that they were going to claim the police had violated their civil rights, the officer regarded it as little more than a commonplace occurrence. Even though they did not relate directly to the investigation, the suspect's remarks and the identity of persons witnessing them were included in the report as a matter of thoroughness. Subsequently, when the Federal Bureau of Investigation investigated the matter of a possible violation of the suspect's rights, the allegation was easily refuted by corroborating statements from the medical personnel identified in the police officer's report.

Well-prepared reports based on a thorough investigation of an offense also promote the rapid apprehension of the suspect, thus preventing further crimes, and the recovery of property. The report also serves as the official memory of the department. Offenses may be placed in an inactive status, receiving no further investigative treatment for some time; or officers may resign from the service, retire, or be transferred to other duties, resulting in the assignment of another person to the case. In such circumstances, the report ensures that complete information will be readily available at future dates to people who may not have been involved in the case originally.

Incomplete or improperly prepared offense reports may, ironically, contribute to complaints that officers often voice about prosecutors and judges. A study revealed that of thirty-nine evidentiary questions prosecutors considered important for effective case presentation, only 45 percent were covered in robbery reports from one police department studied and a mere 26 percent were addressed in a second police department scrutinized.[2] Thus, inadequate reports may contribute to such practices as refusal to prosecute, a weakening of the prosecutor's plea-bargaining position, and lenient sentences. To some extent the absence of the information that prosecutors feel they need but that is missing from police reports may be a comment on the degree to which prosecutors make their informational needs known, the completeness with which those needs are made known to the officers actually initiating reports, the degree to which officers can actually meet those needs, the thoroughness of supervisory reviews of offense reports, and related factors. However, the implication is clear: More thoroughly documented offense reports are necessary to successful prosecutions. Toward that end, prosecutors and police agencies serving the same jurisdictions should jointly develop a list of key questions that can be used by the police and the prosecutor as a checklist for investigating and preparing criminal cases.

Police reports also serve important operational and administrative purposes. In the aggregate, individual reports form the records from which offense rates are determined and personnel distribution needs established. Additionally, by reviewing the reports of subordinates, supervisors are able to review the work performed and make suggestions to correct any deficiencies.

WRITING EFFECTIVE
REPORTS

If reports are to serve the purposes for which they are intended, they must have certain characteristics. Fairly lengthy lists about the traits associated with sound report writing have been developed, such as the following: clear, pertinent, brief, complete, current, accurate, fair, proper classification, informative, objective, use of correct format, and submission on a timely basis.[3] These are sound principles which, when followed, will produce a good piece of writing. There are, however, two indispensable elements of an effective report: (1) communication of that which was intended and (2) accuracy.

Not infrequently the new investigator will, if only at the subconscious level, attempt to impress those who will be reading the report by writing in an elaborate manner in order to display mastery of the English language. Persons reading the report will learn much, or perhaps all, they will ever know about the investigation from what has

been written. Therefore, it is essential to write using a clear and uncluttered style; the report must be written not only so that it can be understood, but more importantly, so that it cannot be misunderstood.

The report must be completely accurate. No detail should be added or deleted; the potential or actual consequences of such deviations, however innocent the motivation, are considerable. For example, at the scene of an armed robbery, a young investigator was conducting interviews necessary to prepare the original report. One of the questions he asked the victim was, "Had you ever seen the perpetrator before this happened?" The response was, "Yes, he works on the loading platform of the grocery on Sixth Avenue." Out of a desire to provide as much detail as possible, the investigator supplemented this statement with information from the telephone directory, writing a portion of the interview in the following manner:

> The victim advised the undersigned officer that the suspect works at Blake's Grocery Wholesale, located at 1425 Sixth Avenue, telephone number 223-3291.

Later the following exchange took place between the officer and the defense attorney in court:

Defense Attorney: Officer, do you recognize this report?

Officer: Yes, I do.

Defense Attorney: Did you prepare it?

Officer: Yes, sir, I did.

Defense Attorney: Would it be fair to say that it represents your investigation?

Officer: That is correct, sir.

Defense Attorney: Then, having conducted the investigation and having prepared the report, your testimony would be that it accurately and completely portrays your actions and what you learned?

Officer: Yes, sir.

Defense Attorney: Would you read from page 5 of this report?

Officer: "The victim advised the undersigned officer that the suspect works at Blake's Grocery Wholesale, located at 1425 Sixth Avenue, telephone number 223-3291."

Defense Attorney: Officer, the complainant in this case has already testified to the effect that she did not, in fact, tell you this. Why are you prejudiced toward the defendant in this case, and what else have you added to the report or subtracted from it in order to strengthen the state's case?

Thus, a seemingly innocuous addition to a report reduced the credibility of the entire investigation. Clear communication and accuracy are the mainstays of effective reports. The absence of one diminishes the other.

ELEMENTS COMMON TO REPORTS

The content of reports varies according to departmental policy, statistical needs, individual case requirements, and the format in use. Even considering these factors, certain crucial elements common to most reports are treated in this section.[4]

NAMES

The full names of complainants, witnesses, and other parties must always be obtained. In recording proper names, the first time an individual is referred to in a report the sequence of names should be last, first, middle. When a person mentioned in the report is commonly known by acquaintances by some name other than the proper name or an apparent derivation, the nickname should also be provided.

RACE AND SEX

Race or extraction should never be documented in such a manner as to cast aspersion on a person; ordinarily race is indicated by use of one of the following abbreviations:

Race	Abbreviation
Caucasian	W
Black	B
Hispanic	H
Oriental	O
American Indian	Ind.
Other	Oth. (along with a specific designation)

Sex is always designated by F for female and M for male. The proper sequence is race/sex, for example, W/F.

AGE

On entries requiring only a person's age, it should be indicated as of the last birthday. However, the first reference to this individual in the narrative portion of the report should give the exact date of birth, if known. When documenting the age of certain parties, such as an unidentified deceased person or a suspect whose identity has not been established, it may be approximated or given in a narrow span of years, for example, "approximately 32 years" or "approximately 31-33 years."

ADDRESSES

This information is particularly important because it helps investigators to find people for additional interviews or related procedures. Each residence and business address should show the street number and, when applicable, the apartment, suite, or room number. If this is not immediately ascertainable, the general location should be described in sufficient detail to make its whereabouts known. When military personnel are involved, the location information should include serial numbers, unit designations, and ship or installation, if applicable. If a person is only visiting a location, both temporary and permanent addresses should be obtained.

TELEPHONE NUMBERS

The telephone numbers of an individual should always be obtained, including area code, residence number, and business number, including any extension number.

PERSONAL DESCRIPTION

A model form for gathering personal descriptions appears and is discussed later in this chapter. Minimally, the following points should be included: sex, race, age, complexion, hair and eye color, physical defects, scars, marks, tattoos, build, and the nature and color of clothing worn.

PROPERTY DESCRIPTION

Elements useful in describing property are: make, model, serial number, color, and type of material from which constructed. Other types of information may also be pertinent. Using the case of a stolen car as an example, the presence of stickers, cracked windows, articles hanging from the mirror, or loud engine noise would be additional information useful in locating the vehicle.

OCCUPATION

The occupation of a person may be of some importance to an investigation. In the case of a suspect it may establish familiarity with the use of certain types of equipment or procedures associated with a particular function, such as banking. It may also lend further credibility to the statement of a witness:

A man exited from a restaurant as two suspects ran about fifteen feet from the bank they had just robbed, entered a vehicle, and rapidly drove around the corner. Despite being presented with only a brief view of the car, the witness was able to give the police a fairly detailed description of it. At the trial the defense was unsuccessful in casting doubt upon the accuracy of the description, as the witness operated an automobile repair service.

Occupation is also useful in suggesting times when a person might be successfully and conveniently contacted by the investigator. If an individual is unemployed, his ordinary line of work is to be given along with the notation "currently unemployed." Certain categories of people may be unemployed but not seeking a position in the compensated labor market; in these instances it is more appropriate to give their exact status, for example, "college student" or "housewife." If employed, the occupation given in a report should be as specific as possible, for example, "brick mason" as opposed to "manual laborer."

VALUE

The value of property stolen may determine whether the offense is a felony or misdemeanor. For articles subject to depreciation, the fair market value should be used, unless new or almost new, when the replacement cost should be utilized. On goods stolen from retail establishments, the merchant's wholesale cost, which constitutes the actual dollar loss, is the proper value to use. The value placed upon nonnegotiable instruments such as traveler's checks or money orders should be the cost of replacing them; negotiable instruments, including bonds payable to the bearer, are valued at the market price at the time of the theft.

When the stolen property is subject to

appreciation from the time of its acquisition by the owner—for example, limited-edition prints—the current fair market value is to be indicated.

The value of recovered stolen property ordinarily equals the valuation placed upon it at the time of theft unless damaged; then it is to be established by the fair market value. In those cases where the value of the stolen article is not readily ascertainable, the conservative estimate of the owner may be utilized.

DATES

These are normally documented in the sequence of day-month-year, using the first three letters of the month and the last two digits of the year, for example, 1 JAN '88.

TIME

For all official business, excluding general public and related information, most police agencies use the military system of hundred hours. Time runs from 0001 hours (12:01 A.M.) through 2400 hours (12:00 P.M.).

THE FLOW OF FIELD REPORTS

Figure 6-1 depicts the sequence of events which comprise the flow of field reports. The majority of incidents which result in a police report's being initiated will come to light by a citizen's telephone call to the complaint desk and the dispatch of a car to the scene. In a lesser number of situations, officers in the field will have the complainant or a witness approach them or see a situation requiring investigation. In any of these cases, following work at the scene the officer or officers involved will, when warranted, initiate a report.

If a department uses a word-processing center, the information pertaining to the report is dictated by telephone and the typed report signed by the officers subsequently, after reviewing it at the end of their tour of duty. Alternatively, if reports are handwritten, the officers responsible for initiating them may, if time permits, prepare them prior to making themselves available for additional calls, write them later during the shift when the pace of work has slowed, or complete them at the police station following the tour of duty. Ordinarily, a supervisor meets with subordinates one or more times during a shift to review and pick up completed reports. The supervisor who approves the report will indicate one of several possible dispositions and then send it to a records unit where a case number would be assigned, the original copy filed, and duplicates of the report routed as may be required by the disposition indicated, such as to the unit providing the latent investigative effort.

REPORT FORMAT

A typical police report form is shown in Figure 6-2. Much of the information pertinent to an investigation is so standard that simple one-line entries or checks within boxes corresponding to applicable phrases are sufficient. Such forms also offer the advantages of being rapidly completed and self-coding for high-speed data processing.

The back of the form illustrated is devoted entirely to a narrative of the case, based on the following organization of information obtained during the course of the investigation:

Suspects

- The listing, description, and, when available, identity of the suspects involved should be provided, along with a notation of whether a pickup order was placed and, if placed, the time of its initiation and the person receiving it.

FIGURE 6-1   Flow Chart for Field Reports

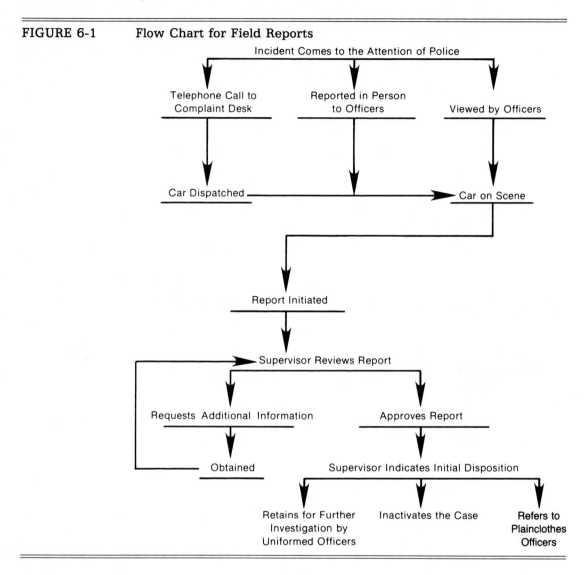

Persons Arrested

- The proper names of any persons arrested should be entered, along with any known aliases.

Witnesses

- All witnesses and pertinent information relating to them, including telephone numbers and addresses, should be listed.

Evidence

- The evidence seized, how it was marked, the chain of custody, and numbers assigned by the property or evidence control room must be recorded.

Crime Scene

- A short, but sufficiently detailed, description of the crime scene should be given to

FIGURE 6-2   **Police Report Form**

(CC 9-10-11-12) UNIFORM CLASS AND DETAIL OF MISC. OFFENSES

FALSE CRIME REPORT	10	02	CARRY CONCEAL WEAPON	15	04	UNLAWFUL ASSEMBLY	24	03
DEFACING BLDGS	14	01	FIREARM	15	05	VAGRANCY	25	00
PRIVATE	14	02	KNIFE	15	06	BEGGING	25	20
PUBLIC	14	03	KNUCKLES	15	07	LOITERING	25	80
DEFACE TOMBS	14	04	OFFNS AGNST FAM/CHILD	20	00	ESCAPE STOCKADE	26	02
DESTROY PROPERTY	14	05	CONT. TO DEL. MINOR	20	01	POSS BURGLARY TLS	26	03
PRIVATE	14	06	DEPRIVE MINOR	20	20	MALICIOUS TRESP	26	04
PUBLIC	14	07	DRUNK ON STREET	23	01	THROW NOX SUBS	26	05
DISCHARGE FIREARM	15	00	BR. OF PEACE DRUNK	23	02	POSS OF EXPLOS	26	06
MANUAL POSS. FIREARM	15	01	DISORDERLY CONDUCT	24	00	ABANDONED ICEBOX	26	07
DISPLAY DEADLY WEAPON	15	02	DISTURBANCE	24	01	BRIBERY	26	08
FELON IN POSS. FIREARM	15	03	PROFANITY	24	02	CAB DEFRAUD	26	09
						CRUELTY TO ANIM.	26	10
						GLUE SNIFFING	26	11
						EXTORTION	26	12
						FALSE FIRE ALARM	26	13
						FUGITIVE	26	14
						HOTEL FOOD DEFR.	26	15
						PEDDLING W/O LIC	26	16
						PEEPING TOM	26	17
						REFUSE TO ASSIST	26	18
						RIOTING	26	19
						SLEEP PVT/PUBL PROP	26	20
						TRESPASSING	26	21
						OTHER CRIME AGNST PERSON	26	23
						OTHER MISC OFFENSE	26	24
						CURFEW VIOLATION	28	00

JUVENILE INFORMATION – No. of Juveniles Arrested _____ (69)

RESTRICTED

NAME_____ SEX/RACE_____ AGE_____

LIGHT CONDITIONS: Daylight / Darkness W/ St. Lights / Dawn / Dusk / No St. Lights

WEATHER: Clear / Raining / Cloudy / Fog / Smoke / Other

IF JUVENILE(S) ARRESTED COMPLETE AND ATTACH T.P.D. 851-R

ADULT ARREST INFORMATION   No. Arrested _____ (70)

Evidence Seized / Diagram Drawn / Photos Taken / Latent Prints Lifted / Other Tests (List In Details of Report) / SAO Notified

(List All Arrests in Detail of Report)

ASSIGNMENT NO. (15-19)   GRID NO (20-23)

MISCELLANEOUS OFFENSE REPORT

(2-7) OFFENSE REPORT NUMBER:

NAME OF BUSINESS / ADDRESS / PHONE

OWNER: (Last-First-Middle) (SEX & COLOR) (34) D.O.B. (35-36) / BUSINESS ADDRESS / RESIDENT ADDRESS / PHONE

COMPLAINING WITNESS: (Last-First-Middle) D.O.B. / BUSINESS ADDRESS / RESIDENT ADDRESS / PHONE

DEFENDANT (Last-First-Middle) D.O.B. / BUSINESS ADDRESS / RESIDENT ADDRESS / PHONE

TYPE OF OFFENSE / LOCATION / (26-27) TIME OF OFFENSE HRS

REPORTED BY / ADDRESS / PHONE / (28) DAY OF WEEK (29-32) DATE

1ST OFFICER ON SCENE / BADGE / DIVISION / TIME REPORTED (8-71-72) HRS DATE

INVESTIGATED BY / BADGE / DIVISION (33) / REFERRED TO / RETAINED BY / BY / DATE

INDEX CARDS / PU VEH SUBJ / 1066 VEH SUBJ / NOTIFIED/OTHER / FHP SO 1066 / ALARM CARDS / COPIES REQUESTED FOR / NO. / ROUTED / ASSIGNED TO

CLOSED BY: (65) ARREST / EXCEPTIONALLY CLEARED / INACTIVE / WARRANT ISSUE

UNFOUNDED / CLASSIFICATION CHANGE / TO: / (66) DIVISION: / (67-68) DATE: / TPD 940-R1

BY:

permit a basic conceptualization of it by persons unfamiliar with it. If a diagram is made, reference is usually made to it at this point. Original diagrams are placed into the property or evidence control room in the same manner as physical articles seized at the scene. Information pertaining to photographs is also included under this point.

Investigation

- This element requires the documentation of all actions taken by the investigator at the scene regardless of whether or not they yielded useful information.

Interviews

- All persons with whom the investigator talked during the course of the inquiry should be identified, even if they could not provide information at the initial contact. On occasion the perpetrator may remain near the scene, usually in property crimes where no witnesses are involved, in an attempt to determine what the police have established. More rarely, the perpetrator or an accomplice will deliberately provide false information in order to misdirect the investigation. The identification of all witnesses is helpful in ferreting out the rare instances of such occurrences. Moreover, people who have actually seen something of value to the inquiry may be reluctant to discuss it with the police at the scene, but will readily reveal it during a follow-up contact.

Reconstruction

- The reconstruction is a narration of the probable manner in which the crime was committed, based on statements made by the suspect, if in custody and cooperating, interviews of witnesses, the examination of the crime scene, and physical evidence.

AIDS TO INFORMATION GATHERING DURING THE ORIGINAL INVESTIGATION

Whenever there are witnesses to a crime, even the most conscientious investigator may fail to elicit all information available. Certain aids, however, can be of critical importance in preventing this.

One tool, shown in Figure 6-3, is a checklist of all pertinent personal description information to be gained by interviewing witnesses. One additional benefit of such a form is that it enhances efforts to cross-reference information from different cases where it appears likely the perpetrator was the same.

One of the most frustrating experiences for investigators occurs when trying to obtain a description of a firearm, as the victim or witnesses are often injured, unfamiliar with firearms or visibly shaken by their experience. One helpful device in such situations is shown in Figures 6-4 and 6-5, which contain photographs of the most commonly encountered firearms. Most frequently even emotionally upset victims or witnesses can make an identification or at least give a good description of the weapon when these are viewed.

THE LATENT INVESTIGATION AND SUPPLEMENTAL REPORTS

Those assigned to the latent investigation function also rely on aids to assist them; one such device is the checklist shown in Figure 6-6, which guides and summarizes the progress of the latent investigation. The elements listed are those common to latent investigations, although they may occur in a different sequence depending on the particulars of a given case, such as when a suspect has been apprehended at the crime scene and is already in custody. The checklist provides a

FIGURE 6-3 Checklist for Obtaining Personal Descriptions

Complainant _____ Nature of offense _____

Address _____ Date _____

Offense # _____ Suspect _____

1. Closest estimate of age _____

2. *Sex*
   Male _____
   Female _____

3. *Race/Nationality*
   White _____
   Black _____
   Indian _____
   Oriental _____
   Hispanic _____
   Other _____

4. *Height*
   Less than 5′ _____
   5′ –5′ 2″ _____
   5′3″–5′ 5″ _____
   5′6″–5′ 8″ _____
   5′9″–5′11″ _____
   6′ –6′ 3″ _____
   6′4″ or over _____

5. *Eye Color*
   Blue _____
   Brown _____
   Gray _____
   Hazel _____
   Green _____

6. *Weight*
   Less than 100 lbs. _____
   100–120 _____
   121–140 _____
   141–160 _____
   161–180 _____
   181–200 _____
   201–220 _____
   221–240 _____
   240 or more _____

7. *Eye Defects*
   Blind _____
   Crossed _____
   Cockeyed _____
   Deep set _____
   Squints _____
   Bulging _____
   Bloodshot _____
   Oriental _____
   Different colored _____
   Contacts _____
   Glasses _____
   Cataracts _____

8. *Hair Color*
   Blonde or strawberry blonde _____
   Brown (light) _____
   Brown (dark) _____
   Black _____
   Gray or partially gray _____
   White _____
   Red or auburn _____
   Dyed, unusual, or added color _____

9. *Hair type*
   Bald _____
   Partially bald _____
   Long straight _____
   Short straight _____
   Long curly _____
   Short curly _____
   Thinning _____
   Bushy _____
   Wavy _____
   Thin or receding _____
   Kinky _____
   Wig or hairpiece _____
   Afro _____

10. *Complexion*
    Fair _____
    Ruddy _____
    Dark _____
    Medium _____
    Light _____
    Sallow _____

11. *Facial Scars*
    Forehead _____
    Eye (right) _____
    Eye (left) _____
    Nose (including broken) _____
    Ear (right) _____
    Ear (left) _____
    Chin _____
    Lips _____
    Right cheek _____
    Left cheek _____
    Eyebrow (right) _____
    Eyebrow (left) _____

12. *Facial Oddities*
    Pockmarked _____
    Freckled _____
    Pimpled _____
    Birthmark _____
    Protruding chin _____
    Receding chin _____
    Thick lips _____
    Thin lips _____

13. *Torso Scars*
    Chest _____
    Shoulder (right) _____
    Shoulder (left) _____
    Upper back _____
    Lower back _____
    Buttocks _____
    Stomach _____
    Hip (right) _____
    Hip (left) _____

14. *Limb Scars*
    Arm (right) _____
    Arm (left) _____
    Hand (right) _____
    Hand (left) _____
    Leg (right) _____
    Leg (left) _____
    Foot (right) _____
    Foot (left) _____
    Wrist (right) _____
    Wrist (left) _____
    Elbow (right) _____
    Elbow (left) _____
    Pockmarked _____
    Bullet or shrapnel wound _____
    Needle marks _____
    Vaccination (right arm) _____
    Vaccination (left arm) _____
    Multiple scars _____

15. *Mustache or Beard*
    Heavy Mustache _____
    Medium Mustache _____
    Thin Mustache _____
    Full Beard _____
    Goatee _____
    Sideburns _____

16. *Deformities*
    Humpback _____
    Lame leg _____
    Crippled hand (right) _____
    Crippled hand (left) _____
    Crippled fingers (right) _____
    Crippled fingers (left) _____
    Bowlegged _____
    Cauliflower ears _____

17. *Amputations*
    Arm (right) _____
    Arm (left) _____
    Leg (right) _____
    Leg (left) _____
    Foot (right) _____
    Foot (left) _____
    Finger (right) _____
    Finger (left) _____
    Other (specify) _____

18. *Teeth*
    All missing _____
    Missing top _____
    Missing bottom _____
    Irregular _____
    Chipped _____
    Protruding upper (rabbit) _____
    Protruding lower _____
    Visible decay _____
    Stained _____
    Very attractive _____

19. *Accent and Speech Pattern*
    Foreign accent _____
    Southern drawl _____
    Northern accent (if possible, specify
    Brooklyn, Boston, etc.) _____
    Vulgar language _____
    Beatnik or jive _____
    Spanish accent _____
    Slurred _____
    Stutter _____
    Mute _____
    Soft _____
    Loud _____
    Refined _____
    Used written note _____

20. *Clothing (MEN)*
    Hat (type) _____
    Jacket (color and type, waist,
    length, etc.) _____
    Shirt (color, pattern, short or
    long sleeves) _____
    Trousers (color, style—flared,
    tight fitting) _____
    Sweaters (color, style, sleeves,
    vest, etc.) _____
    Necktie (color and design) _____
    Shoes (color and style—loafers,
    boots, sneakers, etc.) _____
    Gloves (color and type) _____
    Other pertinent information _____

21. *Clothing (WOMEN)*
    Dress (color, design, length) _____
    Pants suit (color, design) _____
    Blouse (color, design) _____
    Skirt (color, design, length) _____
    Hat (color, type) _____
    Gloves (color, type) _____
    Other pertinent information _____

22. *Disguises*
    Mask (silk stocking) _____
    Mask (Halloween) _____
    Mask (ski type) _____
    False nose _____
    False beard _____
    False mustache _____
    Sunglasses (color, style) _____

FIGURE 6-4   Commonly Used Handguns

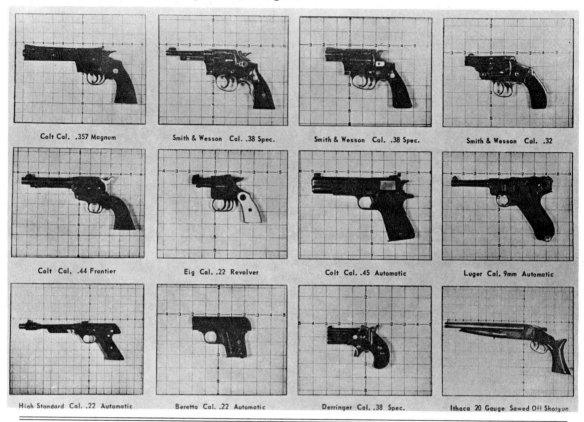

Colt Cal. .357 Magnum   Smith & Wesson Cal. .38 Spec.   Smith & Wesson Cal. .38 Spec.   Smith & Wesson Cal. .32

Colt Cal. .44 Frontier   Eig Cal. .22 Revolver   Colt Cal. .45 Automatic   Luger Cal. 9mm Automatic

High Standard Cal. .22 Automatic   Beretta Cal. .22 Automatic   Derringer Cal. .38 Spec.   Ithaca 20 Gauge Sawed Off Shotgun

visual summary of the status of a case and is an adjunct to any narrative supplemental reports initiated rather than a substitute for them. Investigators may choose to simply check the appropriate column associated with each element. Alternatively, entries can be made under the appropriate column of the time and date an act was accomplished. Additionally, to avoid someone unfamiliar with the case having to read through supplemental reports to find a particular fact, short informational entries could be made, such as for "vehicle released" the notation "to complainant" might be made under the "yes" column.

Periodically during the latent investigation supplemental reports must be initiated. Ordinarily, supplemental or follow-up reports should be written no less frequently than every ten days and the continuance of a particular investigation beyond thirty days should require supervisory approval to ensure proper use of an investigator's time. The purpose of writing follow-up reports is to keep the file current as new or corrected information is generated. Additionally, specific acts or accomplishments might require individual supplemental reports such as the activation or cancellation of a pickup order, the issuance of a warrant, the arrest of a suspect, the complainant's discovery that other prop-

FIGURE 6-5   Assorted Longguns

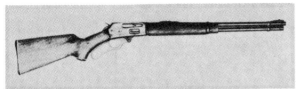

.30-30 CALIBER MARLIN, MODEL 336, LEVER ACTION RIFLE

MOSSBERG PUMP ACTION SHOTGUN, WITH VARIABLE CHOKE

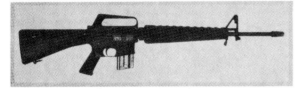

.223 CALIBER COLT AR-15 (M-16) RIFLE

12-GAUGE MOSSBERG BOLT ACTION SHOTGUN

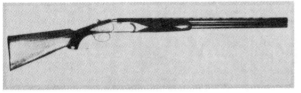

12-GAUGE BERETTA OVER & UNDER SHOTGUN

9MM ISRAELI UZI SUBMACHINE GUN (BELGIAN-MADE)

BROWNING BOLT ACTION RIFLE (NUMEROUS CALIBERS)

.30 CALIBER U.S. M-1 CARBINE

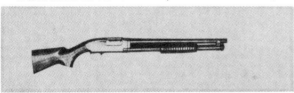

20-GAUGE WINCHESTER, MODEL 12, SAWED-OFF SHOTGUN

.22 CALIBER WINCHESTER, MODEL 69, BOLT ACTION RIFLE

7.62MM RUSSIAN AK-47 ASSAULT RIFLE

.303 CALIBER BRITISH SMLE RIFLE

Source: **Federal Bureau of Investigation,** *A Visual Aid for Firearms Identification*

FIGURE 6-6   **Checklist for Latent Investigations**

	YES	NO	NOT APPLICABLE
Reviewed Offense Report			
Evidence: Viewed			
To Laboratory			
Reviewed Technician's Report			
Records Check of Complainant(s)/Witness(s)			
Crime Analysis Information: MO Check			
Field Contacts			
Known Offenders			
Recap Information			
Visited Crime Scene			
Contacted Complainant(s)			
Contacted Witness(s)			
Mugshot File/Likeness Viewed			
Informants Queried			
Pickup Order Placed			
Pickup Order Cancelled			
Interrogated Suspect(s)			
Lineup Conducted			
Conference with Prosecuting Attorney			
Formal Charge Filed			
Final Disposition			
Vehicle Released			
Evidence Disposed of			
Outside Agency Contact: Probation			
Parole			
Other Agencies			
Supplemental Report Made			
Final Supplemental Report Made			

INVESTIGATOR	BADGE #	APPROVING SUPERVISOR	BADGE #

erty was stolen which was not noticed missing at the time the original report was made, the recovery of all or part of property taken, or a change in the title of the offense, due to improper classification on the original report, e.g., a strong-arm robbery reclassified as a purse snatch.

Other circumstances under which supplemental reports are required include: (1) when the offense is unfounded, that is, when it is established that the offense, in fact, did not occur; (2) when it is exceptionally cleared, meaning that the police know who the perpetrator is but are unable to pursue the case further due to circumstances beyond their control, such as the death of the only witness; and (3) when the case is inactivated.

If the supervisor reviewing the original report inactivates it due to insufficient leads to warrant latent investigation, then a supplemental report is not required. However, if some follow-up work is done, no promising leads develop, and the case is then inactivated, the person assigned responsibility for it must complete a supplemental report to substantiate the basis for inactivation.

As a general concluding note, case files inactivated may in later months or years receive further investigative work which is productive; therefore, it is of considerable importance that at each stage of report-writing care is exercised in presenting all available information.

QUESTIONS

1. Why are field notes important?
2. Of what importance and use are police reports of crimes?
3. What are the two indispensable elements of an effective report?
4. Why might the occupation of a person be of importance in an investigation?
5. Under what circumstances is a supplemental report required?

NOTES

1. Allen Z. Gammage, *Basic Police Report Writing* (Springfield, Ill.: Charles C. Thomas, 1966), pp. 105–108.
2. Jan Chalken, Peter Greenwood, and Joan Petersilia, "The Criminal Investigation Process," in *The Criminal Investigation Process: A Dialogue of Research Findings* (Washington, D.C.: Government Printing Office, 1977), p. 23.
3. Gammage, *Basic Police Report Writing*, pp. 13–14.
4. Establishing the original source material in this section has been difficult. Police departments use verbatim material in training manuals and other documents without any indication as to its source. It is possible that the original source is V. A. Leonard's *Police Records Manual*, an undated eighty-page monograph published by the International Association of Chiefs of Police.

7

LATENT INVESTIGATION

THE DECISION TO INITIATE A LATENT INVESTIGATION

Latent investigation is the police effort to gather information subsequent to the initiation of the original report and until the case is ready for prosecution. After a uniformed officer initiates a report, his or her immediate supervisor makes an initial disposition. Certain crimes such as homicides, rapes, and suicides, invariably receive latent work. Other offenses receive latent investigation depending on department policy. Ordinarily only the most serious offenses and those with potential for conclusive results get investigative effort beyond that necessary to generate the original report.

To eliminate subjectivity in supervisors' decisions about whether to refer cases for latent investigation, some police departments have developed case disposition guides. Several years ago, one component of a study by the Police Executive Research Forum (PERF) of the most effective ways to investigate burglaries and robberies dealt with case disposition guides for robberies and burglaries. The study involved police departments in DeKalb County, Georgia, St. Petersburg, Florida, and Wichita, Kansas.[1]

In two of three departments, patrol officers' burglary and robbery reports were sent to the appropriate investigative supervisors,

usually on the workday following the incident. The assignment of robbery cases differed in DeKalb County, where investigators were generally assigned cases shortly after the patrol officer established that a robbery had occurred. In St. Petersburg, robbery cases were sent to the Personal Crimes section of the Investigative Operations Bureau. In Wichita only commercial robbery reports were sent to the Major Crimes section of Central Investigation; street robbery reports were sent to the teams for latent investigations. Burglary case reports were sent to burglary investigators in DeKalb County and St. Petersburg and to the appropriate team investigator in Wichita.

Although all robbery cases were assigned to investigators for latent investigation in the three departments, many burglary cases received no more than a preliminary investigation by a patrol officer. Burglary case screening procedures were markedly different in the three agencies. Figure 7-1 shows the form used by first-line supervisors for screening burglary cases in DeKalb County. Cases in which more than $1,000 worth of property was stolen also were automatically assigned to investigators. This was the most formalized screening procedure used among the three agencies.

In St. Petersburg, first-line supervisors reviewed patrol officers' burglary reports, with-

FIGURE 7-1   DeKalb County Police Burglary Screening Decision Model

Weight (Circle)	*Information Element*	
	1. Suspect Information	
10	A. Positive Identification	
8	B. Tentative Identification	
6	C. Poor Identification	
	2. Vehicle Information	
10	A. Positive Identification (tag and/or other)	
8	B. Definitive Description	
6	C. Poor Description	
	3. Estimate Time Between Incident - Report	
4	A. Less than one hour	
3	B. One to twelve hours	
2	C. Twelve hours and over	
	4. Method of Reporting	
2	A. Witness and/or victim	
1	B. Officer on-view	
	5. Information Received ⟶	SECTION 5 TO BE USED *ONLY* IF
	A. Confidential Informant and/or victim	INFORMATION AVAILABLE AT
10	1. Definitive information	CODING *OR* TO
8	2. Possible information	ACTIVATE AN
6	3. Poor information	INACTIVE CASE
	B. Information shared from other investigator and/or agency	
10	1. Definitive information	
8	2. Possible information	
6	3. Poor information	
	6. Modus Operandi	
5	A. Definitive pattern	
4	B. Possible pattern	
3	C. Poor pattern	
	7. Fingerprints	
10	A. Identified with suspect	
1	B. Without suspect	

_____   TOTAL   CUT POINT FOR CASE ACTIVATION IS 10

            Case: Active

                  Inactive   (Circle)

Other factors not listed which cause the case to be active.

(Specify) _____

NOTE: *This scale is to be used as a guideline only and is not intended to override nor interfere with the good judgment of a supervisor in assigning cases where there may be considerations not included in the scale.*

CASE NUMBER _____   INVESTIGATOR _____

DATE _____   SCREENER _____

out formal guidelines, to determine what information was present. Cases in which a suspect's name or description appeared and those in which fingerprints were recovered were usually assigned to an investigator for latent investigation. Some cases were assigned irrespective of the information available, cases in which victims had suffered high property losses and in which public relations required an investigation.

The Wichita Police Department also had a policy governing the screening of burglary cases, but adherence to the policy varied by team. According to policy, burglary cases were screened out when no suspect name or description appeared, no property serial numbers or other leads were noted, or when losses were valued at under $500. Letters were sent to victims explaining the decision to curtail further investigation. But the procedure generally followed was to assign a case to an investigator if there was any likelihood of an arrest and then to let the investigator decide how much effort should be expended on the investigation. In some teams, the investigator screened cases and sent investigatory termination letters after the case was assigned to them. In other teams, all cases were worked by recontacting the victim to see if any new information was available. Some of the investigators stated that this procedure was employed primarily for public relations purposes. One team captain stated that all burglary cases were assigned in his team because he felt that it was more important to spend time contacting victims and establishing rapport between the victims and the officers than to save detectives' time by screening out cases unlikely to result in arrest.

In many cases, the investigators recontacted victims to verify patrol officers' reports, to find new information, or merely to appease victims. Generally, no new information was forthcoming, and sometimes the public relation attempts backfired.

In the following example the investigator reinterviewed a victim. Because the victim had assumed that nothing would come of the investigation, he was annoyed at being recontacted by the detective.

An investigator visited the victim of a burglary. Earlier that week the victim's home had been broken into and several hundred dollars worth of electronic entertainment and citizens-band radio equipment stolen. The victim expressed surprise at the appearance of the investigator and stated that he had given the patrol officer all the information. The interview of the victim took approximately 20 minutes, provided no new information, and confirmed the lack of substantial leads. The victim seemed bothered by the amount of time the interview was taking. Finally, taking his cue from victim, the investigator left, having acquired no new leads.

The following example illustrates a case in which recontacting the victim and searching for possible witnesses not only were unsuccessful, but also led the investigator to suspect the victim was not being truthful.

The victim of a commercial burglary in which an expensive set of power tools was stolen was recontacted by the investigator. The tools were highly specialized and were used in only one type of business, that in which the victim was employed. The investigator was shown the crime scene, and the victim recounted how he had discovered the theft. The victim employed numerous high school students and young adults in low-paying jobs; there was a high turnover of employees. The victim said, however, that he suspected no current or former employee of committing the burglary. After interviewing the victim, the investigator canvassed the neighborhood for possible witnesses in the apartments overlooking the crime scene. Although several people had been home at the time, no one had seen or heard anything suspicious. The investigator stated after the canvass that the victim might have reported a false burglary to gain the insurance money. Few people would have had any use for the items taken. No further investigation was conducted.

But some cases which have no good or apparent leads are not so hopeless as the original report may indicate. In this type of case, recontacting the victim is useful:

An investigator checking the address of a strong-arm robbery victim found that he lived in a halfway house for juvenile delinquents. At the victim's residence, the investigator was introduced to the victim by the adult supervisor. The investigator asked the victim to explain in greater detail than was in the patrol report the circumstances of the robbery. After some hesitation, the victim stated that the suspect was known to him, but not by name, and that the victim and suspect had gone to the location of the incident together. After further inquiries, the victim admitted that he had wanted to purchase some marijuana from the suspect, but the suspect had beaten him and taken his money. The victim had not told this fact to the patrol officer, because the victim had been afraid to incriminate himself. The investigator assured the victim that no charges would be brought against him and confirmed the suspect's description as obtained by the patrol officer. The investigator then continued to investigate the case.

NAMED SUSPECTS

Sometimes a suspect is named in a patrol report assigned for investigation. Investigators then may check department arrest records to see if the named suspect has a criminal record. Since the suspect may not have any record, either because he or she has never been involved with the particular agency, or because the suspect is a juvenile, this activity may not always be useful. Indeed, the identification of a suspect in a patrol report is no guarantee that the named suspect committed the offense, or had anything to do with it.

Although a named suspect sometimes can be arrested and charged, often the testimony of victims and witnesses leaves much to be desired. For example, the victim may only be theorizing about who committed the offense. Sometimes victims and witnesses see someone they know in the vicinity of an offense, but no other evidence links the suspect to the offense. Thus a named suspect or a description in a patrol report may provide valuable leads, but they often do not make the investigation easy nor guarantee a solution. The following example illustrates this point.

While conducting a follow-up investigation to a burglary, an investigator found a juvenile suspect listed in the patrol report. The suspect had been named by the victim, who claimed to have seen the suspect near her house shortly after it was broken into. The suspect's parents were contacted by phone and an appointment made for the next day at the suspect's home. At that time, the investigator interviewed the suspect and discussed the case with his parents in their living room. The suspect claimed not to be involved but was aware of the incident; he also claimed that he could name the people who had committed the burglary. The suspect provided the name of another person who he said could verify that he was not involved. The investigator was aware of the activities (not directly related to the offense under consideration) of some of the people named by the juvenile and felt that this suspect probably had had little or nothing to do with the burglary. After warning the juvenile to stay away from some of his associates because of their links to known offenders, the investigator left. The investigator believed that although the suspect might not have been completely innocent, he certainly was not deeply involved in the offense, and his parents seemed to be the type to keep him in line.

GOOD LEADS

The amount of effort required to follow up a good lead is seldom mentioned in research or investigative work. However, as the following example shows, even when good leads are available, the investigation is not a simple matter of arresting suspects.

A burglary victim called an investigator to explain that she thought the offenders were two employees of a firm that the apartment complex had hired to do some work in her apartment. The described suspects, names unknown, had been given a key to perform the necessary work. The burglary had been committed eight days later, and there had been no forced entry. The apartment manager, when contacted by the investigator, denied that the suspects could have conducted the burglary but provided the name of the firm that employed them. The owner of the firm testified to the suspects' good employment records and reliability. A message was left for the suspects to contact the investigator. The suspects called back about a half hour later and gave the investigator their full names, dates of birth, past criminal history, and described the work done on the victim's apartment. The investigator used this information to check his own department's records and also requested a record check on the suspects from a neighboring jurisdiction. The investigator concluded after following up these leads that the suspects were not likely to have been the offenders and closed the investigation.

This example demonstrates that even when apparently good leads are available, additional work is required to check them out, and even then the case still may not be solved.

Although information about a suspect may not be present in a preliminary report, there may be enough evidence to lead to the identification of a suspect. In the following example, the preliminary report included a few tenuous leads that proved very useful. Of particular interest is the fact that at every step of this investigation, the likelihood of identifying the suspect was small.

A patrol report of a robbery included the name and address of a juvenile witness but failed to indicate the nature of the information she might have. The investigator visited the address listed on the patrol report; it was the address of the witness's grandmother. Although the witness had been living there at the time of the robbery, she had just moved back with her parents. The investigator drove to the address provided by the grandmother and interviewed the witness in the company of her parents. The witness thought she recognized the suspect and provided what she thought was the suspect's name. She also stated that she would recognize the suspect if she saw him again.

The investigator returned to the police station and began checking for the suspect's name in department records. Several variations of the name were tried without success. The investigator discussed the case with a youth officer who suggested a different variation on the suspect's name. A recheck of department records provided a photo, description, name, address, and prior record of a suspect who matched the descriptions given by the victim and witness. Furthermore, and as important to the investigator, the suspect had a prior record of assaults and drug offenses.

The investigator then put together a photo lineup of five color photographs of similar-looking people plus the suspect's photo. When the investigator returned to the witness's home, she easily identified the photo of the suspect. Armed with this information, the investigator drove by the suspect's home but did not stop. He then called the dispatcher and asked that a particular patrol officer meet him nearby. When the officer arrived, the investigator gave the information about the suspect to the officer and directed him to arrest the suspect on sight. Shortly thereafter the suspect was arrested by the officer.

CRIME ANALYSIS

Ever since police officers began searching for similarities among reported crimes, there has been some form of crime analysis.[2] Although crime analysis is usually considered to be an esoteric process left to Sherlock Holmes types, a number of recent factors have renewed interest in the process. Certainly increases in crime rates, calls for police service, costs of police operations, and attention to productivity standards have had significant effects. As a result, agencies are beginning to develop crime analysis units, and the use of computers assume ever greater importance.

The effect of crime analysis on a law enforcement agency is impressive. For example, several years ago the Los Angeles Police Department reported that their computerized PATRIC system (Pattern Recognition and Information Correlation) could process 130,000 cases a year and yield over $6 million annually in savings. A further finding showed that in approximately two of every five new cases, the PATRIC data base contained a crime report or related suspect information of immediate interest to the investigator. By comparison, the Chicago Police Department, utilizing their manual handsort system, identified only 1,528 crime patterns in five selected offense categories and, of those, cleared 436. The average pattern consisted of six cases.

SCOPE AND USE OF CRIME ANALYSIS INFORMATION

Crime analysis is a system of identifying patterns or trends. It is one more tool of law enforcement that can serve the needs of different masters. It may help to suppress crime through the early identification of pattern activity and staff recommendations on specific corrective programs. Crime analysis can aid in the apprehension of criminals by providing correlations between offenders and between suspects and offenses. Crime analysis can aid in the prevention of criminal activity through recommendations about security in residences and commercial developments. Crime analysis can aid police administrators to improve community relations by graphically illustrating criminal activity patterns to citizens' groups, homeowner associations, and the like, and thereby enlisting their support in crime-specific programs.

Crime analysis supports police operation through strategy planning, manpower deployment, and investigation assistance. It supports police and criminal justice planning efforts and provides data for program and tactical evaluation. A more definitive overview of crime analysis appears in Table 7-1.

The purpose of a crime analysis is threefold. First, crime analysis should assist in establishing, screening, and ordering lists of suspects for individual crimes, based on characteristics of the crime and the method of operation (MO) of known offenders. Second, crime analysis should assist in assembling and ordering the topics and specific

TABLE 7-1
The Crime Analysis Mission

Support	Activity	Method or Technique	
Detective	Case Investigation	Known Offender	-MO -Associates -Status -Location
Detective	Case Investigation	Offense Correlation—	-Evidence -Location -Day, Week, etc. -Property -Crime Specific -Victim, Witness
Detective Patrol	Special Operations Manpower Allocations	Locational Stake-out Patterns Crime Pattern Information Crime Prediction Profiles	
Patrol	Tactical Assignments	Crime Location Patterns	
Patrol	Suppression	I.D. of Offenders Active in Area	
Patrol	Patrol Effectiveness Improvement	Characteristics—Unique Crimes	
Planning	Strategy Development	Categorize Crime Problems Demographic Correlations Prediction of Future Problem Areas	

Source: George A. Buck et al., *Police Crime Analysis Unit Handbook.* Washington, D.C.: Government Printing Office, 1973, p. 1.

crimes that may involve a suspect already in custody. This function can maximize the number of cases properly cleared by a single arrest. Third, crime analysis should assist in assigning and deploying preventive patrols and other police functions to assure police observation of crimes in progress.

Operational Use. The primary source of raw data for crime analysis comes from the reports prepared by patrol officers. They must have a working understanding of crime analysis.

CRIME ANALYSIS DEVELOPMENT

All police departments perform some crime analysis activity. However, the overwhelming majority have not made any one individual or unit responsible for this activity. Police departments that have designated crime analysis units actually have units performing tasks like compiling crime statistics, making beat surveys, and planning work force allocations. The actual work of crime analysis is being performed in unassociated divisions and details.

Stimulation for crime analysis can be attributed to the development of the idea of *modus operandi* in England in the early 1900s and now found in many police agencies; and to the requirement for traffic analysis as promoted by the Northwestern University Traffic Institute. This development grew out of the need for information on the circumstances that create traffic accidents. It was soon clear that data had to be processed and meaningfully formatted, for example, shown in pin maps, tables, graphs, and summaries for prediction, deployment, and other purposes.

In a discussion of crime analysis concepts, we define both informal and formal crime analysis and discuss the latter in terms of basic and advanced operations.

Informal Crime Analysis. Informal crime analysis, in its simplest sense, is performed by all officers as they investigate crimes. Crime analysis is examining one crime and comparing it with others like it. Basically, officers are walking crime analysis units as they compare their investigations with their own and others' past experiences. Officers' experiences are limited by the number of hours they work and, essentially, their experiences are not coordinated with those of others. The following case illustrates this point:

> A young woman reported to the police that a young black man approximately 18 years of age stole her purse after she had walked out of a grocery store. She said that the man came up behind her and tried to grab her purse. She resisted and held onto her purse, at which time the man punched her in the face several times, knocking her to the pavement. Then he took her purse and fled.

The preliminary report was completed by a patrol officer and forwarded to the robbery bureau for follow-up investigation. The victim's abandoned purse, without its money, was found by some children in a nearby alley the following day and turned over to the police department.

Several days later, a robbery detective returned to the scene to conduct a neighborhood check. The first person to be interviewed was the owner of the grocery store. The owner said that this had been the fifth purse theft of grocery shoppers in three months. The detective advised the merchant that no similar crimes from this area had been referred to the robbery bureau for quite some time, but the merchant insisted that there had been at least five similar crimes, that each had occurred on a Friday night, and that all had been reported to the police department.

The detective checked the police department's handwritten log of reported offenses and found that there had been five purse thefts at the grocery store prior; each had been committed on a Friday night between 7:30 and 9:00 P.M.; each victim's discarded pocketbook had been found in the same alley nearby and turned over to the police; and the suspect in each case was a black male, 15 to 20 years old, 5'11" to 6'1", 155 to 165 pounds.

Part of the reason that this clear pattern had not been detected lay in the referral procedure of the police department. In two cases, victims reported the suspect's age at 15 to 16, and the reports were referred to the Youth Services Bureau. In two other cases, no force had been used, and they had been referred to the Larceny Bureau. (Typically, a purse theft in which no force or fear is involved is classified as a larceny. If force or fear is involved, the crime is classified as a robbery.) In addition, the initial reports and reports of the recovery of the stolen purses of each offense had been taken by different patrol officers.

The area where the purse thefts had occurred was placed under surveillance by detectives for two consecutive Friday nights. The suspect showed up on the second Friday at 7:30 P.M. and stole a purse from a woman who had just walked out of the grocery store. Detectives arrested the fleeing suspect. He was 18 years of age, 5'11", and weighed 160 pounds. The suspect subsequently confessed to having committed all of the other purse thefts.

Larger agencies with crime-specific details also perform informal crime analysis. Because investigators specialize in crime categories, the quality of the informal analysis is generally higher than that of patrol officers. Despite sometimes extensive logging, investigators generally rely on memory for correlating reports and identifying patterns.

Following is a list of characteristics generally associated with informal crime analysis. It is:

- Based on individual officer's memory and past experience
- Hampered by an officer's limited time on duty and interest
- Subjective, biased, and out of date
- Hampered by a large volume of crime
- Time consuming
- Limited in its MO data storage system
- Likely to identify patterns only by unusual MO characteristics
- Limited in ability to recognize a crime picture developing within an area
- Uncoordinated
- Of limited use and hampered by the absence of formal communications

Formal Crime Analysis Operation. A formal crime analysis operation is one in which the responsibility for identifying crime patterns has been given to one or more specific people or units. Few crime analysis units

have a delineated set of operational goals. The essential quality of a formal crime analysis unit is that it views the overall occurrence of crime through "one set of eyes." As a general rule, the crime analysts are selected for their experience and analytical abilities. The following is a list of characteristics generally associated with a formal crime analysis unit. It:

- Provides a more objective, quicker analysis than an informal analysis
- Reviews the overall occurrence of crime
- Identifies crime patterns through MO analysis and systematically stores and retrieves MO data
- Is a staff unit not directly involved in investigation or enforcement
- Links communications among operational units on crime patterns and thereby coordinates staff

Formal crime analysis units may be basic, advanced, or somewhere in between. Factors determining the operational level include:

- Number of personnel assigned
- Hours of operation
- Type of equipment
- Extent of data storage
- Scope of crimes, subgroups, and MO traits analyzed

Basic Operations. Basic crime analysis is characterized by *limited* capabilities. They generally solve current problems, rather than preventing their occurrence, predicting, or suggesting corrective programs. A basic operation is characterized as follows:

- Staffed by one or two people
- Operated during normal business hours
- Analyzes three or four crime categories
- Employs a manual system of filing and storing data
- Has a limited cross-referencing of data storage
- Lacks crime prediction

- Lacks known-offender/MO analysis
- Has limited visual geographical analysis, generally pin maps

Crime analysis depends on a unit's ability to collect and store information from incoming crime reports. The limited staff of a basic crime unit severely handicaps it. In all but small departments, the absence of automated data processing limits crime analysis.

Advanced Operations. Advanced crime analysis operations analyze data for the purpose of identifying future trends and problem areas. Although they are not absolutely essential, computers can form the core of advanced crime analysis. Computers can search numbers of records and use relatively complex search criteria. Computers do not tire of repetitive tasks nor fail to recognize logical associations as a result of fatigue or stress. Advanced operations should have the following characteristics:

- Rapid correlations among offenses
- Names of suspects provided
- Computer-stored data base
- Complex searching criteria
- Large staff
- Twenty-four hour a day operation
- Crime reports reviewed for quality before data base is updated
- Expanded numbers of crime categories
- Complex storage of known offenders information, including descriptions, vehicles, and MOs

Whether formal or informal crime analyses are employed, it is quite possible that in the early stages of the investigative process some important feature or pattern of crimes will be overlooked. The following case illustrates this point:

For several years, *Omaha Magazine,* published in Omaha, Nebraska, had been selecting and then doing feature stories on that city's "Ten Most Eligible Women." In addition to their pictures, the stories gave readers biographies of the women, including their ages, addresses, and places of work. The youngest woman was 24, the oldest 46; some were divorced and had children; others had never married. Early on the morning of March 31, one of the women featured was raped. She reported to police that a man broke into her house, blindfolded her, put duct tape over her mouth, bound her hands and feet, and threatened to kill her. He then raped her. No one thought to ask nor did the victim suggest that there might be some connection between this rape and the magazine story.

On April 14, a second woman featured in the magazine reported an attempted break-in. A connection was still not apparent.

Five days later, another woman reported a brutal rape. She had not been listed in *Omaha Magazine,* but one of the women on the list had moved out of the house a month earlier. Still no connection was made. However, the police saw a pattern in the rapes and suspected they had been committed by the same man because of his bizarre method of operation and abnormal sex acts. On April 27, there was another attempted break-in on another of the women featured in the magazine.

After hours of reviewing case files and reinterviewing victims, the common denominator was found. Police watched each of the women's homes. One week later, the suspect was arrested while attempting to break into the home of another woman. A list of the women's names was found in the suspect's pocket, and the suspect admitted that they were listed in the order in which he had planned to assault them.[3]

Consistency is such an important characteristic of most repeated sexual offenses that any indications of inconsistency must assume a special significance for the investigator. It would be natural to treat the presence of an inconsistency as an indication that a different offender or perpetrator was involved. This was certainly the assumption in the famous Boston Strangler slayings, a series of murders in which sexual aberration had a focal significance. Five of the Strangler's victims had been older women killed within two months in 1962. In each case, the victim had been strangled and an article of clothing, such as a brassiere or a scarf, had been tied around the neck and looped into a decorative bow, but although the bodies bore traces of semen, there was no indication that the victims had been raped by the murderer.

After a lapse of four months, the first of what turned out to be a series of six additional slayings was discovered. In this and subsequent cases, there were indications that the victims had been targets of wild sexual assault. The first set of victims had been, for the most part, women in their 60s, but the second series of victims were young and attractive. The inescapable conclusion seemed to be that because of the difference in MOs, more than one man had to be responsible for these crimes.

Amidst the chorus of agreement on this proposition, there was one dissenting voice: that of Dr. James Brussel, a psychiatrist. He told the members of a medical and psychiatric committee assembled in Boston for the purpose of offering suggestions to the police:

> I think we are dealing with one man. . . . The apparent differences in MO, I believe, result from changes that have been going on in this man. Over the two-year period during which he has been committing these murders, he has gone through a series of upheavals—or, to put it another way, a single progressive upheaval. What has happened to him, in two words, is instant maturity. In this two-year period, he has suddenly grown, psychosexually, from infancy to puberty to manhood. This came about, of course,

in the most horrible way possible. He had to commit these murders to achieve this growth. It was the only way he knew to solve his problems, find himself sexually, and become a grown man among men.[4]

With deep intuitive insight, Dr. Brussel had grasped the most important clue of all in this unspeakable series of sexual atrocities. When Albert DeSalvo, the Boston Strangler, was finally apprehended, he proved to be the slayer of all of the victims.

With regard to trademarks, MO, and consistent characteristics in the case of the Boston Strangler, two of the killer's trademarks were the jaunty bow that he tied around the necks of his victims and the grotesque froglike positioning of their legs. After his apprehension, it was determined that DeSalvo's daughter had been born with a deformity of the legs and had been fitted at the age of two with a "frog" cast—so called because it held the legs spread in a froglike position. DeSalvo had carried out the orthopedist's instructions to massage the little girl's thighs in a particular way several times each day. Often he would tie a ribbon or scarf around the cast in a gay little bow to make the frog cast seem less grim to the child. We can only speculate, of course, on the possible meaning and significance of this act for DeSalvo. Both the bow and the froglike position of the legs were part of the unmistakable pattern of his later crimes, and their persistent presence as an unmistakable feature of the MO inevitably suggests that they were significantly linked to the obscure motivation for these murders.

IDENTIFICATION OF SPECIFIC CRIMES AND DATA ELEMENTS MOST APPLICABLE TO ANALYSIS

Crime analysis is most effectively applied to crimes likely to recur. Single incident crimes do not lend themselves to analysis. Most crimes against persons do not usually benefit from analysis, with the notable exceptions of rape, robbery, and related combinations of offenses (such as kidnap-rape, robbery-attempted murder, burglary-rape, burglary-robbery-kidnap). Analyzing the isolated criminal offense has some value, for one may learn where offenses are likely to recur. However, this knowledge is usually difficult to translate into prevention or suppression.

Crime analysis should be directed at crimes that police can best prevent or suppress or, failing this, those in which the criminal can be apprehended. Information coordination increases apprehension of criminals; analysis and strategy prevent and suppress crime.

Crime analysis must be devoted to crimes on a priority basis. Most analysis sections have limited workforce and budgets, and so priorities based on agency policies, operational needs, and community crime problems should be set.

Many of the offenses reported to any law enforcement agency are committed by persons who have committed similar crimes in the past. If not prevented, these persons will commit similar crimes in the future. These criminals have established an MO based on past successes.

Almost all crimes offer universal factors for analysis. Although these factors vary greatly among crimes, they are important in that once they have been identified and recorded, they are available for analysis. A sample of these factors is presented in Table 7-2. Comparisons among crimes require that information be commonly available. For example, in the analysis of burglaries, a description of one suspect in a particular case may be of less value than a description of the type of property taken or the type of structure entered. This is because the analyst usually does not have a suspect description for comparison purposes, but does have information on similar property losses or structures.

In addition to the above universal factors, an almost infinite number of factors may be considered specific to particular crimes. These factors are data usually recorded during the reporting of a particular offense and are used for analysis. An example of crime-specific analysis factors is presented in Table 7-3.

Crime-specific factors provide information the analyst can use to connect crimes with similar characteristics and also to identify MO patterns. Information regarding physical evidence may have considerable value in the analysis of several crime types, such as burglary and auto theft. Thus the suitability of different crimes to analysis depends on the seven universal factors, specific MO factors, and physical evidence.

INTERNAL INFORMATION SOURCES

Investigators often have information in fragmented form, such as a partial description of a vehicle or a nickname. Such information results in a successful case only when investigators make intelligent use of the many information sources available, including the records of Boards of Education, Bureaus of Vital Statistics, City Directories, Departments of Motor Vehicles, and related agencies. Internally, each police department has a variety of information sources with which investigators must be familiar. The "Daily Crime News Recap" is a list of crimes reported during the previous 24 hours; it provides information on the type of crime, the date, time, location, and evidence seized. The "Daily Confidential Information Bulletin" provides information about wanted persons, missing juveniles, major crime news not reported in the Daily Crime News Recap, and other crime-particular information. Departments large enough to staff a crime analysis unit make it responsible for providing investigators with investigative leads or

TABLE 7-2
Universal Factors for Crime Analysis

- CRIME TYPE
  - Burglary (class: business-commercial, residential, other)
  - Robbery (class: armed vs. not armed)
  - Auto theft (automobile, commercial vehicle, motorcycle, etc.)
  - General larceny (thefts from autos or of auto accessories, scrap metal, dock, etc.)
  - Fraud (forgery, credit cards, confidence games, etc.)
  - Rape and sex crimes (forcible rape, child molesting, indecent exposure)
  - Aggravated assault and murder

- GEOGRAPHICAL
  - Location offense occurred
  - Street address or intersection
  - Block
  - Subreporting area or census tract
  - Reporting area, patrol area, or beat
  - Zone, precinct, or district

- CHRONOLOGICAL
  - Specific time offense occurred
  - Time span in which offense occurred (day-night)
  - Day of week
  - Week of year
  - Month of year

- VICTIM TARGET
  - Victim person (sex, age, race, etc. of victim)
  - Type victim structure (single dwelling house, apartment, high rise, etc.)
  - Type victim premise (commercial, industrial, public, etc.)
  - Victim purpose (sales, service, manufacturing, etc.)
  - Victim knowledge of suspect

- SUSPECT
  - Name of responsible
  - Age of responsible
  - Race of responsible
  - Height of responsible
  - Weight of responsible
  - Clothing and unusual characteristics

- SUSPECT VEHICLE DESCRIPTIVE
  - Specific license number
  - Make of vehicle
  - Model and year of vehicle
  - Color of vehicle
  - Damage to vehicle

- PROPERTY LOSS DESCRIPTIVE
  - Serial number of property loss
  - Make of property loss (brand name, etc.)
  - Model of property loss
  - Type of property loss
  - Purpose of property used for

Source: George A. Buck et al., *Police Crime Analysis Unit Handbook.* Washington, D.C.: Government Printing Office, 1973, p. 33.

TABLE 7-3
Crime-Specific Factors for Crime Analysis

• RESIDENTIAL BURGLARY SPECIFIC	Type premise attacked (house, exterior apt., interior apt., etc.) Occupied vs. unoccupied Point of entry (window, door, etc.) Method of entry (pry door or window, pipe wrench door, break window, etc.) Presence of physical evidence (latent prints, etc.)
• COMMERCIAL BURGLARY SPECIFIC	Type of business attacked (TV store, clothing store, savings & loan, etc.) Alarm information (no alarm, alarm defeated, method, etc.) Point of entry (window, door, roof, wall, floor, vent, etc.) Method of entry (window smash, lock in-break out, peel wall, etc.) Safe attack method (rip, punch, peel, burn, drill, grind, etc.)
• ROBBERY SPECIFIC	Type of business victim (diner, bar, taxi, savings & loan, gas station, etc.) Victim descriptors (sex, race, age, occupation, etc.) Type weapon used (handgun, shotgun, knife, club, etc.) Suspect mask and type (facial area covered) Suspect statement during commission (or note), particular MO
• THEFT FROM PERSON SPECIFIC	Exact location of victim (sidewalk, park, hallway, bar, etc.) Victim person descriptors (sex, race, age, etc.) Victim condition after attack Suspect particular MO (approach, flight, statements, etc.) Object of theft (cash, checks, credit cards, jewelry, etc.)
• AUTO THEFT SPECIFIC	Area stolen vs. area recovered Exact last location (on-street, parking lot, carport, sales lot, etc.) Make, year, and model of vehicle Degree of strippage and parts Presence or absence of physical evidence
• LARCENY SPECIFIC	Type victim property (business, personal, use, purpose, etc.) Location of property (left unattended, in vehicle, etc.) Specific property taken and market potential Suspect particular MO Presence or absence of physical evidence

(Continued on next page)

TABLE 7-3
Crime-Specific Factors for Crime Analysis *(continued)*

• FORGERY SPECIFIC	Check and credit card specifics (how obtained, type, etc.) Type business or person victimized Document descriptors (stolen commercial, personal, etc.) Type of identification used Confidence game specifics (ploy used, etc.)	• AGGRAVATED ASSAULT AND MURDER SPECIFIC — Degree of relationship between victim and suspect Victim personal descriptors Motive Weapon used Physical evidence
• RAPE & SEX OFFENSE SPECIFIC	Victim descriptors (age, race, sex, occupation, etc.) Location of encounter vs. location of departure Suspect statements during commission Suspect particular actions or MO (include relationship) Weapon or degree of force used	

Source: George A. Buck et al., *Police Crime Analysis Unit Handbook*. Washington, D.C.: Government Printing Office, 1973, p. 35.

correlation reports when cases exhibit similarities to other reported offenses.[5]

Of particular importance are the known-offender files and mug shot files.[6] Most police departments attempt to maintain current information on known offenders in their jurisdiction. These offender files may be divided into "known active" and "inactive" and usually contain the suspect's description, MO, and a summary of the suspect's criminal record. They may be categorized further according to special type or location. Such files help personnel to familiarize themselves with known offenders and provide an excellent starting point for selecting mugshots to be shown to victims. Mug shot files are used in conjunction with known-offender files to help victims identify suspects whom they have observed. The mug shot file may consist of inexpensive Polaroid-type photographs, black and whites, or high-quality color slides. Some departments have mug-shot files organized by crime type, along with the race, skin tone, and height of the suspect so that with only a basic description of the suspect, a victim can be shown a selected subset of all the files. In other departments, a computer is programmed to select only those photographs which fit a suspect's description.

Ordinarily, a field interrogation report (FIR) is completed by a uniformed officer, with a copy to the investigator. For example, a police officer may observe a subject carefully watching a business which has been the target of armed robberies. The officer, under such circumstances, would be warranted in conducting a field interrogation if the subject could not provide a satisfactory explanation for his conduct and presence. If the individual had in fact been planning a robbery, the initiation of the FIR might discourage him. The FIR would provide data for checking police records to ascertain whether any offenses committed had recently been committed by a person fitting the description of the individual. FIRs also may identify individuals who have committed offenses that have not yet been reported to police. Thus for a latent investigator, a check of the FIR file may yield a prime suspect or provide a lead on a person who was in the general area at the time a later-reported offense was committed. Generally, routine checks of FIR files infrequently yield information leading to successful clearance of cases. Even so, latent investigators must never fail to check this source. (But FIRs should *not* be employed indiscriminately. This practice may damage community relations. The use of FIRs has raised strong criticism of police, especially by minority groups. At times the criticism has been warranted. Officers must be sensitive to this fact.)

The perfectly normal lifestyles of members of lower socioeconomic groups may seem suspicious by middle-class standards. For example, groups of young men standing in mid-evening in front of a closed store may look suspicious to white, middle-class members. But to members of a minority group on a hot summer night, the sidewalk is cooler than an apartment without air-conditioning. Moreover, it may also merely reflect a form of social organization, the street corner being an extension of the home and an entirely normal place for friends to meet and talk.[7]

THE NATIONAL CRIME INFORMATION CENTER

With the advent of computer technology, high-speed retrieval of investigative information has become a reality. The single most important system of this type is the National Crime Information Center (NCIC) located in Washington, D.C., and operated by the FBI. The NCIC was designed to complement, rather than to replace, local and state crime information systems. Local and state computer information systems contain data which should not and cannot be placed into the NCIC. For example, these systems contain data on in-state vehicle registration, outstanding warrants for traffic violations, and subjects wanted for nonextraditable offenses.

The following types of data may be stored and retrieved through the NCIC: stolen, missing, or recovered guns; stolen articles; wanted persons; stolen vehicles; stolen license plates; and stolen, embezzled, or missing securities. To make an entry into the NCIC, one needs a complete description of the item involved, including its manufacturer, brand name, serial number, model, color, and any other applicable information. The NCIC only places an individual's name into its wanted-persons file if a warrant has been issued and the state involved is willing to extradite for the offense for which the warrant was issued.

Whenever entries are to be made into the NCIC, the police agency must also give the date of the offense, the name of the agency initiating the report, and the case number. Agencies entering crime data also are respon-

FIGURE 7-2   National Crime Information Center Terminal Operator

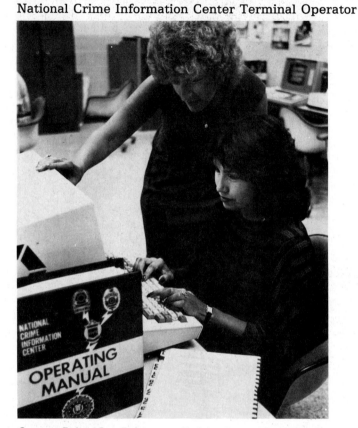

Courtesy Federal Law Enforcement Training Center, Glynco, Georgia

sible for maintaining the accuracy of records, updating information, and removing old data. Generally, requests to the NCIC are answered within one to five minutes.

═══ NEIGHBORHOOD CANVASS ═══

One fundamental aspect of most investigations is the neighborhood canvass of both residential neighborhoods and merchants and others who may have been in the immediate vicinity of a crime and have useful information. It is estimated that a systematic neigh-

borhood canvass soon after the commission of an offense results in positive information of investigative value in approximately 20 percent of all cases. The extent of the canvass depends on variables such as the type of offense, time of day, and characteristics of the crime scene. The timing of a neighborhood canvass is an important consideration. People not only move randomly through areas but also ebb and flow on a variety of schedules. To mistime a neighborhood canvass by 30 minutes, for example, may mean eliminating the possibility of locating persons who regularly catch a bus at a particular time and who, on the day of an offense, might have seen something of considerable investigative value.

Before a neighborhood check, investigators should be given all information relating to the offense, including a full description of the suspect, any injuries sustained by the suspect, and the type of property taken. The possession of these facts is absolutely essential for two major reasons. First investigators then can question witnesses intelligently, increasing the probability that all available information will be elicited. Second, it protects the investigator from unknowingly encountering the suspect and being placed in jeopardy.

Interviews should be conducted first at businesses or dwellings with a clear view of the crime scene and the suspect's avenues of approach and flight. When there are substantial numbers of locations involved, several teams of officers canvassing simultaneously are helpful. When the proprietors or residents are not on site during the canvass, a second contact is necessary. Even when persons interviewed do not provide any useful information, investigators must record the fact that no information was obtained, to eliminate the possibility of duplicating effort later on. Another reason for recording when no positive information has been provided is shown in the following case study:

> On a Sunday morning, a residential burglary of $3,800 in rare coins was reported. The uniformed officer making the original investigation received permission to conduct the neighborhood canvass. Usually the latent investigator did the canvass, but the uniformed officer had extra time that day. The victim's home was situated on a cul-de-sac along with four other homes with some view of the victimized premises. There were no homes to the rear of the victim's residence. After interviewing residents of the four neighboring homes, including a teenage boy,

the uniformed officer recorded the identities and statements of those with whom he had talked in his report. All indicated they had seen nothing. Because of the value of the property taken, the case was referred for latent investigation.

> The detective assigned to the case recently had been transferred from the Youth Services Bureau to the Burglary Bureau and recognized the name of the youth identified in the interview section of the uniformed officer's report as an individual with an extensive juvenile record for breaking and entering. Investigation revealed that the youth had committed the offense, and all coins taken were recovered.

Admittedly, this is an unusual case. Although luck played some part, the neighborhood canvass and adherence to sound reporting procedures not only avoided duplication of effort but cleared the case so quickly that the perpetrator had no opportunity to dispose of the stolen property.

INFORMANTS

Information provided by informants often plays a vital role in making an investigation successful. Such information may provide evidence of an unreported crime or constitute the basis for a legal search or an arrest. Whatever the value of information provided by informants, the attending reality—depending on the motivation of the individual informant involved—is that the informant-investigator transaction is often sordid business. Although relationships with certain informants may approach the genteel, they frequently involve an investigator's finding a point of leverage in the potential informant's values or personal history and applying pressure, ranging from veiled threats to outright coercion.

Not all informants have committed

crimes. They come from all walks of life. In dealing with them, investigators often find it useful to determine their motivations. The list of informant types discussed here is not exhaustive, nor are the categories mutually exclusive.

Mercenary informants provide information to the police for financial reward. Foreign police systems, such as the French, historically have placed great reliance on paid informants, but it is less characteristic here. It is, nonetheless, not an uncommon occurrence. From time to time, individuals who themselves are engaged in illegal activities may wish to eliminate a competitor. The *rival informant* provides information to establish control over the activity in question, using the police to achieve legally what he or she cannot do alone. An individual arrested for a crime may know of criminal activities by others and, in exchange for telling the police, the *plea-bargaining informant* seeks reduced charges or a lenient sentence. Frequently, police departments receive anonymous information either by telephone or in writing. Because the identity of the *anonymous informant* is never known, the motivations are not identifiable. Anonymous information should not be discarded but pursued, so long as it may be fruitful. Many law-abiding citizens have information about crimes, which they will share with the police. In a strict sense, such persons are not informers. But they are designated *legitimate informers* to distinguish them from other types.

The *self-aggrandizing informant* has many contacts in criminal circles and feels important by giving information to the police. When investigators identify this motivation, they should give ample praise each time information is supplied. Otherwise such informants do not continue the relationship. A comparative rarity is the *false informant,* who intentionally provides misleading information to direct attention away from him or herself, friends, or relatives. *Fearful informants* worry that they will be endangered by the criminal activities of an associate. Fearing for their own well-being, they supply information.

Swap shops and pawnshops, however properly operated, occasionally are places where stolen property is recovered. Shop operators may share information about criminal activities with the police to build credit and reduce the likelihood that they will be formally charged if stolen property is found in their possession.

DEALING WITH INFORMANTS

Investigators must observe certain rules in dealing with informants. Breaking these rules keeps investigators from cultivating and retaining informants and fosters a negative image of the police department, reducing the potential flow of information. Investigators must never make promises they cannot or do not intend to keep. When talking with a plea-bargaining informer, investigators cannot promise a lenient sentence or a reduced charge, only support in seeking them. Meetings with informants should not be held in police facilities but where informants will not be identified as having any association with an investigator. In writing to an informant, investigators should never use letterhead stationery or other devices identifying the police department. The practice of leaving a business card on an informant's car or front door unnecessarily exposes the informant. The proper names of informants should never be used in investigative reports; instead, they should be identified by code, such as "A273." The identity of informants should be revealed only to persons designated by the police department, such as an investigator's immediate supervisor. Access to an informant's file should be limited to the fewest persons, and then only on a need-to-know basis. Investigations conducted with the assistance of informants are collaborations, but investigators must always maintain clear control, with the informant playing a supporting role. Regardless of informants' value and reliability, they should never be permitted to act illegally. Informants should be told fully the circumstances that constitute entrapment and advised to avoid them scrupulously.

Informants should be paid only when their information is necessary to clear an investigation or when other procedures would be too lengthy or costly. Many informants begin with a request for payment, but investigators must try to get their cooperation by other inducements. Before agreeing to pay, investigators should assess the reliability and value of information provided by the person in the past, usually by reviewing data in the informer file. Regardless of reliability, no informant should receive payment until the reliability of the information has been verified. All payments should be made in cash, with the informant signing a receipt in his or her code name. The receipt then is to be placed in the informant's file. Whenever possible, reimbursement for expenses, such as meals and rooms, should be made only on presentation of a receipt or within limits agreed on by the investigator and the informant.

SURVEILLANCE

The terms "surveillance" and "following" are often used interchangeably. Properly, *surveillance* is viewing. One may keep a person under surveillance by walking along on the opposite side of the street or by driving several car lengths ahead and observing in a rearview mirror.

Surveillance is an important part of the investigator's repertoire. The keys to successful surveillance are planning and preparation. Once an operation has begun, the need to extemporaneously reorganize presents extreme difficulties. Surveillance is a complex topic, the complete treatment of which is not possible here. For example, sta-

tionary surveillance from an apartment over many months presents problems of logistics, staffing, and cover stories so that the location is not compromised by acquaintances of those being observed. Here we discuss two of the most common types of surveillance used by police departments—foot and automobile surveillance.

All members of a surveillance team must be able to identify the subject, preferably after having seen the subject in person, though they also may study photographs. The advantage of the personal view is to give investigators the opportunity to observe gait and mannerisms. All available information about the surveillance should be shared with the team, including investigative objective, peculiarities of the subject, places frequented, and related particulars. Before initiating the surveillance, members should become familiar with the areas in which it will be conducted and the conditions under which it will be abandoned. Team members also should learn about all equipment and procedures that may be used, including hand signals if radios do not work.

Generally, one person conducting surveillance on foot is ineffective. Ordinarily three or more people are required. There are no specific rules regarding the distance from which a subject under observation may be followed, but a good rule of thumb is to shorten the distance in congested areas or when the subject approaches buses or elevators. Caution is necessary, because subjects occasionally enter a bus, pay, and immediately exit by the rear door. In sparsely peopled areas where the view is good, the distance may be lengthened considerably. If subjects are lost sight of, it may be possible to second-guess them, especially if a great deal is known about their personal habits, such as where he usually eats or visits.

Foot surveillance may be close tailing, loose tailing, or progressive tailing. *Close tailing* may be done with or without the knowledge of the subject, depending on the investigative objective. For example, in a congested area with heavy pedestrian traffic, three investigators may tail closely without being observed, by alternating. However, occasionally investigators want subjects to know that they are being followed, to prevent subjects from making contacts or to create anxiety which may produce an important involuntary revelation. *Loose tailing* is employed when subjects suspect surveillance. Sometimes investigators decide to break off the surveillance in this instance. *Progressive tailing* is conducted in several stages at different times, depending on the degree of caution necessary. For example, on the first day of surveillance, a member of the team might follow the subject from home to a nearby bus stop. On the second day, another member of the team might be waiting at the bus stop and would follow the subject to where he or she leaves the bus. On the following day, yet another member of the team might wait for the subject from after the bus ride when he exits to another point.

When conducting moving automobile surveillance, at least two automobiles are necessary. Ideally, there should be at least three persons in each surveillance vehicle: one team member to drive, one to observe from the front, and the third to sit in the rear, making notes. Although it is possible for one person to operate an automobile surveillance alone, using a tape recorder to make investigative notes, the advantage of three investigators is that, if a foot tail becomes necessary, there are enough people available to undertake it adequately.

Once the subject's vehicle has been spotted, the tailing car should stay several cars away. The other surveillance car should proceed along a parallel route on an adjacent street, ready to take up the tail if the subject becomes suspicious. Standard unmarked police cars should *not* be used; their appearance is too easily recognized by criminals.

= MECHANICAL LIE DETECTION =

The polygraph can be an invaluable investigative aid. Like any scientific instrument, however, its efficacy is limited by the skill of the operator. It has been demonstrated that there is a significant relation between a person's state of mind and his or her physiological state. Fear and anger, for example, increase the rate of the heartbeat, respiration, and the production of perspiration. The polygraph measures these physiological responses to psychological phenomena. It records physiological changes in breathing, blood pressure, pulse rate and amplitude, and galvanic skin reflex (see Figures 7-3 and 7-4).

Properly administered polygraph examinations uniformly yield accurate results. A five-year study of persons tested by a leading polygraph operator indicated an accuracy rate of over 96 percent, 3 percent inconclusive findings, and only a 1 percent margin of possible error.[8]

It is generally agreed that a polygraph examination should not be undertaken until a thorough investigation has been completed and all physical evidence processed by the crime laboratory. Without the benefits of such information, it is difficult for the examiner to formulate important questions and to uncover inconsistencies in a subject's statements.

Polygraphs are used for a variety of reasons. Of these, the most important are to free an innocent person from suspicion; to identify deception easily, quickly, and accurately; to make offenders confess under psychological stress; and to promote effective use of investigative time.

The Psychological Stress Evaluator (PSE) is an instrument that measures and displays indications of stress in the human voice. When an individual speaks, the voice has two modulations: audible and inaudible to the human ear. Stress may be inaudible to the hu-

FIGURE 7-3   A Typical Four-Channel Polygraph

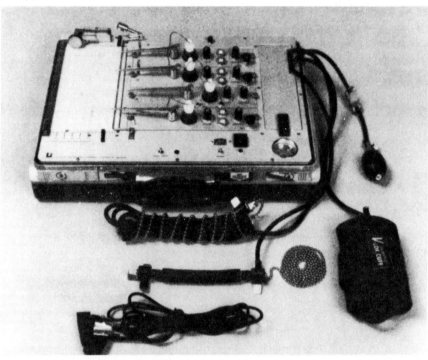

Courtesy Federal Bureau of Investigation

man ear, but it is both detectable and measurable by the PSE. While to the human ear a person may sound entirely normal, free of tremors or other guilt-suggesting qualities, the PSE would identify the involuntary, inaudible indicators of stress.

The key to the use of the PSE is preparation of simple questions keyed to a specific individual and designed to reveal patterns of truth and deception. Once the voice patterns associated with truthfulness and deception have been established, the questioning proceeds to the area of investigation, and analysis of the subject's voice pattern in this area indicates truthfulness or deception.

Proponents of the PSE maintain that it has two advantages over similar instruments. First it is simple; it has few moving parts

and is relatively easy to operate. Second, it is not necessary to have the PSE in operation at the time of the first interview or interrogation; a recording of the initial interview can be fed into the PSE later. The PSE also may be used on tape recordings of telephone conversations.[9]

POSSIBLE EFFECTS
OF TRANQUILIZERS
ON POLYGRAPH RESULTS

Criminal suspects have for years been advised that they can fool a lie detector by taking tranquilizers. Polygraph experts have always denied it. But recently researchers at the Institute of Pennsylvania Hospital pub-

FIGURE 7-4　　**Polygraph Tracings Being Recorded on Paper during Examination**

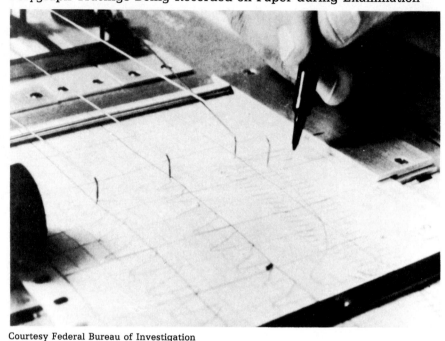

Courtesy Federal Bureau of Investigation

lished a study that reports that a standard 400 mm dose of meprobamate, a common mild tranquilizer sold under the brand name Miltown, reduced physiological responses to stress so that laboratory subjects could fool the polygraph.

The study involved forty-four male college student volunteers who were given the task of memorizing six words. Thirty-three were told to lie when asked to recite and talk about the words on a polygraph test. Of the thirty-three, one-third took a tranquilizer, one-third took a placebo, and the others took nothing. The polygraph operators identified most of the "guilty" subjects in the groups that had taken the placebos or no pills. But the polygraph readings showed erroneously that most who had taken the tranquilizers were telling the truth.

Dr. Martin Orne, the director of the laboratory where the test was conducted, confirmed that his experiment was not done by field polygraphers and was not a field situation. But the study shows that tranquilizers can affect selective responsivity, and polygraph examiners should begin to watch out for tranquilizer effects.[10] Richard O. Arther, Executive Director of the Academy of Certified Polygraphists and Director of the National Training Center of Polygraph Science, had the following reaction to this study as reported in a recent news story:

He called the findings "a big joke" and said the researchers failed to use three out of the four measurements polygraph experts use in conducting tests.

Arther said the Pennsylvania study's

results have been available since 1972, and claimed the study involved only the galvanic skin response (GSR) measurement of the test, and not breathing and cardiovascular measurements, which are standard parts of any lie detector test.

The polygraph specialist said he has "known since the 1950s" that depressants affect the GSR measurement on lie detector tests. "Look, it causes a straight line," he said, pointing to a line on a lie detector chart. "But that should cause 27 bells to go off in the operator's mind. Normally, there's some kind of fluctuation."

Arther said his research has turned up erratic breathing and pulse responses when tranquilized individuals are tested. "I wondered why it didn't show up in these findings. Then I realized—they weren't looking for those measurements. The breathing and cardiovascular responses should get very erratic. The body is trying to throw off this poison."

He said law enforcement and other officials trained in polygraph operation would spot clues for drug use immediately and would judge their results accordingly.

He also took issue with the study's timing, demanding "Why are they publishing now, when they've known about this since 1971?" Similarly, the study's choice of experimental subjects caught flak from Arther.

"They're using students, a bunch of volunteers, who have no stake in the outcome," he said, noting that lie detection relies, to an extent, on the individual having some stake in the outcome.

Arther said there are people with whom the lie detector has trouble, people he called "psychologically dead."

"It doesn't register a response with them. It's difficult to get any kind of response from them."

But he said his research has found that approximately 80 percent of all people can be measured with lie detectors.[11]

LEGAL CONSIDERATIONS

No witness, suspect, or defendant can be compelled to take any mechanical lie-detection test, as this would violate the Fifth Amendment privilege. No one can be required to be a witness against him or herself. However, a suspect may, subject to the legal requirements discussed more fully in Chapter 8, agree voluntarily to submit to a lie-detector test.

Ordinarily tests are administered after an arrest, but before a final decision to lodge formal charges. Frequently police initiate such examinations when evidence is largely circumstantial. Sometimes people under arrest request a lie-detector test in the erroneous belief that they can fool the lie-detection system or when they are earnestly convinced of their innocence.

Occasionally, prosecuting and defense attorneys, after an arrest of a subject but before formal charging, agree to a mechanical lie-detection test pursuant to a stipulated agreement. The prosecuting attorney uses the results to decide whether charges should be made and what they should be. The results of tests taken pursuant to stipulated agreements are generally admissible as evidence in this country. But in general, in those rare instances when trial judges have offered defendants the opportunity to prove their innocence by taking a mechanical lie-detection test, the appellate courts have held this to be improper.[12]

RELATIONSHIPS WITH VICTIMS
AND WITNESSES

The cooperation of victims and witnesses—and the same person may play these two roles simultaneously—is frequently the key to successful investigations. But many police departments neglect to consider the adverse effects which the investigative process may have on it. Cooperation tends to be reduced when people are unnecessarily inconvenienced, repeat testimony needlessly to different investigators, are not informed of the progress of a case, are not thanked for their cooperation, or extended small courtesies, such as interviews scheduled at times and places most convenient for them.[13]

Certain of the preceding obligations clearly belong to the police, others to the prosecutor's office. The distribution of responsibilities should be articulated in a written agreement between the police department head and the prosecutor. However, if the prosecutor's office fails or declines to undertake certain of these responsibilities, they fall to the police.

A Rand Corporation study underscored the importance of providing victims with feedback.[14] Most victims express a very strong desire to learn officially whether the police have solved their case and whether a suspect has been arrested. Most victims also want to be told about progress in the prosecution and adjudication of defendants. Victims are divided in their wish to be informed about when suspects are released from custody. The greater the involvement of a victim in the prosecution of a suspect, the greater the victim's desire to be informed about events in the later stages of proceedings. Most victims prefer to be informed when the police decide to suspend investigation of their case. Victims are divided in wanting to know when a suspect arrested for a crime other than theirs is believed to be responsible for the offense against them. A sizable majority of victims react unfavorably to the police when told of negative developments in the case, for example, that the investigation will be suspended or that their stolen property is unlikely to be recovered, although robbery victims tend to be less troubled about this prospect than do burglary victims. Most victims tend to respect, or at least accept, the

exercise of professional judgment by the police or prosecutor's office.

Despite the fact that certain disadvantages may be created for the police, feedback to victims is important to them. Investigators should bear in mind that the study shows that no matter how distressed by the information they get, few victims act inimicably to police. Although those few instances must be regarded seriously, considerable benefits arise from a system of feedback to victims.

GUIDELINES FOR CONDUCTING LINE UPS

With a line up, the victim of a crime can view a suspect along with others of similar physical appearance. In a line up, those involved must literally line up, side by side, usually behind a two-way mirror or similar device, so that the victim can view the suspect without being seen.

With some jurisdictional variations, the following guidelines for conducting line ups have been suggested by law enforcement agencies:[15]

- All persons in the line up should be of the same general age and race and have similar physical characteristics.
- The clothing worn by each should be similar.
- Statements by persons in the line up should not be requested unless a witness suggests it. If statements are made, all participants should repeat the same words. However, because many states prohibit a defendant from being forced to say anything during the line up, investigators should first consult with local prosecutors.
- Front and profile color photographs of the line up should be taken and developed as soon as possible.
- A witness should be prevented from seeing

FIGURE 7-5   Witness Line Up Identification Form

Offense Number

TO WITNESS: PLEASE READ THESE INSTRUCTIONS CAREFULLY.
The position of the persons in the line-up will be numbered left to right, beginning with
the number one (1) on your left. Take as much time as you wish to view the line-up.
Examine each of the line-up participants carefully. You will be viewing the line-up in a
manner which will enable you to see the participants while <u>they will be unable to see
you.</u> <u>PLEASE DO NOT DISCUSS</u> any aspect of the case or line-up with any other witness
who may be present.

1. If you can identify any of the persons in the line-up as having participated in the
   criminal offense to which you were a witness, place a "X" in the appropriate square
   corresponding to the number of the person in the line-up.

2. If none, place a "X" in the square marked NONE.

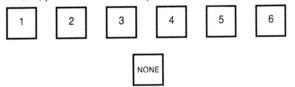

3. Then sign your name and fill in the date and time.

4. When completed, hand this sheet to the officer conducting the line-up.

OFFICER CONDUCTING LINE-UP	WITNESS' SIGNATURE
ATTORNEY FOR THE STATE	DATE TIME
LINE-UP ATTORNEY FOR DEFENDANT	

Courtesy of St. Petersburg, Florida, Police Department.

the defendant in custody prior to the
lineup.

- Witnesses should not be shown a photograph of the defendant before the line up.
- If more than one person is to view a line
  up, they should do so one at a time and
  out of the presence of the other.
- No actions should be taken by investigators or statements made to witnesses to

suggest that a suspect is standing in any
particular place.

- Before entering the line up room, the witness should be given a form on which the
  identification can be made (see Figure
  7-5).
- There should be at least six persons in the
  line up.
- If the suspect's attorney is present, he or

FIGURE 7-6

Offense Number

POLICE LINEUP WORKSHEET

SUBJECT #	1	2	3	4	5	6
NAME						
RACE						
AGE						
HEIGHT						
WEIGHT						
SHIRT						
PANTS						
SHOES						

WITNESS PRESENT AT LINE-UP:

			SUSPECT IDENTIFIED		
NAME	ADDRESS	PHONE	YES	NO	TIME ALLOWED

Did suspect waive right to counsel at line-up?   YES_____ NO_____

NAME OF ATTORNEY PRESENT: _____

ADDRESS: _____ PHONE: _____

OFFICER(S) CONDUCTING LINE-UP: _____

DATE: _____ TIME BEGAN: _____ TIME ENDED: _____ CHARGE: _____

NOTE: All subjects in LINE-UP are numbered from left to right, facing interviewing officer. Officer conducting interview shall fill in description of subjects PRIOR TO LINE-UP BEING CONDUCTED.

REMARKS: _____

Source: Courtesy of St. Petersburg, Florida Police Department

she should be allowed to make suggestions.

- Before the line up, the witness should give a detailed description of the perpetrator and the description put in writing.
- If possible, law enforcement officers should not be used in line ups.
- A suspect has no right to refuse a line up.

Many police agencies now use police line up worksheets to create records of suspects, witnesses, attorneys, and officers present at line ups (see Figure 7-6).

In some cases it is virtually impossible to conduct a fair line up because the suspect's physical appearance and clothing are so distinctive. The following actual case illustrates this point.

A cab driver reported to the police that he had been robbed by one of his passengers. The cab driver made the report immediately after the suspect had fled on foot with the money. The driver reported that the suspect was a black male, approximately 25 years old, 6'6", 285 pounds, armed with a large chrome-plated semi-automatic pistol. The man was wearing an orange silk shirt, blue jeans, and a cowboy hat. Exactly $52 in cash had been taken. Approximately one hour after the crime was reported, the suspect was observed in the vicinity of the robbery by the same two officers who had taken the original report. The suspect was arrested by the police officers. A search produced a chrome-plated .45 caliber semi-automatic pistol and $52.12.

In their effort to conduct a line up, the officers realized that they could not possibly find five people who approximated the suspect in size, race, age, attire, and so forth. The officers decided to use a photo line up instead of a live line up. They had a black and white photo taken of the suspect, minus the cowboy hat, and incorporated it into a packet of five other police photos of black males.

The cab driver was able to positively identify the photo of the suspect, who subsequently confessed to the crime.

SOCIAL NETWORK ANALYSIS: AN AID IN CONSPIRACY INVESTIGATIONS

In conducting a complex conspiracy investigation, police officers must not only identify key participants but grasp the connections among them to determine the scope of an illicit operation. One process, social network analysis, can help them.[16]

Social network analysis is a technique for describing interaction patterns among people to understand and predict their behavior.[17] To perceive this process and its law enforcement applications, consider the following hypothetical example:

Police in a western city received information of an organized fencing operation being run by members of a local gang. The operation appeared to be centered at a tavern, which was also a popular gathering place for gang members. Police also learned that a person identified as Bert Bey recently had indicated that he had access to stolen rifles, which were for sale for $50 each. Because at this stage of the investigation, the police were interested in learning more about the scope of this fencing operation and the people connected with it, they decided to watch the tavern during the evening.

From the surveillance, 18 people believed to be connected with the group were identified. The officers then converted their observations of who came and went at the tavern into a network diagram of personal relations within the group (see Figure 7-7). From this diagram, police began to focus on those suspects and who might know the most about the crimes.

The data sheet for compiling network diagrams is illustrated in Table 7-3. The matrix

FIGURE 7-7   Social Network Diagram

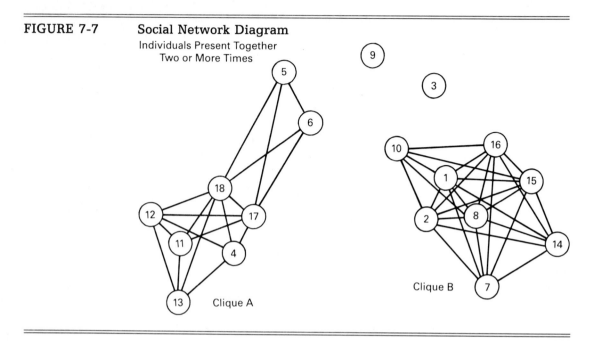

Individuals Present Together Two or More Times

Clique A

Clique B

includes suspects by name and the time periods they appeared at the tavern. With network analysis, the officers then developed the network diagram, Figure 7-7, which disclosed the group connections.[18]

In looking at Figure 7-7, the officers learned that the group was split into two cliques. Bert Bey, the original suspect, was individual 16 and was part of clique B. The core members of clique B (Figure 7-8) and prime suspects to focus on were individuals 2, 7, 8, 14, and 15. Because these individuals were the central members, they might have been controllers of the operation or key links to others who may or may not have frequented the tavern. The technique let the officers focus their efforts early in the investigation on key members and predict who might have been involved in crime.

Network analysis as a law enforcement technique does more, however, than construct a picture of the relationships between people. It allows investigators to use those links to predict criminal behavior and to penetrate deeply into the structure of personal relationships. By comprehending these patterns, investigators can better understand attitudes and behaviors unique to each clique. Other social network characteristics, such as leadership patterns and the nature of information exchanged between individuals, may also be disclosed. Key connections to people not previously linked to criminal acts also may be revealed.

THE CONCEPT

Understanding group structure and analyzing the connections between people involved in illegal activities must begin with an understanding of how group relations evolve. Criminal networks operate in the same way as all other social networks. Relationships among people rest on shared values, interests, characteristics, and goals.[19]

Group structure may be important to in-

FIGURE 7-8   Social Network Diagram of Core Members of Clique B

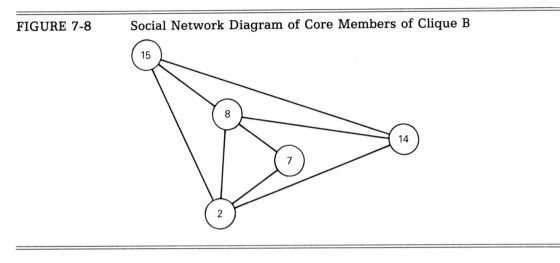

vestigations of racketeering, narcotics operations, illegal gambling, and business frauds. Knowing how conspirators divide their responsibilities to accomplish an illegal task tells investigators how to proceed and whom to target. Members' roles, relationships, and personalities may reveal the nature and extent of conspiratorial involvement.[20]

Important properties of any group are the stabilization of relationships among members and the function each member must accomplish to carry out an activity. A group strongly influences the behavior of its members by setting and enforcing unwritten rules. "If a person wants to stay in a group, that person will be willing to conform to the rules which the group sets up."[21] Take as an example a group cooperating to obtain and dispose of stolen property. If the informal rules of the group require that members help locate buyers or at least show complacency toward that crime, it follows that for a member to continue to be accepted within those circles, the person must participate to some degree, if only passively.

Groups pressure members to conform to certain unwritten rules. That social force eliminates some from the group and filters others into subgroups or cliques bound together in ways which are possible for the

investigator to uncover. Where activities between associates are mutually rewarded, common attitudes, sentiments, and behaviors result. Increased association perpetuates itself. As people drift into subgroups, their values converge and a kind of consensus emerges.[22]

From these social forces that influence people in varying ways to select friends and associates emerge relatively stable patterns allowing the group to accomplish its objectives. This role structure is maintained by rules and social pressures that regulate what, within that group, is acceptable and what is not. These behavior patterns can be used by an investigator as building blocks to understand not only how a group under investigation functions but also those expectations associated with each individual's position in the network and the extent of his or her conspiratorial involvement.

It follows that knowledge of how and through whom social pressure is applied may offer the investigator an advantage in understanding the relations between people involved in crime and in structuring the direction of future inquiries. If criminal activity is suspected of certain individuals within a group, a look at the network associations will offer clues to identify through whom the best

TABLE 7-3
Matrix of Suspects and Time Periods

	Time Periods					
	June 1			June 2		
	8 p.m. to 10 p.m.	10 p.m. to 11 p.m.	11 p.m. to 3 a.m.	8 p.m. to 9 p.m.	9 p.m. to 10 p.m.	10 p.m. to 12 a.m.
1) Fred Corley	0	1	0	1	0	0
2) Richard McGood	0	1	0	1	0	0
3) Gordon Waid	0	0	0	0	0	1
4) Thomas Smith	0	0	0	1	1	1
5) Basil Malone	1	0	0	0	0	1
6) Archy Hope	1	0	0	0	0	1
7) Horace McLain	0	1	1	1	0	0
8) Feltus Robb	0	1	1	0	0	1
9) Simon Henry	0	0	0	0	0	1
10) Justin Harvey	0	1	0	1	0	1
11) Larry Earp	0	0	0	1	1	1
12) Reid Raney	0	0	0	0	1	1
13) John Seitz	0	0	0	0	1	1
14) Silas Weisel	0	1	1	1	0	1
15) Pedro Conner	0	1	0	1	0	0
16) Bert Bey	0	1	0	0	0	0
17) Robert Ensor	1	0	0	1	1	0
18) Alvin Cox	1	0	0	1	1	1

information is available to the investigator and with whom the suspect may conspire to break the law.

Knowledge of an individual's social network provides the investigator some opportunity to better understand the personalities under investigation. One would expect that people in central network positions would be more persistent in involving others and moving the group toward its objectives. A group may also contain socially oriented individuals who are more passive and agreeable and therefore more susceptible to group pressures. A group also may contain selfish, vulnerable individuals who may be targets for development as sources of information.[23]

The information and observations collected by an investigator can be used to chart

TABLE 7-3
Matrix of Suspects and Time Periods *(continued)*

				Time Periods			
	June 3				June 4		
12 a.m. to 2 a.m.	2 a.m. to 3 a.m.	8 p.m. to 10 p.m.	10 p.m. to 12 a.m.	12 a.m. to 1 a.m.	1 a.m. to 3 a.m.	9 p.m. to 11 p.m.	11 p.m. to 2 a.m.
0	1	0	0	0	1	0	0
1	1	0	1	0	1	1	0
0	0	0	0	0	1	0	0
0	0	0	0	0	1	0	0
0	0	0	0	0	0	0	0
0	0	0	0	0	0	0	0
1	1	0	1	0	1	0	0
1	1	0	1	0	1	1	0
0	1	0	0	0	1	0	0
0	0	0	0	0	1	0	0
0	0	1	0	1	1	0	1
0	0	1	0	1	1	0	1
0	0	1	0	0	1	0	0
1	1	0	0	0	1	1	0
1	0	0	0	0	0	1	0
1	1	0	0	0	1	0	0
0	0	1	0	0	1	0	0
0	1	1	0	1	0	0	1

interpersonal relationships between people of investigative interest. Links between people may involve other than criminal connections, but pertinent network relationships, when understood in terms of their meaning to criminal activity, may provide the foundation to measure the extent of suspect involvement. The network links may also help extend the investigation logically along a path built on an understanding of who will probably be involved with whom and to what degree. Network analysis is a tool that constructs this picture of individual involvement or in potential knowledge of criminal activity.

The framework of a network structure is built on a variety of elements that allow the visual display of personal relationships. Influences on group structure are far-ranging.

Psychologists focus on factors that draw people together, such as: role similarities (husband, father, club member), family status, citizenship, nationality, religion, occupation, political party affiliation, economic status, and race. Social scientists also measure the amount and intensity of social interaction between friends, acquaintances, neighbors, or coworkers. They measure people's racial, regional, sex, age, role, educational, class, occupational, religious, and ethnic differences. They chart exchanges, such as greetings, civilities, conversation, information, visits, work assistance, interaction, sentiment, joking behavior, personal service, and cash.[24]

Investigators take more limited measurements: of friendships, common affiliations, business connections, people observed together, help with finances and jobs. When more detailed network analysis is appropriate, investigators may gather and analyze the interpersonal network relationships by counting the number of instances in which people interact and by noting who initiates and terminates the interactions. This analysis provides direction to the network link.[25]

Where people are linked to others through the social relations identified, they are also tied to society through membership bonds with various groups and organizations.[26] People are also the links connecting groups to other groups. Knowledge of these ties between groups may be important sources of investigative information when used to understand conspiratorial links between criminal groups and to measure cooperation and mutual assistance provided to groups of interest.

From the behavioral elements collected, it is possible then to use this information to construct a picture of the important linkages that exist between people under investigation or display the interconnections of targeted groups involved in a criminal enterprise.

SOCIAL DISTANCE

Social distance is a concept that may be usefully applied to investigations. The social distance built on the similarities between people and groups can be measured like the distance between two points. Social distance may be analyzed in terms of people's features in common and features separating people and groups. "Just as the location of a point . . . is determined by values of . . . coordinates, so a [person's] location in social space is determined by the values of many coordinates."[27]

With the application of matrix mathematics to important links among people and groups, group structure can be disclosed, relationships can be put into useful perspective, subgroupings can be displayed in easily understandable form, and the meanings of interpersonal connections not previously suspected can be revealed.

A matrix representation records links between individuals or groups of people and events. Manipulation of this data reveals people in cliques; isolate brokers, flow of information, patterns of influence, and potential coalitions. The steps in constructing a matrix are fully explained in other publications and will not be discussed here.[28]

Once the matrix is constructed, the data may be manipulated by hand or computer. Inexpensive computer programs are capable of constructing network relationships for groups. This scaling process not only shows patterns of relationships hidden in the matrix but also displays them in clear graphs and in terms of meaningful social distance. Manual manipulations are relatively simple for small groups. But as networks grow to over ten to 15 individuals or nodes, the work becomes time-consuming.[29]

On the matrix representation of relationships, the persons represented become "nodes" of a graph, and the lines are links (friendships, helping, influence, personal service). A clearer picture evolves of who is connected with whom, how tightly, and what that connection may mean in terms of illicit activity.[30]

From the introductory example in this section, the clique structure shown in Figure 7-6 was based on people appearing together in one place over a period of time. From this initial representation, the investigator may wish to include additional connections as more information is gathered. To accomplish this, again the investigator would construct a matrix listing names of individuals of interest along the side and across the top or bottom and create a record of known components further linking individuals of interest. (See Table 7-3.) The matrix may be symmetrical, as in Table 7-3, or it may record weighted relationships, such as when one person is observed seeking out another more than he or she is sought. If weighted links are used, the individuals along the side of the matrix should represent those seeking out others and those named across the top or bottom are the ones sought.

For example, if during a surveillance several people were observed arriving or departing together or conserving outside of the tavern, an additional matrix constructing those connections might reveal more of the group's structure. Table 7-4 is a matrix which records the number of times individuals were seen together. From additional matrices, further network diagrams may be developed, showing not only key participants in a crime but also potential communication channels and important people who, though not directly involved, may act as brokers or links between participants and people who are in a position because of their network location to manipulate others.[31] If, for example, Figure 7-8 is constructed from additional observations and Gordon Waid (3) appears connected with Fred Corley (1) in clique B and

Archy Hope (6) in clique A, the investigator should consider Gordon a potential broker who may be the important source through whom stolen property is flowing.

As the investigation develops, persons of interest and their links to associates may be analyzed. Parameters also are set to construct profiles of group attitudes for interview purposes.

FLOW

Flow describes the direction in which exchanges between people move. Flow of information, interaction, influence, or stolen property, though discussed before, should be mentioned here. Knowing who is linked to whom and how closely can be an aid in determining information of importance to an investigation. If an investigator is interested in tracking how stolen property will likely be disseminated within a group, knowledge of the network structure will help. If Figure 7-9 represents an updated network constructed from the original surveillance and adjusted to include subsequent knowledge of known associations and connections, some revealing possibilities exist. If, for example, the investigator learns that individual 15 (Pedro Conner) is offering stolen guns for sale, from the group structure he can hypothesize that the original suspect, Bert Bey (16), is supplied by Pedro. The investigator now can estimate through whom Pedro may be getting his guns or at least who is probably in a position to know about Pedro's activities. Because he is most closely associated with individual 8 (Feltus Robb), Feltus may be a likely suspect. Pedro also is linked, though not as closely, with individual 2 (Richard McGood), individual 14 (Silas Weisel), and individual 16 (Bert Bey), the original suspect. The investigator may want to explore those individuals as suppliers or distributors for individual 15 (Pedro). If stolen property begins to be

TABLE 7-4
Frequency of Meetings Between Individuals

Individual	1	2	3	4	5	6	7	8	9	10	11	12	13	14	15	16	17	18
1) Fred Corley																		
2) Richard McGood	6																	
3) Gordon Waid	3																	
4) Thomas Smith																		
5) Basil Malone																		
6) Archy Hope			2	3	6													
7) Horace McLain		7																
8) Feltus Robb		7					8											
9) Simon Henry			4															
10) Justin Harvey	11		3															
11) Larry Earp																		
12) Reid Raney										9								
13) John Seitz																		
14) Silas Weisel		4											4					
15) Pedro Conner		6					7							5				
16) Bert Bey																		
17) Robert Ensor						6							5					
18) Alvin Cox						6				8	9						7	
	1	2	3	4	5	6	7	8	9	10	11	12	13	14	15	16	17	18

(Note: Numbers across the bottom represent the same individuals listed numerically. All data are hypothetical.)

offered by individuals connected with clique A, then the possibility arises that the people connecting the two groups are brokers.

The network displayed in Figure 7-8 may also aid in developing witnesses and informants as the case progresses and may be of assistance later for explaining in court the complex connections among conspirators. It may be possible to predict who, by virtue of network position, is relatively isolated from information or group activity. If the investigator is receiving information from individual 13 (John Seitz), the investigator knows from John's position in the network that John probably knows more about the activities of clique A and less about clique B and seems to be most closely connected with individual 17 (Robert Ensor). Ensor, in turn, appears to get his information mostly from individual 18 (Alvin Cox) and individual 6 (Archy Hope).

For law enforcement purposes, it may be

FIGURE 7-9　　　**Updated Social Network Diagram**

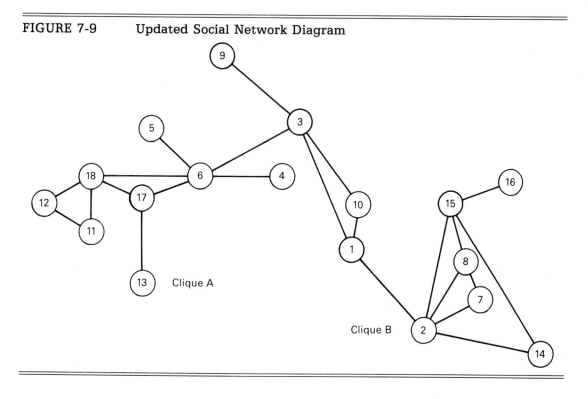

useful to predict who may get an item of information or who may be asked to help and by whom. The network diagram may also aid in focusing efforts to learn what types of messages, in fact, flow between individuals at various points in the network structure and aid in estimating the volume of information a particular person is likely to receive.

RELATIVE INFLUENCE

A suspect's network position and the nature of the transactions between individuals of investigative interest can disclose the degree to which people, at given points, are subject to influence and may allow an estimate for investigative purposes of the likelihood a person at a particular point in the network will be involved in criminal activity. If the investigator knows that Feltus Robb (8) is involved, the accessibility and closer social proximity of individual 7 (Horace McLain) to Feltus Robb (Figure 7-8) affects the likelihood that Horace McLain and probably even Richard McGood (2) not only have important information about Feltus but also may be involved to some extent in his crimes. The greater accessibility and closer social distance of individual 8 (Feltus Robb) to individual 7 (Horace McLain) may also affect Robb's ability to manipulate McLain. Information can be gathered and converted to an interaction matrix measuring, for example, the degree to which individual McLain sought and talked to Robb. If Robb was sought out more frequently, he is in the more powerful and influential position. The reciprocated exchange of interaction (in this case seeking out versus being sought) indicates equal influence, and the unequal flow indicates unequal power and prestige.[32]

CENTRALITY

Centrality is also a network concept with application to police work. It is an index of a person's accessibility and pertains to the number of network paths which pass through him or her. The group from Figure 7-8 is divided into two major clusters, and central individuals exist within and between clusters. From clique B, for example, individual 2 (Richard McGood) is in a position to affect the flow of communication, information, or maybe stolen property to and within that clique, thereby increasing his ability to gain power by manipulating people and information. Individual 3 (Gordon Waid) is also central in the group and is even in a more powerful leadership position. Understanding which people are in the best network position to control information and manipulate others offers a tool for determining the direction an investigation should take. If a case is pursued on a preconceived but inaccurate notion of a group's structure, then the investigative focus may be misdirected. A group's apparent hierarchy need not match its true links.[33]

Centrality has to do with the degree an individual controls the flow of information, goods, and services. Formal and informal leaderships consequently are disclosed in a network representation of interaction and important criminal links. The individuals who appear as leaders in some situations may be unimportant in a criminal investigation. Leadership tends to be differentiated into two functions. The person who appears to be the most liked, the social leader, may be less important to a matter under investigation. "Task specialists," people who are less motivated to be liked and more inclined to move the group toward accomplishing its tasks, may be more important focuses of investigative activity.[34]

GROUP COHESIVENESS

Density is the degree to which members are in touch with each other. The density of relationships, or group cohesiveness, is a measure of a network structure which may become evident from network charting. The degree of connection of an individual to a group illuminates distinctions between cliques, members' attitudes, and criminal involvement.[35]

Cohesive groups have clear boundaries, are difficult to enter and leave, and have members with a stronger sense of belonging. These groups are more difficult to penetrate from within or without.[36] Clique structure pictured in network form becomes especially important in investigations connected with such highly cohesive groups as motorcycle gangs, youth gangs, hate groups, or other groups with ritualized behavior patterns, including initiations, regular meetings, and other ceremonies.

GROUP-TO-GROUP ANALYSIS

Principles of network analysis may also serve law enforcement agencies in examining and understanding intergroup connections. Groups have a network environment similar to individuals' contact networks.[37] The group network may be subjected to analysis for likely conspiratorial connections or sources of information. Groups central in a network may be the logical focus of intensified investigation. The network diagram may help investigators to predict how stolen property is dispersed or where group members would turn for aid in solving a problem or harboring a fugitive from justice.

CONCLUSION

As one can see, networking is more than mapping of links among individuals and groups. It is an investigative technique, along social science principles, that allows investigators deeper understanding of the behavior they observe and allows them to use their observations coherently and systematically to simplify and provide direction to complex conspiracy cases. For law enforcement purposes, investigators may select a few components and break them down into a few significant connections to predict behavior of individuals.

Out of the many elements that link people and determine their social distance, a few can be selected to develop the partial network of investigative interest. Although the elements used to construct the network must be understood only as guides, when the sets of observed relations between individuals of investigative interest are charted as lines or links, conclusions can be drawn about what the patterns mean.

When the network is perceived, the behavior of people within the network can be better understood. The meanings these people attribute to their connections and the implications of those connections for involvement in crime also become clearer. Network analysis is an important part of conspiracy investigation and should not be overlooked as an investigative aid.

QUESTIONS

1. Of what value is the "Burglary Screening Decision Model" employed by the Dekalb County, Georgia Police Department?
2. What is the purpose of crime analysis?
3. What are the seven universal factors of crime analysis?
4. What is the purpose of the field interrogation report?
5. How has the National Crime Information Center (NCIC) improved the crime-fighting capabilities of law enforcement agencies?
6. What type of information should an investigator have before beginning the neighborhood canvass?
7. Describe the major categories of informants.
8. How many investigators should be involved in a surveillance?
9. Discuss the various principles on which the polygraph and psychological stress evaluator work.
10. What are the major legal factors that must be considered when employing any mechanical lie detection test?
11. Discuss some important steps that can be taken by law enforcement agencies to enhance and assure victim and witness cooperation in criminal investigations.
12. What is social network analysis?
13. In what types of criminal activity might an understanding of a gang's structure be of some value?

NOTES

1. John E. Eck, *Solving Crimes: The Investigation of Burglary and Robbery*. (Washington, D.C.: Police Executive Research Forum, 1983), pp. 79–80. This discussion of assigning cases, recontacting victims, named suspects and good leads were obtained with permission from this study.
2. George Buck et al., *Police Crime Analysis Unit Handbook* (Washington, D.C.: Government Printing Office, 1973). The dis-

cussion of the Crime Analysis and the accompanying tables and figures discussed in this section have been taken from this source.

3. Shelly Smith, "Most Eligible' Status Became Nightmare for 10 Women," The *Tampa Tribune-Times*, May 16, 1982, 10-A.

4. James A. Brussel, *Case Book of a Psychiatrist* (New York: Bernard Geis Associates, 1968), p. 152.

5. Buck et al., *Police Crime Analysis Handbook*, p. 50.

6. Peter W. Greenwood et al., *The Criminal Investigation Process, Volume III: Observations and Analysis* (Santa Monica, Calif.: Rand, 1975), pp. 11–12.

7. For additional information see Thomas F. Adams, "Field Interrogation," *Police*, March–April 1963, p. 28. For an in-depth study of the effectiveness of field interrogation reports, see the 1975 study sponsored by the Police Foundation, *San Diego Field Interrogations: Final Report*.

8. Richard O. Arther and Rudolph Caputo, *Interrogation for Investigators* (New York: William C. Copp and Associates, 1959), p. 214.

9. Dektor Counterintelligence and Security, "The Psychological Stress Evaluator" (Springfield, Va., 1975), Advertisement Cover Letter.

10. "Tranquilizers May Affect Polygraph Results," *Police Magazine*, 1981, Vol. 4, No. 3, p. 5. For an in-depth look at the results of this study, see William M. Waid, Martin T. Orne, Emily Carota Orne, and Mary R. Cook, "Meprobamate Reduces Accuracy of Physiological Detection of Deception," *Science*, April 3, 1981, Vol. 2112, No. 4490, p. 71; and William M. Waid and Martin T. Orne, "The Physiological Detection of Deception, *American Scientist*, 1982, Vol. 70, No. 4, pp. 402–404.

11. "Study of Tranquilizers Effect on the Detector Meets Stinging Reply from Polygraph Expert." *Law Enforcement News*, April 27, 1981, p. 3.

12. Thomas J. Gardner and Victor Manian, *Principles and Cases of the Law of Arrest, Search and Seizure* (New York: McGraw-Hill, 1974), p. 133.

13. Block and Weidman, *Managing Criminal Investigations*, p. 15.

14. Greenwood et al., *The Criminal Investigation Process*, p. 15.

15. This discussion and accompanying references was obtained from William W. Daniel, *Georgia Criminal Trial Practice* (Norcross, Ga.: Harrison, 1984), pp. 202–204. Re age: *State* v. *Smith*, 180 S.E. 2d 7 (N.C. 1971); *Bowning* v. *Cox*, 334 F. Supp. 334 (W.D. Va. 1971). Re race: *Young* v. *State*, 243 Ga. 546, 255 S.E. 2d 20; *Smith* v. *State*, 239 Ga. 744, 238 S.E. 2d 884 (1977). Re similar physical characteristics: in *Foster* v. *California*, 394 U.S. 440, 89 S. Ct. 1127, 22 L. Ed. 2d. 402 (1969), the defendant was about 6' tall. The other persons in the line up were about 5'6" tall. The defendant wore a jacket like that worn by the robber. The court held that the lineup violated due process. Re similar clothing: In *United States* v. *Williams*, 469 F. 2d. 540 (D.C. Cir. 1972) only defendant was hatless; in *La Blanc* v. *People*, 493 P.2d 1089 (Colo. 1972), only defendant wore jail overalls; *Arnold* v. *State*, 155 Ga. App. 569, 271 S.E. 2d 702 (1980). Re seeing defendant before line up: *Bradly* v. *State*, 148 Ga. App. 252 S.E. 2d 648 (1979). Re seeing photo of defendant: *Thornton* v. *State*, 238 Ga. 160, 231 S.E. 2d 729 (1977); appeal after remand, 239 Ga. 693, 238 S.E. 2d 376 (1977) cert. denied, 434 U.S. 1073, 98 S. Ct. 1260, 55 L. Ed. 2d 778 (1978), rehearing denied, 435 U.S. 962, 98 S. Ct. 1595, 55 L. Ed. 2d. 812 (1978). Re one witness at a time: *Young* v. *State*, 243 Ga. 546, 255, S.E. 2d. 20

(1979). Re attorney: *Moore* v. *Illinois,* 434 U.S. 220, 225, 98 S. Ct. 458, 54 L. Ed. 2d 424 (1977).

16. Roger Davis, "Social Network Analysis: An Aid in Conspiracy Investigations," *FBI Bulletin,* December 1981. This discussion of social network analysis and accompanying references, charts, and tables was taken with permission from this source, pp. 11–19.

17. Claude S. Fischer, *Networks and Places: Social Relations in the Urban Setting* (New York: Free Press, 1977), p. 33.

18. Matrix data used were collected in a study by Allison Davis, Burleigh B. Gardner, and Mary R. Gardner, *Deep South: A Social Anthropological Study of Caste and Class* (Chicago: University of Chicago Press, 1941) and hypothetically adapted to the examples shown. Ronald L. Breiger, "The Duality of Persons and Groups," *Social Forces,* 1974, Vol. 53, No. 2, p. 181.

19. Jeremy Boissevain, *Friends of Friends* (New York: St. Martin's Press, 1975), p. 33.

20. For an explanation of the technique of determining personality, predicting leadership and probable coalitions from observations of interpersonal relations, see Robert Freed Bales, *Personality and Interpersonal Behavior* (New York: Holt, Rinehart & Winston, 1970).

21. Leon Festinger, Stanley Schacter, and Kurt W. Back, *Social Pressures in Informal Groups* (New York: Harper, 1950), p. 91.

22. William J. Chambliss, "The Selection of Friends," *Social Forces,* 1965, Vol. 43, p. 372; Theodore M. Newcomb, "The Study of Consensus," in *Sociology Today: Problems and Prospects,* eds. Robert K. Merton et al. (New York: Basic Books, 1959), p. 288; Lois M. Verbrugge, "The Structure of Adult Friendships Choices," *Social Forces,* 1977, Vol. 56, No. 2, p. 576.

23. B. M. Bass, *Social Behavior and the Orientation Inventory: A Review,* Technical Reports G, Contract NONR-624 (14), November 1965.

24. Fred Attneave, "Dimensions of Similarity," *The American Journal of Psychology,* 1950, Vol. 63, No. 4; Boissevain, *Friends of Friends,* pp. 26, 28; Pitirim Sorokin, *Social and Cultural Mobility* (New York: Free Press, 1959), p. 5; Emory S. Bogardus, "A Social Distance Scale," *Sociology and Social Research,* 1933, Vol. 17, p. 265 and *Social Distance* (Yellow Springs, Ohio: Antioch Press, 1959), pp. 30–78; George C. Homans, *The Human Group* (New York: Harcourt, Brace & World, 1950), p. 34; B. Kapferer, "Norms and the Manipulation of Relationships in a Work Context," in *Social Networks in Urban Situations,* ed. J. A. Mitchell (Manchester, Eng.: Manchester University Press, 1969), p. 181.

25. Charles H. Hubbell, "The Effect of Weighted Links in Communication Networks," *Sociological Theories in Progress,* eds. Joseph Berger et al. (New York: Houghton Mifflin, 1972), p. 260.

26. Erving Goffman, *Relations in Public Microstudies of Public Order* (New York: Harper & Row, 1971), p. 100.

27. David D. McFarland and Daniel J. Brown, "Social Distance as a Metric: A Systematic Introduction to Smaller Space Analysis," in *Bonds of Pluralism: The Form and Substance of Urban Social Networks,* ed. Edward O. Laumann (New York: John Wiley, 1973), p. 214–215. Quote is from Sorokin, *Social and Cultural Mobility,* p. 5.

28. Leon Festinger, "The Analysis of Sociogram: Using Matrix Algebra," *Human Relations,* 1949 Vol. 11, No. 2. See also Breiger, "The Duality of Persons and Groups," p. 181; James L. Stinsor and Edward S. Heyman, "Analytic Approaches for Investigating Terrorist Crimes," *Clandestine Tactics and Technology Series*

(Gaithersburg, Md.: International Association of Chiefs of Police, 1980); and Walter R. Harper and Douglas H. Harris, "The Application of Link Analysis to Police Intelligence," *Human Factors,* 1975, Vol. 17, No. 2, p. 158.

29. Festinger et al., *Social Pressures.* Joseph B. Kruskal and Myron Wish, *Multidimensional Scaling* (Beverly Hills, Calif.: Sage, 1978). Duncan MacRae, Jr., "Direct Factor Analysis of Sociometric Data," *Sociometry,* 1960, Vol. 23, No. 4, pp. 360–371. See also Louis Guttman, "A General Nonmetric Technique for Finding the Smallest Coordinate Space for a Configuration of Points," *Psychometrika,* 1968, Vol. 33, No. 4, pp. 469–506; Ronald L. Breiger, Scott A. Boorman, and Phipps Arabie, "An Algorithm for Clustering Relational Data with Applications to Social Network Analysis and Comparison with Multidimensional Scaling," *Journal of Mathematical Psychology,* 1975, Vol. 12, pp. 328–381.

30. J. Clyde Mitchell, *Networks in Urban Situations* (Manchester, Eng.: Manchester University Press, 1969), p. 10.

31. Norman E. Whitten, Jr., and Alvin W. Wolf, "Network Analysis," in *Handbook of Social and Cultural Anthropology,* ed. John J. Honigmann (Chicago: Rand McNally, 1973), p. 724.

32. Hubbell, "The Effect of Weighted Links," p. 260.

33. Boissevain, *Friends of Friends,* p. 42. See also Robert L. Moxley and Nancy F. Moxley, "Determining Point Centrality in Uncontrived Social Networks," *Sociometry,* 1974, Vol. 37, No. 1, pp. 122–130. For an analogy of group structures with urban structure, see Christopher Alexander, "A City Is Not a Tree," in *Surviving the City: A Source Book of Papers on Urban Livability,* ed. John Gabree (New York: Ballantine Books, 1973).

34. Boissevain, *Friends of Friends,* p. 42. R. F. Bales, "Task Status and Likeability as a Function of Talking and Listening in Decision Making Groups," in *The State of Social Sciences,* ed. L. D. White (Chicago: University of Chicago Press, 1956), p. 148.

35. Boissevain, *Friends of Friends,* p. 42.

36. John W. McDavid and Herbert Harari. *Psychology and Social Behavior* (New York: Harper & Row, 1974), p. 293.

37. S. F. Nadel, *The Theory of Social Structure* (London: Cohen and West, 1957), p. 91; Richard H. Hall, *Organizations, Structures and Process* (Englewood Cliffs, N.J.: Prentice Hall, 1972).

8

INTERROGATION

INTRODUCTION

To many authorities, interrogation is the most important aspect of a criminal investigation, because if offers the possibility of determining, by the statements of suspects themselves, whether the suspects committed particular crimes. The principles and techniques discussed in this chapter are similar to those presented in Chapter 5, "Interviews," although the degree of importance and the time spent on each factor may vary for interrogations. At the outset, it is necessary to explore the differences in objectives of interviewing and interrogation.

OBJECTIVES OF INTERROGATION

Interviewing has been defined as the process of obtaining information from people who possess knowledge about a particular offense, as part of the process of investigation.[1] The interrogation is designed to match acquired information to a particular suspect to secure a confession.[2] Another way to describe this difference is that interviewing is primarily for the purpose of gaining information while interrogation is the process of testing that information and its application to a particular suspect.

There are four commonly recognized objectives to the interrogation process. They are:

1. to obtain valuable facts
2. to eliminate the innocent
3. to identify the guilty
4. to obtain a confession

As the investigator moves from the preliminary task of gathering valuable facts to the concluding task of obtaining a confession, there is an increase in the difficulty of acquiring information. That difficulty, however, is rewarded by an increase in the value of the information.[3] Figure 8-1 illustrates these relationships.[4] It may also be observed that the first three objectives listed above may be equally applied to interviews and interrogations. Thus in attempting to obtain a confession from a suspect, the interrogator also gains information about the facts and circumstances surrounding the commission of an offense. In seeking such information, the investigator must be concerned with asking the basic questions (as identified in Chapter 6) that apply to all aspects of the investigative process: who? what? where? when? how? with what? why? with whom? how much?

FIGURE 8-1   Objectives of Interrogation

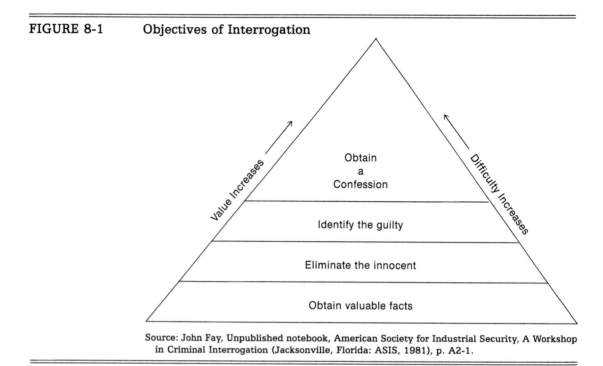

Value Increases

Difficulty Increases

Obtain
a
Confession

Identify the guilty

Eliminate the innocent

Obtain valuable facts

Source: John Fay, Unpublished notebook, American Society for Industrial Security, A Workshop
in Criminal Interrogation (Jacksonville, Florida: ASIS, 1981), p. A2-1.

INTERVIEWS AND INTERROGATIONS: SIMILARITIES AND DIFFERENCES

As in interviewing, the success of an interrogation depends on a number of personal characteristics and commitments of the investigator. Planning for and controlling the events surrounding both interviews and interrogations are important but are generally viewed as more critical to the success of an interrogation. Establishing rapport, asking good questions, careful listening, and proper documentation are elements common to both forms of obtaining information. Table 8-1 illustrates the similarities between interviews and interrogations.

Besides the difference in purpose between interviewing and interrogation, many other distinctions exist. Of paramount importance are the myriad of legal requirements attendant to interrogations that are absent in interviews. Because of the criticality of confessions and their use in obtaining convictions, it is not surprising that numerous legal guidelines and standards apply in the interrogation that would not be needed in interviewing witnesses or victims. Of course, it is more likely that a hostile and adversary relationship will exist between an interrogator and suspect than between an interviewer and a victim or witness. The differences between interviews and interrogations are noted in Table 8-2.

PREINTERROGATION LEGAL REQUIREMENTS

Before delving into the specifics of interrogations, it is important to discuss the legal requirements. This issue became of critical

TABLE 8-1
Similarities between Interviews and Interrogations

Interviews	*Interrogations*
Planning important	Planning critical
Controlling surroundings important	Controlling surroundings critical
Privacy or semi-privacy desirable	Absolute privacy essential
Establishing rapport important	Establishing rapport important
Asking good questions important	Asking good questions important
Careful listening	Careful listening
Proper documentation	Proper documentation

concern during the 1960s and, as a result, the Supreme Court handed down two landmark decisions that have dramatically affected the conditions under which interro- gations take place. The issues in both cases revolved around the Fifth Amendment protection against self-incrimination and the Sixth Amendment guarantee of the right to

TABLE 8-2
Differences between Interviews and Interrogations

Interviews	*Interrogations*
Purpose to obtain information	Purpose to test information already obtained
Minimal or no pre-interview legal requirements; no rights warning	Extensive pre-interrogation legal requirements; rights warning required
Cooperative relationship between interviewer and subject likely	Adversarial or hostile relationship between interrogator and suspect likely
No guilt or guilt uncertain	Guilt suggested or likely
Moderate planning or preparation	Extensive planning and preparation
Private or semi-private environment desirable	Absolute privacy essential

Source: American Society for Industrial Security, A Workshop in Criminal Interrogation (Jacksonville, Florida: ASIS, 1981), p. A1-1.

counsel, both as made applicable to the states through the due-process clause of the Fourteenth Amendment.

ESCOBEDO V. ILLINOIS

The first case came to the Supreme Court in 1964. Danny Escobedo was arrested for the murder of his brother-in-law. After an unsuccessful interrogation he was released. Ten days later, the police acquired additional information and rearrested him. During the second interrogation Escobedo's lawyer appeared at the police station and asked to confer with his client. Even though the attorney requested numerous times to see Escobedo, the police consistently denied him access. At the same time, Escobedo, while being interrogated by police, asked to see his lawyer but was repeatedly told that his lawyer did not want to see him. On one occasion, the lawyer was even permitted to look into the room where Escobedo was being interrogated but was not permitted to enter. Escobedo subsequently confessed to the crime and was tried and convicted in the Illinois courts. His appeal to the state supreme court was denied and the conviction upheld. He then appealed to the United States Supreme Court, contending that his confession should not have been admitted as evidence into his trial because his right to counsel was denied, in violation of constitutional guarantees. In a five-to-four decision the Supreme Court reversed the conviction and said:

> We hold, therefore, that where, as here, the investigation is no longer a general inquiry into an unsolved crime, but has begun to focus upon a particular suspect, the suspect has been taken into police custody, the police carry out a process of interrogation that lends itself to eliciting incriminating comments, the suspect has requested and been denied an opportunity to consult with his lawyer, and the police have not effectively warned him of his

absolute constitutional rights to remain silent . . . the accused has been denied the assistance of counsel in violation of the Sixth Amendment of the Constitution as made obligatory upon the states by the Fourteenth Amendment . . . and that no statement elicited by the police during the interrogation may be used against him at a criminal trial.[5]

The decision of the Supreme Court in the Escobedo case was so significant that state supreme courts tended to interpret it in a very narrow constitutional context by holding that it only applied where the suspect had been refused counsel after specifically requesting to consult with a lawyer, or when the attorney specifically requested to confer with his or her client. Hence, the Escobedo case left many questions unanswered. This condition existed in the state courts for a period of two years until 1966 when the Supreme Court again was asked to examine this procedure.

MIRANDA V. ARIZONA

The Supreme Court, in another five-to-four decision, spelled out the requirements and procedures to be followed by officers when conducting an in-custody interrogation of a suspect.

In March 1963, Ernest Miranda had been arrested for kidnapping and rape. After being identified by the victim, he was questioned by police for several hours and signed a confession which included a statement indicating that the confession was given voluntarily. The confession was admitted into evidence over the objections of Miranda's defense counsel, and the jury found him guilty. The Supreme Court of Arizona affirmed the conviction and held that Miranda's constitutional rights had not been violated in obtaining the conviction because, following the *Escobedo* ruling, Miranda had not specifically requested counsel. The Supreme Court, in reversing the decision, attempted to clarify its intent in the *Escobedo* case by spelling out specific guidelines to be followed by police before they interrogate persons in custody and attempt to use their statements as evidence. In clarifying the requirements of *Escobedo,* the court felt compelled to include the Fifth Amendment requirements against self-incrimination in the decision. The guidelines require that after a person is taken into custody for an offense and prior to any questioning by law enforcement officers, if there is any intent to use a suspect's statements in court, the person must first be advised of certain rights. (See Figure 8-2.) These rights include:

1. The right to remain silent.
2. The right to be told that anything said can and will be used in court.
3. The right to consult with an attorney prior to answering any questions and the right to have an attorney present during interrogation.
4. The right to counsel. If the suspect cannot afford an attorney, the court will appoint one.[5]

SUSPECT'S RESPONSE: WAIVER AND ALTERNATIVES

It is common practice for the officer to ask the suspect if he or she understands the rights as they have been explained. If the answer is yes, then the officer may ask if the subject wishes to talk with the officer. At this point, the alternatives open to the suspect are four:

1. The suspect may choose to remain silent, not wishing even to respond to the officer's question. The courts have held that choosing to remain silent does not imply consent to be interrogated.

FIGURE 8-2   **Warning Rights Card in English and Spanish**

THE EXPLANATION OF THE ADMONITION AND USE OR WAIVER OF YOUR RIGHTS	LA EXPLICACION DEL AVISO Y EL USO O NO DE TUS DERECHOS
1) You have the right to remain silent—you do not have to talk.	1) Tienes el derecho de quedar en silencio—no tienes que hablar.
2) What you say can be used, and shall be used against you in a court of law.	2) Lo que digas se puede usar y se usará en contra de ti en la corte de ley.
3) You have the right to talk with an attorney before you talk with us, and you have the right to have the attorney present during the time we are talking to you.	3) Tienes el derecho de hablar con un abogado antes de hablar con nosotros, y tienes el derecho de tener el abogado presente durante el tiempo que nosotros estamos hablando contigo.
4) If you do not have the funds to employ an attorney, one shall be appointed to represent you free of charge.	4) Si no tienes el dinero para emplear un abogado, uno sere fijado para que te represente, sin pagar.
5) Do you understand these rights as I have explained them to you, yes or no?	5) ¿Comprendes estos derechos como te los expliqué, si o no?
6) Do you want to talk to us about your case now, yes or no?	6) ¿Quieres hablar con nosotros de tu caso ahora, si o no?
7) Do you want an attorney present during the time we are talking to you, yes or no?	7) ¿Quieres un abogado presente durante el tiempo que estamos hablando contigo, si o no?

Courtesy Los Angeles County Sheriff's Department

2. The suspect may request counsel. At that point, the investigator must not undertake any questioning of the suspect, for anything said will not be admissible in court.

3. The suspect may waive his or her rights and agree to talk with police without the benefit of counsel. The waiver of rights is a sensitive topic for police, as it is upon their shoulders and those of the prosecutor to prove in court that the waiver was validly obtained. A valid waiver must be voluntarily, knowingly, and intelligently given by the suspect. The burden is upon the prosecution to prove that the suspect was properly advised of his or her rights, that those rights were understood, and that the suspect voluntarily, knowingly, and intelligently waived those rights, before the court will allow the introduction of any incriminating testimony in the form of a confession. The waiver cannot be presumed or inferred. It must be successfully proved by the prosecution. Therefore, it is preferable for the investigator who secures a waiver of rights from a suspect to attempt to get the waiver in writing with sufficient witnesses to substantiate its voluntariness. Figure 8-3 shows a sample waiver form. One additional fact should remain under consideration. Even though the suspect has waived the rights, he or she is free to withdraw that waiver at any time. If this occurs during questioning, the investigator is under a legal obligation to cease the interrogation at that point and either comply with the suspect's request for representation or simply cease the interrogation if the suspect refuses to talk.

4. The suspect may indicate a desire not to talk with the investigators. At this point, the police have no choice but to refrain from attempting to interrogate the suspect concerning the events of the crime for which the suspect has been arrested.

In this event, the case must be based on independent evidence, which may or may not be sufficient to warrant prosecution.

Since the responsibility is on the prosecution, supported by evidence provided by the investigators, to substantiate the voluntariness of the waiver and the propriety of the warnings given the suspect, many police agencies provide printed cards with the exact wording of the required warnings. They further recommend or require that when warnings are given they be read verbatim from the printed card. In this manner the officer, when testifying in court, can positively state the exact words used in advising the suspect of his or her constitutional rights. Such a procedure avoids any confrontation with the defense as to the exact wording and contents of the *Miranda* requirements.

A person being subjected to in-custody interrogation often chooses not to answer any questions posed by the police or at least not until an attorney is present. When counsel is made available to the suspect prior to or during interrogation, it is almost universal practice for the attorney to advise the client not to say anything to the police. Therefore, the effect of the *Miranda* decision has been to reduce significantly the number of valid interrogations by police agencies in this country today. For the most part, however, confessions obtained in compliance with prescribed rules are of better quality and are more likely to be admissible.

It must be impressed upon investigators that the failure to properly advise a suspect of the rights required by *Miranda* does not invalidate an otherwise valid arrest nor does it necessarily mean that a case cannot be successfully prosecuted. Even in light of the line of court decisions discussed in the next section indicating that *Miranda* warnings may not be re-

FIGURE 8-3   **Rights Waiver Form**

<u>YOUR RIGHTS</u>

Date_____

Time_____

<u>WARNING</u>

Before we ask you any questions, you must understand your rights.

You have the right to remain silent.

Anything you say can and will be used against you in court.

You have the right to talk to a lawyer for advice before we ask you any question and to have him with you during questioning.

If you cannot afford a lawyer, one will be appointed for you.

Geauga County has a Public Defender. Before answering any questions, you have a right to talk with the Public Defender.

If you decide to answer questions now, without a lawyer present, you will still have the right to stop answering at any time. You also have the right to stop answering at any time until you talk to a lawyer.

Do you understand these rights? _____

Signed: _____

Witnesses:

_____

_____

<u>WAIVER OF RIGHTS</u>

I have read this statement of my rights and I understand what my rights are. I am willing to make a statement and answer questions. I do not want a lawyer at this time. I understand and know what I am doing. No promises or threats have been made to me and no pressure or coercion of any kind has been used against me.

Signed: _____

Witnesses:

_____

_____

Date: _____

Time: _____

Courtesy Geauga County, Ohio, Sheriff's Department

quired in all interrogation situations, good practice or departmental policy may require that all suspects in custody be advised of their rights.

IN-CUSTODY INTERROGATION DEFINED

For investigators to understand the proper application of *Miranda* requirements, it is essential that they understand the meaning of *in-custody interrogation*. The *Miranda* case involved simultaneous custody and interrogation. Subsequent police actions revealed that all cases were not so nicely defined and that the meanings of "in custody" and "interrogation" required clarification. Although it may be difficult to separate the custody from the interrogation in certain factual situations, the two concepts must be considered separately. The cases cited in the following paragraphs should be examined from the standpoint of the subheading under which each is included.

CUSTODY DEFINED

Analyses of case decisions show that there is not yet a universally accepted definition of custody. Rather, case by case analysis is used to determine the applicability of *Miranda* requirements.

In *Beckwith v. United States,* agents of the Internal Revenue Service interrogated the defendant, who was the subject of a tax fraud investigation. The defendant was not under arrest at the time but was advised of all the *Miranda* warnings except the right to a court appointed attorney. He waived his rights, subsequently furnished incriminating evidence, and was convicted. On appeal, the defendant claimed that the complete warnings had not been given and therefore incriminating statements should not have been ad-

mitted. On appeal, the Supreme Court held that the agents were not required to apply *Miranda* in those circumstances. *Miranda* application depends on custodial police interrogation, involving questioning in a coercive, police-dominated atmosphere. Those conditions did not exist in this case.[6]

In a 1977 case, the court again emphasized that something more than suspicion or focus of an investigation is necessary before *Miranda* applies. In *Oregon v. Mathiason,* the defendant was asked to come to the state patrol office to be interviewed about a burglary. Mathiason was told that he was not under arrest but was informed that the police believed he had participated in the burglary. No *Miranda* warnings were given. He confessed, was convicted, and appealed. The Oregon Supreme Court reversed the conviction, finding that the defendant was interviewed in a "coercive environment," and *Miranda* applied.[7] The U.S. Supreme Court disagreed with the state court, pointing out that the defendant had not been formally arrested, nor was his freedom of locomotion restrained in any significant way and, without the presence of any of these factors, *Miranda* does not apply. The court said:

> Any interview of one suspected of a crime by a police officer will have coercive aspects to it simply by virtue of the fact that the police officer is part of a law enforcement system which may ultimately cause the suspect to be charged with a crime. But police officers are not required to administer *Miranda* warnings to everyone whom they question. Nor is the requirement of warnings to be imposed simply because the questioning takes place in the station house, or because the questioned person is one whom the police suspect. *Miranda* warnings are required only where there has been such a restriction on a person's freedom as to render him "in custody." It was that sort of coercive environment to which *Miranda* by its

terms was made applicable, and to which it is limited.[8]

In 1983, the Supreme Court again addressed the *Miranda* custody issue. In *California v. Beheler,* the defendant and several others attempted to steal a quantity of hashish from the victim, Dean, who was selling the drug in the parking lot of a liquor store. While resisting the robbery, the victim was killed by one of the perpetrators. Shortly afterward, defendant called the police and told them who had killed the victim. Later the same day, the defendant voluntarily agreed to accompany police to the police station and was specifically told he was not under arrest. During the 30-minute interview, Beheler told police what had happened. He was not advised of his rights under the *Miranda* decision. After the interview, Beheler was permitted to return home. Five days later he was arrested for aiding and abetting first-degree murder. He was advised of his rights, which he waived, and confessed. Both confessions were used against him in his conviction. The California Court of Appeals reversed the decision, holding that the first interview was "in-custody" because it took place in the station, Beheler was a suspect at the time, and the interview was designed to elicit incriminating information.

The U.S. Supreme Court reversed the California appellate court decision and, following its previous holding in *Oregon v. Mathiason,* held that in determining whether custody exists for purposes of *Miranda,* the inquiry is simply whether there is a formal arrest or restraint on freedom of movement usually associated with a formal arrest. Finding that no such restraint existed in this case, the court added that the amount of information possessed by the police concerning the person to be questioned and the length of time between the commission of the crime and the time of questioning are not relevant to the issue of whether custody exists for purposes of applying *Miranda.*[9]

All interviews do not have to take place in a police station to have a coercive effect. In *Orozco v. Texas,* the court held inadmissible a confession given after the defendant was questioned in his bed in the middle of the night by four police officers. The court concluded that the defendant had been deprived of his freedom in a significant way.[10]

Similarly, the defendant in *United States v. Lee* was questioned by two federal agents in a government car parked in front of Lee's home. The questioning concerned the death of Lee's wife. Lee agreed to answer questions and was told he was free at any time to terminate the interview and leave. The conversation lasted between an hour and an hour and one half, during which time the agents advised Lee of the incriminating evidence they possessed. Lee finally confessed to killing his wife but was not arrested until the next day, when he voluntarily appeared at the police station for further questioning. At no time was he advised of his rights. Using a test called the "totality of the circumstances," a federal appeals court upheld the trial court's decision to exclude the statements on the basis that Lee was in custody and was not free to decline the interview under the circumstances, even though he had not been formally arrested.[11]

Other courts using the totality of circumstances test have come to conclusions different from that in the *Lee* case, but perhaps because of different factual conditions. In *United States v. Dockery,* a 24-year-old female bank employee was questioned by FBI agents concerning the theft of bank funds. She was questioned for just over 15 minutes in a small vacant room in the bank. Dockery was told at the outset that she did not have to answer any questions, that she was not under arrest nor was she going to be arrested, and that she was free to leave at any time. Dockery denied any involvement in the thefts. After the interview ended, Dockery was asked to wait outside the interview room. A few minutes later, she asked to see the agents, who again advised her that she did not have to talk to them and that she was free to leave whenever she desired. Shortly thereafter, Dockery gave a signed statement implicating herself in the thefts. The federal appellate court reviewing the conviction ruled that Dockery was not in custody during the interviews, and therefore, her confession was properly admitted at her trial.[12]

To fully comprehend the definition of custody, it is necessary to explore additional case decisions. For example, in *Mathis* v. *United States,* the defendant was convicted of filing false claims against the government. Part of the evidence used to convict consisted of statements made by the defendant to a federal agent while the defendant was in prison serving a state sentence. At the time of questioning, the government agent did not advise the defendant of his rights. On appeal of the conviction to the Supreme Court, the defendant argued that the statements used against him had been obtained in violation of *Miranda.* The government countered with the argument that *Miranda* did not apply because the defendant had not been put in jail by the agents questioning him, but was there for a much different offense. The court, in reversing the decision, held that it was immaterial why a person has been arrested or by whom. It is the coercive aspect of the custody itself, coupled with the police interrogation, that triggers the application of *Miranda.*[13]

A 1984 decision of the Supreme Court for the first time recognized a "public safety" exception to *Miranda.* The facts in the case of *New York* v. *Quarles* involved an officer who entered a supermarket looking for an alleged rapist who was supposed to be armed. The officer spotted the suspect, Quarles, who, upon seeing the officer, ran toward the rear of the store with the officer in pursuit. The officer lost sight of Quarles for a few seconds. Upon regaining sight of the suspect, the officer ordered him to stop. While frisking Quarles, the officer discovered an empty shoulder holster. After handcuffing him, the officer asked Quarles where the gun was. Quarles nodded in the direction of some empty cartons and stated, "The gun is over there."

After retrieving the gun, the officer formally placed Quarles under arrest and advised him of his rights. Quarles waived his rights and, in answer to questions, admitted ownership of the gun and where he obtained it. In the prosecution for the criminal possession of the weapon, the trial court suppressed all the statements about the location or ownership of the gun and suppressed evidence of the gun on the grounds that the officer had failed first to advise the suspect of his constitutional rights and that the information acquired after the arrest and subsequent *Miranda* warnings were tainted by the first omission.

In reversing the decision, the Supreme Court agreed that Quarles was subjected to custodial interrogation without proper advisement and waiver of his rights. However, the court ruled that the statement concerning the location of the gun and the gun itself were admissible under a "public safety" exception to the *Miranda* rule. The court said that the need for answers to questions in a situation posing a threat to the public safety outweighs the need for protecting the subject's Fifth Amendment privilege against self-incrimination. The court conceded that this exception lessened the clarity of the *Miranda* rule but that it also would keep police officers from the untenable position of having to consider, often in a matter of seconds, whether it best serves society for them to ask questions without providing the *Miranda* warnings and chance having the evidence excluded or to give the warnings and chance not getting the evidence at all.

The court further indicated it had confidence that law enforcement officials could easily determine the applicability of the "public safety" exception but cautioned that the burden is on the police later to articulate the specific facts and circumstances justifying the need for questioning, without the warnings, in order to protect themselves, fellow officers, or the public. Furthermore, because this is a very narrow exception to the *Miranda* rule, once the reason for the public safety exception ends, any further questioning should be preceded by the warnings and waiver.[14]

The question of whether *Miranda* applies to misdemeanor arrests has been the subject of controversy for many years. In 1984, the Supreme Court settled this issue once and for all. The Court ruled in *Berkemer* v. *McCarty,* that *Miranda* applies to the interrogation of an arrested person regardless of whether the offense is a felony or a misdemeanor. The justices found that to make a distinction would cause confusion because many times it is not certain whether the person taken into custody is to be charged with a felony or a misdemeanor.[15]

In 1968, the Supreme Court ruled in the case of *Terry* v. *Ohio* that law enforcement officers may constitutionally detain persons against their will for short periods of time and in a reasonable manner to investigate and resolve suspicious circumstances indicating that a crime has been or is about to be committed. Such "Terry stops" or "stop and frisk" situations often require questioning the person detained, because that is often the most effective method of resolving suspicious activities quickly and reasonably.[16] The question has long been asked whether such questioning may be conducted without meeting the requirements of *Miranda*.

Berkemer v. *McCarty* squarely addressed that issue. In this case, a state trooper observed McCarty's car weaving in and out of traffic. The vehicle was stopped and, upon getting out of the car, McCarty had difficulty

standing. McCarty was asked to take a "balancing test," which he was unable to do without falling. His speech was slurred. The trooper asked if he had been using any intoxicants. McCarty replied that he had had two beers and had smoked several marijuana joints. At that point, McCarty was arrested and transported to the police station where he was administered a test that showed no alcohol in the blood. Upon further questioning by the trooper, who was seeking information to complete his report, McCarty again admitted that he had been drinking and also indicated in writing that the marijuana he had smoked did not contain angel dust (PCP). He was then charged with operating a motor vehicle while under the influence of alcohol and/or drugs. At no time was McCarty advised of his rights. At trial, McCarty moved to have his incriminating statements excluded as violating *Miranda* requirements. The trial court refused. After his conviction and a series of appeals, McCarty's case was heard by the Supreme Court. Two issues were presented. The first was described earlier, in which the court held that *Miranda* applies to misdemeanor arrests as well as to felonies. The second question concerned the application of *Miranda* to roadside questioning. The court ruled that an investigative detention does not constitute custody if it meets the test of reasonableness. Therefore, *Miranda* does not apply.[17]

The cases cited clearly show that the statement offered in the beginning of this section is still correct. There are no universally accepted definitions of custody and, with as much direction as the courts are trying to provide, many decisions are still subject to case-by-case scrutiny.

INTERROGATION DEFINED

For many years following the *Miranda* ruling, there was considerable confusion over what constituted questioning or interrogation. For example, in a 1977 case the Supreme Court found an impermissible interrogation occurred when a detective delivered what has been called the "Christian burial speech" to a man suspected of murdering a young girl. While the suspect was being transported between cities, the detective told the suspect to think about how the weather was turning cold and snow was likely. He pointed out how difficult it would be to find the body later. The detective went on to say that the girl's parents were entitled to have a Christian burial for the little girl, who had been taken from them on Christmas Eve and murdered. Subsequent to this little speech, the suspect led the detectives to the spot where he had disposed of the body. The Supreme Court held this to be an interrogation within the scope of *Miranda,* even though direct questions had not been asked of the suspect.[18]

The Supreme Court faced the question of what constitutes interrogation for the first time in a 1980 case. In that case a robbery suspect was arrested after the victim had identified him from photographs. The prisoner was advised several times of his constitutional rights and was being transported by three officers who had been specifically ordered not to question the suspect. During the trip, two of the officers were having a conversation about the case, and one commented how terrible it would be if some unsuspecting child found the missing shotgun (used in the robbery) and got hurt. The conversation was not directed at the suspect, nor did the officers expect a response from the suspect. However, the suspect interrupted the conversation and, after again being advised of his rights, led the officers to the shotgun. The Supreme Court stated the rule regarding interrogation as follows:

> We conclude that *Miranda* safeguards come into play whenever a person in custody is subjected to either express questioning or its functional equivalent. That

is to say, the term "interrogation" under *Miranda* refers not only to express questioning, but also to any words or actions on the part of the police (other than those normally attendant to arrest and custody) that the police should know are reasonably likely to elicit an incriminating response from the suspect. The latter portion of this definition focuses primarily upon the perceptions of the suspect, rather than the intent of the police. This focus reflects the fact that the *Miranda* safeguards were designed to vest a suspect in custody with an added measure of protection against coercive police practices, without regard to objective proof of the underlying intent of the police.[19]

By applying this rule to the facts of the case, the court held that the conversation between the officers did not amount to an interrogation and was properly admissible. Consequently, the current rules appear to be that if a suspect is in custody or otherwise deprived of freedom in a significant way, and if the suspect is to be asked pertinent questions, or if an officer uses words or acts in such a way that the officer should know would be reasonably likely to elicit incriminating responses from the suspect, the warnings must be given.[20] It is also fairly clear that volunteered statements, such as those given when a person walks into a police station and confesses to a crime, and general on-the-scene-questioning by an investigator, such as "What happened?" do not fall within the scope of *Miranda* requirements.[21]

=== **WHY PEOPLE CONFESS** ===

There are two basic categories of people who tend to confess to crimes. First, there are those guilty parties who seek some psychological motive for "getting it off their chest." The second category is comprised of those who are not guilty but who act under some urge to confess. It is to protect this latter category of people that some procedural safeguards are provided. For example, a conviction cannot be based solely on a confession, and there must be some other independent corroborating evidence to support the conviction.

The psychological and physiological pressures which build in a person who has committed a crime or who suffers from guilt feelings concerning any other type of conduct are best alleviated by communicating. Talking is the best means of communicating. Therefore, in spite of having been advised of certain protections guaranteed by the Constitution, some people feel a need to confess. Even confirmed criminals suffer from the same pangs of conscience as first-time offenders. However, "the fear of the various punishments which await them naturally contributes to their remaining silent. But, they pay for their silence with bodies and minds, their souls, their entire existence shrunken and warped in fear, anxiety, and other emotions that tear and rip at them all the time."[22] Those who do confess rarely regret it, for it gives them peace of mind. It permits them to look at themselves and life differently and to live with themselves. Research indicates that most guilty individuals who confessed were, from the outset, looking for the proper opening during the interrogation to communicate their guilt to the interrogator.[23] The good interrogator will seek out and be able to recognize individuals who desire to confess and will approach the interrogation in such a way as to provide the accused with the proper opening for the relief of the psychological and physiological pressures which have built up.[24]

THE INTERROGATOR

The qualities of a good interrogator are fundamentally those of a good interviewer. Thorough preparation should precede the interrogation and include reviews of the offense report, statements of witnesses, laboratory reports, all file information pertaining to the suspect, and kindred data. It is also essential that the interrogator know all the elements of the offense involved. Failure to possess this information may preclude obtaining a complete confession which, by definition, must contain admissions by the suspect of the commission of each and every element. In the interview, persuasiveness and perseverance are essential. The investigator must have a flexible personality; must be able to convey anger, fear, joy, and sympathy at various times; and must subdue all personal prejudices, keeping an open mind, receptive to all information, regardless of its nature. The investigator must carefully evaluate each development during the interrogation while studiously avoiding the pitfall of underestimating the capabilities of the subject being interrogated. Screaming or shouting, belittling the subject or the information, sneering, and other such unplanned and uncontrolled reactions most often adversely affect the interrogation. The investigator must at all times maintain control of the interrogation without being openly domineering, by being a good listener, by being serious, by being patient, and most important, by being persistent. An ability to categorize the psychological and emotional traits being manifested by the suspect helps the investigator react in a manner which enhances the possibility of conducting a successful interrogation.

The success of the interrogator and the interrogation will often be determined by the time, dedication, and success committed to preparing for the interrogation.

PLANNING FOR THE INTERROGATION

At the outset of this chapter, one definition of interrogation made reference to the objective of checking already acquired information against that information which can be gleaned from a suspect. This definition implies that all the information possessed has been passed on to and is known by the interrogator. The key to the effective utilization of the aggregate information is in planning for its use during the interrogation.

To carry out the four objectives described earlier, the interrogator must learn as much as possible about:

1. the offense
2. the victim(s)
3. the suspect

The Offense. It is necessary that the investigator know specifically what crime or crimes were allegedly committed. This knowledge includes a working familiarity with the elements of each offense and some understanding of the kind of information necessary to prove each. Accurate information on the date, time, place, and method of the crime, including tools used, points of entry and exit, method of travel to and from the scene, complete description of any property involved, weapons used, modus operandi, and physical evidence recovered all are essential. The investigator should also obtain a full description of the crime scene and the surrounding area. Any and all possible motives should be identified.[25]

The Victim. If the victim is a person, the investigator should learn as much as possible about his or her background, the nature of the injury or loss, attitudes toward the investigation, and any other useful information, such as the existence of insurance in a property crime case. If the victim is an organization or business, a determination of any practices that would make the organization a criminal target could be extremely valuable. In addition, the investigator should determine if the business is insured against losses, if relevant.[26]

The Suspect. The investigation should reveal as much personal background information on the suspect as can be obtained. This should include: aliases, Social Security number, date and place of birth, education, marital status, employment history, financial history and current circumstances, prior offenses, past and present physical and mental health, any drug or alcohol abuse or addiction, relationship to the victim or crime scene, possible motive, biases and prejudices, home environment, sexual interests (if relevant), and hobbies. Additionally, the investigation and preparation for an interrogation should determine if the suspect had the capability and opportunity to commit the offense and should confirm or disprove an alibi. Last, before beginning an interrogation, the investigator should attempt to determine the suspect's attitude, to anticipate levels of hostility or cooperativeness during the interrogation.[27] Figure 8-4 can serve as a review and checklist for the investigator planning an interrogation.[28]

SETTING: THE INTERROGATION ROOM

Unlike the interview, which may take place in any number of different locations and at various times—which may or may not be advantageous to the investigator—interrogation is a controlled process, controlled by the interrogator. The interrogator is in command of the setting. The interrogator governs the number and kinds of interruptions. The most critical factor in controlling the interrogation is to insure privacy. Privacy guarantees that any distractions, planned or otherwise, are controlled by the interrogator. In addition, privacy may be used as a psychological tool: the suspect may feel willing to unload the burden of guilt in front of only one person.

The room should be sparsely furnished, usually with only two chairs. There should

FIGURE 8-4   **Pre-Interrogation Checklist**

	Do You Have these Facts Regarding the Crime?	Check Here
1	The legal description of the offense	
2	The value and nature of loss	
3	Time, date, and place of occurrence	
4	Description of crime scene and surrounding area	
5	Physical evidence collected	
6	Weather conditions at time of offense	
7	Specific entry/exit points of perpetrator	
8	Approach and departure routes of perpetrator	
9	Methods of travel to and from scene	
10	The modus operandi of the perpetrator	
11	The tools or weapons used	
12	Names of persons having knowledge	
13	Possible motive	
14	Details from other case files that a. point to particular suspects	
	b. show matching modi operandi	
	c. suggest a pattern of criminality	

Source: American Society for Industrial Security, A Workshop in Criminal Interrogation (Jacksonville, Florida: ASIS, 1981), p. A4–1.

be no physical barriers, such as tables or desks, between the investigator and the suspect. From the officer's standpoint, such barriers may create an unwanted feeling of psychological well-being on the part of the suspect.

Notice the arrangement of the table and chairs in Figure 8-5. They are corner to corner rather than on opposite sides. This arrangement permits the interrogator to move both chairs away from the table and eliminate the barrier.

The two-way mirror, although still a useful tool for allowing others to observe the interrogation, is widely known and may cause some subjects to refuse to cooperate in the interrogation. If a two-way mirror is to be used, it should be small and unobtrusive. As a standard practice, the interrogation room should be equipped with a microphone

FIGURE 8-5   Interrogation Room

Photo courtesy of F. D. Hand, Jr., Director, Public Safety Department, Dekalb County, Georgia

connected to a recording device located somewhere nearby, unless prohibited by state law.

BEGINNING THE INTERROGATION: CONTROLLING AND EVALUATING THE SUSPECT

It is essential that the interrogator be in complete command of the interrogation and that this be made absolutely clear to the suspect at the outset. The interrogator must project competence and self-confidence in making a first impression on the suspect. As an example, if the interrogator perceives that the suspect considers him or herself superior to the interrogator, the suspect may be addressed by last name only, instructed to sit, instructed not to smoke, and manipulated in other ways.

At this stage, it is important for the interrogator, using personal observations and known facts about the suspect, to evaluate the mental capacity of the suspect. Intelligence is an important aspect of this process. Generally speaking, physiological changes in the suspect's body will be stronger in persons of higher intelligence. This is not always true and often such changes may not be immediately visible. On the other hand, an individual of very low intelligence may be less likely to experience physiological changes due to a lack of understanding of the danger he or she confronts, or when the interrogator cannot communicate the extent of that danger through the conversation. Emotional stability or instability is also important to evaluate. However, caution must be exercised. The emotionally unstable person can often produce reactions completely opposite from that which might be expected, thus making it difficult to assess the emotional stability of the suspect.

In evaluating the suspect, the interrogator also must consider the cultural and ethnic background of the suspect. Often, behavioral signals have cultural roots. What might appear as a deceptiveness signal may, in fact, be quite the opposite. Drugs or alcohol can also cause a suspect to produce a deceptive reaction, like delaying answering a question.[29]

COMPOSING AND ASKING QUESTIONS

Effective interrogators, like interviewers, must be skilled in psychology, persuasiveness, and acting. They must be capable of giving the appearance of empathy, sympathy, and objectivity when those characteristics are most appropriate to accomplishing their objectives. The character one assumes as an interrogator must be determined from the reactions of the suspect and the approach that will obtain the best response. A successful interrogation requires the investigator to sell himself or herself to the subject. In part this is done through skillful questioning. There are certain basic rules an interrogator should keep in mind when composing and asking questions.

Questions should not be complex, because they will be difficult to understand; they should be short, direct, and confined to one topic. They must be clear and easily understood. Only words that the suspect can understand should be used. Questions should avoid legal terms—larceny, homicide—and, unless intended, accusatory questions should be avoided. Leading questions (those which are asked in such a manner as to suggest the answer desired, e.g., "You don't mean to tell me that you're actually denying pulling the trigger?") should be avoided unless necessary to facilitate the questioning process. Adherence to these basic rules ensures that interrogator and suspect understand what the other is talking about.

Identical techniques do not work for all interrogations. Approaches and questions differ with the type of suspect being questioned. Questioning a suspect whose guilt is certain requires a different approach from questioning a suspect whose guilt is uncertain. Similarly, different approaches would be used to interrogate an unemotional and an emotional suspect.

When a suspect's guilt is certain, the interrogator should display confidence in this fact, perhaps by asking the suspect *why* rather than *if* he or she committed the crime, by pointing out the futility of telling lies, and by asking the suspect, "Aren't you sorry to have become involved in this mess?" Warning the suspect to tell the truth and pointing out some of the circumstantial evidence of guilt are also techniques to be used when guilt is certain. Calling attention to psychological and/or physiological symptoms of guilt can also work. A sympathetic approach can often be successful: telling the suspect that anyone would have reacted as he or she did under the same circumstances, minimizing the moral seriousness of the offense, suggesting a less offensive motive than the one known or suspected, or condemning victims, accomplices, or anyone else who might be seen by the suspect as being morally responsible for the crime.

When a suspect's guilt is uncertain, the interrogator should begin with an indirect approach, assuming that the interrogator already possesses all necessary facts. By using all physical evidence, photographs, and sketches, and challenging all lies, the interrogator may make this method extremely productive.

To the emotional suspect, the interrogator may call attention to physiological and psychological symptoms indicating guilt while pointing to the futility of resistance and appealing to the suspect's pride.

Just as in interviewing, it is important to establish rapport with the person to be questioned. Rapport can be established by showing a sincere interest in the person and his or her personal problems. Complimenting the suspect on some outstanding trait or characteristic often gets the suspect talking. That, of course, is a prime objective—to get the subject talking. Small talk can often accomplish the same objective.

RECOGNIZING AND COPING WITH DECEPTION

As in the pursuit of any other kind of information, the interrogator's objective is to establish the truth, to know what is going on in the subject's mind. A good interrogator, like a good interviewer, must be able to distinguish between truth and falsehood. One writer has observed that normally the interrogator relies on "common sense, experience and knowledge of human behavior to determine whether the subject is giving him true information, is misleading him with evasions and false statements, or is actually ignorant of the facts as he claims."[30] Deception may be expressed verbally and nonverbally.

VERBAL SIGNALS

Verbal signals are generally easier for a deceptive subject to control than nonverbal signals. Verbal signals may take the form of changes in voice quality as well as specific statements. Stuttering or slurring words may be an indication of deception, as may a change in the speed of talking. Rapid speech may indicate nervousness while abnormally slow speech may suggest a careful planning of each word to avoid incriminating statements. An unusually high pitch or cracking

of the voice may indicate deception.

Religious statements such as "Honest to God" and qualified answers to questions beginning with such phrases as "to be perfectly honest" are potential indicators of deception and should be pursued by the attentive interrogator.

NONVERBAL SIGNALS: KINESICS

The body of a person who is being deceptive—lying—usually experiences certain physiological and psychological changes. The changes occur because of an inherent fear of detection. Although not true for all people being interrogated, the deceptive person's fears intensify as questions tend to focus on those investigative details having the greatest threat to the suspect's personal welfare. Thus the body language indicating deception tends to become more pronounced the closer the interrogator's questions come to incriminating the suspect. Often the deceptive person who attempts to disguise body language and to create an impression of nonconcern produces the opposite result. When this occurs, the body language is accentuated and more easily interpreted as signs of deception. Although not all persons who act deceptively are in fact deceptive, kinesics can supplement common sense, experience, and hunches for the investigator who wants to determine truth and deception.

Everyone experiences and participates in nonverbal communications with others every day. Most people are capable of making gross interpretations of this body language, but the skillful interrogator looks for more—specifically, for signs of deception. The qualified interrogator understands that what may seem to be a sign of deception may in fact be nothing more than natural nervousness or may indicate an emotional illness unrelated to the subject of the interrogation.

Among the more common symptoms which may appear as a result of pressure produced by lying are: an increase in sweating; changes of color in the skin; a dry mouth, shown when the subject frequently swallows, wets the lips, or constantly indicates thirst; an increase in the pulse rate; an observable change in the breathing rate. A good investigator is constantly alert for the manifestation of such symptoms to use them to advantage. Such manifestations should be pointed out to the suspect as indications of lying. The interrogator should never allow a suspect to lie and get away with it. If this occurs, the suspect will be in control of the interrogation, an intolerable condition.

Body language is extremely difficult to control. One's body reacts naturally to a situation, and these reactions cannot be fabricated without a great deal of training. Body language indicating deception can be a reaction to a verbal statement, question, remark, photograph, or the sight of evidence. It can occur in response to a body language message sent by the interrogator. The entire body or any part or parts of the body can be involved in body language—the arms, legs, shoulders, lips, eyes, nose, the entire face, posture, and gestures. To illustrate, the sitting posture of a deceptive individual may differ significantly from that of a nondeceptive one. The deceptive individual often slouches rather than sitting upright, sits rigidly instead of relaxedly, does not face the interrogator but looks to the side, sits with arms or legs crossed, and shifts sitting positions often and in a very jerky manner. Gestures indicating tension include wringing the hands, popping knuckles, chewing nails, picking lint from clothes, and clearing the throat, to name but a few.

Facial expressions including eye movement, can tell much about an individual's thoughts and feelings and can indicate deception if one knows how to properly evaluate those expressions. Facial expressions can display fear, anger, confusion, pleasure, and a myriad of other emotions. [31]

Many qualified interrogators have been using kinesics as part of interviewing and interrogation processes for years. *Body language* may be the current term used to refer to this technique, but its concepts are not new. Rather, closer scientific study has been made of these concepts in more recent years. Some experts now claim that it would take two years to teach a trained social scientist the skills needed to properly evaluate kinesics. [32]

Proximics, like kinesics, is not new to the experienced interrogator. For years, experts have urged the "knee-to-knee" method of interrogation; close enough to touch without being too close and without any object such as a chair or desk between subject and interrogator. "It seems, for example, that around 27 inches is the limit of proximity for white American middle-class males. . . . If you move closer, people become uncomfortable . . . further away than 27 inches, you can't read a person's face well." [33]

THE IMPORTANCE OF LISTENING

At the risk of being repetitive, the authors stress the importance of active listening as an essential characteristic of the truly effective interrogator. (See Chapter 5.) Listening is also critical if the interrogator is to apply the techniques of kinesics, proxemics, or any of the other scientific principles discussed.

DOCUMENTING THE INTERROGATION

Documenting an interrogation consists of three main phases: note taking, recording, and obtaining written statements. All three of these phases are geared to accomplish two basic functions: to retain information for the benefit of the interrogator and the continued investigation and to secure a written statement or confession from the accused for later use as evidence in court.

The three most widely accepted methods of keeping notes during an interrogation are: mental notes, written notes, and notes taken by a third party. There are advantages and disadvantages to each. The two advantages of making mental notes are that it permits the subject to communicate with the interrogator without being interrupted constantly while the interrogator makes notes, and it is not distracting to the suspect. The disadvantage is apparent: if the interrogation continues for any period of time, details which might have proved of considerable importance are likely to be lost in the maze of information.

Written notes are more advantageous in that they permit the interrogator to document salient information. However, even a well trained interrogator can only record a certain amount of information during an interrogation, and there is a tendency to concentrate on the major points while disregarding minute but salient details. In addition, making written notes requires thought and concentration. The interrogator may not fully concentrate on what the suspect is saying and may miss something important. Note taking may also distract the subject, who may be hesitant to convey the truth, knowing that the information is being taken down.

Although the presence of a trained third party, such as a stenographer, to take notes during an interrogation has the advantage of allowing for the documentation of a great deal more information, it has the major disadvantage of being a distraction to the subject. Again, the subject may not wish to communicate openly with the interrogator if the subject knows that a third party is present and that complete notes are being taken.

The situation dictates which, if any, of these methods are to be used. The interrogator should keep in mind that the primary

objective is to communicate with the subject. If note taking will hinder that function, the advantages and disadvantages must be weighed.

Recording an interrogation is the best means of documentation. Audio, video, or a combination may be used but, because of the absence of case law to serve as a legal guide, local requirements should be checked. The determination should include whether it is necessary to inform the suspect that the interrogation is going to be recorded. A sound videotape that can be shown on a television set or a sound motion picture that can be introduced into court is best. It can be used to overcome charges of coercion. It permits a jury to see the actual manner in which the interrogation was conducted, to observe the demeanor of the interrogator and the suspect, and to hear any incriminating statements directly from the suspect's own mouth.

Because the law concerning the use and admissibility of video taping is still in the developmental stages, many courts allowing its use require expert testimony of a qualified technician or operator as a condition of admissibility. The technician must be sufficiently knowledgeable and experienced with the equipment and process of videotaping to assure the court that all the equipment was in working order, that the tape was not edited, and that a proper chain of custody was maintained. Despite every effort to insure fairness and accuracy in the taping process, a court may find other reasons to suppress a tape. Therefore, it has been suggested that, when possible, it is best to obtain a statement first and then have it repeated on tape. Then if the tape is suppressed, the confession may still be admissible. Video documentation is a means of reinforcing not substituting for established and proven procedure.[34]

Quality equipment and tapes should be used to insure a quality product. It should be remembered that the purpose behind this effort is to convince a jury. The higher the quality, the more convincing it will be. Interrogators and technicians must be aware that little things can affect the message on the tape. For example, it is important to select a location for taping that exudes an atmosphere of fairness and nonhostility. A background filled with handcuffs, firearms, wanted posters, and sounds of blaring sirens is not likely to portray the kind of impression to the jury that the law enforcement agency or prosecutor desires.[35]

Audio documentation is the second best method for recording. Its introduction in court necessitates establishing the identity of the people involved in the interrogation and what each had to say. One disadvantage arises if the subject does not know that the interrogation is being recorded. The individual is likely to point out things or make statements that an interrogator can see but no one else will be able to identify from the audio recording. For example, the suspect may hold up a knife and say, "I held it like this." The interrogator knows what is meant, but to a third party listening to the recording later, the words may be meaningless.

Documenting information incriminating the accused may take a number of forms. All of them are generally admissible, but the weight they carry with the jury is likely to vary. The most convincing method that can be used is an audio-visual recording of a confession or admission given by a suspect during an interrogation. Barring the use of this technique, the next best form would be a signed statement written in the first person by the suspect in his or her own handwriting. Frequently, however, it is not possible to convince a suspect to prepare such a statement.

Other forms in which statements may be admitted into evidence, listed in descending order of the credibility which they are likely to have with a jury, are: a typed or handwritten statement by someone else which is signed in the accused's own hand; a typed or otherwise prepared statement which the accused does not sign but which is acknowledged in front of witnesses; or the oral testimony of some person who was present and overheard the subject give a confession or admission. In this last case, even though admissible, the testimony is likely to carry little weight with the jury. Table 8-3 shows each of the methods of documentation in descending order of preference and the advantages and disadvantages of each.

The distinction between confessions and admissions is important. A confession is defined as an acknowledgment by an accused that he or she has committed a crime. It includes an acknowledgment of the commission of all the elements of the crime and the individual's involvement in their commission. The burden is on the prosecution to prove that a confession was obtained freely and voluntarily. An admission is an acknowledgment by the accused of certain facts which tend to incriminate him or her with respect to a particular crime but which are not sufficiently complete to constitute a confession. The burden of proving that an admission was obtained involuntarily is upon the defense, should they seek to have it suppressed.

The form and content of a written statement should include a heading, which incorporates the data identifying the circumstances under which the statement was taken, the body of the statement, and a verification. The statement should open with an indication of the place where it was taken, the date, time, city, county, and state, and an identification of the person giving the statement by name, address, and age. The heading must also include a definite statement to the effect that the subject is giving the statement freely and voluntarily after having been appropriately advised of his or her constitutional rights.

The body of the statement, which acknowledges the subject's involvement in the

TABLE 8-3
Methods of Documenting a Confession and Their Advantages and Disadvantages (In Descending Order of Believability to Juries)

Method	Advantages	Disadvantages
1. Video/audio tape or movie	Shows all, including fairness, procedures, and treatment; easy to do; can be relatively inexpensive	May be legal constraints; quality equipment may be costly
2. Audio recording	Can hear conversations; can infer fairness	Some words or descriptions may be meaningless without pictorial support; necessitates identifying people and things involved
3. Statement written and signed in suspect's own handwriting	Can be identified as coming directly from suspect	Can't see demeanor or hear voice inflections; suspect may not agree to procedure
4. Typed statement signed by suspect	Signature indicates knowledge of and agreement with contents of statement	Less convincing than methods described above
5. Typed unsigned statement acknowledged by suspect	Contents of confession or admission are present; acknowledgment helps show voluntariness	Reduced believability of voluntariness and accuracy of contents
6. Testimony of someone who heard confession or admission given	Contents admissible	Carries little weight with juries

crime under investigation, should, if possible, be phrased in the first person, allowing the suspect to include his or her own ideas in a free-flowing manner. However, if this is not possible or practical, then the question-and-answer format is permissible. The terminology used should include the words, grammar, idioms, and style of the person making the statement. The body of the statement should be arranged so that its content follows the chronological order of the subject's involvement in the case under investigation.

At the end, the statement should indicate that the subject has read the statement or has had it read to him or her, that its contents and implications are understood, and that the subject attests to its accuracy.

Other suggestions for the interrogator to keep in mind include:

Each page of the statement should be numbered consecutively with an indication that it is page ———— of ———— pages. If the pages get separated, they can later be easily restored to order.

The interrogator should ensure that each page is initialed by the subject. If the subject is unwilling to sign, the statement should be acknowledged by him or her. In instances when the subject cannot write, another identifying mark may be used.

If the suspect cannot read, the statement must be read to him or her, and the interrogator must ensure that the suspect understands its contents before the suspect is allowed to attest to its accuracy.

All errors in the statement should be corrected on the final copy and initialed by the suspect. The interrogator may accommodate the suspect by allowing small errors if this will help to obtain the suspect's initials on each page of the statement.

The interrogator should make sure that the suspect understands all the words used in the statement. If there are some words which are confusing, their meanings should be explained to the subject, and the subject should be required to explain them back in front of witnesses in order to establish understanding.

During the process of drafting and attesting to a statement derived through interrogation, there should be at least one additional witness who can testify to the authenticity of the statement and the circumstances under which it was obtained. After the suspect signs the statement in ink, the witnesses should sign their names, addresses, and positions.[36]

ADMISSIBILITY OF CONFESSIONS AND ADMISSIONS

Prior to 1936 the only test for the validity and admissibility of a confession or admission was its voluntariness. However, the determination as to whether it was given volun-tarily by the suspect was subject to very loose interpretation. There were no rules restricting the method by which police obtained "voluntary" statements. Physical violence, psychological coercion, empty promises, and meaningless guarantees of rewards were not considered objectionable procedures.

THE FREE AND VOLUNTARY RULE

The first notable incidence of Supreme Court intervention into interrogation practices came about in *Brown* v. *Mississippi*.[37] In this case, the Supreme Court held that under no circumstances could a confession be considered freely and voluntarily given when it was obtained as a result of physical brutality and violence administered by law enforcement officials against the accused. The reaction to this decision by police was not unexpected. Many threw up their hands and claimed that they could no longer function effectively because "handcuffs had been put on the police." However, as was true with many other decisions placing procedural restrictions on law enforcement agencies, the police found that they were able to compensate by conducting thorough criminal investigations.

Subsequent to the *Brown* decision the Supreme Court, in a succession of cases over the next thirty-five years, indicated that any kind of coercion, whether physical or psychological, would be grounds for making a confession inadmissible as being in violation of the free and voluntary rule. This includes such conduct as threatening bodily harm to the suspect or members of the suspect's family,[38] psychological coercion,[39] trickery or deceit, or holding a suspect incommunicado. Investigators are also cautioned about making promises to the suspect which cannot be kept. All these practices were condemned in *Miranda* v. *Arizona*.[40] Despite the appearance that *Miranda* has eliminated all techniques previously used in interrogations, such is not actually the case. What *Miranda* seeks is to abolish techniques which would prompt untrue incriminatory statements by a suspect. Thus, unlike physical coercion, psychological coercion, threats, duress, and some promises, the use of trickery, fraud, falsehood, or other techniques are not absolutely forbidden. If such methods are not likely to cause an individual to make self-incriminating statements or to admit to falsehoods in order to avoid a threatened harm, confessions or admissions so obtained are admissible.[41]

THE DELAY IN ARRAIGNMENT RULE

In 1943 the Supreme Court delivered another decision concerning the admissibility of confessions. Even though the free and voluntary rule was in effect in both the federal and state courts, another series of statutes seemed to have gone unheeded. Every state and the federal government had legal provisions requiring that after arrest a person be taken before a committing magistrate "without unnecessary delay." Before 1943, if there was an unnecessary delay in producing the accused before a committing magistrate, the delay was merely one of a number of factors which the courts were required to take into consideration in determining whether the confession was freely and voluntarily given. The facts of *McNabb* v. *United States* reveal that McNabb and several members of his family were involved in bootlegging. They were arrested following the murder of federal officers who were investigating their operation in Tennessee. McNabb was held incommunicado for a long period of time and was not taken before a committing magistrate. He subsequently confessed, and the confession was admitted into evidence at his trial. He was convicted, and on appeal to the Supreme Court the conviction was reversed. The court held that the failure of federal officers to take the prisoner before a committing officer without unnecessary delay automatically rendered his confession inadmissible. The significance of this case is that for the first time the court indicated that failure to comply with this procedural requirement rendered the confession inadmissible regardless of whether it had been obtained freely and voluntarily. Thus, instead of examining the facts of the case to determine the voluntariness of the confession, the court ruled, as a matter of law, that the procedural violation alone rendered the confession inadmissible.[42] The holding in the McNabb case was emphatically reaffirmed in 1957 by the Supreme Court in *Mallory* v. *United States*.[43]

As the mandate of the Supreme Court in the McNabb and Mallory cases had applicability only to federal prosecutions, the states were free to interpret their own statutes on unnecessary delay as they saw fit. Few chose to follow the McNabb-Mallory rule; the majority have continued to require that there must be a connection between the failure of police to produce the accused before a committing magistrate without unnecessary delay and the securing of a confession. Although the issue of the applicability of the delay in arraignment rule to the states through the due-process clause of the Fourteenth Amendment was touched on in the *Miranda* decision, it is not yet clear whether it is applicable to the states.

QUESTIONS

1. How does interrogation differ from interviewing?
2. Trace the development of due process and
   right to counsel in interrogation cases.
3. What requirements are imposed on the police by *Miranda* v. *Arizona*?

4. Why do some people confess?
5. What are the qualities of an effective interrogator?
6. Describe the importance of planning for the interrogation.
7. How does an interrogator evaluate and thus control a suspect?
8. Describe the conditions under which an interrogation should take place.
9. Of what significance is the investigator's ability to compose proper questions?
10. What is the science of kinesics and how does it relate to the criminal interrogation process?
11. What is the science of proxemics and how does it relate to the criminal interrogation process?
12. How may an interrogation be documented?
13. Why is it important to number pages in a statement?
14. What is the evidentiary test for admissibility of confessions and admissions?

NOTES

1. Paul B. Weston and Kenneth M. Wells, *Criminal Investigation: Basic Perspectives* (Englewood Cliffs, N.J.: Prentice-Hall, 1970), p. 151.
2. Charles E. O'Hara with Gregory L. O'Hara, *Fundamentals of Criminal Investigation,* 5th ed. (Springfield, Ill.: Charles C. Thomas, 1980), pp. 111–112.
3. John Fay, Unpublished notebook from a Workshop In Criminal Interrogation, November 17–18, 1981, sponsored by the Jacksonville, Florida Chapter, American Society for Industrial Security, p. A2-1.
4. *Escobedo v. Illinois,* 378 U.S. 478 (1964).
5. *Miranda v. Arizona,* 384 U.S. 436 (1966).
6. 425 U.S. 341 (1976).
7. 429 U.S. 492 (1977).
8. 429 U.S. 492, 495 (1977).
9. 103 S.Ct. 3517 (1983).
10. 89 S.Ct. 1095 (1969).
11. 699 F.2d 466 (9th Cir. 1982).
12. 736 F.2d 1232 (8th Cir. 1984).
13. 391 U.S. 1 (1968).
14. 104 S.Ct. 2626, 81 L. Ed. 550 (1984).
15. 82 L. Ed. 317 (1984).
16. 392 U.S. 1 (1968). For additional references, see C. E. Riley, III, "Finetuning Miranda Policies," *FBI Law Enforcement Bulletin,* January, 1985, pp. 23–31, and R. Jacobs, "The State of *Miranda,*" *Trial,* January, 1985, pp. 45–48.
17. 82 L. Ed. 317 (1984).
18. 430 U.S. 387 (1977).
19. 100 S. Ct. 1682 (1980).
20. Klotter and Kanovitz, *Constitutional Law,* p. 343.
21. Robert L. Donigan, Edward C. Fisher, David H. Hugel, Robert H. Reeder, and Richard N. Williams, *The Evidence Handbook,* 4th ed. (Evanston, Ill.: The Traffic Institute, Northwestern University, 1980), p. 44.
22. Arthur S. Aubrey, Jr., and Rudolph R. Caputo, *Criminal Interrogation,* 3rd ed. (Springfield, Ill.: Charles C. Thomas, 1980), p. 45.
23. Aubrey and Caputo, pp. 44–45.
24. Fred E. Inbau and John E. Reid, *Criminal Interrogation and Confessions* (Baltimore: Williams & Wilkins, 1962), p. 1.
25. Fay, p. A3-1.
26. Ibid., p. A3-2.
27. Ibid., p. A3-1.
28. Ibid., p. A4-1.
29. Ibid., pp. A5-1–A5-2.
30. O'Hara and O'Hara, *Fundamentals of Criminal Investigation,* p. 119.
31. See Daniel Goleman, "People Who Read People," in *Psychology Today,* July 1979. See also Daniel Goleman, "The 7000 Faces of Dr. Ekman," in *Psychology Today,* February 1981, p. 43; John Leo, "The

Fine Art of Catching Liars," *Time,* April 22, 1985, p. 59.

32. Forest E. Kay, Jr., "Detecting Deceptions During the Criminal Interview," *The Police Chief,* May 1979, p. 57.

33. William Hart, "The Subtle Art of Persuasion," *Police Magazine,* January 1981, p. 10.

34. William H. McDonald, "The Use of Videotaping in Documenting Confessions," *The Police Chief,* February, 1983, p. 43.

35. Ibid.

36. For an excellent reference on police interrogation and confessions see Yale Kamisar, *Police Interrogation and Confessions* (Ann Arbor: University of Michigan Press, 1980).

37. 297 U.S. 278 (1936).

38. *Payne* v. *Arkansas,* 356 U.S. 560 (1958).

39. *Miranda* v. *Arizona,* 384 U.S. 436 (1966).

40. Ibid.

41. Donigan, Fisher, et al., *The Evidence Handbook,* pp. 47–48. See also *Frazier* v. *Cupp,* 394 U.S. 731 (1969), and *Oregon* v. *Mathiason,* 429 U.S. 492 (1977).

42. 318 U.S. 332 (1943).

43. 354 U.S. 449 (1957).

9

THE CRIME LABORATORY AND THE CRIMINAL INVESTIGATION PROCESS

INTRODUCTION: PURPOSE OF A CRIME LABORATORY

A crime laboratory is a scientific organization with a closely dedicated mission of aiding the process of criminal justice. It provides this aid by answering, or helping to answer, the vital question of whether a crime has been committed, how and when it was committed, who committed it, and, just as important, who could not have committed it. The crime laboratory seeks answers such as these through the scientific analysis of physical material collected primarily from the scene of crimes or from suspects.[1]

To understand the role of crime laboratories, one must understand their relationship to the scientific community and to the functions of the criminal justice system. There are two distinct activities involved in labo-

ratory work. One is the gathering of evidence at the scene of the crime by evidence technicians or investigators. The second function is the scientific analysis of evidence, which occurs in the laboratory.[2] The effectiveness of the latter activity depends on the efficiency with which the first operation is performed.

FORENSIC SCIENCE AND CRIMINALISTICS DEFINED

The terms *forensic science* and *criminalistics* are often used interchangeably. Forensic science is that part of science applied to answering legal questions. It is the examination, evaluation, and explanation of physical evidence in law. Forensic science encompasses pathology, toxicology, physical anthropology, odontology (dental structure, development, and diseases), psychiatry, questioned documents, ballistics, tool work comparison, and serology, among other fields.[3]

One of the branches of forensic science, criminalistics, deals with the study of physical evidence related to a crime.[4] From such a study, a crime may be reconstructed. Criminalistics too is interdisciplinary, drawing on mathematics, physics, chemistry, biology, anthropology, and many other scientific endeavors. The late Paul L. Kirk, a leader in the criminalistics movement in the United States, once remarked, "Criminalistics is an occupation that has all of the responsibilities of medicine, the intricacy of the law, and the universality of science."[5]

CRIME LABORATORIES: DISTRIBUTION, CAPABILITIES, LIMITATIONS

As depicted in Figure 9-1, there are 319 federal, state, and local crime laboratories in this country. The oldest crime laboratory in the United States was established in 1923 and the most recent in 1982; 55 percent were established between 1968 and 1978, just after Supreme Court decisions limited police interrogations and while funds were available from the now defunct Law Enforcement Assistance Administration. Seventy-nine percent of the laboratories are within public

FIGURE 9-1

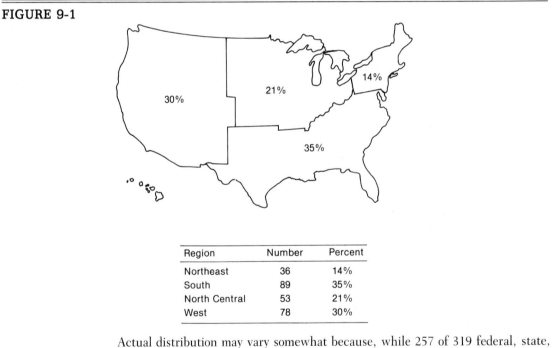

Region	Number	Percent
Northeast	36	14%
South	89	35%
North Central	53	21%
West	78	30%

Actual distribution may vary somewhat because, while 257 of 319 federal, state, and local laboratories responded to a survey, 18 percent did not respond.

Source: Joseph L. Peterson, Steven Mihajlovic, and Joanne L. Bedrosian, "The Capabilities, Uses, and Effects of the Nation's Laboratories," Journal of Forensic Sciences, 1985, Vol. 30, No. 1, Figure 1, p. 4.

safety and law enforcement agencies; the remainder are distributed in medical examiners' offices, prosecutors' offices, scientific and health agencies, and other private and public institutions.[6]

Most crime laboratories have developed in response to a particular need in a community or region. The areas of scientific concentration in particular laboratories are based on those needs and also on the interests and skills of the people available.

> Not all crime laboratories have the same capabilities. Some can do much more than others. Laboratories also tend to emphasize and build up expertise in particular areas. The manner of collection of some types of physical evidence . . . will vary according to the type of test procedures the laboratory applies. Therefore, it is important that police investigators familiarize themselves with the capabilities of the crime laboratories supporting their jurisdictions, as well as with the requirements of the national forensic science laboratories.[7]

Table 9-1 reflects the variation in crime laboratory capabilities. Only a few (5 percent), for example, examine voiceprints; nearly all (93 percent) examine drugs. In an effort to overcome some of the problems caused by varying specializations and concerns, and because of the absence of agreement on what should be the purpose, function, and services of crime laboratories, the American Society of Crime Laboratory Directors was formed. This organization provides a means for laboratory directors to discuss problems and work out ways to provide the services needed to support law enforcement efforts.[8]

UNREALISTIC EXPECTATIONS

It is not unusual to find situations in which investigators, not acquainted with the ser-

TABLE 9-1

Percentage of Crime Laboratories with the Capability to Examine Various Categories of Physical Evidence

Type of Evidence	Percent
Drugs	93
Semen	81
Bloodstains	81
Fibers	79
Hairs	79
Accelerants	76
Paint	79
Toolmarks	75
Firearms	73
Glass	70
Alcohol	67
Explosives	61
Fingerprints	62
Documents	45
Gunshot residue/powder patterns	43
Toxicology	42
Polygraph	30
Voiceprints	5

Source: Joseph L. Peterson, Steven Mihajlovic, and Joanne L. Bedrosian, "The Capabilities, Uses, and Effects of the Nation's Criminalistics Laboratories," *Journal of Forensic Sciences,* 1985, Vol. 30, No. 1, Table 4, p. 14. The data are based upon questionnaires returned by 257 of 319 federal, state, and local crime laboratories.

vices of the crime laboratory, expect too much from scientific analysis. Some expect the crime laboratory to provide a solution in every criminal case.

When investigators do not receive answers to the questions they pose through the submission of physical evidence, they are not only disappointed, but more than occasionally reluctant to use the technical assistance of the laboratory again. To some extent, investigators must be selective in collecting and preserving evidence that they believe can be profitably submitted for scientific analysis to a crime laboratory. It should always be kept in mind that the laboratory was never intended to replace a complete field investigation. The function of the laboratory is to support the investigator and the primary line units of the police agency. The laboratory is sometimes capable of lightening the burden of the investigator, but it can never completely assume that burden. Too often personnel collect evidence at the scene, send it to the laboratory, and then allow the investigation to linger until the laboratory report is received, expecting the laboratory to come up with some magical solution. This is an unrealistic expectation and largely results because the investigator does not understand what is and is not evidence subject to laboratory examination. The analysis of evidence can be no better than the samples submitted. The investigator therefore has a vital role to play in the success of laboratory examinations. James Osterburg, another criminalistics leader, summarizes why there is underutilization or total neglect of crime laboratories:

1. Lack of knowledge about how the laboratory can aid the criminal investigator.
2. Unfamiliarity with the more esoteric varieties of clue material, resulting in evidence not being preserved for examination.
3. Failure to collect physical evidence. This may be caused by a fear of cross-examination on some technical, legal, or scientific requirement that may be overlooked. It may be due to inadequate training or experience or to the overcautiousness of field investigators and the fear of destroying evidence.
4. Overrepresentation of laboratory capabilities.
5. Inconvenience to the investigator when there is no local laboratory available or backlogs are so great as to prohibit timely reports of laboratory results.[9]

This list is accurate and complete. The second and fourth points are especially important. If investigators do not know how the most minute or insignificant-looking item can be processed at a properly equipped laboratory, critical pieces of material go uncollected, unprocessed, and unused in substantiating guilt or innocence. In addition, if the capabilities of a crime laboratory are overrepresented so that investigators, uniformed officers, prosecutors, and judges all believe it can produce results that it, in fact, cannot produce, these people eventually will underuse the laboratory. Too often scientists fail to keep justice personnel informed of the state of the art in forensic work.[10]

The laboratory can be an extremely valuable investigative tool if the field investigator uses it intelligently and understands its capabilities and limitations. The investigator must also assume responsibility for providing the laboratory with evidence that is properly collected, marked, and preserved so that laboratory analysis, to the effective limits of present technology, can be successful.[11]

James K. Stewart, Director of the National Institute of Justice (NIJ) states: "Forensic sciences give us a notable example of how the justice system weds the recondite and the practical: the laboratory is dependent on the policeman and detective; the prosecutor is often dependent on the laboratory."[12] Some findings of a research study clearly illustrate the relations among investigative efforts, laboratory processing, and successful prosecutions. An NIJ project revealed that clearance rates for robberies and burglaries were significantly higher in cases where physical evidence was examined than in those cases where it was not and that forensic evidence has its greatest effect in cases that traditionally have the lowest solution rates. Those are the cases in which suspects have not been identified or are not in custody during the initial investigation.[13]

FIGURE 9-2   **Laboratory Personnel at Work**

Photo courtesy of the New Jersey State Police

TECHNICAL CAPABILITIES

The technical capabilities of the scientific community also affect how fully laboratories answer the questions posed by investigators. Although technical advances develop rapidly, there are still a great number of things that science cannot do in analyzing and individualizing evidence.

Additional techniques and instrumenta-tion are needed to establish such things as the "refractive index of glass and for a better individualization of hairs, fibers, and body fluids. Several authorities recognize the urgent need to more specifically identify bullets, gun powder, automobile headlights, glass of all types, safe lining, paint, and petroleum products."[14]

A number of authorities are of the opinion that the capabilities of crime laboratories could be greatly enhanced and articles could be more easily identified specifically if manufacturers would deliberately mark items with individualized trace elements, rare earth, or fluorescent stains. For example, the examination of a deformed bullet could be immeasurably enhanced if the manufacturers would identify the different calibers with trace elements that could be detected by instrumentation; the job of the investigator could be greatly improved if laboratories know with certainty the year and the type of cars in hit and run accidents because broken headlights or paint samples contained trace elements. Additionally, they suggest such things as mandatory licensing of commercial laundry and dry cleaning establishments and registration of jewelry identification marks and symbols to make identification and individualization much easier for the police.[15] Manufacturers are reluctant to provide trace elements because they would increase manufacturing costs.

Although the instrumentation industry is constantly devising new ways to analyze samples with greater speed and precision, the Task Force on Science Technology of the President's Commission on Law Enforcement and the Administration of Justice called for massive research activity in existing and new laboratories to improve technological capabilities as rapidly as possible.[16]

Several proposals of interest have been initiated by federal law enforcement agencies to enhance the identification of trace elements and to foster the sharing of information between law enforcement agencies. The Bureau of Alcohol, Tobacco and Firearms (ATF) of the Department of the Treasury has, since 1972, operated the National Firearms Tracing Center, a centralized title history tracing service available at no cost to law enforcement agencies. The center will trace any firearm to the original purchaser and provide the buyer's identity to the requesting

agency. Transfers from the original buyer usually must be done by the requesting agency.

The FBI has developed a Criminalistics Laboratory Information System (CLIS) tied in with the computer network comprising the National Crime Information Center (NCIC). The CLIS currently houses a General Rifling Characteristics File. This file can aid in the identification of questioned firearms and ammunition by providing data on caliber, type of firearm, manufacturer, model, number and width of lands and grooves, direction of twist, firing pin shape, and extractor-ejector relationship. This file is available to other crime laboratories in computer printouts (see Figure 9-3).

Budget considerations largely determine the level of service that a crime laboratory can deliver. A lack of understanding of the extent to which efficient crime laboratory programs can contribute to the effectiveness of a police agency has led many police administrators to channel financial resources into more traditional kinds of police operations.

"The most important resource in any crime laboratory is the scientific staff. Without an adequately trained, competent staff, the best organized and equipped laboratory will not be efficient."[17] Historically, there has been a shortage of qualified personnel with scientific backgrounds interested in working in a criminalistics laboratory. Many who are qualified shun police laboratory work, particularly on a local level, because private industry can offer much more attractive salaries.[18]

= MEASURES OF EFFECTIVENESS =

The effectiveness of crime laboratory services can be measured in terms of three criteria: quality, proximity, and timeliness.[19]

QUALITY AND PROXIMITY

Quality is judged largely on the availability or unavailability of the factors discussed in the previous section. It is understood, if not accepted, that most police departments cannot afford to staff and maintain a crime laboratory. In light of this fact, however, police agencies which desire and will utilize the facilities of a crime laboratory should not be denied the opportunity to have such services at their disposal. "Past experience indicates that police investigators rarely seek laboratory assistance when the facility is inconvenient. There are areas where the technician or investigator must travel an unreasonable distance to obtain laboratory services. Studies have shown that evidence submission decreased sharply as the distance from the crime scene to the laboratory increased."[20] The solution to this dilemma lies in adequate planning on the state level to provide needed laboratory services.

Studies have indicated that a unified state system can best serve the needs of the law enforcement community by providing a parent, or core, laboratory on the state level capable of delivering most laboratory services and strategically located regional laboratories that respond to immediate less sophisticated analytical needs and funnel evidence when more sophisticated analysis is required. Texas, for example, has its headquarters laboratory located under the auspices of the Texas Department of Public Safety in Austin, with field laboratories in Dallas, Tyler, Houston, Corpus Christi, Midland, El Paso, Lubbock, and Waco. The Division of Consolidated Laboratory Services in Richmond, Virginia, serves as a parent laboratory with regional facilities located in Norfolk, Roanoke, and Fairfax. Other states adopting the regionalized concept include Alabama, California, Florida, Georgia, and Illinois. Figure 9-4 shows the location of regional and local crime laboratories subsidized by one state into a regional network.

Several studies have addressed the issue of proximity of crime labs. One recommended that a regional crime laboratory should be established to serve each population group of 500,000 to 1,000,000 in an area where at least 5,000 Part I crimes are committed each year. (Part I crimes are serious offenses categorized by the FBI's *Uniform Crime Reports* into the following eight categories: murder, forcible rape, robbery, aggravated assault, burglary, larceny, arson, and auto theft.) Another study recommended that regional laboratories be located within a 20-mile radius of 90 percent of the law enforcement agencies' sworn personnel who would use the facilities. A third recommendation is that a regional laboratory be located within 50 miles of any agency that it routinely serves.[21] Local laboratories, such as those serving large cities, continue to provide the level of services within their capabilities and also serve as regional laboratories for surrounding agencies.

TIMELINESS

Timeliness is also extremely important to the investigator and is the third measure of effectiveness of a crime laboratory. A major portion of the case load of most laboratories today results from requests from investigators for analysis of suspected or known samples of narcotics or dangerous drugs.[22] Even in areas where officers carry and are trained to use presumptive test kits that are available on the commercial market, the results of laboratory analysis provide conclusive evidence necessary to the success of cases. Unlike many other articles or items submitted to a laboratory for examination, which only corroborate evidence possessed by the investigator, the analysis of suspected narcotics or

CARTRIDGE TYPE	FT	MANF	MANUFACTURER NAME		MODEL	TWT	LAG	LWIDTH	GWIDTH	FPN	EXT	EJR	BOB	SRC
17 BUMBLEBEE	PS	THM	THOMPSON	US	CONTENDER	R	06	044045	044045				S	H
17 HORNET	PS	THM	THOMPSON	US	CONTENDER	R	06	044045	044045				S	H
17 K-HORNET	PS	THM	THOMPSON	US	CONTENDER	R	06	044045	044045				S	H
17 REM	RB	REM	REMINGTON ARMS		M700BDL	R	06	026026	063063				S	H
17 REM	PS	THM	THOMPSON	US	CONTENDER	R	06	044045	044045				S	H
5MM REM RF	RB	REM	REMINGTON ARMS		592 REPEATER	R	06	022023	082082				S	H
5MM REM RF	RB	REM	REMINGTON ARMS		591 REPEATER	R	06	022023	082082				S	H
5MM REM RF	PS	THM	THOMPSON	US	CONTENDER	R	08	039040	039040				S	F
218 BEE	RL	WIN	WINCHESTER	US	64 65	R	06	040040	074074				S	H
218 BEE	PS	THM	THOMPSON	US	CONTENDER	R	06	057058	057058				S	F
219 ZIP	RL	WIN	WINCHESTER	US	43	R	06	040040	074074				S	F
219 ZIP	RB	WIN	WINCHESTER	US	64 65 94	R	06	040040	074074				S	F
22 EX L	RB	WIN	WINCHESTER	US	THUMB TRIGGER SS	R	06	046046	069069				S	C
22 EX L	RB	WIN	WINCHESTER	US	02 SINGLE SHOT	R	06	046046	069069				S	C
22 HORNET	RB	SAV	SAVAGE	US	23D	R	04	077078	092094	H			S	F
22 HORNET	RB	SAV	SAVAGE	US	23D	R	04	080080	090090			9	S	H
22 HORNET	RB	SAV	SAVAGE	US	23D	R	04	083083	090090				S	I
22 HORNET	RB	ST	STEVENS	US	322A	R	06	020021	092093	H	3	7	S	C
22 HORNET	RB	SAV	SAVAGE	US	322 STEVENS 342 SAV	R	06	029029	087087		3		S	H
22 HORNET	R	ITH	ITHACA	US/CD	22/410 USAF SURVIVAL	R	06	044045	069070	H	3	3	S	C
22 HORNET	R	ITH	ITHACA	US/CD	22/410 USAF SURVIVAL	R	06	044046	068070	H	3	3	S	C
22 HORNET	R	ITH	ITHACA	US/CD	22/410 USAF SURVIVAL	R	06	044046	068070	H	3	3	S	C
22 HORNET	RB	WIN	WINCHESTER		70	R	06	045045	068068				S	F
22 HORNET	R	ITH	ITHACA	US/CD	22/410 USAF SRUVIVAL	R	06	045046	068070	H	3	3	S	C
22 HORNET	PS	THM	THOMPSON	US	CONTENDER	R	06	057058	057058	H			C	H
22 HORNET	RB	SAV	SAVAGE	US	340 C	R	06	057059	059060	H	39	9	S	R
22 K-HORNET	PS	THM	THOMPSON	US	CONTENDER	R	06	057058	057058	H	3	7	S	H
22 LR	PI	CLT	COLT	US	WOODSMAN	L	06	030030	080080	W	3	7	P	R
22 LR	PI	CLT	COLT	US	WOODSMAN	L	06	032032	078078	W	3	7	S	C
22 LR	PR	CLT	COLT	US	OFFICIAL POLICE	L	06	033034	075076	L			S	C
22 LR	PI	CLT	COLT	US	WOODSMAN	L	06	033034	075077	RO4	3	7	P	R
22 LR	PS	HAA	HOPKINS & ALLEN	US	XL1	L	06	033034	075080				S	C
22 LR	PR	CLT	COLT	US	OFFICIAL POLICE	L	06	034035	075080	R			S	C
22 LR	PI	CLT	COLT	US	WOODSMAN	L	06	034036	074077	RO3	3	7	S	R
22 LR	PI	CLT	COLT	US	WOODSMAN	L	06	034036	075076	RO3	3	7	S	R
22 LR	PI	CLT	COLT	US	WOODSMAN	L	06	034036	075077	RO3			S	R
22 LR	PI	CLT	COLT	US	WOODSMAN MATCH TRGT	L	06	035035	077077	W	3	7	S	R
22 LR	PI	CLT	COLT	US	HUNTSMAN	L	06	035036	072074	RO4	3	7	S	R
22 LR	PI	CLT	COLT	US	HUNTSMAN	L	06	035036	073074	RO4	3	7	S	R
22 LR	PI	CLT	COLT	US	CHALLENGER	L	06	035036	073075	RO3	3	7	S	R
22 LR	PI	CLT	COLT	US	WOODSMAN	L	06	035036	074075	RO3	3	7	S	R
22 LR	PI	CLT	COLT	US	WOODSMAN	L	06	035036	074075	RO4	3	7	S	R
22 LR	PI	CLT	COLT	US	WOODSMAN	L	06	035036	075076	RO4	3	7	S	C
22 LR	PI	CLT	COLT	US	WOODSMAN	L	06	035037	072073	RO4	3	7	S	R
22 LR	PI	CLT	COLT	US	WOODSMAN	L	06	035037	073074	RO4	3	7	S	R
22 LR	PI	CLT	COLT	US	WOODSMAN	L	06	035037	074076	RO3	3	7	S	R
22 LR	PR	CLT	COLT	US	FRONTIER SCOUT	L	06	035037	076078	CO7			S	C
22 LR	PI	CLT	COLT	US	ACE	L	06	036036	080080	RO3	3	7	P	R
22 LR	PR	CLT	COLT	US	TARGETSMAN	L	06	036037	071073	RO3	3	7	S	R
22 LR	PI	CLT	COLT	US	WOODSMAN	L	06	036037	079080	RO4	3	7	S	R
22 LR	PI	CLT	COLT	US	HUNTSMAN	L	06	036038	070071	RO2	3C	7	S	C
22 LR	PR	CLT	COLT	US	BUNTLINE SCOUT	L	06	036038	071072	H			P	R

GENERAL RIFLING CHARACTERISTICS

9/21/82

CARTRIDGE TYPE	FT	MANF	MANUFACTURER NAME		MODEL	TWT	LAG	LWIDTH	GWIDTH	FPN	EXT	EJR	BOB	SRC
22 LR	PI	CLT	COLT	US	MATCH TARGET	L	06	036038	071072	RO4	3	7	S	R
22 LR	PI	CLT	COLT	US		L	06	036038	072074	RO3			S	R
22 LR	PI	CLT	COLT	US	CHALLENGER	L	06	036038	072075	RO3	3C	7	P	C
22 LR	PI	CLT	COLT	US	MATCH TARGET	L	06	036038	074076	W	3C	7	S	C
22 LR	PR	CLT	COLT	US	OFFICERS MATCH	L	06	036039	072073	RO2			P7	C
22 LR	PI	CLT	COLT	US	WOODSMAN	L	06	036039	072075		3	7	S	R
22 LR	PI	CLT	COLT	US	WOODSMAN	L	06	036039	073074	RO4	3	7	S	R
22 LR	PI	CLT	COLT	US	WOODSMAN SPORT	L	06	036040	071075				S	H
22 LR	PR	CLT	COLT	US	TROOPER	L	06	036040	071075				S	I
22 LR	PI	CLT	COLT	US	TARGET MATCH TARGET	L	06	036040	071075				S	I
22 LR	PR	CLT	COLT	US	POLICE POSITIVE	L	06	036040	071075				S	I
22 LR	PR	CLT	COLT	US	OFFICIAL POLICE	L	06	036040	071075				S	I
22 LR	PR	CLT	COLT	US	OFFICERS TARGET	L	06	036040	071075				S	I
22 LR	PR	CLT	COLT	US	OFFICERS MATCH	L	06	036040	071075				S	I
22 LR	PI	CLT	COLT	US	CHALLENGER	L	06	036040	071075				S	H
22 LR	PS	CLT	COLT	US	CAMP PERRY	L	06	036040	071075				S	I
22 LR	PI	CLT	COLT	US	ACE CONVERSION	L	06	036040	071075				P	R
22 LR	PI	CLT	COLT	US	TARGETSMAN	L	06	037038	071072	RO3			S	R
22 LR	PI	CLT	COLT	US	CHALLENGER	L	06	037038	071072	RO4			P	R
22 LR	PI	CLT	COLT	US	CONVERSION UNIT	L	06	037038	072074	CO4			C	C
22 LR	PR	CLT	COLT	US	MATCH TARGET	L	06	037038	072074	W	3	7	P	R
22 LR	PI	CLT	COLT	US	FRONTIER SCOUT	L	06	037039	070072	H			S	R
22 LR	PI	CLT	COLT	US	WOODSMAN	L	06	037039	071073	RO3	3	7	P	R
22 LR	PI	CLT	COLT	US	WOODSMAN	L	06	037039	071074	RO4			S	R
22 LR	PI	CLT	COLT	US	COURIER	S	06	037039	072073	RO3			P	R
22 LR	PI	CLT	COLT	US	CHALLENGER	L	06	037039	073074	RO4	3	7	P	R
22 LR	PI	CLT	COLT	US	WOODSMAN	L	06	037039	073075	RO4	3		P	R
22 LR	PI	CLT	COLT	US	HUNTSMAN	L	06	037039	073075	RO4	3	7	S	R
22 LR	PI	CLT	COLT	US	WOODSMAN	L	06	037039	073075	S			S	R
22 LR	PR	CLT	COLT	US	FRONTIER SCOUT	S	06	037040	069071	RO3	3	7	P	R
22 LR	PI	CLT	COLT	US	WOODSMAN	L	06	038039	070071	RO2			S	R
22 LR	PI	CLT	COLT	US	HUNTSMAN	L	06	038039	070072	RO4	3	7	S	R
22 LR	PI	CLT	COLT	US	WOODSMAN	L	06	038039	071072	RO3	3	7	P	R
22 LR	PI	CLT	COLT	US	CHALLENGER	L	06	038039	071072	RO3	3	7	P	R
22 LR	PI	CLT	COLT	US	WOODSMAN	L	06	038039	071073	RO3	3	7	S	R
22 LR	PI	CLT	COLT	US	TARGET MASTER	L	06	038039	071073	RO4	3	7	P	R
22 LR	PI	CLT	COLT	US	WOODSMAN	L	06	038039	072073	RO5	3	7	P	R
22 LR	PR	CLT	COLT	US	FRONTIER SCOUT	L	06	038040	069071	H			S	R
22 LR	PI	CLT	COLT	US	FRONTIER SCOUT	L	06	038040	070071	H			P	R
22 LR	PR	CLT	COLT	US	FRONTIER SCOUT	L	06	038040	070071	H			S	R
22 LR	PI	CLT	COLT	US	HUNTSMAN	L	06	038040	070071				P	R
22 LR	PI	CLT	COLT	US	WOODSMAN	L	06	038040	070071	RO2	3	7	S	R
22 LR	PI	CLT	COLT	US	HUNTSMAN	L	06	038040	070072	RO4	3	7	P	R
22 LR	PI	CLT	COLT	US	HUNTSMAN	L	06	038040	070072	L			P	R
22 LR	PI	CLT	COLT	US	HUNTSMAN	L	06	038040	070072	RO3			P	R
22 LR	PI	CLT	COLT	US	WOODSMAN	L	06	038040	070072	RO3			S	R
22 LR	PI	CLT	COLT	US	WOODSMAN	L	06	038040	070072	RO4	3	7	P	R
22 LR	PR	CLT	COLT	US	FRONTIER SCOUT	L	06	038040	071072	RO4	3		S	R
22 LR	PI	CLT	COLT	US	WOODSMAN	L	06	039040	069071	H			P	R
22 LR	PR	CLT	COLT	US	FRONTIER SCOUT	L	06	039040	069070	H			S	R
22 LR	PI	CLT	COLT	US	WOODSMAN	L	06	039040	069070	RO3			P	R

PAGE 2

Source: Courtesy of the Federal Bureau of Investigation

231

FIGURE 9-4   Location of crime laboratories in Florida.

● Regional Laboratories–State System

Escambia (Pensacola)
Leon (Tallahassee)
Duval (Jacksonville)
Orange (Orlando)
Hillsborough (Tampa)

✳ Local Laboratories–State Subsidized

Dade (Miami)
Broward (Fort Lauderdale)
Palm Beach (West Palm Beach)
Indian River (Vero Beach)
Pinellas (Clearwater)

dangerous drugs can be a key to a successful prosecution. Its identification can significantly affect early stages of the judicial proceedings, such as the probable-cause hearing; and very often it is an essential piece of corpus delicti evidence. Hence, it is necessary that the results of laboratory examina-tions be made available to the investigator as quickly as possible. The National Advisory Commission recommended that laboratories operate round the clock when necessary to handle the existing caseload and that, when-ever possible, analyses be completed within 24 hours of submission.[23] Of course, meeting these goals would require adequate budgeting and staffing.

INSTRUMENTAL ANALYSIS

As noted in Chapter 4, the kinds of evidence subject to laboratory examinations are many and varied. For laboratory purposes, examinations generally fall into the following categories: chemical examinations, biological examinations, physical examinations, personal identification, firearms identification, documentary examinations, and photography.

In a textbook of this nature it is not practical to present a detailed discussion of the technical intricacies of various scientific instruments. However, it is appropriate to acquaint readers with some of the capabilities of instruments used in scientific analysis of evidence.

Emission Spectrograph: Each element, such as tin, iron, and copper, when properly burned, will give off light which is characteristic of itself and different from the light produced by all other elements. Emission spectrography is capable of identifying these elements from the light which is produced. Its uses include rapid analysis of all metallic constituents in an unknown substance; detection of traces of metallic impurities in residues such as oils, ashes, glasses, or metals; testing the purity of a substance; detection of rare metals; and the examination of paint specimens. Emission spectrography has the advantage of allowing a complete analysis of metallic elements in an unknown substance through one operation. In addition, analysis requires only a relatively small sample, and it provides positive identification of the elements present in the substance.[24]

Mass Spectrography: A mass spectrograph is an instrument which ionizes a sample under examination, separates the ions according to their characteristic masses, and records the spectrum. It is used for the detection of trace elements present in extremely low levels in metals, glasses, ashes, and other normally inorganic materials. It is capable of analyzing unknown metallic substances and can produce comparisons of known and questioned metallic substances. The advantages of mass spectrography are that it gives positive identification of most elements present in a sample, detects elements present at a parts per million level, and provides qualitative and quantitative analysis.

Visible Spectrophotometer: This instrument is used for studying color and coloring agents such as dyes and pigments. For example, all the colors of the rainbow are paraded through a dye in solution. The instrument records the percentages of each color that pass through the solution. The variation in the amount of each color that can pass through the solution is characteristic of the dye. The instrument can also be used to measure the amount of each color reflected from a colored surface. The visible spectrophotometer is often used in comparing dyes and coloring agents in materials such as cloth, paint, and glass. The instrumental analysis of colors can eliminate personal error in color comparisons. Small samples can be examined and studied and the instrumentation provides rapid analysis.

Infrared Spectrophotometer: This instrument passes a narrow beam of infrared energy through a thin film of the substance being studied. As the wavelengths change, the amount of energy transmitted by the specimen is measured and recorded on a chart. The chart is a "fingerprint" of the organic material being subjected to study. Infrared spectrophotometry is a primary means for the identification and comparison of plastics, rubber, paint, and other organic compounds. It has the advantage of being able to detect slight differences in composition and molecular arrangements of minute amounts of material.

Atomic Absorption Spectrophotometer: Atomic absorption spectroscopy is a quantitative technique whereby elements in a sample are placed in a vapor state which allows them to be analyzed by means of a flame. It is used to determine concentrations of specific elements in a sample. This procedure is not used for a survey type analysis to establish which elements may be present, but rather to determine proportional concentration of each known element in the sample. The advantage of atomic absorption spectroscopy is that it is a very accurate and sensitive method of determining elemental concentration, especially where many samples are involved and when a sample can be readily placed in solution. It also provides a relatively economical and normally rapid procedure for determining the concentrations of elements.

Gas Chromatograph: Essentially used as an analytical method for separation and identification of gases or liquids from complex mixtures or solutions, the gas chromatograph can analyze organic material such as narcotics, explosives, paints, plastics, inks, or petroleum products (see Figure 9-6). Since the crime laboratory rarely will receive evidence of a chemical nature that is pure, separation methods are essential to the proper identification of constituent components, liquids, or gases. The gas chromatograph is able to provide in one operation a complete analysis of all the organic materials present in the sample for comparative tests. It can also be used for solving a wide variety of analytical tasks through the analysis of volatile solids, high-boiling liquids, or gases. The

recording and evaluation of the analytical results of the testing are not time consuming.

X-ray Diffraction Spectrophotometer: This instrument is used to identify and compare unknown crystalline substances (see Figure 9-6). Crystals which differ in chemical composition also differ in size and shape and will diffract X-rays differently, thus permitting the identification of crystalline material in comparison with known standards. Only small samples are required, and the sample is not consumed in using this technique.

Neutron Activation Analysis: One of the most sophisticated instruments that has been developed for laboratory use is a laboratory-sized nuclear reactor that bombards evidentiary samples with neutrons to cause the elements of the sample to become radioactive. This process, known as neutron activation analysis, can analyze samples up to 100 times more minute than those capable of being analyzed through spectrographic techniques. The various elements in the sample react to the radiation by giving off different levels of energy intensity, and the decay of radiation proceeds at different rates. These indications allow for identification of the individual components of the sample. Most often used in the analysis of gunshot residue, neutron activation analysis has fallen into disuse because it is extremely expensive and the equipment is only available in a few locations in the country. It has for the most part been replaced by atomic absorption.

The above defines some of the more sophisticated equipment presently being used in full-service crime laboratories. The list excludes some of the more obvious or technical examination methods, such as many chemical analyses, fingerprint identification, firearm identification, physical and chemi-

FIGURE 9-5

The X-ray Fluorescence Spectrometer is used in the elemental analysis of metals and other inorganic materials. It utilizes an X-ray beam for the excitation of the sample constituents, whereupon the excited elements reemit X-rays unique to themselves and are detected and measured. Illustrated in the lower portion of the photograph is the X-ray generator and immediately above the generator are the electronic controls for the scaler, detector, and power supply.

Courtesy Federal Bureau of Investigation

FIGURE 9-6　　The Gas Chromatograph

Courtesy Wichita Police Department

cal documentary examinations, photographic techniques and equipment, and microscopy.

THE FBI CRIME LABORATORY AND ══ IDENTIFICATION SERVICES ══

Of importance to the investigator is the fact that the facilities of the FBI laboratory are available without charge to all state, county, and municipal law enforcement agencies of the United States. There are two provisos concerning the submission of evidence for examination to the laboratory. The first is that the evidence be connected with an official investigation of a criminal matter and that the laboratory report be used only for official purposes related to the investigation or a subsequent criminal prosecution. Laboratory investigations and reports cannot be used in connection with civil proceedings. The second proviso is that the laboratory will not make examinations if any evidence in the case has been or will be subjected to the same type of technical examination by another laboratory or other experts. This policy is designed to eliminate duplication of effort and to ensure that evidence is received in its original condition, allowing laboratory personnel to interpret their findings properly and to ensure meaningful testimony and presentation of evidence in subsequent court cases.

In addition to analysis, the bureau furnishes experts necessary to testify in connection with the results of their examination in

FIGURE 9-7   **X-Ray Dispersive Analysis System**

Portion shown is computer "end." This system is capable of comparisons or analyses of specimens by determining elemental compositions or ratios of elements. The results are visible on the CRT—similar to a television—screen; results may also be stored on tape or printed out on a teletype in various formats. Once programmed, the system will run itself through 16 specimens and print out the results.

Courtesy Federal Bureau of Investigation

either state or federal courts. Again, there is no charge to local law enforcement agencies for this service.[25]

The FBI Identification Division, separate from the Laboratory Division, was established by an act of Congress on July 1, 1924. The act combined the fingerprint records of the National Bureau of Criminal Identification and of Leavenworth Penitentiary, a total of 810,188 files, to form the nucleus of the FBI files, which serve as the national repository of criminal identification data. There are now over 173 million civil and criminal prints, representing 64 million persons in the file. Approximately 24,000 fingerprints are

received each day by the division for processing. The Fugitive Program of the division places wanted notices on fingerprint records for law enforcement agencies. Over 200,000 fugitive notices are on file; an average of 1,500 are added each month and 1,500 identified each month.

The Identification Division also maintains two important reference files in the Latent Fingerprint Section. The single fingerprint files contain known prints of persons who have committed certain major crimes, such as bank robbery, bank burglary, bank larceny, kidnapping, extortion, interstate transportation of obscene materials, and fraudulent

FIGURE 9-8   Instrument Analysis of Metallic Elements in Paint from a Hit-and-Run Vehicle by the Use of the Emission Spectrograph

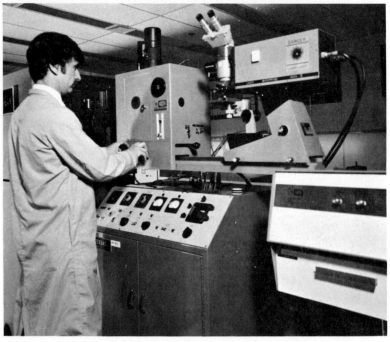

Courtesy Federal Bureau of Investigation

check passing. The second file, the National Unidentified Latent File, contains unidentified latent prints from crime scenes in FBI-investigated major crimes.

The Laboratory Division provides a comprehensive array of forensic services. Serology examinations provide identification and characterization of blood and other body fluids. Laboratory personnel also conduct microscopic examinations of hair and fiber, fabric, tape, rope, and wood. (Review Chapter 4.) Chemical examinations are conducted on many substances, often to supplement examinations conducted by other sections. Examinations are conducted on poisons (toxicology), paint, ink, tear gas, dyes, flash and water-soluble paper, blood, and urine, among others.

Mineralogy examinations are conducted on soils and combinations of mineral substances such as safe insulation, concrete, plaster, mortar, glass, ore, abrasives, gems, industrial dusts, and building materials.

Firearms examiners may be asked to determine if firearms are operating properly or to conduct gunpowder shot pattern tests. In addition, examinations of questioned bullets or cartridge cases may assist in ascertaining the type of weapon used in a crime. Utilizing the same basic principles of firearms examination, the identification of telltale marks left at crime scenes by punches, hammers, axes, pliers, screwdrivers, chisels, wrenches, and other objects can be made. The explosives specialist can analyze fragments of explosives to determine their original composition and possible sources of raw materials.

The metallurgy unit is called on to restore obliterated or altered numbers on such things as firearms, sewing machines, watches, outboard motors, slot machines, automobiles, tools, and other metallic items. Tests can show whether two or more pieces of metal are related, the possible cause of metal separation, and whether production specifications for metals have been met.

Handwriting examiners agree that no two individuals write exactly alike. Even though there may be superficial resemblances in the writing of two or more persons as a result of similar training, the complexity of writing is such that individual peculiarities and characteristics appear. These characteristics can be detected by a documents expert, who then can arrive at a scientific opinion.

REFERENCE FILES

To aid examiners in their work, the FBI laboratory in 1932 established what is now one of the largest reference collections for helping solve cases. These files are of two types: standard reference files and collections, which contain known samples of items, generally of manufactured products; and reference files of questioned materials, which are composed of items actually arising from cases worked and which may form the basis for subsequent identification of individuals or their MOs.

The Cigarette Identification File is used by examiners to identify cigarette butts received as evidence and is currently composed of over 185 different types of American cigarettes. A Standard Ammunition File contains over 10,000 specimens of domestic and foreign manufacturers' samples. The Firearms Reference Collection contains over 2,000 handguns and 800 shoulder weapons and is used for identifying gun parts and locating serial numbers. The Reference Fired Specimen File contains test bullets and cartridge cases from weapons which have been in the laboratory.

The National Automobile Altered Numbers File is composed of selected specimens, including replica plastic impressions of altered vehicle identification numbers (VINs) found on stolen cars, trucks, and heavy equipment. The file helps investigators to identify recovered stolen cars and link them with commercialized theft rings nationwide or other FBI investigated cases. The National Vehicle Identification Number Standard File maintains standards of VIN plates from each factory of the major manufacturers of American automobiles. The file allows laboratory personnel to determine if a submitted VIN plate is authentic. In the event that bogus VIN plates are being prepared in an automobile factory, the factory as well as the particular machine used can be identified.

The Typewriter Standards File consists of original samples of typewriting from numerous styles of type made in this country as well as in foreign countries. The file permits classification of questioned typewriting on the basis of make and model. The Watermark Standards File is an index of watermarks and brands used by paper manufacturers and aids in tracing the source or origin of paper. Original samples of safety paper used for checks are the contents of the Safety Paper Standards File. These can be used to determine manufacturers. The Checkwriter Standards File is a collection of original checkwriter impressions and permits classification of questioned checkwriter impressions as to make and model. As an aid in determining the manufacturers of office copying machines (either photocopy or duplicator), the laboratory maintains an Office Copier Standards File.

The Shoe Print File contains photographs of designs used in soles and heels made by major U.S. manufacturers. The Tire Tread File contains blueprints, drawings, or photographs of tire tread patterns furnished by tire manufacturers.

The National Motor Vehicle Certificate of Title File consists of original state motor vehicle certificates of title, manufacturers' statements of origin, and vehicle emission stickers. This file also contains photographic copies of fraudulent titles, statements, and stickers. The National Fraudulent Check File contains over 100,000 samples of checks, writings, and other documents. The Anonymous Letter File consists of photographic copies of kidnap notes and extortion and threatening letters. The Bank Robbery Note File contains photocopies of writings of known bank robbers and holdup notes. A Pornographic Materials File is kept of materials submitted to the laboratory; it assists in determining the production and distribution sources of the material. The Explosive Reference Files contain technical data, known standards of explosive items, and bomb components on commercial and military explosives and improvised explosive devices or homemade bombs.

Other files maintained by the FBI are the Automotive Paint File, Hairs and Fibers Collection, Blood Serum Files, Safe Insulation Files, and the Invisible Laundry Mark File.

CHANGE

It has been said that the only thing that remains constant in this world is change. So it is with forensic science and criminalistics.

Major changes are occurring all the time in both scientific techniques and in the quality and proficiency of crime laboratories. For example, as discussed in Chapter 4, scientists are making significant advances in identifying genetic markers in blood and other body fluids. The computer has increased the proficiency of identification. Deblurring and other computer image enhancement techniques developed by the FBI can often make usable evidence out of previously worthless photographs, typewritten specimens, and fingerprint patterns.

The application of techniques from other disciplines has been of enormous assistance to the criminalist. For example, laboratory technicians with archeological skills in body recovery cases.

Laboratories themselves are getting better, through support from each other, from the American Society of Crime Laboratory Directors, and from the National Institute of Justice. Proficiency testing programs have been instituted, technical assistance is provided, education and training programs have blossomed, and, in some small measure, even funding may be improving. As progress continues to be made, it is likely that the utilization of labs will increase, thus contributing to the increased efficiency and effectiveness of the justice system.

QUESTIONS

1. Define forensic science.
2. What are the two main functions of a crime laboratory?
3. Define criminalistics.
4. What are the patent limitations of crime laboratories?
5. Describe the relationship that must exist between the criminal investigator and the crime laboratory.
6. Briefly describe the uses of the following instrumentation:
   (a) spectrograph
   (b) chromatograph
   (c) neutron activation analysis
7. Describe the measures of effectiveness of crime laboratories.
8. How can the criminal investigator make use of the following FBI files?

(a) National Fraudulent Check File
(b) Standard Ammunition File
(c) General Rifling Characteristics File
(d) Explosive Reference File
(e) Tire Tread File
(f) Watermark File

NOTES

1. Florida Bureau of Law Enforcement, *Crime Laboratory,* unpublished document, p. 2.
2. The President's Commission on Law Enforcement and the Administration of Justice, Task Force Report: *The Police* (Washington, D.C.: Government Printing Office, 1967), p. 90.
3. Marc H. Caplan and Joe Holt Anderson, *Forensics: When Science Bears Witness,* National Institute of Justice, Washington, D.C.: Government Printing Office, October 1984, p. 2.
4. Richard Saferstein, *Criminalistics: An Introduction to Forensic Science,* 2nd ed. (Englewood Cliffs, N.J.: Prentice-Hall, 1981), pp. 1–3.
5. Paul L. Kirk, "The Ontogeny of Criminalistics," *Journal of Criminology and Police Science,* 1963, Vol. 54, p. 238.
6. Joseph L. Peterson, Steven Mihajlovic, and Joanne L. Bedrosian, "The Capabilities, Uses, and Effects of the Nation's Criminalistics Laboratories," *Journal of Forensic Sciences,* 1985, Vol. 30, No. 1, p. 11.
7. Richard Fox and Carl L. Cunningham, *Crime Scene Search and Physical Evidence Handbook.* (Washington, D.C.: U.S. Department of Justice, 1985), p. 1.
8. Kenneth S. Field, Oliver Schroeder, Jr., Ina J. Curtis, Ellen L. Fabricant, and Beth Ann Lipskin, *Assessment of the Forensic Sciences Profession: Assessment of the Personnel of the Forensic Sciences Profession,* Vol. II, National Institute of Law Enforcement and Criminal Justice, Law Enforcement Assistance Administration, U.S. Department of Justice, (Washington, D.C.: Government Printing Office, March 1977) for a complete discussion of continuing problems.
9. James W. Osterburg, *The Crime Laboratory* (Bloomington: Indiana University Press, 1968), p. 3.
10. *Forensics: When Science Bears Witness,* p. 19.
11. For a discussion of working relationships between police investigators and crime laboratory personnel, see Joseph L. Peterson, *The Utilization of Criminalistics Services by the Police, An Analysis of the Physical Evidence Recovery Process,* Law Enforcement Assistance Administration, National Institute of Law Enforcement and Criminal Justice (March 1974).
12. *Forensics: When Science Bears Witness,* Foreword.
13. Ibid., p. 18.
14. O'Brien and Sullivan, *Criminalistics Theory and Practice,* p. 6.
15. Ibid., pp. 6–7.
16. The President's Commission, Task Force Report: *Science and Technology,* p. 18.
17. National Advisory Commission on Criminal Justice Standards and Goals, *Police* (Washington, D.C.: Government Printing Office, 1973), p. 303.
18. Field et al., *Assessment of the Forensic Sciences Profession,* pp. I-4 through I-9.
19. The President's Commission, *The Police,* p. 91.
20. National Advisory Commission, *Police,* p. 302.
21. Ibid.
22. Peterson, *Utilization of Criminalistics Services,* p. 6.

23. National Advisory Commission, *Police,* p. 302.

24. Federal Bureau of Investigation, *Handbook of Forensic Science,* October 1978 revision (Washington, D.C.: Government Printing Office). This discussion of the equipment used by crime laboratories was taken with permission from pp. 63–64 of this source.

25. Federal Bureau of Investigation, *Handbook of Forensic Science,* October 1984 revision. This discussion of the FBI Crime Laboratory and Identification Services was taken from pp. 20–83.

10

INJURY AND DEATH INVESTIGATION

INTRODUCTION

Felonious injuries and criminal homicides are viewed as among the most serious offenses committed in our society. The seriousness is reflected in all state statutes, which impose severe penalties for acts resulting in the grave bodily injury or death of a human being. It is therefore appropriate that all available resources be employed in their investigation.

THE LAW

The various state statutes contain different names for felonious assaults, such as aggravated assault, assault with intent to commit murder, felonious battery, and so forth, but all have certain common legal elements; namely, that the assault was committed for the purpose of inflicting severe bodily harm or death. In most such assaults, a deadly weapon is employed.

Police officials and members of the public often use the terms homicide and murder interchangeably. In fact, murder is only a part of the broad category of homicide, and *homicide,* defined as the killing of a human being by another human being, is divided into two broad classifications of homicides:

nonfelonious homicides and felonious homicides.[1]

NONFELONIOUS HOMICIDES

Nonfelonious homicides may be justifiable or excusable. Justifiable homicide is the necessary killing of another person in performance of a legal duty or the exercise of a legal right when the slayer was not at fault. Excusable homicides are those committed during the act of self-defense or in nonnegligent accidents.

FELONIOUS HOMICIDES

Felonious homicides are treated and punished as crimes and typically fall into two categories: murder and manslaughter. *Murder* is defined by common law as the killing of any human being by another with malice aforethought. Most states now provide for varying degrees of murder. *Manslaughter* is a criminal homicide committed under circumstances not severe enough to constitute murder, yet it cannot be classified as either justifiable or excusable homicide.[2]

MOTIVES FOR MURDER

The identification of a criminal's motives has both legal and investigative implications. By identifying the motive for a crime, investigators can begin to focus investigative efforts in a specific direction. If a motive cannot be identified, the range of possible suspects is broad and the investigation therefore more difficult. Murders tend to fall into eight general categories: spontaneous, profit, felony, jealousy, sex, revenge, elimination, and political.

SPONTANEOUS MURDERS

This type of murder occurs most frequently and tends to follow a set pattern; it is quite likely to present a combination of certain factors:

- The victim and the assailant were married, living together in a common-law arrangement, relatives, friends, or casual acquaintances.
- The victim and/or the assailant were under the influence of alcohol at the time of the offense.
- The weapon used to commit the murder was perhaps a cheap hand gun, rifle, or shotgun.
- The victim was younger than the assailant.
- The victim and assailant were from a low socioeconomic group.
- The incident that led to the assault was trivial.
- The victim and assailant were of the same race.
- The assailant has been implicated in earlier violent incidents.
- The victim precipitated his or her own death by making the first menacing gesture or striking the first blow.[3]

Because spontaneous murders are not carefully planned, but instead spring from volatile emotions spontaneously acted on, there are often witnesses and considerable evidence. Spontaneous murders have a high clearance rate. The assailant frequently is arrested at or near the scene, at home, or at the home of a relative or friend. The murder probably would not have happened if a gun had not been readily available, although it is likely that some type of assault would have occurred.

PROFIT MURDERS

Profit murders generally occur between individuals who are professionally or personally involved in such a manner that the perpetrator stands to benefit materially from the victim's death. The material benefit can take many forms. In some instances, a business partner gains control over a jointly owned business or receives payments as the beneficiary of a "key man" type of insurance policy.* In other cases, the murderer may stand to gain a sizable inheritance. One of the key questions that the investigator must ask is: Who stands to gain the most from the victim's death?

The investigator should never overlook the possibility that the actual murder was committed by someone hired by the beneficiary of the victim's death. These types of murders present an extraordinary challenge to the investigator. When they are solved, often it is because the actual murderer was apprehended and agreed to provide testimony against the individual employing his or her services. Such cooperation by the murderer is not due to guilt or altruism, but rather to an agreement with a prosecutor for immunity from prosecution or for a plea to a lesser offense.

Profit murders are usually carefully planned, and the perpetrator sometimes goes to great lengths to make the death appear

---

* This type of policy may be issued on the life of a business partner or employee whose death can cause a severe economic loss to the business.

natural or accidental. In some instances, the murder plan involves having the victim killed during the commission of some other crime, such as burglary or robbery, thus giving the impression that it resulted as a secondary factor associated with the original crime.

FELONY MURDER

The felony murder is committed during the commission of another crime, such as robbery or burglary. By definition it is not a planned part of the crime but occurs, for example, when a victim unexpectedly appears or resists efforts to be robbed. This type of murder is among the most difficult to solve, because there are seldom witnesses, much physical evidence, or immediate suspects. When felony murders are cleared, it is generally because the perpetrator was located at or near the scene or because the perpetrator was arrested later for a similar crime. In the latter situation, the investigator linked the crimes, perhaps because the suspect's physical description or MO was similar, or a weapon or tool was found in the possession of the suspect which could be linked to the earlier crime. In other instances, an informant may provide information leading to the identification and arrest of the suspect.

JEALOUSY MURDERS

Like spontaneous murders, jealousy murders have a high clearance rate, because the assailant is primarily concerned with injuring or killing the person on whom his or her emotions have become fixed, rather than with escaping apprehension. The murderer is often a rejected spouse or lover, and the victim may be either the person who has done the rejecting or some third party involved in a lovers' triangle. Jealousy murders are sometimes followed by the suicide of the perpetrator.

SEX MURDERS

These murders may have been preplanned by the perpetrator or may have occurred as a secondary aspect of a sex crime. The actual murder of the victim may occur before, during, or after the sex act; it depends to a great extent on the idiosyncrasies of the perpetrator and the actions of the victim. In some instances, the victim is murdered as a psychologically integral part of the sex act. In other cases, the victim is murdered to eliminate a witness or is killed accidentally as the perpetrator attempts to stop efforts to resist or scream.

REVENGE MURDERS

The background of the victim may provide valuable insight into revenge murders. For example, judges and police officers, organized crime figures and drug dealers may be victims of revenge. In some instances the act of revenge is inflicted indirectly, such as on some member of the target person's family. Thus, the victim may not have been the real object, but only a convenient and effective means of revenge. The successful investigation of such murders depends in large measure upon the cooperation of the person to whom the act was supposed to cause pain.

ELIMINATION MURDERS

Elimination murders are committed to eliminate persons who are considered an obstruction to some desired end. For example, a spouse may eliminate a mate to marry a lover, or underworld figures may murder a competitor to acquire a monopoly over a lucrative criminal activity. The most important leads are ordinarily uncovered in thorough checks of the victim's background and character.

POLITICAL MURDERS

Murders of this type are often committed by individuals or members of groups who are fighting for a particular political or social cause. They are carefully planned and are intended to remove individuals considered to be real or symbolic impediments to goals of the movement. In many instances, these murders are also calculated to obtain publicity for the cause espoused by the individual or group. Success in clearing politically motivated murders generally occurs when investigators can infiltrate the group or when an informant supplies information.

=== RESPONDING TO THE SCENE ===

In responding to the scene of a suspected homicide or assault, fundamental rules must be followed. The officer should proceed with deliberate but not reckless speed. As the officer approaches the scene, he or she should be observant for a suspect fleeing either on foot or by vehicle. The dispatcher may have been able to obtain and relate specific details to the responding officer about the offense and suspect. If not, the officer has to rely on discriminating observations, training, and past experience. The officer should be suspicious of: a vehicle being driven away from the crime scene at a high rate of speed or in an erratic manner; an individual who attempts to hide from view; or a person whose clothing indicates recent involvement in a struggle.

=== ARRIVAL AT THE SCENE ===

When conditions permit, certain procedures should be completed at the scene. The tag numbers of vehicles parked in the immediate area should be recorded. First, a vehicle at the scene may belong to a suspect who is still in the area but who for some reason has been unable or unwilling to return to it. Second, it may belong to someone who has witnessed the offense. Third, once the officer initiates the investigation, there may not be time to record the tag numbers.

On entering the crime scene, the officer should use caution in case the perpetrator is still at the scene. In assault offenses, there may also be a potential danger from the victim, especially if the victim has been injured or is frightened. Thus even if the suspect is known to have fled the scene, the officer should be cautious, especially when entering a darkened home or business.

The responsibility of the first officer to arrive at the scene is to render assistance to the victim. With certain notable exceptions, it is unsound to assume that a person is dead. Unless there is a physician or other medically certified person at the scene who has pronounced the victim dead, acceptable procedure dictates having the victim transported to a hospital as rapidly as possible. If the victim is conscious but has not been interviewed at the scene, an officer should accompany the victim to the hospital and conduct an interview in the ambulance. Efforts to interview the victim in the hospital emergency room are generally futile, particularly if the victim is critically injured, because emergency treatment will begin immediately upon the victim's arrival.

If there are witnesses at the crime scene, identification should be obtained from them as early as possible. This action is especially important if the scene is a public place, such as a bar or restaurant, because some of them may leave. In such instances, personnel should be assigned to block off the exits temporarily. All witnesses should be requested to show documented proof of their identity because some will attempt to provide fictitious names and addresses to avoid being further involved.

The questioning of witnesses should be

brief and out of hearing of other witnesses. Detailed questioning is best accomplished away from the crime scene and preferably in the police buildings. If the suspect is still at the scene when the police arrive, the following steps should be taken: the suspect should be searched for weapons and handcuffed so that he or she cannot escape or inflict injury to self or others; and the suspect should be advised of his or her constitutional rights and removed from the scene as quickly as possible. If the suspect is willing to discuss the crime, the officer should not attempt to conduct an in-depth interrogation at the scene but should wait until they are at police headquarters. This is not to suggest that the officer should discourage the suspect from making a statement, but most crime scenes are not conducive to detailed interrogations. If the suspect indicates that he or she committed the crime in self-defense, then the officer should indicate in the report all the facts that either substantiate or fail to substantiate this claim. For example, if the suspect claims to have been first assaulted by the victim, the officer should record any injuries to the suspect. In addition, it is a good practice to photograph in color all injuries that the suspect states were sustained at the hands of the victim. It may be that the injuries sustained are internal and therefore not visible or perhaps covered by the suspect's clothes and not readily subject to observation or photography. In such cases, it is wise to request the suspect to submit to an examination by a physician. If the suspect agrees, then the information obtained from the examining physician is included in the report. If the suspect refuses, this refusal too should be noted.

PROTECTING THE CRIME SCENE

The protection of the crime scene is a vital part of the investigation of injury and death cases. The scene of any crime itself is evidence, and the testimony of an officer concerning his or her observations may be vitally important to obtaining a conviction. Improper protection of the crime scene usually results in the contamination, loss, or unnecessary movement of evidence, any one of which is likely to render the evidence useless. Therefore, the first officer at the scene of the crime automatically incurs responsibility for securing it from unauthorized intrusion.[4] People may intentionally or unintentionally disrupt or destroy physical evidence at a crime scene, including the suspect, victim, relatives or friends of the suspect or victim, witnesses, curious onlookers, news media personnel, and other officers, including superiors. The basic rule for handling pedestrian traffic in and out of the scene is to exclude all individuals whose presence serves no specific function.

DEATH SCENE CHECKLIST

In cases where a medical examiner or medical examiner investigator is not at the crime scene or where the police officer cannot be present at the autopsy, it is essential that certain information be furnished to the pathologist before this autopsy is performed. A death scene checklist may have to be forwarded to the medical examiner with the deceased's body. The checklist also serves as a readily available source of essential information. Such a list would be most helpful in jurisdictions where pathologists performing autopsies have little contact with investigating officers (see Figure 10-1).[5]

THE MEDICO-LEGAL EXAMINATION

The medico-legal examination brings medical skill to bear upon injury and death investigations. The medical specialist frequently

FIGURE 10-1   Death Scene Checklist

DEATH SCENE CHECKLIST

(This form is to be used as a supplementary source sheet for readily available information and is not intended to replace conventional reports. Copies should be distributed to investigating officers and medical examiners.)

Name of Deceased:

First   Middle   Last

Address:

Age: **Race**:   White   Black   Hispanic   Asian   American   Indian   Unknown

Sex: Male   Female

Telephone number:

Marital status: S   M   W   D   Separated   Unknown

Next-of-kin:

    Name:

    Address:

    Telephone number:

Police Notified by:

    Date: Time:

    Name:

    Address:

    Telephone number:

    Relationship to deceased:

Deceased found:

    Date: Time:

    Address: (if different from above)

    Location: Apartment   House   Townhouse   Other (describe):

    Entrance by: Key   Cutting chain   Forcing door   Other (describe):

    Type of lock on door:

    Condition of other doors and windows: Open   Closed   Locked   Unlocked

Body found:

Living Room   Dining Room   Bedroom   Kitchen   Attic   Basement   Other (describe):

Location in room:

Position of body: On back   Face down   Other:

Condition of body:

Fully clothed   Partially clothed   Unclothed

Preservation: Well preserved   Decomposed

Estimated Rigor: Complete   Head   Arms   Legs

Liver: Front   Back   Localized

Color:

Blood: Absent   Present   Location

Ligatures: Yes   No

Apparent Wounds: None   Gunshot   Stab   Blunt force

Number:

Location: Head   Neck   Chest   Abdomen   Extremities

Hanging: Yes   No   Means:

Weapon(s) present: Gun (estimate caliber)

Type:

Knife:

Other (describe):

Condition of surroundings: Orderly   Untidy   Disarray

Odors: Decomposition   Other:

Evidence of last food preparation:

Where:

Type:

Dated material:

Mail:

Newspapers:

TV Guide:

Liquor Bottles:

(Figure 10-1 continued on next page.)

Figure 10-1 *(continued)*

Last contact with deceased:

Date:

Type of Contact:

Name of Contact:

Evidence of robbery: Yes   No   Not determined

Identification of deceased: Yes   No

If yes, how accomplished:

If no, how is it to be accomplished:

Evidence of drug use: (prescription and nonprescription)   Yes   No

If drugs present, collect them and send with body.

Evidence of drug paraphernalia: Yes   No

Type:

Evidence of sexual deviate practices: Yes   No

Type: (collect and send with body)

Name and telephone number of investigating officer:

called to assist in such cases is the forensic pathologist. Pathology is the branch of medicine involved in the scientific study of abnormal changes in body tissues and afflictions caused by disease. The forensic pathologist receives additional training in the study of sudden, unexpected, and violent deaths.[6] Physicians specializing in forensic pathology are ordinarily employed by some unit of government and are not in private practice.

THE AUTOPSY

All violent and suspicious deaths require an autopsy to determine the time and precise cause of death.[7] The autopsy may also answer the following questions:

- What type of weapon was employed?
- If multiple wounds were inflicted, which wound was fatal?
- How long did the victim live after the injury?
- What position was the victim in at the time of the assault?
- From what direction was the force applied?
- Is there any evidence of a struggle or self-defense?
- Is there any evidence of rape or other sex-related acts?
- Was the deceased under the influence of alcohol or any type of drug?[8]

Answers to all or even some of these questions increase the possibility of bringing the death investigation to a successful conclusion.

If any of the clothing is damaged, the investigator should determine whether the damage was related to the assault or was caused by hospital personnel giving emergency treatment. When a determination is made of the cause of the damage, it should be recorded in the investigation report.

The victim should be fingerprinted, even if there is positive proof of identification. If circumstances dictate, palmprints and footprints should also be obtained. They may prove useful if later found in the suspect's home, business, car, or some other location. In those instances of possible physical contact by the victim with the assailant or contact with some object employed in the attack by the assailant, standard specimens of hair should be removed from the victim's head, eyebrows, pubic area, anus, armpits, legs, and chest.

IDENTIFICATION OF THE DEAD PERSON

Personal identification is one of the most important functions of an investigation. The inability to identify a deceased person greatly complicates the investigative process. The major problem attending the failure to identify a deceased person is the difficulty in focusing the investigation toward, for example, the victim's enemies or those who would most stand to gain from the death. These and other important questions cannot be answered until the victim's identity is established.

A number of techniques contribute to establishing the deceased person's identity, including fingerprinting, forensic odontology, physical description, surgical history, viewing by possible identifiers, occupational trademarks, and personal belongings. On any unidentified body, fingerprints should be obtained if possible.[9]

Identification based on examination of teeth, fillings, inlays, crowns, bridgework, and dentures is valuable inasmuch as the teeth are probably the most durable part of the human body.[10] Physical description data—sex, age, weight, height, build, color of hair, color of eyes, race, amputations, deformities, or tattoos—help in the checking of missing-persons reports in an effort to locate individuals who fit the description of the victim.

The medical examiner should search for the presence of evidence of surgery on the victim. In some cases, scars are readily visible, such as in the case of an appendix operation. However, in other instances, surgical scars may be completely internal. The medical examiner should also note the surgical removal of any internal organs.

Visual inspection leaves much to be desired for two reasons. First, if the victim has sustained severe facial injuries, they may cause gross distortion of the face. This is also true if putrefaction has begun and the face is swollen. Second, this method of identification results in a certain amount of psychological trauma for relatives and friends called on to view the body. Sometimes there is no choice but to use this method, but if other options are available, they should be used.

Valuable indicators may be obtained by close examination of the victim's body, especially the hands. For example, the occupational trademarks of a bricklayer's hands will be distinctly different from those of a clerk. Also, one frequently finds that an auto mechanic has hard-to-remove grease stains under the fingernails. An examination of personal belongings may prove to be of value in establishing where they were purchased or cleaned. Clothing may prove to be of particular assistance. If the victim was wearing a watch, the internal portion of the watch may possess the unique markings left by a watchmaker who repaired it. In some instances, the victim's jewelry, such as rings or

watches, may have the victim's initials in-
scribed.[11]

PERSONALITY RECONSTRUCTION
FROM UNIDENTIFIED
REMAINS

The identification of deceased persons takes
on additional difficulty when the body is
badly decomposed. However, remarkable
work has been done in recent years by scientists in identifying such victims. The following case, investigated by an East coast
police department, provides an excellent example of the state of the art.

The badly decomposed remains of a human were found in an isolated wooded
area adjacent to an industrial park. The
crime scene investigation disclosed that
the skeletal remains had been dragged a
few feet from the location, and it was
suspected that this dislocation of the remains resulted from animal activities. An
intensive search produced only a few
strands of hair, a medium-sized sweater,
and a few pieces of women's jewelry. The
physical remains were taken to the medical examiner's office where the time of
death was estimated to be three to six
weeks prior to the discovery of the body.
A subsequent review of missing-person
reports for the pertinent time period produced no additional clues.

With the question of the victim's identity still unresolved, the remains were
forwarded to the Curator of Physical Anthropology at the Smithsonian Institution
in Washington, D.C. Based upon an examination of the skeletal remains (see
Figure 10-2), it was concluded that the
skeleton was that of a Caucasian female
approximately seventeen to twenty-two
years of age, who was of less than average
stature. She had broader than average
shoulders and hips, and was believed to

be right-handed. Her head and face were
long; the nose high bridged. Also noted
was the subcartilage damage to the right
hip joint, a condition which had probably
caused occasional pain and suggested occupational stress. An irregularity of the
left clavicle (collarbone) revealed a healed
childhood fracture.

Local police officials then began a social and personality profile of the deceased
based upon an analysis of the physical
evidence obtained through the crime
scene search and related photographs,
medical examiner's reports, and reports
from the FBI laboratory. In addition,
aided by a physical anthropologist from
the Smithsonian Institution, a police artist was able to sketch a photograph (see
Figure 10-3). The sketch was then published in a local newspaper and police
officials immediately received calls from
three different readers who all supplied
the same name of a female whom they all
knew. They advised that she resembled
the sketch and they further advised that
she had been missing for approximately
four months.

A search of the local police files disclosed that the individual with this name
had been previously photographed (see
Figure 10-4) and fingerprinted. These
prints were compared with the badly decomposed prints from one of the victim's
fingers, and a positive identification was
made.

Further investigation by the police determined the victim was 20 years of age.
Associates related that when she had
worked as a nightclub dancer, she occasionally had favored one leg. It was further determined that she had suffered a
fracture of the left clavicle at age 6.[12]

The lessons learned from this case have
significantly contributed to forensic anthropology and crime scene technology. When
police investigate a crime scene where skeletal remains are located, extreme caution

FIGURE 10-2   Skull of Murder Victim

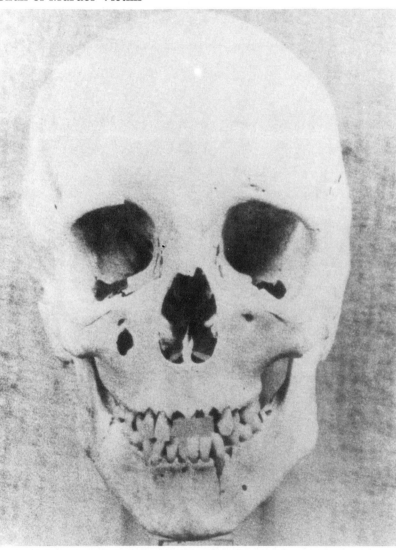

Courtesy Donald G. Cherry and J. Lawrence Angel, "Personality Reconstruction from Unidentified Remains," in *FBI Law Enforcement Bulletin*, August 1977, Vol. 46, No. 8, pp. 14 and 15

should be exercised in the search. Because animals may have disturbed parts of the body, the search should be conducted over a fairly large area. It may be significant to know that dogs, coyotes, or hogs consume bones; rodents gnaw or nibble on skeletal remains. Although murderers may scatter or burn parts of victims, enough bone fragments may

FIGURE 10-3   **Police Artist Sketch Based on Information Provided by the Physical Anthropologist**

Courtesy Donald G. Cherry and J. Lawrence Angel, "Personality Reconstruction from Unidentified Remains," in *FBI Law Enforcement Bulletin*, August 1977, Vol. 46, No. 8, pp. 14 and 15

FIGURE 10-4   Police Photograph of Victim

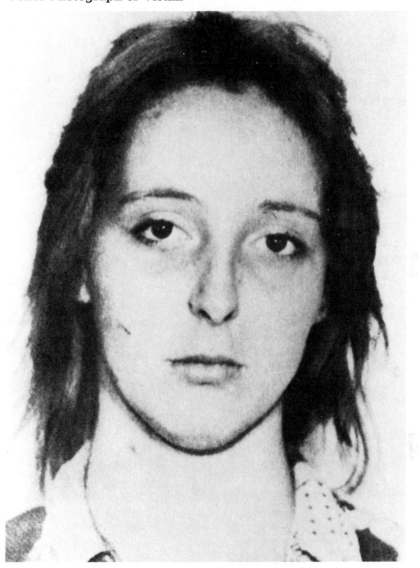

Courtesy Donald G. Cherry and J. Lawrence Angel, "Personality Reconstruction from Unidentified Remains," in *FBI Law Enforcement Bulletin,* August 1977, Vol. 46, No. 8, pp. 14 and 15

survive to be useful for identification. A victim's facial features, however, can be reconstructed only when the skull is virtually complete, with lower jaw and teeth.

Depending on the composition of the ground beneath the remains, there may be an outline of the body. If so, this area should be recorded with precise measurements and photographs, and if possible, plaster casts of the site should be considered. Through the use of such techniques, valuable clues to tissue thickness may be found, indicating whether the deceased was plump or thin. Clothing sizes are helpful, too. If a skeleton is situated on an incline, a very careful search should be conducted downhill from the original site because the action of rain, wind, animal activity, and even gravity may have caused some parts to separate from the main skeleton.

The skeletal remains themselves must, of course, be carefully measured and photographed. After the bones have been recovered, the ground under them should be sifted for additional bits of evidence.

The artistic team, having made a thorough analysis of all physical evidence, must then strive to recreate a living likeness.

The case described earlier provides an excellent example of what can be accomplished when the police artist, scientist, and investigator pool their talents to reconstruct a face, lifestyle, and personal history—a personality—from skeletal remains.

THE SEARCH FOR BURIED BODIES

The multitude of problems an investigator faces at the scene of a murder case is compounded when the victim has been buried.[13] These cases are not common, but they are common enough to warrant training in their proper handling.

PREPLANNING

One important facet of major case investigations is administrative preplanning, an area that is frequently and unfortunately neglected.

The case supervisor usually is confronted with a series of problems in the initial stage of the investigation, most of them requiring immediate decisions and actions. Often the result is confusion, which can hinder the successful completion of an investigation. However, on-scene confusion can be avoided by good planning of details from how to run a command post in a wooded area to establishing written policy dealing with written confessions.

DISCOVERY

Many buried bodies come to light accidentally. Occasionally, information is received that a body is buried at a particular location; these cases will be considered later.

The first duty of an officer responsible for such a case is to establish a list of priority items, despite pressures from both within and without the department. Officers should not allow themselves to be rushed or misdirected from orderly procedures. Upon notification of a body's discovery, efforts should be made to safeguard the entire scene before the arrival of law enforcement officials. Generally, a hunter, passer-by, or construction worker will find the buried body and notify a police agency. The entire area should be cordoned off, as with any scene, and access refused to *anyone* prior to the arrival of the investigator in charge, who can appraise the situation before any damage is done.

If the body has already been removed from the burial site, an archaeologist as well as a forensic pathologist and evidence technician should be called to the scene. This example of preplanning is critical: these experts should have been contacted previously and contingency plans formulated so they are on call when the need arises. Generally, these doctors look with enthusiasm toward such an opportunity, especially when the crime scene remains undisturbed.

The archaeologist is proficient in the careful and systematic excavation of a burial site. Most of the excavation phase of the investigation should be left to the archaeologist's direction, while others of the team assist as necessary.[14]

Forensic pathologists are the experts most familiar to law enforcement officers, and their work is becoming more prevalent throughout the country as a replacement for the coroner. They can provide valuable and impartial expertise when investigating the various forms of death.

Unless some extremely unusual circumstances exist, there is generally no need to hurry at this stage. If, for example, the weather is inclement, guards should be posted about the area until the weather improves. If there is need for immediate excavation, the erection of a tent over the site should be adequate. (This item should be included in preplanning equipment.) The same rule would apply during hours of darkness. Nothing is to be gained, and all may be lost by a premature excavation. After the area is secured, all team members assembled, and plans completed, the actual work may commence. The golden rule of homicide investigation—Never move, touch, or alter anything until it has been noted, sketched, and photographed—is especially applicable in this type of case.

Prior to a thorough search and processing of the area, the entire site should be mapped. Then the search may continue, both visually and with mechanical assistance (metal detectors, and the like), and any items noted, sketched, and photographed.

Photographs should be taken of the entire area, including aerial views if possible. The team can then move in slowly to the actual site. Photographs, both black and white and color, are to be taken at intervals up to and including the actual burial site. If possible, as with any discovered body, determine the path taken to the site by the finding party, mark it, and then use *only* this way in for the initial investigation in order to preserve as much of the general area as possible. The photographer should be accompanied by the crime scene technician or investigator, who can note and preserve any item of evidentiary nature on the way to the site—tire tracks, articles of clothing, possible weapons, or anything that might possibly be connected to the crime.

Photographs should not include any persons standing around the scene or any items not originally located there. At the same time, any item of evidence that has been moved, even accidentally, must never be replaced for purposes of photographing. It can never be put back exactly as found, and the fact that it was moved and replaced for photographing could be damaging in subsequent court testimony. Items should be photographed with and without identifying numbers, a scale, and an arrow pointing to magnetic north.

The definition of *site* is important in the buried body case. When a grave is dug and the excavated soil is placed near the grave, the surface of the soil is disturbed, so that the grave site is considered to be the entire disturbed area. If an average-size body had been buried, the entire site of grave and disturbed section would easily measure six feet wide and eight feet long. The depth of the excavation generally depends on soil composition and the amount of time the subject spent burying the body.

When the excavated soil is placed on the surface, vegetation may be compressed or broken off. When the grave is refilled, some

FIGURE 10-5   Site Prior to Excavation

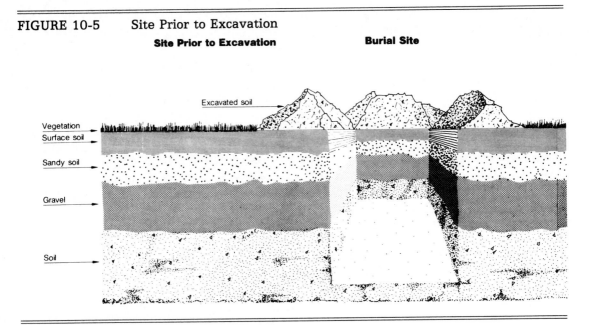

Site Prior to Excavation   **Burial Site**

Excavated soil

Vegetation
Surface soil

Sandy soil

Gravel

Soil

of this surface vegetation goes back into the grave (see Figure 10-5). Here another expert may be of value—the botanist—who can estimate when the vegetation was damaged by observing the height, distribution, and depth of root systems. If a botanist is not available, measurements and samples should be taken for later study. Damage done by digging and refilling a grave may be visible and measurable for years. If any dead insects are recovered from the grave, an entomologist may give information about them. (An expanded discussion of the role of the entomologist is discussed later in this chapter.)

EXCAVATION

The surface of the grave should now be carefully cleared of extraneous material with a flat-bladed spade or hand trowel so that the boundary of the actual grave may be visible.

Then the dimensions should be recorded on the map and excavation begun.

Extreme care should be taken to preserve the exact limits of the original grave or the undisturbed remains, if part of the site has been damaged during the discovery. When the soil was originally removed and then thrown back into the grave, the various layers and compositions of soil and vegetation may have become mixed or mottled. Slow and careful removal of this material may reveal the tool marks made on the outside edges; it may even show the type of blade involved, whether curved or straight, with enough definitions to make tool mark identification later on.

Before actual excavation and after the photographs have been taken of the burial site in its original condition, additional maps should be made of the site to show both plane and elevation views of the grave and to tie in

FIGURE 10-5   Site Prior to Excavation *(continued)*
Refilled Site

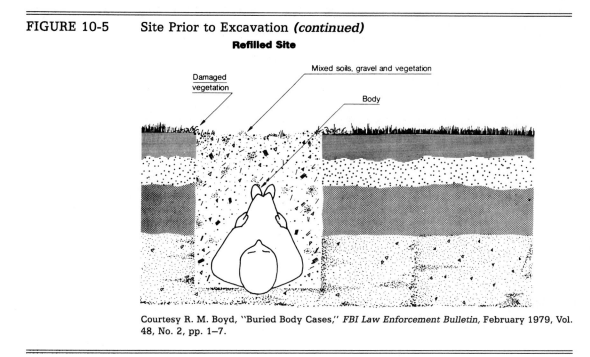

Courtesy R. M. Boyd, "Buried Body Cases," *FBI Law Enforcement Bulletin,* February 1979, Vol. 48, No. 2, pp. 1–7.

items found both by horizontal location and depth (see Figures 10-6 and 10-7). Expert help may be available through a county or state highway department engineer or surveyor, who would have the tools necessary to do the job properly. (Items such as a compass, plumb bob, string, protractor, and string level are necessities.)

The soil should be removed in even layers of 4 to 6 inches and all material sifted through two screens. The first screen should have quarter-inch mesh; the second should be standard window screen. As items are located and recovered, they should be plotted on the elevation or side view of the drawings. The completed drawing then accurately reflects the various vertical levels of items in the grave, and the plane view indicates their horizontal distances apart. For comparison, soil samples should be taken where each item is recovered, and each should be accurately

documented. Recovered items may still bear latent fingerprints.

THE BODY

When the body is uncovered and has tissue remaining on it, the forensic pathologist may make an on-scene cursory examination. When this examination is completed and photographs taken, a freshly laundered or new sheet should be available and the remains carefully placed in it so as to preserve any evidence not immediately visible but which might be lost in transit. Next the sheet's edges should be folded over and placed with the remains in a body bag or container for removal to a proper place of autopsy. The sheet and physical evidence are separately marked for identification and carefully packaged.

After removal of the body, the grave should

FIGURE 10-6   Plan View of Site

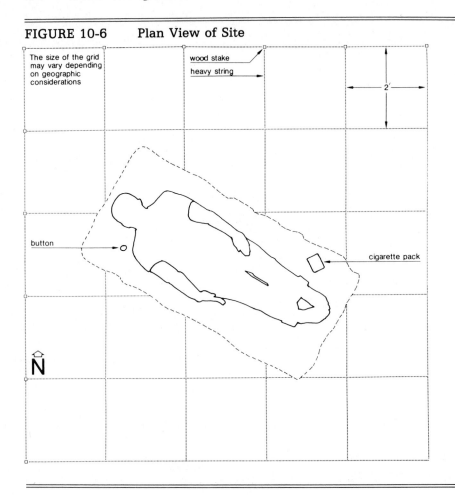

The size of the grid may vary depending on geographic considerations

wood stake

heavy string

2′

button

cigarette pack

N̂

Illustration of lanes laid out in north-south direction.

Then a cross-grid is laid out when body is located.

Smaller grids may be used when small objects are found in the grave.

Courtesy R. M. Boyd, "Buried Body Cases," *FBI Law Enforcement Bulletin,* February 1979, Vol. 48, No. 2, pp. 1–7.

FIGURE 10-7   Elevation View of Site

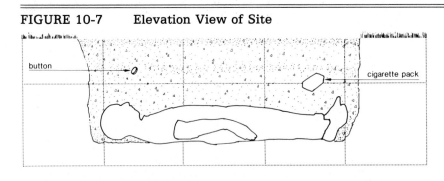

button

cigarette pack

Photograph items of evidence with ruler and north indicator.

Courtesy R. M. Boyd, "Buried Body Cases," *FBI Law Enforcement Bulletin,* February 1979, Vol. 48, No. 2, pp. 1–7.

again be photographed and the area under the body carefully searched and excavated to a depth of several more inches. A metal detector is useful if bullets were fired into the body after it was placed in the grave or to find other metal objects.

SEARCH FOR A BURIED BODY

In some cases, information is received through an informant, citizen, or through a confession that a body has been buried, and an approximate location is given. The grave site may be identified precisely or as in an area as small as a city lot or as large as several hundred acres. In either case, it is critical to establish security quickly around the entire suspected area to prevent access by unauthorized persons.

Good planning is vital. The more known about the circumstances of the crime and burial, the greater the chances for locating the site. For example, if it is known or believed the victim was killed and then buried elsewhere, the grave may not be too far from a road. However, if the killing was alleged to have taken place at the site, then the victim could have been made to walk a considerable distance. The time since the killing affects vegetation around the site and the grave itself; the grave may have sunk, or the surplus dirt may still be in a mound. A botanist can give approximations on damaged plant life that started growing again. Areas of sparse vegetation offer little to go on. Buried insects may be useful. When the surface has been cultivated, the only remaining visual indicator of a grave may be a depression in the surface.

An aircraft, especially a helicopter, may be used before a foot search to spot soil or vegetation disturbance. Thermal infrared photography may be of help. Infrared film detects heat, and a decomposing body emits heat. However, very soon and very long after a body has been buried heat is not generated, and nothing will show on infrared film. Aerial photographs should be taken of the area before a search and, if the search is successful, after it.

When it becomes necessary to conduct a foot search in a suspected area, mechanical aids become essential, especially if a visual search has been negative. Probing is the first step. Before probing begins, the coordinator of the search must formulate the plans carefully by having a map of the area, making a grid overlay tied into known landmarks, and preparing lanes with stakes and string for the searchers. In areas of woods or heavy underbrush, the establishing of grids is more difficult, and the case coordinator will have to be especially watchful to ensure that locations are checked properly. The area should be probed in not more than two-foot squares and in a staggered pattern. Coordinators must also keep their maps posted on the search area that has been completed. As probing is difficult and requires the use of generally unused muscles, care should be taken to plan for shifts of searchers and frequent rest periods.

Probing is done with a steel rod, preferably stainless steel, approximately five-sixteenths of an inch in diameter and four and one half to five feet long. A "tee" handle is welded to one end; the other end is sharply pointed. Probing works by detecting differences in disturbed and undisturbed subsurface soil. Investigators need to practice in the immediate area to get a feel for the soil.

When a soft spot is located, indicating a possible grave, the probe should be left in the ground, and no further probing done to the area. At that point a second mechanical aid is employed, an instrument to verify the presence of a body without the need of excavating. One such instrument, using methane gas as a primary source of verification, operates on the detection of hydrogen sulfide, hydrogen phosphide, carbon dioxide, ammonia, and methane gases formed by a decomposing body. The gas formation is minimal at low temperatures, 32 degrees to 35 degrees, but at these low temperatures the ground also would likely be frozen, and probing would not be attempted. At warmer temperatures, gas forms.

After a suspected site is located, a temperature-sensing probe is inserted and a reading taken to adjust the gas instrument to the correct sensitivity. Gases from a buried body penetrate the soil upward in a V-shape, with the greatest concentration directly over the body. A probe inserted beside a body or too deeply could therefore miss the gas area. Consequently, several probings are made at different depths to ensure complete coverage (see Figure 10-8). This probe can be an invaluable aid in checking suspected areas without an excavation at each one. It can also be used to check under concrete—roadways, patios, floors—after a small hole is drilled through the concrete. This instrument or one like it should be a part of a crime lab's equipment, especially where rural areas are included in the jurisdiction.

The discovery and excavation of a buried body tax abilities and patience and require firm control over the entire investigation. There is no place in these cases for the investigator who grandstands, lacks training, or is unaware of available resources. Expert help should be summoned if possible. Generally, delays in starting to process crime scenes in order to marshal necessary resources ensures more successful investigations.

It must be remembered that the ultimate goal is to recreate as accurately as possible the circumstances of the crime committed, identify and apprehend the perpetrator(s), and successfully guide the case through the criminal justice system.

POLICE RESPONSIBILITIES AT THE MORGUE

A number of tasks should be completed by law enforcement personnel at the morgue. The pathologist should be briefed on all pertinent information relative to the case. The body should be photographed before the removal of the victim's clothing. The sheets or blanket used in covering the victim's body should be considered potentially valuable physical evidence, especially if trace evidence from the victim may be adhering to it. If this possibility does exist, then the item should be handled with extreme care to avoid the loss of evidence. After the victim's clothing is removed, each item should be properly tagged and packaged separately in appropriate containers, such as plain brown paper bags. At one time, clear plastic bags were widely used for packaging, but their heat retention and air tightness sometimes caused mold and bacteria to grow on the garments, interfering with efforts to identify and classify blood and other body fluids.

ESTIMATING TIME OF DEATH

The ultimate responsibility for estimating the victim's time of death lies with the medical examiner. One indicator used for this estimate is loss of body heat. The normal body temperature of human beings is a constant 98.6 degrees; this temperature remains constant except in cases of illness. After death the rate at which the body cools depends on variables such as air temperature, air currents, body size, amount of clothing, surface on which the body has lain, and body temperature at the time of death.

The medical examiner usually obtains the body temperature rectally or by cutting an incision in the abdomen and placing the ther-

FIGURE 10-8   Vapor Detector

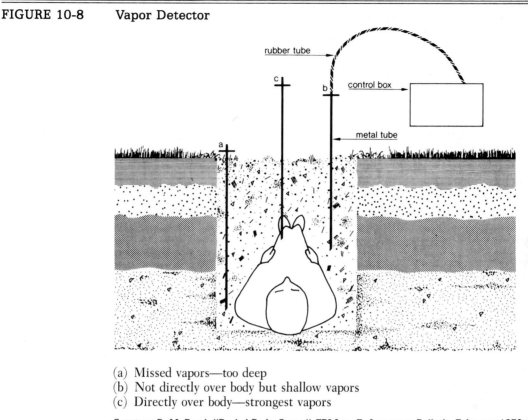

(a) Missed vapors—too deep
(b) Not directly over body but shallow vapors
(c) Directly over body—strongest vapors

Courtesy R. M. Boyd, "Buried Body Cases," *FBI Law Enforcement Bulletin,* February 1979, Vol. 48, No. 2, pp. 1–7.

mometer in the liver. The average loss of body heat in an environment of 70 degrees is 1.5 degrees per hour.[15]

RIGOR MORTIS

Rigor mortis is a general stiffening of the body muscles caused by significant changes in the post-mortem chemical composition of the muscle tissue.[16]

The time of onset varies considerably with atmospheric temperature, humidity, and movement of air around the body. Authorities vary in their pronouncements as to the usual timetable of appearance and disappearance of rigor, but all agree that so many variables are present that a firm timetable cannot be established. However, there are some broad time frames with which most authorities tend to agree. For example, there is general agreement that rigor mortis begins within two to seven hours after death; that the entire body is affected within ten to 18 hours; and that rigor mortis most often disappears within 24 to 36 hours. Because of differential muscle mass, rigor mortis appears to afflict the smaller muscles first. Smaller muscle masses freeze up faster and therefore relax faster after the rigor has passed. Larger muscle masses, such as in the upper arms and upper legs, take longer to develop and relax from rigor. This phenomenon explains why it is sometimes said that rigor begins in the upper parts of the body (smaller muscles at the head and neck) and exits at the lower parts of the body. However, the fact remains that if there is rigor in the fingers, the toes are also generally stiff.[17]

Conditions at the time of death may accelerate the onset of rigor. Some of these are: violent exertion shortly before death; surroundings of moist heat; death by convulsant poisons; septicemia, wasting diseases or enfeeblement; violent deaths, such as throat cutting or electrocution; poisoning by alkaloids; and heatstroke. The greater muscle mass in the more developed person requires a longer time for the entire muscle to be affected.[18]

POSTMORTEM LIVIDITY

A purplish color that appears under the skin on those portions of the body closest to the ground denotes *postmortem lividity*. The discoloration is caused by the settling of the blood. It may begin as early as one half hour after death and is pronounced four hours after death. The officer who is unfamiliar with this condition could erroneously conclude that the discoloration resulted from an assault. However, there are certain differences between the discoloration caused by lividity and that caused by bruising; a bruise may have swelling or abrasions around the wound, whereas lividity does not; the coloring of bruises may vary, being black, blue, yellowish-green, and so forth, but lividity color remains uniform; and finally, bruises may appear on numerous parts of the body, while lividity appears only on the portions of the body closest to the ground, unless the body was moved before the blood completely clotted.

Postmortem lividity is extremely important for three reasons: 1. When considered with other factors, it may help estimate the time of death. 2. Because the skin must be relaxed and not lying flush against any surface, object, or even clothing folds for the lividity coloration to develop, it may indicate whether the body has been moved or even slightly disturbed after death. It is for this reason that exact measurements, sketches, and photographs must be made at the scene before and as a body is being recovered. 3. The actual coloration of the skin may indicate the cause of death, as in the case of carbon monoxide poisoning, certain forms of cyanide poisoning, or extreme cold, when the color of the lividity is not purplish, but a cherry red color.[19]

The following case illustrates that in some instances lividity and rigor mortis can provide valuable clues in determining if a body has been moved after death.

A young woman failed to report to work one morning, and a female coworker and close friend became concerned after telephoning the victim's home and receiving no answer. The friend left work and went directly to the victim's apartment. She knocked on the door several times, and when no one answered she tried the doorknob and discovered that the door was unlocked. She entered the apartment, went through the living room, and into the bedroom, where she discovered the victim clad in her nightgown lying in bed on her back. She tried to revive the victim but couldn't. She then called for the police and an ambulance. When the medical personnel arrived, they examined the victim and pronounced her dead. There were no signs of foul play but the police did discover some barbiturates on the nightstand and suspected, quite correctly as it turned out, that the victim had died of an overdose of drugs. There was a small amount of blood approximately two inches in diameter on the

FIGURE 10-9

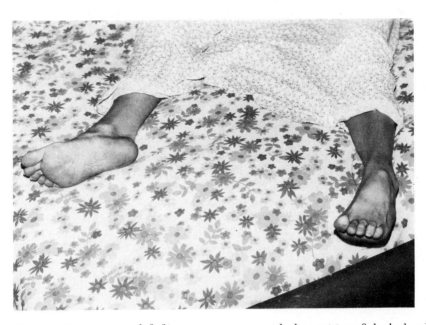

Rigor mortis pattern in left foot not consistent with the position of the body when discovered.

Courtesy Leon County Sheriff's Department, Tallahassee, Florida

front of the victim's nightgown in the pubic area, and as would later be determined, it was blood from her menstrual period.

The body was removed and taken to the morgue where a visual examination revealed the presence of postmortem lividity on the front and back of the victim's body. In addition, rigor mortis had begun and the victim's left foot was extending straight out (see Figure 10-9). The position of the foot was not consistent with the rigor mortis patterns that would normally result when someone was lying on her back but rather would be consistent with someone who was lying on her stomach. These inconsistencies along with the presence of the menstrual blood on the front of the victim's nightgown rather than on the back strongly suggested that

the victim had likely been lying face down for several hours after death and that someone had moved the body.

The autopsy revealed no signs of foul play, however, semen was found in the victim's vagina. The cause of death was determined to be from an overdose of drugs.

The subsequent investigation and interviews of her friends revealed that the victim was last seen alive in a nearby bar the evening before. She was drinking quite heavily and was also taking some barbiturates. During the course of the evening she met a man who bought her several drinks. Around midnight she left the bar with the male companion. The witnesses who were at the bar were able to provide the police with the name and address of the man. The male companion, who was married, provided the police with the following information.

After leaving the bar, he and the woman had gone directly to her apartment. They went to her bedroom, disrobed, and had sexual intercourse in her bed. The man fell asleep and was awakened when the alarm clock went off at 7:30 A.M. When he woke up, the woman was lying face down on the floor next to the bed in her nightgown. He picked her up and put her back in bed. When he realized that she was dead, he became frightened, got dressed, and left the apartment.

The fact that this woman's body was moved is really inconsequential in this specific case, but in other instances the knowledge that a body was moved, especially from one location to another, can be profoundly important. This is so because important physical evidence may be available at the first location which is totally absent from the second location. On occasion, postmortem conditions may provide important clues to determine if in fact the body was moved after death.

CADAVERIC SPASM

Although firm statements are frequently made concerning the instantaneous tightening of an extremity or other part of the body at the time of death (commonly called a "death grip"), there seems to be a general failure to explain its mechanism. The literature typically describes a decedent's hand tightly clutching a weapon, usually a gun or knife, as occurring at the moment of death. However, the actual cases of cadaveric spasm are few and far between. To date, the precise physiologic mechanism of "cadaveric spasm" remains unknown.[20]

PUTREFACTION

The rate at which a body decomposes depends to a great extent on moisture, air temperature, the body's own bacteria and enzymes, and insects. There tends to be agreement that for every 10-degree rise in temperature, the speed of the chemical reaction is doubled. The early signs of putrefaction are a greenish discoloration of the abdomen and external genitals, darkening of the entire body until it turns completely black or brown, thickening of the features, liquid and gas blisters on the skin, and an unpleasant odor. The stomach contents may be forced through the mouth.[21]

DETERMINATION OF TIME OF DEATH BY MEANS OF CARRION INSECTS

The entomologist can help in estimating the time of death by examining the various carrion insects, because different carrion insects successfully attack the body at various stages of decomposition and under certain environmental conditions.[22]

The following case illustrates how a qualified entomologist can assist investigations in death cases.

> Dr. Bernard Greenberg, of the University of Illinois (Chicago), helped to solve a double murder that had occurred in the basement of an apartment house. The only evidence he had to work with was a photograph of the bodies at the scene. He examined the photograph, which clearly depicted the advanced pupae (the developmental stage immediately after full maturity), under a microscope. He then obtained National Weather Service Information for the period when the murders took place and determined how long it would have taken the flies to develop to the stage shown in the photograph. His estimate of the time of death came within two days of the actual murders, and this evidence linked the suspect to the murders. The suspect was eventually convicted.

Collection of Carrion Insects from a Clothed and Decomposing Body. When an entomologist is to assist, the investigator must, before examining the body, take several photographs of the body, including close-ups of the areas of insect activity. Then the investigator should record the present air temperature, relative humidity, and environmental setting (shaded wooded area, open field, and the like).

Collection of the insects should begin in the facial area of the decomposing body, because it is the first to undergo degradation by insects. Only an open wound attracts insects more readily. The investigator must be sure to collect as many different insect forms as possible and all life stages (egg, larvae, pupae, and adult).

If time or other complications limit insect collection, the investigator should collect at least fly larvae. With fly larvae the largest specimens should be obtained, because they represent the earliest attacking insects. Examination of the folds in the clothing and underlying soil for pupating larvae or pupae cases is very important. If there is no evidence of hatched pupae cases, one may assume that the fly larvae collected represent the first life cycle.

Collected insect specimens should be placed in a container of preservative solution of 85 percent alcohol. Duplicate samples should be placed in aerated containers with small amounts of soil. Each specimen container should be labeled with the date, time, and area of the body from which it was collected.

As the clothing is removed from the body, many more insects are observable. Efforts should be made to collect samples from within the folds of the clothing. If the decomposed body has been placed in a disaster bag and transported to a morgue, insects still can be easily collected. Some insects drop off the body before it is placed in the disaster bag, but most continue feeding on the body. Upon opening the disaster bag, the investigator will observe many beetle forms. The darkness in the disaster bag causes the fly larvae to migrate into the various body orifices and the beetles to surface from the clothing and body orifices. The same procedure as described above for collecting insects should be followed after the body is removed from the disaster bag. (See Figure 10-10 for areas of the body to collect insects.)

After a complete examination of the body, collected insects should be taken immediately to an entomologist for identification and determination of how long the insects have been feeding on the human remains.

Collection of Carrion Insects from Human Skeletal Remains. As a body decomposes, it is attacked by many insect forms. Most belong to the insect orders Diptera (flies) and Coleoptera (beetles). These insects feed on decomposing tissue or on other carrion insects.

Some of the carrion insects that attack a body shortly after death themselves die after laying eggs or after being caught in the viscous and putrefying liquids of the decaying corpse. The insect remains (exoskeletons) of these insects, however, remain intact for long periods in the many skeletal cavities or underlying soil. Close examination of the cavities of a skeleton (before it is removed from the crime scene) usually produces numerous insect remains.

The best area to find these remains is the skull, particularly inside the cranial vault (see Figure 10-11). The examination can begin when the skull is placed carefully on a white sheet or on a large piece of paper. Then with forceps and a penlight, the investigator probes the eye orbits, nasal opening, and external auditory meatus for insect remains. The remains most commonly belong to carrion and rove beetles and blow flies. Sometimes the remains are obscured by mud or dried debris within the skull. In this case, the skull should be carefully placed into a plastic bag to avoid the loss of any insect remains. Later the skull should be removed from the bag and washed over a fine screen

FIGURE 10-10   Body Areas from which to Collect Insects

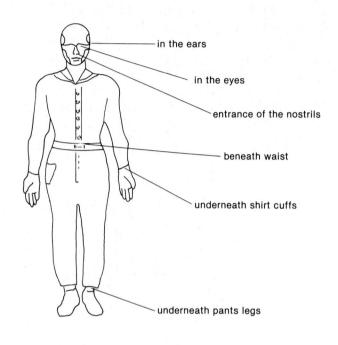

in the ears

in the eyes

entrance of the nostrils

beneath waist

underneath shirt cuffs

underneath pants legs

tray. The mud and debris along with the insect remains will become separated and caught on the screen. After recovery of the insect remains, they should be air dried, placed in cotton in a small container, and taken to an entomologist for identification. The entomologist can also provide information on the developmental timing of the insects, from which can be inferred a fairly accurate estimation of time since death.

In certain instances, when a consulting entomologist is not available, an investigator must rely on taxonomic and entomological texts for identification of the insect remains. Many states publish entomological bulletins with good information on seasonality, developmental rates, and geographical ranges.

Entomologists may also be able to assist investigators in other types of criminal investigations. The following case illustrates this:

In a case referred to as the "Cocklebur Caper," a woman was raped near her apartment by a man wearing a ski mask. Investigators found such a mask in the apartment of a suspect who said he had not worn it since the previous winter. A small cocklebur was embedded in the mask, and inside it was a beetle. It was determined that a beetle larva in the cocklebur could not possibly have survived from the previous winter, and therefore the mask had been worn outside during the current summer. The cocklebur was

FIGURE 10-11   Areas of Skeleton Most Likely to Harbor Insects

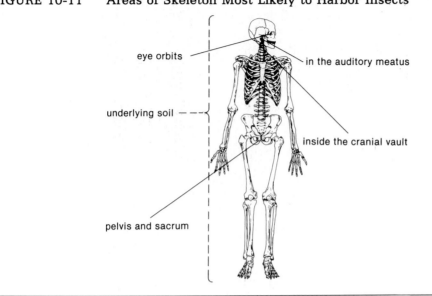

eye orbits

in the auditory meatus

underlying soil

inside the cranial vault

pelvis and sacrum

of the same species as others found near the rape scene. The suspect was ultimately convicted of the rape.

EVIDENCE FROM WOUNDS

A basic knowledge of wounds is of great assistance to officers who are responsible for injury and death investigations. It helps them reach preliminary conclusions. The five most common types of wounds encountered by police officers in injury and death investigations are: gunshot wounds, incised wounds, stab wounds, puncture wounds, and lacerations.

GUNSHOT WOUNDS

A variety of factors affect the type of wound inflicted from a firearm, such as the caliber of the firearm, the distance between the victim and the firearm, and whether the bullet first ricocheted off some object before striking the victim.

ENTRY AND EXIT WOUNDS

Whether a gunshot wound is an entry or exit wound can be a paramount consideration in determining whether or not a death was accidental, homicidal, or suicidal. The medical examiner makes the final determination, but if he or she does not come to the scene, then the officer at the scene has to make a preliminary determination so that the investigation may proceed.

The typical gunshot entry wound has certain characteristics. The wound is ordinarily smaller in diameter than the projectile causing the wound because the elastic quality of the skin causes it to expand as the projectile passes through and to contract afterwards. There is generally not a great deal of bleeding from the entry wound. The wound frequently has a gray ring around it, particularly if inflicted at close range (see Figure 10-12).

FIGURE 10-12   Pistol Gunshot Wound

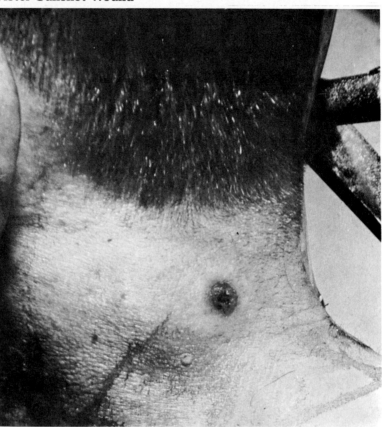

Note the gray ring around the wound, typical of gunshot entry wounds inflicted at close range.

Courtesy Kentucky State Police Department

The ring results from the residual gunpowder being deposited around the wound and is referred to as *smudging*. This deposit can be wiped away. However, in some cases where the firearm is discharged at close range, the flesh around the wound may actually have been burned by the heated gunpowder. This burning is called *tattooing* and cannot be wiped away. The extent of both tattooing and smudging depends in part on the distance from which the weapon was fired and the amount of clothing the victim was wearing. If a person is shot in an unclothed portion of the body at close range, 18 inches or less, there often is both tattooing and smudging. If the victim is struck in a portion of the body that was clothed, then much of the expended powder is absorbed by the clothing. However, even in such situations there may still be an even gray ring around the wound because, as the projectile passes through the outer layer of clothing, some of the gunpowder and grime deposited on it are rubbed off by the skin.

The presence or absence of powder burns is especially significant in investigations involving serious questions about whether the death is a suicide or homicide. Close and careful examination of these markings around the wound may indicate the distance from which the firearm was discharged. The laboratory may also be able to provide supporting data by conducting a series of test shots at varying distances with the recovered firearm to establish the powder pattern.

CONTACT ENTRY WOUNDS

The contact entry wound typically is much larger than the noncontact entry wound and results when the firearm is held against the body, usually the head, and fired. See Figs. 10-13 and 10-14. It is commonly found in both suicides and execution murders. The officer unfamiliar with such wounds might mistake a self-inflicted wound for a homicidal wound, because the contact entry wound might seem to have been made by a larger caliber firearm than the one found at the scene. The larger size of the contact wound is caused in part by the gases released when the weapon is discharged. In noncontact entry wounds the gases dissipate into the atmosphere, whereas in a contact wound the gases cannot escape. Thus as the projectile enters the body, the gases enter, too. In head wounds, the gases quickly build up between the scalp and the skull, with the flesh of the scalp bursting outward, leaving a gaping hole. Such wounds are not always found in self-inflicted gunshot wounds, because the end of the barrel may not have been held firmly against the head.

GUNSHOT EXIT WOUNDS

Gunshot exit wounds also have distinct characteristics. They are frequently larger than entry wounds, bleed freely, are irregular in shape, and occur most commonly when the ammunition used is of a high-velocity, metal-jacket type or when the projectile strikes a limb or a glancing blow.

SHOTGUN WOUNDS

A shotgun is a smooth-bore, shoulder-fired firearm and is usually used to fire multiple pellets, rather than a single slug. The most common gauges with their corresponding bore diameters are:[23]

Gauge	Diameter (Inches)
12	.729
16	.662
20	.615
410	.410

The pellets fired range in size from .08 inches for No. 9 shot to .33 inches for 00 Buck. A "wad," which may be either paper or plastic, lies in between the shot pellets and the powder. Most modern shells use plastic wads. A shotgun shell can contain anywhere from a couple of hundred pellets, to nine for 00 Buck, or one large lead slug.

ENTRANCE WOUNDS

From contact to 12 inches, there is a single round entrance three fourths to one inch in diameter. The edge of the wound shows an abrasion ring. As the distance between muzzle and skin increases, powder tattooing appears. Powder blackening is most prominent at less than 12 inches. Powder tattooing is considerably less dense than in pistol wounds (see Figure 10-15).

When discharged at from between three and six feet of range, the single entrance wound widens to one and one-half to two inches in diameter and shows "scalloping" of the edges. At about six feet, the pellets begin to separate from the main mass of pellets.

FIGURE 10-13   Contact Bullet Wound

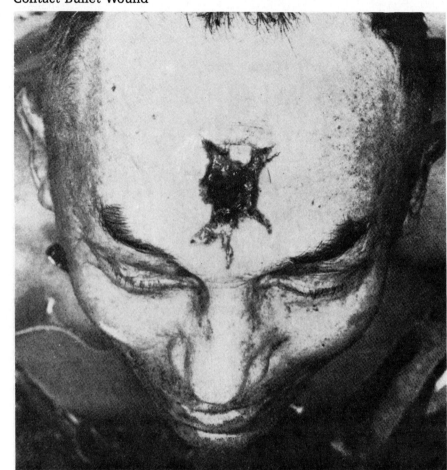

Homicidal contact bullet wound of forehead. Notice the charring of the edges and the star-shaped tears of the skin due to undermining of the scalp.

Courtesy Santa Ana, California, Police Department.

Beyond ten to 12 feet, there is great variation in the spread of the pellets.

THE WAD

At close ranges, the wad will be propelled into the body through the large single en-trance wound. Beyond ten to 15 feet, the wad will have separated from the pellets and will not enter. However, it may mark the body. The gauge of the shotgun and the size of the pellets can be obtained from the wad and pellets, respectively. On occasion, a plas-tic wad may be marked by the choke or ir-

FIGURE 10-14

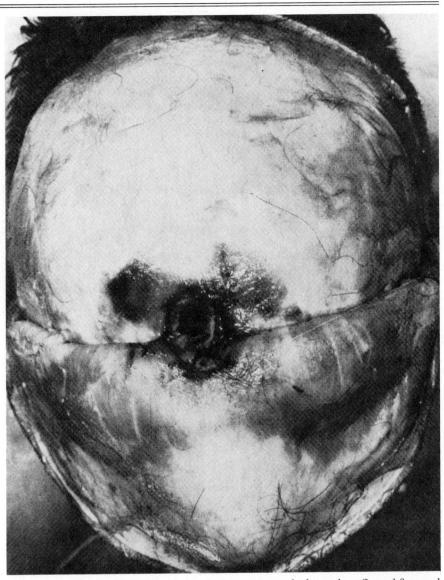

The same bullet wound as shown in Figure 10-13 with the scalp reflected forward over the face. Notice how the blast has undermined the scalp, singeing and blackening the surface of the skull.

Courtesy Santa Ana, California Police Department.

FIGURE 10-15   Close Range Wound from a 12-Gauge Shotgun

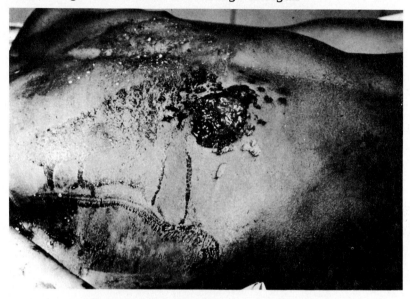

regularities at the end of the barrel, making ballistic comparison possible.

RANGE DETERMINATION

Range determinations can be made later if the size of the shotgun pattern was described at autopsy and duplicated on paper. The same weapon with the same type of ammunition must be used in duplication of the pattern if accurate results are desired. Range formulae do *not* work.

X-ray patterns of the shot in the body are useless for range determinations as are patterns on the body in which the shot first struck the target.

The size of the shot pattern on the body depends primarily on the choke of the gun. The type of ammunition and barrel length are secondary factors. The size of the pellet pattern is independent of the gauge of the shotgun and an increase in gauge just increases the density of the pattern.

EXIT WOUNDS

Shotgun pellets very rarely exit except when used as instruments of suicide in the region of the head.

FIREARM RESIDUES

Detecting firearm residues on the hands of an individual may be of great importance in evaluating deaths due to gunshot wounds. Detection of such residues on the hands of a deceased individual is often confirmatory evidence of a suspected suicide.[24]

One of the earliest methods of determining whether an individual discharged a weapon, the paraffin test or dermal nitrate test, was based on the detection of nitrates on the surfaces of the hands. Paraffin was employed for the removal of powder residues from the hands. Diphenylamine was the reagent used to detect the nitrates picked up by the paraffin. This test is no longer considered valid, because no distinction can be made between nitrates of gunpowder origin and those from other sources, which are quite commonly encountered in day-to-day living.

In 1959 Harrison and Gilroy developed a series of chemical spot tests for detection of metallic components of firearm discharge residues. Such metallic substances mainly originate from the primer, though they can also come from the bullet or cartridge case. Spot tests were developed for the presence of antimony, barium, and lead, substances found in most primers. These tests are inconclusive, because they are essentially qualitative rather than quantitative.[25]

The concept of detecting metallic primer components led to more sophisticated approaches now in general use. Compounds of antimony, barium, and lead are used in modern noncorrosive primers. When a handgun is discharged, discrete particulate matter containing these elements is deposited on the thumb, forefinger, and connecting web (the back of the hand holding the weapon). The metallic compounds are removed from the hand, either with paraffin or, more commonly, with cotton swabs saturated with a dilute solution of acid. This material is then submitted for analysis.

ATOMIC ABSORPTION ANALYSIS AND NEUTRON ACTIVATION ANALYSIS

Discussed in a more general context in Chapter 9, the two methods for the detection of firearm discharge residue which have received the greatest attention in recent years are atomic absorption analysis and neutron activation analysis. However, atomic absorption analysis has emerged as the test of choice, in part because the necessary equipment is less expensive. Most modern crime laboratories now offer atomic absorption analysis. Both methods of analysis have been employed to detect the trace elements of antimony and barium deposited on the hands

when a gun is discharged. Atomic absorption analysis, however, is also able to detect lead deposits in gunshot residue, thus giving it one more advantage over neutron activation analysis.[26]

REMOVAL OF GUNSHOT RESIDUE

Whatever the system of analysis to which the pathologist has access, the procedures for removal of firearm discharge residues from the hand are the same. The solution most commonly used is of dilute acid. Four cotton swabs are used to remove the firearm discharge residues from the hands. Two swabs are used on each hand; one for the palm, the other for the "back" of the hand. The swabs of the nonfiring hand and the palm of the hand suspected of discharging the weapon act as controls. A control swab dipped in the acid also should be submitted as a blank. Cotton swabs with plastic shafts should be used. Those with wood shafts should not be used because the wood may be contaminated with metallic elements. Because wood shows great variation in the concentration of such elements, no blank can be used.

If a person has discharged the handgun, firearm discharge residues should appear only on the back of the hand that fired the weapon, not on the palm of that hand or on the other hand. Some people, because of their occupations, may have high levels of barium, antimony, or lead on their hands. Thus if the back of the hand were the only area submitted for examination, a misleadingly positive report would come back. If analysis reveals firearm discharge residues only on the palms, it strongly suggests that the individual's hands were around the weapon at the time of the discharge or were trying to ward off the weapon.

It must be realized that determining whether an individual fired a gun cannot be based on absolute quantities of primer residue on the hands. Rather, it is based on contrast of the levels of these compounds from right to left and from palm to back.

═ INCISED AND STAB WOUNDS ═

The incised wound—more commonly referred to as the cutting wound—is inflicted with a sharp-edged instrument such as a knife or razor. The weapon typically employed in inflicting both incised and stab wounds is a pocket knife, although kitchen knives are also common. In comparison with shootings, fewer cutting assaults result in death, largely because the perpetrator's intention was to injure or disfigure, rather than kill the victim. Cutting wounds are often found on the arms, face, and legs. Even in these "friendly" cuttings, as they are sometimes referred to, death may occur. When the victim does die from a cutting wound, it generally is found around the throat. The severity of most incised wounds is directly related to the shape and sharpness of the weapon, the part of the body being cut, and the amount of force used in striking the victim. The incised wound is typically narrow at the edges and gaping at the center, with considerable bleeding. The inexperienced investigator may conclude that a gaping incised wound was inflicted by a large cutting instrument. However, a small knife with a honed blade is capable of causing very severe wounds.

Most frequently, death is caused after a stab results in severe damage to a vital organ, internal bleeding, shock, or fatal secondary infections which develop several days after the attack. Any of these factors may itself be fatal; they often occur in combination. The shape, size, and keenness of the blade all determine a wound's shape and depth as is the manner in which the knife is thrust into and pulled out of the body. One noticeable aspect of multiple stab wounds is their different shapes when made with the same

knife. The proximity of the wounds in a multiple stabbing assault may be helpful in determining the actions of the victim prior to death. If the wounds are concentrated within a small region of the body, then there is a good possibility that the victim was immobilized at the time of the assault, that is, held down, asleep, or intoxicated.

CHARACTERISTICS OF PUNCTURE ═ WOUNDS ═

The weapon most frequently used in assaults resulting in puncture wounds once was the ice pick. It is less common today. Leather punches and screwdrivers also are capable of producing puncture wounds, which are normally small and have little or no bleeding (see Figure 10-16). Such wounds can be easily overlooked, particularly if they are in hairy parts of the body. Infliction of a puncture wound produces death in the same way as do stab wounds.

═ LACERATIONS ═

When used in an assault, clubs, pipes, or other such blunt objects can produce open, irregularly shaped wounds termed *lacerations*. Such wounds bleed freely and characteristically are accompanied by bruising around the edges. There is no necessary relationship between the shape of the wound and that of the weapon employed. Occasionally, such force will be used in an attack that an impression of the weapon is left on the victim's skin. Most frequently, when death results from an assault in which lacerations were inflicted, the cause is severe head injuries. Laceration wounds may be inflicted accidentally as in the case of an intoxicated person who falls and strikes his head against a curb or step. In other instances, circumstances may appear more suspicious.

FIGURE 10-16   Victim of Multiple Ice Pick Stab Wounds

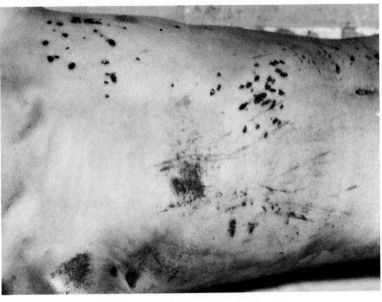

Checking the back doors of businesses at about 9:30 P.M., an officer found the proprietor of a jewelry store dead at the open rear entrance to his store. He had sustained a large laceration on his forehead and had bled considerably. It appeared that a murder had taken place during a robbery or burglary. Careful processing of the scene yielded traces of blood and one small skin fragment from the brick wall near the rear entrance.

Nothing was established as missing from the business. The medical examiner found the cause of death to be a heart attack. The head laceration contained minute traces of brick. Thus a reconstruction of events showed that as the owner was closing his business, he suffered a heart attack and convulsions, striking his head against the brick wall. The lacerations he suffered made it look as though he had suffered a fatal head wound.

DEFENSE WOUNDS

Defense wounds are suffered by victims attempting to protect themselves from an assault, often by a knife or club. These wounds are commonly found on the palms of the hands, the fingers, or the forearms (see Figure 10-17). In the most aggravated form, the defense wound may sever one or more fingers.

THE UNCOOPERATIVE VICTIM

Officers sometimes find victims uncooperative in identifying assailants and in providing details about offenses. When the victim is uncooperative, it is often for one of the following reasons:

- The assailant is a husband or boyfriend, wife or girlfriend whose arrest would undo

FIGURE 10-17   Defense Wounds

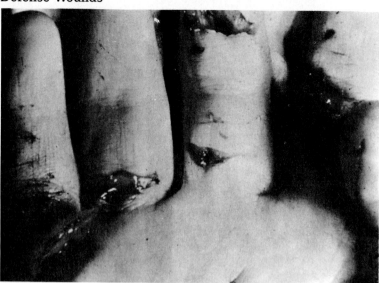

This victim received severe defense knife wounds on the hands while trying to stop his assailant from stabbing him to death.

an arrangement from which the victim benefits.

- The victim wants to settle the dispute personally.
- The victim believes that he or she deserved the assault and therefore does not want the assailant punished.
- The victim fears revenge if charges are pursued.

The uncooperative victim creates both legal and investigative difficulties. All states consider felony assaults to be crimes against the people of the state; thus the state is legally considered the aggrieved party. Technically, the victim has no legal right to decide whether the offense will or will not be prosecuted. This decision is the prosecutor's. However, many prosecutors are reluctant to

pursue the prosecution of a felony assault when the victim is going to be uncooperative, especially when the victim's injuries are not critical and when the parties involved are related. Because victims often do not know that the usual practice is not to prosecute such cases, victims may be uncooperative or even fabricate a story about how the offense occurred. The officer's dilemma is to get the uncooperative victim to provide facts about the crime. There are a number of ways in which this may be done, but they generally revolve around convincing the victim that no legal action will be taken against the assailant. The laws vary from state to state, but in many jurisdictions informal arrangements have been worked out between the prosecutor's office or the courts and the police department, and under carefully controlled conditions the police may be given authority to have the victim sign a complaint-withdrawal affidavit, which includes the following:

- The name of the assailant
- The victim's total satisfaction with the investigation by the police department
- The victim's desire not to have the state pursue prosecution

There are those who object to these practices because they believe that it tends to encourage assault offenses. They base their objection on the assumption that persons who commit assaults and are not punished will be encouraged to commit other assaults. Nevertheless, overcrowded court dockets and the difficulties associated with prosecuting cases with reluctant victims obviate any benefits that might derive from the full prosecution of such cases.

Many state and local governments provide statutes and ordinances which make it unlawful either to withhold information relating to a crime intentionally or to provide false and misleading information about it. The victim who is uncooperative or who is suspected of not being completely truthful should be advised of such laws and of the penalties associated with them.

Incapacity may also be the cause of noncooperation. If the victim is intoxicated at the time of the initial interview, then it may be necessary to wait until he or she is sober before continuing. Naturally, if the severity of the injury makes any delay in interviewing unwise, then the investigator must proceed with the interview, while recognizing the inherent limitations.

SUICIDE

For the investigator, a major concern in an apparent suicide case is to make certain that the death was self-induced and not the result of a homicide. In some cases, the investigator finds overwhelming evidence to this effect at the scene. In other cases, important information about the victim's behavior before death can be obtained from relatives, friends, coworkers, and employers. Suicide is often committed for the following reasons:

- Ill health or considerable pain
- Severe marital strife
- A recent emotionally damaging experience, such as an unhappy love affair, separation, or divorce
- Financial difficulties, including the threat of a much lower standard of living or failure to meet some significant and past-due financial commitments
- Perceived or actual humiliation
- Remorse over the loss of a loved one or over an act of the victim
- Revenge, a frequent motive for adolescents who have serious difficulties with parents and for spurned lovers[27]

These factors are far from all-inclusive, but the investigator will find a significant number of suicides associated with them. Conversely, if there is an apparent suicide and thorough scrutiny fails to produce a solid motive, then the investigator's suspicion should be thoroughly aroused. Thus, in all apparent suicides the possibility of a homicide should never be lightly discarded.

METHODS OF SUICIDE

Eight methods are most commonly employed in suicides: firearms, hanging, sleeping pills and other pharmaceuticals, drowning, cutting and piercing instruments, ingestion of poisons, gases, and jumping from high places.[28]

Although all of these can be stimulated in the commission of murders, there are important differences in physical evidence that distinguish suicides from murders.

SUICIDE BY GUNSHOT

It is sometimes difficult to determine whether a gunshot wound was self-inflicted or resulted from the actions of an assailant. However, there are certain indicators which may be helpful in reaching a conclusion. One of these is the location of the wound and the trajectory of the projectile upon entering the body. The most common method of committing suicide with a firearm involves the victim's placing a handgun to the temple and firing a shot into his or her head. Frequently, there is no exit wound, and it will be impossible for the investigator to determine the precise angle at which the projectile entered. This information is obtained during the autopsy, but it may be several days before it is performed. The investigator must therefore make some preliminary determination. The following case illustrates some of the points discussed thus far:

> A man telephoned the police hysterically, reporting that his wife had just shot and killed herself. When the police and an ambulance arrived, the victim was dead of a bullet wound in her upper left temple. The husband was holding the gun with which he alleged his wife had shot herself. He stated that he had arrived home from work just before the incident but that neither his wife nor their three preschool-age children had been there. His wife had arrived home a short while later, and she had been drinking heavily. When he questioned her about the whereabouts of their three children, she had told him they were at her mother's home. A heated argument then followed about her neglect of their children, her drinking, and her seeing other men. According to the husband, his wife then slapped him in his face, and he slapped her back. At that point, she walked over to a nearby desk drawer where he kept a revolver. She removed the revolver from the desk drawer, placed the barrel against her

head, fired a single shot, and fell to the floor. No one else was home at the time this incident occurred.

The following set of facts were revealed by the medical examiner's autopsy report:

- The bullet entered the upper left portion of the head, traveled downward through the brain, and continued downward through the victim's body, coming to rest in her chest.
- There were no powder burns present around the gunshot wound.
- Death occurred immediately.
- If the wound had been self-inflicted, the victim would have been holding the weapon in her left hand, at least two feet from her head, and had to have used her thumb to pull the trigger.

The relatives of both the victim and her husband provided the police with the following information.

- To their knowledge, the victim had not been despondent, nor had she ever previously attempted or discussed suicide.
- The victim and her husband had been having serious domestic difficulties because she was seeing other men, spending the house money on liquor, and not properly caring for their three young children.
- Both parties were known to have assaulted each other in domestic disputes in the past.

These facts tended to indicate that the victim's death was perhaps not a suicide, but a criminal homicide. An interrogation of the husband established what the facts suggested. The husband related that he had been truthful about the events leading up to the argument but that after his wife slapped him, he angrily had knocked her to the floor, removed the revolver from the desk drawer, and went back to his wife, who was now on her knees.

Standing over her, he fired a single shot into her head. After shooting her, he became frightened and fabricated the story of his wife's suicide.

This case demonstrates the importance of two factors in the investigation of an alleged suicide. The first is the importance of the location of the wound on the body and its trajectory upon entering the body. Second is the presence or absence of evidence indicating that the victim was predisposed to committing suicide.

In certain rare instances there may be more than one self-inflicted gunshot wound in the body. In an investigation conducted by a West Coast police department, a suicide victim was found with three gunshot wounds in the right temple, but the handgun reviewed at the scene had only two spent shells. Although there was considerable physical evidence at the scene, along with supporting historical data to suggest that the death was a suicide, the presence of the three wounds was an apparent contradiction of this evidence. The medical examiner's autopsy report revealed that two of the wounds were gunshot entrance wounds and that one wound was a gunshot exit wound. After establishing the nature of the three wounds, the medical examiner concluded that the victim first fired a single shot into his right temple. The bullet had failed to penetrate the skull, but instead slid under the scalp for a distance of approximately two inches and then exited. The victim's second shot into his head penetrated the skull and lodged in the brain. Death resulted as soon as the second shot was fired. The medical examiner hypothesized that the first shot did not penetrate the skull because of the angle at which the victim was holding the gun.

SUICIDE BY HANGING

Certain misconceptions associated with suicidal hangings can lead to erroneous conclu-sions. The first is that the victim's neck gets broken and, second, that the feet are off the floor. Although both of these conditions *may* occur, they are exceptions rather than the rule. The first misconception is related to the circumstances of legal executions by hanging. In legal executions the procedures involved in inflicting death are intended to result in the neck's being broken. This is accomplished by the use of a specific type of noose and a gallows with a trap door through which the person will drop some distance before being abruptly stopped. However, in a suicidal hanging, even when the feet are suspended, the neck is rarely broken, because the noose is not properly tied, and the fall is not long enough to cause the jolt necessary to break the neck.

It is also common in suicidal hangings for the victim's feet or even the knees to be touching the ground. Occasionally, the victim is found in a sitting position. (See Figure 10-18.) Finding victims in these positions often creates suspicion because it is difficult for inexperienced investigators to understand how anyone could remain in these positions while slowly choking to death. They might improperly conclude that the victim first was rendered unconscious or was killed and placed in the hanging position. It is more likely, however, that the victim did not slowly choke to death, but rather first tied the rope around some supporting device and then around his or her neck. Pressure was then applied by the victim either by crouching down, if in a standing position, or leaning forward, if in a sitting position. This initial pressure painlessly cuts off the flow of blood to the brain, which results in unconsciousness. When unconsciousness does occur, the full weight of the body is then applied to the noose, whereupon all oxygen is cut off to the brain and death follows. There is very little physical pain associated with suicides of this type. If one considers that many suicidal hangings occur in victims' homes, then it is

FIGURE 10-18　　Various Positions in Hanging

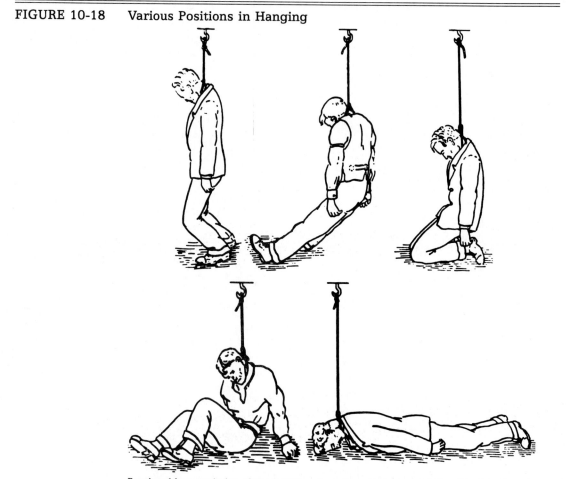

Reprinted by permission of the publisher from Arne Svensson and Otto Wendel, *Techniques of Crime Scene Investigation* (New York: Elsevier North-Holland, 1973), p. 352.

logical to expect the feet not to be suspended above the floor because few household objects in a house are strong enough to hold the weight of a fully suspended body or one that has fallen several feet from a chair or table.

Postmortem lividity is most pronounced in the lower portion of the arms and legs and around the face, lips, and jaw. There may be some variations in the location of the discoloration, depending on the position of the body. When death occurs in this manner, one frequently finds petechial hemorrhaging in the eyes, caused when small blood vessels in the eye bleed because blood pressure increases in response to compression around the neck (see Figure 10-19).

Occasionally, hangings are accidental and not suicidal. The individual may have himself in a modified hanging position while masturbating, and accidentally fall, slip, and knock over the object upon which he is standing, resulting in an accidental death,

FIGURE 10-19   Petechial Hemorrhaging in the Eye

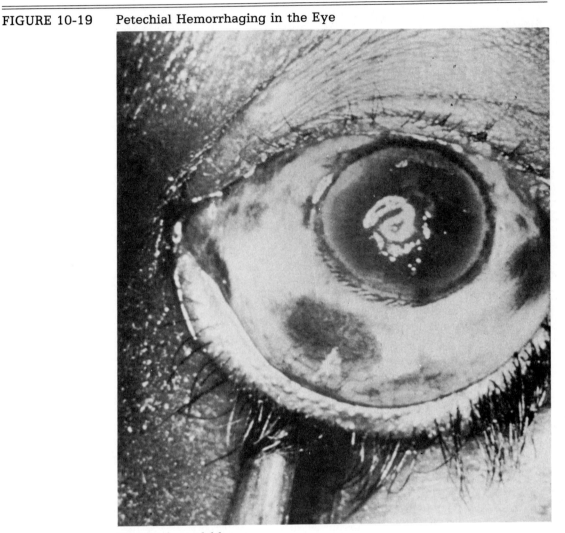

Victim of suicidal hanging.

known as autoerotic death or sexual asphyxia; the intent is sexual rather than suicidal. In these cases, the genitals are exposed and semen may be present. Chapter 11, "Typology of Rape," provides an in-depth explanation of autoerotic death. The presence of feces and urine is common because of the total relaxation of the bladder and bowel muscles at the time of death.

SLEEPING PILLS AND OTHER PHARMACEUTICALS

Sleeping pills and other pharmaceuticals have for many years been a common means of committing suicide. However, some deaths resulting from the ingestion of sleeping pills or tranquilizing drugs may be accidental and not suicidal. The investigator has an obligation to determine whether the death was accidental or suicidal. Certain types of medication, such as barbiturates, when mixed with alcohol have a synergetic effect which increases the potency of the drug beyond its normal strength. One should not be too quick to decide that the death is a suicide until the investigation is completed and some evidence is available to support this conclusion. In these cases, the investigator should seize as evidence any remaining medication and its container. Frequently, the container identifies the medication, the drug store dispensing it, and the physician prescribing it. There is always the possibility that the medication was purchased or obtained illegally, thus complicating the investigative process. As in all apparent suicides, the investigator should conduct interviews of relatives, friends, or neighbors who may be able to provide background information about the victim.

DROWNING

The majority of drowning incidents are either accidental or suicidal, but some are homicidal. There are three questions which must be answered in apparent drowning cases before any final conclusions can be reached: Was the cause of death due to drowning, or was the victim first killed and then placed in water? If the cause of death was drowning, did it take place in the water where the body was recovered, or was the victim drowned elsewhere and then placed in the water where found? Was the victim conscious when placed in the water? Answers to these questions can be obtained by external examination of the body by the investigator. External signs to indicate that the victim was alive and conscious before drowning include:

- Objects clutched in the hand, such as grass or bottom soil commonly found in water

- Fingernail marks on the palms of the hands
- White foam extruding from the nose and open mouth
- Postmortem lividity most marked in the head and neck because the body settled with these parts in a dependent position.[29]

An internal examination by a physician serves to establish whether death occurred by drowning. In drowning cases:

- The chest cavity and the lungs are distended and soggy, with fine foam in the trachea and bronchi.
- The heart is flabby, with its right side dilated and filled with dark red fluid. The blood is unclotted and usually hemolyzed due to the absorption of the drowning fluid into the system.
- There is water in the stomach and duodenum.
- Algae and other marine particles may be found in the stomach and adhering to the sides of the air passages.
- If the victim has drowned in salt water, the chloride content of blood taken from the left ventricle of the heart will be considerably greater than that in the blood of the right ventricle. If the victim has drowned in fresh water, then the chloride content in the left ventricle will be less than that in the right.

If there is reason to believe that the victim may have been intentionally drowned in fresh water, such as in the bathtub, and the body then deposited in salt water, a request for the appropriate blood analysis should be made by the investigator.

In removing the body from the water, the investigator may notice considerable damage to portions of the victim's body, especially around the head and face. This should not cause the investigator to conclude prematurely that the victim was the object of foul play. Some bodies of water contain many rocks and shells; a free-floating body which is subject to strong currents can be repeatedly slammed into and dragged across such objects, causing severe damage, especially to the forehead, knees, tops of the feet, and backs of the hands. In addition, if the water is rich with fish, crabs, and other marine life, these too can cause damage. It is not unusual for the lips, ears, and nose to be at least partially eaten away. The extent of damage from the objects or marine life in the water varies, but understanding what can result from their presence minimizes the possibility of premature conclusions. But the investigator must not prematurely conclude either that all damage resulted after the body was placed in the water. The medical examiner can help draw conclusions about the actual nature of wounds.

CUTTING AND PIERCING INSTRUMENTS

The instruments ordinarily employed in suicides by cutting are razor blades, knives, and occasionally glass. One of the common characteristics of suicides inflicted by these instruments is the presence of hesitation marks. Hesitation marks are a series of lesser wounds inflicted by the victim in the general region of the fatal wound, often the wrists, forearms, or throat. In certain throat cuttings, it may be possible to reach a conclusion about whether the injury was self-inflicted or resulted from an assault. If a wound is self-inflicted, it tends to be deep at the point of entry and to shallow out at its terminus, which is near, or slightly past, the midline of the throat. In a homicidal throat cutting, the wound appears deep from the start to the terminus. It is not unusual for a victim to inflict a series of severe cuts on different parts of the body to ensure death. The reasons vary, sometimes involving the influence

of alcohol or hallucinogenic drugs. The ingestion of drugs may have been a planned prelude to the act of self-destruction. Self-inflicted wounds can be surprisingly brutal and tend to make people disbelieve that they were self-imposed, particularly when mutilation of the sexual parts is involved. In one recent case, a twenty-eight-year-old man used a single-edged razor blade to cut off his penis. When questioned by paramedics, the man said: "Its just been eating away at me for so long and when I thought about it, I heard voices saying 'do it, do it.' I was just angry at myself. I had it all planned out and I did it."[30]

INGESTION OF POISONS

The ingestion of liquid poisons is sometimes clear from outward signs on the body. Powerful caustic lyes or acids may produce vomiting once the liquid reaches the digestive tract. There is considerable damage to lips, tongue, and mouth, and there may be blood in the vomitus, along with pieces of the esophagus and stomach (see Figure 10-20). Usually, death does not occur rapidly, and victims may employ another means of suicide to stop the excruciating pain.

Cases of suspected poisoning frequently pose very difficult problems to the police investigator and to the medical examiner. Many poisons produce symptoms similar to those of certain diseases, a fact that can complicate determination of whether a crime has been committed. However, if there is any reason to suspect poisoning, the investigation must proceed along the lines of a possible homicide, suicide, or accidental death, until death due to natural causes is established.[31] To compound the problem, suicides and accidental deaths by poisoning are sometimes very difficult to distinguish from homicide. Alcohol, when consumed with certain medications, may result in an accidental (possibly suicidal) death by respiratory failure. An ex-

FIGURE 10-20   Ingestion of a Caustic Drain Cleaner

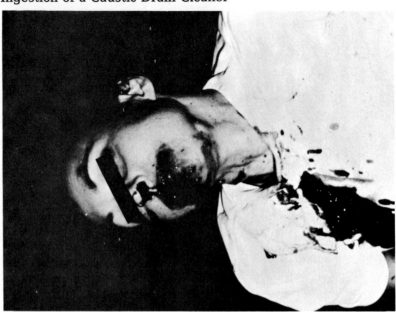

This victim committed suicide by ingesting a strong caustic drain cleaner. Upon ingestion vomiting was induced, thereby causing severe burns to nose, chin, and chest area.

ample is the combination of amphetamines and alcohol. When the alcohol level in the blood reaches about half the lethal dose, most individuals lose consciousness and thus stop drinking. But with the addition of a stimulant, such as an amphetamine, this effect may not occur, and individuals may drink a lethal dose of alcohol before they fall into a coma.

Actually, poisons are now rarely used in homicides because their physical properties usually alarm the intended victim. In addition, modern laboratory techniques can readily detect most poisons, thus unmasking an intended homicide. But when they are used, poisons cover a very wide range of possibilities.

Even though the crime scene investigators seldom can identify the chemical compound which caused the death, they should be alert to the general range of possibilities and the potentially hazardous environmental factors that may be connected with a poisoning.

Regardless of the nature of the incident—homicide, suicide, or accident—the symptoms of death by poison are the same. The field investigator should attempt to determine if the victim had any of the symptoms—vomiting, convulsions, diarrhea, paralysis, rapid or slow breathing, contracted or dilated pupils, changes in skin color, or difficulty in swallowing just prior to death. These symptoms are general manifestations of systemic poisoning. They do not provide proof of poisoning but can be meaningful in relation to other evidence. Someone who observed the victim just before death provides the best source of information concerning his or her symptoms. If no witness is available, the investigator must rely all the more on physical evidence from the crime scene. Table 10-1 lists common poisons and their associated physical manifestations.

The investigator should collect all available information concerning the activities of the victim during the last three days of life. Information on types of medication taken, when the last meal was eaten, and where it was eaten can be very important in determining the type of poison involved. Medical history may indicate that death was due to natural causes.

The toxicologist is concerned with the identification and recognition of poisons, with their physiological effects on humans and animals, and with their antidotes. Crime laboratories usually provide some toxicological support but vary considerably in the amount and type that they can furnish. However, full toxicological support is always available through a combination of hospital and medical examiner, coroners' and criminalistics laboratories. Crime laboratories can direct police to local facilities.

If the investigator suspects that poison was ingested, a diligent search should be conducted for the container. In suicides and accidental poisonings, the container frequently is close at hand. Even though a container appears empty, it should be processed for fingerprints, packaged, marked, and forwarded to the laboratory for examination.

TABLE 10-1
Poisons and Associated Physical Manifestations

Type of Poison	Symptom or Evidence
Caustic Poison (Lye)	Characteristic burns around lips and mouth of victim
Carbon Monoxide	Victim's skin takes on an abnormally bright cherry-red color
Sulfuric Acid	Black vomit
Hydrochloric Acid	Greenish-brown vomit
Nitric Acid	Yellow vomit
Silver Salts	White vomit turning black in daylight
Copper Sulfate	Blue-green vomit
Phosphorous	Coffee-brown vomit, onion or garlic odor
Cyanide	Burnt almond odor in air
Ammonia, Vinegar, Lysol, etc.	Characteristic odors
Arsenic, Mercury, Lead Salts	Pronounced diarrhea
Methyl (Wood) Alcohol, Isopropyl (Rubbing) Alcohol	Nausea and vomiting, unconsciousness, possibly blindness

Source: Richard H. Fox and Carl L. Cunningham, *Crime Scene Search and Physical Evidence Handbook* (Washington, D.C.: Government Printing Office, 1985), p. 126.

Additionally, any other object that could reasonably relate to the poisoning should be collected, such as unwashed dishes and glasses, wastebasket contents, envelopes, and medicine containers.

GASES

The gas most frequently involved in medicolegal investigations is carbon monoxide. When a death does result from this gas, it is generally accidental or suicidal. Carbon monoxide is found in automobile exhaust fumes and improperly ventilated space heaters in homes. In a death caused by auto emissions, the individual may have started the engine of the vehicle in the garage after closing the garage door or may have extended a flexible hose from the exhaust pipe into the vehicle and then closed the windows.

When death occurs from carbon monoxide poisoning the victim's skin takes on an abnormally bright cherry-red color because of the reaction of the red blood cells to the gas. The red blood cells have a very high affinity for carbon monoxide molecules, absorbing them rapidly, making them incapable of absorbing oxygen, and thereby rendering them dysfunctional in the life-sustaining process. Death will usually occur when the red blood cells have reached a saturation level usually above 40 percent, although this varies, the level sometimes going higher before death results if the victim was asleep, due to the body's reduced oxygen needs.

JUMPING FROM HIGH PLACES

The major question to be answered in death resulting from jumping is whether the victim voluntarily leaped or was thrown or pushed. Often, there are witnesses who can provide this information, suicide notes, or background information which indicates previous suicide attempts or a predisposition toward suicide.

VEHICLE SUICIDE

The motor vehicle as a means of suicide, although not as common as the means previously discussed, is one which police officers should be sensitive to. Usually a vehicle suicide entails a single occupant speeding into an off-road obstacle. Physical evidence to look for in these accidents includes a lack of skid marks, indications that the person did not attempt to stop or avoid the obstacle, and shoe sole imprints.

Shoe sole imprints can provide information regarding the position of a driver's feet and thus his or her action. Most imprints are found on soft-soled shoes, but some are found on hard leather soles. These shoe imprints are clear and indisputable impressions; they are not simply dust marks which may be easily erased by rubbing the sole with a finger or cloth. A word of caution to the police officers—these marks are evidence and must be handled properly. For laboratory personnel to properly examine the sole imprint, control pedals from the car need to be removed. Routinely officers should examine the brake, clutch, and accelerator. These pedals, as well as other floor-mounted controls such as the dimmer switch, should be collected as evidence. Figure 10-21 shows an accelerator pattern imprinted on a tennis shoe sole. The driver and only occupant committed suicide by crashing the motor vehicle against a concrete support next to a highway. The imprint comparison provided evidence that it had been a suicide, and follow-up investigation revealed the suicidal tendencies of the deceased.

All of the deceased's clothing should be retained as evidence. Officers need to alert the personnel in the hospital emergency room that the person's clothing must not be discarded, regardless of their condition. Additionally, officers at the crash scene must find any shoes which may have been torn off during the force of the crash and strewn about

FIGURE 10-21   Accelerator Pattern Clearly Imprinted on Tennis Shoe Sole

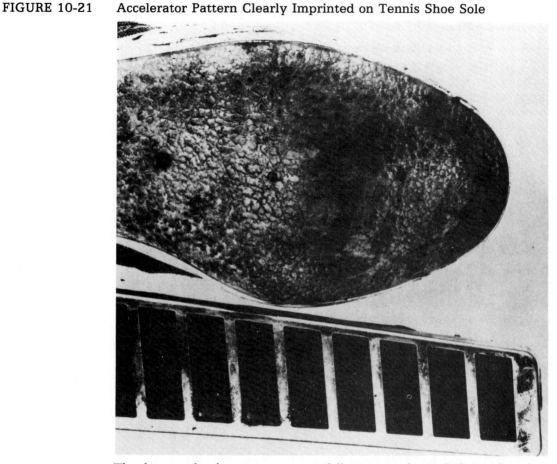

The driver and only occupant successfully committed suicide by crashing her motor vehicle against a concrete support of an elevated highway.

Reprinted by permission of the *Journal of Police Science and Administration,* © 1973 by Northwestern University School of Law, March, Vol. 1, No. 1, p. 3.

the area. At the laboratory, the clothing is examined. Marks on shoe soles are compared with patterns on the control pedals.

It is only after painstaking investigation that a death is determined to be a suicide. By recognizing some of the important evidence of self-inflicted wounds, investigators contribute to the successful solution of the death investigation.[32]

THE SUICIDE NOTE

Research indicates that suicide notes are not left in most suicides. One study revealed certain facts about those who do and do not leave notes. Generally there are no differences between the two groups in age, race, sex, employment, marital status, history of mental illness, place of suicide, reported causes or unusual circumstances preceding the act, medical care and supervision, or history of previous suicidal attempts or threats. However, the note writers differed from the non-note writers in the methods used to kill themselves. The note writers used poisons, firearms, and hanging more often as a means of death than non-note writers.[33]

SEXUAL DIFFERENCES IN SUICIDAL BEHAVIOR

Studies of suicide in the United States indicate that the suicide rate is higher for men than for women, whereas the attempted suicide rate is higher for women than men. There is some evidence to suggest that there are often differences between men and women in the methods employed to commit suicide, women preferring barbiturates and poisons. If women do use a firearm, the fatal wound is frequently in the body rather than the head. It has been suggested that these methods are used because they are not disfiguring and that women appear to be concerned more often about their appearance after death than men. It is not uncommon for a female to leave a note to her female friends or relatives requesting in detail the clothes she wishes to be buried in along with details relating to facial cosmetics.[34]

In contrast, some males kill themselves where their body will not be discovered by family members. These types of suicides can create investigative problems, especially if a note is not written. For example, if a passerby is tempted to steal a gun and valuables from a suicide victim, the police may think that the death was a murder and robbery rather than suicide.

SUICIDE-INSURANCE SCHEMES

Sometimes individuals take their own lives and try to convey the impression that the death was accidental or even homicidal. Generally, they try to create this impression because they have invested in insurance policies that will not pay out money to the beneficiary if a death is self-inflicted. The following case illustrates such an instance:

> Several years ago an Armenian man from Iran died in the Marina del Rey area of Los Angeles, California, when a bomb blew up his car. At first investigators believed that it might have been a terrorist killing. However, after a long investigation, the investigators concluded that the man had killed himself in a way that looked like a terrorist attack to allow his father to collect more than $1 million from newly secured insurance policies.[35]
>
> Victor R. Galustian, 42, had lived in Los Angeles since 1950, when his father returned to Iran. His father had sent him money illegally from Iran for safekeeping against the day when the father would come to the United States. Galustian used the money to entertain acquaintances at lavish restaurant dinners, passing himself off as a real estate businessman or sometimes an engineer.

Because the money entered this country illegally, it is impossible to know just how much Galustian received, but investigators estimate that he spent at least $600,000 of the money his father had sent. Desperate when he learned that his father was planning to return to this country, Galustian began planning how to regain the money he had spent. He took out numerous insurance policies shortly before he died, with his father as beneficiary. All the policies had double indemnity clauses, which double the benefits if the policyholder dies an unnatural death. The policies prohibit payoff if the policyholder commits suicide.

Early one morning, Galustian was driving his car near his apartment when a powerful explosive under his front seat went off, propelling Galustian's body 25 feet from the demolished auto and spewing debris for 600 feet. The explosion occurred after an outbreak of violence involving local Armenian and Iranian families. Authorities initially believed that the explosion, too, might be political. A few days before his death, Galustian had told a security guard in his apartment building that he had found a bomb in his car. That and other clues, including his lack of political activity in the Armenian community, convinced investigators that Galustian's death was not the result of a political attack. It took investigators several months to piece it together, but they eventually concluded that it was a suicide.

ASSAULTS AGAINST CHILDREN

The most common cause of children's death is physical abuse, often by their own parents. The clinical term commonly used to describe physically abused children is the "battered child syndrome." This possibility should be considered in any child exhibiting evidence of bone fracture, subdermal hematoma, failure to thrive, soft-tissue swelling, or skin bruising, in any child who dies suddenly, or when the degree and type of injury is at variance with the history given regarding the occurrence of the trauma.[36]

Abuse of children takes on various forms, from minor assaults to flagrant physical torture. Many times these injuries cannot or will not be explained by the parents, or the story seems inconsistent with the injuries received. For example, bruises in various stages of healing generally vary in color. Thus, one should be suspicious of an explanation of such injuries as being from a fall from a bike. Intentional injuries tend to occur most frequently on the face, back, ribs, buttocks, genitals, palms, or soles of the feet. Although abusers use a wide variety of instruments, the two most common are the belt (see Figure 10-22) and electric cord. The two

most common areas of intentional burning are the palms of the hands and soles of the feet (see Figures 10-23 and 10-24).

One father who caught his young son playing with a cigarette lighter inflicted several third-degree burns on the palms of the child's hands with the lighter to teach his son the hazards of playing with fire. On being questioned by the police, the father explained that his father had caught him doing the same thing when he was a child and had burned his hands.

Children have also received intentional burns from being pressed against a radiator or immersed in hot water. These burns often are distinguished as intentional by a clearly defined line or mark separating the burned and unburned area (see Figure 10-25).[37]

The problem the investigator often encounters in such cases is that the victim is either too young to explain what has occurred or is too intimidated to cooperate. In injuries or deaths of young children, investigators find radiologists, physicians who specialize in the interpretation of X-rays, especially helpful. It is common for those abused to be brought to the hospital emergency room by their parents or relatives, who tell hospital personnel that the child was injured in a fall or some other accident. When there is a discrepancy between the characteristics of the injury and the explanation, X-rays can be useful in determining whether the injuries were accidental. X-rays of the entire body reveal not only the presence of fractures and other injuries to joints and bones but also the existence of older injuries in various stages of healing.

Careful questioning of those bringing the child to the hospital may be sufficient to confirm the need for a complete investigation. The following facts about child abuse are helpful in such questioning:

- In many cases, only one of a number of children in the family is chosen as the

FIGURE 10-22   **Boy Beaten with the Buckle End of a Belt**

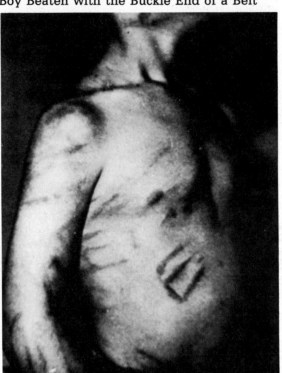

Courtesy Tampa Police Department.

target of abuse, and frequently that child was conceived or born extramaritally or premaritally.

- The marital partner tends to protect the abusive parent through denial of the facts.
- Occasionally, an abusing father also assaults his wife, but more frequently he restricts the gross abuse to a child.
- In over half the cases in which child abuse results in hospitalization, there was a preceding incident of abuse of equal severity.
- Not infrequently the battered child is taken to a different hospital after each abuse in order to conceal the recurrence of injuries.[38]

The families of battered children cover the entire socioeconomic spectrum. The investigator cannot assume that the injured child from what appears to be a "good home" is not the victim of child abuse.

In cases where medical examination is inconclusive but abuse is strongly suspected, interviewing becomes even more significant. The rule is to leave no source unexamined. To fail to do so places the actually abused child back into a defenseless position in which death could occur. The interviewing of baby-sitters, neighbors, teachers, and others must be conducted sensibly and sensitively. The aim is not to "get the person

FIGURE 10-23   Burn Injury—Palm

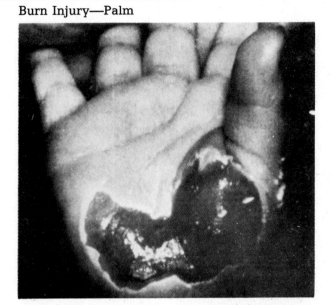

Courtesy Milwaukee County Department of Social Service.

FIGURE 10-24   Burn Injury—Sole

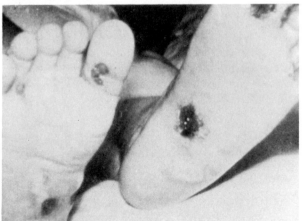

Courtesy Milwaukee County Department of Social Service.

FIGURE 10-25   Burn Injury—Legs

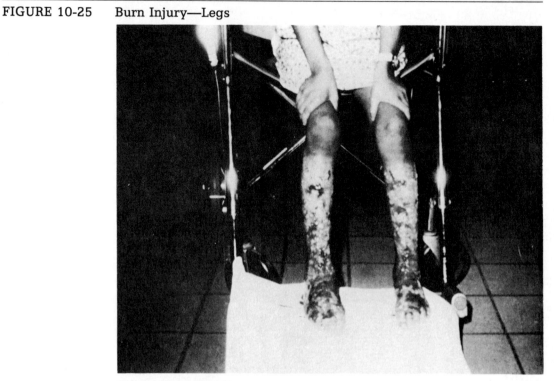

Courtesy Tampa Police Department.

who did it," because there may not in fact have been an abuse incident. The primary objective is to get the information so that if there is an abuse case the child is protected.

SUDDEN INFANT DEATH SYNDROME (SIDS)

Health professionals in the past had limited contact with SIDS families because SIDS rarely occurs outside of the home. A few babies have died of SIDS while hospitalized, but the usual case involves a baby who is brought to the hospital emergency room and is pronounced dead on arrival. As a result, many physicians and nurses have had little knowledge of SIDS.[39]

WHAT IS THE SUDDEN INFANT DEATH SYNDROME?

Simply defined, SIDS is the sudden and unexpected death of an apparently healthy infant that remains unexplained after the performance of a complete autopsy. In the United States, approximately 7,000 infants die each year as a result of this syndrome. On the average, 2 of every 1,000 infants born alive succumb to SIDS, and it is the leading cause of death among infants one week to one year of age.

In the majority of instances, the baby is apparently in good health prior to death and feeds without difficulty. Although there may be evidence of a slight cold or stuffy nose, there is usually no history of serious upper respiratory infection. In most cases, the infant is placed in a crib for sleep and is found dead several hours later.

Most SIDS deaths occur between November and March. Sudden changes in temperature may trigger SIDS. The risk of SIDS appears to be highest in: crowded dwellings; among the infants of young mothers; males; nonwhites regardless of socioeconomic status; families of lower socioeconomic status regardless of race; and premature infants. Twins have an increased risk of SIDS, likely a consequence of their low birth weight and premature birth. SIDS occurs in both breast-fed and bottle-fed babies. Most victims are between the ages of one and six months, with the highest frequency of occurrence between two and four months.

Characteristic Appearance of SIDS Victims:

- Usually normal state of nutrition and hydration
- Blood-tinged, frothy fluids around mouth and nostrils, indicative of pulmonary edema
- Vomitus on the face
- Diaper wet and full of stool
- Bruise-like marks on head or body limbs (postmortem pooling or settling of blood in dependent body parts)

Characteristic Autopsy Findings on SIDS Victims:

- Some congestion and edema of the lungs
- Petechial hemorrhages in thymus, heart, and lungs
- Minor evidence of respiratory tract inflammation

MISCONCEPTIONS ABOUT SIDS

Suffocation. Many people believe that the babies have suffocated because they are often found with their faces pressed into the mattress or with the bedclothes covering their heads. Studies have repeatedly disproved these ideas as a cause of death.

Aspiration, Choking. These babies do not inhale or choke on their feeding.

Unsuspected Illness. Particularly if the baby had a cold, the parents may feel guilty about not having taken the child to the doctor. If the baby was checked by the doctor, the parents (and the doctor) may wonder what the doctor missed. In any case, neither is at fault.

Freezing. Although the body may be cold when discovered, this is a postmortem change.

Accidental Injury, Neglect, or Abuse. Law enforcement officers should not jump to the wrong conclusions because of the appearance of the infant. The results of accusations of wrongdoing have been tragic. A few innocent and grief-stricken parents have been accused of murdering their babies and put in jail. Appearances can be deceiving.

SIDS RESEARCH

Currently, the most widely recognized theory about the mechanism of SIDS is spontaneous, protracted apnea, or cessation of breathing. Considerable progress has been made by the SIDS Institute at the University of Maryland in the past five years. In comprehensive tests of 1,000 babies, it was found that fully 10 percent stopped breathing for periods longer than 15 to 20 seconds, or their heart rate dropped below 80. Detected in time, such infants are considered at risk for SIDS and are monitored with an electronic device which sets off an alarm if the child's breathing or heart rate drops below a certain level.

Perhaps the most significant research supporting the apnea theory is the work of Dr. Richard Naeye of the Pennsylvania State University College of Medicine. Dr. Naeye began to look for structural changes in the infant's body at autopsy which would indicate chronic lack of oxygen attributable to repeated and relatively long periods of apnea. He found the following changes in a large group of SIDS victims:

1. The walls of the small arteries in the lungs were thicker than normal.
2. The wall of the right ventricle of the heart was thicker than normal.
3. The relative retention of brown fat around the adrenal gland was greater than normal.
4. There was abnormal retention of fetal capacity for the production of red blood cells in the liver.

Dr. Marie Valdes-Dapena, University of Miami School of Medicine, has confirmed Naeye's observations with respect to the two latter changes and is currently working on the first two.

THE OFFICER'S ROLE

The law enforcement officer serves a key role in the SIDS case and is often the first person to encounter the shock, grief, and guilt experienced by the parents.

It may be an experience such as this: The officer responds to a call, entering a house where an infant has just died. The mother is hysterical, incoherent, and unable to clarify what happened. The father is dazed yet tearless; he is confused and responding evasively. As the officer proceeds, the mother continues to sob, blaming herself. The infant is in the cradle, its head is covered with a blanket. When the blanket is removed, the officer notes a small amount of blood-tinged fluid in and around the mouth and nose and bruise-like marks on the body where the blood settled after death.

Was the death a result of illness, abuse, neglect, or unexplained causes? The officer will make a preliminary assessment based on the information obtained at the scene.

With care and sensitivity, the officer can obtain the necessary information concerning the circumstances of the death. Suspicious questioning or accusation in investigating a potential SIDS case can result in reinforcing blame and lifelong feelings of guilt in innocent parents. Law enforcement officers are encouraged to approach the parents in a positive, sympathetic manner. Emphasis should be placed on interviewing with dialogue as opposed to interrogation. It is recommended that the officer avoid immediately asking questions such as: Have you ever hit the baby? Have you dropped the baby recently? Has anyone in the family been ill lately? If it is a crib death, questions such as these reinforce the parents' conviction that they were somehow to blame for the death.

If the circumstances are unclear, an autopsy may establish the need for criminal investigation. In some jurisdictions, even the medical examiner's office is unaware of the problem of SIDS. If the death is unexplainable, the officer can do a great service to the family by telling them that their baby was possibly a victim of SIDS. The officer can explain that it is the leading cause of death in infants after the first month of life and can tell them that there are organizations to provide them with information and assistance. By knowing about this disease and being able to provide sympathy and information to parents, the law enforcement officer serves a key role in the management of a SIDS case.

═══ VEHICLE HOMICIDES ═══

Few drivers in fatal hit and run accidents intended the accident to occur. The driver generally fails to stop for one or more of the following reasons:

- The driver had been drinking.
- The vehicle was stolen.
- The driver had a suspended or revoked operator's license.

- There was someone in the car whose presence, if discovered, could cause additional problems (for instance, someone else's spouse).
- The driver had no liability insurance.
- The driver or a passenger was injured, requiring a trip to the nearest emergency room.
- The driver did not realize that he or she had hit anyone.
- The driver had committed a crime before the accident and still had evidence of it in the vehicle.

PHYSICAL EVIDENCE FROM HIT AND RUN ACCIDENTS

The physical evidence created by hit and run accidents is located at the scene, on the victim's body, and on the hit and run vehicle. The physical evidence left by the vehicle typically is broken glass from headlights, paint fragments, and underbody debris. Chapter 4, "Physical Evidence," provides an in-depth explanation of the potential of these items as physical evidence. The investigator may also find broken equipment which can provide extremely valuable clues in identifying the make, model, and year of the hit and run vehicle, especially if the equipment was manufactured for a specific model. Broken equipment at the scene can often be matched to parts on the hit and run vehicle.

Tire marks typically are found in mud, clay, dirt, snow, warm tar, and sometimes on the body of the victim. If a good negative impression is left and the hit-and-run vehicle is recovered, it can often lead to a positive identification. As with all other physical evidence, the tire prints should be protected, photographed, and measured before any efforts are made to make a cast.

Skid marks show the direction of travel before the accident and allow for estimates of the speed of the vehicle. Skid marks, unlike tire marks, provide clues regarding direction of travel prior to the accident and the estimated speed of the vehicle. The absence of skid marks at the point of impact suggests a variety of things. The driver may not have seen the victim ahead of time, possibly because the driver fell asleep at the wheel or was intoxicated or because visibility was poor. This would also be the case if the skid marks appear only after the point of impact. If there are no skid marks at all, the investigator should consider the possibility of planned vehicular assault. However, some vehicles are equipped with antiskid braking systems, another possibility to consider in the absence of skid marks.

The investigator is looking for complementary physical evidence between the hit and run vehicle and the victim. Because the physical evidence may be quite small, such as paint fragments or a few fibers from a victim's clothing, the investigator must take painstaking efforts in searching for, collecting, and preserving such evidence. If the accident involved a pedestrian, his or her clothing may be of value in two ways. First, fibers from the victim's clothing may adhere to the vehicle, and these can be compared and matched. They are likely to be found on or near the part of the vehicle first striking the victim. If the victim was rolled under the vehicle, pieces of cloth, blood, hair, and skin may adhere to the undercarriage. Second, fiber marks from the victim's clothing may be embedded in the paint of the hit-and-run vehicle.

The medical examiner should obtain blood from the victim for possible comparison with blood found on the hit-and-run vehicle. In addition, the victim's blood should be analyzed for the presence of alcohol or drugs, because the victim's condition at the time of the accident may have contributed to the accident.

Headlight Examination in Hit and Run Accidents. On occasion, it may be important to determine if the headlights of a hit and run vehicle were on or off at the time of the accident. For example, a driver suspected of being involved in a night-time hit-and-run collision claimed that the damage to his car was done in a previous day-time accident. Examination of the damaged headlight showed that they were on at the time of the collision. This finding by the investigator suggested that the damage to the suspect's vehicle was done during the evening hours and not during the day-time as stated by the driver. Determining whether a vehicle's headlights were on or off at the time of impact is done by examining the filament. The effect of a crack on a filament is quite different when the filament is incandescent and when it is cold. This fact gives two bases for judging whether the lamp was on or off. First, if the glass breaks and air replaces the nitrogen surrounding the filament, oxygen in the air has no effect on a cold filament, but quickly blackens an incandescent one. Second, if the glass does not break, collision shock may sharply fracture a cold, brittle filament, but stretch out and uncoil an incandescent filament which is quite elastic in this condition.[40] Investigators therefore should be certain to preserve not only the external glass lens of the lamp but its internal components as well, especially when there is a question of whether the headlights were on or off at the time of the accident.

SEARCH FOR THE VEHICLE

The steps to be taken in searching for a hit and run vehicle depend mainly on information provided by witnesses, victim, and physical evidence located at the scene. In the absence of eyewitnesses or physical evidence that readily identify the suspect or the vehicle, the investigator may have to use logic and deductive reasoning. For example, the investigator may often safely assume that the driver of the vehicle was at the scene of the accident because the driver was coming from someplace and going to another place by apparently the best route. But in some cases, drivers are lost or otherwise unaware of where they are and what they are doing. These cases are exceptions.

Three significant factors should be determined by the investigator in seeking to discover the driver's objective: first, the time of the accident; second, the direction of travel; and third, if it can be learned, the direction of travel after the accident.[41] Every area has certain features that investigators must consider in making tentative assumptions. For example, let us assume that a hit-and-run vehicle was described by witnesses as a flashy sportscar driven by a man approximately 20 years old. The accident occurred during a weekday at 9:00 A.M. Before the accident, the vehicle was traveling in the direction of a nearby college. In the absence of other evidence, the investigator might assume that the vehicle was being driven by a student from the college. Of course, this assumption could be totally erroneous, but when there are no solid leads, then the only initial course of action may be to apply logical and deductive reasoning.

Repair Shops, Garages, and Parts Stores. If the investigator can locate physical evidence or a witness who can identify the make, model, year, and color of the vehicle, a detailed notice should be sent out to area repair shops, garages, and parts stores. If the damage to the vehicle is severe, the driver generally does one of several things. First, the driver may try to keep the car concealed in a private garage. Second, the driver may take the vehicle to a repair shop. Third, the driver may try to purchase the replacement parts from a dealer or junkyard.

In some situations, investigators ask for help from the news media and, through them, help from the public. They may do so when existing clues are sparse.

FIRE DEATHS

Frequently, the human remains are found at the scene of a fire. Properly examined, these remains may provide important data to the investigator about the facts surrounding the fire and the cause of death. Investigators should ask these questions:

- Was the decedent accidentally killed by the fire (whether or not the fire was caused by arson)?
- Was the decedent deliberately killed by the fire?
- Was the decedent already dead when the fire occurred?

To answer these questions, investigators should determine certain facts. These facts are outlined in the remainder of this section.[42]

COORDINATION AND COOPERATION

Coordination of and cooperation between police and fire investigators are of paramount importance in the successful investigation of any questioned fire. As with other forms of physical evidence at a fire scene, a body should never be moved until fully examined at the scene unless there is some possibility that the person is still alive, or there is danger of further destruction of the body if it remains where it is. Also, because a dead human being is probably the most complex and rapidly changing type of physical evidence at a crime scene, cooperation between medical personnel (preferably forensic pathologists) and investigators is essential. This coordination should extend from the scene of the fire to the medical facility where the postmortem examination is conducted.

DEGREES OF BURNING

Burns are medically classified into four types. The extent of burns may provide information about the proximity of the body to the point of origin of the fire, the length of time the body was exposed to the fire, and the intensity of the fire.

First degree burns are superficial and limited to the outer layers of skin. Although the burned area is red and swollen, blisters do not form and peeling may follow. Second degree burns involve blistering and the destruction of the upper layers of skin. Scarring occasionally results in living victims. In third degree burns, the entire thickness of the skin (epidermis and dermis) is destroyed. In living victims with third degree burns pain is usually absent as nerve endings are destroyed; scarring results and skin grafting is usually necessary. Fourth degree burns completely destroy (char) the skin and underlying tissue.

The degree of incineration of the body should be considered in comparison with other facts and circumstances of the fire. Are the burns of the decedent consistent with the nature of the fire and other burned areas? Body mass should be considered, keeping in mind that faster and greater destruction occurs to smaller, lighter bodies. Less destruction may be expected in ordinary house fires (usually of 1,200 degrees or less) than in fires accelerated, for example, by certain chemicals. Complete incineration of a body, as in cremation, usually takes one and a half hours at temperatures of 1,600 to 1,800 degrees, resulting in an ash weight of two to three pounds for an adult.

IDENTIFICATION OF REMAINS

Because fire destroys human tissue, identification of the remains may be especially difficult. Yet because identification of a decedent is a key factor in any questioned death investigation, an orderly, sequential approach must be used in the identification process. The five methods that follow should be considered in sequence, from the "best" identification means to the "worst."

Fingerprints. Although considered the best means of identification because of centralized files of fingerprints, fingerprint identification may not be possible in fire death cases due to the destruction of the skin.

Dentition. Being the hardest substance in the human body, teeth are frequently the best form of identification for fire victims. The only drawback is that in order to make a dental comparison, one must have something to compare the decedent's teeth with. The investigator must have some idea of who the decedent was.

Scars, Marks, or Tatoos on the Exterior of the Body. These abnormalities on the skin, like fingerprints, are frequently obscured or destroyed by the fire.

Scars, Marks, Abnormalities, or Appliances Inside the Body. Bone abnormalities, surgical appliances, or operative scars may be helpful, but the investigator must have some idea of who the victim was so that appropriate medical records may be examined.

Identification, Jewelry, and Clothing on the Body. The least desirable method is a last resort due to the possibility of substitution. Indeed, in some arson and/or murder cases, the body is often disguised to look like someone else.

SCENE CONSIDERATIONS

As with any physical evidence, burned bodies must be sketched, measured, and photographed in place and in relation to other evidence at the scene of the fire. The actual location of the bodies may be of crucial importance to the investigation. Determination as to whether the decedent was a smoker is important for establishing the cause of the fire and whether he or she was alive at the time of the fire.

EXAMINATION OF THE EXTERNAL BODY

The body of the deceased should be examined in detail both at the scene and again at the morgue. Significant areas for examination include the following:

Signs of Trauma. Any sign of injury to the external body should be carefully noted, sketched, and photographed. The use of a five-power magnifying glass (as a minimum) is required, because fire obscures signs of injury.

Skull Fractures. Skull fractures that could indicate blunt force trauma should be sought in all fire death cases. They are difficult to find, however, because extreme heat from the fire may have caused the skull to explode slightly to allow the escape of expanding gases. This explosion frequently produces a skull fracture that looks like one from externally applied force.

Skin Splits. Heat dries the skin and may cause it to split. These splits may look like incised or other wounds from a sharp instrument. Conversely, a stab wound may be overlooked as a skin split. Again, careful examination under magnification and a good knowledge of the nature of incised wounds are necessary.

Noncranial Fractures. If enough heat is applied, bones shrink, warp, and fracture. Determining whether fractures were caused by a trauma or heat requires painstaking examination.

Pugilistic Attitude. This so-called pugilistic attitude of the body is a natural occurrence of the dehydrating effect caused by the heat from the fire and is not related to the cause or manner of death. The arms and legs will be drawn into a posture resembling that of a boxer.

EXAMINATION OF THE INTERNAL BODY

After the body has been closely examined, sketched, and photographed, an internal examination of the body should be conducted by a forensic pathologist. Investigators should attend this procedure to get information about the facts, to correct discrepancies in data (such as measurements), and to recover evidence from the body. Significant areas for examination include:

Soot, Other Debris or Burning in the Air Passages. These findings may indicate that the decedent was breathing while the fire was burning.

Pulmonary Edema. Frothy substance in the lungs may result from irritants breathed in during a fire.

Epidural Hemorrhages. Hemorrhages above the tough membrane covering the brain (the dura mater) and under the skull may occur at the rear of the head due to heat. These hemorrhages should not be mistaken for the hemorrhages associated with blunt-force injuries.[43]

Internal Injuries. All internal injuries should be closely examined, measured, and photographed, with samples taken by the pathologist for later microscopic examination.

Foreign Objects. Any foreign objects found in the body, such as bullets, should be recovered as evidence by the investigator. Because these objects are frequently small and difficult to locate, X-ray examination of the body before internal examination is recommended.

TOXICOLOGY EXAMINATION

The pathologist should take samples for later examination by a toxicologist. Toxicologic results may be of extreme importance to the investigation.

Alcohol. Alcohol in blood indicates whether the decedent was incapacitated at the time of the fire and thus unable to escape. A finding of high levels of alcohol raises questions for the investigator about the decedent's habits.

Other Drugs. Indications of other possibly incapacitating drugs may provide new leads. The possibility that drug interactions combined—barbiturates with alcohol, for example—should also be considered.

Carbon Monoxide. Generally, some carbon monoxide is found in the blood of deceased persons, and elevated levels may be found merely because the person lived in a polluted inner-city environment or was a smoker. Frequently, high carbon monoxide levels (usually above 40 percent) are the cause of death in fire situations. A less than fatal level of carbon monoxide in the blood may indicate that the decedent was dead at the time of the fire.

Presence of Other Chemicals. Chemicals given off by burning materials may indicate the accelerant of the fire and that the decedent was breathing them in at the time of the fire. Hydrogen cyanide or hydrogen sulfide found in the blood may contribute to death. Nitrous oxides may indicate the presence of nitrogen-containing fuels; acrolein may indicate the destructive distillation of fats and oils. Refrigerants and other chemicals such as ammonia, freon, methyl chloride, or phosgene may indicate the nature of the fire.

HISTOLOGIC EXAMINATION

Microscopic examination of tissues is also an important part of the postmortem examination and is carried out by the pathologist after selected tissues from the victim have been placed in a fixative, usually for ten to 14 days. Frequently, injury sites are microscopically examined for signs of white blood cells at the injury. White blood cells may indicate that the injury was inflicted at least several hours before death.

"FLASH" FIRES

Concentrated burns in one area of a body may indicate the nature and cause of death. Such example would include a spray of burning fuel as in a motorcycle accident or the application of a device such as a blowtorch to a particular area of the body (face or hands) to obscure identification.

MOTIVES OF FIRE DEATHS

In fire deaths, the following motives should be kept in mind by investigators:

- Destruction or mutilation of the body to conceal the identity of the decedent.
- Destruction or mutilation of the body to conceal the true cause or manner of death.
- Incineration of the body with homicidal intent.
- Insurance fraud—the incineration of a body to collect on an insurance policy. For example, a decedent may have committed suicide but have an insurance policy prohibiting collection after death by suicide. Beneficiaries may burn the body to indicate accidental death by fire.
- Suicide with an accelerant.
- An attempt by a suicide victim to hide the cause of death.
- Victim trapped in building burned by an arsonist or by accident.

QUESTIONS

1. Briefly discuss the differences between felonious and nonfelonious homicides.
2. What basic procedure should be used in responding to the scene of a suspected homicide or assault?
3. What are the purposes of an autopsy?
4. Why is the personal identification of a victim so important in homicide investigation?
5. What roles can be played by archeologists, forensic pathologists, and botanists in the search for and discovery of buried bodies?
6. What role can be played by entomologists in estimating time of death?
7. Why should the investigator be knowledgeable about postmortem conditions?
8. Briefly describe the typical entrance and exit gunshot wound.
9. What are the basic differences between

neutron activation analysis and atomic absorption analysis in testing for firearm residues?
10. Describe an incised wound, stab wound, and laceration.
11. What are defense wounds, and where are they most commonly found?
12. Which misconceptions are associated with suicidal hangings?
13. Why are poisons rarely used in homicides?
14. What are the two most common instruments used in child abuse?
15. Discuss the differences in suicidal behavior between men and women.
16. What types of children are most frequently the target of child abuse?
17. Describe the appearance of a SIDS victim.
18. What are the most common reasons that hit-and-run drivers fail to stop?

19. In regard to human remains at a fire, what three broad questions should investigators keep in mind?
20. Burns are medically classified into four types. Briefly describe each type.

21. What are the common motives in fire deaths?

NOTES

1. Neil C. Chamelin and Kenneth R. Evans, *Criminal Law for Policemen* (Englewood Cliffs, N.J.: Prentice-Hall, 1971), pp. 76–78.
2. Ibid., pp. 78–83.
3. Don C. Gibbons, *Society Crime and Criminal Careers* (Englewood Cliffs, N.J.: Prentice-Hall, 1973), pp. 359–365.
4. U.S. Department of Justice, Law Enforcement Assistance Administration, National Institute of Law Enforcement and Criminal Justice, *Crime Scene Search and Physical Evidence Handbook,* prepared by Richard H. Fox and Carl L. Cunningham (Washington, D.C.: Government Printing Office, 1973), p. 11.
5. James C. Beyer and William F. Enos, "Death Scene Checklist," *FBI Law Enforcement Bulletin,* 1981, Vol. 50, No. 8, pp. 15–18.
6. Charles E. O'Hara, *Fundamentals of Criminal Investigation* (Springfield, Ill.: Charles C. Thomas, 1973), p. 502.
7. Wisconsin Crime Laboratory, *Criminal Investigation and Physical Evidence Handbook* (Madison: Department of Justice, State of Wisconsin, 1968), p. 10.
8. John J. Horgan, *Criminal Investigation* (New York: McGraw-Hill, 1974), p. 292.
9. Lemoyne Snyder, *Homicide Investigation* (Springfield, Ill.: Charles C. Thomas, 1973), p. 62.
10. Horgan, *Criminal Investigation,* p. 294.
11. Wisconsin Crime Laboratory, *Criminal Investigation and Physical Evidence Handbook,* p. 11.
12. Donald G. Cherry and J. Lawrence Angel, "Personality Reconstruction from Unidentified Remains," *FBI Law Enforcement Bulletin,* 1977, Vol. 46, No. 48, pp. 12–15. Much of the information dealing with personality reconstruction was obtained from this article.
13. R. M. Boyd, "Buried Bodies," *FBI Law Enforcement Bulletin,* 1979, Vol. 48, No. 2, pp. 1–7. Much of the information dealing with the search for buried bodies was obtained from this article.
14. William M. Bass and Walter H. Birkby, "Exhumation: The Method Could Make the Difference," *FBI Law Enforcement Bulletin,* 1978, Vol. 47, No. 7, pp. 6–11.
15. International Association of Chiefs of Police, *Estimating Time of Death: Training Key #79* (Washington, D.C.: International Association of Chiefs of Police, 1967), p. 2.
16. For a more in-depth and scientific explanation of these chemical changes see *Dorland's Illustrated Medical Dictionary* (24th ed., 1965), pp. 37 and 1231; and Cyril John Polson and D. J. Gee, *The Essentials of Forensic Medicine* (Oxford: Pergamon Press, 1973), p. 21. The information in this chapter on rigor mortis and cadaveric spasm was obtained from the unpublished paper by Brian F. (Karlovich-) Smith, "The Cadaveric Spasm—Fact or Fiction?" Unpublished research paper, George Washington University/Armed Forces Institute of Pathology, 1974.
17. Brian F. (Karlovich-) Smith, "The Cadaveric Spasm—Fact or Fiction?"
18. Cyril John Polson and D. J. Gee, *The

Essentials of Forensic Medicine, p. 18. See also Alan Richards Moritz, *The Pathology of Trauma,* 2nd ed. (Philadelphia: Lee and Febiger, 1954), p. 399. Y. Yamase, abstract of *Far East, Science Bulletin,* 1942, pp. 1, 52. Edgar Rentoul and Hamilton Smith, eds., *Glaister's Medical Jurisprudence and Toxicology,* 13th ed. (London: Churchill and Livingstone, 1973), p. 117.

19. Francis E. Camps, ed., *Gradwohl's Legal Medicine,* 3rd ed. (Bristol: John Wright and Sons, 1976), p. 83.

20. There is no mention of cadaveric spasm in either *Dorland's Illustrated Medical Dictionary,* 24th ed. (Philadelphia: W. B. Saunders, 1965) or the voluminous and comprehensive work of Werner V. Spitz and Russell S. Fisher, eds., *Medico-legal Investigation of Death,* 2nd ed. (Springfield, Ill.: Charles C. Thomas, 1980).

21. *Estimating Time of Death: Training Key #79,* p. 3.

22. W. C. Rodriguez and William C. Bass, *Determination of Time of Death by Means of Carrion Insects.* A paper presented at the 35th annual meeting of the American Academy of Forensic Sciences, Feb. 15-19, 1983, Cincinnati, Ohio. (This discussion and accompanying figures were taken, with modification, from pp. 1–6.)

23. The information on shotgun wounds was obtained from material developed by Vincent J. M. Di Maio, M.D., Medical Examiner, Dallas County, Texas.

24. The information on firearm residue included in this chapter was developed by the Southwestern Institute of Forensic Sciences at Dallas, Texas.

25. R. C. Harrison and R. Gilroy, "Firearms Discharge Residues," *Journal of Forensic Sciences,* 1959, No. 4, pp. 184–199.

26. S. S. Krishnan, K. A. Gillespie, and E. J. Anderson, "Rapid Detection of Firearm Discharge Residues by Atomic Absorption and Neutron Activation Analysis, *Journal of Forensic Sciences,* 1977, No. 16, pp. 144–151. See also I. C. Stone and C. S. Petty, "Examination of Gunshot Residues," *Journal of Forensic Sciences,* 1974, No. 19, pp. 784–788.

27. Jacques Charon, *Suicide* (New York: Charles Scribner's Sons, 1972), p. 56.

28. Ibid., p. 39.

29. Snyder, *Homicide Investigation,* p. 228.

30. Donna Newson, "Doctors Perform Rare Surgery," *Tampa Tribune,* July 25, 1980, 1-A and 10-A.

31. Richard H. Fox and Carl L. Cunningham, *Crime Scene Search and Physical Evidence Handbook* (Washington, D.C.: Government Printing Office, 1973), pp. 124, 126. This discussion of poisons was taken from this source.

32. *Suicide Investigation, Part II, Training Key #196* (Gaitherburg, Md.: International Association of Chiefs of Police, 1973), pp. 4–5.

33. J. Tuckman et al., "Credibility of Suicide Notes," *American Journal of Psychiatry,* June 1960, No. 65, pp. 1104–1106.

34. David Lester, *Why People Kill Themselves* (Springfield, Ill.: Charles C. Thomas, 1972), p. 36.

35. D. Hastings, "Long Investigation Uncovers Suicide Scheme." *Tampa Tribune-Times,* January 22, 1984, p. 24A.

36. C. J. Flammang, *The Police and the Unprotected Child* (Springfield, Ill.: Charles C. Thomas, 1970), p. 90; Harold E. Simmons, *Protective Services for Children* (Sacramento, Calif.: General Welfare Publications, 1968), p. 45.

37. James D. Regis, "The Battered Child," *Police Work,* April 1980, p. 6.

38. Ibid., pp. 41–42.

39. *A Resource Handbook: Sudden Infant Death Syndrome* (Tallahassee, Fla.: Department of Health and Rehabilitative Services, 1978), pp. 1–2. Much of the information dealing with SIDS was taken from this source.

40. J. Stannard Baker and Thomas Lindquist,

Lamp Examination for On or Off in Traffic Accidents, 3rd ed. (Evanston, Ill.: Traffic Institute, Northwestern University, 1983).

41. International Association of Chiefs of Police, *Hit and Run Investigation: Training Key #7* (Washington, D.C.: International Association of Chiefs of Police, 1967), pp. 2–3.

42. Brian F. (Karlovich-) Smith, "Fire Death Case Notes and Procedures," unpublished research notes and materials, 1974–1982, passim.

43. Francis E. Camps, ed., *Gradwohl's Legal Medicine,* p. 358; and Lester Adelson, *The Pathology of Homicide* (Springfield, Ill.: Charles C. Thomas, 1974), p. 610; Richard Lindenberg, "Mechanical Injuries of the Brain and Meninges," in Werner U. Spitz and Russell S. Fisher, *Medicolegal Investigation of Death,* 2nd ed., pp. 447–456.

11
SEX-RELATED OFFENSES

CLASSIFICATION OF SEX OFFENSES

Sex offenses may be grouped into three classifications: serious, nuisance, and mutually consenting. With the exception of murder, few crimes generate greater public concern and interest than serious sex offenses.

SERIOUS SEX OFFENSES

The term serious is used because not all sex offenses are a significant threat to the individual or to the public. Sex offenses of this type, such as rape, are high priority offenses because they constitute the greatest physical and psychological injury to the victim.

This chapter concentrates on the serious sex offenses that most frequently come to police attention: forcible rape, child molestation (pedophilia), homosexual-related offenses, and incest.

NUISANCE SEX OFFENSES

Included in this classification are such acts as voyeurism and exhibitionism. Usually such acts present no personal danger to anyone except the offender, who may fall prey to an angry father, husband, or boy friend. Few perpetrators of nuisance sex offenses

physically injure anyone. But instances do occur:

The police were called to an apartment complex by tenants who had become concerned after not having seen their next-door neighbor for two days. The neighbor was an attractive twenty-five-year-old woman. The police entered the apartment of the woman and discovered her dismembered body stuffed in a clothes trunk in her bedroom.

The investigation resulted in the arrest of a suspect. He stated that a few days before the murder, he had seen the victim hanging some undergarments on a clothesline. The suspect returned a few hours later at dark and stole two of the victim's panties and bras off the clothesline.

The victim mentioned the incident to a neighbor but not to the police. Later, the suspect returned to the victim's home and saw her, through a bedroom window, disrobe and put on a nightgown. He became sexually aroused and entered the house through an unlocked, rear kitchen door. He picked up a knife from a table in the kitchen and went directly to the victim's bedroom. When she saw him she became frightened. The perpetrator told her not to scream or he would kill her. He ordered her to take off her nightgown and get into bed. He got into bed with her, still clutching the knife. While having sexual intercourse with her, for some reason he could not explain, he started choking her. When she started to resist he plunged the knife into her heart, killing her instantly. He then dressed the victim in undergarments and a dress, propped her in a chair in the bedroom, and talked to the deceased victim for approximately forty-five minutes. Then he disrobed and dismembered the body and stuffed it in the clothes trunk. The suspect admitted to the police that he had acted as a voyeur on other occasions but had never before assaulted any woman.

SEX OFFENSES INVOLVING MUTUAL CONSENT

Sex offenses of this nature involve consenting adults whose behavior is deemed illegal by various state and local laws; examples include adultery, fornication, prostitution, and certain homosexual activities. Except for commercial prostitution and public solicitation by homosexuals, many police agencies assign these acts low investigative priority. When enforcement action is taken, it is generally because of a citizen complaint or because the act was performed in a public place and observed by the police or a private citizen.

TYPOLOGY OF RAPE

Extensive interviews with 133 convicted rapists of adult females and rape victims raised three major factors in understanding the rapists' behavior. These three factors—power, anger, and sexuality—seemed to operate in all rapes, but the proportion varied. In any given rape, one factor seemed to dominate. By ranking each offender and each victim's

account for the dominant issue, the following typology of rape emerged:

1. Power rape—sexuality used in the service of power.
2. Anger rape—sexuality used in the service of anger.
3. There were *no* rapes in which sex was the dominant issue; sexuality was instead always used for other motives.[1]

POWER RAPE

In power rape, the offender achieves power over his victim through intimidation with a weapon, physical force, or threat of bodily harm. Physical aggression is used to subdue the victim. To effect sexual intercourse, many power rapists kidnap or tie up their victims.

This type of offender shows little skill in negotiating personal relationships and feels inadequate in both sexual and nonsexual areas of his life. With few other avenues of personal expression, sexuality becomes the core of his self-image and self-esteem. Rape becomes the means by which he reassures himself of his sexual adequacy and identity. In that it is a test of his adequacy, the rape fills the rapist with anxiety, excitement, and anticipated pleasure. The assault is premeditated and preceded by an obsessional fantasy in which, although his victim may initially resist him, she submits gratefully to his sexual embrace and responds with wild abandon. In reality, many power rapists are handicapped by failure to achieve or sustain an erection or by premature ejaculation and find little sexual satisfaction in rape. The assault never lives up to the fantasy. Further, they do not feel reassured by their own performance or their victims' response and, therefore, look for another victim—this time the "right one."

Power rapes become repetitive and compulsive. The amount of force used in the assault may vary, and there may be an increase in aggression over time as the offender becomes more desperate to achieve what continues to elude him. Usually there is no conscious intent on the part of this offender to hurt or degrade his victim.

The victim is typically near the age of the offender or younger. Hospital examination generally shows minimum or inconclusive evidence of physical or sexual injury. Clinical evidence of intercourse—presence of active sperm—may be absent. Victims often report being questioned by the offender about their sexual lives, their reactions to the rapist's sexual performance, and their identities with the implication of expected further contact.

Power Rape Subtypes. Power rapists are subdivided into two groups according to whether the major goal in the offense is assertion or reassurance.

The *power-assertive* rapist regards rape as an expression of his virility, mastery, and dominance. He feels entitled to "take it" or sees sexual domination as a way of keeping "his" women in line. The rape is a reflection of an inadequate sense of identity and effectiveness. The following are examples of power-assertive rapes.

Warren is a twenty-year-old single male. While at home on leave from the Coast Guard, he picked up an eighteen-year-old hitchhiker and drove her to a secluded beach. She begged to be let go, but he grabbed her, saying, "You don't want to get hurt, baby. You want to get laid. You want it as much as I do." He forced her to submit to intercourse and then offered to buy her dinner. Arrested and convicted for this rape, while out on bail, he committed an identical offense. As an adolescent Warren had been involved in a number of sexual incidents involving exhibitionism and sexual play with children. He was treated at a local mental health clinic. As an adult he had no

steady girlfriends. In the service, he lived with and was supported by a thirty-year-old man in exchange for sexual favors, although he did not regard himself as homosexual. Apart from his two rape offenses (and two earlier ones for which he was never apprehended), he had been arrested for driving without a license, driving under the influence, and speeding. Although of above-average intelligence, his academic and vocational accomplishments were mediocre. The only activity he had pursued diligently was body-building.

Nancy is a forty-five-year-old divorced woman. While at home on a Friday evening, she was visited by a former boyfriend who arrived with a bottle of gin. He asked her to share drinks with him and Nancy agreed. Later in the evening, she refused to have sex with him and her account of what happened follows: "He messed me over the street way. I'm not supposed to tell. He said he'd beat me if I told and he gave me a sample tonight to show me. They work you over to control you so they can have you sexually anytime they want. He hit me on the ear, pulled my hair, hit me in the back by my kidneys—very strategic. But its not the physical part that's the thing. It's mental—to control you. They project onto you. Violence and sex—they think you want that—they project onto you what they want." On follow-up, Nancy reported that she had dropped the rape charge, saying, "He knows I mean business. As long as he doesn't put his hands on me is all I care about. I reported it and have pointed him out to people so that they know him."[2]

The *power-reassurance* rapist commits the offense to resolve disturbing doubts about his sexual adequacy and masculinity. He aims to place a woman in a helpless position so that she cannot refuse or reject him.

Steve is a twenty-four-year-old married man who pleaded guilty to six charges of rape. In every case, he approached the victim in a shopping mall with a gun. His fantasy was that the woman would say, "You don't need a gun. You're just what I've been waiting for," and then "rape" him. He would kidnap them, force them to submit to intercourse, and then asked them whether they had enjoyed the sex and whether he was as good as other sex partners they had had. In every case, he tied up his victims. Steve had no other criminal history. His background was unremarkable, but Steve felt that he had never done particularly well in any area of life (academic, social, vocational, marital) with the exception of his military service, which had been the most satisfying area of his life. He had dated actively as a teenager and indulged in sexual play but stopped short of intercourse. He finds intercourse unsatisfying, partly because of premature ejaculation and partly because it never lived up to his expectations. He saw marriage as a solution, but because he could not be attentive to anyone else's needs, his marriage floundered. Just before his offense, Steve discovered that he was sterile and began to have disturbing homosexual thoughts. He described the offense as a compulsion. Although he realized the consequences of what he was doing, he found that he could not control himself.

Arlene, a 21-year-old single woman, had just stepped off a bus and was walking down a well-lit street. A man approached her from behind, held a knife to her back, pushed her into some bushes, and pulled her sweater over her head so that she would not see him. He raped her, asking her questions such as: "How does it feel? Am I as good as your boy friend?" Arlene said, "He seemed as if he needed to be reassured, and so I tried to reassure him. I was lying on my back in the gravel. He

was odd saying those things, and then I had to bargain with him to get my clothes back. He also wanted my address and to know if he could come and do it again. I felt that if I could convince him I was being honest, he would let me go. He had my pocketbook and would know who I was so I told him where I lived but not the right apartment."

The medical record indicated abrasions on lower and upper back; no other signs of bleeding or trauma.

ANGER RAPE

In this type of sexual assault, the offender expresses anger, rage, contempt, and hatred of his victim by physically beating her, sexually assaulting her, and forcing her to perform or submit to additional degrading acts. The rapist assaults all parts of the victim's body. The rapist often approaches his victim by striking and beating her; he tears her clothing; and he uses profane and abusive language. The rapist vents his rage on his victim to retaliate for perceived wrongs he has suffered at the hands of women. His relationship to important women in his life is frought with conflict, irritation, and irrational jealousy, and he is often physically assaultive toward them. His offenses tend to be episodic and sporadic, triggered by conflicts in his relationships to significant women in his life (mother, girlfriend, wife) but frequently displaced onto other individuals. Sex becomes a weapon, and rape is a means of hurting and degrading.

This kind of offender considers women unloving, ungiving "whores and bitches." Sex is regarded as base and degrading; this offender finds little sexual satisfaction in the rape. Frequently he feels revulsion and disgust and often has difficulty in achieving erection or ejaculation.

Because the rape is one of conscious anger

or sadistic excitement, the assault is brutal, violent, sometimes homicidal.

The angry rapist finds it difficult to explain his rapes and often rationalizes them by saying that he was under the influence of alcohol or drugs. Often the details of the assault are vague to the rapist because during the attack he was blind with rage. His satisfaction and relief result from the discharge of anger rather than from sexual gratification.

Older women may be particular targets for this type of rapist, although victims may be of any age. Medical examination generally reveals considerable physical trauma to all areas of the body, often requiring X-rays and consultation with other medical specialists. Victims report experiencing the rape as life-threatening; symptoms following rape are disruptive to physical, social, psychological, and sexual life.

Victims indicate that initial contact with the assailant generally is cordial and non-threatening. For example, the rapist may pick up a woman hitchhiking, or vice versa; or the rapist may use some confidence ploy to gain access to the victim's home (pretends to need to use the phone, poses as a salesman, and so forth). However, once the rapist feels confident that the victim is under his control, he lashes out suddenly and violently. The victim is often physically immobilized and unable to fight back. The offender may use humiliating language, and perverted acts may become a major aspect of the assault.

Anger Rape Subtypes. The rapists who fall into the anger-assault category subdivide into two groups.

The *anger-retaliation rapist* commits rape as an expression of his hostility and rage toward women. His motive is revenge, and his aims are degradation and humiliation.

Derek is a white, twenty-five-year-old married man and father of four. His mother abandoned the family shortly after his birth. Throughout his life, Derek's father reminded him that his mother was "a whore, and never to trust any woman; they are no good." During his adolescence, Derek became acquainted with his mother. Once, while she was drunk, she exposed herself to him and asked him to fondle her. He fled, terrified. In a vain effort to win his father's recognition and approval, Derek put a premium on physical toughness. In high school, he played sports "like a savage" and then entered the Marine Corps. He had an outstanding service record and after discharge got married and attended college. One day he got into a dispute with his female history teacher over the merits of the Vietnam war and felt that she was ridiculing and humiliating him in front of the class. He stormed out of the room, thinking "women are dirty, rotten bastards" and went to a bar to drink. On his way to his car, he spotted a forty-year-old woman (who he thought was older) in the parking lot. He grabbed her by the throat, hit her in the mouth, ripped off her clothes, and raped her. Before this offense, Derek had been arrested for gambling, loitering, and drunkenness.

Shortly after midnight, Catherine, a thirty-three-year-old mother of two, was in bed reading and waiting for her husband to return from work. A man known to the family for ten years knocked at the door. The fourteen-year-old son let him in. He said that he was leaving town the next day and wanted to say goodbye. Catherine talked to him from the bedroom and wished him well on his trip. Suddenly the man ordered the son to his room, grabbed Catherine, and forced her to go outside with him to another building. He beat her, choked her, and sexually assaulted her. It was only after the man fell asleep that Catherine was able to escape and return home.

On follow-up, Catherine reported considerable physical pain from the beatings. She had pain and swelling to her face, neck, arms, and legs; she also reported loss of appetite, insomnia, nightmares, crying spells, restlessness, and a fear of being followed as she walked home from work. She was unable to carry out usual household tasks. Her relationship with her husband suffered, and she had flashbacks to the assault.

Charges were pressed against the offender, who "copped a plea" for the charges of rape, unnatural acts, and kidnapping. The judge sentenced him to three years on probation. One year later, the offender committed two rapes of teenage girls.

The *anger-excitation rapist* finds pleasure, thrills, and excitation in the suffering of his victim. He is sadistic; his aim is to punish, hurt, and torture his victim.

Eric is a thirty-year-old divorced man charged with first degree murder. His victim, a twenty-year-old woman he picked up in a singles bar, was tied to a tree, whipped, raped, sodomized, and slashed to death. Although found to be sane, Eric claimed that he was high on drugs and could not remember what had happened. His criminal record included assault and battery, breaking and entering, nonsupport, and motor vehicle violations. At the age of 17, he had tied a 13-year-old neighbor girl to a bed and assaulted her. He beat his children and during intercourse, burned his wife with cigarettes. Shortly after his conviction, Eric committed suicide.

Mary, an 18-year-old single woman, described being sexually assaulted by her boyfriend's uncle as follows: "I had met him three times before; I felt I knew him. He seemed like a nice man. He was taking me home from the airport, and he said he had to stop and pick something up from the house and asked me to come in. Inside

he told me to get into the bedroom. . . . I tried to get away. I cried. He was slapping me around. At one point I blacked out, and when I woke up he had ripped all my clothes off. He was so brutal and degrading. He made me do things to him and it was just terrible. I could never be normal again." The offender sodomized Mary and also picked her up by her breasts. She had multiple bruises on her body and rectal bleeding. On follow-up, Mary reported that the man's wife and children had been calling her begging her not to press charges. Mary said, "I dropped the charges and then found out he raped his little girl and two other girls right in the neighborhood. He robbed a store and almost killed the man by hitting him in the head with a brick. I can't press charges. He could kill me." Mary left the state two weeks following the rape.

SEX-RELATED INVESTIGATIONS

Rape, or sexual battery as it is also called, is a legal term defining the crime of a person having sexual relations with another person under the following circumstances: (1) against the person's consent, (2) while the person is unconscious, (3) while the person is under the influence of alcohol or drugs, (4) with a person who is feebleminded or insane, and (5) with a child who is under the age of consent as fixed by statute. A number of state statutes include men as victims of rape.

When the police and medical examiner are dealing with dead bodies, no story from the victim can be confirmed or denied. Investigators often must rely on their initial impression of the scene, such as the state of the clothing, items found, the presence or absence of injuries related to sexual intercourse (fingernail scratches, bite marks, hickeys, direct genital injury, etc.), in deciding whether sexual intercourse (or attempted intercourse) was related to death. But investigators must be careful, because the victim might have had sexual intercourse with another person before death, and the intercourse might not be related to the death.

When investigating a homicide and the victim is a female, the question frequently arises of whether rape also has been committed. But similar questions should arise when the victim is a male and especially if it is a child.[2] Sex is a major motivator and modifier of human behavior. Therefore, a determination of sexual activity may be of great value not only in the classic rape-murder case but also in natural, suicidal, or accidental deaths. Careful observation of the scene and the body may indicate a need for a rape investigation. Even if sexual intercourse does not seem to have any direct bearing on the cause of death, it may explain motives, timing of death, or simply provide a check on the veracity of a suspect or witness. The following cases illustrate these points.

A fifty-three-year-old businessman was found dead in a motel room. There was no evidence of foul play. The bed was in slight disarray, with one of the pillows on the floor. The bed covers were bunched in an unusual position. The body on the floor was dressed in a shirt, loosened tie, trousers, underclothes, and socks. Shoes were neatly laid out next to a chair, and a jacket was on the back of a chair. Examination of the contents of the deceased's trouser pockets revealed the usual items, except for a pair of female panties. Autopsy revealed a massive heart attack and no vaginal cells on the penis. A logical reconstruction of the events preceding death suggested: sexual foreplay with a female, in the course of which a wrestling match ensued during which the man took the woman's panties and then suffered a heart attack.

Although establishing the absence of sexual intercourse in this case did not significantly add to the medical solution of the problem, it did explain why the victim was found at a motel when he was supposedly having lunch.

A furnace repairman was found dead, slumped over the front seat of his van. There was no evidence of foul play, and the medical examiner was not called to the scene. Observation at the morgue revealed that there were peculiar parallel linear abrasions over the victim's knees, tearing of the overalls at the same region, and no underwear. His boots were reversed and loosely laced. Penile washings were positive for vaginal cells. Further investigation disclosed that he had visited a woman at 7 o'clock in the morning under the pretext of cleaning her furnace and had been stricken by a heart attack during intercourse. The woman hastily dressed him and dragged him across the back alley to his truck, not realizing that his underwear was neatly tucked under her bed.

A fifteen-year-old girl's body was found in a vacant lot. The absence of clothing on the lower body suggested sexual intercourse immediately before or at the time of death. Faint abrasions were present on the back of the neck, and marked hemorrhages were present in the eye. The medical examiner believed that this was a case of rape/murder. Autopsy confirmed recent sexual intercourse. The scratch on the back of the neck, however, proved to be superficial, and there were no deeper injuries. Reconstruction of the events immediately preceding death confirmed that the girl had had sexual intercourse with her boyfriend (who lived nearby), in the course of which (according to the boyfriend's testimony) the girl started making choking noises. She reported pain in her chest but said that it was going away. The boyfriend resumed intercourse. The girl started making even more violent noises. He assumed these to be related to orgasm. After intercourse, he noticed that the girl was motionless and unresponsive. After a few minutes, he decided that she was dead and became very scared. He escaped from the scene and told investigators that he had not seen his girlfriend on the night of her death.

The body of a missing preadolescent boy was found in the woods, face down, with his hands tied behind his back by laces removed from the boy's sneakers and his belt. His trousers and jockey shorts were pulled down below the buttocks. The ligature on the hands consisted of laces removed from the boy's sneakers and the boy's own belt. He had been tied around the neck with a torn piece of his shirt. The scene suggested homosexual rape/murder. However, the investigation revealed no evidence of sexual assault. Although there was a depressed groove under the ligature, no subcutaneous hemorrhages were associated with it. A contusion on the back of the neck was associated with deep hemorrhages in the muscles and around the base of the skull and cervical spine. Reconstruction of the case directed suspicion to the boy's stepfather, who had discovered the body. The subsequent investigation revealed that after finding the boy, who frequently played hooky from school, wandering through the woods, the stepfather had hit him with a karate chop to the neck, killing him. The stepfather then tied and disrobed the child to convey the impression of homosexual assault.

INTERVIEW OF THE RAP VICTIM

The interview requires intimate communication between a police officer and a victim who has been physically and psychologically assaulted. As such, the investigative nature of the interview represents only one dimension of the officer's responsibility. By conducting the interview tactfully and compassionately, the officer can avoid intensifying emotional suffering. At the same time, the cooperation of the victim is gained and the investigative process is thereby made easier.[3]

The psychological reactions of rape victims vary. For many, the psychological trauma is worse than the physical injury. One psychiatrist believes that victims of rape experience depression, shock and anxiety which may last only an hour or may persist for several months.[4]

A psychotherapist notes that submitting to rape does "something to a woman, you have no sense of self; once you are used and raped you are a thing, an object, a non-person . . . the victim feels shock, feelings of being apart, split from humanity."[5] Thus, the investigator must be sensitive to the psychological state of the victim. Insensitivity can have two ill effects. First, from a practical standpoint, it might diminish the ability or the willingness of the victim to cooperate in the investigation. Second, it might cause serious psychological aftereffects. Certain steps make the interview less painful for the victim and more effective for the investigator.

INTERVIEW PROCEDURES AND INVESTIGATIVE QUESTIONS

The attitude of the officer is extremely important and makes a lasting impression on the victim. The initial interview of the victim should not be excessive. It is frequently best to obtain only a brief account of events and a description of the perpetrator for the pickup order. Rapid placement of the pickup order is essential. Unless the circumstances of the offense make it unwise to delay the investigation, the detailed interview should be conducted the following day, when the victim has calmed down. When threats have been made against the victim, protection should be provided. The interview should be conducted in a comfortable environment with absolute privacy from everyone, including husbands, boyfriends, parents, children, friends, or anyone else personally associated with the victim. Without privacy the victim's reluctance to discuss the details may be magnified greatly.[6]

There is some question about whether the investigator interviewing the victim should be male or female. Some argue that a female victim feels more at ease in discussing the details of the assault with another woman. Others argue that an understanding male may help the victim to overcome a possibly aversive reaction to men, especially if the victim is relatively young or sexually inexperienced. The major criterion, regardless of whether the investigator is male or female, is that the person have the ability to convey trust and confidence to the victim, while possessing considerable investigative ability. Many police departments have moved toward male-female teams in rape investigations.[7]

The investigator should use language that the victim will understand. For example, if the victim uses slang terms to describe the sex act or parts of the body, it may be because she does not know the proper terms. Thus an investigator may find it necessary to use slang terms to interview the victim effectively. Judgment must be used in such cases, but if it becomes necessary to use slang, then the investigator should do so unhesitatingly and without embarrassment. Slang should be used only when it is the only language the victim understands.

There are certain questions which are totally inappropriate and unnecessary for the investigator to ask, both in the legal and ethical sense. Such questions as, "Did you enjoy it?" or "Did you have an orgasm?" are im-

proper and do nothing to facilitate the course of the investigation.

When the victim has had an opportunity to compose herself, the investigator should make inquiries into the following areas.

Type and Sequence of Sexual Acts During An Assault. To determine the motivation behind a rape, it is imperative to ascertain the type and sequence of the rape.[8] This task may be made difficult because of the victim's reluctance to discuss certain aspects of the crime out of fear, shame, and humiliation. Often, however, investigators can overcome victims' reluctance with a professional and empathic approach. It has been found that although interviewers are likely to ask about vaginal, oral, and anal acts, they do not often ask about kissing, fondling, use of foreign objects, digital manipulation of the vagina or anus, fetishism, voyeurism, or exhibitionism by the offender.[9] In a sample of 115 adult, teenage, and child rape victims, researchers have reported vaginal sex as the most frequent act, but they also reported 18 other sexual acts. Repetition and sequence of acts are infrequently reported. Most reports state, "the victim was raped," "vaginally assaulted," or "raped repeatedly."

By analyzing the sequence of acts during the assault, the investigator may determine whether the offender was acting out a fantasy, experimenting, or committing the sexual acts to punish or degrade the victim. For example, if anal sex were followed by fellatio (oral sex—mouth to penis), the motivation to punish and degrade would be strongly suggested. In acting out a fantasy, the offender normally engages in kissing, fondling, or cunnilingus (oral sex—mouth to female genitals). If fellatio occurs, it generally precedes anal sex. If a rapist is experimenting sexually, he is moderately forceful and verbally profane and derogatory. Fellatio may precede or follow anal sex.[10]

Verbal Activity of Rapist. A rapist reveals a good deal about himself and the motivation behind the assault through what he says to the victim. For this reason, it is important to elicit from the victim everything the rapist said and the tone and attitude in which he said it.

A study of 115 rape victims revealed several themes in rapists' conversations, including "threats, orders, confidence lines, personal inquiries of the victim, personal revelations by the rapist, obscene names and racial epithets, inquiries about the victim's sexual 'enjoyment,' soft-sell departures, sexual put-downs, possession of women, and taking property from another male."[11]

Preciseness is important. For example, a rapist who states, "I'm going to hurt you if you don't do what I say," has threatened the victim, whereas the rapist who says, "Do what I say, and I won't hurt you," may be trying to reassure the victim and gain her compliance without force. A rapist who states, "I want to make love to you," has used a passive and affectionate phrase, and may not want to harm the victim physically. But a statement such as, "I'm going to fuck you," is much more aggressive, hostile, and angry. Compliments to the victim, politeness, expressions of concern, apologies, and discussions of the offender's personal life, whether fact or fiction, indicate low self-esteem in the offender. In contrast, derogatory, profane, threatening, or abusive language suggest anger and the use of sex to punish or degrade the victim.

When analyzing a rape victim's statement, the interviewer is advised to write down an adjective that accurately describes each of the offender's statements. For example, the interviewer might record, "You're a beautiful person" (complimentary); "Shut up, bitch" (hostility); "Am I hurting you?" (concern). The interviewer then has better insight into the offender's motivation and personality.

Verbal Activity of Victim. The rapist may make the victim say certain words or phrases that enhance the rape for him. By determining what, if anything, the victim was forced to say, the interviewer learns about his motivation and about what gratifies the rapist. For example, a rapist who demands such phrases as "I love you," "Make love to me," or "You're better than my husband" suggests the need for affection or ego-building. One who demands that the victim plead or scream suggests sadism and total domination. If the victim is forced to demean herself, the offender may be motivated by anger and hostility.

Sudden Change in Rapist's Attitude During Attack. The victim should be specifically asked whether she observed any change in the attitude of the rapist during the time he was with her. She should be asked whether he became angry, contrite, physically abusive, or apologetic, and whether this was a departure from his previous attitude. If the victim reports such a change, she should be asked to recall what immediately preceded the change. A sudden behavioral change may reflect weakness or fear. Factors that may cause such sudden behavioral changes include a rapist's sexual dysfunction, external disruptions (a phone ringing, noise, or a knock on the door), the victim's resistance or lack of fear, ridicule or scorn, or even completion of the rape. An attitudinal change may be signalled verbally, physically, or sexually. Because the rape is stressful for the rapist, how he reacts to stress may become important in future interrogations, and knowing what caused the change can be a valuable psychological tool to the investigator.

In attempting to determine the experience of the rapist, the investigator should ask the victim what actions the offender took to protect his identity, remove physical or trace evidence, or facilitate his escape. It may be possible to conclude from the offender's actions whether he is a novice or an experienced offender who may have been arrested previously for rape or similar offenses. Most rapists take some action, such as wearing a mask or telling the victim not to look at them, to protect their identity. But some go to great lengths to protect themselves from future prosecution. As in any criminal act, the more rapes a person commits, the more proficient he becomes in eluding detection. If a person is arrested because of a mistake and later repeats the crime, he is not likely to repeat the same costly mistake.

The offender's experience level can sometimes be determined from the protective actions he or she takes. Novice rapists are not familiar with modern medical or police technology and take minimal actions to protect their identity. Some wear a ski mask and gloves, change their voice, affect an accent, or blindfold and bind their victims. The experienced rapist's modus operandi can indicate a more than common knowledge of police and medical developments. The rapist may walk through the victim's residence or prepare an escape route prior to the sexual assault, disable the victim's telephone, order the victim to shower or douche, bring bindings or gags rather than using those available at the scene, wear surgical gloves during the assault, or take or force the victim to wash items the rapist touched or ejaculated on, such as bedding and the victim's clothing.

Theft During Rape. Almost without exception, police record the theft of items from rape victims. All too often, however, investigators fail to probe the matter unless it involves articles of value. But knowing about the items stolen may provide information about the criminal and aid in the investigative process. In some cases, the victim initially may not realize that something has been taken. For this reason, the victim should be asked to inventory items.

Missing items fall into one of three categories: evidentiary, valuables, and personal. The rapist who takes evidentiary items—those he has touched or ejaculated on—suggests prior rape experience or an arrest history. One who takes items of value may be unemployed or working at a job providing little income. The type of missing items may also provide a clue as to the age of the rapist. Younger rapists have been noted to steal items such as stereos, televisions; older rapists tend to take jewelry or items more easily concealed and transported. Personal items taken sometimes include photographs of the victim, lingerie, drivers' licenses, and the like. These items have no intrinsic value but remind the rapist of the rape and the victim. A final factor to consider is whether the offender later returns the item to the victim, and if so, why. Some do so to maintain power over the victim by intimidation. Others wish to convince the victim that they meant her no harm and wish to convince themselves that they are not bad people.

Rapists often target their victims beforehand. A series of rapes involving victims who were either alone or in the company of small children is a strong indication that the offender had engaged in peeping or surveillance. He may have entered the residence or communicated with the victim prior. For this reason, the investigator should determine whether the victim or her neighbors experienced any of the following before the rape:

1. calls or notes from unidentified persons
2. residential or automobile break in
3. prowlers or peeping toms
4. feelings of being watched or followed

Frequently, rapists who do target their victims have prior arrests for breaking and entering, prowling, peeping, or theft of women's clothing.

Delayed Reporting. If the victim has delayed making a complaint, the investigator should establish the reason. It may be that the victim was frightened, confused, or apprehensive. However, delays of several weeks or several months reduce the likelihood of apprehending the suspect and tend to weaken the state's case should a trial be held. Nevertheless, such a complaint must be investigated in the same way as all other similar complaints, until or unless it is substantiated or considered unfounded. An unfounded case does not go forward for prosecution for such reasons as lack of medical evidence, delay in reporting, intoxication of the victim, previous relationships between victim and offender, or because the victim is too embarrassed or too upset to cooperate.[12]

WHY WOMEN DO NOT REPORT RAPE TO THE POLICE

Studies have shown that there is considerable reluctance on the part of many women to report rape to their local police. Victims do not report the crime out of

- Lack of belief in the ability of the police to apprehend the suspect
- Worries about unsympathetic treatment from police and discomforting procedures
- Apprehension, a result of television programs or newspaper reports, of being further victimized by court proceedings
- Embarrassment about publicity, however limited
- Fear of reprisal by the rapist

Unfortunately, some complaints about the criminal justice system's treatment of rape victims are justified. In many jurisdictions, efforts are being made to correct deficiencies. Many corrections have come about through legislative changes.[14] In other instances, women's groups have worked with local police departments to educate the public, especially women, about the crime of rape and to correct much of the misinformation that

may be transmitted via television programs and the news media.

The failure of victims to report rapes has serious implications, because without such information, the effectiveness of the police to protect other women is considerably diminished. A case in point occurred recently in San Francisco.

> A young woman who was raped turned first to her friends for help and comfort, then sought aid from a local Women Against Rape group. No one encouraged her to make a police report; she was indecisive and did nothing. Several days later, she read a news account describing a rape similar to her own. She immediately notified the police and learned that the rapist had attacked three other women. With the additional information that she provided, the police located and arrested the rapist by the end of the day.[15]

FALSE RAPE COMPLAINTS

During the past several years, police agencies have been more selective in assigning personnel to rape investigations. They are now more sensitive to the emotional trauma experienced by victims. However, although the vast majority of rape complaints are legitimate, investigators must remain alert to the possibility of false rape complaints.

In the rape investigation, officers have a responsibility to the legitimate victims of rape and to men who are falsely accused of rape. There are no hard and fast rules to guide the investigator to the truth, but experienced investigators generally find it by carefully questioning all parties involved and scrutinizing the circumstantial and physical evidence. Investigators should conduct a complete check on the background of the victim and all suspects. If the victim is a prostitute or promiscuous, these facts should be considered in the search for the truth. But once it is evident that the legal elements for rape are present, the victim's character should be disregarded. The following case shows the importance of the victim's background in rape complaints:

An eighteen-year-old woman reported that she had been walking past a vacant house at night when three young men leaped from behind some bushes and dragged her, kicking and screaming, into the house. She claimed that she resisted. But while two men held her down, each of the three had sexual intercourse with her. When the last one had finished, they fled. She went to a nearby store and called the police.

The officer assigned to the case had reservations about the validity of the victim's complaint for the following reasons:

The occupant of the house next to the vacant house said that he had heard no scream even though his house was only 20 feet away and his windows were open.

Sand examined near where the men supposedly had leaped from behind the bushes was undisturbed, although there were a number of shoe impressions in the sandy path leading into the house.

The woman's clothing showed no indications of struggle.

The interior of the house was examined and a large piece of cardboard found on the floor in a back room. The woman stated that she had been forced to lie on this while the men raped her. There was a considerable amount of dirt in the room and near the cardboard but, except for some shoe impressions, there were no tracks that would indicate that a person had been dragged through the house and to the cardboard.

Physical examination indicated that the victim had recently had sexual intercourse, but there were no injuries or other traumas. The investigator assigned to the case went to the suspects' hangout, a pool hall. The pool hall manager reported that the victim had voluntarily left the pool hall with the three suspects earlier in the evening.

The manager said that the girl frequently came into the pool hall to pick up men; he said that he had been told by patrons that she was a prostitute who took her customers to an abandoned house nearby to have sexual intercourse. The manager was asked to call the police if any of the men returned. The following day one of the young men, who had heard that the police were looking for him, voluntarily came to police headquarters. He said that he and two other young men had agreed to pay the girl $1 each for her sexual services, to which she agreed. They were directed by her to a nearby abandoned house, and each had sexual intercourse with her. When they finished, one of the men stole her brand new shoes to give to his girlfriend. The victim was reinterviewed and admitted that she had lied to the police because she was angry with the men for cheating her out of the money they had agreed to pay her and because they also had stolen her shoes.

Had the victim actually been assaulted, then her background would have been immaterial.

Some inexperienced investigators are not suspicious of false complaints because of the victim's youth or advanced age. This complacency is an error, as the following two cases illustrate:

A nineteen-year-old woman reported that she had caught her nineteen-year-old boyfriend raping her nine-year-old sister. The woman provided the police with the following details. Her boyfriend had come to visit her. The only other member of the family at home had been the 9-year-old sister. Soon after the boyfriend arrived, the young woman went to a nearby store to buy soft drinks. Her boyfriend and sister remained at home alone. She had been gone for approximately 15 minutes when she returned and saw her boyfriend and her sister having sexual intercourse on the living room couch. The boyfriend jumped up when he saw her; the sister said that the boyfriend had forced himself on her. The woman called the police, and the man was arrested. The man advised the police that he had not forced himself on the young girl and that she had seduced him.

The physician who examined the young girl suggested that she was sexually experienced, and she later admitted this. Interviewed away from family members, the young girl admitted that she had been having sexual intercourse for the past two years. She also admitted that she had lied about her sister's boyfriend forcing himself upon her because she became frightened when her sister caught them.

A sixty-five-year-old great-grandmother reported that a nineteen-year-old neighbor had raped and robbed her in her home. The woman advised police that she had invited the young man over for a cup of coffee. After a while, he told her that he wanted to have sexual intercourse with her. She refused his request, whereupon he slapped her in the face and told her he would kill her great grandson, who was asleep in a nearby bedroom, unless she had sexual intercourse with him. The woman said she agreed because of her concern for her great grandson's safety. She went into her bedroom, disrobed, and had sexual intercourse with the man. When they were finished, he demanded that she give him some money and again threatened to injure the child if she failed to comply with his wishes. She gave him more money, and he left.

A police pickup order was broadcast for the man. The woman was questioned and admitted that she had invited the young man to her home and had suggested that they have sexual intercourse; he had

agreed. When they were finished, he demanded money from her. She refused, and he threatened her great grandson. The woman said that she became frightened and gave the man the rent money. Because she now had to explain to her husband why the rent money was gone, she made up the rape complaint. Although the rape complaint was unfounded, a robbery had occurred.

Conversely, at least occasionally, legitimate rape complaints are not deemed credible by the police.

Upon arriving home late one evening, a thirty-year-old woman checked all windows and doors and went to bed. Shortly thereafter, she was awakened by a man who told her not to make any noise or attempt to resist or he would kill her. After raping her, he directed her to the bathroom, ordered her to douche, and flushed the toilet. The suspect then fled by the front door. When the police arrived, they could find no signs of forced entry into her home; the hospital examination revealed no signs of sexual intercourse or the presence of semen. The police called the case unfounded, believing that for unknown reasons the woman had fabricated the incident. Two months later, a man was arrested in the same area as the woman lived in after he had broken into a woman's house and tried to rape her. In his possession were a number of keys, one of which belonged to a home that the suspect and his family had lived in several months earlier. It turned out to be where the first rape victim lived. The suspect had unlocked the front door and committed the rape.

THE VICTIM AND PHYSICAL EVIDENCE

Victims of sex offenses provide important investigative details and ordinarily are a major source of physical evidence. Certain investigative procedures must be followed to ensure that physical evidence is not lost or accidentally destroyed.

INSTRUCTIONS TO THE VICTIM

The victim of a rape attack should be instructed not to douche, because douching could result in the loss of valuable physical evidence, such as semen and pubic hairs.

+ Hair

SEMEN AS EVIDENCE

The discovery of semen is valuable in two ways. First, if the assailant was a secretor, then a clean seminal stain may be useful in identifying his blood type.[16] Second, the presence of semen in the absence of other physical evidence, such as bleeding, bruising, or trauma in or near the vaginal area, tends to substantiate that sexual intercourse did occur. Naturally, the presence of semen is not evidence that a rape occurred, nor does its absence mean that a rape did not occur. For example, because rapists sometimes experience sexual dysfunction, the examining physician may find no semen during the pelvic examination. In the interviews of the 133 convicted rapists previously discussed, 50 (30 percent) admitted some sexual dysfunction. Twenty-three of the rapists stated that they were unable to achieve an orgasm during the sex act; twenty-two experienced difficulty in achieving and sustaining an erection (impotency), and five experienced premature ejaculation.[17]

It must be pointed out that the terms *semen* and *sperm* are not synonymous. Semen is the grayish-white fluid, produced in the male reproductive organs, ejaculated during orgasm. In liquid form, it has a chlorine-like odor; when dried, it is stiff and has a starch-like consistency. Sperm are the tadpolelike organisms contained in and that travel through semen, to fertilize the female egg. This distinction is important because the laboratory examinations and tests to search for each are quite different. Thus, if a rape were committed by a male who was sterile (having no sperm in his ejaculate) then semen but not sperm may be present. Thus the physician examining the victim for sperm in the vagina aspirates the vagina—removes fluids with a suction device—and microscopically examines them for sperm. The motility of sperm in the vagina is short, measured in hours rather than days; motility decreases to zero in about three hours. Menstruation may prolong motility to four hours. If large numbers of highly motile sperm are aspirated from the vagina, one may conclude that sexual intercourse had been one to two hours before the examination. If a few motile sperm remain, one may conclude that sexual intercourse had been within three hours of the examination. Nonmotile sperm may be found in a living female in small numbers up to 48 hours after sexual intercourse. Nonmotile sperm have been found in dead bodies for up to several hours after death.[18]

When sperm cannot be found, a second test may be employed to identify the presence of acid phosphatase. Acid phosphatase, an enzyme, is a component in the liquid portion of semen. The test should be conducted by experienced crime laboratory personnel and interpreted with care. Routine hospital laboratory techniques are not applicable to this type of examination and may be erroneously interpreted as significant. Only strong reactions should be considered evidence of semen, as mild positive reactions have been noted with vegetable matter, feces, and many other types of organic substances. Experiments have been conducted to determine the persistence of a significantly positive reaction to the acid phosphatase test over variable lengths of time following sexual intercourse. In the living, acid phosphatase may be lost from the vagina after 12 to 40 hours. There is little written on the subject with respect to deceased persons.

Recently scientists have discovered a new enzyme in human semen that is expected to help identify rapists and to clear innocent suspects. Because genetic markers in semen tend to disintegrate quickly, it is important that specimens of semen be obtained from the victim within several hours of the assault. The new enzyme, named *sperm diaphorase,* was discovered by accident during research on known genetic markers in semen. According to researchers, the enzyme exists in several distinctive forms that make it possible to classify men into three groups. The most common form is found in about half the male population, the second appears in 40 percent, and the third in only 10 percent. Once crime experts can zero in on genetic markers in sperm and seminal fluids, they will be able to make accurate comparisons of sperm and seminal fluid obtained from the victim and those from the suspect. The procedures employed would be like those presently employed in grouping blood.[19]

INFORMATION FOR
THE EXAMINING PHYSICIAN

The physician responsible for examining the victim should be provided with all of the available facts before the physical examination. Frequently, a gynecologist is called in to examine a living victim; a forensic pathologist should examine a deceased victim.

Usually certain hospitals in a community are designated as the ones to which rape victims are taken for a physical examination. These hospitals frequently have both specially trained staffs and the necessary technical facilities. Under no circumstances should a male investigator be present in the hospital room when a physical examination is being made. If a male investigator believes

that some physical evidence may be adhering to the victim's body, he should instruct the examining physician to collect such evidence and turn it over to him. The collection of physical evidence in this manner must conform to all guidelines for preserving chain of custody.

COLLECTION OF
THE VICTIM'S CLOTHING

The victim's clothing should be collected as soon as possible. Even if the victim was forced to disrobe prior to the sexual attack, it is possible that hair, semen, or fibers from the suspect's clothing have been deposited on her undergarments. Great care should be employed in collecting and packaging the victim's clothing because the physical evidence adhering to it may be minute and fragile. Underpants should not be the only item of a victim's clothing recovered, because they often offer only limited physical evidence and are likely to be contaminated with other stains, such as vaginal secretions or urine, that interfere with the laboratory examination. Other garments, such as the dress, slip, or coat may be of greater value in providing physical evidence. The evidence most frequently obtained from the victim's clothing are fibers from a suspect's clothing and loose pubic hairs. If the assault occurred in a wooded or grassy area, there will often be soil, seeds, weeds, and other vegetation adhering to the victim's clothing.[20] The following actual case illustrates the importance of a careful search for physical evidence:

> The partly dressed body of a sixteen-year-old female was discovered by two young boys traveling through a wooded area. The victim's slacks and underpants were pulled down around her ankles, and her brassiere was pulled up around her head. A check of the missing persons file revealed that a female fitting her descrip-

tion had been reported missing by her parents 18 hours earlier. The body was later identified as the missing female.

The victim's body was removed from the scene in a clean white sheet and transported to a local hospital. The medical examination of the victim revealed that she had died from brain damage after being struck repeatedly with a blunt object. In addition, she had a large bruise on her right cheek, also caused by a blow from a blunt object, possibly a fist. The examination of the deceased's person and clothing yielded the following:

- her clothing
- pubic hair samples
- blood samples for typing
- grease stains on the inside of her thighs
- a single human hair clutched in her hand, mixed with considerable dirt, leaves, twigs, and so forth
- no semen either in or on her body, clothing, or the immediate area

Physical evidence also was obtained from the crime scene:

- tire impressions
- samples of soil, leaves, weeds, and other vegetation

A suspect who had been the last person seen with the victim and who also had an arrest record for a similar offense was taken into custody and his vehicle impounded. The vehicle's entire interior, including steering wheel, dashboard, door panels, seats, floor mats, and visor, were removed, as were all four wheels. These items were transported to the FBI laboratory along with all of the evidence collected from the victim and the crime scene. A pair of blood-stained trousers and hair samples were obtained from the suspect. The results of the laboratory examination revealed the following:

- The victim's brassiere had several fibers caught in the hooks which were iden-

tical to those of the terry cloth seat covers in the suspect's car.
- The grease stain on the victim's thighs was compared with grease found under the dashboard and near the ignition switch in the suspect's vehicle and found to be identical. An examination of the ignition switch revealed that the car could only be started if someone reached under the dash and crossed the ignition wires, which had grease near them. The subsequent confession by the suspect indicated that in starting the vehicle earlier in the evening he had dirtied his hands and later transferred the grease to the victim when he was trying to force her legs apart.
- The single hair found in the victim's hand was similar in all characteristics to that of the suspect.
- Samples collected from the victim's hair at the morgue were similar to those recovered from the floorboard of the suspect's vehicle.
- Fibers from the victim's underpants were identical to fibers recovered from the suspect's vehicle.
- A tire impression at the scene matched a tire on the suspect's vehicle.
- Debris collected from the scene matched debris recovered from the interior of the suspect's car and dirt extracted from the rims of the wheels of the suspect's car.
- Human blood was found on the steering wheel of the suspect's car, but various contaminants meant that the blood could not be typed accurately.
- Because the suspect had soaked his trousers in cold water overnight, blood typing was impossible.

The suspect confessed to murdering the victim after abducting her from a teenage dance, although his confession was not needed in view of the physical evidence.

He identified the murder weapon as an automobile master cylinder, which he had disposed of after the crime. It was never located. He had killed the victim after she violently resisted his efforts to assault her sexually.

This case clearly illustrates the importance of recognizing, collecting, and preserving even the smallest piece of physical evidence. Except for the tire impression, the evidence had only class characteristics. However, the preponderance of it, coupled with the particulars of the case, made a compelling case against the suspect.

ERRORS MOST COMMONLY MADE IN COLLECTING EVIDENCE

The importance of identifying, collecting, and preserving physical evidence in sex-related offenses cannot be overstated. Yet, evidence continues to be mishandled or not recovered. The FBI crime laboratory indicates a number of common errors in collecting physical evidence. It cites the failure to:

- Obtain fingernail scrapings from the victim
- Obtain all of the victim's and suspect's clothing worn at the time of the offense
- Obtain samples of soil and other vegetation at the crime scene
- Mark each item of evidence properly for future identification purposes
- Obtain saliva and blood samples for blood grouping determination and secretor status
- Remove obvious, visible hair and package it properly when the location of the hair may be germane to the investigation
- Obtain hair samples from suspect and the victim. Hair samples are extremely important because in rape-murder cases the victim is soon buried, and obtaining samples

after the burial presents serious problems.[21]

The FBI also cites faulty handling and packaging of evidence, which results in contamination during shipment.

Sexual Battery Exam

RECORD OF INJURIES

A careful record should be made of the victim's injuries and included in the report. Photographs of the victim's injuries serve two purposes. First, if a suspect is arrested and tried for the offense, the photographs tend to corroborate the victim's account of the attack. Second, the injuries may be of an unusual nature—bite marks, scratches, or burns from cigarettes—and may provide data valuable for developing the suspect's MO. In some cases, the injuries are readily visible to the investigator. In other cases, the injuries are concealed by the victim's clothing. The examining physician can provide details of injuries not readily noticeable. Color photographs should be taken if the victim has sustained visible severe injuries. If the injuries are in a location that requires the victim to disrobe partially or completely, to be photographed, then it is essential that a female nurse, policewoman, or some other female officially associated with the police department or the hospital be present. If possible, a female police photographer should photograph the victim.

HOMOSEXUALITY AND CRIME

Frequently, homosexual activities become known to the police only because the homosexual is the victim of crime. Certain types of crimes are more commonly associated with homosexuality. For example, homosexuals may be respected members of their community, with good jobs, families, and excellent reputations. If their homosexuality became known, it could result in social stigmatization and other painful consequences. Thus they are vulnerable to blackmail. Occasionally blackmailers have been murdered by those from whom they sought to extort money. Often they fear making a police report because it could expose their sexual preference. Homosexuals also are the victims of robbery, larceny, and other crimes. The homosexual who is victimized and reports the crime is entitled to professional, courteous treatment. Sometimes, however, police take the position that the victim "got what he deserved." This unfortunate attitude may compel the victim to fabricate details that destroy any chance of a successful investigation.[22]

This case illustrates some of the barriers encountered when a homosexual is victimized:

The body of a man was discovered in a motel room by a cleanup woman. The man was nude, and there were what appeared to be cigarette burns on his body. He was bound with a three-foot length of rawhide which extended from his ankles to his throat. The hands were bound with a separate length of rawhide. There was no wallet, money, keys or jewelry in the room. The victim had registered at the motel with a fictitious name and address, but he had indicated the correct auto tag number on the motel register. A check with the auto tag agency provided the police with their first lead to the victim's identity. The victim's vehicle was missing from the motel; it was assumed that the perpetrator had stolen the car. A pickup order was placed on the vehicle.

At the address provided by the tag agency, the investigators learned that the victim had lived with two other men. The man who met the investigators at the front door said that he thought they were members of the vice squad. With some effort, the occupants were convinced that the investigators were members of the homicide bureau and that their roommate had been murdered. Once they were convinced of this, they cooperated.

According to the roommates, they and the victim had been in a local gay bar the night before when the victim got into a conversation with a known male prostitute. A few minutes later, the victim and the male prostitute left the bar. Neither had been seen again. A pickup order was put out on the suspect; he was arrested three days later, still driving the victim's car. He confessed to having strangled the victim with rawhide after having bound the victim's hands and torturing him.

Some aging homosexual men become so depressed over their loss of physical attractiveness that they kill themselves. A homosexual whose sexual identity is secret may commit suicide out of anxiety and guilt over being forced or seduced into homosexual acts or over the threat of exposure to family and friends. The following note left by a young serviceman who committed suicide at his parents' home illustrates this point:

My Dear Parents:

I have been trying to find a way to write this ever since I came home. I am sick, not physically, but mentally. I have known for some time that I would take my own life but did not know it would be so soon. I needed help, but you could not help because you could never understand. I enjoyed being gay. I just got sick of life. I came home to die. Please do not mourn for me, for I was sick, and this is my way out of a sick life.

I love you both and I am sorry I had to do this.

Love,
Your son

P.S. I brought everything I own with me. The rest was all a fairy-tale, like my life.

Ordinarily, male prostitutes frequent gay locations looking for patrons. When one is found, a price is agreed upon and the act consummated. Some prostitutes "roll" the patron—steal his valuables. Contrary to popular depictions, the gay world is often violent; if the victim offers any resistance, a severe beating or even deadly assault may take place. In some instances, the violence ensues because the patron suggests to the hustler that the hustler reciprocate the sex act. Such an invitation is a direct threat to the prostitute's denied homosexuality. Thus he externalizes his fears and anger into physical violence. People arrested for these types of murders tend to provide very similar explanations for their actions. They frequently state a lack of knowledge that the man "befriended" was a homosexual and that when they were alone and the improper advances were made, they became angry, striking the victim to stop him but not to kill him.

Accidental deaths of homosexuals have been known to occur during fellatio, either as a result of aspiration of ejaculate with subsequent asphyxiation, or by asphyxiation due to impactation of the penis in the hypopharynx. Although this type of death is rare, the trachea should be checked for semen and sperm if the case has sexual overtones. Accidental deaths may also occur during sodomy. One partner may grasp the neck of the other, twist a towel around the neck, or strangle the other.[23]

CHILD MOLESTATION

Beyond the taboo against sexual acts with children, the vulnerability of children and their general inability to defend themselves arouse considerable public anger against the pedophile, or child molester. However, many of the stereotypes that exist about child molesters are not supported by the available facts. From a study of 148 child molesters conducted in Massachusetts emerged findings that tend to contradict many popular notions:[24]

Myth #1: The child molester is a "dirty old man." The majority of the offenders (71 percent) were under the age of 35. At the time of their first known offense, 82 percent were 30 years of age.

Myth #2: The offender is a stranger to his victim. In the majority of cases (71 percent), offender and victim knew each other at least casually. In 14 percent of the cases, the offender was a member of the child's immediate family.

Myth #3: The child molester is retarded. On the basis of their performance on a standard intelligence test (the Wechsler Adult Intelligence Scale), there was no significant difference between the convicted child molester and the general population in regard to intellectual ability, or scholastic achievement.

Myth #4: The child molester is an alcoholic or drug addict. Drug use was essentially nonexistent among the subjects, and less than one third were dependent on alcohol.

Myth #5: The child molester is a sexually frustrated person. It is sometimes thought that children are turned to because the offender has no other outlet for sexual gratification. The researchers found that many child molesters were married (70, or 47 percent). In fact, the sexual encounters with children coexisted with sexual contacts with adults. For example, in the incest cases that were studied, the offenders were having sexual relations with their daughters or sons in addition to rather than instead of sexual relations with their wives. For those offenders who confined their sexual activities to children, this was through choice. There was no one for whom no other opportunity for sexual gratification existed. In describing the frustration they experienced, the child molesters described this less in terms of sexual needs and more in regard to feelings of intimacy, competency, and adequacy. It was determined that sexuality is not the underlying issue in pedophilia, but instead the distorted expression of identification and affiliation needs, power and control issues, and hostile and aggressive impulses.

Myth #6: The child molester is insane. One of the most frightening stereotypes of the child molester is that of the demented "sex fiend." It appears that such cases are rare exceptions. Of this study group, only 7 (5 percent) showed clinical evidence of some psychotic process operating at the time of their offense.

Myth #7: Child offenders progress over time to increasingly violent acts. The assumptions that the child molester will repeat the act is a legitimate one; however, there does not appear to be any reason to assume that an offender will necessarily become more dangerous over time. This was evident in the majority of cases. Only a small number (27, or 18 percent) of the subjects exhibited an increase in the use of force over time.

Myth #8: Children are at a greater risk of sexual victimization from "gay" (homosexual) adults than from straight (heterosexual) adults. It has been alleged that homosexual males actively recruit and indoctrinate young boys into their life styles since they cannot reproduce. In fact, 75 (51 percent) of the men selected only female children as their victims; 42 (28 percent) selected only male children; and 31 (21 percent) selected boys and girls as their victims. Female children were victimized almost twice as often as male children. Further, it is a faulty assumption that if an adult male selects a young boy as his victim that this constitutes a homo-

sexual orientation on the part of the offender. The research on these offenders found that some 73 (49 percent) offenders responded to children—boys, girls, or both—exclusively, and showed no interest in adults or age mates for sexual gratification. These men were pedophiles in the true sense of the word. Other offenders (75, or 51 percent) showed no persistent sexual preference for children but turned to them as a result of conflicts or problems in their adult relationships. Although this group reverts to sexual encounters with children, their predominant sexual orientation was toward adults. In examining their adult sexual life styles, it was found that the larger majority of these subjects (63, or 83 percent) led exclusively heterosexual lives, and the remaining 13, or 17 percent, were bisexually oriented—that is, their adult sexual activities involved both female and male partners—although, here too, their preference was for women. It appears that the heterosexual adult constitutes a higher risk of sexual victimization to the underaged child than does the homosexual adult. The offender who selects young boys as his victim has either done that exclusively in his life, or does so having regrets from adult heterosexual relationships. Offenders attracted to boy victims typically report that they are uninterested in or revolted by adult homosexual relationships and find the young boy's feminine characteristics and absence of secondary sexual characteristics such as body hair appealing.

In conclusion, the child molester is a relatively young heterosexual male who is not insane, retarded, nor sexually frustrated. He seeks to control rather than to injure the child and usually poses more of a psychological than a physical threat. His behavior is highly repetitive, often to the point of a compulsion, rather than being the result of a temporary lapse of judgment while in a state of intoxication.

INTERVIEWING THE MOLESTED CHILD

The reaction of a child to molestation is affected by a number of variables, each of which in turn has implications for the interviewing procedures to be used. As with rape victims, the investigator must employ considerable sensitivity and compassion and must take into consideration the extent of physical injuries sustained by the child and the child's emotional state.

Experience has shown that physically brutalized children most often can provide only a minimum of information. Beyond this, it is difficult to predict the quality and quantity of their information. Even relatively young children may have strong and accurate recollections, while older children may be so traumatized that obtaining useful information is extremely difficult.

It is best to interview children with one of the parents present. Before the actual interview, parents must be advised that they should not suggest responses to the child or interrupt while the facts are being provided. They should be advised that they will have time after the interview to fill in or correct information provided by the child. Parents also should be cautioned not to display strong emotions during the interview. The investigator must be prepared to deal with the feelings of the parents. Some parents feel guilt, particularly if they feel—even wrongly—that they could have done something to prevent the molestation. Frequently, parents blame the other for creating the opportunity for molestation. The ability of the parents to help the child markedly decreases if they are dealing with these personal issues. Therefore, the role of the investigator includes at-

tempting to relieve parental guilt feelings and reducing tension between the parents.

The detailed interview should be conducted at a comfortable location. The home is a good place if the crime did not occur there. The home is an extension of the self, and if the interview can be done privately there, it often adds to the child's sense of safety and security.[25]

EMOTIONAL REACTION TO THE PEDOPHILE

Because many investigators themselves are parents, they react strongly to the pedophile. However, for legal and pragmatic reasons, such feelings must never be translated into physical or verbal abuse. Physical abuse by police is unlawful and should result in criminal and civil charges. Verbal abuse or open expressions of revulsion minimize the possibility of obtaining the suspect's cooperation and, perhaps, of obtaining a much-needed voluntary statement.

> A 5-year-old girl told her mother that the man next door had taken her into his home, removed her underpants, placed his penis between her legs, and rubbed her vagina with it. After putting her underpants back on, he had sent her home. The mother called the police, but when they arrived the child was very hesitant to repeat the story.
>
> Careful handling of the interview by the officer provided enough information to justify probable cause for an arrest, although the suspect denied the offense. Supplementing the child's statements were those of neighbors who had seen the man taking the child into his house, where she had remained for about ten minutes.
>
> The child was taken to the hospital and given an examination. The examining physician could find no injuries, se-

men, or pubic hair. The victim's clothing was normal in appearance. The situation at this juncture was a shy young child who probably would not be a good witness, an absence of physical evidence, a suspect who denied the charges, and witnesses who saw the child enter the suspect's house but saw no molestation. A voluntary statement was imperative if a successful prosecution were to result.

The suspect was interrogated and at first denied the charges. But when confronted with the child's and the neighbors' statements, he admitted molesting the child in the manner she described. He said that he had been drinking heavily at the time and attributed his actions to intoxication. The suspect agreed to give a full statement under oath to the state prosecutor.

Before the suspect was sworn in, the prosecutor was advised, outside the presence of the suspect, of the facts in the case. The prosecutor requested that the suspect be brought into his office. In an angry voice, he told the suspect, "If that had been my little girl, you son of a bitch, I would have broken your goddamned neck." The prosecutor then asked the suspect if he would like to make a statement. The suspect replied, "I have nothing to say to you." Subsequently, he pleaded guilty to contributing to the delinquency of a minor, a misdemeanor.

The reason for this misdemeanor rather than the felony charge was insufficient evidence. The prosecutor was not new to his job, and had an excellent reputation. What he had done was to identify the victim with his own daughter.

CHILDREN AND "CHICKEN HAWKS"

Some pedophiles are classified as "chicken hawks." The target of the pedophile's atten-

tion, a young boy, is the "chicken" upon whom the "hawk" preys. He engages in homosexual practices with a boy and typically prefers boys within an age span of two or three years. A profile of chicken hawks, which may aid officers in identifying suspects, is as follows:[26]

- Has an identifiable sexual preference for children and frequents locations that attract them;
- May seek employment or volunteer work involving children of his sexual preference;
- May have a genuine interest in children;
- Relates far better to children than adults;
- Pays more than a normal amount of attention to a child in his company;
- Sexually pursues children by eye contact, furtive glances, or staring at the genital area of a prospective victim;
- Usually photographs his victims;
- Collects child pornography and uses it for self-gratification and for lowering the inhibitions of victims;
- May use narcotics to lower the inhibitions of victims;
- Usually gives the child presents or money;
- Often rationalizes any involvement, emphasizing the positive impact on the victim and repressing the harm;
- Often portrays the child as the sexual aggressor;
- Talks about the child as someone might talk about an adult lover or spouse;
- May go to great lengths to conceal the illicit activity;
- Is usually intelligent enough to recognize his personal problem and to understand the severity of it;
- Is often a nonviolent middle-aged man who was molested at an early age; may be single or have a "protective" marriage;
- Associates with few adults except other pedophiles.

No instance of a relationship between a boy and a chicken hawk is isolated. Often the relationship extends over a period of time and involves a whole network of people. In these cases, an analysis should be made of who else could be involved. Chicken hawks constantly seek new boys. A single incident can provide information that extends the investigation to many other cases.

Chicken hawks have a genuine interest in children. They usually seduce the boys through attention and affection, and the relationship may be close enough to give the impression of a parent-child relationship. The child may, in fact, believe that nothing is wrong with the relationship.

The victims of chicken hawks tend to have these characteristics:[27]

- Be between 8 and 16 years old and unsupervised;
- May be runaways;
- May be from an unstable home, with poor family ties and an absent parent;
- Be underachievers at school and at home;
- May be from low- or average-income families;
- Be subject to abrupt changes in mood, attitude, and behavior;
- Be without strong moral or religious values;
- Are not necessarily delinquent;
- Seek attention, affection, praise, rewards, and approval;
- Have more money than usual, new toys, new clothes (rewards from the chicken hawk);
- Spend more than the usual amount of time at recreation areas, theaters, and other juvenile hang outs and in the company of adults

The sexual exploitation of children must be distinguished from other sexual crimes against youngsters, such as rape and molestation. Unlike cases of rape and molestation, the young victims of illicit sex are typically willing participants who may not cooperate with the police in the investigation of such incidents.

INCEST

THE DEFINITIONS OF INCEST

Almost every state has some mention of incest in its statutes. However, the focus of these statutes varies broadly. Many states describe the biological relationship and the kind of sexual contact that occurred (e.g., intercourse); other states refer only to the prohibition of marriage between biologically related persons, with no mention of sexual activity with a minor child. These statutes appear to have two purposes: to prevent marriage and sexual relations between too closely related people and to protect children from sexual abuse by adult relatives. Some state laws do not recognize stepparents, foster parents, or adoptive parents in their incest statutes and handle these cases of sexual abuse under their sexual assault or rape statutes.[28]

In this chapter we define incest broadly, to include any sexual abuse of a minor child by an adult perceived by the child to be a family member. The sexual behaviors include genital fondling, indecent exposure, oral and anal sexual contact, finger insertion and intercourse. The perpetrator may be a biological parent, stepparent, foster parent, adoptive parent, mother's boy friend, other parent surrogate or relative in a caretaking relationship to the child, including extended family members such as grandparents or uncles. Sibling relationships are included when there is exploitation, assault, or a large age gap between parties. We do not discuss incest between consenting adults.

Because the most frequently reported form of sexual abuse is between father and daughter, we use the pronoun *he* to refer to the perpetrator and *she* to the victim. However, it is important to be aware that the child may be male and the adult, female.

SOME CHARACTERISTICS OF INCESTUOUS FAMILIES

What kinds of families are involved in incest? All kinds. There are many kinds of incestuous families, and there is much discussion in the professional literature about how the family members got the way they are. In this section, we briefly describe some of the common behavior and attitudes of incestuous families.

The incestuous family is often reclusive. The child victim lives in a secretive home environment and frequently cannot have friends in, especially as overnight guests. Further, she is discouraged from mingling with neighbors, developing close relationships, or taking part in outside activities or events. The family may be zealously religious. There may be heavy dependency on the closeness of the family relationships, with extreme authority residing in the father figure. The family may have strong beliefs about right and wrong, good and evil, and these beliefs may be superimposed on the children by the authoritarian parent. Fear is often used to control the child's behavior.

Overt incest is an example of tension-reducing acting out in a dysfunctional family. Yet the family maintains a facade to outsiders. Many factors can contribute to the incest: family breakdown due to some sort of stress, such as unemployment, alcoholism, or the physical or mental illness of one parent; an emotionally immature parent or parents; and a lack of understanding of adult nurturing roles within the family. The parents may come from poor family backgrounds.

Serious disorganization in family roles often occurs before the beginning of the incestuous relationship. Usually the mother becomes passive or absent. The victimized daughter becomes the mother substitute, supporting the mother in her housework but giving in to the father, whom she perceives as having been turned away by her own mother. In turn, the father, unrelieved in his sexual drives, turns to the daughter to maintain the family unit. The incest may be reported only after some outsider notes evidence of it or of other maltreatment of the children in the family.

It is not uncommon for more than one child to be sexually exploited in the same family. When a series of children are being abused, disclosure may occur when the oldest child becomes aware that her younger siblings are also being victimized. In one such case, the eldest daughter had kept her own abuse a secret in exchange for her father's promise that he would not touch her younger sisters. When she discovered that they, too, were being abused, she reported to the authorities out of her desire to protect them.

Although the stereotype of the perpetrator is that he is mentally ill or mentally retarded, uneducated, poor, and probably an alcoholic, only a small percentage fit this description. Most perpetrators are middle-class men with above-average income and intelligence, although until recently perpetrators from low-income families were much more likely to come to the attention of law enforcement and social service personnel. Although they may abuse male children, research suggests that most male perpetrators have a heterosexual orientation in their adult sexual activities. The use of alcohol is often involved in acts of incest, but it is not clear whether the alcohol precipitates the abuse or whether drinking simply lessens the feelings of guilt for the abuser who would be involved in incest even if he were not drinking.

The abusive man may not recognize or may have denied to himself the damaging aspects of his behavior. He frequently denies the allegations totally or attempts to minimize or justify his actions. Many abusers develop complex, sophisticated rationalizations (such as that he is providing sex education to his daughter) to justify his behavior. These rationalizations reflect not only his unwillingness to face the criminal justice system's response to his behavior but also his unwillingness to accept responsibility at a personal and emotional level. The sexual abuse may conflict with his image of himself as a good father, good provider, and law-abiding citizen.

Although incest has a negative effect on all family members, the involved child develops the most serious problems. When a child is assaulted by a stranger, there is usually consensus that it is a crisis, that she is an innocent victim, and that she was not responsible for the assault. Her family and the community usually rally around to support her through her experience. But when a child is sexually abused by a family member, disclosure is met with much more ambivalence. The child may even be chastised by family members for informing the authorities, may be accused of initiating the abuse, may be viewed with jealousy as the "other woman" by the mother, or may simply be met with disbelief by family members. All these responses add to trauma to the child.

BEHAVIORAL SIGNS

A number of behavioral signs can be observed in the child victim of sexual abuse. She may frequently be without parental supervision and be exposed to teenage siblings and teenage babysitters with great frequency. The father or mother's boy friend is often in the home alone with the child, especially when the mother is a working parent. The man, in contrast, is often unemployed. The child may be shy, withdrawn, or socially aloof. She may express defiance and hostility toward her

parents and other adults. She may have difficulty concentrating at school. The child may demonstrate an inappropriate interest in the opposite sex and may be sexually aggressive and provocative. The adolescent victim may be pregnant and allege false paternity to divert attention from the true abuser. Involvement in criminal activities or socially unacceptable behavior may also be an indication of victimization. Older victims may attempt suicide or homicide or report a rape. In this way, the victim hopes indirectly to expose the incestuous relationship.

THE MOTHER'S ROLE

The role of the mother in incestuous families has been a controversial subject. Mothers have been accused of setting up opportunities for the incest to occur and of working against authorities attempting to end it. For effective intervention to occur, it is important for investigators to realize the difficulties a woman confronts when she must cope with these behaviors in her family. It is very easy to judge a mother's lack of support for the child victim as indicating a lack of love or caring. However, this judgmental attitude merely alienates the mother further from helping systems. It is important to recognize that the mother is often emotionally and financially dependent on the abuser. She fears public disclosure and embarrassment, loss of economic support, loss of partnership, disruption of the family, and incarceration of her partner or spouse.

Even when a mother reports the abuse, she will have ambivalent feelings, and her support for the child may waver over time. It is helpful to have some understanding of what precipitated the mother's report. It may surface that she made the report in the heat of anger without considering the consequences. It is possible that she had been aware of the sexual abuse for some time and reported it out of anger because of other events in the relationship. It is also possible that she genuinely had no idea that abuse was taking place. She may start out very supportive of the child and yet, as her anger dissipates, her support may waver.

Often the mother experiences the disclosure of the information as a reflection on her adequacy as a wife, sexual partner, and mother. She may feel guilty, ashamed, and inadequate. She may begin to place pressure on the child to drop the charges or may give overt or covert messages to the child until the child decides on her own to end cooperation with the authorities. In some cases, mothers have taken extreme measures to avoid cooperation with authorities, including taking the child out of the state, providing negative information about the child to discredit her statements, or expressing a willingness to testify against the child.

THE POLICE OFFICER'S ROLE

A police officer and protective service worker may interview a child jointly. In such an interview, the role of the police officer is to investigate the suspected incest and to compile evidence for a case against the abuser. The role of the protective service worker is to assess the validity of the abuse complaint and the needs of the family. It is also important to be aware that people working on cases of childhood sexual abuse often have strong feelings about the information they receive from the children. Many express anger, discomfort, and embarrassment when they first encounter sexual abuse. To intervene effectively in these cases, they must be aware of their feelings and keep them in check during the interview.

Before the interview with the child, it is important to obtain answers to the following questions: Who reported it? What is that person's relationship to the child? How did he or she come to know? Information about the child's personality is helpful. Is this child very verbal and expressive, readily showing her feelings, or is she controlled and closed? It is an advantage when a child makes a self-report, because it indicates that she looks at the police officer as a helping resource and that she has decided to take action to end the sexual abuse. Other children may interpret the presence of a police officer to mean that they are the ones who are in trouble. The police should reassure the child that telling about the abuse, in the long run, will do good, for her and her family.

Because it is extremely important not to make the child confront the abuser during the interview, it is best if the social worker and police officer can interview the child alone, in a place that is comfortable for her. Tape recording the interview can be a very efficient way of gathering information without distracting the child. If a child has first gone to a trusted person, such as a school counselor or pastor, the child may request that person's presence during the initial interview to allay her fears and provide emotional support. A child who is extremely frightened and fearful of strangers may be unwilling to communicate without such support.

There are three important considerations in interviewing children. First, it is important to be aware of how the child may be viewing the sexual experience(s) and her interview. Some children have no idea that the behavior was wrong or inappropriate. Consequently, it is important not to convey by attitude or words, negative judgments about what happened. The incestuous activity may have been the only affection the child has known, and she may have very strong positive feelings about the abuser.

Second, children have their own terms for body parts. It is important to learn what their words are and to use them. If the child will not say the words (she may have been told they are naughty words), she may point to her body or use pictures to describe what

FIGURE 11-1   Anatomically Correct Dolls

Courtesy of Eymann Anatomically Correct Dolls, Sacramento, California.

happened. Some police officers use anatomically correct dolls as props in their investigations (see Figure 11-1). Leading questions should be avoided because children may not be clear on what behaviors were sexual; time must be spent to explore all behaviors.

Third, it is important to realize that children have a different sense of time than adults. "A long time ago" could mean two weeks. Concepts like *before, after, yesterday,* and *tomorrow* may be beyond their comprehension. Children remember events in personal frames of reference, such as birthdays, holidays, school days, or weekends, whether it was dark or light, before or after dinner, or what was on TV. The interviewer should move at the child's own pace from general information about the sexual activity to specific details. In situations of multiple incidents, it may be easiest for the child to talk about the most recent and work backwards. The interviewer should find out if the child has told anyone else and who that person is.

If the incest has been undetected for a long time, the child may have built up catastrophic expectations about what will happen when she tells. The interviewer can find out what she has been told will happen to her if she tells. Frequently children have been threatened with physical harm or harm to their family. They may have been told that telling will destroy the family, put Daddy in jail, cause Mother to have a nervous breakdown, and send the children to a foster home. They also may have been bribed to keep silent through special favors, presents, or money. For other children, the authority of the adult involved, plus assurances that there is nothing wrong with the sexual behavior, may have been enough to have ensured the child's silence.

MEDICAL NEEDS

Medical intervention is necessary in some incest cases. In all cases of incest, the officer must consider the potential that gonorrhea or syphilis has been contracted by the victim, and, depending on the age of the child, there is the possibility of pregnancy. Most communities have a social hygiene clinic or sexual assault treatment center for venereal disease testing. If such a clinic is not available and the family has a private physician, they should be encouraged to follow through on an appointment.

If the sexual contact has occurred within 48 hours, much more medical evidence can be obtained. A physical examination, and possibly a pelvic examination, could be done to look for the following: genital or anal bruises; genital or anal bleeding; swelling or red cervix, vulva, or perineum; semen on the genitals or clothing; gonorrhea and/or syphilis; or pregnancy. Although a broken hymen may be an indicator, it cannot be considered absolute. In the male child, there may be blood, bruises, hematoma, or lubricant traces at the anal area. A sample can be taken for sperm in the rectal area, vaginal area, cervix, and uterus. In obtaining medical information, the medical personnel must separate parent and child and obtain separate stories.

THE CHILD AS WITNESS

A police officer can assess the child's ability to perform as a witness. The success of incest cases in court depends on the child's ability to testify—her credibility and her ability to stand up emotionally to the stress of questioning. Frequently it is the adult's word against the child's, and there is little corroborating evidence. How well the child is able to describe the event and isolate it in place and time are important considerations. Young children especially cannot distinguish between relevant and irrelevant facts. But with careful and sensitive interviewing, they can give accurate accounts. Most children cannot describe explicit sexual experiences unless they have been exposed to them. Children who are functioning normally on an emotional and intellectual level are not likely to fabricate such experiences.

Because legal proceedings are frightening and confusing even to many adults, it is extremely important that a child witness receive a great deal of support throughout the legal process. Someone must accept responsibility for explaining the legal process to her in language she can understand and provide an orientation to the courtroom. This function can be handled by the police officer, the social worker, or an advocate or counselor from a rape crisis center.

=== AUTOEROTIC DEATHS ===

Death from accidental asphyxiation occasionally occurs as a result of masochistic activities of the deceased. This manner of death has been described as autoerotic death or sexual asphyxia.

Typically, a white male is found partially suspended and either nude, dressed in women's clothing, women's undergarments, or with his penis exposed. A ligature, suspended from a point within his reach, is affixed to his neck; it is padded to prevent bruising and visible evidence of his activity. There is no indication of suicidal intent, and the death surprises friends, relatives, and associates. Usually, the deceased has no history of mental or sexual disorder.[29]

The death is attributable to asphyxia. The most common method is neck compression; more exotic forms involve chest compression, airway obstruction, and oxygen exclusion with gas or chemical replacement. Neck compression is illustrated in the first and

FIGURE 11-2   Autoerotic Death

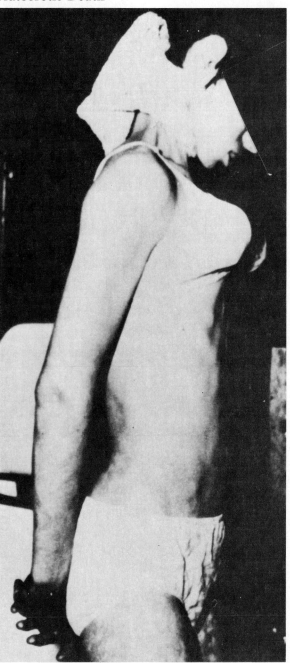

Note female undergarments being worn by male victim with oranges stuffed into the cups of the brassiere. A towel was wrapped around the rope to keep it from bruising his neck.

chest compression in the second of the cases that follow.

A thirty-three-year-old government employee was found dead in a rented motel room. He was in an upright position, and his feet were resting on the floor. A T-shirt around his neck suspended him from a room divider. He was attired in a skirt, sweater, brassiere padded with socks, panties, panty hose and high heels. In the room were two suitcases. One contained men's trousers, shirts, socks, and undergarments. The second contained a knit sweater, skirt, slip, panties, bra, panty hose and high heels. Investigators determined that he was married, had two preschool children, had recently been promoted in his job, and was well thought of by his associates.

The victim was a forty-year-old commercial airline pilot who was married and the father of two small children. On his day off, he left home, telling his wife that he was going to target practice. A fisherman discovered him a short time later, crushed against the left rear fender of his 1968 Volkswagen in a large turn-around area at the end of a secluded road. The left door was open and the motor was running. The steering wheel was fixed in an extreme left turn position and the automatic transmission was in low gear. Tire tracks indicated that the automobile had been moving in concentric circles. The body was held against the car by heavy link chain and was totally nude except for a chain harness. The harness had a moderately tight loop around the neck and was bolted in front. The chain passed down the sternum and abdomen and around the waist to form a second loop. From the waist loop, strands of chain passed on each side of the testicles and into the gluteal fold and was secured to the waist loop in the small of the back. A ten foot length of chain was attached from the waist loop to the rear bumper and had become wound around the rear axle five times. It is not known whether he jogged behind the car or was dragged; however, when he tired of the exercise, he approached the car intending to turn off the motor. In so doing, the chain became slack and the back tire rolled over it, causing the chain to become wound onto the rear axle. The trunk of the car contained his clothing, a zippered bag holding locks, bolts, chains, and wrenches. A lock and key were on the ground beside the body and another lock was found 20 feet from the body.[30]

Airway obstruction is illustrated in the following case:

The victim, a middle-aged male, was discovered dead in his apartment. He was totally nude and held to a pole which had been fitted into his apartment floor. Several black leather belts had been permanently affixed to the pole. These belts supported the victim from the neck, waist, and legs. Leg irons connected his ankles, handcuffs dangled from one wrist, and a gag was over his mouth. The belt around his neck was so tightly buckled that it lacerated his neck. Upon removal of the gag, it was found that he had placed so much paper in his mouth that he had been asphyxiated. Evidence of masturbation was also present.

The following is a case of oxygen exclusion with gas replacement.

A fifty-year-old dentist was discovered dead in his office by an assistant. He was lying on his stomach, and over his face was a mask that he used to administer nitrous oxide to his patients. The mask was connected to a nitrous oxide container and was operational. His pants were unzipped, and he was thought to have been fondling himself while inhaling the gas.

Each of these cases was ruled accidental, and each occurred while the victim was involved in autoerotic activities. Although the motivation for such activity is not completely understood, asphyxia appears to be the cardinal feature of the act: "A disruption of the arterial blood supply resulting in a diminished oxygenation of the brain . . . will heighten sensations through diminished ego controls that will be subjectively perceived as giddiness, light-headedness, and exhilaration. This reinforces masturbatory sensations."[31] In autoerotic deaths, there does not appear to be a conscious intent to die, although the danger of death may well play a role. The masochistic aspect of this activity is evidenced by the elaborate bondage employed. Another masochistic practice associated with sexual asphyxia is the practice of infibulation or masochism involving the genitals. The fantasies of the individuals who engage in sexual asphyxiation are heavily masochistic, involving such thoughts as one's own "penis being skewered with pins; being tied up in an initiation rite; being the leader of an imperiled group; and being raped by cowboys."[32] Evidence of the fantasy involvement may be found in the form of diaries, erotic literature, pornography, films or photographs of the individual's activities, or other such paraphernalia.

It appears that this phenomenon is quite rare among females, but the following case illustrates that it certainly does occur.[33]

This case involved a thirty-five-year-old woman, a divorcée with a nine-year-old daughter. The mother was found by the daughter deceased in the morning after the child arose from a night's sleep in an adjoining room.

The child had gone to bed at 10:00 p.m. the night before and upon awakening noticed a strange humming noise coming from her mother's room. After entering the room she found her mother hanging deceased in a small closet off the bedroom.

The victim was found completely nude

lying on a small shelved space at the rear of the closet. Her feet were against the wall and her body was extended in a prone position, head downward, thus placing her legs and thighs in a horizontal position, resting on the shelved area from her feet to her waist. There was a folded quilt placed on the front portion of the shelf that was immediately under her abdomen and upper thighs. Behind the quilt and toward the rear of the shelf area was a broken cardboard box containing numerous books and other personal or family items. Her lower legs and feet were lying on these boxes, causing them to be at a slight upward angle from her waist.

It was estimated that the victim had been dead ten to twelve hours, as there was evidence of scattered post-mortem lividity on the body. She died of strangulation. An electric vibrator connected to an extension cord was found running. The vibrator was positioned between her thighs with the hard rubber massaging head in contact with the victim's vulva. There was a string-type clothespin on the nipple of her right breast, compressing the nipple, and another clothespin of the same type was found in a basket, immediately below her left breast.

In front of the shelved area, on the floor of the closet, was a laundry basket containing dirty clothes and another quilt was folded and placed on top of the dirty clothes. The victim's hands were resting on this folded quilt in an arms down position. The palms were facing upward. Over the place where the body was lying on this shelved area was a small narrow shelf sixty-six inches above the floor. This was attached to the wall by two steel brackets and the one closest to the shelved area had a nylon hose tied around it which formed a long loop. The victim had placed her head in the loop and placed a hand towel between her neck and the nylon hose. Her face was turned toward the wall and lying against it.

FIGURE 11-3   Victim of Accidental Sexual Asphyxiation

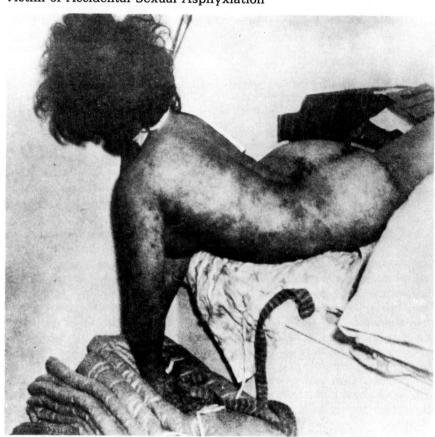

Courtesy *Journal of Forensic Science,* Vol. 20, No. 1, 1975, pp. 181-185

The investigating officer made several important observations based on the body's position and condition at the time of discovery.

1. Because of the position of the clothespin on the nipple of her right breast and the depressed or flattened nipple on the left breast, it appeared that this second clothespin had fallen off and dropped into the basket.
2. It was felt that the hand towel beneath the nylon stocking served as a padding to prevent damage to the neck. The padding in the form of the quilt on the shelved area in the closet was probably placed there to make the deceased more comfortable.
3. The victim placed herself in this position, placed clothespins on her nipples to cause discomfort, and used the electric vibrator for additional sexual gratification. The victim intended to support part of her weight with her arms, as in a push-up, but passed out. This relaxed her arms and the full weight of her body then came to rest on the nylon stocking around her neck, causing the strangulation (see Figure 11-3).[34]

THE PSYCHOLOGICAL AUTOPSY

Occasionally the medical examiner or police investigator is confronted with a death that may be the result of autoerotic or suicidal intent on the part of the deceased. For resolving questions about the death, there is a technique employed called the psychological autopsy described as follows:

> Resolution of unexplained death has long been of concern within law enforcement activities and for the past quarter century, an object of inquiry within the mental health specialities. The term "autopsy" is usually associated with postmortem examination of human remains to determine the cause of death. The psychological autopsy is an analytical statement prepared by a mental health professional based upon the deceased's thoughts, feelings, and behavior.
>
> Its specific purpose, therefore, is to form a logical understanding of death from tangible physical evidence, documented life events, and intangible, often illusive, emotional factors. To accomplish its purpose, the psychological autopsy is structured to address three questions: What was the deceased like? What occurred in his/her life that could have been stressful? What were his/her reactions to those stresses? To accomplish this, structured interviews are conducted with friends, relatives, and associates of the deceased in the hope of developing psychological motivation for the death and pinpointing patterns of life-threatening behavior.[35]

QUESTIONS

1. Briefly discuss the major characteristics of men who are classified as power rapists and anger rapists.
2. Briefly discuss the major factors that should be considered in interviewing rape victims.
3. What are some of the major reasons that women do not report rape?
4. Why do women sometimes make false rape complaints?
5. Why is the discovery of semen valuable in rape investigations, and why is the absence of semen fairly common in rape offenses?
6. What errors are most commonly made in collecting evidence on rape investigations?
7. What types of crimes may be associated with homosexuality?
8. Describe the profile of child molesters.
9. What is the profile of most perpetrators of incest?
10. What are some behavioral signs in children who are sexually abused?
11. What factors should indicate to the investigator that a death may have resulted from accidental sexual asphyxiation?
12. What is a psychological autopsy?

NOTES

1. A. N. Groth, A. W. Burgess, and L. L. Holmstrom, *Rape, Power, Anger and Sexuality.* A paper presented at the LEAA Conference on Rape, Atlanta, Georgia, March 1977. The information from this study was collected from a random sample of 133 convicted rapists of adult victims. The rapists were committed to the Massachusetts Treatment Center for Clinical Assessment. The victim sample population

was derived from a one-year counseling and research study conducted at Boston City Hospital, which included all persons admitted to the emergency service with the chief complaint, "I've been raped." This discussion of the "Typology of Rape" has been derived from this paper. In 1971, Menachem Amir published the results of a study similar to the one more recently conducted by Groth et al., 1977. The Amir study, titled *Patterns in Forcible Rape* (Chicago: University of Chicago Press, 1971), served to dispel some of the most erroneous beliefs and myths about rapists, the most common of which was that they were sexually unfulfilled men carried away by a sudden uncontrollable surge of desire. Data collected by Amir showed that 90 percent of group rapes were planned in advance and 58 percent of the rapes committed by a single man were planned. As for the belief that rapists were sexually unfulfilled, 60 percent of the men in Amir's study were married and led normal lives. Another popular myth is that rapes occur in dark back alleys or to women who hitchhike; however, Amir's study showed that one-third of all rapes are committed by a man who forces his way into the victim's home, and over half of all rapes occur in a residence. Further results of Amir's study showed that in fully 48 percent of the cases, the rapists knew the victim either as casual friends or close relatives. Rapes also tend to be overwhelmingly intraracial. This was so in 93.2 percent of the cases studied by Amir.

2. The information discussed in this section of the chapter was obtained from material developed by Peter Lipkovic, M.D., Medical Examiner, Jacksonville, Florida.

3. International Association of Chiefs of Police, *Interviewing the Rape Victim: Training Key #210* (Gaithersburg, Md.: IACP, 1974), p. 1.

4. The Georgia Commission on the Status of Women, *Rape and the Treatment of Rape Victims in Georgia* (Atlanta: The Georgia Commission on the Status of Women, 1974), p. 5.

5. Ibid.

6. Ibid., p. 13.

7. Morton Bard and Katherine Ellison, "Crisis Intervention and Investigation of Forcible Rape," *The Police Chief,* May 1974, Vol. 41, No. 5, pp. 68-74.

8. This discussion and accompanying references came from R. R. Hazelwood, "The Behavior-oriented Interview of Rape Victims: the Key to Profiling." *FBI Law Enforcement Bulletin,* September 1983, pp. 13–15.

9. L. L. Holmstrom and A. W. Burgess, "Sexual Behavior of Assailants During Rape," *Archives of Sexual Behavior* Vol. 9, No. 5, 1980, p. 437.

10. Ibid., p. 427.

11. L. L. Holmstrom and A. W. Burgess, "Rapist's Talk: Linguistic Strategies to Control the Victim," *Deviant Behavior* Vol. 1, 1979, p. 101.

12. C. LeGrande, "Rape and Rape Laws: Sexism in Society and Law," *California Law Review,* 1973, p. 929.

13. Queens Bench Foundation, Rape Victimization Study (San Francisco: 1975), pp. 81–87; E. L. Willoughby and James A. Inciardi, "Estimating the Incidence of Crime," *The Police Chief,* 1975, Vol. 42, No. 8, pp. 69–70; The President's Commission on Law Enforcement and the Administration of Justice, *Task Force Report: Crime and the Impact* (Washington, D.C.: Government Printing Office, 1967), p. 80.

14. The state of Florida recently repealed its previous statute on Forcible Rape and Carnal Knowledge 794, with a new statute, titled Sexual Battery 794. The new law provides for various penalties for sexual battery depending upon the amount of

force used and the injuries sustained by the victim. In addition, the statute provides that specific instances of prior sexual activity between the victim and any person other than the defendant cannot be admitted into evidence.

15. Queens Bench Foundation, Rape Victimization Study, p. 86.

16. As noted in Chapter 4, a secretor's blood type may be discovered in body fluids. Approximately 80 percent of the population are secretors. A genetic factor determines whether or not a person will be a secretor.

17. A. N. Groth and A. W. Burgess, *Rape: a Sexual Deviation,* 1976, p. 4. A paper presented to the American Psychological Association Meeting, Sept. 5, 1976, Washington, D.C. This deals with the same group of rapists discussed earlier by Groth and Burgess.

18. J. H. Davis, "Examination of Victims of Sexual Assault and Murder." Material developed for a homicide seminar offered by the Florida Institute for Law Enforcement, St. Petersburg, Florida, 1965.

19. Tampa Tribune, "Enzyme Discovered to Help Rape Suspect," March 27, 1976.

20. Arne Svensson and Otto Wendell, *Techniques of Crime Scene Investigation* (New York: American Elsevier, 1973).

21. FBI National Academy, *Collection of Physical Evidence in Sex Crimes* (Quantico, Va.: 1975), p. 2.

22. Frank A. Sass, *The Influence of Homosexuality on Crime* (Quantico, Va.: FBI National Academy, 1975), pp. 2, 6.

23. J. C. Rupp, "Sudden Death in the Gay World," Florida Police Chiefs *Bulletin,* January–February 1972, p. 17.

24. A. Nicholas Groth, Ann W. Burgess, H.

J. Birnbaum, and Thomas S. Gary, "A Study of the Child Molester: Myths and Realities," *LAE Journal of the American Criminal Justice Association,* 1978, Vol. 41, No. 1, pp. 17–22.

25. Bard and Ellison, "Crisis Intervention and Investigation of Forcible Rape," pp. 72–73.

26. S. Goldstein, "Sexual Exploitation of Children: Ignorance vs. Innocence," *Journal of California Law Enforcement,* Vol. 14, No. 3, January 1980, p. 117.

27. Ibid.

28. Marianne Ewig, Lynne Ketchum, and Carolyn Kott Washburne, "Incest," *Police Work,* April 1980, pp. 11–18. (The discussion was taken with modifications from this source.)

29. R. R. Hazelwood, "Autoerotic Deaths." (Quantico, Va.: Behavioral Science Unit, FBI Academy 1984.)

30. J. Rupp, "The Love Bug." *Journal of Forensic Science,* pp. 259–262, 1973.

31. H. L. P. Resnick, "Eroticized Repetitive Hangings: A Form of Self-Destructive Behavior." *American Journal of Psychotherapy,* p. 10, January 1972.

32. R. Litman and C. Swearingen, "Bondage and Suicide." *Archives of General Psychiatry,* pp. 82, vol. 27, July 1972.

33. R. D. Henry, Medical-Legal *Bulletin,* Office of the Chief Medical Examiner, Department of Health, State of Virginia, 1971, vol. 20, No. 2, Bulletin 214.

34. F. A. Sass, "Sexual Asphyxia in the Female," pp. 182–184.

35. N. Hibbler, "The Psychological Autopsy." *Forensic Science Digest,* pp. 42–44, vol. 5, September 1978.

12

ROBBERY

IMPORTANCE OF THE PROBLEM

Robbery is defined as the illegal taking of something of value from the control, custody, or person of another by threatening, putting in fear, or through the use of force. Because of this face-to-face confrontation between perpetrator and victim, the potential for violence is always present and, when it does occur, may range from minor injury to loss of life. Because of its personal and often violent nature, robbery is one of the crimes most feared by the public, a fear which may be heightened by perceptions of police inability to deal effectively with these offenses. Police solve about one in four reported robberies. The importance of robbery resides in economics, its frequency, the fear created, the potential for violence, and its frequent resistance to investigative efforts.

THE LAW OF ROBBERY

There are two basic methods of robbery—armed and unarmed—but the targets are innumerable and range from purses to banks.[1] Legislative enactments have also produced such variants as train robbery, truck hijacking, safe robbery, robbery of bank vault, and violent robbery. These variants reflect differences in methods of commission, techniques, victims, and objects of attack. The primary reason for such diversified classifications of conduct which constitutes robbery has been to allow for the legislation of increased or decreased penalties for the commission of these acts depending upon their seriousness and the threat posed to the welfare of society. Nevertheless, the elements of the basic crime of robbery remain constant throughout and have undergone few changes.

ELEMENTS OF THE CRIME

Robbery consists of the following elements: taking, carrying away, personal property, of another, with the intent to deprive permanently, by the use of force, fear, or threat of force.

TAKING

The property taken in a robbery must be taken illegally by the robber. Someone who has the right to take such property cannot properly be convicted of robbery. This illegal taking is called "trespassory." The property must be taken from the custody, control, or possession of the victim and, as will be seen later, from the victim's presence. This element of the crime is satisfied once the robber has possession of the property; until posses-

FIGURE 12-1   A Bank Robbery in Progress

The man in the foreground glances over his shoulder at the entrance while he keeps bank employees and patrons covered. His female accomplice is stuffing money into a briefcase held in front of her. Note the bills that have dropped to the floor.

Courtesy of the Atlanta Police Department

sion has occurred, only an attempt has occurred.

CARRYING AWAY

Once the element of taking has been satisfied, the robber must then have carried away the property. As is true in the crime of larceny, this element can be satisfied simply by showing that the accused totally removed the article from the position which it formerly occupied. It is not necessary to show that any great distance was involved in the carrying away.

PERSONAL PROPERTY

The object of the robbery must be personal property as opposed to real estate or things attached to the land. Again as in larceny, any tangible property and some forms of intangible property represented by tangible items, such as stocks and bonds, gas, electricity, minerals, and other such commodities can be objects of robbery.

ANOTHER

The property taken must belong to another, not to the accused. This again relates to the first element of taking. If the taking is trespassory—illegal—then the property must be the rightful property of one other than the robber.

THE INTENT
TO DEPRIVE PERMANENTLY

Robbery is a crime of specific intent and requires that the prosecution establish, in court, that the defendant, at the time of taking the property by force or threat of force from the victim or the victim's presence, did, in fact, intend to deprive the victim of the use and enjoyment of that property permanently. In most cases this can be concluded from the facts and circumstances surrounding the case, but in specific-intent crime cases juries are not permitted to assume this particular fact. Thus, the police officer's investigation must be geared to establishing this as an essential element of the crime. The fact that force or the threat of force was used to secure the property from the victim is often enough to convince a jury of the accused's intent to deprive permanently.

THE USE OF FORCE,
FEAR, OR THREAT OF FORCE

This element of the crime requires that the force or threat of force was directed against the physical safety of the victim rather than his or her social well-being. Thus threats to expose the victim as a homosexual or an embezzler do not satisfy this element of the crime. Proof that force was used or, at the very least, that threats were made such that the victim feared imminent bodily harm is essential for successful prosecutions of robbery cases. The taking of property without force is the crime of larceny. However the force used to separate the victim from his or her property in robbery need not be great.

Serious injury to the victim of a robbery usually presents little difficulty in convincing the investigator or the jury that force was used. However, difficulties may arise in the case of a victim who claims to have been robbed under the threat of force when no actual injury occurred. In this case, the skill of the investigator in determining the facts of the case becomes of crucial importance to successful prosecution.

There are also more subtle situations in which the investigator must know legal requirements as well as investigative techniques. The typical purse-snatching case is an illustration. Often, the force element of the crime of robbery can be satisfied only by determining whether the victim attempted to resist the force used, and if so, the extent of that resistance. It is generally accepted by courts that a woman who puts her purse next to her on the seat of a bus without keeping her hand on it or loosely holds it in her hand is not the victim of robbery if someone quickly grabs the purse and runs. In these cases, the woman has not resisted. However, if she were clutching the bag tightly and someone managed to grab it from her after even a slight struggle, sufficient force and resistance would have occurred to constitute robbery. A good rule for the investigator to follow in cases of uncertainty is that the removal of an article without more force than is absolutely necessary to remove it from its original resting place constitutes larceny. If any additional force, no matter how slight, is used, it is then robbery, provided the object is taken from the presence or person of the victim. The property does not have to be held by the victim physically or be on his or her person. It merely has to be under the victim's control. Control in this sense means the right or privilege to use the property as the victim sees fit. Neither is it necessary or essential that the property be visible to the victim when the crime is committed.

The force or threat of force must precede or accompany the taking. Force applied after the taking does not constitute robbery. Thus a victim who realizes that his or her property has been stolen and attempts to recover that property, at which time force ensues, is not the victim of a robbery if the property was originally taken surreptitiously and without force.

When force is not used but is substituted by a threat to the physical well-being of the victim, it is not necessary that the victim actually be frightened to the point of panic. It is enough that the victim is reasonably apprehensive and aware of the potential for injury.

OVERVIEW: THE OFFENSE, THE = VICTIM, AND THE OFFENDER =

When generalizing about offenses, victims, and offenders certain limitations must be acknowledged. Research findings are occasionally inconclusive and conflicting. A variety of factors account for this. For example, a study of the various aspects of robbery in one city has limited generalization power because, while cities may share certain characteristics, such factors are not precisely duplicated from city to city or perhaps not even in the same city over time. If we attempt to compensate for this factor by using national data, a general picture emerges, while individual differences disappear. If we use an intensive scrutiny of a smaller number of cases, their profile may not be like that of other intensive studies or the general profile. Additionally, a limitation common to most studies of crimi-

nals is that we are focusing upon those who "failed," i.e., those who were caught, and whose resemblance to those not apprehended is a matter of conjecture. Despite such issues, information concerning offenses, victims, and offenders is useful in providing a qualified frame of reference.

Robbery is essentially a problem of large cities. Cities with populations of 100,000 or more bear the brunt of this offense; six of every ten reported offenses occur in them.[2] Robbery occurs most frequently in the northeastern states, where the rate is 262 per 100,000 people, and the least in the southern states, where the rate is 163.[3] (Table 12-1 indicates the location of reported robberies nationally.)

In terms of weapons used, a firearm is involved in 36 percent of the cases, a knife or cutting instrument is used 13 percent of the time, some other weapon, such as a blunt object, in 10 percent of the offenses, with the remaining 41 percent of the robberies involving the use of physical force only.[4] Together these data reveal that approximately six of every ten robberies are armed and the balance strong-armed. One study showed that armed robbers had carried handguns (60 percent), knives (40 percent), sawed-off guns

TABLE 12-1
Locations of Reported Robberies

Type	Percent of Total
Street/Highway	54.5
Commercial house	11.5
Gas or service station	3.3
Convenience store	5.5
Residence	11.0
Bank	1.4
Miscellaneous	12.8
Total	100.0

Source: FBI, *Crime in the United States.* (Washington, D.C.: Government Printing Office, 1985), p. 18.

(15 percent), unmodified shoulder weapons (11 percent), and assorted other weapons, such as brass knuckles, explosives, and martial arts weapons (16 percent).[5] The percentages total more than 100 percent because 25 percent of the offenders had carried at least two weapons—most often a handgun and a knife—and 10 percent revealed that they had carried three or more weapons.[6] Thus, officers should continue to exercise great caution when approaching a robbery suspect who has thrown down a weapon.

Findings on the frequency of injury to robbery victims vary.[7] A study of three local jurisdictions reported that in one jurisdiction victims had minor injuries in only 12 percent of the cases; another jurisdiction reported that 45 percent of its victims had minor injuries.[8] When the data for all three jurisdictions studied are combined the results are as follows: no injuries (64 percent), minor injuries (24 percent), received treatment and released (7 percent), hospitalized (3 percent), and killed (2 percent).[9] A 13-year study of robbery in another city revealed that the risk of death in a robbery situation was one in 100 and that firearms were the cause of fatalities in 72 percent of the cases.[10]

When victims are injured in a robbery, men and women are equally likely to have minor injuries, but men are three times more likely to suffer serious injuries.[11] The self-protective measures most associated with injury to the victim are his or her use of physical force or a weapon and trying to get help or to frighten the offender.[12] In contrast, the self-protection strategy most associated with noninjury is nonviolent resistance, including evasion.[13] When victims know the robber, they are more likely to use self-protection measures and to be injured. Victims know robbers in about 19 percent of cases.[14] The likelihood of injury is greatest when a lone victim is confronted by several youthful offenders employing strong-arm tactics. The use of violence by young perpetrators may

simply be part of an unvarying technique in which the ability or willingness of the victim to resist is not even considered, but rather the object is to create a fear which paralyzes the victim and bystanders, to get a perverse "kick," or to be part of a hostile act in which the victim is a convenient and symbolic target:

> There is no doubt in my mind that I would have killed any victim who tried to cross me. You have to understand, I was fighting a full-fledged war against "them." "Them" was anyone—the establishment, whites, police, anyone. I did seriously hurt a couple of victims and I actually felt pretty good about it. I thought I was getting back at "them." At times I thought I might be winning the war. They would do something to me, and I'd do something back. It was kind of a game. You see I wanted to make "them" pay for all the shit I had to put up with. Oh yeah, there is no doubt that, especially in my earlier years, I was out to bust some heads.[15]

Robberies are highest in the winter months, peaking in December, and the lowest during the summer months, bottoming during June.[16] The average dollar loss nationally per robbery is $609, with an average loss for banks of $2,690.[17] Crime and drugs are intimately related; in some instances, offenses are committed to support a drug habit, and in others the use of drugs or alcohol may reduce inhibitions and fears about committing crime.[18] One study showed that 49 percent of convicted robbers admitted to being dependent on alcohol or drugs, and 57 percent had been high when they "went out on a job."[19] As a practical matter, drug use poses potentially difficult situations for investigators because people who mix drugs and alcohol may react in unpredictable and suddenly violent ways.

Robbery is basically an intraracial crime; in one study, blacks said that they were robbed by blacks 85 percent of the time, and whites said that they were robbed by whites 51 percent of the time.[20] Nationally among those apprehended for robbery, 93 percent are males, 61 percent are blacks, and 67 percent are under twenty-five years of age.[21]

The circumstances under which robberies occur range from the mundane, to the bizarre, to the tragic:

> In New York City, a salesman in his private car was forced to the side of the road and robbed at gunpoint of jewels worth $30,000.[22]
>
> A police officer was robbed and disarmed by two men posing as detectives.[23]
>
> Occupants of a luxury San Francisco hotel were startled to see a sawed-off shotgun emerge from the elevator hatch above their heads; a mail sack dropped out, and they were ordered to put their cash, jewelry, credit cards, and wallets in it. They were left helpless, stranded between floors, while the robbers made their escape.[24]
>
> A gunman, enraged by the size of his loot, ran amok in a Savannah store . . . killing two persons and wounding two others. "This is not very much money," the bandit screamed. "Somebody has to die!"[25]

Despite these variations, three styles of robberies—the ambush, the selective raid, and the planned operation—can be classified according to the amount of planning conducted by the perpetrators. The ambush involves virtually no planning and depends almost entirely on the element of surprise. A prime example would be robberies in which victims are physically overpowered by sudden, crude force and in which "scores" are generally small.[26] The lack of planning does not mean, however, that there is no premeditation, a distinction made by one offender:

> I never really did any planning, as you see it. I pulled robberies at random . . . without disguises or anything. . . . But you must understand one thing, just because I didn't do "planning" as you describe it doesn't mean I didn't think about crime a lot. I had to get myself mentally ready to do crimes. This doesn't mean I planned . . . but . . . I was thinking and preparing for crime constantly; I simply waited for the right circumstances to occur. When I saw the time was right, I would pull the job.[27]

The selective raid is characterized by a minimal amount of casual planning. Sites are tentatively selected, very briefly cased, and possible routes of approach formulated. "Scores" vary from low to moderate, and several robberies may be committed in rapid succession:

> When I get ready to fall in for one, I visit the place a couple of times in one day. I want to see how it's laid out, how to get away as quick as possible and what kind of people work there . . . women are bad to rob because they get all emotional . . . if the man there looks hard, I might not even mess with the place. You can tell what people are like by the way they present themselves. . . . I wouldn't want to just blow a family man away, but if it's me or him, that's business. I like to do pharmacies because besides the money, there's drugs and on the streets that's the same as cash. You can't ever worry about being caught because that is negative thinking, and most likely you'll end up being caught right after. I don't mess with no disguises, I just go to someplace like about 25 or 30 miles away where nobody knows me and do it, sometimes a couple real quick if I'm on a roll. Before I go out to do one, I try to relax and fish or make love a lot. You want your head to be right because it could be your life or someone else's. I don't do no pills or drink until after the work for the same reason . . . but if I need the money and have been doing some of that shit, I'll just go ahead and pull one, but working that way is dangerous.[28]

The planned operation is characterized by larger "scores," no force, less likelihood of apprehension, and careful planning:

> The reason I was never apprehended in five years was because I never had any partners, I worked alone, kept my own counsel, I wasn't on an ego trip—I wasn't shooting my mouth off to the girls I went around with, I changed my name like I changed my socks. I had four different aliases during that period—legitimate aliases where I would go down and get a California driver's license in a different name and tell them that I was retired military or had just gotten discharged after thirteen years and didn't have a current license, and the only license I had was a military license. With the driver's license, I opened up savings accounts, checking accounts, and so forth. As far as the friends I had at the time, I never knew a thief in my life. Not even when I was robbing banks. I never knew a thief until I went to prison.
>
> I would go into the bank well dressed—suit and so forth, dyed hair and moustache, a couple of sweatshirts under the suit to make me look heavier, a hat to make me look taller . . . never sunglasses . . . and an attaché case and so forth. And I would go into the manager's outer office where his secretary was by saying I had an appointment or something like this. To make an impression on her, I would take that .38 Colt Cobra. I wanted him to call his chief teller or whoever he considered the most reliable and tell him to take my attaché case into the vault and come out with all the larger bills—no ones, fives, or tens—which, incidentally, led to my downfall, that little old line, because I may just as well have signed my name to every bank I ever robbed. So the guy would go out and bring the money back, and then I would have him open the attaché case in front of me to make sure that there wasn't a bug or little hom-

> ing device which could trace me or whatever, and I would get an idea of how much money was in it. If it looked like a considerable sum of money, then I had transacted my business. Very rarely was anyone in the bank aware of what was going on. I wanted to be in and out of there in three minutes flat.
>
> The way I left the bank is—I never stole a car in my life—I bought a clunker for $150 two weeks before I robbed that bank. This guy advertised in the paper, and you go, give him the money, sign the slip, and that's all there is to it. You never reregister it; you use it two times—driving it from where you bought it and the next time when you rob the bank. Then you ditch it within one minute, however far you can get. I used to pick a shopping center within a mile or whatever of the bank, and there I'd have my other car, and I'd switch cars. And I would be wearing these dishwashing type gloves so there would be no fingerprints. Sometimes I'd let the car be running with the key in it, hoping some kid would steal it. I'd be tickled to death if he'd run off with it! And then of course I would change clothes and sometimes take the old clothes and throw them in a convenient garbage can, Goodwill box, or whatever. Then I'd take cover, more or less, whether it be a local hotel, motel, crowded part of town, and I'd just stay inside.[29]

═══ TYPOLOGY OF ROBBERIES ═══

In addition to knowing the broad profile of the offense, the investigator must be familiar with the various types of robberies.[30]

VISIBLE STREET ROBBERY

Visible street robberies take place in open areas, frequently on side streets or in parking lots, and are characterized by physical force, the element of surprise, and speed. Research indicates that visible street robbery is more likely to involve a chance occurrence with little or no planning by the perpetrator. Generally, street robberies can be classified in one of three ways: armed, unarmed, and the purse snatch. In some jurisdictions the purse snatch is classified as grand theft.

Because most visible street robberies occur quickly, the victim is unlikely to be able to provide anything beyond a limited physical description. Purse snatches and muggings are the most common of visible street robberies, and studies indicate that the perpetrator is not likely to be armed. However, the use of physical force is not uncommon, and the victim may be knocked to the ground or beaten by the perpetrators. In particular, younger offenders often use their numbers as a weapon and consider the commission of a robbery as an act which enhances their status within the peer group. In many instances the major reward is peer admiration rather than money. Most street robberies occur at dusk or after dark, although some form of artificial light is usually present. Subjects who commit visible street robbery are likely to number two or more, be young, black, and have a previous record of involvement with authorities. Preparation for the act is generally minimal, and it would appear that the decision to commit a robbery is based largely on opportunity. In many instances the robbery is a group decision, frequently on the spur of the moment. However, it is not unusual for two or more youths to set out with the idea of committing a purse snatch or "mugging."

The older robber is more interested in the financial aspect of the robbery and is therefore more likely to plan the robbery although not the victims. Perpetrators frequently stake out a night depository box at a bank, an automatic teller location or look for shopkeepers who close late at night. The more sophisticated street robbery involves some planning, and the victim may be someone known to carry large amounts of money. In such cases, the perpetrator is usually armed and works with an accomplice, who drives the get-away car. Statistically, the armed street robber is rare, with the exception of nonvisible street robberies, where knives appear to be used more frequently.

NONVISIBLE ROBBERIES

Although there are many similarities between visible and nonvisible robberies, certain aspects give the latter a character of their own. Nonvisible robberies occur off the streets, usually in a residential or commercial building, a public transportation facility, or some similar location. They are generally committed by youths, but the average age of the perpetrator is slightly higher than in visible robberies. The use of a weapon is more common, especially in robberies occurring in residential lobbies, hallways, and elevators; knives are the principal weapon employed. Frequently, perpetrators have "graduated" from visible street robbery. They generally work alone or in pairs, particularly in residential buildings, and both planning and intent to commit robbery are more common.

Victims in public areas, such as train stations and bus terminals, are likely to be elderly men and women. Robberies in residential buildings, particularly apartments and high-rise buildings, are committed against anyone who comes along.

The tendency toward violence is heightened in nonvisible robberies, particularly when the victim refuses to submit. Unfortunately, data rarely reveal the mobility of suspects, but few travel great distances to commit the crime. Most are familiar with the neighborhood and escape on foot or in public conveyances. Perpetrators are likely to have criminal records.

RESIDENTIAL ROBBERIES

Residential robberies, in which the perpetrator actually enters a home, account for 11 percent of reported robberies.[31] One study indicates that 55 percent involved housebreakers who were discovered in the act of burglary. In 45 percent of the cases, the perpetrator gained entrance by knocking on the door and forcibly entering.[32] In residential robberies victim and suspect may have known each other slightly. Some victims of robbery are chosen because they are thought to keep money or valuables. In wealthy neighborhoods, victims are apt to be chosen randomly.

Perpetrators of residential robberies are likely to be armed with either knives or hand guns. They also will typically have a prior criminal record. Similar occurrences may be the work of a relatively small number of subjects working together.

VEHICLE ROBBERIES

The vehicle robbery generally involves the holdup of commercial drivers. Taxicabs, buses, and delivery vans are the most frequent targets. There is a correlation between the probability of robbery and the area a driver works; those working in the inner city are most likely to be victimized.

Most vehicle robberies occur during evening hours. Only delivery vans appear to be robbed more frequently during the afternoon. Unlike street robbers, perpetrators are generally armed, in their late teens or early twenties, and have set out with the intention to commit a robbery. Little or no thought is generally given to the individual victim, although plans are made for the method of escape. In the case of a taxicab, the driver is frequently given an address in a quiet or secluded area and robbed at the destination. Perpetrators of vehicle robberies tend to be violent, and taxicab drivers are often injured or killed. Plexiglass screens in cabs may reduce holdups and injuries.

COMMERCIAL ROBBERIES

Most commercial robberies are of small businesses and stores that are open in the evening and night hours, such as convenience stores, service stations, bars, and package stations. Robbers also invade restaurants or other premises and take money and valuables from patrons, including cash, watches, wedding bands, and other jewelry. Victimization studies indicate that while 53 percent of robberies happen between 6:00 P.M. and 6:00 A.M., 67 percent of all serious injuries (broken bones, loss of teeth, internal injuries, and all other injuries resulting in hospitalization of two or more days) occur during this time period.[33] Thus commercial robbers—who are typically armed with firearms—appear to contribute disproportionately to violence done to victims. Victims may resist because of the stakes involved, and robbers then may use force.[34]

Perpetrators of commercial robberies are more likely to be experienced robbers. Since a commercial robbery suspect is more likely to have a criminal record, the possibility of developing information from his modus operandi is heightened. The number of adults committing commercial robberies is higher than those involved in street crimes.

═══ ARREST PROBABILITIES ═══

Robbery bears a comparatively low clearance rate: only 26 percent.[35] The reasons for this are several: physical evidence may not be found; the time of perpetrators at the scene is limited; witnesses are usually shaken, so that their information runs from minimal to completely erroneous. Physical descriptions are the most common evidence, but these are

FIGURE 12-2 The Robbery of a Convenience Store

Working as a pair, one robber takes the cash from the till while his accomplice controls the clerk by using physical force and holding a weapon in the clerk's back.

Courtesy of the Phoenix, Arizona, Police Department

of limited use when offenders enjoy geographic mobility.

INVESTIGATIVE TECHNIQUES

The police response to the report of a robbery can be divided into the following components: responding to the scene, tactical situations at the scene, the original investigation, and latent work.

RESPONDING TO THE SCENE

The time between receiving the call reporting the robbery and arriving at the scene must minimize the possibility of injury to the officer while maximizing the possibility of apprehension. The arrival at the scene should be as rapid as safety permits while avoiding excessive noise. If responding alone to an "in progress" call, the investigator should attempt to coordinate his or her arrival at the scene with that of a backup car.

However, because robbery is a violent crime with high potential for physical harm to the victim, the officer must attempt to arrive as soon as possible.

The investigator must ensure that all information available from the dispatcher has been obtained, including the answers to the following questions: What is the exact location of the offense, including the type of business? Is the offense in progress? How many suspects are involved? What type and how many weapons were displayed? What description of the suspect is available? By what method and in what direction did the suspect flee? What is the description of the means of transportation used by the suspect?

In approaching the scene, the investigator must be alert for several possibilities:

- Based on information provided by the dispatcher, the suspects may be observed fleeing from the direction of the scene, either on foot or in a vehicle.
- If the dispatcher cannot supply any information other than the nature of the call, the officer assigned to respond should review information from recent robberies about target, MO, suspects, vehicles, weapons used, and other factors to recognize the suspects if they are moving away from the scene on the street along which the officer approaches.
- The fleeing suspects may, as the officer approaches them on the way to the scene, abruptly turn off, fire at the officer, or otherwise suddenly reveal themselves.
- Both as the officer approaches the scene and at the scene, officers should avoid action, physical, or situational stereotyping.[36]

Action Stereotyping. Action stereotyping occurs when the officer's expectations are so set to see one thing that he or she fails to perceive the event accurately. For example, the responding officer may expect the suspect to come rushing out of the store, hop into a

"souped up" car, and speed away. Although this may be the case, there are also other possible behaviors:

Two robbers who confessed to over twenty "quick mart" robberies had been apprehended during a police surveillance. While being interrogated, the pair revealed that they had come close to being caught on several occasions when responding units arrived at the scene very quickly. They said they had escaped apprehension at those times by simply walking away in a normal manner. This proved to be an embarrassment for one officer who remembered the pair walking past his car. This officer said they just appeared to be "normal" citizens and that there was nothing extraordinary about them.[37]

In Los Angeles, a young bank robber arrived at the scene to evaluate his target and left after the robbery by the same method—a rented chauffeur-driven limousine.[38]

Officers responding to a robbery call arrived at the scene as several people ran out of the business involved. When the people ignored orders to halt, one officer shot and killed one of them and injured several others. All of them were witnesses or victims running to escape from the robber, who was still inside.

A silent alarm was triggered, and officers were dispatched to the scene of a possible robbery in progress. As the officers got out of their cars, a man calmly walked out and waved at them, stating that the alarm had accidentally been set off. The officers left. Later it was found that the robber had killed a pharmacist and shot a clerk, who survived to identify the robber-murderer as the man who had greeted the police.

Physical Stereotyping. Physical stereotyping is an officer's expectations that the robber will be of a particular description. Such ster-

FIGURE 12-3

Here is an illustration of an exception to the notion that robbers approach the crime scene with care and flee with abandon. Here two robbers calmly count their "take" while still on the premises. Off camera, two accomplices are standing guard over employees.

Courtesy of the Austin, Texas, Police Department

eotypes may allow the suspect to escape or be fatal to officers:

An officer entered a convenience store in response to an alarm; his gun was drawn, but he started to put it away when he didn't see anything out of the ordinary. As he approached the two clerks behind the counter, the younger one yelled a warning: the other "clerk" was an armed robber whose appearance—he was 60

years old—did not fit with the officer's stereotype of a robber.[39]

A luxury hotel in mid-Manhattan was held up. The two men who replaced the night manager and his assistant were dressed for the role, wearing tuxedos. But they wore guns at their waists. They simply opened their coats to expose them when they wanted cooperation from guests of the hotel as they robbed them.[40]

Situational Stereotyping. In situational stereotyping, the officers' previous experience with and knowledge of a particular location increases their vulnerability:

A silent alarm went off at a bar; the call was dispatched and as the assigned unit drove toward the bar, the two partners joked about the inability of the owner to set the alarm properly as he was continuously tripping it accidentally, creating frequent false alarms. The officer operating the police car parked it in front of the bar and as the two officers began to saunter casually up to the front door of the bar, two suspects burst out with guns in hand and began shooting. Miraculously, neither officer was hit. One of the suspects was wounded and arrested at the scene; the other one escaped and was not apprehended until several weeks later.

Returning to some earlier points, although the suspects may be observed fleeing the scene or reveal themselves in some manner to the officer assigned to respond to the call, such encounters do not take place with any regularity. In addition, deviating from the assignment to become engaged in a "pursuit," instead of proceeding directly to the call, will often be unproductive. In such instances the "suspect," especially one driving an automobile, may merely be acting in a suspicious manner, because he may have committed some minor traffic violation and is fearful that the officer is going to write him a traffic citation. The officer actually assigned to the robbery call should not normally deviate from the assignment without significant reason; the officer's responsibility is to get to the scene and to get accurate, detailed information for the preliminary pickup order as rapidly as possible. By doing so, more resources then are brought to bear on the offense, and the likelihood is reduced that other officers may unknowingly stop armed suspects for what they think is only a traffic violation. It

is not wise to assume that the suspects have left the scene, even if the dispatcher has so indicated. Panicky suspects may double back to the scene and take a hostage; they may even hide at or near the scene in the belief that they can escape detection. In such circumstances the responding officer is particularly vulnerable to attack. The investigator must exercise caution even when there is no apparent need for it.

If not assigned to the call as the primary backup unit, other officers should not respond to the scene. Instead they should patrol along a likely escape route such as entrances to expressways. They should avoid transmitting routine messages, as the primary unit will need to transmit temporary pickup orders concerning the offense.

TACTICAL SITUATIONS AT THE SCENE

Units assigned to a robbery call should plan the actions to be taken at the scene. Two-officer units should face their car directly toward the business involved; one-officer units should park with the passenger's side toward the business. This allows the vehicle to be used as a shield in the event of gunfire. Particular attention must be given to the possibility that not only may the suspect be inside, but that confederates may also be in the immediate area and they could easily assail the unwary officer from another direction.

If a suspect is observed, the investigator should determine the person's most likely avenue of flight and where any accomplices might be located. If the investigator is fired upon by the perpetrator, he or she should not return the fire unless able to do so without needlessly endangering the victim or passersby. The dispatcher should immediately be advised of all gunshots so that arriving units will not unknowingly be placed in jeopardy. It is far better to allow the escape of the perpetrator than to kill an innocent person by the premature or careless discharge of a weapon. With a suspect who is not attempting to flee or to take aggressive action but who refuses to drop his weapon when so directed, the investigator is not authorized to open fire, as some have suggested.[41] Instead, the officer should remain alert for some sign that the suspect intends to discharge the weapon or flee. Assistance will arrive rapidly, and at that time the suspect can be disarmed by standard cover-and-disarm techniques. Deadly force must be used only as a last resort.

When the subject is barricaded or holding hostages, the officer assigned to the call should immediately advise the dispatcher of this and proceed as provided by departmental policy. Usually this entails dispatching a supervisor and special tactical units, and sealing off and evacuating the area.

THE ORIGINAL INVESTIGATION

Although a robbery may produce a great variety of physical evidence—hair samples, blood, fingernail scrapings, fibers, buttons, notes, and similar materials—such evidence may be discovered only through diligent effort. Therefore, the investigator must always conduct a thorough crime scene search. The most common type of evidence is produced by careful interviews of victims and witnesses. It usually includes a description of the perpetrator and the weapon, directions given in committing the offense, the direction of approach and flight, and, less usually, a description of the means of fleeing the scene. Thus, the interview phase of a robbery is critically important to a successful conclusion. Because of the availability and importance of this type of evidence in robbery cases, the investigator must be thoroughly familiar with principles of witness perception and identification. The investigator must remember that identifications are made by human beings who perceive things differently. The whole approach to the investigation must be directed toward securing the most accurate identifications and descriptions humanly possible, because no less is acceptable in the courtroom. A number of departments use a checklist for obtaining personal descriptions, such as the one in Chapter 6. Even experienced investigators will, on occasion, inadvertently fail to obtain a full description, resulting in lost information and a consequent reduction in opportunity for apprehension. A description report also offers the possibility of computerizing the information so that, by means of periodic "searches" and the correlation of information from offenses involving similar descriptions, the probability of apprehension can be increased.

Typically, robbers approach the scene with care. After the robbery, however, they may flee recklessly. The investigator should take great care to establish and check the avenues of flight and approach to locate dropped articles that might help in the identification of the suspect. The immediate area should be canvassed by a "neighborhood check" to locate witnesses to the offense or to the flight of the perpetrator. In the latter case the investigator is occasionally able to locate persons who observed an individual matching the suspect's description enter a vehicle about which they can provide considerable information.

In addition to obtaining a description of the offense and offender, the interview of the victim should elicit information concerning: the exact words spoken by the offender, which may constitute an identifiable MO; the physical condition of the perpetrator, including anything which would suggest the use of alcohol or drugs; the possibility that a disguise was used; any nervous mannerisms of the perpetrator, such as tics or stutters; the possibility that the perpetrator recently had visited the victimized premises and said, did, or wore something which would assist in identification.

FIGURE 12-4

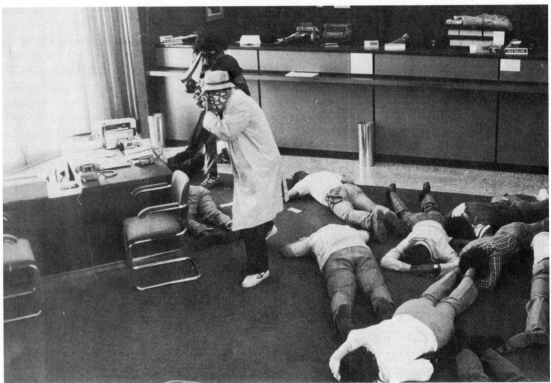

The dress of these two bank robbers is intended to hamper the original investigation: the wig, hat, and masks can be readily discarded. Wearing an overcoat, which can also be easily discarded, allows the robber to more easily get weapons into the bank; it also makes it more difficult for witnesses to describe the physical build of the robber.

Courtesy of the Atlanta Police Department

If resources permit, a likeness of the suspect should be assembled using one of several types of kits. One kit has over 500 plastic transparencies, each of which measures 4 by 5 inches. It consists of a series of overlays, each bearing a single facial characteristic. Every slide is coded by a letter or a number according to twelve categories: age lines, beards and moustaches, chin lines, eyebrows, eyes, facial tones, glasses, hairlines, headgear, noses, lips, and scar tissue. When the transparencies are properly layered in a plastic "sandwich," a likeness of the suspect is produced. The overlays can produce 62,000,000 different faces for any racial group. Additionally, tinting of the transparencies permits the duplication of the suspect's coloration. To learn to operate these types of kits, a basic course of 20 to 40 hours is required; a skilled officer can produce a

FIGURE 12-5 Identi-Kit

Courtesy Identi-Kit

likeness of a suspect in 20 minutes, more rapidly than an artist can draw. Being numerically coded, the keys may be transmitted nationally or internationally to any qualified operator, who in turn can assemble an exact likeness. In departments where such kits are used regularly, it is not unusual to have a likeness assembled, reproduced, and circulated to patrolling units and investigators within two to four hours. (See Figure 12-5.)

LATENT WORK

The latent investigator should review a copy of the original offense report to become familiar with the case. The investigator should consider facts that suggest an MO, such as the target of the robbery, weapons, type of property taken, the exact words spoken by the perpetrator, the number of suspects and the tasks they performed, needless or vicious force, and similar elements. All physical evidence should be personally examined by the officer assigned to the follow-up investigation. A file check should be made of the victim's name in case the person has a history of making crime reports. For instance, certain types of businesses—such as economy gasoline stations—often do not conduct even a minimal background investigation of employees. Given the availability of cash and long periods of isolation during the night hours, an untrustworthy employee occasionally pockets the cash for his personal gain and covers its absence by claiming a robbery was committed. A file check on the complaining witness may suggest such a pattern.

The investigator should reinterview the victim and witnesses if it appears that there may be information that was not obtained due to incomplete questioning or insufficient recall of the event. Occasionally witnesses will remember some detail and not go to the "trouble" of looking up the police department's listing. Therefore, the investigator should leave a card with his name and departmental phone number. If a likeness of the suspect has not been made, this should be done immediately. Additionally, the victim and witnesses should review the "mug-shot" file of known and active robbery perpetrators. The investigator should return to the crime scene at exactly the same time that the offense was committed and attempt to locate additional witnesses; at the same time, the neighborhood check should be reconducted.

An attempt should be made to tie the offense to other robberies, as the combined information from several offense reports may result in sufficient detail to identify a perpetrator. Reliable informants should be contacted by the investigator. However, this should be done judiciously, as they should not be called on to provide information on every open case regardless of its importance. Table 12-2 summarizes typical investigative activities for the day following a robbery.

THE CRIME SCENE TECHNICIAN AND THE LABORATORY

In many departments, the uniformed officer is responsible for processing the crime scene. Other departments are fortunate enough to have the services of a special crime scene technician trained in procuring evidence at the crime scene. It must be borne in mind that such technicians are not miracle workers—they cannot develop evidence which simply does not exist. Likewise, laboratory personnel can contribute little if they have not been given something substantive with which to work. Evidence must be collected, preserved, and identified according to established procedures for the laboratory to process it and for it to be usable in a court proceeding. To ensure the admissibility of physical evidence, responsibility must be firmly fixed for maintaining the chain of custody of each item with a view toward accurate and appropriate identification of the item in court.

FORENSIC PHOTOGRAPHY ANALYSIS

The Bank Protection Act of 1968 prescribed certain minimum security requirements for financial institutions. This along with the security consciousness created by the crime

TABLE 12-2
Frequency of Detective Activities during First Robbery Follow-up Investigation Day

Activities Conducted	Percentage Frequency
Routine Activities	75.7%
Interview Victims	
Secondary Activities	
Discussions with Detectives	31.9
Check Department Records	26.2
Interview Witnesses	21.8
Canvass for Witnesses	19.3
Discussions with Patrol Officers	17.9
Interview Others*	17.7
Discussions with Supervisors	16.3
Interview Suspects	14.9
Check Crime Scenes	13.2
Tertiary Activities	
All Other Information Gathering Activities	9.9
Checked Other Files or Records	8.8
Checked Computer Files/NCIC	7.7
Discussions with Others in Department**	5.7
Physical Evidence Collection	4.5
Interview Informants	3.9
Stakeouts	0.5

* Interviews are of persons *not* employed by the police agency.
** Discussions with persons *employed* by the police agency.

Source: John E. Eck, *Solving Crimes: the Investigation of Burglary and Robbery* (Washington, D.C.: The National Institute of Justice and The Police Executive Research Forum, 1983), extracted from Table 5.14, p. 137. The data in this table were gathered in three different cities.

prevention movement, which began during the early 1970s in this country, has resulted in a widespread use of surveillance cameras not only by financial institutions but also by many other types of businesses.[42] As a consequence, it is not uncommon to have pictures of an actual robbery. In some banks, the number of photographs may be as high as 800 to 1,000, although fewer than a dozen ordinarily yield information of investigative significance. When the robber has not worn a mask, it is possible to compare the forensic photograph with file pictures of suspects. The comparison may be a simple visual check or laying a photographic transparency over the file pictures to compare the size, shape, and symmetry of the eyes, eyebrows, nose, mouth, ears, facial creases, scars, marks, and head shape.

Even when robbers wear a mask, the analysis of forensic photographs may yield useful information, such as the height of the suspect and defects in clothing. In Figure 12-6, the clothing worn during a robbery is shown

FIGURE 12-6

Comparison of identifying clothing show common characteristics from bank surveillance photograph and pose with clothing subsequently recovered.

Courtesy Federal Bureau of Investigation

next to clothing found in the possession of the suspect. Note that the paint spot on the leg and the crease in the jacket appear in both pictures. Despite the fact that analysis of forensic photographs has already demonstrated their utility on a number of occasions, it is a field from which additional determinations can be expected as the quality of forensic photographs improves and as new methods of analysis are applied.

THE INVESTIGATOR'S EDUCATIVE RESPONSIBILITY

Investigators and their departments should not only be prepared to identify and locate the perpetrator and recover stolen property, but should also prevent as many offenses as possible. Toward this end a number of police departments have undertaken antirobbery campaigns which focus on preventing the offense rather than reacting to its commission. Typically the programs take one of the following forms: seasoned investigators speak before community groups; uniformed patrol officers visit businesses in their geographic area of responsibility, offering observations based upon the individual premises that will make the businesses less attractive to robbers, coupled with the distribution of handout materials; or convicted robbery offenders speak to groups about the determinants for selecting a business to be "hit."

Regardless of their form, such presentations usually cover three broad areas: preventive measures, anticipatory strategies, and reactive measures.[43]

PREVENTIVE MEASURES

Business operators can reduce the likelihood of being victimized by a robbery through several basic "target hardening" measures: the interior and all entrances to the premises should be kept well lighted; the windows of the establishment should not be used to display large advertisements which would block a clear view into the building; the rear and side doors of the premises should be locked at all times; and alarm systems should be periodically inspected and properly maintained to provide maximum effectiveness.

All businesses should keep "bait money"— currency of which the serial numbers and related information, such as denominations, have been prerecorded—to hand over in the event of a robbery.

The daily schedule of a business is an important variable. Owners and operators should avoid opening or closing the premises outside of normal working hours and should immediately contact the police if a request, however valid it may seem, is received to open the business after normal working hours. Bank deposits should be made, always with a companion, at various times and by various routes to avoid establishing a routine.

The amount of cash on the premises, especially in the register, should be kept to a minimum. Unnecessary exposure of cash should be avoided, and daily receipts should never be counted in public view. Business operators should be alert for suspicious persons on or near their premises. If a vehicle is involved in any such suspicious observation, a full description, including license plate number, should be obtained and all information immediately transmitted to the police.

ANTICIPATORY STRATEGY

All business people must recognize that, as a matter of statistical probability, they are likely to be victimized. They can minimize the impact of a robbery, however, by making certain decisions in advance, one of the most important of which is how the individual proprietor or operator will respond. Typically store operators are ill-prepared, by virtue of experience, training, and mental set, to resist a robbery. Therefore, they should be prepared to cooperate with the robbery perpetrator and follow directions carefully.

REACTIVE MEASURES

Robberies are usually completed in 60 seconds. The person victimized should be prepared to study the perpetrator quickly to provide a full description to investigators. If several offenders are involved, it is best to concentrate on one of them. If several employees are usually on the premises, the business operator should assign each one a responsibility, such as calling the police, observing the perpetrator's direction and method of flight, protecting any available physical evidence, and detaining and separating witnesses. There also should be a prearranged division of responsibility for studying perpetrators when more than one is on the premises.

QUESTIONS

1. What are the elements of the crime of robbery?
2. Describe the type of robbery in which the victim is most likely to be injured.
3. When and where do most robberies occur?
4. On the basis of the amount of planning involved, describe three robbery styles.
5. What considerations are required as you approach the scene of a robbery?
6. Of what importance is it to establish the exact words spoken by a robber?
7. What actions are required on the part of the investigator assigned to do the latent work on a robbery?
8. Define and give examples of preventive measures, anticipatory strategies, and reactive measures.

NOTES

1. Because this text is directed primarily toward criminal investigation, detailed case citations and references to the legal aspects of the crime of robbery have been omitted by the authors.
2. FBI, *Crime in the United States.* (Washington: D.C.: Government Printing Office, 1985), pp. 17, 164.
3. Ibid., p. 17.
4. Ibid., p. 18.
5. James D. Wright and Peter H. Rossi, *The Armed Criminal in America* (Washington, D.C.: National Institute of Justice, 1985), pp. 4 and 14.
6. Ibid., p. 14.
7. For longitudinal data see David Burnham, "Bronx Police Aim at Indoor Crime," *New York Times,* December 24, 1969; Andre Normandeau, "Patterns in Robbery," *Criminologica,* November 1968, Vol. 6, No. 3; and Donald J. Mulvihill and Melvin Tumin, *Crimes of Violence,* Vols. 11, 12, 13, staff study reports to the National Commission on the Causes and Prevention of Violence (Washington, D.C.: Government Printing Office, 1970). Normandeau found that 44 percent of his cases produced no injury; of the 56 percent resulting in injury, 16 percent were minor, 25 percent received treatment with discharge immediately following, and the remaining 5 percent ended with the victim's being hospitalized.

8. John E. Eck, *Solving Crimes: the Investigation of Burglary and Robbery* (Washington, D.C.: The National Institute of Justice and The Police Executive Research Forum, 1983), Table 3.9, p. 58.
9. Ibid. These data were calculated from the data in Table 3-9, p. 58, and the percentage for no injuries is the reciprocal for reported injuries.
10. Franklin E. Zimring, "Determinants of the Death Rate From Robbery: A Detroit Time Study," *Journal of Legal Studies,* 1977, Vol. 6, No. 2, pp. 317–332.
11. Bureau of Justice Statistics, U.S. Department of Justice, *Crime Victimization in the United States, 1982* (Washington, D.C.: Government Printing Office, 1985), Table 3, p. 23.
12. Ibid., Table 67, p. 59.
13. Ibid., Table 67, p. 59.
14. Ibid., Table 36, p. 45.
15. Joan Petersilia, Peter W. Greenwood, and Marvin Lavin, *Criminal Careers of Habitual Felons* (Washington, D.C.: Government Printing Office, 1978), p. 103.
16. Ibid., p. 17.
17. Ibid., p. 18.
18. Wright and Rossi, *The Armed Criminal in America,* p. 7. Also see Bernard A. Gropper, *Probing the Link between Drugs and Crime,* NIJ Reports, November 1984, pp. 4–7.
19. Ibid., p. 7.

20. Bureau of Justice Statistics, *Crime Victimization in the United States, 1982,* Table 49, p. 51; these percentages apply to offenses involving multiple offenders.

21. FBI, *Crime in the United States,* p. 20; also see Bruce Harry, "A Diagnostic Study of Robbers," *Journal of Forensic Sciences,* 1985, Vol. 30, No. 1, pp. 50–80.

22. *Atlanta Constitution,* December 14, 1972.

23. *Atlanta Constitution,* November 27, 1972.

24. *The Atlanta Journal,* December 20, 1979.

25. *Atlanta Constitution,* December 22, 1972.

26. See Werner J. Einstadter, "The Social Organization of Armed Robbery," *Social Problems,* Vol. 17, No. 1, p. 76. The broad categories are those identified by Einstadter; some of the content has been extended by the authors.

27. Joan Petersilia, Peter W. Greenwood, and Marvin Lavin, *Criminal Careers of Habitual Felons* (Washington, D.C.: Government Printing Office, 1978), p. 61.

28. Interview by Charles Swanson with convicted armed robber, January 19, 1983, Clarke County, Georgia, Jail.

29. Petersilia, Greenwood, and Lavin, *Criminal Careers of Habitual Felons,* pp. 60–61.

30. The material in this section is taken with permission from Richard H. Ward et al., *Police Robbery Control Manual* (Washington, D.C.: Government Printing Office, 1975), pp. 5–10. Any changes are the responsibility of the present authors.

31. Federal Bureau of Investigation, *Crime in the United States,* p. 18; also see Table 12-1 in this chapter.

32. Lawrence Gunn, "Commercial Robbery in a Medium-Sized City: Columbus, Georgia," draft. (Washington, D.C.: The Mitre Corp., November 1973), p. xi.

33. Bureau of Justice Statistics, *Crime Victimization in The United States, 1982,* Table 53, p. 3 and p. 98.

34. Ibid., Table 79, p. 65.

35. Federal Bureau of Investigation, *Crime in the United States,* p. 20.

36. The distinction between these types of stereotyping is taken from Jerry W. Baker and Carl P. Florez, "Robbery Response," *The Police Chief,* October 1980, Vol. XLVII, No. 10, pp. 46–47.

37. Ibid., p. 47.

38. "Police Say Teen Used Limo as Getaway," *The Atlanta Journal,* June 22, 1981, p. 19A.

39. Baker and Florez, "Robbery Response," p. 47.

40. John Barbour, "Manhattan Hotel Thieves Pull High-Paying Capers," *The Atlanta Journal and Constitution,* November 28, 1976, p. 19B.

41. For example, see Charles O'Hara, *Fundamentals of Criminal Investigation* (Springfield, Ill.: Charles C. Thomas, 1964), p. 324; to do so would represent an extrajudicial execution for which an officer may create a personal legal culpability.

42. For a more detailed analysis of this technique see Joseph M. Avignone and Daniel Rielly, *FBI Law Enforcement Bulletin,* November 1979, Vol. 48, No. 11, pp. 21–25, from which the material in this section was drawn.

43. Much of this information is taken from a report of the Small Business Administration, *Crime Against Small Business* (Washington, D.C.: Government Printing Office, 1969), pp. 242–245. Also see Jan M. Chaiken et al., *The Impact of Police Activity on Crime: Robberies on the New York City Subway System* (New York: New York City Rand Institute, 1974), and for a study on the impact of policing practices on the rate of robbery in thirty-five large American cities, see J. Q. Wilson and B. Boland, "The Effect of the Police on Crime," *Law and Society Review,* 1978, Vol. 12, pp. 367–390 and Michael S. McCampbell, "Robbery Reduction Through Directed Patrol," *The Police Chief,* February 1983, pp. 39–41.

13

BURGLARY INVESTIGATION

THE OFFENSE

Two important aspects of burglary are its frequency and its economic impact. Nationally, if reported burglaries were distributed evenly in time, one would occur every eleven seconds.[1] Residential burglaries account for two-thirds of this category of crime with the rest being attacks on various types of commercial establishments.[2] Despite the fact that in terms of sheer numbers there are more residential than commercial burglaries, the risk of being victimized is greater to a business since there are much fewer of them.[3] To some extent, this average loss figure for burglaries is deceptive; a national victimization study reported that in 5.7 percent of the cases, victims reported no loss, and in another 24.4 percent, the loss was less than $50. Thus, in roughly one-third of the offenses, burglars committed a felony for little or no gain.[4] The total annual loss due to burglaries is $2.7 billion, with an average loss of $900.[5] In nearly two-thirds of all instances where property is stolen as a result of a burglary, the items can be categorized as hard salable items, such as televisions or stereos. Trailing behind these, in rank order, are cash, jewelry and furs, soft salable items such as clothing, firearms, negotiable instruments, drugs, and items from inside of a

safe.[6] When considering the differences between items taken in residential versus nonresidential burglaries, the most significant differences are that money is about twice as likely to be taken from a commercial establishment, jewelry and furs are seven times more likely to be taken from a home, firearms are two times more likely to be taken from a residence, and drugs and items from a safe about ten times more likely to be obtained from a place of business.[7]

Nationally, among reported burglaries, 73 percent involve a forcible entry in which an instrument such as a pry bar, screwdriver, or axe is employed; 21 percent of the cases were entries obtained without the use of force, such as through the employment of a master key or lockpicking, with the remaining offenses being made up of attempted entries.[8] Two-thirds of all burglaries are characterized by a door rather than a window as the point of attack, and in comparison to homes, burglaries of businesses are more likely to involve the use of a tool to produce a forcible entry in which damage is done to the premises.[9] In general, commercial establishments are attacked at the rear while for residences it tends to be the front. Although burglars prefer to be invisible, attempts to gain entry at the front of a house have a certain logic to them. Burglary of homes tends to be a daytime crime; neighbors who remain at home are used to seeing salespeople or political workers approach front doors. Thus, to see a pedestrian approaching a door is not an abnormal occurrence, although a stranger going to the rear of a house would be. Further recommending this tactic are the speed with which many doors can be compromised and the fact that doors set back from the main plane of the house's front serve to limit visibility, except to a particularly well-positioned neighbor.

Although national data for reported burglaries vary by month, with December the high and April the low, there does not appear to be seasonal fluctuations, each month being within two percentage points of the others.[10] In a study of over 8,000 burglaries in six cities, it was found that residential burglaries are most often a daytime attack during a weekday, a time when many homes are not occupied. Although most commercial burglaries are also committed on weekdays, they are overwhelmingly an act done at night when the absence of people can be predicted accurately.[11] While statistically both burglaries of homes and businesses occur during weekdays, on weekends a burglary is one-and-one-half times more likely to occur at a business than at a residence.[12]

Burglary has a low clearance rate; somewhat less than one in five is cleared. As a rule of thumb, very low and high losses are associated with a greater clearance rate than are the more frequently reported midrange losses. One study revealed that approximately 34 percent of burglaries with losses in the $0 to $9 range were cleared, 21 percent in the $10 to $49 range, and 16 percent in the $50 to $99 range. The clearance rate continued to decline until reaching the $500 to $999 range where a slight upswing was noted. Of burglaries with reported losses of $5,000 to $9,999 and $10,000 or more, 25 percent and 10 percent, respectively, were cleared by arrest. Burglaries in which the value of property taken was $200 to $499, were most frequently reported, but resulted in clearances in only 12.3 percent of the cases.[13] These data are interpreted as meaning that less sophisticated offenders commit the petty burglaries and are more easily identified, while cases which involve losses of $5,000 or more receive more attention than do midrange loss burglaries, which accounts for their respectively higher and lower clearances.

OFFENDERS

Burglars are not the product of modern society; the tomb of the Egyptian Tutankhamen was broken into shortly after his death, and during the Middle Ages churches and abbeys were constantly victimized.[14] Burglary does, however, change with time. Types that flourished even in the recent past have disappeared; the transom, coal-slide, and dumbwaiter burglars are virtually extinct.[15] A rapidly vanishing type is the so-called "step-over" burglar.[16] Apartment dwellers often place screening or other impediments over windows which open onto fire escapes, but don't do so with the windows next to them. The "step-over" burglar crosses from the fire escape to the ledge and works his way to an unprotected window. The advent of interior fire escapes has led to a steady decline in the use of this technique.

While burglars tend to spring from the lower socioeconomic class and are often not well educated, investigators must never let the higher social status of a suspect deflect from a thorough scrutiny of that person. Cases illustrating this point include burglaries by a professor of sociology, a probation officer, police officers in several cities,[18] and a psychiatrist:

A South Carolina psychiatrist, who also held a law degree, earning up to $100,000 annually, was arrested for burglary. Authorities believe the $500,000 in recovered stolen goods may be linked to as many as 150 burglaries in a single county.[17]

Since so few burglaries are cleared, it is difficult to make sweeping generalizations, but based on arrest statistics, burglary is overwhelmingly a male endeavor, with females representing only about 6 percent of those arrested for this offense.[18] Of those arrested for burglary 74 percent are less than twenty-five years old.[19] About two-thirds are Caucasian, with arrests of whites representing a ratio of about two to one over blacks; arrests of American Indians, Chinese, and Japanese for burglary are negligible.[20] Burglary, in slightly more than two-thirds of the offenses, involves multiple perpetrators, and within this framework women were significantly more likely to have "worked" with one or more partners.[21] Females are also more likely to commit burglaries at greater distances from their homes; in one study only 31 percent of the females, as compared to 54 percent of the males, had burglarized a building within one mile of where they lived.[22]

While burglars may be classified according to a number of variables, such as preferences for premises to be attacked and types of property which they will, or will not, take, the most useful classification is skill. Conceived as a continuum, the two extremes would be the amateur and the professional. The largest number of burglars would be clustered toward the less skilled end of the continuum, with progressively fewer toward the skilled end.

Professional burglars commit only a few offenses per year, going for the "big score":

Burglars in Miami, Florida, were described as "hitting the mother lode" after they successfully circumvented a sophisticated alarm system and removed nearly $8 million worth of gold and silver from one of the nation's largest wholesalers of precious metals. One investigator said that the crime, which resulted in 800 pounds of gold in addition to the silver being stolen, was a "monster hit" and a "masterpiece."[23]

During one weekend telephone service on Chicago's northside was disrupted for thousands of customers when numerous cables were cut. Police officials speculate that it may have been a diversion for a burglary by highly skilled criminals whose break-in at a jewelry manufacturing firm resulted in the loss of gold and uncut diamonds valued at more than $2 million.[24]

While professional burglars may only commit a few offenses a year, they are of considerable interest to investigators because of the large value of cash or property taken and their intimate knowledge of sophisticated fencing systems, which are often detected, and therefore investigated, only following the apprehension of a professional. In addition to the "big score," the hallmark of the professional is the thorough planning which precedes each burglary. Professionals refuse to place themselves in jeopardy for anything other than sizable gains and do so only after weeks or even months of painstaking study of the target selected. Knowing exactly what they want in advance, professionals do not ransack premises. Thus, if they have employed surreptitious methods of entry, articles taken may not be missed for some time. Working nationally, or at the very highest professional level, internationally, this type of burglar often operates for long periods of time without being arrested. When arrested such burglars are often released without being charged due to a lack of physical evidence, coupled with their own adroitness in responding to the questions of investigators. When operating in elegant hotels or apartment buildings the professional will use a businesslike appearance and manners to talk his way out of a situation. Should an occupant return unexpectedly,

> he may confidently pull out a card, say that he is the house security officer, reprimand the guest for leaving the door open, state that he found it so on his routine inspection tour, and explain that, because the hotel had recently had a number of burglaries, he was worried this might be another, thus explaining his presence inside the room. . . . If a guest comes back to his hotel room—for example, Room 721—and finds the burglar there, [the burglar] may pretend to be drunk and stagger around. When asked by the guest if he knows what room he is in, the burglar will reply "Room 821," and feign surprise at being in 721. If the legal occupant of the room has asked how he got into the wrong room, he'll say he found the door open and thought he forgot to lock it.[25]

However, should these or similar ploys fail or if the burglar's real intent is apparent, the professional will employ violence if necessary to escape:

> A well-known cardiologist was shot to death when he walked into the burglary of his home in a fashionable section of Washington, D.C. The police arrested a man who was alleged to be a "superthief" for the crimes. Upon searching the suspect's swank suburban home, the police found some $4 million worth of allegedly stolen property. It took the police 472 manhours and 400 legal-sized pages to count, tag, and describe the property. The eighteen-foot truck in which the seized property was transported away contained fifty-one large boxes and two smelters which were believed to have been used to melt down precious metals.[26]

In addition to the "big scores," their intimate knowledge of sophisticated fencing systems,

their careful planning, and their capacity to use violence, professional burglars are significant adversaries because of the restraint that they can call upon when needed:

> A burglar broke into an apartment in Manhattan, taking a credit card with the victim's signature on it and a bank book showing deposits of $18,000. Left behind was $600 in cash as a ruse to avoid detection of the theft of the bank book. The burglar, avoiding the difficulties of closing the account, wrote a withdrawal slip for $5,250. Then, using a rented office as a cover, he placed an ad in a newspaper for a secretary; the first girl to apply was hired. Among her first chores was to go to the bank and withdraw some money for her "boss." As the secretary exited from the bank, the boss "just happened" to be passing by. On learning she had the money, he thanked her, took the bank book, identification and money, and told her to go back to the office, which he, himself, never did.[27]

The amateur burglar often operates on the basis of impulse or reacts to a suddenly presented opportunity. Such burglars tend to work not only in one city, but often in a relatively small segment of it. The amateur may cruise in a car looking for a business to victimize, prowl hotels seeking an unlocked door, or try to locate doors whose locks can be easily slipped using a celluloid strip. While the amateur may occasionally enjoy a relatively "big score," it is the absence of preplanning which sharply differentiates him from the professional. If a narcotics addict, the amateur must often work four or more days per week, committing several offenses each day, in order to support a habit; if not an addict this may still be necessary to support his life style. Frequently using sheer force to enter, the amateur crudely ransacks a business or residence to find anything of value. Occasionally, unlike his discerning professional counterpart, he takes costume jewelry in the belief that he has found something of considerable value. When confronted by an unexpectedly returning business owner or occupant of a residence, the amateur may become immediately violent, and secondary crimes, such as murder or rape, unintended in the original concept of the offense, will occur. Finally, the amateur burglar often has a lengthy record and is frequently in and out of jail.

THE LAW

The crime of burglary generally consists of the following elements: (1) breaking and (2) entering (3) a dwelling house or other building (4) belonging to another, (5) with the intent to commit a crime therein. The common-law crime of burglary necessitates the act to be committed in the nighttime. This element has been deleted in a number of state statutes.

Burglary and related offenses are classified as crimes against the habitation, dwelling, or building itself; no force need be directed against a person. The breaking element may be satisfied through acts which constitute a breaking into, a breaking out of, or a breaking within. Generally, the slightest force used to remove or put aside something material which constitutes a part of the building and is relied on to prevent intrusion can be the object which is broken, e.g., doors or windows. This element can be satisfied whether accomplished at the hands of the perpetrator, through the use of some inanimate object like a brick, or by the participation of an innocent third party. Similarly, the element of entry is satisfied once the slightest intrusion has taken place by the perpetrator, the use of an inanimate object, an animal, or by an innocent third person.

The character of the building at which the breaking and entering takes place will largely determine the type of offense committed. The most serious offense is breaking and entering of a dwelling house; that is, a place used by another person as a residence. The nature of the dwelling itself is not determinative, but rather the manner in which it is used. Hence, a hotel room can be considered a dwelling house.

The other major ingredient controlling the nature of the crime is the intent with which the perpetrator unlawfully breaks and enters the building. The more serious the crime intended to be committed after entry, the more serious becomes the breaking and entering itself. Thus, the most serious breaking and entering offense is that which is done with the intent to commit a felony.

APPROACHING THE SCENE AND INITIAL ACTIONS

When responding to a burglary-in-progress call, uniformed officers should drive rapidly while avoiding excessive noise such as the dramatic but unnecessary use of the siren. The last several blocks to the scene should be driven at lower speeds for two reasons. It will eliminate the possibility that the squealing tires of the police vehicle will give the perpetrators, if still on the scene, the advantage of crucial seconds of warning. Additionally, it allows opportunity for observation. A vehicle driving away from the vicinity of the scene may be seen and its description and license plate number noted as a possible investigative lead. Under such conditions, late model, expensive cars, such as Cadillacs or Continentals, should not be discounted. Burglars often select these, not only because of the large amounts of equipment and stolen property they can hold, but also because they recognize the fact that the police often act with deference to the occupants of such vehicles because of the implied social status.

When dispatched to a burglary-in-progress call, the uniformed officer working alone should attempt to coordinate his or her arrival time and position with the backup unit. This will enable the building to be secured immediately. One unit can arrive positioned so that it can watch two sides of the building, for example the north and east sides, while the other unit can observe the west and south sides. When a two-officer unit is dispatched to a burglary-in-progress call, the operator of the police vehicle should drop his or her partner off in a position to view two sides of the building and position the vehicle to allow observation of the remaining two sides. When working alone, if it is necessary to begin checking the building immediately, the uniformed officer should drive around the building to determine if there is a readily observable break. If this is not possible, the officer should check rapidly, but cautiously, on foot. When using a flashlight during the hours of darkness, it should be held away from the body as the suspect is most likely to aim at the light source if firing at the officer. If a point of entry is established, under no circumstances should an officer attempt to enter, as it needlessly exposes him or her to extreme danger. Most burglars prefer to go unarmed because, in many states, breaking and entering while armed is a more serious offense than an unarmed breaking and entering. However, occasionally burglars are armed and willing to use their weapons to avoid apprehension. The fact that no point of entry was established by riding or walking around the building does not mean that a forcible entry has not occurred; whenever possible, the roof should be checked, particularly vents and skylights.

Even if there is an alarm sounding, there may not be a burglary. Such alarms frequently malfunction, particularly during inclement weather. However, officers must never become complacent about checking a premises with a reputation for false alarms. If a breaking and entering has occurred, additional cars, if available, should be brought into the general area. Burglars often park their vehicles some blocks from the building to be attacked and the perpetrator may not yet have had time to flee the area. "Lovers" parked in the general area should not go overlooked by the police. Burglars often use couples as lookouts or have their girl friends remain in the car while they commit the offense. The perpetrator may have reached the car but was not able to flee the immediate area; the use of a "just parked lovers" story may allow him to escape detection.

If a burglary has been committed and the police department has a dog unit, the uniformed officer at the scene should request its presence prior to entering the building. The alarm servicing company will ordinarily have a representative at the scene fairly rapidly to provide officers with access to the building. If there is no alarm, then the owner must be contacted either from information usually posted on the door or from other sources. Before beginning the crime scene search, the building must be thoroughly checked to ensure that the burglar is not hidden on the premises. In order to achieve the proper degree of caution, the building check should be conducted as though it were known that the burglar was still there.

INVESTIGATIVE CONSIDERATIONS AT THE SCENE

Caution must be exercised to avoid the accidental destruction of physical evidence while attempting to make a determination whether the burglar is still in the building. Officers should be sensitive to the possible presence of physical evidence, but not act in a manner which might jeopardize the most important value, the officer's safety. If gross physical force has been used in gaining entry, the point of attack is easily established. However, one cannot assume that it is also the point of exit. Often burglars will break into a building at a particular point and then leave by opening a door. Where gross physical force is used, the point of attack is of particular importance because it may yield the types of physical evidence discussed in Chapter 4. In combination, the determination of the points of attack and exit will suggest the avenues of approach and flight traveled by the perpetrator, which also must be explored for the possible presence of physical evidence.

Investigators must be particularly attentive for unusual signs which may be of investigative value. Juvenile burglars commonly commit destructive acts of vandalism. Also, their age may be implied by the choices of what is taken and what is left behind:

> . . . friends of mine convinced me that I was too old to return to petty stuff like stealing bikes, and I participated in my first housebreaking, along with two other boys who showed me how easy it was to make entry through windows, how . . . to determine if a house was vacant, how . . . to pose as a person seeking odd jobs, knocking on doors to see if anyone was home to answer. On that first burglary, as with those that immediately followed, the valuables we sought were cash . . . stamp books . . . radios, clocks, typewriters, record players, sewing machines, and television sets. . . . We disregarded jewelry and furs for two reasons. First, we didn't know the difference between a piece of glass and a diamond, or between ermine and rabbit, and second, we didn't have the connections to unload such goodies.[28]

The sudden removal of trophies or other prized possessions by their owner from a business or residence, followed by a burglary for the purpose of committing an arson, should raise certain questions in the investigator's mind. Further, the weight or dimensions of property taken in a burglary may suggest, if only roughly, the number of people involved in the offense. Articles or tools left behind, combined with other specifics of the crime, may be useful in the identification of an MO. The choice of target may in and of itself be revealing; one study found that 75 percent of those apprehended for burglary of pharmacies were dependent upon or addicted to drugs.[29]

Many commercial establishments keep check imprinters on their premises. A not uncommon occurrence is for a burglar to gain entry to a commercial building, tear several checks from the company checkbook, imprint them and cash them the next day. Thus, it is of particular importance to have the proprietor ensure that no checks have been taken. Normally, when a burglar employs this practice the checks will be taken from the very rear of the book or from several different series in order to lessen the likelihood of detection.

RECOGNITION OF BURGLARY TOOLS

Most often when tools used in the commission of a burglary are recovered at the scene, they will not be greatly differentiated from those found in many households. A partial list includes knives, screwdrivers, crowbars, tire irons, pipe wrenches, chisels, sledge hammers, hack saws, hydraulic jacks, bolt cutters, vice grips, axes, and glass cutters. In the crude "smash and grab" burglary, where the display window of a jewelry store is broken and articles immediately available taken, the "tool" may be as unsophisticated as a brick in a paper sack. However, tools left at the scene may have been subject to certain adaptations to facilitate their use in a burglary (see Figure 13-1, for an example). Screwdrivers or crowbars may be carefully sharpened or shaped to increase their effectiveness in attacking doors and windows; nippers can be transformed into lock pullers if they are honed in a manner which permits firmer biting ability on exposed lock edges.[30]

FIGURE 13-1   An Array of Tools Commonly Employed by One Burglar Who Specialized in Attacking Safes

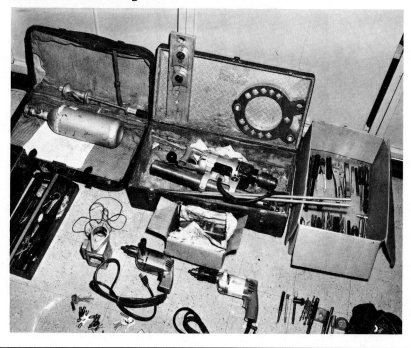

Burglars will also apply masking tape in the shape of a cone to the end of a flashlight so that it emits only a very thin light beam.

Apprehension of a suspect not in the act of burglary but in possession of lock picks, specially modified tools, or standard tools which can be used in burglaries may permit a felony charge of possession of burglary tools. Some states require that a person must have a prior conviction for burglary in order for this charge to be placed. Even where this requirement does not exist, proof of intent to commit burglary is essential for conviction.

SURREPTITIOUS ENTRIES

Occasionally, the investigation of a burglary cannot establish a point of entry or exit.

What happens in such instances is in large measure determined by the knowledge and thoroughness of the investigator, who may initiate a report indicating "entrance by unexplained means," decline to take a report due to lack of evidence, take a report knowing that due to departmental policy it will subsequently be designated "unfounded," or attribute it to an "inside job." Complaints of this nature frequently involve surreptitious entries; that is, a burglary has occurred, but there was no apparent force used. Excluding the case of closed but unlocked doors, the most common explanations are that the door was "loided," the lock picked, or the premises victimized by someone who has unauthorized possession of a key.

"Loiding" is the act of slipping or shimming, by using a strip of celluloid, a spring

FIGURE 13-2   A "Ball-Point Pen" Container for Concealing Lock Picks

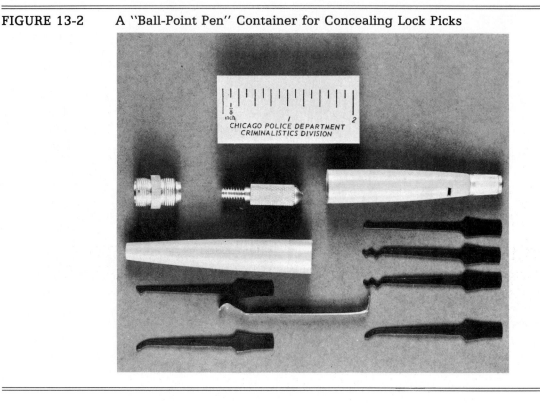

bolt lock which does not have an anti-shim device. Technically, a spring bolt without an anti-shim device should be considered a privacy, rather than a security, device. Simply stated, picking is a process of manipulating a lock into an unlocked position using picks rather than a key. When picking is suspected as the means used to gain entry, the lock should be submitted to the laboratory for examination. By examining the lock, the laboratory will be able to determine whether or not the lock was picked. From the marks alone on a lock, the laboratory cannot state the type of picking device used, except in general terms. If, however, a pick is seized as evidence, it is possible to make an individual identification by comparing the marks on the lock with test marks made by the seized pick. To facilitate the reassembly of the lock

following its examination by laboratory personnel, the key should also be submitted. The laboratory cannot determine whether a lock was loided, due to the lack of physical evidence associated with this technique.

Officers must be familiar with privacy and security devices, as it increases their investigative effectiveness and the credibility of their testimony, assists in the construction of MO files, generates data to support crime prevention legislation, and allows them to talk knowledgeably before community groups.

Besides stealing or making an impression there are other ways in which burglars can obtain keys:

Long before a new building is ready for occupancy, its locks are delivered to the construction site. Burglars have been able

FIGURE 13-3   Lock Picks Concealed in an Eyeglass-type Case

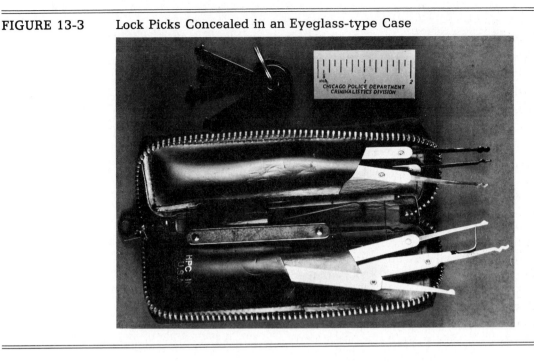

to steal two or more of these locks and then make—or have made—a key which will open every apartment in the building.[31]

Five men and a woman flew to New York City and took up residency at a cheap hotel. Shortly after they arrived, one of the men and the woman registered at a good hotel. After checking in, their accomplices were called on a pay telephone, so as to avoid leaving any record on their room bill. Subsequently, the accomplices arrived one by one so as not to attract attention. A local lock expert with whom arrangements had previously been made also showed up. He removed the entire cylinder from the door and within an hour had manufactured a key that would open a number of rooms in the hotel. The cylinder was then replaced. In the evening, when most of the guests were out, the burglars let themselves into a couple of

dozen rooms and gave them a thorough but choosy going over.

Burglars are seldom so methodical, but . . . a burglar may stay in different rooms of a hotel over a period of time until he has accumulated enough keys to give him a choice of rooms to burglarize.[32]

FRAUDULENT AND DISTORTED COMPLAINTS

While most citizens are honest in reporting burglaries, there are others who initiate fake reports. Says one person in alluding to the publicity value:

If you were a young singer and hired me as your press agent, you'd have a nice big burglary the day before your next nightclub opening. Your loss would be uninsured of course, so when you later "found" the stolen jewelry, you wouldn't have any explanations to make to a skeptical insurance company . . . also . . . an uninsured burglary makes for a better and more sympathetic news story.[33]

A second type of fraudulent complaint occurs when a financially troubled individual fabricates an offense, often going so far as to plant physical evidence and create signs of a forced entry. Armed with a police report of large but believable loss, he or she then collects from the insurance company. Even if a publicity ploy is not suspected, the fact that an individual does not have insurance should not be automatically taken as an indicator that an offense actually occurred. Schedule "A" of the Internal Revenue Service's Form 1040 provides for deductions for casualty losses, including thefts. Perhaps the most widespread and insidious form of distortion involves the legitimately victimized complainant who inflates the value of property taken or overstates the number of things actually taken. False reports, those involving inflation of the value of the property taken, and misrepresentations of the number of articles stolen are not easily detected, although occasionally individuals who seek to create signs of a forced entry on their own homes do so in such a manner as to give themselves away, e.g., broken glass at the alleged point of entry will all be on the outside instead of the inside of the residence. Such reports cause the waste of large numbers of investigative hours. Insurance companies are aware of fake or distorted reporting practices and, in losses involving sizeable amounts, are increasingly requiring the insured to take a polygraph or psychological stress evaluator examination. Overall, about 2 percent of all original reports of burglaries are subsequently unfounded.[34]

IMPORTANCE OF THE TIME FACTOR

An important aspect of taking burglary reports is attempting to determine when the offense took place. One study found that 37.9 percent of all burglaries were reported within three hours of their occurrence; at the other end of the continuum is the 11 percent reported two or more days after their commission.[35] This late reporting is largely attributable to the circumstances of businesses closed for the weekend and homeowners away for short trips or extended vacations. Summer communities, populated by people living some distance away who visit their mountain or lake-front vacation homes only intermittently, represent a large problem for the police. Such residences are particularly vulnerable to burglars, who may take all the furniture and dispose of it several months before the offense is detected. In such instances, the estimate of the time-frame in which the offense occurred will of necessity be very broad. Frequently, however, it is possible to identify a range of time during which the perpetrator attacked the premises; this can then be correlated with other data for investigative leads and to include or exclude certain persons as suspects. For example, a person known to employ an MO similar to the one used in a particular offense would be a suspect. If, however, a field interrogation report was initiated on him some distance away from the scene at about the same time as the offense occurred, his presence there would have been virtually impossible, thus excluding him as a suspect. While the example is an unusual occurrence, it is the essence which is important: as the time range in which the offense could have taken place narrows, the more useful other information becomes.

TYPES OF SAFES

While relatively few items are actually taken from safes as a result of burglaries, a good many more attempts to do so are made each year. Because of the fact that higher losses are often associated with successful attacks

FIGURE 13-4   Important Features of a Typical Fire-Resistant Safe

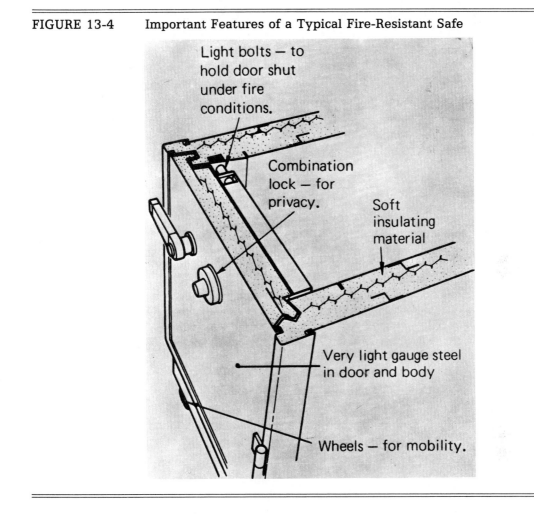

Light bolts — to hold door shut under fire conditions.

Combination lock — for privacy.

Soft insulating material

Very light gauge steel in door and body

Wheels — for mobility.

on safes, and special knowledge is needed to investigate them, the complete investigator should be prepared to handle such incidents.

The term *safe* is often used with little appreciation of the difference between fire-resistant safes and those intended to be burglar resistant. Victimized business owners will lament, "How could this happen to me, how could they have gotten into my safe?" In fact, what has been compromised is a fire-resistant safe, the construction of which is intended to protect the contents from heat, with a lock system intended for privacy, rather than security.

To the uninitiated, the appearance of safes is very much alike: they are relatively large, have combination locks, and look heavy.[36] Safes, however, can be divided into two distinct classes: the fire-resistant safe and the money chest, which is intended to be burglar resistant. In general, fire-resistant safes have square or rectangular doors, while money chests have round ones (see Figures 13-4, 13-5, 13-6). There are, however, a few money chests with square or rectangular doors; a check of the manufacturer's label which is attached to the inside of the door will resolve any confusion in classifying the

FIGURE 13-5   Money Chest

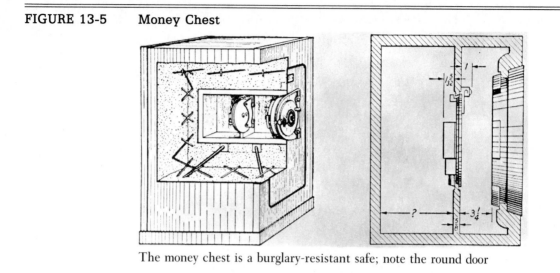

The money chest is a burglary-resistant safe; note the round door

safe (see Figure 13-7). The walls of the fire-resistant safe are of comparatively light metal with a thick insulation between the inner and outer walls to protect the contents from heat. The money chest has thick walls and a strong door. Fire-resistant safes are graded by the period of time they can protect their contents from a particular level of heat. In contrast, money chests are classified by the amount of time they can protect their contents from attack by an expert burglar using common hand tools, mechanical tools, torches, and explosives. The fire-resistant safe provides protection from fire, but only a minimum amount of security. Security and reasonably good protection from fire are given by the money chest.

= ATTACK METHODS FOR SAFES =

Knowledge of methods of safe attack is important because it allows the investigator to make judgments about the skill and knowledge of the perpetrator, an important contri-

bution to narrowing the focus of the investigation. The methods covered in this section include the punch, pulling, the peel, ripping, blasting, drilling, burning, the thermal burning bar, manipulation, prying, and the carry-off. Less commonly encountered methods have been included because in those few instances when they are used, investigators must be prepared to respond properly.

THE PUNCH

Also known as "drifting" and "knob knocking," the punch is a popular technique because it requires little skill or knowledge of safe construction. It is used successfully when attacking fire-resistant safes or money chests which do not have relocking devices or spindles constructed to eliminate this approach, the spindle being an axle which rotates the safe's tumblers or locking wheels to the right or left.[37]

The first step in a punch is removal of the combination dial; this is accomplished by striking it with a heavy hammer, swinging

FIGURE 13-6   Dual-Unit Money Safe

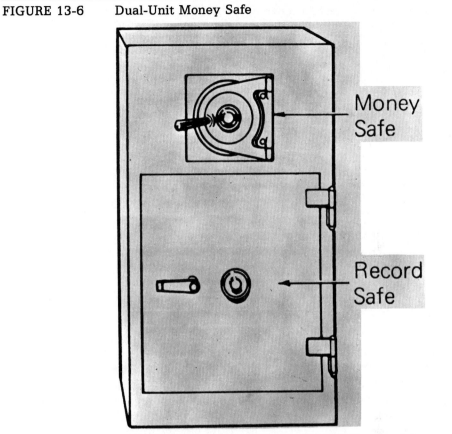

Money
Safe

Record
Safe

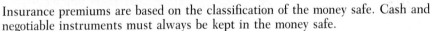

Insurance premiums are based on the classification of the money safe. Cash and negotiable instruments must always be kept in the money safe.

downward parallel to the face of the safe (see Figure 13-9). Alternatively, a cold steel chisel is placed on the top center portion of the combination dial and struck with a hammer. A drift, or punch, is then placed over the exposed end of the spindle and hit with a hammer (see Figure 13-10), driving the spindle back through the locking case and forcing the locking mechanism out of position so that the door can be opened.[38] The principal disadvantage in using the punch is the noise the hammering makes; occasionally materials such as cloth or strips cut from inner tubes are used to muffle these sounds, and constitute important physical evidence useful for comparisons, if a suspect is apprehended.

PULLING

The pull method is infrequently encountered. The effect of pulling is the same as punching, but the two are differentiated by the direction of force. Punching forces the spindle inward, while pulling relies upon the

FIGURE 13-7   Examples of the Manufacturer's Label

The "TL-15" designation indicates that the safe is burglar-resistant for fifteen minutes when attacked by an expert using common hand tools. The Safe Manufacturer's National Association Class "C" shows the safe protects records from damage by fire up to 1,700° Fahrenheit for one hour.

use of a type of wheel-puller tool to extract the spindle. Alternatively termed the "drag" or "come along," the pull will work on a few models of safes with spindles specially constructed to resist punching.

THE PEEL

The peel is a common safe attack method and is often employed when a punch attempt fails; it requires a moderate knowledge of safe construction. In general, the amount of damage done to a safe and the perpetrator's skill are inversely correlated: the greater the damage, the less skill possessed. Additionally, if the safe bears evidence of numerous places at which the attacker sought to begin the peel, then a less knowledgeable perpetrator is suggested (see Figures 13-11 and 13-12).

The initial move in a peel is to gain some small grip on the door of the safe so the metal sheet can be peeled away to expose the bolt system or locking mechanism, either of which may then be compromised and entry

to the safe gained. Often the peel will begin at the upper left-hand corner of the safe, as it is viewed from the front, and the metal face will be curled toward the lower right corner. A sectional jimmy, made from several lengths of automobile axles which are bolted together at the scene, may be used for the peeling.

Several methods may be used to create the opening where the peel begins: the safe door may be crudely pounded; cold steel chisels and metal wedges may be used; a hole might be drilled—ordinarily about three-quarters of an inch in diameter—or an acetylene torch may be employed. When simple pounding is used, the door hinges will often be the attack point, and when they are successfully struck, the torque may force the door to curl. Even if the door does not curl, removal of the hinges exposes the door edge so the peel is still possible. Once the door edge is exposed, a hammer and cold chisel can be used to pop the rivets or spot welds holding the metal plate to the door frame.

FIGURE 13-8 Safe Recognition Report

SAFE RECOGNITION REPORT
CRIME LABORATORY DIVISION/CHICAGO POLICE

1 VICTIM	2 ADDRESS OF OCCURRENCE		DATE OF INVESTIGATION DAY / MONTH / YEAR	TIME
3 DIST OCCUR	4 RD NUMBER	5 CRIME LAB OR F-1 NOTIFIED	6 PHOTOS TAKEN	7 LATD TAKEN

8. DRILL SIZE OF HOLE
1
2 CORE DRILL SIZE OF HOLE
3 TORCH SIZE OF HOLE
4 PRY (PRY DOOR OPEN)
5 PEEL (PEEL OFF OUTER METAL)
6 (DIAL KNOCKED OFF PUNCH SPINDLE PUNCH OUT OF CASE)
7 CHOP (HOLE CHOPPED IN SAFE)
8 NO FORCE
9 REMOVED
10 OTHER

9. POINT OF ATTACK (MEASURE FROM TOP AND FROM LEFT SIDE) __ X __

10. ALARMS (AREA OF SAFE) YES / NO
PROTECTING SAFE YES / NO
ON SAFE YES / NO

11. TYPE OF SAFE
1 MONEY CHEST (ROUND DOOR)
2 FIRE RESISTANT (SQUARE OR RECT DOOR)
3 COMBINATION MONEY (MAKE INDIVIDUAL REPORTS)
4 VAULT (WALK IN SAFE)
5 INSULATED FILE
6 ROTARY DEPOSITORY
7 FLOOR SAFE
8 OTHER

12. TYPE OF LOCK
COMBINATION
ONE KEY
TWO KEYS
COMBINATION AND KEYS
RELOCKING
TIME DELAY
OTHER

13. MFR MODEL SERIES

14. UNDERWRITERS LABELS

15. INSTALLATION
1 FREE STANDING
2 EMBEDDED IN WALL
3 EMBEDDED IN FLOOR
4 FASTENED TO WALL
5 FASTENED TO FLOOR
6 WALL MOUNTED
7 OTHER

16. EXTERIOR DIMENSIONS HIGH / WIDE / DEEP
17. INTERIOR DIMENSIONS HIGH / WIDE / DEEP
18. DIMENSIONS OF ROUND DOOR DIAMETER; **DIMENSIONS OF RECT DOOR** HIGH / WIDE / THICKNESS

19. LOCATION OF DOOR OPENING
1 TOP
2 FRONT
3 FRONT & BACK
4 TOP & FRONT
5 OTHER

20. NUMBER OF DOORS
21. NUMBER OPENED

ROUND DOOR SAFE DATA:
22. LOCATION OF DOOR
22A HINGES
1 RIGHT SIDE
2 LEFT SIDE
3 POST HINGE
4 HORSE SHOE HINGE
5 RING HINGE
6 OTHER
22B HINGE PINS HEADS
7 FLAT
BALL
ACORN
OTHER

22D DIALS (ROUND DOOR)
STANDARD
KEY LOCK
SPY-PROOF
DIAL AND HANDLE COMBINED
OTHER
22D HANDLES (ROUND DOOR)
ROUND TAPER
FLAT TAPER
RIB TAPER
T-HANDLE
OTHER

SQUARE OR RECTANGULAR DOOR SAFE DATA:
25. LOCATION OF DOOR
23A HINGES
RIGHT SIDE
LEFT SIDE
SURFACE MOUNTED
SURFACE MOUNTED ON DOOR PART OF SAFE
SURFACE MOUNTED ON SAFE PART OF DOOR
OTHER
23B HINGE PINS HEADS
FLAT
BALL
ACORN
OTHER

28 DIALS
STANDARD
KEY LOCK
SPY-PROOF
DIAL AND HANDLE COMBINED
OTHER
29 HANDLES
ROUND TAPER
FLAT TAPER
RIB TAPER
OTHER
29 CORNERS ON SAFE
ROUNDED
SQUARE
OTHER
29 CORNERS ON DOOR
ROUNDED
SQUARE
OTHER
29 WHEELS
FIXED-MOVE LEFT OR RIGHT
FIXED-MOVE FRONT OR BACK
SWIVEL FRONT AND BACK
OTHER

The diverse features of a safe are illustrated by this report form; when completed it provides considerable investigative information.

FIGURE 13-9   An Attempted Punch

Note the dial on the floor. Occasionally a punch will be found in this position when it was slightly too large, indicating an inexperienced safe burglar.

Courtesy Tampa Police Department

FIGURE 13-10   **Chisel Marks**

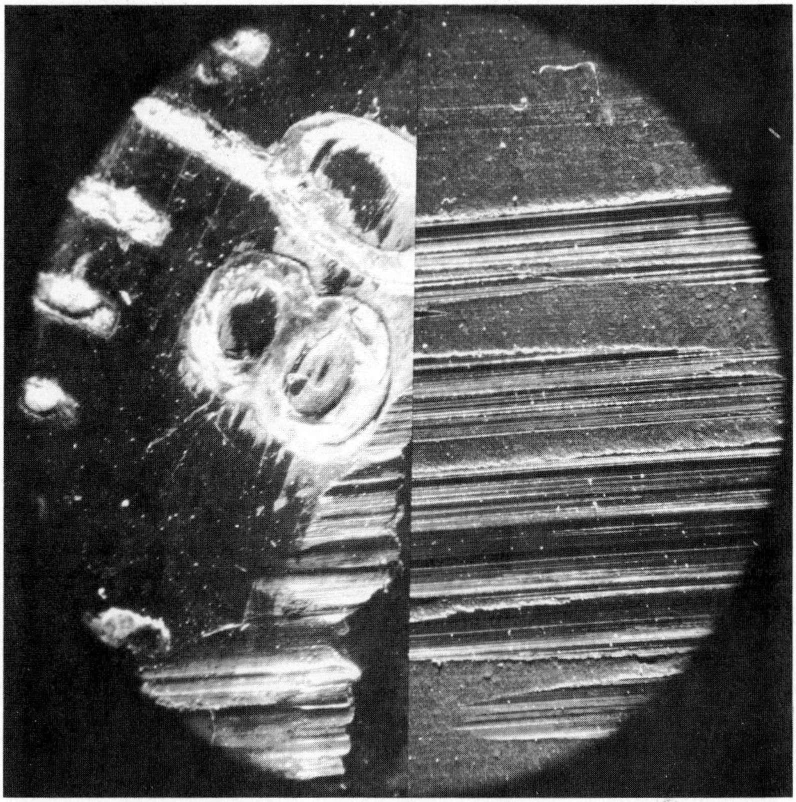

The striae on the left were created when a hammer was used to strike a cold chisel positioned at the center top of the combination dial as the first step in a punch. The striae on the right were made by the laboratory examiner using the chisel after it was seized from the suspect's custody.

Old models of fire-resistant safes are most successfully attacked using this method, but burglar-resistant safes cannot be compromised with a peel. Presently, most safe manufacturers use seam welds to compensate for the inadequacies of rivets or spot welds.

THE RIP

The terms *peel* and *rip* are sometimes erroneously used synonymously. While the peel curls the metal backward to gain access to the bolt system and locking mechanism, the rip uses crude force to penetrate the metal face of the safe (see Figure 13-13). The "chop," occasionally viewed as an entirely separate attack method, is actually a rip applied to the bottom of the safe until a hole is made large enough to insert a hand to remove the contents. In its most elementary form, a rip attack on the bottom of a safe—its weakest point, especially in older fire-resistant models—is accomplished with an axe.

Because of the degree of force required,

FIGURE 13-11   A Peel Preceded by an Unsuccessful Punch

Note the combination dial on the floor and the pry marks on the exposed locking bar.

Courtesy Tampa Police Department

FIGURE 13-12

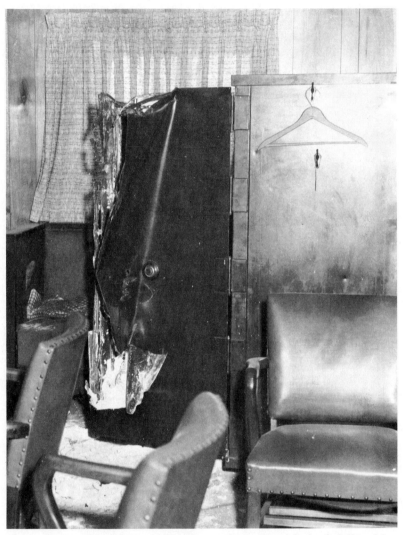

The extensive damage created by this peel suggests a lack of skill and knowledge of safe construction by the perpetrator.

Courtesy Tampa Police Department

FIGURE 13-13   A Rip Attack

Note the hammer and exposed insulation on the floor.

rips often leave a great deal of physical evidence, including shoe impressions in safe insulation and broken edges from tools. The rip or chop attack will not succeed with burglar-resistant safes.

BLASTING

Blasting, or "soup jobs"—using explosives to attack a safe—was once popular, but has almost disappeared. Its disappearance is attributed to the more severe penalties associated with burglaries committed while carrying explosives, the inherent danger to the safe-man, the noise as compared to other methods, and the stringent federal penalties for the sale, possession, use, transportation, or manufacture of explosives for illegal uses. Blasting can compromise both fire- and burglar-resistant safes.[39]

In those rare instances when explosives have been used, extreme caution must be used in processing the scene to avoid accidental detonation of explosives which may have been left behind. In cases where explosives have been placed, but the safe has not been blown, the investigator must take certain precautions:

- Exclude all persons from the scene until qualified ordinance personnel arrive.
- Never pick up or handle anything or operate any light switches in the room housing the safe or adjoining rooms.
- Do not allow anyone, other than ordinance personnel, to attempt to deactivate any devices.
- Avoid smoking; Avoid walking about the scene.
- If possible, avoid radio transmissions within one mile of the scene.
- Do not place explosives recovered at the scene in water.[40]

DRILLING

Burglar-resistant safes are most successfully attacked using a high-torque drill equipped with diamond- or carbide-tipped bits. Successfully employed drilling implies a thorough knowledge of safe construction and considerable skill. Drilling requires precision and perpetrators, after carefully measuring and marking the appropriate attack points, will often attach the drill to a chain, or bolt-mount onto the safe a drill attached to a jig, to steady their aim (see Figure 13-14). Even the most skilled safe-man will occasionally break bits while drilling, and these should be seized as evidence. Moreover, the drill bit, as illustrated in Figure 13-15, will leave microscopic striae on the metal shavings, which must also be collected, as individual class evidence.

A variant of drilling involves the use of a cystoscope. The cystoscope is a medical instrument about one-eighth inch in diameter which has its own light source and permits examination of confined areas. Occasionally safe burglars will drill a hole, insert the cystoscope, and manipulate the lock's tumblers.

The core drill is a hollow tube which removes from the safe a solid plug of sufficient size for the safe-man to reach inside and take the safe's contents (see Figures 13-16 and 13-17). Most frequently, the door, which is most resistant, will not be attacked, the bottom or sides being preferred. Because of the ease with which core drill bits break, the drill will be attached to the safe in one of the manners previously described. If a safe-man does not have a core drill, but favors that technique, he may repeatedly drill in the same area using a high-torque drill with a large bit until a hand-size hole is made.

BURNING

Once on the wane, burning—the use of an acetylene torch—is becoming more common and may compromise both fire- and burglar-resistant safes. One reason for the increase in the popularity of burning is the availability of smaller, easily portable, concealable oxygen and acetylene tanks, as illustrated in

FIGURE 13-14   Attempted Drilling with a Jig-Mounted Drill

Figure 13-18. In examining burning jobs, investigators must make two important determinations:

First, how much does the safe-man know about the use of the torch? Second, how much knowledge of safe construction does the attack demonstrate? A skilled torch operator takes pride in his cuts, which are usually straight and clean. Unskilled torch operators may make rough, uneven cuts, start a fire by improper running of the slag or try to cut with the improper

oxygen-acetylene mixture (see Figure 13-19). The last is indicated by black soot in the area of the attempted burn.[41]

As a rule, the use of burning on a fire-resistant safe indicates a novice who went to more trouble than was necessary and applied a more advanced technique than was required. Samples of the slag—the now cooled metal which ran off the safe while the burning was in progress—must be seized as evidence for comparison if a suspect is apprehended. While perpetrators almost invariably

FIGURE 13-15   Marks on Drill Bit Shavings

Comparison of striae on drill bit shavings found at the scene of a safe burglary with those obtained in the laboratory after the drill and bit were seized from the suspect's custody.

wear gloves when burning, they occasionally roll their sleeves up and may sustain spot burns from the molten slag. Suspects with such marks should be carefully investigated, particularly if their occupation or unverified statements do not explain the presence of the burns.

THE THERMAL BURNING BAR

One of the most effective devices for penetrating money chests, safes, and bank vaults is the thermal burning bar.[42] It consists of a three-eighths-inch steel pipe filled with twelve rods, eleven of which are steel and one of which is aluminum-magnesium alloy (see Figure 13-20). Additionally, such an instrument may be constructed by filling an ordinary three-eighths-inch pipe with welding rods. Commercially manufactured thermal burning bars are produced in ten-foot lengths with a coupling at one end which is hooked to an oxygen bottle. The bar is ignited by heating a point at the open end with an

FIGURE 13-16   Core Drill

A core drill in a specially constructed box designed to muffle the noise of its operation.

acetylene torch; as the oxygen from the bottle filters through the pipe, it produces an effect, when applied to a surface to be penetrated, similar to that created by fireworks sparklers. The heat intensity ranges from 4,500° to 10,000° Fahrenheit. Its efficacy is demonstrated by its ability to sever a railroad rail completely in thirty-seven seconds, pierce a six-inch thickness of tempered steel in fifteen seconds, or cut a hole approximately two inches in diameter through three and one-half feet of reinforced concrete in approximately five minutes. Sold throughout the country, the thermal burning bar is in use by construction companies, steel industries, shipyards, demolition companies, and related industries. Although it is a relatively inexpensive item burglars ordinarily prefer to steal the device rather than to purchase it themselves, so as to minimize the possibility of its being traced.

Beyond its efficacy in penetrating various materials, the thermal burning bar offers the additional advantage of generating relatively little heat, except around the immediate point of attack, negating the value of heat sensors which are utilized to protect some safes.[43] Despite the significant advantages of the thermal burning bar, relatively few instances of its use are reported.[44] This is due to a number of factors which complicate its use in safe attacks, including the feature that it rapidly consumes large amounts of oxygen, necessitating the availability of several tanks, which may be a logistics problem for the burglar. Other disadvantages are that several ten-foot lengths of the bar may be required to make a hole large enough for a hand to be inserted to remove the contents of the safe; a fire hazard is created by the large amounts of slag which are burned off; and large amounts of smoke are given off, making it

FIGURE 13-17   Core Drill Attack on a Money Chest

difficult to see and increasing the possibility of detection. (See Figure 13-21.)

MANIPULATION

Combination manipulation involves such extraordinary sensitivity that one can hear or feel the tumblers falling into position, so that the safe can be opened. Genuine manipula-

tion of a safe's combination is such a rarity that few investigators will ever encounter it, although popular depictions give it life in the public's mind. Alleged manipulations usually prove to have involved an unlocked safe, the cooperation of a dishonest employee, the leaving of the combination in a place so obvious that the perpetrator found it, or an employee's dialing two of the three numbers

FIGURE 13-18   Portable Oxygen-Acetylene Units

after closing the safe, in order to open it more rapidly next time. In this last instance, to open the safe's door the burglar needs only to turn the dial slowly until the third number is found.

THE PRY

An amateurish method which can be used to compromise fire-resistant, but not burglar-resistant, safes is the pry. It simply involves creating a large enough gap so that the door, by employing a jimmy-type tool, can be pried open. The gap may be made by pounding the safe—which may also open it—by tightening a logging chain around the safe using a hydraulic jack, or by any of a number of other methods (see Figure 13-22).

THE CARRY OFF

The carry off is not strictly a method of attack. Rather, it refers to the removal of a safe—most often fire resistant—to a location where it can be compromised at the burglar's leisure using any of the methods previously described. Often carry offs will be attacked, compromised, and left in isolated wooded areas. In such instances there is an excellent opportunity to locate physical evidence, particularly shoe and tire impressions.

SAFE INSULATION AS EVIDENCE

Whenever an attack on a safe has exposed the safe insulation, samples should be collected as evidence. Depending on circumstances, particles of insulation may be found on the perpetrator's tools, adhering to his clothing, under his fingernails, in his shoes, pants cuffs, or pockets, on the floormat of his car, or embedded in his shoes.[45] In a number of cases safe insulation has been found in the nail holes of shoe heels several weeks after the commission of the offense.

FIGURE 13-19   A Crude Attempt at Burning a Money Chest

Note the bottom left of the door area where a peel attempt was abandoned. The techniques and cuts suggest lack of knowledge. The burning unit was taken in a previous burglary of a hardware store.

Courtesy Tampa Police Department

FIGURE 13-20   Thermal Burning Bar in Carrying Case

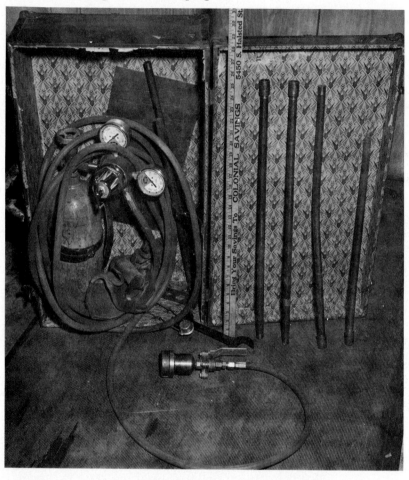

It is the variation among insulations which makes them valuable as class evidence. Many safes made prior to 1930 contain an insulation of natural cement made by burning to a powder certain claylike limestones, used without gravel or cement only as safe insulation. A number of more recently made safes use an insulation of diatomaceous earth, portland cement, and vermiculite mica, a combination only used in safe insulation. Many brands of safes contain distinctive insulation, samples of which are kept in the FBI laboratory files. It is, therefore, possible to compare insulation found on a suspect's tools or person with those in the file and name the make of safe from which it came. Some safe manufacturers use material for insulation, such as gypsum mixed with wood

FIGURE 13-21   Results of Thermal Burning Bar Attack on Fire-Resistant Safe

chips, which is not peculiar to safe insulation. In such instances, however, laboratory examination can establish consistency or the lack thereof, between insulation samples from the scene and the suspect.

As a final note on the value of safe insulation as evidence, establishing intent is important in charging a person with possession of burglary tools. Tools found with what can be conclusively established as safe insulation on them may be the basis for proving that intent.

DIALOGUE WITH A SAFE BURGLAR

The following dialogue took place with a twenty-three-year-old convicted safe burglar serving a sentence in a state penitentiary.[46]

FIGURE 13-22   Express-Type Fire-Resistant Safe Compromised by Pry Attack

Note the bent hinges and the pry marks on the edge of the safe.

While he did not regard his skill as unusual, he demonstrated it by opening, through the use of a truck tire iron, a large fire-resistant safe in only six minutes.

Q: Where do you get your tools?

A: I buy them at stores such as Western Auto, Sears, and Montgomery Ward. That way, you have the most suitable tools for the job.

Q: Where do you obtain tanks for burning a safe?

A: We steal them or go to rental companies. By doing it that way we can get the best equipment, and after the job, return it. Obviously, it's best not to use your name.

Q: Do you use your own car for carry-off jobs?

A: No. We buy an old junker from a used-car dealer for about $100, use it on the job, and then sell it a day or two later for $75 to $80. We've gotten our money out of it.

Q: How do you identify a business to hit?

A: We try to avoid large shopping centers; they are patrolled more often. We case a business which is somewhat isolated, determine the volume of business, the method of transporting money to the bank, look for alarm devices, closing hours, and frequency of patrol. For example, if the business employs an armored car service, we watch the time of pickup, the business volume for the remainder of the day after the pickup, and the business that the store will be prepared to handle on the following day prior to the armored car pickup. We determine if the owner or store manager is bonded for transporting monies to a night deposit box at the bank. We observe the police officer, the time sequence of his patrol, whether or not there is a foot policeman in the area, and if so, we avoid the business. Casing generally requires ten days to two weeks.

Q: How is entry gained?

A: It depends on the building itself and such things as alarm devices and barred windows. If entry is gained through the roof we attach ropes to exhaust pipes and climb down, generally into a small hallway. On occasion, a building next door is entered, and we break through a wall. If the door is secured by use of a padlock, entry is fairly simple. We take a second padlock, break the original lock off, enter the building, unlock a window, climb out, replace the lock, climb back through the window, and close it.

Q: How does a lookout system operate?

A: Generally, we have lookouts in telephone booths in the area, with the lookout dialing all the numbers of the business's telephone number except the last number. Then, by a prearranged signal, the number of rings on the telephone, the people in the building can know if a police officer is approaching, whether it is a routine patrol, or if they have been discovered, and then they can act accordingly.

Q: How is the time selected to make a break?

A: Generally, the best times are between 10:00 and 12:00 o'clock in the evening, after the business closes. At that time, people are on the street so that we do not attract any unnecessary attention. Also, the on-duty policeman has usually worked a complete tour of duty and is anxious to get off work. He doesn't check the buildings, and the first thing the oncoming police officer does is stop for a cup of coffee.

Q: How do you hide your car when you break a safe on the premises?

A: We usually park it in the driveway of a home in the area, where all the lights are out. When people are asleep, they don't ask any questions.

Q: How do you learn about how a safe is constructed?

A: These insurance companies, in describing rates to businesses, list various types of safes, explain their operation, so we just pick up a copy of these books. We also get catalogues from safe companies.

Q: Do you carry a gun?

A: No. Very few safe burglars carry a gun. They have no need for it. They are operating on the assumption that their plans have been made, that they are foolproof, and the gun would be excess weight—it could get you in trouble.

Q: What type of lighting do you use?

A: If we are operating in a darkened building, we would need light, which might be noticeable from outside. So we prefer a business that leaves night lights on.

Q: How do you cope with tear gas in a safe?

A: Most of the literature on safes indicates that tear gas is used frequently, so we just assume it is in all of them, and go at it. You can work for a while before it bothers you. Occasionally, you can use an exhaust fan to draw it away.

Q: On occasion, the locking device and the tumblers from the safe have been found carefully laid out on the floor. What is the reason for that?

A: A new man will go with us, and we try to show him what makes those things work.

=== THE ROLE OF INFORMATION ===

Information is of critical importance to burglars and an appreciation of the means they utilize to gather it is essential for investigators. Burglars are naturally worried that the law of averages will catch up to them eventually and they will be apprehended. Thus, they tend to search for information which will maximize their "score" while reducing unnecessary exposure to "the bitch of chance."[47]

Some of the information is gathered by watching public announcements such as those for weddings and funerals, with the burglar entering residences left vacant while the occupants attend such functions.[48] Alternatively, the society column of a newspaper may be used to identify wealthy persons planning vacations which may leave their residences unattended. A slight variation on this method is to obtain a list of a ship's passengers and victimize the residences of those on a cruise, particularly the first-class passengers.[49] Burglars may also regularly read, or subscribe to, journals in the entertainment field to learn which performers are

coming to town and where they will be staying, assuring themselves of a good "mark."[50] In other instances, the burglar may personally "case" the premises to be attacked:

He carefully prepared himself in workman's clothes with his first name stitched on a chest patch . . . hung a tool pouch on his belt . . . carried a lightweight tool box in his right hand, a flashlight in his left, and swept into a "secure" manufacturing plant . . . the guard took note of his casual greeting and thought he was a candy machine repairman. This occurred at 8:30 on a Friday morning . . . the burglar took a total of five hours casing the entire premises complete with diagrams for the burglary that would take place the following Thursday night. At various times and areas in the plant, the burglar appeared to be someone else to each person he met. The nurse closed the ladies' washroom while he "repaired" the hot water control in the washup sinks—he actually located and jumped an alarm contact, allowing access from the roof through the washroom. . . . He entered an occupied conference room, leisurely traced an alarm circuit and departed with little notice from a trio of impatient and irritated executives. Throughout the day . . . the burglar successfully masqueraded as an electrician, a repairman, a plumber, a phone repairman, and as an employee. He carefully diagrammed alarm circuits, located the payroll and valuable property items. . . . When the burglars entered the plant, they took their time, making off with a strongbox and thousands of dollars in material goods.[51]

Tipsters, also designated as spotters, fingermen, or setup people, are also an important source of information to burglars. Burglars, as well as other types of criminals, tend to have ambivalent feelings about tipsters: "on the one hand they are suspicious and fearful, lest they be an unwitting recipient of grossly exaggerated information or information planted by the police."[52] Conversely, there is a need to rely on such information because it may give them the additional edge which they are always seeking. The reality that burglars do rely on tipsters for information was underscored by a study which revealed that 61 percent indicated that they had received one or more tips with respect to a premises to be burglarized.[53] Tipsters, it should be emphasized, are not confined to any particular social strata, coming from all walks of life; among the specific types of tipsters mentioned in the autobiographical literature of burglars are night watchmen, window cleaners, prostitutes, attorneys, catering service employees, jewelers, used-car dealers, and police officers.[54]

Alternatively, the burglar may take an active role in seeking persons who have the kind of information he needs; in such cases, he exchanges cash for information:

> This particular place was here in town. I knew a girl that knew a girl that worked there, so I approached this girl and said, "Hey, I'd like some information about this place, why don't you ask her and see what she says," 'cause they cash company payroll checks . . . then I sent back for some specific information, what kind of safe it was and how the alarm was tied in . . . we got the place and then I gave this other girl $500 and I never heard any more about it.[55]

Additionally, there are friends and even acquaintances of many burglars who either know or suspect their occupation:

> I have a lot of friends who know I was a burglar. Hell, if you haven't worked for two and a half years, just about anybody that knows you, knows you're stealing.[56]

From this realization that someone is a thief, it is only a short step to the conveyance of information or the placement of a standing order for some desired piece of merchandise.[57]

TRACING AND RECOVERING STOLEN PROPERTY

Investigators attempt to recover stolen property through a variety of techniques. Once individual suspects are identified and arrested, legal searches pursuant to the arrest and/or a search warrant are carried out in the hope that property taken in a burglary may be found. Pawn shop records are monitored, flea markets are observed for visits of known and active burglars or for booths operated by them, and classified advertisements in newspapers are checked. As discussed more fully in the next chapter, efforts are made to identify the receivers of stolen property or "fences" who act as go-betweens for the actual thieves and those who purchase the property. Since the mid 1970s the police have enjoyed significant success in disrupting stolen property markets and in identifying burglars and other types of thieves by going undercover and posing as illegal receivers of stolen property in "sting" operations. (See Figure 13-23.) Additionally, as noted in Chapter 6, the National Crime Information Center (NCIC) and complementary state and local computer systems provide a means of checking to see if property is stolen. One of the most intriguing applications of automated information systems to the identification and recovery of stolen property deals specifically with office equipment.[58] A five-state pilot project matched automated stolen property files with repair records of new and used equipment. In California, a statute was enacted which required all repairers of new and used office equipment to report identifying information about the machines worked on to law enforcement officials. These data were then checked against existing stolen

FIGURE 13-23

Property valued at $3.5 million recovered from an undercover "sting operation" coordinated between the FBI, Florida Highway Patrol, and Polk County (Florida) law enforcement officials.

Courtesy John L. Beale, retired FBI agent

property files. Among the five cooperating states in this project, 10,000 pieces of stolen office equipment were recovered. In California the recovery of typewriters alone amounted to 2,100 machines valued at $1 million.

The places at which typewriters were located is shown in Table 13-1; note that information was not available for all typewriters and thus the pattern may actually be somewhat different than depicted. However, it is significant that 13 percent of the type-

writers were recovered in public institutions. Among the possible explanations for this is a looseness in procurement practices and the possibility of procurement frauds by purchasing agents who are dealing either with fences or directly with thieves.

One of the principal difficulties police departments encounter when they seek the assistance of other police departments or merchants in recovering stolen jewelry is providing them with an accurate description of the stolen pieces.[59] Recently, members of

TABLE 13-1
Settings Where Stolen Typewriters Were Located

Settings for Stolen Typewriters	Number of Typewriters Found in Setting	Percentage of Typewriters Found in Setting
Business Establishments	340	63%
Wholesalers/Retailers	(58)	(11%)
Financial Institutions (banks, mortgage and insurance companies)	(53)	(10%)
Light Manufacturing Firms	(40)	(8%)
Heavy Industrial Firms	(40)	(7%)
Management Consultant/ Investment Firms	(29)	(5%)
Service Businesses (temporary/secretarial services, janitorial, security firms)	(29)	(5%)
Laboratories/Research Organizations	(17)	(3%)
Realtors	(16)	(3%)
Publishers/Print and Electronic Media	(16)	(3%)
Transportation Firms	(16)	(3%)
Travel and Tourism Firms	(12)	(2%)
Construction Firms	(10)	(2%)
Public Institutions	69	13%
Elementary/Secondary Schools	(26)	(5%)
Hospitals/Clinics	(20)	(4%)
Colleges/Universities	(14)	(3%)
Churches	(9)	(2%)
Professional Offices/Firms	54	10%
Laws Firms	(28)	(5%)
Physicians' Offices	(20)	(4%)
Other Professionals	(6)	(1%)
Private Residences	29	5%
Government Agencies	26	5%
Private Organizations/Associations	20	4%

Source: Marilyn E. Walsh, *Computerized Tracking of Stolen Office Equipment* (Washington, D.C.: Government Printing Office, 1979), p.84, Table 10.

one police department, investigating a burglary/homicide involving a female victim, faced such a problem. During their investigation of this crime, they learned from the victim's daughter that five pieces of jewelry could not be located in the house and were quite likely stolen by the murderer. The police department was given a verbal description of the jewelry by the victim's daughter and prepared a crime information bulletin for distribution to area police departments, pawnshops, and jewelry stores. Prior to its distribution, there was general agreement among the detectives who were investigating this crime that the bulletin would be of limited value without sketches or photos of the stolen jewelry. With the cooperation of a large jewelry store in their area, they were able to locate a photograph of a piece of jewelry that was identical to one of the pieces stolen. In addition, with the assistance of the victim's daughter, an artist was able to sketch a color facsimile of the other stolen pieces. Color prints were then made of the original photograph provided by the jewelry store and of the artist's color facsimiles; these were incorporated into the police bulletin. The bulletins were then distributed to area police departments, pawnshops, and jewelry stores.

Within twenty-four hours, the police recovered all of the jewelry and arrested and charged a suspect. The first break in the case came when the suspect pawned all of the stolen pieces in four different pawnshops in two nearby cities. The pawnshop dealers had recognized the jewelry from the police department's bulletin.

The two cities in which these pawnshops were located had ordinances that required all persons pawning items to show identification. The suspect provided each pawnshop dealer with identification that accurately identified his correct name and address. He was arrested several hours later after pawning the jewelry and was charged with not only the murder of the victim in this case but also two other murders that were committed in similar ways.

Based upon their experience and success with this case, the police department proceeded to develop the jewelry identification kit depicted in Figure 13-24 it called the "Catch-A-Thief" Kit, or "CAT Kit." The kit consists of 16 sections with 116 transparency pages. Over 1,800 different pieces of jewelry are depicted, along with rings, bracelets, chains, and charms. Included are approximately 160 overlays for constructing jewelry involving a combination of features. These include examples of gold coins and other decorative items used in the manufacture of jewelry. A system of transferring various cuts and sizes of stones from a printed sheet to a particular item of jewelry is included. In addition, a chart that illustrates the array of colors of precious metals, gems, and birthstones with color-coordinated pencils has been provided.

As a final note, one of the most vexing and troublesome issues in tracing and recovering stolen property has to do with the person who just may actually have been an innocent and unknowing purchaser of stolen goods. Among the indications of a lack of good faith by the purchaser are: (1) buying at prices below a "good bargain"; (2) purchasing from people who are unknown to them and whom they "don't know how to reach"; (3) taking delivery of the merchandise under unusual conditions or at unusual times; (4) accepting the property without a sales receipt; (5) buying property when its identifying numbers have been removed or apparently altered or when there are unusual identifying stickers such as state inventory numbers; and (6) the record of the individual who purchases the property with respect to a past history of receiving.

THE INVESTIGATOR'S CRIME PREVENTION ROLE

While at the scene of a burglary, investigators should tell those victimized the precautions they can take to decrease the likelihood of their being "hit" again.

While on vacation, home owners and apartment dwellers should stop deliveries of mail and newspapers or have a neighbor pick them up daily, and arrange for a special

FIGURE 13-24   The "CAT Kit"

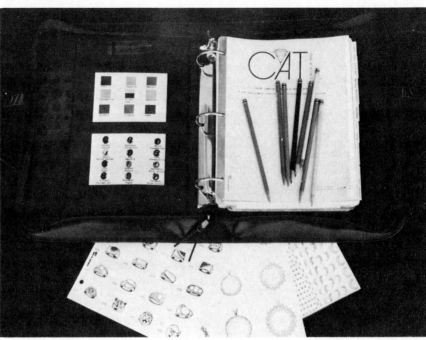

Courtesy, Chief John H. Jamason, West Palm Beach (Florida) Police Department

watch on their residence by the police. The use of timing devices on lights and a radio— set to go on and off at different times—will give the appearance of occupancy. Whether on vacation or not, neighbors should be requested to report any suspicious circumstances immediately. Day-to-day security will be increased by the use of double cylinder dead bolt locks, solidly constructed door frames, solid wooden doors at least two inches thick, locks on windows and sliding glass doors, exterior night lights, by ensuring that doors are hung in a manner which does not expose the bolt, and by keeping bushes neatly trimmed to avoid giving a burglar a concealed point of entry. Additionally, in the event that another burglary does occur, the owner's recording of serial numbers, colors,

and other descriptive information about valuable items will increase the chances for property recovery. Residents should also be made aware that the permanent marking of items with their social security number may cause a burglar not to take them. While home owners can do all of these things for themselves, apartment occupants cannot. However, acting in concert, apartment dwellers may be able to persuade the property owners to be responsive to their security needs.

Operators of businesses should be told to prevent easy access to their roofs by securing all vents and roof openings; to use security-providing locks, frames, and doors properly; to light the exterior of the building; to use, if feasible, an alarm system and surveillance

FIGURE 13-25   Sample Office Security Checklist

	Yes	No
1. Do you restrict office keys to those who actually need them?	☐	☐
2. Do you keep complete, up-to-date records of the disposition of all office keys?	☐	☐
3. Do you have adequate procedures for collecting keys from terminated employees?	☐	☐
4. Do you secure all typewriters, adding machines, calculators, photocopiers, etc., with locks?	☐	☐
5. Do you restrict duplication of office keys, except for those specifically ordered by you in writing?	☐	☐
6. Do you require that all keys be marked "Do not duplicate" to prevent legitimate locksmiths from making copies without your knowledge?	☐	☐
7. Have you established a rule that keys must not be left unguarded on desks or cabinets, and do you enforce that rule?	☐	☐
8. Do you require that filing-cabinet keys be removed from locks and placed in a secure location after opening cabinets in the morning?	☐	☐
9. Do you have procedures which prevent unauthorized personnel from reporting a "lost key" and receiving a "replacement"?	☐	☐
10. Do you routinely obliterate numbers on all keys to prevent unauthorized duplication?	☐	☐
11. Do you have some responsible person in charge of issuing all keys?	☐	☐
12. Are all keys systematically stored in a secured wall cabinet of either your own design or from a commercial key-control system?	☐	☐
13. Do you keep a record showing issuance and return of every key, including name of person, date, and time?	☐	☐
14. Do you use telephone locks to prevent unauthorized calls when the office is unattended?	☐	☐
15. Do you provide at least one lockable drawer in every secretary's desk to protect purses and other personal effects?	☐	☐
16. Do you have at least one filing cabinet secured with an auxiliary locking bar so that you can keep business secrets under better protection?	☐	☐
17. Do you leave a night light on?	☐	☐

FIGURE 13-25   **Sample Office Security Checklist** *(continued)*

	Yes	No
18. Do you record all equipment serial numbers and file them in a safe place to maintain correct identification in the event of theft or destruction by fire?	☐	☐
19. Do you shred all important papers before discarding in wastebaskets?	☐	☐
20. Do you lock briefcases and attache cases containing important papers in closets or lockers when not in use?	☐	☐
21. Do you insist on identification from repairmen who come to do work in your office?	☐	☐
22. Do you deposit incoming checks and cash each day so that you do not keep large sums in the office overnight?	☐	☐
23. Do you clear all desks of important papers every night and place them in locked fireproof safes or cabinets?	☐	☐
24. Do you frequently change the combination of your safe to prevent anyone from memorizing it or passing it on to a confederate?	☐	☐
25. When working alone in the office at night, do you set the front door lock to prevent anyone else from getting in?	☐	☐
26. Do you have the police and fire department telephone numbers posted and handy?	☐	☐
27. Do you check to see that no one remains in hiding behind you at night if you are the last to leave the office?	☐	☐
28. Are all windows, transoms, and ventilators properly protected?	☐	☐
29. Do you double check to see that all windows and doors are securely locked before you leave?	☐	☐
30. Are all doors leading to the office secured by heavy duty, double cylinder, dead bolt locks?	☐	☐
31. If your office is equipped with a burglar alarm system or protected by a guard service, do you make sure the alarm equipment is set properly each night?	☐	☐
32. If you employ a guard or watchman, do you check his watch-clock tape or dial every morning to be certain he is doing his job properly?	☐	☐
33. Do you have a periodic security review by a qualified security expert or locksmith?	☐	☐

Courtesy Bolen Industries, Hackensack, New Jersey

camera; to use a money chest rather than a fire-resistant safe and to set the safe in concrete in open view at a place which can be lighted at night. Completion of the office security checklist depicted in Figure 13-25 will serve two purposes: it will provide the owners with useful information about how to improve their security, and may provide important investigative leads, particularly if a surreptitious entry is involved.

QUESTIONS

1. Describe the dimensions of the crime of burglary.
2. What is the profile of those arrested for burglary?
3. How are professional and amateur burglars distinguished?
4. What are the elements of the crime of burglary?
5. What considerations are important in approaching the scene of a burglary?
6. What is "loiding"?
7. How are fire-resistant safes and money chests differentiated?
8. What are "knob-knocking" and the "drag"?
9. What special actions are required if there has been a "soup job"?
10. What is the method most likely to succeed when attacking a burglar-resistant safe?
11. How do burglars get their information?
12. With respect to the possible illegal receiving of stolen property, what are some indicators of the absence of good-faith purchasing?
13. What measures can home owners and business operators take to lessen their chances of being burglarized?

NOTES

1. Federal Bureau of Investigation, *Crime in The United States* (Washington, D.C.: Government Printing Office, 1985), p. 5.
2. Ibid., p. 25.
3. Carl E. Pope, *Crime Specific Analysis: The Characteristics of Burglary Incidents* (Washington, D.C.: Government Printing Office, 1977), p. 18.
4. FBI, *Crime in The United States*, p. 25.
5. Bureau of Justice Statistics, *Criminal Victimization in the United States, 1983* (Washington, D.C.: Government Printing Office, 1985); note that the reported average loss of $900 is for calendar year 1984 while the victimization data is for 1983.
6. Pope, *Crime Specific Analysis: The Characteristics of Burglary Incidents*, Table 14, p. 31. For all types of offenses the figures by percent are: (1) hard salable items, 62.6; (2) cash, 17.2; (3) jewelry and furs, 8.2; (4) soft salable items, 6.8; (5) firearms, 3.6; (6) negotiable instruments, 0.7; (7) drugs, 0.5; and (8) items from inside of a safe, 0.4.
7. Ibid., Table 14, p. 31. The list which follows gives the specific figures by percentage; in each category the first figure is for residential burglaries and the second for nonresidential: cash (15.0 v. 25.0); negotiable instruments (0.6 v. 0.7); jewelry and furs (10.5 v. 1.5) soft salable items (6.6 v. 7.4); hard salable items (63.0 v. 61.6); drugs (0.1 v. 1.5); firearms (4.3 v. 1.2) and items from inside of a safe (0.1 v. 1.2).
8. FBI, *Crime in The United States*, p. 25.

9. Pope, *Crime Specific Analysis: The Characteristics of Burglary Incidents*, Table 15, p. 32.

10. FBI, *Crime in The United States*, p. 25.

11. Pope, *Crime Specific Analysis: The Characteristics of Burglary Incidents*, p. 25.

12. Ibid., Table 16, p. 33. Also see John E. Conklin and Egon Bittner, "Burglary in a Suburb," *Criminology*, August 1973, Vol. 2, No. 2, pp. 206–232.

13. Ibid., Table 16, p. 33. Relatedly, see L. J. F. Smith and T. F. Marshall, "Who Gets Away with Crime? A Study of Unsolved Burglaries," *Police Journal*, 1981, Vol. 54, No. 2, pp. 105–118.

14. Susan Black, "A Reporter at Large: Burglary—1," reprinted by permission, copyright 1963 *The New Yorker Magazine, Inc.*, p. 69. Also see John Bowers, "Big City Thieves," *Harper's*, February 1967, pp. 50–54, and Pedro R. David, ed., *The World of the Burglar* (Albuquerque: University of New Mexico Press, 1974).

15. Ibid., p. 79.

16. Ibid., p. 79.

17. *The Atlanta Constitution*, July 7, 1979.

18. FBI, *Crime in The United States*, p. 27.

19. Ibid., p. 27.

20. Ibid., Table 37, p. 182.

21. Carl E. Pope, *Crime Specific Analysis: An Empirical Examination of Burglary Offender Characteristics* (Washington, D.C.: Government Printing Office, 1977), p. 21.

22. Ibid., p. 22.

23. " 'Masterpiece' Burglary Yields 'Mother Lode,' " *The Dallas* (Texas) *Morning News*, March 12, 1980, 8A.

24. "Jewel Burglars Get $2 Million," *The Atlanta Journal*, September 9, 1980, 7A.

25. Black, "A Reporter at Large: Burglary—1," p. 114.

26. "Loot Jams Va. Home of Alleged Superthief," *Atlanta Constitution*, December 16, 1980, 20D.

27. Black, "A Reporter at Large: Burglary—1," p. 78.

28. Robert Earl Barnes, *Are You Safe From Burglars?* (Garden City, N.Y.: Doubleday, 1971), p. 3.

29. A. Kreuzer, "Burglary of Pharmacies and Related Offenses," *Kriminalistik*, 1973, Vol. 27, No. 11, pp. 500–503, and No. 12, pp. 548–553.

30. Chicago Police Department Training Bulletin, "Burglary—Physical Security Devices," Part 1, May 7, 1974, Vol. 15, No. 9, p. 2.

31. Black, "A Reporter at Large: Burglary—1," p. 84.

32. Ibid., pp. 84–86.

33. Ibid., pp. 133–134.

34. Pope, *Crime Specific Analysis: The Characteristics of Burglary Incidents*, Table 8, p. 26.

35. John E. Conklin and Egon Bittner, "Burglary in a Suburb," *Criminology: An Interdisciplinary Journal*, 1973, Vol. 11, No. 2, p. 222.

36. The information in this paragraph is drawn from Arthur Paholke, "Safe Recognition" (Paper presented to the Association of Firearm and Tool Mark Examiners, 1970).

37. Donald G. Webb, *Investigation of Safe and Money Chest Burglary* (Springfield, Ill.: Charles C. Thomas, 1975), p. 42. This book is an excellent source of detailed information on safe burglaries.

38. Ibid., p. 42.

39. Ibid., p. 62.

40. Ibid., pp. 63–64.

41. Ibid., p. 58.

42. The description of the thermal burning bar is largely taken from "The Thermal Burning Bar," *FBI Law Enforcement Bulletin*, February 1968, Vol. 37, No. 2, pp. 10–11.

43. Webb, *Investigation of Safe and Money Chest Burglary*, p. 61.

44. *Ibid*, p. 61, discusses these disadvantages more fully.

45. The information on safe insulation as evi-

dence is taken from "Safe Insulation and Its Value in Crime Detection," *FBI Law Enforcement Bulletin,* November 1974, Vol. 43, No. 11, pp. 23–25.

46. The subject of this paragraph appeared at a seminar on burglary held at Mount Dora, Florida. The information was incorporated into a five-page handout identified only as "Revelations of a Safe Burglar."

47. Neal Shover, "Structures and Careers in Burglary," *The Journal of Criminal Law, Criminology and Police Science,* 1972, Vol. 63, No. 4, p. 546.

48. For detailed information see Lawrence S. Conner, "When Mourners Go To Services Robbers Break in Some Homes," *National Observer,* January 4, 1971, p. 12.

49. Black, "A Reporter at Large: Burglary—1," p. 98.

50. Ibid., p. 98.

51. Grady P. Hunter, "Exposure: The Most Certain Deterrent to Public and Private Crime," *Security Register,* 1974, Vol. 1, No. 2, pp. 21–22.

52. Shover, "Structures and Careers in Burglary," p. 546.

53. Ibid., p. 547.

54. Ibid., p. 547.

55. Ibid., p. 547.

56. Ibid., p. 546.

57. Ibid., p. 546.

58. The description of the stolen office equipment project is taken from Marilyn E. Walsh, *Computerized Tracking of Stolen Office Equipment* (Washington, D.C.: Government Printing Office, 1979); also see Mary V. McGuire and Marilyn E. Walsh, *The Identification and Recovery of Stolen Property Using Automated Information Systems: An Investigator's Handbook* (Washington, D.C.: Government Printing Office, 1981).

59. John H. Jamason, "Police Chief Designs New Method to Identify and Recover Jewelry," *The Florida Police Chief,* Vol. 9, No. 3, 1983. This information was obtained in part from this source, pp. 111, 113, and 114. Persons interested in obtaining additional information about the "CAT Kit" may do so by contacting the West Palm Beach (Florida) Police Department.

14

LARCENY OFFENSES

INTRODUCTION

The legal definition of larceny contains five essential elements: (1) taking, (2) carrying away, (3) personal property, (4) of another, (5) with the intent to deprive permanently.[1] Many criminal offenses may be classified under the general heading of larceny. This chapter discusses the most frequently encountered: auto theft, boat theft, fraud by credit card and check, buying, receiving and distribution of stolen property, shoplifting, and confidence games. The chapter also discusses acquiring, laundering, and concealing illicit funds, as well as computer crimes.

A look at the FBI Uniform Crime Reports quickly shows the dollar loss suffered by the American public from larceny. Frequently, the dollar loss is directed back to consumers in the form of higher prices. Yet except for very large cases, larceny tends not to generate the same public interest as certain other crimes.

INVESTIGATIVE PROCEDURE

For theft to occur, two elements must be present: opportunity and desire. Investigative procedure depends on the facts of each case. Thus the theft of an item from a home—possibly by a guest—would be handled differently from business thefts by employees.

However, certain inquiries are common to most theft cases:

- At what time, as accurately as possible, did the theft occur? This information is valuable in identifying individuals who were in the area when it occurred and who had the opportunity to commit the crime and in eliminating suspects.
- Who had access to the item and, if the item was not readily visible, who knew its location?
- If the stolen item was not readily visible, did the perpetrator go directly to the item, or was a general search made of the area? Experienced criminals who know where an item is concealed attempt to convey the impression that the item was discovered during a general search. They disrupt drawers, closets, and so forth.
- Who discovered the theft? Is discovery by this person usual or unusual?
- Does anyone with access to the item have financial difficulty? Checks of credit and local pawnshop files might provide indications.
- Has anyone expressed a strong interest in the item lately?
- Is the stolen item likely to have been retained by a suspect, pawned, sold, or given to someone as a gift?
- Has the victim reported similar thefts to the police in the past?

- Was the item insured? If so, was the dollar amount of the policy sufficient to cover the total value of the item, or will the owner lose a considerable amount of money as a result of the theft?
- Do any circumstances about the case suggest that the victim is making a false or misleading report?

The following case illustrates one example of a suspected misleading report:

A coin dealer reported that he and his wife had been participating in a dealers' show at a local hotel. At the conclusion of the show the coin dealer placed his rare coins, valued at $5,000, in the trunk of his car and drove to a nearby supermarket. He told the police that he took the coins in an attaché case into the supermarket with him. His wife accompanied him into the supermarket.

When they returned to their car, they were confronted by three armed men. One ordered the coin dealer to surrender the attaché case, which he did. The three men then got into a vehicle parked nearby and sped away. The police were called and the coin dealer related what had happened.

The coins were insured for their full value, but a clause in the insurance policy nullified the coverage if the coins were stolen from an unattended vehicle. This information came to light only when the insurance policy was carefully reviewed by the investigator assigned to the case.

The supermarket cashier and the boy who bagged the groceries reported to the investigator that they were certain that neither the coin dealer nor his wife had been carrying an attaché case in the store. Therefore, there was reason to suspect that the coins had been left unattended in the car and were stolen from it—although there was no indication of forced entry into the vehicle—or that the coins had been stolen while unattended at some other location, or that the dealer had sold the coins, or that he was concealing them.

The coin dealer was requested to submit to a polygraph examination in order to corroborate his report. He refused. Upon his refusal, the initial pickup order on the three alleged suspects and the vehicle was cancelled. A copy of the police report was forwarded to the insurance company.

There are many ramifications to a case like this one. The first consequence, of course, is that a police investigation and pickup order were sent in a completely erroneous direction, wasting time and presenting the specter of arresting innocent people. Criminal fraud also was attempted by the complainant, and so further investigation was required. Hence, if there is some serious doubt about the legitimacy of a complaint, every effort should be made to investigate thoroughly.

THE NATIONAL AUTO THEFT BUREAU

The National Auto Theft Bureau (NATB) is a nonprofit organization supported by associated insurance companies. It maintains a national stolen-vehicle file and helps police to prevent and investigate motor vehicle thefts. The NATB helps in the identification of vehicles bearing altered or obliterated identification numbers, investigation of professional motor vehicle theft rings, and educates police in investigative techniques of vehicle identification and theft.

The NATB has regional files at New York, Atlanta, Dallas, and San Francisco. The Chicago office has a national stolen-vehicle file and microfilm records of motor vehicle assembly and shipping data. This office is open 24 hours a day, seven days a week for urgent inquiries. Routine calls are directed to divisional offices. The NATB Chicago and

Dallas offices can be reached through the National Law Enforcement Teletype System.

Any law enforcement agency may request help from the NATB in tracing or establishing the true ownership of a vehicle under investigation or obtain field services from their special agents. The NATB publishes the *Passenger Vehicle Identification Manual*. It provides the following information:[2]

- NATB directory
- Summary of vehicle laws
- Domestic vehicle information
- Identification charts for vehicle identification numbers, engine identification data, transmission identification data, attachment methods, motorcycle identification data
- Imported vehicle information

STOLEN VEHICLE REPORTS

In taking stolen vehicle reports, the first consideration is whether the vehicle was actually stolen.[3] Because repossession of vehicles for nonpayment is common, one of the first questions to ask is whether the complainant was behind on car payments. If so, then contact should be made with the company financing the car. Many finance companies notify police when they repossess a car.

In some instances, the vehicle has been taken by a member of the family without notifying anyone.

A young woman had taken her family's second car without permission while her parents were visiting relatives. Although she had a valid license, her parents felt that one of them should be with her when she drove because of her lack of driving experience. The young woman picked up two of her girl friends and took them for a ride. It started to rain, and the streets were slippery. While driving down a steep

hill, she attempted to turn. The vehicle slid into a curb and blew out a front tire. Two detectives in an unmarked police car observed the incident and stopped to help. The three young women jumped from the vehicle, and the driver excitedly ran to the detectives and asked them to help her move the car before the police came, because she had taken her father's car without permission. If he found out, she said, she would be in trouble.

Now let us assume hypothetically that the father had returned home earlier and found the car missing. He might have made a stolen-vehicle report.

Occasionally a complainant knows who has the vehicle but fails to tell the police officer because of a desire to get the person into trouble. This situation may stem from some personal conflict or a prank. The officer should tell the complainant the consequences of providing false and misleading information to the police.

In domestic disputes and divorces, serious conflicts may revolve around property rights, especially if the matter is still in litigation. Thus in most states neither a husband nor wife can be charged with the theft of the other's property, so long as no final legal judgment has been made regarding the disposition of jointly owned property.

Occasionally the owner of a vehicle falsely reports its theft to cover up a hit-and-run accident. The owner abandons the vehicle at or near the scene, returns home, and reports it stolen. Stolen-vehicle reports made soon after such accidents should be scrutinized, especially if there is no physical evidence that the vehicle was stolen, that is, no indication of forced entry or ignition manipulation.

Still other owners stage the theft of their car and falsely report it stolen to collect insurance. For example, a generally honest individual is hard pressed for cash because of a job layoff, doctor bills, or the like. He delivers and sells his car to a "special" body shop, fully aware that within hours it will be stripped of its parts and the body rolled out to the streets to be found by the police. He then reports his car stolen, the police verify it, and an insurance claim is submitted for the car's value. The owner has thus received a sum of money from his insurance company as well as from the body shop, which resells the parts at a profit. The following are some facts relating to car thefts presented by various authoritative sources[4]:

- The National Auto Theft Bureau estimates that of the 1.1 million vehicles stolen each year, 10 to 15 percent are fraudulent thefts.
- The Insurance Information Institute estimates losses attributed to fraudulent vehicle thefts to be between $300 million to $400 million per year.
- The cost to the insurance industry of all car thefts is almost $4 billion a year. In the New York area alone, one-third of all vehicles reported stolen represent insurance frauds, indicating that as many as 30,000 people in this area tried to cheat insurance companies.

TYPES OF VEHICLE THEFT

Auto theft may be grouped into four categories:

- Joy rides
- Thefts for use in other crimes
- Thefts for transportation
- Professional thefts

JOY RIDES

Joy riders are most often teenagers—15 to 19 years old—who steal a car for a joy ride, on a dare, as initiation into a gang, or sometimes for parts and accessories. Many youths arrested for car theft have been involved in previous thefts. Any juvenile arrested in a stolen car should be questioned carefully. Particular investigative attention should be

given to such factors as the similarity of makes of cars, and place and time of theft and abandonment. Careful questioning can clear many car thefts and identify other car thieves. Many joy riders have a favorite location for abandoning stolen cars. If stolen cars are repeatedly recovered in certain areas, then thought should be given to conducting surveillance in those areas.[5] Cars taken for joy riding are usually recovered within a few hours or days.

THEFTS FOR USE IN OTHER CRIMES

Criminals planning another crime often steal cars that can be abandoned immediately after the crime and that cannot be traced to them. The criminals try to steal the cars as close to the time of the other crime as possible, reducing chances that the owner will discover the theft, report it to the police, and that a pickup order will be broadcast.

THEFTS FOR TRANSPORTATION

This type of theft generally involves transients, hitchhikers, and runaways. They abandon the cars at their destination or when they run out of gas.[6]

PROFESSIONAL THEFTS

A comprehensive study by the U.S. Department of Justice showed that car theft increasingly has become the province of professional thieves. Statistics for those under the age of 18 arrested for vehicle theft decreased from 56 percent in the early 1970s to 40 percent in the 1980s. In the past, most cars stolen were passenger cars. But recently, thefts of more expensive vehicles have been increasing. For example, in the early 1970s, 91 percent of the vehicles reported stolen were cars, 2 percent were trucks, and 7 percent were motorcycles and other vehicles. In the early 1980s, only 75 percent of stolen vehicles were cars, 14 percent were trucks and buses, and 11 percent were motorcycles and other vehicles.[7]

The recovery rate also has dropped significantly. Owners of stolen vehicles once could expect to recover them. But today the chances of recovery are lower; the rate of recoveries declined from 84 percent to 55 percent in just ten years.

All of those factors—increasing adult involvement, increasing thefts of trucks and commercial vehicles, and declining recovery rates—strongly indicate that vehicle theft has become the province of professionals. The professional auto thief steals to make a profit, either by cannibalizing the vehicle for parts to sell or by altering it for resale. There is evidence to suggest that organized crime is behind the growing $4 billion a year steal-to-order car theft industry. Several years ago, the Senate Permanent Investigations subcommittee held hearings on this growing problem. The hearings revealed that although a 1966 law intending to make cars more theft-resistant had been effective against teenage joy riding, it had not stopped professional auto thieves.[8]

The committee looked into the operations of "chop shops"—garages that strip a stolen car of usable parts for sale to auto repair shops (see Figure 14-1). Ordinarily an auto

FIGURE 14-1   Chop Shop Operation

Note that all of the vehicles, some of which still bear registration plates, are in a partial state of disassembly. When this photo was taken, several of the vehicles had not been reported stolen.

Courtesy Nassau County (New York) Police Department

repair shop calls a salvage yard for parts. Yard owners get parts from auctions at which insurance companies sell wrecks not worth repairing. If the yard does not have the part, it can call on a network of other yards across the country.

In an illegal operation, a salvage yard offers a price below cost and delivery date. The yard owner then contacts a thief, instructing him to steal the car or truck from which the part is needed. After it is stolen, the vehicle is dismantled in a chop shop in a matter of hours and the part delivered to the yard owner who has requested it. The high cost of replacing parts for automobiles—$26,000 to buy separately what went into an $8000 car—is considered a prime factor in the emergence of chop shops.

One law enforcement official, who was the head of the Northern Illinois Auto Theft Unit, testified before the committee:

> Most body parts for late model automobiles used in the Midwest are supplied by mob-dominated Chicago yards. Detroit, Kansas City, St. Louis, Iowa City, Milwaukee, Indianapolis, Cincinnati, Louisville, Nashville, and many other areas all received a large number of their body parts from Chicago. . . . They operate in specific territories and specialize in specific makes and models. A thief who specializes in Cadillacs, for example, will be assigned to steal all the Cadillacs needed by a yard while another thief fills the demands for Fords.[9]

However, not all autos are stolen for their parts. Many are altered and sold intact. The thief may acquire the title to a late-model car which has been damaged beyond repair. Then he, or someone working with him, steals the same model car and transfers the license plates and the vehicle identification number to the new car after its license plates and vehicle identification number have been removed. With the appropriate equipment and skills, the engine identification number and transmission identification number of the new car can be altered to match those of the wrecked car. Although the alterations can be detected by a careful examination, they are not readily noticeable to the inexperienced observer.

METHODS OF IDENTIFYING AUTOMOBILES

There are five general methods by which automobiles can be identified: (1) license or registration number, (2) general description and personal identification, (3) engine number, (4) vehicle identification number (VIN), and (5) hidden number or component part numbers.[10]

LICENSE NUMBER

The license number is the way most stolen cars are identified and recovered. However, changing license plates or altering them is a simple task. Therefore officers who are looking for stolen vehicles must also use the color of the vehicle, ornaments, special hubcaps, dents, scratches, decals, and other facts from the pickup order.

ENGINE NUMBERS

The engine number is die stamped on a smooth, raised boss, although on a few models the number is die-stamped into the rough surface of the block. Motor numbers are always indented, not raised.[11] Because different manufacturers place the engine numbers on different parts of the block, searching for them is made easier by reference to the NATB *Passenger Vehicle Identification Manual*.

VEHICLE IDENTIFICATION NUMBER

Since 1954 American automobile manufacturers have used a Vehicle Identification

Number (VIN) instead of the engine number for identification. Before 1968 the VIN plates were not uniformly located on American vehicles; since then all VIN plates have been attached to the left side of the dashboard or instrument panel, visible through the windshield (see Figure 14-2). There are two exceptions: the Corvette carries the VIN attached to the left windshield post and all 1968 Fords use the right side of the instrument panel. Valuable information can be obtained from a VIN number.

FIGURE 14-2

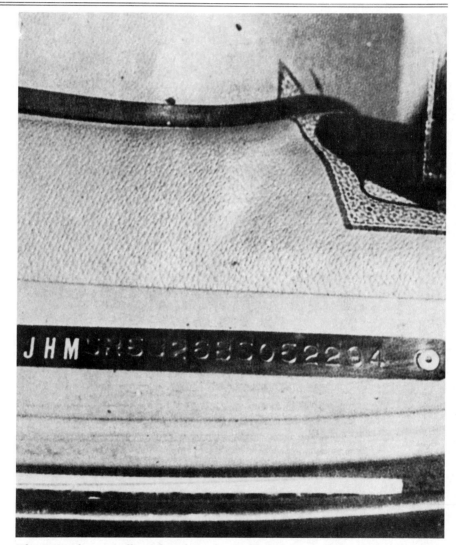

The VIN plate usually is found on the dashboard on the left side of the car in vehicles manufactured after 1968.

Courtesy The National Centurion

In 1981, the U.S. government passed legislation to standardize the format for identifying cars sold in the United States by creating a 17-digit VIN requirement. The VIN had previously been 13 digits for General Motors, 11 digits for Ford and Chrysler, and various other lengths for cars made in other countries. The first 11 digits of the new 17-digit VIN contain letters that identify the manufacturer, make, model, body style, type of restraint, engine, model year, and assembly plant, as well as the country where the assembly plant is located. The ninth digit is a check digit—a mathematical representation of the other 16 digits.

In recent years, motor vehicle thieves have increasingly resorted to the altering of VIN numbers in order to minimize the possibility of the police discovering that a vehicle was stolen.

The burden of reconstructing the correct or true VIN (TVIN), given only the altered VIN (AVIN), rests with the auto theft investigator. Until recently, this reconstruction could only be accomplished manually by use of manufacturers' data published by organizations such as the National Automobile Theft Bureau (NATB).

In an effort to simplify VIN reconstruction and expand effective use of available manufacturers' data, a computer program called "VINSLEUTH" was created by a Special Agent assigned to the Detroit, Michigan, office of the Federal Bureau of Investigation. Following is a non-technical summary of how this program works and how it can be practically applied by the auto theft investigator.

Stolen automobiles may come to a police officer's attention because the driver is violating a speed law, the car is not legally parked, or an informer points out the stolen car. The officer notes the license plate number and runs that number in a license plate data base, such as those operated by the state Department of Motor Vehicles. The officer may obtain a "hit" on a stolen car, but in most cases involving professional car thieves the officer will not identify the car as stolen because the thief has taken the precaution of installing legitimate license plates.

At best, the officer may receive a report that the license was sold for a car that does not resemble the car being stopped. The officer should then note and check the VIN. If the car thief has taken the proper precautions to disguise his deed, the VIN will have been altered and the officer will not get a "hit." The report simply will state that there is no record of the car in the computer. The report may also indicate that the check digit is in error. At this point, the officer has enough probable cause to confront the driver with the fact that the car is not titled. As yet, depending on the laws of the individual state, the officer may not have probable cause to seize the car from the driver and inspect it for the TVIN. But if the officer were able to confront the driver with the name of the true owner and the fact that the car had been reported stolen, the driver might be more likely to admit his part in the theft and identify others.

DETERMINING TVINs

One task of VINSLEUTH is to decipher or correct VIN digits altered by a car thief who has disguised the TVIN on a vehicle for which a theft report exists. VINSLEUTH then provides a limited number of true VINs to "run" in search of the theft report.

The VINSLEUTH program divides the VIN into two parts. The first 11 digits, the "Vinstem," identify the type of car. The last six digits are used by the manufacturer to number the car as it is being made. For example, assume someone has stolen a 1985 Chevrolet Corvette, and its true VIN, IGIYY0784F5123456, has been entered into a computer as stolen. Entering this VIN into the VINSLEUTH program would produce the following:

VINSLEUTH

1G1YY0784F5123456

1	1 ORIGIN	USA
2	G MANUFACTURER	GENERAL MOTORS
3	1 MAKE	CHEVROLET
4	Y MODEL	PASSENGER CAR
5	Y MODEL	CORVETTE
6	O BODY TYPE	2
7	7 BODY TYPE	DOORS
8	8 ENGINE	5.7 LITER, V8, TPI
9	4 CHECK DIGIT	
10	F YEAR	1985
11	5 PLANT	BOWLING GRN.
12-17	SEQ. PROD. NR.	123456

THE DIGIT SUM IS 400
THE CHECK DIGIT IS 4
THE CALCULATED DIGIT IS 4

Suppose the car thief had altered this VIN to read 1G1YY0734F8123456. The eighth digit, which represents the type of engine, has been changed from an 8 to a 3, and the eleventh digit, which represents the assembly plant, was changed from a 5 to an 8. If the police officer radioed this altered VIN to the dispatcher and the dispatcher used VINSLEUTH, the following would be reported:

VINSLEUTH

1G1YY0734F8123456

1	1 ORIGIN	UNKNOWN
2	G MANUFACTURER	GENERAL MOTORS
3	1 MAKE	CHEVROLET
4	Y MODEL	PASSENGER CAR
5	Y MODEL	CORVETTE
6	O BODY TYPE	2
7	7 BODY TYPE	DOORS
8	8 ENGINE	ERROR DIGIT
9	4 CHECK DIGIT	4
10	F YEAR	1985
11	5 PLANT	ERROR DIGIT
12-17	SEQ. PROD. NR.	123456

THE DIGIT SUM IS 374
THE CHECK DIGIT IS 4
THE CALCULATED DIGIT IS 0
ALTERED

VINSLEUTH compared each of the first 11 digits with data supplied by General Motors and found that GM did not put a number 3 engine into the Corvette. It therefore declared this digit to be in error. The program also found that GM did not make the Corvette at plant number 8. Since the digit representing the assembly plant was in error, the program could not determine whether the first digit, which represents the country where the assembly plant is located, was correct. Thus, the car's origin was unknown.

VINSLEUTH is divided into three separate programs: Compuvin, Vinstem, and Carent. Compuvin computes a check digit for the entered VIN and compares it with the entered VIN digit nine; audits the VIN for alterations in the first 11 digits, which identify the car; calculates the sequence by changing one or two digits at a time; prints the digit calculations on the entered VIN; and handles the administrative portion. Vinstem allows the user to build one or more TVINs if alterations were found in the first 11 digits; and Carent allows entry or alteration of the car data on which the program relies.

Through the Vinstem, the TVIN 1G1YY0784F5123456 could have been built, or the AVIN 1G1YY0734F8123456 corrected. Vinstem will also build the TVIN given only the confidential VIN (in this case, 1F5123456).

Since most car thieves prefer to alter one of the last six VIN digits rather than change the identity of the car, VINSLEUTH attempts to decipher their alterations. The primary objective of VINSLEUTH is to obtain a reasonably small number of TVINs that may be entered into a stolen car data base, such as the National Crime Information Center (NCIC), in search of a car theft report. Suppose the car thief left the first 11 digits unaltered, but changed the 14th digit from a 3 to an 8. The VIN now reads 1G1YY0784F5128456. When this VIN is entered, VINSLEUTH will report the following:

VINSLEUTH

1G1YY0784F5128456

THE FOLLOWING ARE THE ONLY POSSIBLE TRUE
VINS IF ONE OF THE LAST SIX DIGITS WAS ALTERED:

1G1YY0784F5178456
1G1YY0784F5123456
1G1YY0784F5128656
1G1YY0784F5128446

VINSLEUTH calculated all possible calculations of the last six digits, then calculated a check digit for each of these combinations and compared the calculated check digit with the check digit 4, which is the 9th digit in the above VIN. If the calculated check digit was also 4, the whole VIN was saved and reported as shown above. The above four TVINs are the only ones possible. The investigator will receive a theft report when entering the second of the above VINS.

VINSLEUTH will also calculate all possible TVINs if two of the last six digits were altered. The program will further correct al-

---

FIGURE 14-3

A false VIN may be punched onto a tape, which may then be painted black and glued over the true VIN plate.

Courtesy The National Centurion

terations in the first 11 digits and in the last six; however, the program will report up to 20 possible TVINs in this case.[12]

It is not easy to remove the VIN plate without damaging it. Therefore, if a VIN plate appears to have been tampered with, investigative action should be taken. (See Figures 14-3 and 14-4.)

Many foreign cars are now sold and registered in the United States. In earlier years, most foreign cars were produced in a series without regard to model years. But recently many foreign manufacturers have adopted systems similar to that of the United States, whereby the VIN is descriptive and furnishes complete information about the vehicle. In some instances, the model year is determined by the beginning and ending sequential serial number. Occasionally the VIN plate is removed from a salvaged vehicle and affixed to a stolen vehicle (see Figures 14-5 and 14-6).

FIGURE 14-4

VIN plates are never glued on, so a peeling VIN plate is probably false and should be a clue that the vehicle is stolen.

Courtesy The National Centurion

FIGURE 14-5

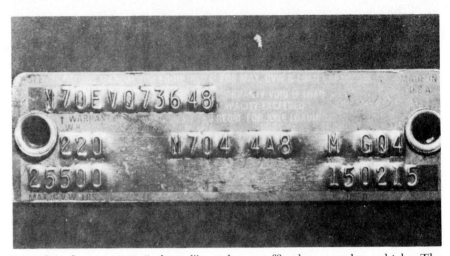

VIN plate from a 1973 "salvaged" truck was affixed to a stolen vehicle. The outward appearance of both vehicles is virtually identical.

Courtesy Nassau County (New York) Police Department

FEDERAL SAFETY
CERTIFICATION LABEL

All American and foreign cars manufactured after 1970 must have a federal safety sticker (see Figure 14-7). If the sticker has been removed, the word "void" is sometimes visible where the sticker should have been (see Figure 14-8).

The federal safety sticker should be located on the driver's door or on the chassis next to it. The VIN number for the vehicle is duplicated on the safety sticker. Although the safety sticker should not be relied on for identification, it can often be used to cross check license plates, registration, or metal VIN plates and to catch a car thief who overlooked it. (see Figure 14-9).[13]

HIDDEN NUMBERS
OR COMPONENT PART NUMBERS

Each car manufacturer stamps a unique identification number into the body of every car it produces. The locations of the numbers vary and are well concealed, making detection and alteration difficult. The location of these numbers is available to the NATB and police agencies. A unique number is also stamped into the transmission case. The location of the number varies depending on the type of transmission and the manufacturer. The NATB manual provides illustrations to assist in locating these numbers which, like the VIN and engine numbers, yield detailed descriptive data.

INDICATIONS OF A STOLEN
VEHICLE

Certain readily observable indications should raise suspicions about the possibility of auto theft.

CONDITION OF VEHICLE

- Missing or damaged locks in ignition (see Figures 14-10 and 14-11).

FIGURE 14-6 **VIN Plate on Duped Truck**

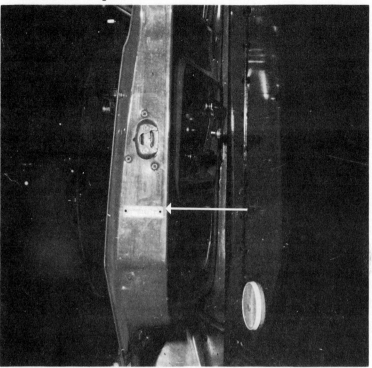

In this instance the duped VIN plate had been affixed after the stolen truck was repainted.

Courtesy Nassau County (New York) Police Department

- Damaged doors, glove compartments, and trunks.
- Broken or missing door glass, particularly vent glass.
- Vehicle operated without lights at night.
- Vehicle being pushed or towed at night.
- Pry marks around windows, doors, glove compartment, or trunk.
- Vehicle parked or hidden in remote areas.
- Missing parts, such as wheels, engine, or transmission.
- Missing accessories, such as radio or spare tire.
- Vehicle illegally parked or abandoned long

enough to accumulate dirt or debris under the wheels.
- Vehicle contains bullet holes.
- Vehicle used in other crimes.
- Windows open in inclement weather.
- Components such as four-speed transmission, bucket seats, or high-performance engine from a late-model vehicle on an older model.
- Vehicle showing evidence of having been lived in.
- Vehicle abandoned at the scene of an accident.
- Vehicle parked with engine running and no one around it.

FIGURE 14-7

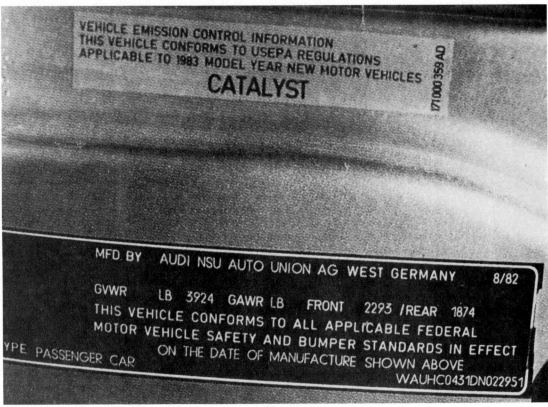

A federal safety sticker on an Audi. The number in the lower right corner is the VIN and should match the permanent VIN on the car.

Courtesy The National Centurion

- Vehicle with a new or used car lot identification number or sticker on it.
- Vehicle with license plates bent down, covered, fastened with wire, new bolts on old plates, or vice versa.
- Vehicle with no front license plate or nonmatching front and rear plates.
- Impacted insects on rear license plates.
- Out of state plates attached with a local dealer's license plate holders.[14]

State license plates have specific colors, numbers, and letters that may vary among passenger, commercial, disabled persons' vehicles, and so on. Investigators must therefore know the unique coding of the state in which they work and of any nearby states.

SUSPICIOUS DRIVER BEHAVIOR

Any of the following suspicious acts by a driver may be indications of a stolen vehicle:

- The driver seems extremely nervous or attempts to avoid police vehicles.

FIGURE 14-8

All American or foreign cars manufactured after 1970 are required to have a federal safety sticker. If the label is removed, the word "void" is sometimes visible.

Courtesy The National Centurion

FIGURE 14-9

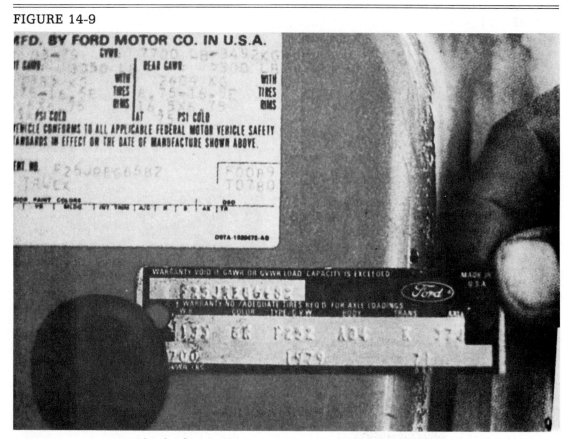

Federal safety sticker on a Ford truck. The permanent VIN plate shows that the two numbers match.

Courtesy The National Centurion

- The driver appears unfamiliar with the operation of the vehicle.
- The driver is wearing gloves in warm weather.
- The driver leaves a service station without paying for gasoline.
- The driver has little or no regard for the property of others or for the vehicle.
- The driver does not fit the vehicle. Usually a vehicle reflects its owner's economic status and his or her personal characteristics.

- The driver attempts to escape from minor traffic violations.[15]

CONFIRMATION OF OWNERSHIP

When a police officer suspects that a vehicle is stolen, and neither the officer nor the agency has a record that the suspicious vehicle was stolen, it may have been recently stolen and not yet reported. If the driver cannot provide proof of ownership, then the officer may wish to ask the driver to provide

FIGURE 14-10

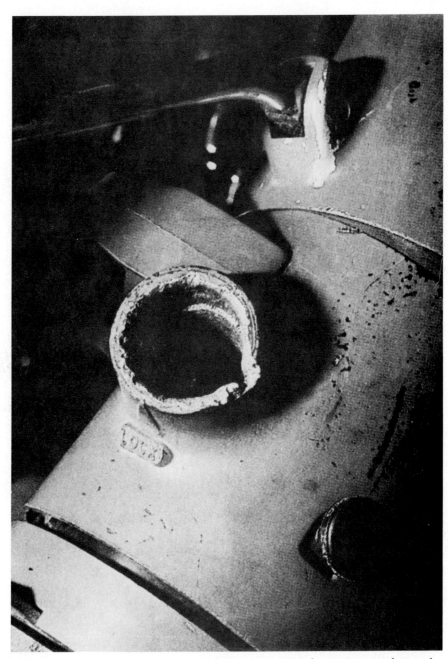

After hotwiring the ignition system, the suspect must destroy or punch out the original ignition switch to destroy the locking steering column mechanism.

Courtesy The National Centurion

FIGURE 14-11

After hotwiring and punching out the ignition, the suspects attempted to conceal the damage with a rag.

Courtesy The National Centurion

certain information which would normally be known either by the vehicle's owner or regular driver. The following information should be solicited after the driver has stepped from the vehicle:

- Description of the contents of the glove compartment and the trunk

- Approximate mileage of the vehicle
- When the vehicle was last serviced for lubrication and the name of the business that serviced the vehicle
- The name and address of the registered owner. If there are passengers in the vehicle, they should be separated and interviewed individually. They then can be

questioned in conjunction with information provided by the driver

- Where the vehicle was purchased
- Model year and make of the vehicle.

EXTERIOR PROCESSING

Latent Prints. Fingerprints and palm prints belonging to the suspect or accomplices may be found on exterior portions of a stolen vehicle such as side mirrors on both the driver and passenger side, tops and undersides of door handles, trunk lid, hood, exterior windows, especially on the driver's side, and the roof immediately above the driver and passenger doors.

Tool Marks. If the vehicle was not stolen by the use of duplicate keys but by forcible entry and ignition switch manipulation, then valuable tool marks may be present. Tool marks most frequently are found at the point of entry and near the ignition switch. Close-up photographs should be made of these tool marks for later comparison.

HIGH TECH RESPONSE
TO VEHICLE THEFT

During the past decade, law enforcement officials have relied ever more heavily on technical—"high tech"—equipment to solve crimes and to apprehend criminals. For example, many now rely on integrated communications and computer networks of the FBI, state, and local police to identify and locate stolen vehicles. One unique system uses a small device called a micromaster which is installed at random in a vehicle's electrical system. The micromaster is a microprocessor-controlled transceiver with its own unique code.

If a vehicle is stolen, the owner reports the theft to the local police in the usual way. The owner also tells the police that the vehicle is equipped with a micromaster. The police then announce through normal channels and the National Crime Information Center that a micromaster equipped vehicle has been stolen. A computer then activates a transmitter that sends a signal with the stolen vehicle's own code. (The present system can manage up to 8 billion discrete micromaster codes.) The signal activates the micromaster's transceiver; it starts sending a signal identifying it as a stolen vehicle. The activation and tracking of the micromaster signal is under the control of law enforcement authorities. They have a homing device that gives them information about the location of the car. The system also allows police officers to identify micromaster signals and determine whether the stolen car has been involved in a crime.[16]

LARCENY AT THE SCENE OF
TRAFFIC ACCIDENTS

Like natural disasters, traffic accidents present opportunities for larcenies by individuals who do not ordinarily commit crimes. The investigator must be sensitive to these possibilities. When a theft occurs at a traffic accident, it is usually committed by people who happen by, such as curious drivers. Before police arrive at the scene, victims may need emergency first aid or be unable to prevent theft from the vehicle or themselves.[17] In one reported case, an ambulance attendant removed a diamond ring from the finger of the deceased victim of an automobile accident while transporting the body to the hospital. Members of the family noticed that the ring was missing and reported it to police. Tow truck operators sometimes steal, too. Once the police arrive on the scene, they become the focus for a great deal of attention, and someone standing in the crowd might remove an article without being detected.

Theft at the scene of traffic accidents can be prevented by several practices. First, if the operator of the motor vehicle is uninjured, then he or she can take immediate custody of valuable items. If the driver is injured, a member of the family may be asked to come and take custody of the items. Second, police may make a complete inventory, which is signed by the operator of the tow truck. The inventory is then attached to the accident report and a copy given to the victim, who can use it to check the contents of the car when it is released by the tow truck operator.

=========== **BOAT THEFT** ===========

The theft of boats and marine equipment has become an increasingly serious problem in recent years. Estimates of the dollar loss annually vary widely, but there is a general agreement that a loss of $60 million per year is a conservative figure.[18]

Two factors contributing to this increase are the jurisdictional problems among law enforcement agencies which deal with marine theft and the absence of uniform state titling and licensing laws. In addition, the absence of statistical data hampers law enforcement administrators. In sum, there is a general lack of knowledge about and a subsequent lack of resources with which to address the problem. Marine theft has been called a high profit, low risk kind of crime.[19]

There are many groups which have an interest in boat thefts, including boat manufacturers and their associations, owners, and various law enforcement agencies. All address the matter in their own way.[20]

BOAT TITLING

Several years ago, the National Law Enforcement Telecommunications System, Inc., conducted a boat registration survey. It revealed that 45 states have statutes requiring the titling or registration of boats; 14 states have an on-line stolen boat file; 15 states have

on-line boat registration files for law enforcement investigations. Several groups are working to promote the adoption of uniform boat titling. It would make all states more effective in determining valid ownership and in curtailing thefts.

HULL IDENTIFICATION NUMBER

The 1971 Federal Boat Safety Act mandated that every boat manufactured for sale in the United States have a 12-character Hull Identification Number (HIN) permanently affixed to the hull (see Figure 14-12). Manufacturers have latitude in its placement on boats.

The HIN was primarily designed to protect the consumer and to assist boat manufacturers in quality control. Before 1971 boats were manufactured without any means for the consumer to identify the model year. The HIN is a tremendous aid to law enforcement officers trying to determine ownership of stolen boats. The National Automobile Theft Bureau's 1981 *Passenger Vehicle Identification Manual* briefly describes the HIN for police officers and is readily available to most law enforcement officers.[21]

NCIC BOAT FILE

In the absence of centralized data, law enforcement agencies can get them from two sources: the insurance industry and the NCIC Boat File. Insurance companies cannot provide a total picture of the problem. The NCIC Boat File has shown the growth of boat thefts since July 1969. There is no way to determine how many boats are stolen that are not listed in NCIC.

For NCIC purposes, a boat is defined as a vessel for transport by water, constructed to provide buoyancy by excluding water, and shaped to give stability and permit propulsion. A stolen boat which has a registration number, document number, or a permanently affixed HIN may be entered in the

FIGURE 14-12   HIN Format

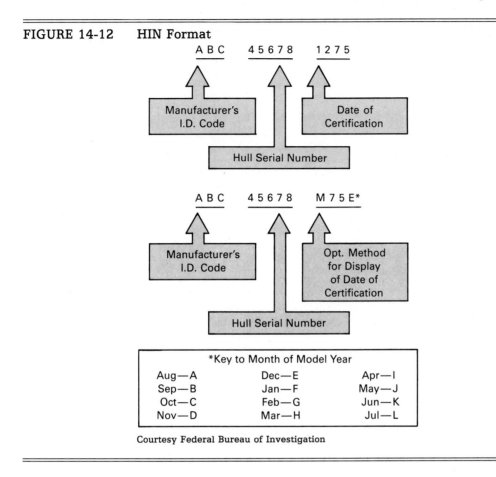

Courtesy Federal Bureau of Investigation

NCIC Boat File by the agency that has taken the theft report. A loaned, rented, or leased boat that has not been returned also may be entered by an authorized agency if an official police theft report is made or a filed complaint results in the issuance of a warrant charging embezzlement, theft, or the like.

The boat file contains the following information:

- The identity of the agency holding the theft report
- The registration or document number of the boat
- The identity of the states of registry or United States, indicating that the U.S. Coast Guard issued the registration or document number
- The year the registration or document number expires
- The construction material of the outer hull, for example, metal, plastic, wood
- The hull serial number
- The type of propulsion (inboard, outboard, sail)
- The type of boat (airboat, houseboat, hydrofoil, sailboat, yacht)
- The overall length of the boat
- The color of the boat
- The date of the theft

- The case number of the agency receiving the theft report
- The manufacturer's complete name, model name, and/or number, and any other information that may be used to identify the boat

The information required for a law enforcement agency to make an inquiry of the NCIC Boat File is complete registration or document number, complete hull serial number, or both registration or document number and hull serial number. NCIC policy requires that any agency receiving a positive response to a boat file inquiry immediately contact the agency that entered the record to verify that the status of the record has not changed and that the boat of inquiry is identical to the boat on record.

Since the boat file became operational, records have been entered with the word BOAT in the Make (BMA) Field. The manufacturer of each boat entered in the file is to be identified in the Miscellaneous (MIS) Field. Studies of the boat file have revealed that many records contain misspelled or unintelligible names of manufacturers. Other records contain the model name instead of the manufacturer's name, and some records do not contain a manufacturer's name at all. Records such as these cause problems for agencies attempting to identify boats. However, the main search parameter is the hull serial number. These problems are currently under study by NCIC, and the results of these studies are expected to improve greatly the quality and usefulness of NCIC Boat File records.

FRAUD BY CREDIT CARD AND CHECK

It is estimated that 26 billion checks are used each year in the United States, and there are about 300 million credit cards in circulation. Fraud involving these payment mechanisms are a monumental problem.

CREDIT CARD FRAUD

Credit cards are obtained for fraudulent purposes in a variety of ways. The results of a survey of fraud by one group of credit card issuers show that:

- 20 percent were issued after false applications.
- 20 percent were issued to but never received by legitimate applicants.
- 60 percent of the cards had been lost or stolen from cardholders.[22]

The counterfeiting of credit cards is a steadily increasing problem and is of growing concern to card issuers. As traditional methods of credit card fraud become less successful, counterfeiting may increase.

One false application procedure is to observe a user's card number and name during a credit card transaction or to get them by retrieving the carbons of credit card charge slips from trash containers. Public records are then studied to gather background information about the card holder. This information is then used to obtain a card from another issuer. In another technique, the defrauder notifies the issuer of the card that he or she is changing addresses and simultaneously requests an additional card "for my wife" or "husband."

Occasionally, a fictitious name is used on the application, along with the fictitious occupation of doctor or lawyer in the belief that issuers are less likely to conduct a thorough check of people in these professions. The credit references selected are stores known to be unresponsive to inquiries about their customers. Less frequently, employees of card issuers are bribed to approve false applications. Cards obtained through false applications have been used for as long as two months in conjunction with counterfeit identification documents.

Cards issued to but never received by legitimate applicants may have been stolen at the manufacturing stage, from the mails, or after delivery but before the applicant opens this mail. Cards acquired in this fashion usually are used for about 28 days.

Users lose their cards or have them stolen in hotels or motels most frequently, according to one authority. Pickpockets rank a distant second, and thefts from glove compartments of cars rank third in frequency. Credit cards may be taken from owners in restaurants and bars. The owner may forget the card, and a waiter might hide it under a plate or napkin in the hope that the customer will forget it. An alternative gambit is for the waiter to return from the cashier with a previously misappropriated card which has outlived its usefulness, in the hope that the user will not note the switch. Another tactic is for a waiter or waitress to pocket the cash received for a large food bill, use a misappropriated credit card to account for the bill by preparing a charge slip in the amount of pocketed cash, and forge the card holder's signature.

Waiters, gas station attendants, or other persons sometimes imprint two sets of charge slips from a customer's credit card. One is honestly filled out and signed by the card holder, who also gets the card back. But the other set is used by forging the card holder's signature.

Credit card fraud takes many forms, and the investigator must be familiar with the most common. One involves collusion between a merchant and the holder of a lost or stolen credit card. They engineer a "purchase," for example, of a $500 television set. The credit card transaction then proceeds in usual fashion, except that the confederate, in fact, gets not the TV but $250 in cash. The merchant collects the $500 from the card issuer on the bogus sale. Reportedly, at one time, 60 to 65 percent of the very small outlets in a major city were involved in this type of fraud. Collusion of this nature is cited by issuers of credit cards as being responsible for most of their losses.

It is also important for the investigator to be familiar with how misappropriated cards

are disposed of. They are given to dishonest merchants or employees who turn them in to the issuer to collect a recovery award. They are deliberately left where they will be recovered by a passerby who tries to use it and is accused of the previous unauthorized uses, temporarily slowing and confusing the investigation. Cards also are sold to second parties, some of whom are fences.

CHECK FRAUD

Check fraud is a problem of considerable magnitude, causing losses in excess of $1 billion annually. One tactic is for a person posing as the president of a local company to call a bank and state that it is urgent that an assistant en route to the bank call the office immediately. The assistant then calls, perhaps to a phone booth or other location. Thus supposedly identified, the assistant is often allowed to cash a company check which later is identified as counterfeit. Another ploy involves opening a bank account by depositing cash and in turn receiving a stamped duplicate of the deposit slip. Returning at various times that day to two or three different tellers at the same bank or its branches, the perpetrator presents the deposit slip to prove that funds exist to cover the check being presented. Even if bank procedure calls for a telephone verification of the amount of the check, the newness of the account makes it impossible for the teller to detect this tactic. Thus money far in excess of the initial deposit is withdrawn.

Another technique is to represent oneself as new in the community and ask to open a checking account. One then opens an account, making a deposit with a worthless check of $250 less $100 in cash. One does this several times in rapid succession in one community and then leaves for another community.

Raising the face amount of a legitimate check is a common deception. Numbers and wording are altered such that a check for $6 might become $60 or even $600. Passers may establish a phony company and issue bogus payroll checks to a confederate who cashes them with local merchants or banks. If they call the "company" for confirmation, they are assured that the person presenting the checks is, in fact, an employee. Another trick is to open a checking account by using counterfeit identification and to make a cash deposit. The person then returns and writes a check requiring the approval of a bank officer. Once the initials of the bank officer are on the legitimate check, the perpetrator forges them on a second counterfeit check, cashes it, cleans out the legitimate account, and disappears. In an actual case, an employee was able to prepare and successfully pass $1,100,000 in fraudulent checks by gaining access to the firm's checkwriting machine, executive signature imprinter, and blank checks.

PREVENTING CREDIT CARD AND CHECK FRAUDS

Investigators often are asked how to prevent such fraud. They can make a number of suggestions. Merchants should be cautioned not to accept cards that have expired, are not yet valid, or that have been altered. Merchants should check to see if the card presented is on the list of cancellations distributed by card issuers. They should compare the signature on the reverse of the card with that on the charge slip. Furthermore, certain types of behavior by the person presenting the card suggest a potential fraud. The card holder may split the purchase between charge slips to circumvent the need for authorization. The card holder may attempt to explain this by saying that he or she is close to the credit limit and would prefer not to suffer the embarrassment of being turned down. A parallel tactic is for the card holder to move through the store, making multiple charges for purchases with the credit card,

but doing them separately so that they remain under the amount that requires authorization by the issuer.

Indicators of possible check frauds include irregularly spaced blots, erasures, or variations in color or thickness of lines, different spellings of the payee's name on the handwritten endorsement and on the face of the check; glib or distracting talk by the person presenting the check; attempts by the person to rush the transaction.

When speaking to merchants, the investigator should stress the need for adequate identification. One piece of identification should contain a photograph of the person, and not only should the signatures on the identification be checked, but the physical description should be examined when no photograph is available. In no case should Social Security cards, business cards, club cards, bank books, birth certificates, library cards, voter registration cards, or personal letters be accepted as identification.

The traveler's check division of American Express has prepared a detailed educational package for banks on conducting check and credit card fraud prevention clinics for their commercial customers. Some credit card issuers pay all expenses to transport witnesses to court to testify; some automatically revoke the card of card holders needed as witnesses and who refuse to testify.[23]

RECEIVING STOLEN PROPERTY

One of the most infrequently prosecuted criminals is the receiver, defined as one who knowingly purchases, sells, or otherwise traffics in stolen merchandise. A fence is a professional receiver who serves as a go-between by funneling stolen property purchased from thieves to various outlets which sell the goods to the actual consumer.[24]

However, the importance of the role of

fences and other receivers has been spotlighted by the Senate Select Committee on Small Business, whose chairman isolated the crux of the problem: "Not until the fence's ability to market stolen goods is blunted will we ever be able to stay that one jump ahead of the thieves plaguing businessmen." Without fences and other receivers to play the pivotal role in the criminal system of distributing stolen goods, most incidents of burglary, hijacking, and pilfering would become unprofitable. The objective of most thieves is not the merchandise per se, but the cash for which the merchandise can be sold.

However, as one thief has testified, most receivers are legitimate businesspeople:

> The distribution of stolen property is not easily achieved without connections with so-called legitimate businesspeople to funnel the . . . stolen property that is taken each day, so that it can be resold to legitimate consumers through an outlet that is seemingly legitimate.

OPERATIONS OF RECEIVERS

Excerpts from testimony on fencing before the Select Committee on Small Business shed light on the scope, methods, and importance of fences and criminal receivers.[25]

Chairman: Now are there master fences in New York City? Chief fences, big fences, whatever you want to call them?

Witness: . . . well, off hand, I know about four big fences that can come up with $100,000 in cash, no sweat.*

Chairman: Four big fences that can come up with $100,000 in cash?

Witness: Yes. On the okay level, without

even seeing the stuff. Without even seeing it.†

Chairman: Now, who generally purchases the stolen property? . . .

Witness: Legit people. You know, stores.

Chairman: Stores do buy?

Witness: Yes. Then you got big stores, department stores, you got cut-rate stores.

The following statement, given to the committee by an assistant district attorney of an eastern city, is particularly enlightening.

> "Mack," as we will refer to this fence, is a gnomelike man in his sixties who maintained three electrical outlet stores. . . . An analysis of Mack's books and records revealed that in 1970, Mack purchased stolen electrical construction materials valued at approximately $1 million, an amount which must be multiplied in terms of the loss to the construction industry in labor costs, delay, and replacement of the stolen property.
>
> Mack's operation is typical because, as a fence, he would only deal in his specialty, that is, electrical construction materials. . . .
>
> In addition, Mack was also typical in that he acted as a catalyst in causing certain materials to be stolen at certain times. When he was overstocked in certain materials, he would so advise thieves. . . . But when one of his clients needed particular materials, Mack would put out a contract for the theft of the particular items, and take great pains to see that his customers, who paid cash, would receive the property at the time requested.
>
> Generally, there appears to be a hier-

---

* The rule of thumb is that to earn $100,000 a fence would have to handle $750,000 to $1,000,000 in stolen merchandise.

† Master fences do not come into physical possession of goods or inspect them; they are "arrangers" for the distribution of the merchandise, not its handlers.

archy among fences. Some fences may deal directly with a thief and openly sell to a buyer. This type of fence . . . deals primarily with small amounts of property. He is the "neighborhood connection.". . .

Some fences may never see or touch the stolen property. . . . Their transactions are all consummated over the telephone. This type of fence is known as the "master fence." . . .

Organized crime figures will very often "stake" a fence with a large sum of money, if he will use his connections to move stolen property for them. This is usually the relationship that exists since a fence, especially a master fence, of necessity has the required legitimate contacts and travels in the highest business circles.[26]

Fences and other receivers deal in a vast array of merchandise: securities, steel, credit cards, forged or stolen identification documents, office equipment, meat, shavers, airline tickets, shoes, clothing, and appliances of all kinds, to name a few. As the Los Angeles district attorney has testified:

Much of this merchandise also goes to . . . liquor merchants who rely on access to stolen liquor and cigarettes to increase their profit margin, jewelers who mix stolen diamonds in with stock which they have legitimately purchased, restaurateurs who serve stolen meat. . . .

Because of his [dealer in heavy equipment tires] ability to obtain stolen . . . tires—which sell for as much as $3,500 each—this individual enjoys a net profit annually of 18 percent of his gross, compared to an average 4 percent net profit among legitimate dealers.

Other outlets for stolen property in Los Angeles County include weekend swap meets which attract hundreds of people and where knowledgeable buyers can contact a fence and actually purchase stolen property with relative [freedom] from surveillance.

Ethical businesspeople are doubly penalized. First, they suffer the loss of stolen goods and endure many consequent dislocations. Production and advertising schedules may suffer, sales may be lost or delayed, and insurance premiums and deductibles may increase. Second, their prices and terms have to compete with those of firms which achieve an illegal competitive edge by purchasing cut-rate goods from criminals.[27]

POSSIBLE INDICATORS OF FENCES AND OTHER RECEIVERS

The larceny investigator should talk to businesspeople or appear before their groups to educate them about fences and other receivers. They should be told about the possibility of unwittingly dealing with fences; the possibility that competitors are dealing with fences; or the possibility that company purchasing agents or buyers work directly with fences, if for no other reason than to impress management with their adroitness at obtaining favorable rates on merchandise.

Investigators should remind businesspeople that by setting unrealistically high performance standards for buyers and purchasing agents, they may pressure employees to deal with fences. Other indicators which businesspeople should examine carefully include: offers to provide merchandise to the retailer at extremely low wholesale prices provided the sale is made in cash. Reports that other retailers are buying or selling a product at abnormally low prices; small neighborhood outlets that offer considerable savings to customers, do a large volume of business, and then suddenly close after a few weeks or months.

PREVENTIVE MEASURES

In the words of a former fence, the placement of identification numbers on products "would stop a lot of burglars from burglarizing, a lot of receivers from receiving." Indeed, the greatest problem confronting prosecutors and police in apprehending and convicting receivers is that stolen merchandise frequently cannot be identified by its owners. If businesspeople cannot distinguish between their goods that were legitimately and illegitimately marketed, their business presents a tempting target to criminals.[28]

Manufacturers play a vital role in devising methods by which identification numbers can be stamped on or otherwise affixed to products and merchandise. However, product identification achieves little if manufacturers, wholesalers, retailers, and consumers do not take the time and expense of recording them. Such numbers are invaluable to investigators, who can enter them into computerized criminal information systems, such as the NCIC's.

Company personnel—especially salespeople—can be instructed to remain alert for the sale of products at unusual discounts or through unusual channels. Other employees who have frequent external contacts could be given the serial numbers of items stolen from their firm. In one instance, a typewriter repairman noted that the serial number on the equipment he was servicing was on his employer's list of stolen equipment.

"Sellbacks"—when victims of theft or their insurers are approached by receivers who offer the return of the stolen merchandise for a small percentage of its replacement value—are not infrequent. Occasionally people yield to such a temptation. But in addition to the legal hazards they risk, such action is hardly in their firm's best long-run interests. Perhaps most important of these is that the implied reciprocity compromises the business and offers the potential for coerced cooperation in other matters involving stolen merchandise.

Routine inspection by investigators of outlets that might traffic in stolen merchandise also may reveal problems. If certain types of outlets are commonly associated with selling stolen property, state or local governments should ban or at least regulate them. In one city, the police are charged with enforcing regulations of over 50 types of businesses, and some forms, such as flea markets, are banned altogether.

SHOPLIFTING

The National Retail Merchants Association indicates that twelve cents of every dollar spent by a consumer is an incremental cost due to shoplifting—which produces losses exceeding $3.5 billion per year.

- The dollar amount of the merchandise recovered has substantially increased over the past few years.
- The total number of apprehensions has also increased substantially.

Shoplifters can be classified into two groups: commercial shoplifters or "boosters," who steal merchandise for resale, and pilferers, who take merchandise for private use.

There are two patterns emerging in shoplifting: Many more people are shoplifting, and the vast majority, as many as 95 percent, are amateurs. Many have no real personal need for the merchandise.[29]

As might be suspected, professional shoplifters are not only apprehended less frequently than amateurs, but also steal more at each theft. Professionals frequently are members of skilled and organized groups. Three to five young men and women set out on carefully planned tours throughout the United States. Their itinerary includes the names of stores to visit. They are trained in shoplifting techniques and wear special clothing designed for concealing and carrying stolen merchandise. For example, a "booster box" can be designed to hold shoplifted items. To the observer the box looks like an ordinary gift wrapped package. But a slot in

FIGURE 14-13

Booster box operation being demonstrated to a store clerk by Palm Beach, Florida, police Sgt. Henry Marchman.

Courtesy Chief J. L. Terlizzese

the side or bottom allows the shoplifter to insert items swiftly and surreptitiously (see Figure 14-13). "Booster skirts" or "booster bloomers" are occasionally used by women. Under the booster skirt is a hammocklike bag suspended between the shoplifter's legs. Booster bloomers (old-fashioned bloomers with double rows of tight elastic at the knees) can be worn under booster skirts. Slits, pockets, or an elastic waistband allow merchandise to be stuffed in. Coat linings also are tailored to hold merchandise. Large handbags, briefcases, and shopping bags are other trademarks of shoplifters.[30]

The techniques employed in shoplifting are legion and the appearance and types of shoplifters innumerable. The following cases are but a few among the many thousands that occur each year, and tend to illustrate the heterogeneity of shoplifters.[31]

A teenage girl was picked up outside a department store because a detective noticed that she seemed to have gained a lot of weight in half an hour or so. A search revealed that she was wearing two bathing suits, three bras, two girdles, four dresses, and a coat and was hiding under her coat two new pocketbooks and a jewel case.

A sixteen-year-old boy walked into a book and record store with a large paper shopping bag containing nothing but a couple of grocery store items. Four minutes later he walked out with one dozen books and eight records, more or less adequately concealed by the grocery store selections. He admitted modestly that he had probably the finest library and record collection of any kid his age.

Police in Philadelphia were obliged to arrest an armless man for shoplifting. What had he been stealing? Shoes. He also confessed to having stolen other items as well. Shoes had been his first choice after a sawmill accident had deprived him of his arms and his livelihood. As he had developed new skills, he had stolen jackets, hats, and overcoats. Sympathetic salesmen helped him, gave him all the time he needed to decide what he wanted, and let him admire himself in the clothes. Then he waited for a propitious moment and casually walked out of the store.

Local police usually become involved in shoplifting cases either to organize crime prevention programs for merchants or to respond to businesses that have been victimized or that have a violator in custody. The greatest security deterrents are often accomplished through security education programs for employees, basic display controls relating to the type of merchandise displayed and its physical location, and the utilization of highly trained security personnel both in civilian clothes and in uniform.

CONFIDENCE GAMES

The confidence artist is a recurring figure in history and in fiction, police annals, and the literature of criminology. The confidence artist steals by guile in a person-to-person relationship. Most confidence artists have insight into human nature and its frailties, not least among which is the desire to get something for nothing or for a bargain.

Many people who read the details of some of the confidence games below will find them hard to believe. How, they will ask, can anyone be so easily "conned"? But the police reports speak for themselves. The monetary loss and the number of confidence games very likely exceed the recorded figures because many victims are too embarrassed to make a police report.[32]

THE PIGEON DROP

This swindle is operated by two people. A lone victim, usually elderly, is approached on the street by one of the swindlers, who strikes up a conversation. A wallet, envelope, or other item which could contain cash is planted nearby. The second swindler walks past, picking up the wallet or envelope within full view of the pair. The swindler approaches the partner and victim, saying that he or she has found a large sum of money and is willing to divide it with them. But first the two must produce a large sum of money to show good faith. The victim is given no time to ponder and is urged to withdraw money from a savings account to show good faith. When the money is withdrawn by the victim, he places it in an envelope provided by the first swindler. It is then shown to the second swindler who, by sleight of hand, switches envelopes, returning an identical envelope filled with paper slips to the victim. Both swindlers then depart. The victim does not know that he or she has been conned until he or she goes to redeposit the savings.[33]

THE BANK EXAMINER SCHEME

The bank examiner scheme is one of the more sophisticated con games and requires knowing where targets bank. The con artist, usually a man, calls the victim—let us say an elderly woman—and introduces himself as a federal bank examiner to say that there has been a computer breakdown at the bank and that he wants to verify when she last deposited or withdrew money and her current balance. If she replies, for example, that there should be $8,000 in the account, then the caller indicates that the bank records show a deposit of some lesser amount, perhaps $2,000. The caller then suggests that a dishonest teller may be tampering with the account and asks for help in apprehending the teller. Once the victim agrees, the caller says that a cab will come and bring her to the bank. She is instructed that she should withdraw $7,000. One con man stays near the woman's house and observes her enter the cab. Another waits at the bank to verify

the withdrawal and to be certain that bank officials or police are not alerted. After withdrawing the money, the woman gets back into the waiting cab and returns home. One of the con men then telephones her to discuss the next phase of the bank's "investigation." While she is still on the phone, the second man knocks on the door. The man at the front door identifies himself as a bank employee, the woman lets him in, and lets him talk to the "bank examiner" on the telephone. After a short conversation, the con man hands the phone back to the woman. The caller instructs her to give her money to the bank employee so that he can redeposit it with the suspected teller. Victim and money are soon parted—she may even be given a receipt.

TV AND LIQUOR SCAMS

A stranger telephones and advises that there has been a vast overshipment of TVs or liquor and that it must be sold at dramatically reduced prices. The victim is instructed to meet the stranger in front of some well known liquor or appliance store. At the meeting, a price is agreed upon. The victim may insist on seeing the merchandise, at which point the victim is led to the rear of the store, where there are the appropriate types of cartons, which usually contain bricks in the case of TVs or water-filled liquor bottles in the case of liquor. Money is exchanged, the con artist leaves, and the victim is left with the worthless boxes.

HOME REPAIR FRAUD

The home repair fraud is perpetrated by individuals who go door to door offering their services for a nominal fee. The home repair may involve painting, repairs of roofs or furnaces, and so forth. Although actual repair work may be done, workmanship and materials are deficient. Due to the large volume of complaints they generate, home repair swindlers do not remain in a single community for long.[34]

SPANISH CHARITIES

This confidence game is similar to the pigeon drop, but instead of playing on the victim's greed, it plays on sympathy. The scheme has many variations, but in a recent case it was worked something like this: A man stood crying outside a Miami Cuban Medical Clinic. A man in his 60s stopped and asked the crying man, "What's the matter? Can I help you? Are you sick?" By showing concern, the man identified himself as a potentially good victim. The crying man said that he had just arrived from South America, where his father was dying. The man then explained that some years ago, while living in Miami, his father had stolen a lot of money, but that since then he had made a great deal of money and wanted to make amends. He explained that his father had given him $10,000 in cash to give to charities in Miami in his name, but because he was a stranger, alone, and grief-stricken over the pending loss of his father, he didn't know what charities to choose. Meanwhile another stranger, actually an accomplice, joined the conversation. After a few minutes, the bereaved man said, "You both seem like fine people. I'll give you the money to distribute, but how do I know I can trust you?" The second accomplice insisted that he could be trusted and was willing to take some money out of his savings account at the bank as a gesture of good faith. The would-be victim agreed to do likewise and withdrew several thousand dollars from the bank. All three men then placed their cash in an envelope, and the envelope which was supposed to contain the cash was turned over to the sympathetic stranger. The men parted, and the victim discovered that the envelope contained newspaper.

"WE'LL MAKE YOU A STAR"

Many proud parents put up hundreds of dollars for a promise that their child will get a big break in the movies or TV commercials. One man staying at a posh Miami Beach motel advertised for children to appear in his movies. He claimed affiliation with a major movie studio, and eager mothers invested hundreds of dollars on the production, which never shot a foot of film.

INHERITANCE SCAM

In this scam, the victim's phone rings and, on the other end, a sweet-sounding person says, "You may be the recipient of a huge inheritance. But first some questions must be answered, such as birthday, birthplace, mother's maiden name, Social Security number"—all the information needed to withdraw money from the victim's bank account. When the victim answers the questions, the con artist says that he or she will deposit the inheritance in the victim's bank account. In the morning, a fraudulent check is deposited into the victim's account. In the afternoon, before the fraudulent check can be discovered, a withdrawal is made, and the victim has lost money.[35]

One variation of the inheritance scam involves a victim who pays an inheritance tax before the inheritance is paid. Sometimes the caller tells the victim to mail the inheritance tax. Sometimes a well dressed, official-looking gentleman collects the inheritance tax in cash before awarding the victim a phony cashier's check.

JAMAICAN SWITCH

Victims and suspects in this scam often are black men or immigrants from a foreign country. The name "Jamaican Switch" has become popular because many of the participants have been from Jamaica or other Caribbean and Central American regions.

The suspects often work near check cashing locations, such as banks, liquor stores, and unemployment offices. They usually pose as a confused and helpless seaman from a foreign country who speaks broken English and is looking for a nonexistent address. The suspect voices his distrust of banks and seeks the victim's help in hiding what appears to be a large amount of money wrapped in a handkerchief or in a paper bag. The suspect insists that the victim show his trustworthiness and his ability to withdraw cash from a U.S. bank. Once the victim withdraws his money, the suspect puts it in the handkerchief or paper bag. When the victim is distracted, the money is switched and the victim gets a container of clipped newspaper.

Several suspects can be involved in this scam. One variation of the "Jamaican Switch" involves a suspect spotting a newcomer and asking the immigrant to keep his money and valuables for safe keeping. In order to prove his trustworthiness, the immigrant must depart with his valuables as collateral. Later, the suspect and the money disappear.

THREE-CARD MONTE

This scam is similar to the traditional shell game. The crook, using three "marked" playing cards, shuffles the cards and coaxes the victim to pick the Ace, Queen of Hearts, or whatever. In this case, the hands of the crook are usually quicker than the eyes of the victims. The cards are "marked," sometimes by feel, such as folded edges with some way that is recognizable to the shuffler. The victim is initially permitted to win and his ego is cajoled before he is cheated out of his money.

C.O.D. SCAM

The suspects usually pose as delivery employees. In an affluent neighborhood, the suspect spots an empty house and finds the resident's name. After writing a phony mailing label, the suspect goes next door and asks the neighbor to accept a perishable package for the absent neighbor and to pay cash for C.O.D. charges.

A variant carried out on weekends involves demanding that a naive teenage gas station attendant take cash register funds to pay for a package his boss supposedly ordered. Hoping to please the boss, the young employee pays the money. Of course, the boss ordered nothing, and the money is lost.

MONEY MAKING MACHINE SCAM

In this scam, a couple of con artists visit a local dice game to look for victims. They tell the victim that they have smuggled a secret formula out of West Germany (or some other foreign country) that will bleach the ink on $1 bills. Then the blank paper can be pressed against $100 bills to form another $100 bill. In one case reported in Philadelphia, a victim brought 150 $100 bills from his bank to a motel room, where the money was washed and stuck in between pieces of tissue paper with "bleached" dollar bills. While the victim went drinking with some of the con artists, one went back to the motel room and took the money. Another promised to look for the thieves and kept the victim from calling the police for a week. When the victim finally did call the police a week later, the suspects were long gone.

PREVENTION RECOMMENDATIONS

The modus operandi of many swindlers is consistent over a long period of time. For example, they resort to using the same name of a fictitious lawyer, the same amount of money in envelopes, the same addresses on the envelopes, the same style of note found inside the envelope, the same locations. Comprehensive MO files help in the eventual apprehension of the confidence artists and can be used to alert other agencies in the region. The single most potent weapon against confidence schemes is public awareness. Local civic groups and news media provide the platform, and their assistance should be aggressively sought by the investigator.

One essential element of many confidence games is that a victim withdraw money from a savings account, because few people keep large amounts of money at home. Bank officials should be encouraged to inform their customers of con games and to question large cash withdrawals, especially by older citizens.[36]

PONZI SCHEMES AND LAUNDERING: HOW ILLICIT FUNDS ARE ACQUIRED AND CONCEALED

In 1949 a new type of crime was brought to the attention of law enforcement when Professor Edwin H. Sutherland defined *white collar crime* as "a crime committed by a person of respectability and high social status in the course of his [or her] occupation."[37] The definition of white collar crime has since been expanded to include people of lower status. It is an illegal act or series of illegal acts committed by nonphysical means and by concealment or guile, to obtain money or property, to avoid the payment or loss of money or property, or to obtain business or personal advantage.[38]

For a successful prosecution, law enforcement officials must show that one or more criminal statutes have been violated. They must prove an illegal activity rather than concentrating on the offender.

It is important, therefore, for officers to understand how white collar crimes are committed. Knowing the identity of the perpetrator of a fraud is not enough. The law enforcement officer must be able to understand, explain, and show conclusively how

and why the activities are illegal. In this portion of the chapter, we look at two types of white-collar crime and demonstrate their complexity and fraudulence. Ponzi, or pyramid, schemes and the laundering of funds are only two examples of the briberies, kickbacks, payoffs, bankruptcy, credit card, check, consumer, and insurance frauds that occur each year.

PONZI AND PYRAMID SCHEMES

Pyramid sales schemes, otherwise known as chain referral schemes or Ponzi schemes, have mushroomed across the United States and may be operating in other countries. There is no way of calculating the exact amount of money lost by the victims, but it is estimated to be well over half a billion dollars in the United States alone. Some officials contend that pyramid sales schemes are the leading consumer fraud problem today. Despite the scope of the problem, many people still do not know what pyramids are.

A pyramid scheme is a marketing program by which people buy the right to sell others the right to sell a specified product. The promoters select a product, such as household items, cosmetics, or safety devices, and sell large inventories to distributors with the incentive of permitting the distributor to sell new distributorships. The real profit is earned as recruiters develop new recruits. In all of this activity, little or no real concern is given to the direct public sale of products or services. Consumer distribution is a sham.[39]

One of the earliest known examples of a pyramid scheme appeared in 1920, in Boston. Charles Ponzi, an Italian immigrant and financial wizard, established the Securities and Exchange Company. The corporation consisted of only Ponzi, who started his company with a few hundred dollars borrowed from two silent partners. The company promised investors substantial returns on their investments in Ponzi's company.

Within forty-five days investors were promised their original investment plus 50 percent interest; in ninety days, they would double their original investment. By June 1920 Ponzi claimed to be receiving $500,000 and paying out $200,000 a day.

Ponzi explained to doubters that knowing how to take advantage of the varying currency exchange rates in different parts of the world was how he made his profit. He started his company upon receiving a business letter from a conspirator in Spain, who enclosed a reply coupon which, if exchanged at any U.S. Post Office, was worth $.06. In Spain, the cost of the coupon to a buyer was only $.01. Ponzi reasoned that by buying the coupon in Spain and redeeming it in the United States, he made a $.05 profit. Thereafter, Ponzi began operations in nine different countries, with his agents traveling back and forth between these countries and the United States to take advantage of the disparity in currency value.

A *Boston Post* reporter was convinced that Ponzi had never purchased any coupons and that he was taking money from one investor to pay off another. This reporter turned up information that Ponzi, under his real name of Charles Bianchi, had been sentenced to prison in Canada for forgery several years earlier. By the end of 1920, Ponzi's world collapsed, and he was convicted in Massachusetts. Of the $15 million that Ponzi had taken in, there was no accounting for $8 million. Such schemes became known as Ponzi schemes.

Today, a pyramid scheme has hit the United States in which one needs only a chart and $1,000 in cash (see Figure 14-14). With the $1,000, you can buy a slot on the bottom line. You give $500 each to the investor above you (position 8) and in the 0 position. Pyramid success occurs when all the slots on the player's line are filled and the player progresses up the chart. When an investor finally moves into the zero position, he or she can begin collecting up to $16,000.

At the heart of each pyramid scheme is the expressed or implied representation that a new participant can recoup his or her original investment by simply inducing two or more prospects to make the same investment. Promoters fail to tell participants that this is mathematically impossible, because some people drop out of the pyramid, and others recoup their original investment and then drop out. This misrepresentation constitutes the heart of the fraud. *If* each investor recruits two additional investors and no one drops out, everything works according to plan. If there are 15 investors at the meeting to start a pyramid and one person at the top level, the number of new members doubles each day thereafter until, at the end of two weeks, 262,143 people are involved and, at the end of three weeks, there are 33,554,431 participants. The whole scheme collapses before this. Therefore, the earlier one gets in on the pyramid, the better the possibility to collect the $16,000. For everyone to win, an infinite number of investors would have to fill the chart.

PROBLEMS FOR LAW ENFORCEMENT

When companies promote Ponzi schemes, auditing becomes difficult, expensive, and time consuming. Many promoters in an area makes prosecution impractical. By the time police have all the information they need, most promotions have run their course.

The problem of establishing criminal liability is made more difficult by the need to separate victims from promoters. It is in the victim's best interest to become a promoter and transfer his or her loss to another. For this reason, useful victim testimony is limited. Only victims who invested in the pyramid for reasons other than participation in the chain referral provide useful testimony.

One immediate answer to reducing the effectiveness of pyramid schemes is to increase public awareness of the impossibility of succeeding. Law enforcement should not

FIGURE 14-14   The Pyramid Scheme

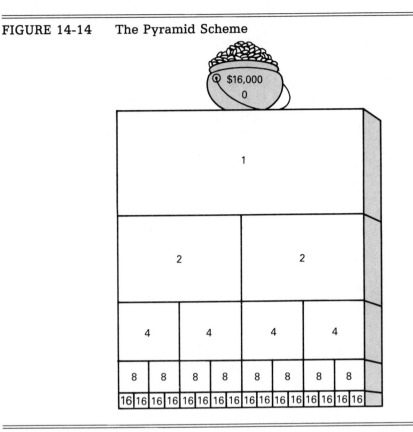

---

rely solely on adverse publicity during or after disclosure of a Ponzi scheme to combat the crime.

DEFINITION OF LAUNDERING

Al Capone, the infamous gangster of the 1920s, is said to have amassed a fortune of $20 million in ten years through bootlegging and gambling. Yet when Capone was sentenced to 11 years in prison in 1931, it was for income tax evasion. The conviction of Capone taught other organized crime members an important lesson: Money not reported on an income tax return is money that cannot be spent or invested without risk of detection and prosecution.

Because most money collected by organized crime is from illegal sources, such as loansharking, prostitution, gambling, and narcotics, criminals are reluctant to report the income or its sources on tax returns. Before spending or otherwise using these funds, they must give the money an aura of legality. This conversion is known as *laundering*. To combat organized crime successfully, law enforcement officials must understand how money is laundered.[40]

THE LAUNDERING OF MONEY BY ORGANIZED CRIME

At the end of the 1800s, most money earned by the American underworld was gained through extortion, blackmail, and dock racketeering. By the 1920s, most came from bootlegging, and some believe that Prohibition supplied organized crime with the funds and skills to operate multimillion-dollar ventures. Today, it is estimated that organized crime has invested more than $20 billion into 15,000 to 50,000 businesses in the United States and takes in at least $48 billion annually in gross revenues, with about $25 billion in untaxed profits.[41]

DOMESTIC LAUNDRIES

Certain businesses lend themselves to laundering money. For example, the business must be capable of absorbing a large volume of cash income, because most illicit income is received as cash. The purpose of laundering funds is to commingle licit and illicit monies so that they cannot be separated and to prevent the discovery of the introduction of illegal money into the business. Because most checks and credit card receipts are traceable by law enforcement officials, businesses such as restaurants, bars, and massage parlors, which take in a high proportion of cash, tend to be more desirable as laundries than businesses that receive most of their income as checks or other traceable instruments.

Another favorable characteristic for a laundry is expenses that do not vary with sales volume. An example of such a business is a movie theater that shows pornographic films. The expenses of such a business (rent, electricity, wages) are almost constant, regardless of whether the theater is full. Illicit income can be introduced and camouflaged in this type of business quite easily, because the additional sales do not increase expenses. Law enforcement officials who examined the records of such a theater would have trouble proving that the legitimate income generated by the theater was lower than that recorded.

Businesses that experience a high rate of spoilage or other loss of goods also may be used to launder money. Groceries and restaurants are good examples. Money is introduced into the business and recorded in its general income accounts as if it had been received from customers. Fraudulent invoices for produce or other perishable items are issued to these businesses by companies acting as suppliers. The grocery or restaurant issues checks to these "suppliers" or records the transaction as a cash payment and charges it to an expense account, such as cost of goods sold. The undelivered produce or perishable items listed as spoiled and discarded are written off the books (see Figure 14-15). The grocery store or restaurant thus avoids tax liability and the funds paid to "suppliers" seem legal and may be spent or invested with little risk of discovery. Within a week of the transaction, it is almost impossible for law enforcement officials to disprove the story of the grocer or restaurant owner.

The above techniques have been used to launder funds successfully for a number of years, and large numbers of domestic businesses controlled by organized crime are still being used for this function. Recently, however, law enforcement officials have adapted new methods, such as sampling, ratio analysis, and flow-charting, to discover laundering operations and to prosecute the people involved in them.

Sampling is a statistical procedure in which the number of customers of an establishment is randomly counted, a conservative estimate made of the amount of money spent by each customer, and a projection made of how much money is actually received by an enterprise in the ordinary course of operation. If the projected income is materially smaller than that reported to taxing authorities, it is a good indication that the business is being used to launder funds.

Ratios to evaluate businesses have been used for many years by accountants, investors, and lending institutions. There are four basic types of ratios:

FIGURE 14-15   Laundering of Money from Illicit Sources

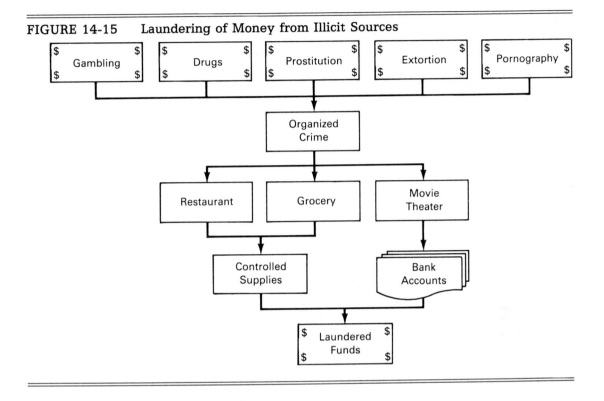

1. Liquidity ratios, which indicate the ability of an enterprise to satisfy its immediate (short-term) financial obligations
2. Operating ratios, which indicate the efficiency of the business
3. Profitability ratios, which indicate the effective use of assets and the return of the owner's investment in the business
4. Leverage ratios, which indicate the extent to which the enterprise is financed by debt

By using ratio analysis, an investigator can compare the past performance of a business with that of the industry in which the business operates. This comparison can be used to spot significant deviations from the norm, and these may indicate the existence of a laundering operation.

Another method used to uncover laundering involves researching the corporate and ownership structures of both the suspected business and all the companies with which it deals. The relationship between the various companies may be illustrated visually by the process of flow charting which allows investigators, prosecutors, and juries to grasp more easily the sometimes complex relationships which exist in laundering operations.

Although law enforcement agencies have been relatively successful in exposing domestic laundering operations, underworld leaders have perfected international laundering operations that have traditionally been immune from exposure. Although international laundries vary greatly in form, organization, and complexity, their object is still to disguise the true nature and origin of illegal funds.

International laundering schemes often involve the use of dummy corporations, numbered bank accounts, or financial instruments issued by banks located in countries where banking regulations are lax (often referred to as "off-shore banks").

FOREIGN LAUNDRIES

Much of the money invested by organized crime in legitimate businesses in the United States is first routed through secret numbered bank accounts in countries such as Switzerland, Liechtenstein, West Germany, Panama, and the Bahamas. This arrangement is ideal for the racketeer who wishes to clean large amounts of cash. Often it involves depositing illicit funds in a secret numbered account and then bringing them back into the United States as a loan from the foreign bank or from a dummy corporation set up under the laws of a foreign country. Not only are the illegal income and its sources hidden from the Internal Revenue Service and other law enforcement agencies, but the interest on this supposed loan is often deducted as a business expense on the tax return of the racketeer.

In many cases, organized crime members have not been content with merely using secret numbered accounts in foreign banks. As early as the 1960s, it was recognized that many banks in Switzerland and the Bahamas had been taken over by Americans known to be associated with organized crime activities.[42] Not only did the American ownership protect the identity of bank customers and allow for the falsification of bank records, but it also enabled the racketeers to bring apparently legitimate money back into the United States in the form of various financial instruments issued by these banks and by foreign governments. Owners realized that controlled banks could also be used to generate illicit income by issuing fraudulent financial instruments that are used in this

country as collateral for loans and in other fraud schemes. Enforcement agents working for the U.S. Comptroller of the Currency now estimate that the volume of phony financial instruments issued by offshore banks is in the hundreds of millions of dollars.[43]

IMPLICATION
FOR LAW ENFORCEMENT

Investigation has shown that laundering operations actually are not complicated and can be understood by law enforcement officers willing to use sampling, ratio analysis, flow charting, and traditional methods.

The success of organized crime in laundering funds through secret numbered bank accounts, foreign corporations, and offshore banks has resulted from their immunity to law enforcement agencies operating in the United States. Although investigating these laundering operations remains expensive, difficult, and time consuming, investigators have new jurisdictional tools to combat this problem. On January 23, 1977, a Mutual Assistance in Criminal Matters Treaty between the United States and Switzerland became effective. U.S. law enforcement authorities are now able to obtain previously secret bank information where organized crime is involved. Investigators are further aided by the passage of the Currency and Foreign Transactions Reporting Act (U.S.C., Title 31, Sections 1051–1143). This act and Treasury Department regulations set forth reporting requirements for anyone importing or exporting currency or other financial instruments totaling more than $5,000. Banks and financial institutions also must report currency transactions over $10,000 to the Internal Revenue Service. This act also requires all U.S. citizens having a financial interest in or signature authority over bank securities or other financial accounts in foreign countries to report this relationship annually to the Treasury Department.[44]

In the final analysis, white collar crime, like traditional crime, has existed for hundreds of years. Our system of jurisprudence has, however, concentrated on those crimes involving violence, threats to person and property, and overt theft. For this reason, laws were passed to deal with the poorer, more visible criminal element. But following the massive securities swindles and bank failures of the 1930s, government leaders and criminologists began to address the problem of white collar crime and passed the first laws to deal with it. The general public and the law enforcement community have come to perceive these activities as illegal.

Few police officers, however, have had experience and training in this subject. The two types of white collar crime just discussed are intended to help law enforcement efforts to combat this crime. If the rapid increase in white collar crime is to be dealt with effectively, law enforcement officials must understand the nature of these crimes and develop new techniques to investigate them.

COMPUTER CRIME INVESTIGATION

In the last thirty years, the use of computers has become widespread; in the federal government alone the number of computers in use has risen from 2 to 10,000.[45] Computers are used to register students, calculate grade averages, and prepare transcripts; to check for stolen articles and wanted persons; to assist in air traffic control and navigation; to prepare credit cards and drivers' licenses; to ascertain if a check given a merchant is backed by sufficient funds; and countless other uses. "Computer" has come to connote efficiency and correctness in the minds of many people and to make them feel frustrated when they feel that the computer has

not treated them fairly or there has been a computer error.[46]

The persuasive power of the computer is illustrated by the following case:

Mrs. Jones visited the local shopping center near her Cincinnati, Ohio, home. She made purchases in several shops and paid by check. Each time, she presented her bank check card to the clerk to identify herself and guarantee that the check would be honored. She was unaware that a man had been watching her every move.

"I was chatting with a neighbor on the way to my car when this man came up and accused me of passing a phony check," Mrs. Jones told the Better Business Bureau investigators. "I was terribly embarrassed. I had paid by check in Woolworth's, and I knew there was money in the bank to cover it. But having him say that it was bogus in front of my friend just confused the life out of me. I was tongue-tied."

The man had been convincing. He said politely, "We've had a negative report on your bank check card from the computer." The use of the word computer was the key. It instantly implied that an infallible machine had caught Mrs. Jones in a misdeed.

"Let me have your bank card and checkbook, please," the man said next, "and enough cash to cover the check you gave Woolworth's. This will show your good faith. Perhaps I can clear up the matter for you."

Mrs. Jones and her friend waited in the parking lot nearly half an hour. Then the girl suggested that something must be wrong and they ought to go to Woolworth's.

No one in the store knew anything about her checkbook or bank card. The store manager, who was familiar with this kind of swindle, told her to telephone her bank and the police. By the time she reported the matter to her bank, $170 worth of goods had been bought by the man and his accomplices with her checks.

"I didn't lose the money personally," Mrs. Jones said sadly. "My bank covered the loss because I informed them immediately. But I was so upset by being conned that I had nightmares about it for more than a month."[47]

In Olympia, Washington, someone fired shots into the state unemployment office's computer. In Johannesburg, South Africa, someone shot a tax processing computer. Antiwar demonstrators in Melbourne, Australia, "shotgunned to death" an American-made computer.[48]

A variety of terms are used to describe computer crime, including computer abuse, computer fraud, computer-related crime, automated data processing (ADP) crime, and electronic data processing (EDP) crime. Whatever the term implies, computer crime has reached a staggering level. With only 15 percent of computer crimes detected and reported, exact losses are unknown. Estimates of losses range from $100 million to $300 million annually, although some experts maintain that this is a conservative figure. The average loss in a computer crime is $430,000 (compared to $19,000 in a manual accounting operation). One factor compounding the difficulty in dealing with computer crime is that the risk of prosecution is only one in 22,000, a fact that may encourage prospective violators.[49]

Other factors related to the flourishing number of computer crimes include:

- The potential for gains may be great; for example, a single computer in New York City is known to contain more than $8 billion worth of negotiable assets.
- Managers disassociate themselves from computer operations, believing that they cannot understand them. Alternatively, they simply do not take the time to become familiar with such systems.

- Computer security often is lax.
- There is insufficient caution in hiring, training, and assigning personnel.
- Certain types of computer crime are easily accomplished by persons with little skill. Conversely, when committed by a thoughtful, skilled, and careful perpetrator, detection may take years and even then only take place by accident, through an informant's tip, or on information from a disgruntled coconspirator.
- Obtaining necessary evidence may be difficult.
- Unusual situations may be identified not as crimes but as machine, operator, or program error.
- Executives may be reluctant to prosecute an offense if it would raise questions about the adequacy of their own performance or create discontent among stockholders.[50]

Computer crimes may not be prosecuted by executives who may see a double advantage in not doing so—personal gain and the elimination of a rival company:

The office manager of a New York brokerage firm programmed a computer to siphon assets from his company into the accounts of him and his wife. Over an eight-year period, he stole about $250,000. When it was detected, his employer not only helped him to cover it up, but together they used their computer to communicate with that of a competing firm. They put assets into dummy accounts they established for themselves, accumulating enough to force their competitor into bankruptcy.[51]

TYPES OF COMPUTER CRIMES

A computer-assisted crime can take the form of any traditional crime, such as theft or embezzlement, as well as misappropriation of computer time or obtaining information for personal gain. In general, "computer crimes" fall into the following categories: 1. theft of services; 2. informational; 3. financial; 4. property; and 5. crimes against the person.[52]

Theft of Services. Theft of services occurs when an authorized person uses computer time for unauthorized purposes, or an unauthorized user successfully penetrates the system. In the first instance, an elected public official may obtain the names and addresses of registered voters from a public computer, for an ostensibly legitimate reason and then use the information to solicit campaign contributions. In the second instance, a former computer operations employee may successfully cajole the information needed for access from a present employee and then use computer time to calculate the best odds to bet on a slate of football games.

Informational Crimes. These are offenses in which people use computerized information for personal profit. For example, three computer operators at the offices of Encyclopedia Britannica sold a list of 3 million "most valuable" customers to a competitor. In another case, people with poor credit ratings were charged $1,500 each to have a clerk alter their credit files in the computer of a nationwide credit reporting company.

Financial Crimes. Financial crimes occur when computers used for financial processing are used to obtain assets.

> One employee managed to cheat the federal government out of an estimated $500,000. The employee had access to the Social Security Administration computer that processed disability checks. She included the names of some accomplices on eligible lists, and checks were dispensed to them. The checks were picked up in Philadelphia and Washington, then purged from the computer. It is estimated that this went on for approximately two years. The employee steadfastly refused to cooperate, and therefore

no one is sure exactly how much money was stolen. Investigators have traced only $99,504.10. Government agents suspect that much of the money is in bank accounts under fictitious names in Philadelphia and Washington. Two were also arrested and convicted.[53]

More than $20 million was stolen from a Beverly Hills, California, branch of Wells Fargo Bank by an official who recorded fictitious deposits for a sports promoter.[54]

Several years ago the FBI uncovered a group of young computer "hackers" who had broken into a San Francisco company's files and filled them with obscenities. Damage was estimated at $260,000, and it cost the company $100,000 in lost revenues to trace the culprits. The group was nabbed when they tried to break into the records of a thoroughbred listing service in Kentucky.

From a computer in his parents' home in Virginia, a young man accessed files of Credit Bureau, Inc., of Atlanta. He allegedly used information about other people's credit card accounts to order $50,000 worth of computer and electronic gear from mail order businesses. The delivery man became suspicious when the young man accepted many of the packages addressed to different people.[55]

The Equity Funding Insurance fraud is another example of a case in which a computer served as an essential tool for accomplishing a major fraud with $100 million in losses to stockholders, customers, and reinsurers and involved over $2 billion in money and assets.

> This fraud involved mass conspiracy and continued for many years. To sustain its image as a successful company and satisfy its need for cash during a recession when sales of its special mutual fund/insurance package dropped alarmingly, the Equity Company produced fake insurance policies. The fake policies, which were re-

corded in the computer, were sold for cash to reinsurance companies. The company was thus able to report steadily increasing earnings during a recession, and the price of its stock rose considerably. After viewing the computer printouts, auditors for the reinsurers asked to see the original policy applications and policies. They were stalled until forgeries could be produced by a special division of the company. Equity executives could tell which documents had to be forged by a secret code number on the computer printout. The computer was also programmed with a special code that kept the computer from billing on fake policies.[56]

A final example of this type of crime involves a consultant and physicians.

A management consultant providing doctors with services, such as obtaining payment for back medical billings (for which he received a 25 percent fee), learned through acquaintances in Blue Shield and through examination of Blue Shield's computer manuals that the computer system was programmed to examine the dates, as well as the other specifics, on requests for payment. If the date on the request for payment was less than a year old, the computer was programmed to recognize it as a possible duplicate, on the presumption that monthly bills are sent out and that the most recent could have been sent while payment was in the mail. However, if the date was over a year old, even though all other information was the same, the computer was not programmed to consider the possibility that the request was a duplicate. The consultant conspired with the claims supervisor to submit duplicate claims from his clients dated over one year old. The conspirators ran a test claim, found that it worked, and started to file duplicate claims.

The fraud was discovered during hearings held by a commission investigating fiscal management in the state's department of health. The investigation involved all standard investigative procedures, including:

- interviews with the doctors and their office personnel
- interviews with Blue Shield personnel
- identification of the suspect, criminal history check, and identification of associates
- submittal of marked claims to the claims supervisor to further test the system and gather evidence of the insider's operations
- search warrants on suspect's house, Blue Shield, and all banks used by conspirators

A state government computer consultant, interviews with Blue Shield computer personnel, and interviews with the defendants for the purpose of making recommendations for changes in the Blue Shield claims processing system were also used.

The investigator's attention is particularly directed to the following facts:

- No computer program changes were required to commit the fraud.
- Collusion by an insider was required.
- The investigation was performed by investigators with no special qualifications in computers.

Property Offenses. One of the most famous cases of a computer being used in a property crime occurred several years ago.

A graduate student with expertise in computers found a telephone company's computer system instructions in a garbage can. These documents gave him the entry code into the telephone company's computer and also the quarterly loss figures allowed by the company on various materials and repair parts distributed to personnel in the field. Using a touch-tone telephone, the schemer entered orders for items from the company's systems manual, which he had obtained by befriending some telephone company personnel. To prevent detection by establishing a pattern, he varied the parts orders by quantity and location. He also kept the orders within the loss allowance programmed into the computer. The fraud continued for two years and involved over $1 million. It was discovered only through the report of an informant. The defendant at his trial rationalized that he really had not been stealing because there had been no loss.[57]

Crimes against the Person. Although unusual, computers may also be involved as a tool in crimes against the person.

In Tokyo, a perpetrator opened a bank account under a fictitious name and tested several of the bank's remote money dispensers to ensure that he could access his account. He then kidnapped the infant daughter of a well known Japanese actor and demanded that the ransom be placed in the previously opened account. The police learned that the kidnapper could get the ransom from any of 348 computer-controlled cash dispenser stations. However, even if all of them were under observation, the police could not tell when the perpetrator had made a withdrawal for twenty minutes. By reprogramming the computer, bank authorities were able to turn the kidnapper's apparent advantage to a liability: the instant the kidnapper's account was used the police would know which station was involved. The subject was subsequently apprehended as he stepped from a cash dispenser, and the child was returned unharmed to the parents.[58]

COMPUTERS AND COMPUTER SYSTEMS

A computer is an electronic machine capable of accepting data, performing mathematical and logical operations on them, and supplying the results of these operations. When a computer is used in a variety of applications, it is a *general purpose unit.* When its use is fixed and unvarying, such as to control the navigation of an airplane, it is called a *dedicated* or *special purpose computer. Hardware* refers to the collection of electronic devices that make up a computer system, such as the central processor, printers, and magnetic tape drives. *Software* is the collection of computer instructions, or programs, that direct the computer.[59]

Figure 14-16 depicts the arrangement of a computer system. A typical computer system uses programs to enter data via an input device into a central processing unit (CPU), where the data are processed and output produced, which ultimately becomes information. This input-processing-output flow is basic to all computer systems. There is some form of auxiliary storage, such as a magnetic disk and/or tape; a console unit which allows the computer operator to communicate with the CPU; and terminals which allow remote access to the system. The areas of vulnerability in a computer system are indicated by Figure 14-17. As this figure suggests, the input can be altered; computer programs can be altered or created; CPUs can be misused; the data contained in the auxiliary storage files can be added to, changed, or deleted; the output can be altered; operating systems can be penetrated; and computer communications can be intercepted or altered. The areas of vulnerability can be ranked in ascending level of technical complexity:

1. Input/output alteration
2. Computer operations
3. Computer programs

FIGURE 14-16   The Arrangement of a Computer System

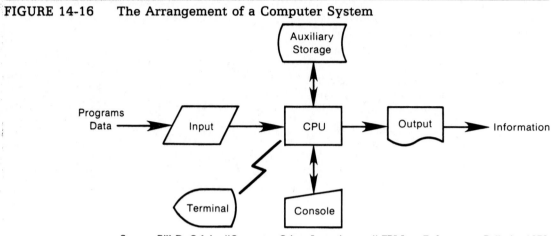

Source: Bill D. Colvin, "Computer Crime Investigators," FBI Law Enforcement Bulletin, 1979, Vol. 48, No. 7, Figure 1, p. 10, with modifications.

FIGURE 14-17   Areas of Vulnerability in a Computer System

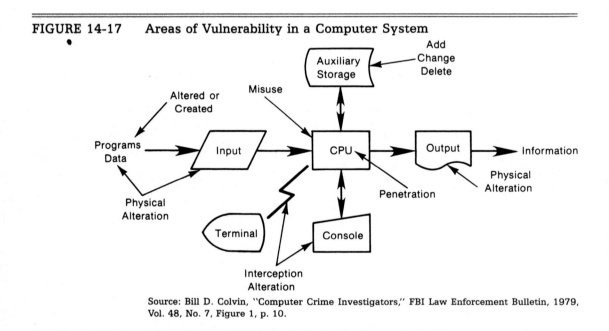

Source: Bill D. Colvin, "Computer Crime Investigators," FBI Law Enforcement Bulletin, 1979, Vol. 48, No. 7, Figure 1, p. 10.

FIGURE 14-18 **Correlation of Technical Capabilities and Types of Operations Relating to Computer Crime**

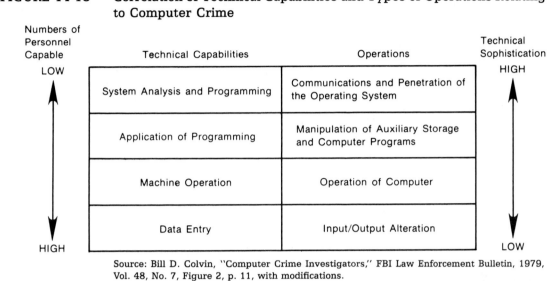

Numbers of Personnel Capable	Technical Capabilities	Operations	Technical Sophistication
LOW ↑	System Analysis and Programming	Communications and Penetration of the Operating System	HIGH ↑
	Application of Programming	Manipulation of Auxiliary Storage and Computer Programs	
	Machine Operation	Operation of Computer	
HIGH ↓	Data Entry	Input/Output Alteration	LOW ↓

Source: Bill D. Colvin, "Computer Crime Investigators," FBI Law Enforcement Bulletin, 1979, Vol. 48, No. 7, Figure 2, p. 11, with modifications.

4. Auxiliary storage manipulation
5. Operating system penetration
6. Interception and/or alteration of communications.[60]

Suspects in a computer crime scheme can be developed by analyzing the technical capabilities required to accomplish a particular manipulation. Within a computer unit, four basic functions are performed: 1. data entry; 2. machine operation; 3. application of programming; and 4. systems analysis. Figure 14-18 relates these functions, or technical capabilities, to various computer crimes. Note that the greater the technical sophistication required, the fewer possible suspects. People with higher technical skills also have the lower skills. Thus a system analyst might be involved in any of the four types of operations, but someone who can only enter data is unlikely to be involved in penetrating an operating system. However, because some people are overqualified for their jobs the investigator should not make an absolute presumption that a person holding a lower level technical job does not have the more advanced skills. Suggestions of possibilities are ordinarily obtained from a review of work history, education, technical training, and job performance.

The investigation of computer crime requires special awareness. As the complexity of crimes increases, it also requires technical capabilities. The nature of evidence in computer offenses creates special difficulties. For example, such evidence is dense; a single tape may contain more information than an entire shelf of books. Not only does this make evaluation more difficult, but the evidence can be destroyed easily, or "booby trapped" so that an attempt by the investigator to reproduce it results in its automatic loss. Nevertheless, investigators can be trained to successfully handle 93 percent of all inquiries into computer offenses.[61]

=== QUESTIONS ===

1. What two elements must be present for a larceny to occur?
2. What is the National Auto Theft Bureau, and what functions does it perform for law enforcement?
3. Discuss some situations in which complainants fraudulently report the theft of vehicles.
4. Discuss the four broad types of auto thefts.
5. Describe how "chop shops" work.
6. Describe the five general methods by which automobiles can be identified.
7. What are some readily observable indications of a stolen car?
8. What two factors contribute to the increase in marine thefts?
9. What information is needed for a law enforcement agency to make an inquiry of the NCIC Boat File?
10. What can be done to assist merchants in preventing credit card and check frauds?
11. Discuss the possible signs that people are acting as fences and other receivers.
12. Describe the techniques employed in the "pigeon drop" and "bank examiner" scheme.
13. Describe a pyramid sales scheme.
14. What is the purpose of laundering money?
15. Why are groceries and restaurants considered good businesses for laundering money?
16. In general, computer crimes fall into five major categories. What are they?

=== NOTES ===

1. Neil C. Chamelin and Kenneth R. Evans, *Criminal Law for Policemen* (Englewood Cliffs, N.J.: Prentice-Hall, 1971), p. 121.
2. These manuals are available from Station Distributing House, P.O. Box 207, Port Jefferson Station, N.Y. 11776.
3. George F. Payton, *Patrol Procedures* (Los Angeles: Legal Book Corp., 1967), p. 357.
4. "Fake Auto Thefts—Guess Who's Paying," *Athens* (Georgia) *Banner-Herald,* February 13, 1982, 11.
5. International Association of Chiefs of Police, *Auto Theft: Training Key #19* (Gaithersburg, Md.: IACP, 1966), p. 2.
6. John J. Horgan, *Criminal Investigation* (New York: McGraw-Hill, 1974), p. 185.
7. Beverly N. W. Lee and Giannina P. Rikoski, *Vehicle Theft Prevention Strategies* (Washington, D.C.: U. S. Government Printing Office, June 1984), pp. 1, 2.
8. "Senate Probing Car Theft Industry," *The Atlanta Journal,* November 26, 1979, 24.
9. Horgan, *Criminal Investigation,* pp. 190, 191.
10. Ibid., p. 191.
11. National Automobile Theft Bureau, *Passenger Vehicle Identification Manual* (Downers Grove, Ill.: 1974), pp. 88 and 96.
12. Charles A. Poplinger, "VINSLEUTH: Outsmarting the VIN Changes," *Police Chief,* May 1986, pp. 56 and 57.
13. Nancy E. Hawkins, "Recognizing Stolen Vehicles," *The National Centurion,* Vol. II, No. VI, July 1984, 34.
14. Hawkins, "Recognizing Stolen Vehicles," p. 32.
15. Hawkins, "Recognizing Stolen Vehicles," p. 32.
16. This information has been provided by the Lo-Jack Corporation of Boston, Mass.
17. Stannard J. Baker, *Traffic Accident Investigator's Manual* (Evanston, Ill.: Northwestern University Traffic Institute, 1970), pp. 125, 126.

18. George J. Lyford, "Boat Theft—A High-Profit/Low Risk Business," *FBI Law Enforcement Bulletin,* May 1982, pp. 1–5. This discussion of boat theft and the accompanying figures were taken from this source.

19. "Boat and Marine Equipment Theft," summary report of a 1979 National Workshop (University of Rhode Island Marine Advisory Service, Narragansett, R.I., 1980), p. 5.

20. U.S. Coast Guard, *Commandants' Instruction # 1620.3* (June 24, 1977).

21. *National Automobile Theft Bureau Passenger Vehicle Identification Manual,* 52nd annual ed. (Palos Hills, Ill.: National Auto Theft Bureau, 1981), pp. 172–173.

22. Chamber of Commerce of the United States, *White Collar Crime* (Washington, D.C.: Chamber of Commerce, 1974), pp. 33–39.

23. Ibid., pp. 75–77.

24. Chamber of Commerce, *White Collar Crime,* pp. 45–48.

25. Ibid., pp. 45–46.

26. Ibid., p. 46.

27. Ibid., pp. 46, 47. Additional details about fences and other receivers are capsuled in *Cargo Theft and Organized Crime* (Washington, D.C.: Government Printing Office, October 1972). Also see *Criminal Redistribution Systems and Their Economic Impact on Small Business, Part I* (hearings before the Senate Select Committee on Small Business, May 1–2, 1973), (Washington, D.C.: Government Printing Office, 1973).

28. Ibid., pp. 80–82.

29. Schuyler M. Meyer, "A Crusade against Shoplifting," *The Police Chief,* June 1974, Vol. 41, No. 6, p. 34. Mary Owen Cameron, *The Booster and the Snitch* (New York: The Free Press of Glencoe, 1964), p. 39. S. J. Curtis, *Modern Retail Security* Springfield, Ill.: Charles C. Thomas, 1972), p. 80.

30. Ibid. and Cameron, *The Booster and the Snitch,* pp. 46–47.

31. Alfred Alexander and Val Moolman, *Stealing,* © Russell Humphries, 1969, pp. 80–81.

32. "Con Men—A Sucker's Sampler of the Games People Play," *The Miami Herald,* April 21, 1977, 15.

33. Ottie Adkins, "Crime against the Elderly," *The Police Chief,* January 1975, Vol. 42, No. 1, p. 40.

34. Ibid., p. 40.

35. R. Griffin, "Bunko schemes—The art of flim flam," *The National Centurion,* October, 1983. (The remainder of this discussion of confidence games was obtained with modification from this source, pp. 38–42.)

36. Theodore Farace and Andrew Camera, "Operations Confidence Game," *The Police Chief,* January 1975, Vol. 42, No. 6, pp. 37–39.

37. Edwin H. Sutherland, *White Collar Crime* (New York: Dryden Press, 1949), p. 9.

38. U.S. Department of Justice, LEAA, *The Nature, Impact, and Prosecution of White-Collar Crime* (Washington, D.C.: Government Printing Office, 1970), pp. 4–6.

39. Vincent P. Doherty and Monte E. Smith, "Ponzi Schemes and Laundering—How Illicit Funds Are Acquired and Concealed," *FBI Law Enforcement Bulletin,* November 1981, pp. 5–11. This discussion was taken from this source.

40. Wayne Moquin and Charles Van Doren, *The American Way of Crime—A Documentary History* (New York: Praeger Publishers, 1976), p. 68.

41. August Bequai, *Organized Crime, The Fifth Estate* (Lexington, Mass.: D. C. Heath and Company, 1979), p. 183. Lawrence J. Kaplan and Dennis Kessler, *An Economic Analysis of Crime* (Springfield, Ill.: Charles C. Thomas, 1976), p. 275. "The Mafia—Big, Bad and Booming," *Time,* May 16, 1977, p. 33.

42. James Cook, "The Invisible Enterprise," *Forbes,* October 13, 1980, p. 125.

43. Jim Drinkhall, "Con Men Are Raking in Millions by Setting Up Own Caribbean Banks," *The Wall Street Journal,* March 23, 1981, p. 1.

44. Robert E. Chasen and Arthur Sinai, "Currency and Foreign Transactions Reporting Act—A New Law Enforcement Tool," *FBI Law Enforcement Bulletin,* August 1979, pp. 1–5.

45. C. R. Swanson and Leonard Territo, "Computer Crime: Dimensions, Types, Causes, and Investigation," *Journal of Police Science and Administration,"* September 1980, pp. 304–311. Much of this discussion on computer crime was taken from this source.

46. Committee on Government Operations, *Staff Study of Computer Security in Federal Programs* (Washington, D.C.: Government Printing Office, 1977), p. 6.

47. Robert Farr, *The Electronic Criminals* (New York: McGraw-Hill, 1975), pp. 2–3.

48. Donn B. Parker, *Crime By Computer* (New York: Charles Scribner's Sons, 1976), p. 18.

49. Bill D. Colvin, "Computer Crime Investigators," *FBI Law Enforcement Bulletin,* 1979, Vol. 48, No. 7, p. 9. "Computer Crime at Staggering Level, Fraud Experts Say," *LEAA Newsletter,* December 1979–January 1980, Vol. 9, No. 1, p. 3. "Computer Coverage," *Security World,* 1980, Vol. 17, No. 1, p. 44. "Computer Crime at Staggering Level," p. 3. In contrast to an average loss of $430,000 is an analysis of sixty-nine federal computer crimes which produced a loss of about $2,000,000; see Committee on Government Operations, *Staff Study of Computer Security in Federal Programs,* p. 18.

50. These five reasons are identified in Jerome Lobel, "Computer Related Crimes," in *Crimes Against Businesses: Proceedings of a Seminar Held in Phoenix, Arizona,* U.S. Department of Commerce (Washington, D.C.: Government Printing Office, 1976), p. 24. Robert V. Jacobson, "Computer Related Crimes," in *Crimes Against Business: A Management Perspective,* U.S. Department of Commerce (Washington, D.C.: Government Printing Office, 1976), p. 90. Farr, *The Electronic Criminals,* p. 8. Also ripe for abuse are decision-making companies in the federal government which make determinations about authorizations for payment, the issuance of checks, requisitions, and related matters, which involve about $1.7 billion annually. See Committee on Government Operations, *Staff Study of Computer Security in Federal Programs,* p. 14.

51. Farr, *The Electronic Criminals,* p. 15.

52. The first four of these categories are taken from August Bequai, "Computer Crime: A Growing and Serious Crime," *Police Law Quarterly,* 1976, Vol. VI, p. 23; additional comments and citations have been inserted by the present authors.

53. Dan Rodricks, "Money Machine . . . What Did Janet Blair Do with the Fortune She Stole Via Government Computer?" *The Tampa Tribune,* July 25, 1980, p. 1A.

54. Louis Friedland, "Getting a Lock on Computer Crime," *State Legislature,* Vol. 10, No. 8, September 1984, pp. 9–10.

55. Ibid., p. 10.

56. Donn B. Parker, *Crime by Computer* (New York: Charles Scribner's Sons, 1976), pp. 118–174. This book presents a comprehensive picture of the methodology and challenge of the criminal who exploits the vulnerability of computer technology.

57. Herbert Edelhertz, *The Investigation of White Collar Crime* (Washington, D.C.: Government Printing Office, 1977), pp. 206–208.

58. Sadatoshi Suzuki, "Computer Catches Kidnapper," *FBI Law Enforcement Bulletin,* 1975, Vol. 44, No. 6, pp. 14–18. There is

also speculation that in the future, given our growing dependency on computers in hospitals and elsewhere, a computer could be utilized as part of a criminal homicide; see "Computer Coverage," p. 45.

59. Edelhertz et al., *The Investigation of White Collar Crime,* p. 202. Parker, *Crime by Computer,* p. x.
60. Colvin, *Computer Crime Investigation,* p. 9.
61. Jay Becker, "The Investigation of Computer Crime," a paper presented at the First Comprehensive Training Course on White Collar Crime Enforcement Strategies and Techniques (Seattle, Wash.: The Battelle Center, September 17–23, 1978), p. 9. On this point, Becker notes that in the Equity Funding Company Fraud, some 3,000 reels of computer tape were potential evidence; also see "A Reconsideration of the Admissibility of Computer Generated Evidence," *University of Pennsylvania Law Review,* 1977, Vol. 126, pp. 425–451. Colvin, "Computer Crime Investigators," p. 12.

15

AGRICULTURAL AND WILDLIFE CRIMES

INTRODUCTION

A conventional wisdom is that crime is fundamentally, if not almost exclusively, an urban phenomenon. Yet, like most matters, there are some aspects of crime which do not immediately meet the eye. Seventeen percent of our nation's farms—or roughly one in every five—are located within Standard Metropolitan Statistical Areas (SMSAs), and thus crime on and against them contributes to the magnitude of reported crime in urban areas.[1] Additionally, crimes are committed against wildlife which have significant value and single instances of them may yield more profit to the offender than for single episodes of conventional crimes such as burglary, robbery, or larceny. The purpose of this chapter is to call attention to the nature and extent of crimes against agriculture and wildlife and to provide information regarding the proper investigation of them.

AGRICULTURAL CRIME AND ITS CITY CONNECTION

There is a natural but mistaken view that crimes against agriculture are of little overall economic consequence and are not within the sphere of interest for urban police officers. Although these themes are examined in detail from various perspectives in subsequent portions of this chapter, a few observations are warranted here. Estimates of the economic impact of rural and agricultural crime are as high as $3 billion annually.[2] This figure may be modest when the size of the agricultural enterprise is considered; it is one of our nation's largest industries and its assets of $531 billion amount to about 60 percent of the capital assets of all manufacturing corporations in America.[3] Additionally, with 3.6 million workers employed on almost 3 million farms, agriculture is one of our nation's largest employers.[4]

There is also irrefutable evidence that urban-based criminals and criminal groups are involved as both planners and perpetrators of crimes in rural areas and on farms. In some instances these crimes are raid-like actions where city-dwelling street gang members enter the rural setting, commit their crimes, and return to their familiar urban habitat swiftly on the interstate highways that are so conveniently positioned. Urban centers are also conduits for the disposal of some property stolen in rural areas; some portion of the extensive amount of farm machinery and equipment which is stolen is rapidly passed through big city ports and shipped for sale in foreign countries, particularly those located in South America. Illegal "killer plants" or slaughter houses have also been located in some cities and are used as part of a distribution system for stolen animals which are processed and sold as meat.

Further, it is quite clear that city-based organized crime has moved into agricultural crimes. One official of the Florida Farm Bureau Federation maintains that organized crime has moved extensively into Florida agriculture enterprises,[5] and the experience of other states substantiates this claim. In Wisconsin, the Badger State Cheese Company, in which four New Yorkers with strong organized crime ties [6] purchased 70 percent ownership several years ago, apparently defaulted in payments to 120 dairy farmers totaling over $500,000.[7] In South Bend, Indiana, this same group, in a business venture involving Valley Lea Dairies, a sixteen-member cooperative for marketing members' products, was involved in a default of $850,000.[8] In South Dakota, the attorney general requested and received a grant to investigate organized crime activity in a multistate grain fraud and the thefts of herbicides and cattle.[9]

Another direct connection between rural crime and city dwellers results from the changing composition of labor used by farmers. There was a time when the principal source of farm labor was provided by the immediate family of the farm owner, neighbors, or laborers who lived in the vicinity of the farms. With the growth of large conglomerate farms and large citrus orchards, the reliance on labor has by necessity shifted more and more to both migrants and city-based labor. When workers from the cities are employed, they will typically travel to the farms or orchards on a daily basis and return to their homes in the cities at night. In some cases, these workers have returned to the farming areas for the purpose of committing crimes and have also, for a fee, tipped active criminals as to specific opportunities there.

Altogether, such illustrations provide substantial evidence that rural and agricultural crimes are economically significant and of concern to both rural and urban police agencies.

SOME DIMENSIONS OF AGRICULTURAL CRIME

A precise analysis of the nature and extent of agricultural crime is not possible because there does not exist any single source of authoritative information on the overall subject or any particular dimension of it. Therefore, we simply do not know the value of crop losses due to thefts and vandalism or the impact that such activities ultimately have on the prices charged to consumers. However, from the fragmentary information that is available, we can conclude that the problem is costly and widespread. For example, vandalism and thefts of farm products are problems which can be illustrated throughout this country. In one year, approximately $21 million worth of property was stolen from rural and unincorporated areas in Florida, of which only one-fourth was ever recovered, with less than $1 million worth ever returned to the owners, because of a lack of identification.[10] Citrus growers in Florida's Polk County alone suffered $5 million in thefts of, and vandalism to, crops and farm machinery. In Imperial County, California, irrigation equipment valued at more than $900,000 was stolen and resold throughout the West.[11] Rustling cases in California increased 79 percent in one recent year,[12] and that state's farm bureau calculates annual theft losses to farmers at $30 million.[13] Due to the strong demands for it in West Germany and Japan, along with their dwindling supply, black walnut wood is in demand. One

200-foot tall tree may bring $25,000.[14] In Iowa, thefts of trees have been reported in the Yellow River State Park and Des Moines' Grandview Park.[15] In Illinois, brazen thieves waited until a farmer went to church one Sunday morning and then stole his prize walnut tree.[16] One Illinois forester speculates that only 10 percent of tree thefts are reported,[17] while in western Washington where thefts from, and vandalism to, forests reach $1 million annually, the reporting rate is calculated to be around 30 percent.[18]

Near Plainfield, Wisconsin, a farmer suffered the theft of his portable irrigation system, creating a replacement cost of $10,500, and near Coloma, Wisconsin, seven tons of corn were stolen from the cribs on one farm.[19] In Jasper County, Iowa, vandals destroyed $10,000 worth of property on a farm,[20] and during a single nine-day period the Sheriff's Office in Hardee County, Florida, received reports of thefts of citrus crops, ranch equipment, and assorted items totaling $10,000.[21] According to a spokesman for International Harvester, officials in one midwestern state estimate equipment losses to farmers in that state at about $1 million annually.[22] A single theft ring operating in Kentucky, Alabama, Georgia, and Tennessee is credited with stealing at least $400,000 in farm equipment, primarily tractors, over a two-year period.[23] In Georgia, during one five-month period, more than $300,000 in losses from theft of farm equipment, livestock, chemicals, and seeds were reported.[24] U.S. Department of Agriculture statistics reveal 2,633 fires of an incendiary origin in National Forest Protection areas occurring in one year, producing damage estimated at nearly $11 million.[25] Illustrative of other segments of agriculture which have experienced losses due to criminal activity are mango and avocado growers, poultry ranchers, and bee keepers, a number of whom have reported the theft of entire colonies.[26] Together such incidents reveal that agricultural crime is costly, complex, and widespread.

FARM EQUIPMENT THEFT: THE IDENTIFICATION PROBLEM

Heavy construction equipment and farm equipment are commonly referred to as "off-road" equipment.[27] Owners of such equipment have, and contribute to, a unique theft problem: there is generally no registration or title required for such equipment, and owners have traditionally resisted such requirements because they fear that such records could be used to levy taxes on expensive property and because they believe that it could impede their ability to move equipment rapidly and freely about the country. Compounding the issue is the fact that off-road equipment, unlike conventional motor vehicles, has no standard, permanently affixed identification number. Historically, each manufacturer has used its own numbering system, which varies from as few as four to as many as fifteen characters. These identification numbers vary in location, size, and composition and the identification plates are easily removed. Some off-road equipment also has identification plates for each separate component piece to the machinery, creating confusion or entirely misleading the inexperienced investigator. The equipment is also easily stolen; a single key may be used to start all models produced by a particular manufacturer, and where key locks are in place, the machinery can be jumped by placing a common pocket knife or screwdriver across the electrical posts on the starter. Although manufacturers offer anti-theft devices, they are costly options which add to the base price of the equipment.

For several years the International Association of Auto Theft Investigators and the Construction Industry Manufacturers Association have been addressing these problems with one key goal being the adoption of standard, industry-wide identification plates which will be permanently affixed to the equipment, rather than spot-welded as is the current practice.

THE NCIC
EQUIPMENT MARKING PROGRAM

In order to help compensate for some of the difficulties associated with identifying off-road equipment, the Federal Bureau of Investigation (FBI) has authorized a numbering system to be used in conjunction with its National Crime Information Center (NCIC).[28] Under this system every state and county is assigned a five-digit number which is recorded in NCIC files and a directory containing these numbers; the corresponding state and county names are available to law enforcement agencies. Individuals interested in participating in an identification program contact their county sheriff to receive a unique number which has a total of ten characters; the first five are the standard state-county designations supplied by the FBI; the remaining five are designations made by the sheriff's office which identify the individual. For example, the number FL 001 0306 D is correctly read in the following fashion:

FL	designates Florida
001	designates Alachua County
0306	designates the 306th person in
D	Alachua County who signed up
	for the identification program
	and whose last name begins with a D

This number can be used to check law enforcement files to find the exact name and other information about the owner of record. Farmers marking their property are encouraged to do so both in a standard readily visible spot, as illustrated by Figure 15-1, and in a second, hidden place. When ownership of equipment changes, the new owner can stamp his or her identification on the equipment just under the prior owner's number, avoiding possible problems and providing a trail of ownership. It is essential in such cases that the seller notify the sheriff's office of the sale.

This system has been actively promoted by a variety of organizations including sheriffs' associations and state farm bureaus; in some areas 4-H members have taken on marking programs as a project. Regardless of how it is accomplished, the program is voluntary. Thus, to encourage participation, the organizations which have promoted it will provide a guide as to how to correctly mark the property, loan an engraver or other tool, provide forms on which to inventory marked property, give decals to display which announce that the property is marked, and provide other helpful suggestions—for example, that the farmer take photographs of all equipment and keep them readily available, but in a secure place, with the inventory forms. Beyond the area of farm equipment, these principles of identification also apply to other property found on farms; for example, bags of seeds can be marked using stencils.

EXTENT AND COST OF FARM
EQUIPMENT THEFTS

Table 15-1 summarizes the amount of unrecovered stolen farm and construction vehicles by state as of the month of September over a six-year period. It is important to note that this is only the unrecovered property and that it combines both major categories of off-road equipment. In Table 15-2, unrecovered stolen off-road equipment in the fourteen states with the highest theft activity is depicted, and construction versus farm equipment is differentiated. In Table 15-2 it is seen that in these high-activity states, farm equipment accounts for 43 percent of all unrecovered off-road equipment, or 5,231 pieces of machinery. Based on an estimated average value of $33,215 at any point in time there may be as much as $173,747,665 worth of unrecovered stolen farm machinery from these fourteen states alone. Because of the way in which reported crime statistics are tabulated, just how many pieces of equip-

FIGURE 15-1   Illustrative Positions for Marking Farm Equipment

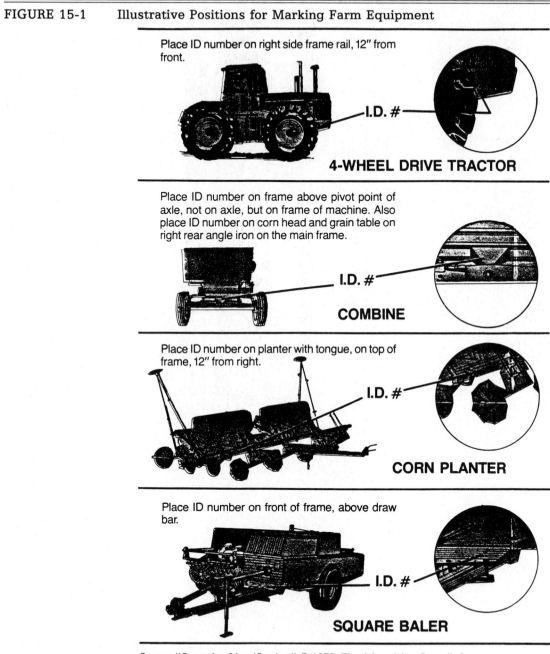

Place ID number on right side frame rail, 12" from front.

I.D. #

4-WHEEL DRIVE TRACTOR

Place ID number on frame above pivot point of axle, not on axle, but on frame of machine. Also place ID number on corn head and grain table on right rear angle iron on the main frame.

I.D. #

COMBINE

Place ID number on planter with tongue, on top of frame, 12" from right.

I.D. #

CORN PLANTER

Place ID number on front of frame, above draw bar.

I.D. #

SQUARE BALER

Source: "Operation Identification," © 1979, The Advertising Council, Inc.

ment are actually recovered is not generally known, but it is believed to be in the range of 6 to 10 percent.[29]

MO OF EQUIPMENT THEFTS AND THEIR INVESTIGATION

MO OF EQUIPMENT THEFTS

It takes experienced tractor thieves approximately four minutes to invade a farm, start and load the tractor, and drive away, according to an informant who worked with a theft ring.[30] For pull-type equipment which does not have to be started, the amount of time required for the average theft is less than two minutes. Farm equipment thefts are frequently committed by professional operatives who steal for profit. They may steal on order, for stripping, or for export.[31] One offender was caught with a notebook filled with photographs he had taken of machinery on various farms; when interrogated he stated that he had roamed the countryside obtaining the photographs in the notebook. The notebook was then used as a "sales catalog" when meeting with prospective buyers and as a means of instructing thieves working with him as to exactly what equipment from a particular location was to be taken. This arrangement made it possible for the equipment to be consigned or sold before it was even stolen, minimizing the amount of time that the equipment was in the thieves' hands and therefore their risk.

INVESTIGATION

The investigation of farm equipment thefts can be an extremely frustrating task given the current low rate of property recovery. Yet investigators are not impotent and can increase their effectiveness by a variety of means. They must recognize that thieves are often skilled and dedicated individuals who approach their work thoughtfully and who have certain advantages working for them such as the problem of identifying equipment, the speed of their operations, and the fact that thefts are often not detected for from twelve hours to several days. This requires that investigators approach their task professionally.

Specialized knowledge can be obtained from a combination of resources. Training seminars which focus on agricultural crimes are being conducted; these are of such quality that even experienced investigators attending them have acquired helpful new information and techniques. In terms of publications which could help facilitate professional growth, the International Association of Chiefs of Police (IACP) has developed the Tractor Identification Manual and manufacturers have produced investigators' guides such as *Serial Numbers: How to Find Them on John Deere Equipment*. Additionally, directors of corporate security for manufacturers of farm equipment have frequently had successful careers in policing and are willing to provide their advice, loan training films, and other assistance. For example, because John Deere insures much of the equipment it sells, in the past that company has provided "buy money" in support of significant investigations.

Another way to become knowledgeable about farm equipment is to visit local dealers and ask them to brief you on their numbering systems and give you the opportunity to examine at some length the pieces they have on hand.[32] Dealers are often willing to supply catalogs which have color photographs of their products and detailed descriptions of their characteristics. Because most investigators are unfamiliar with off-road equipment, these can be useful in knowing what to look for when pickup orders for stolen machinery are broadcast. Although most people have an idea of what a bulldozer looks like, there is also a substantial amount of less

TABLE 15-1

Unrecovered Stolen Farm and Construction Vehicles By State

	Sept 1980	Sept 1981	Sept 1982	Sept 1983	Sept 1984	Sept 1985
Alabama	227	248	244	259	268	248
Alaska	7	9	11	19	19	18
Arizona	350	389	428	351	398	399
Arkansas	132	147	167	196	219	208
California	1718	1655	1824	1830	1681	1451
Colorado	77	94	120	144	152	159
Connecticut	62	75	83	75	72	70
Delaware	17	22	25	29	28	33
Dist. of Columbia	6	5	9	7	8	8
Florida	323	430	601	682	741	776
Georgia	390	446	521	503	518	512
Hawaii	15	18	19	21	28	43
Idaho	20	23	31	36	39	39
Illinois	607	653	710	675	606	584
Indiana	473	480	463	466	398	303
Iowa	87	91	102	111	127	128
Kansas	126	148	175	186	204	207
Kentucky	360	390	457	463	448	425
Louisiana	118	137	149	193	194	220
Maine	9	9	7	7	8	10
Maryland	162	177	228	219	212	259
Massachusetts	127	143	146	130	129	143
Michigan	491	552	555	547	568	552
Minnesota	106	130	152	179	189	215
Mississippi	119	104	141	137	132	141
Missouri	457	534	601	618	568	576
Montana	14	16	21	20	29	26
Nebraska	67	64	69	68	55	66
Nevada	41	53	63	53	52	42
New Hampshire	9	9	11	14	23	25
New Jersey	207	221	252	266	247	238
New Mexico	22	21	28	31	34	43
New York	235	236	260	285	238	231
No. Carolina	264	287	319	386	387	369
No. Dakota	10	17	20	13	16	12
Ohio	552	567	611	612	629	508
Oklahoma	388	462	643	887	963	1003
Oregon	88	109	129	149	156	158
Pennsylvania	363	398	399	377	349	365
Rhode Island	17	15	15	18	21	15
So. Carolina	90	112	170	180	195	196
So. Dakota	16	17	16	12	16	16
Tennessee	336	360	345	426	387	284

TABLE 15-1

Unrecovered Stolen Farm and Construction Vehicles By State
(*continued*)

	Sept 1980	Sept 1981	Sept 1982	Sept 1983	Sept 1984	Sept 1985
Texas	2130	2471	2917	3147	3510	4231
Utah	48	44	44	50	37	38
Vermont	2	2	3	5	2	1
Virginia	163	173	196	191	193	181
Washington	119	132	145	163	184	182
West Virginia	57	56	61	69	70	65
Wisconsin	107	106	126	132	122	122
Wyoming	6	8	6	7	11	8
Misc.	4	8	16	33	40	47
TOTALS:	11938	13073	14854	15677	15920	16199

Compiled by W. E. Rutledge, California Highway Patrol, Chairman-Heavy Equipment Theft Committee, International Association of Auto Theft Investigators. Printed courtesy of Associated Equipment Distributors, Oak Brook, Illinois.

TABLE 15-2

A Comparison of Unrecovered Stolen Construction versus Farm Equipment in Fourteen States as of September 1985

State	Construction Equipment		Farm Equipment		Total
	Outstanding	Percentage	Outstanding	Percentage	
Texas	2568	61%	1663	39%	4231
California	1146	79	305	21	1451
Oklahoma	414	41	589	59	1003
Florida	382	49	394	51	776
Illinois	377	65	207	35	584
Missouri	205	36	371	64	576
Michigan	335	61	217	39	552
Georgia	223	43	289	57	512
Ohio	245	48	263	52	508
Kentucky	157	37	268	63	425
Arizona	322	81	77	19	399
No. Carolina	103	28	266	72	369
Pennsylvania	222	61	143	39	365
Indiana	124	41	179	59	303
TOTALS:	6823	57	5231	43	12,054

Compiled by W. E. Rutledge, California Highway Patrol, Chairman-Heavy Equipment Theft Committee, International Association of Auto Theft Investigators. Printed courtesy of Associated Equipment Distributors, Oak Brook, Illinois.

familiar equipment, such as wheel loaders, backhoes, front-end loaders, loader backhoes, truck loaders, mounted corn planters, and several types of balers. These catalogs can be kept in the briefcase which investigators carry in their cars and can be quickly referred to for accurate and detailed information.

It is important that investigators become familiar with the workings of the NCIC system in order not to enter information erroneously and to be alert to the possibility that others may have entered information incorrectly. Although NCIC has implemented procedures to help control for such problems, inaccurate entries have hindered some investigations in the past. For example, front-end loaders have, after NCIC editing, been found to have been entered as backhoes with loaders attached, loaders with backhoes, shovels, tractor crawlers, farm tractors, bulldozers, and motorized farm equipment.[33] When checking out suspicious equipment, investigators should not stop with an NCIC check if the grounds for suspicion are well founded. Beyond the possibility of the occasional NCIC entry error is the possibility that the machine has not even been discovered missing yet. If there is any reason to believe that the machinery was obtained under anything other than legitimate circumstances, the manufacturer or dealer should be contacted and requested to supply all identification numbers and the purchaser so that ownership can be verified.[34]

Beyond responding to the needs of a specific investigation, there is an obligation to determine how stolen property is being disposed of and to disrupt those networks by the arrest of the principals involved. By closing down these networks, the immediate incentive to steal is reduced since the means of profit is eliminated; although new networks will evolve, they can be dealt with successively. These networks may take many forms. In Georgia, equipment was being offered for sale at a bargain price through the *Farmers & Consumers Market Bulletin,* published by that state's department of agriculture. On investigation, it was determined that brazen thieves were using a state publication to dispose of stolen property. It should also be noted that farmers are not only victims but may be thieves or receivers of stolen property themselves. In one instance a farmer dug a pit on an isolated portion of his property, stole a tractor from a dealer some eighteen miles away, placed the tractor in the pit, covered it with canvas, and refilled the pit. Deputies working the area in a light plane had observed the pit being dug and later noticed tracks leading to the covered-over area, resulting in the case's being solved. In North Dakota a farmer bought equipment under such unusual conditions that it subsequently resulted in his being convicted in federal district court of receiving stolen property.[35] The equipment, which had been stolen in Indiana and transported interstate to North Dakota, was sold under the following conditions: the equipment—two Case tractors and a John Deere loader—with a fair market value of at least $188,000 was conveyed for $70,000; the payment had to be in cash; and there were no warranties, no sales documents, and no information on the origin of the machinery. Despite these obvious warning signs, the farmer's conviction was overturned on legal grounds on appeal.

A technique which was developed in urban areas and has also proven successful in the rural setting is the sting operation; one such effort operated by law enforcement officials from a business called "The Gold Mine Trading Post" resulted in $150,754 worth of stolen property, including twenty-eight vehicles, being recovered at a cost of $11,043 and led to numerous felony arrests.[36] Stolen property markets may be disrupted by the "reverse sting," so called because instead of posing as receivers of stolen property, police officials pose as sellers of stolen property to identify illegal receivers. Although this case did not involve farm equipment, it is illustrative: using a truck and 1,000 pounds of donated fruit, police undercover agents in Florida approached seventeen citrus dealers in a single county.[37] Posing as fruit pickers, the agents offered oranges for sale. When it became apparent to the dealers that the "pickers" did not have trip tickets—which are issued by the state department of agriculture, are required by law, and have extensive information about the origin of the fruit, the seller, the vehicle in which the fruit is transported, and other matters—the "pickers" would then tell the dealers that the fruit was stolen. Four dealers accepted the oranges and were arrested for dealing in stolen property. It is interesting to note, however, that none of the remaining thirteen dealers who declined to make a purchase actually reported the attempted illegal sale to the sheriff's office. The use of this technique must be carefully planned and executed when its employment is contemplated as the defense of entrapment could potentially be raised. According to a generally accepted view, entrapment occurs when a law enforcement officer, or an associated operative acting in conjunction with the officer, originates the idea of a crime and then induces a defendant to commit it by employing methods of inducement such as would cause innocent persons who would normally not commit the offense to do so.[38] At the risk of oversimplification, if the person is persuaded or seduced by argument to commit a crime otherwise not contemplated by him or her, then entrapment has occurred.

TIMBER THEFT

During the 1970s it was clear that the theft of U.S. government timber had assumed serious proportions. The volume of standing timber in the states of Oregon and Washington is alone worth more than $50 billion, and it has been estimated that several million dollars' worth of timber is stolen annually from U.S. government land in just Oregon.[39]

In a ranger district located within the Mount Hood National Forest, U.S. Forest Service employees discovered three separate theft sites where standing green western red cedar had been felled and removed. The dollar loss was estimated to be $12,000. One of the serious ecological side effects of the cutting down of cedar trees is the fact that they are considered a nonrenewable resource. Cedar trees might take 200 to 300 years to grow to maturity, and as yet no way has been devised to grow them from seedlings. The individuals responsible for this cutting had attempted to conceal the tree stumps by covering them with broken boughs and stems; however, the area surrounding the stumps was cluttered with empty oil containers and discarded beer cans. FBI agents who investigated the theft were able to trace large sales of cedar to local mills, and cancelled checks from the sales bore the names of those people later developed as suspects. Further inquiry determined that rental agencies had leased equipment that was used in logging operations to the suspects. Finally, interviews of close associates of the suspects placed them at the crime scenes on the same weekend that they had rented the equipment. After extensive investigation, which took over a year to complete, two individuals were indicted for theft, destruction, and sale of government property, and they subsequently pleaded guilty in U.S. District Court, Portland, Oregon.

INVESTIGATIVE TECHNIQUES

Investigations into illegal cutting of cedar trees, Douglas fir, and species of timber for the commercial firewood market involves a full range of investigative techniques. Examination of crime scenes continues to result in the discovery of evidence of paint transfers and tool marks being found on wood debris left behind by suspects. These marks and paint transfers result from the use of axes, wedges, and splitting mauls and serve to tie a suspect to a crime. Examination of tool marks on wood are based on established principles that it is possible to identify a suspect tool with the mark it leaves on a surface. In several cases, containers left at the scene of a timber theft have been processed and fingerprints developed. These fingerprints have been useful in identifying and placing suspects at the scene. In addition, plaster casts of both shoe and tire impressions which were later identified as belonging to a particular suspect and vehicle have been found at some crime scenes.

Although the crime scene examinations at the site of timber thefts are important, they are supplemented by the long and tedious process of interviewing potential witnesses to the crime, conducting investigations to develop witnesses in resort type areas where thefts have occurred, and checking possible outlets where forest products might be sold. In order to conduct investigations concerning timber sales, law enforcement officers must become familiar with the variety of terms and techniques pertaining to timber sales, from its inception to its eventual purchase and through completed logging operations. Such information is available from the U.S. Forest Service.

GRAIN THEFTS AND FRAUDS

THEFTS

While perhaps the most common association to the word *grain* is *wheat*, grain products encompass a range of other commodities such as soybeans. Depending on market conditions, the theft of grain products can be a lucrative enterprise. For example, the 2,500 bushels of soybeans stolen from elevators in Jasper, Minnesota, several years ago were worth approximately $15,000. Theft of grain products has been characterized as coming very close to being the "perfect crime" because access to them is easy and they are readily sold and virtually impossible to identify. In an effort to provide some means of identifying grain as coming from a particular farm, a system of grain identification has been developed.[40] It consists of small tabs of paper 3/8" wide and 3/4" long, each containing an individual code number, which are mixed with the grain. An example of the coding is as follows:

46-20-040

46 = State (North Dakota)

20 = County (Griggs)

040 = Individual Producer (B & W Ranch)

The name and assigned number of the grain producer are recorded in the registry of all producers by state and county. Periodically, a list of all producers is mailed to all sheriffs and county agents in those areas where the product is being used. In addition, each grain producer using the confetti receives an individual registration card.

The confetti may be mixed in with the grain when the bins are filled by throwing small amounts in with the grain as it is being augered into the bin. It will blend into the grain when it is moved out of storage. When the first bushel is removed the confetti is evident, and with a cost estimated to be one-fourth of a cent per bushel, this method provides an economical and practical deterrent to theft. The registration card is carried by the grain producer and presented to the buyer when the grain is marketed. Posters are supplied by the manufacturer of the confetti and they may be placed on the granaries or displayed in some manner near the stored grain as a warning to prospective thieves. The confetti may be used with barley, corn,

FIGURE 15-2

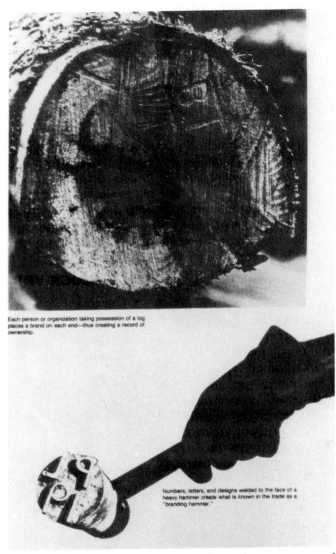

Each person or organization taking possession of a log places a brand on each end—thus creating a record of ownership.

Numbers, letters, and designs welded to the face of a heavy hammer create what is known in the trade as a "branding hammer."

Branding of logs enhances identification and creates a record of ownership.

Courtesy FBI Law Enforcement Bulletin, *"Timber Thefts,"* Terry D. Turchie and Billy Bob Williams, *May 1979, Vol 48, No. 2, p. 3.*

durum, flax, oats, peas, rice, rye, soybeans, and wheat. The confetti is not objectionable to the grain trade or the Pure Food and Drug Administration and can be easily removed by milling companies.

Part of the difficulty in preventing grain thefts is that the grain is frequently stored in bins away from the house or may even be dumped in a field on a temporary basis. In addition, the theft of grain is frequently not noticed immediately. For example, one North Dakota sheriff reported that thieves using a two-ton pickup truck and portable elevator were stealing a few hundred bushels at each of many different farms. Thus, the thefts went unnoticed by the farmers. In other instances farmers have virtually asked to become victims by loading up trucks with a harvest and leaving them in the fields with the intention of driving them to market the next day, only to find both the trucks and the crops gone the next morning.

FRAUDS

Grain frauds may take a variety of forms; in one notable grain fraud case, a large amount of wheat was being exported from the United States. The contract called for a certain grade of wheat to be sent. Those delivering the wheat loaded their rigs with a lesser grade of wheat than was required. Employees of the exporting firm were bribed $50 per load to surreptitiously substitute a sample of higher quality wheat when they took their quality control samples at delivery. Before this activity was discovered in the country receiving the wheat, that country had paid for wheat worth millions of dollars more than that which it actually got.

One of the most common types of grain frauds involves weighing practices; nationally one of the most significant investigations was conducted in the Rocky Mountain area by the FBI:[41]

Four principals associated with a Colorado grain hauling firm were convicted in Federal District Court in Denver of defrauding both buyers and sellers of grain. The convictions were the culmination of a twenty-month long investigation by the FBI. The investigation centered on illegal scale-weighing techniques utilized by truck drivers who hauled grain. These techniques were used to victimize farmers, co-ops, feedlots, and ranchers throughout the Rocky Mountain area. The investigation revealed that the firm had systematically been stealing from its various customers during its past three years of operation. The illegal weighing techniques allowed the truckers to falsely weigh less when purchasing grain and to falsely weigh more when selling it. Thus, an illegal profit could be realized at both the buying and the selling ends of a transaction.

The truckers used mechanical devices capable of shifting weight from one axle to another; the result was false weight gains of from 5,000 to 22,000 pounds. Those most consistently victimized did not have scales capable of weighing an entire tractor-trailer rig in one sitting. Many of the largest weight deviations were obtained by drivers pulling double trailers. "Split weighing" was therefore necessary, meaning that the tractor and the first trailer were weighed, then the rig was driven forward until only the rear trailer remained on the scale for weighing. An inflatable rubber air bag device was secretly mounted in the tongue area of the rear trailer and was hidden by the trailer frame and other supports. The driver regulated the inflation of the air bag from a control in the tractor cab. By inflating the air bag, the reinforced tongue, where connected to the rear trailer, was forced down. In see-saw fashion, the tongue, where connected to the front trailer, was thereby moved upward.

This system was capable of lifting the rear axle of the front trailer high enough that the tires could come off of the ground. That particular axle could feasibly weigh nothing while the rear trailer would weigh thousands of pounds above its true weight since the weight was shifted from the front trailer to the rear trailer once the front trailer was lifted upward. The inflation capacity was powered by the tractor's air brake system; once activated it was not necessary for the driver to remain in the cab. In order to weigh light when purchasing grain, the drivers would attempt to have one or more of the wheels off the scale. This enabled them to falsely weigh light even on full-length scales.

As some farmers and ranchers did not have their own weight scale, the drivers also obtained blank scale tickets and a stamping kit; using these materials they would simply enter on the scale ticket a weight which was to their own advantage.

THEFT OF AGRICHEMICALS

Agrichemical is a broad term whose meaning encompasses a variety of products used on farms including pesticides, fertilizers, and herbicides. As a rule of thumb, fertilizers are not a target of theft because of their bulk and relatively low cost. In contrast, pesticides and herbicides can be costly—certain types may cost as much as $150 to $200 per gallon container—and even a small pickup truck's load can be worth thousands of dollars. Although the theft of agrichemicals is a multimillion dollar per year problem nationally, the exact type of agrichemical taken varies by geographic region, depending on what the predominant crop is.

Some observers thought that agrichemical thefts crested during 1972–1975 when a short supply and high demand combined to produce high prices. It does, however, remain as a problem. In general, manufacturers do not have a theft problem because they can maintain tight security. As the product moves from the manufacturer to the distributor to the dealer to the ultimate consumer, the farmer, the problem increases. Distributors in particular have been vulnerable to the hijacking of trucks carrying agrichemicals, with resulting losses of $50,000 to $60,000 per incident. Dealers typically have been victimized by burglaries. By the late 1970s, when many distributors and dealers adopted target-hardening crime prevention measures, farmers became the focus of more thefts. In 1982, more than $600,000 worth of farm chemicals were stolen from Iowa farmers.[42] Consequently, some farmers have adopted at least some basic crime prevention measures such as lighting. One tactic which is often recommended to farmers is buying agrichemicals only in quantities which can be immediately used. While some farmers have adopted this practice, many have found it to be impractical given the time, inconvenience, and cost of repeated trips to make purchases.

Although some losses of agrichemicals are the result of dishonest individual warehouse or farm employees, the most substantial losses are consistently caused by organized rings of criminals. One dealer who was victimized had the following observation on the burglary of his premises:

> This wasn't any helter-skelter operation. They knew our simazine inventory within 100 pounds and they were accurate on our Treflan inventory. They knew just about everything we had in stock . . . they also knew when the police patrolled the area and who was on duty. They drove Cadillacs equipped to monitor police radio broadcasts and brought in semitrucks to haul it all away.[43]

The sheriff of Washington County, Mississippi, investigated an agrichemical theft ring which had operated for over two years, netting one member $30,000 in black-market sales:

> They were very thorough and took no chances. We learned later that they threw away their shoes after every job. When they got home they washed their clothes in case any chemicals had spilled on them. They always used gloves which they also threw away after every burglary. They would break into a building, set the chemicals outside and then signal for the truck to come. They could load the truck in two or three minutes. Sometimes they would drive right through a farmer's yard and take chemicals from a building less than 50 feet from the house.[44]

Because the theft or illegal taking of agrichemicals may take the form of any of several different criminally chargeable acts, it would be possible for investigators in different parts of the same agency to be working on various activities by the same ring without knowing it. For example, the hijacking of a truck might be worked on by robbery investigators, the burglary of a dealership by the property section or burglary investigators, while personnel assigned to the ranch and grove unit might be working on the theft of pesticides from a local farmer. Although one ring might not exhibit a wide range of difference in criminally chargeable behavior, it may be sufficiently different to cause the fragmentation of investigative information. In such circumstances, the formal crime analysis function discussed in Chapter 7 can be particularly helpful in insuring that all relevant information is unified.

To be effective in the investigation of agrichemical thefts, the investigator must become familiar with the legal supply channels and the principal agrichemicals which are used in his or her region. In particular it is important to know that the same basic chemical or formulation may be sold by several different manufacturers under different product names. For example, atrazine is manufactured and sold by Ciba-Geigy as AAtrex®; it is used as a corn herbicide. Imagine the difficulty created for an investigation if a victim reports the theft of "50 gallons of atrazine" and it is entered into police records that way, when the victim was using *atrazine* as a synonym for *AAtrex*. Another aspect of agrichemicals which requires a specialized knowledge is awareness of various security measures which have been taken by manufacturers, such as coded lot numbers and ultraviolet and chemical coding. Finally, because of their precarious economic situation, some farmers will engage in the theft of agrichemicals or will readily purchase such commodities at "bargain prices." Because farmers are the end users of many agrichemicals, they know that a multigallon plastic jug of agrichemicals can be emptied in less than a minute, the jug readily and totally burned due to its high density, and the product immediately applied, making detection difficult. One method of identifying farmers who are possible illegal receivers of agrichemicals is to determine those whose purchasing patterns through legal supply channels are inconsistent with their crop needs.

LIVESTOCK AND TACK THEFT

It is sometimes difficult for police officers, prosecutors, juries, and judges to comprehend that a society which can land people on the moon and safely return them still has a serious rustling problem. Yet, rustling did not disappear with the closing of the American frontier in 1890. While new and often sophisticated methods of theft are now used, the object of attack—livestock—remains the same, as do the motivations: profit or food.

Cattle, horses, sheep, goats, hogs, mules, and jackasses are illustrative of species falling within the meaning of *livestock*. *Tack* refers to saddles, bridles, harnesses, and related equipment. Certain generalizations can be made with respect to livestock and tack thefts:

1. Most livestock thefts are committed by persons who have been or are currently employed in some aspect of a livestock business. One significant exception to this broad observation is that in economically hard times rural areas adjacent to urban centers experience more thefts in which the physical evidence suggests that the motivation was food rather than profit. Such so-called freezer crimes typically involve only one or a few head of cattle, and when they are butchered at the scene it is often in a manner which reflects only a crude understanding of that process.[45]

2. It is common for livestock to be stolen, transported, and disposed of before the theft is discovered. While the theft of horses may be discovered in a day to two weeks, theft of range cattle may go undetected for months.

3. Except for small roadside slaughters committed as freezer crimes, livestock is stolen to be sold for economic gain. The excellent interstate systems which cross the country lend themselves—like the famous trails of frontier days—to transporting the stolen livestock rapidly for sale in states other than the one in which the crime took place.

4. Because horse owners are typically very attached to their animals, such thefts are often very emotional situations.

5. Horse thieves also tend to be tack thieves; statistically for every stolen horse there are approximately twenty cases of tack theft.

As awareness of the livestock theft problem develops, law enforcement agencies have created specialized investigative units or designated a particular individual as the agency's specialist in such matters.[46] In some areas of the country, the specialized units have a substantial history; the Horse Theft Detail of the Los Angeles County Sheriff's Department was established in 1912, although more recently it has been known as the Livestock Unit. Regardless of whether the investigator works out of a specialized unit or as the sole specialist, he or she must have or develop an expertise in the various aspects of livestock identification, including breeds, markings, blemishes, scars, marks, tattoos, and brands. In short, the investigator must be able to speak "livestock" in order to be effective.

The heaviest burden in livestock investigation often falls on the uniformed officer who takes the original offense report; this is true because such officers may have no knowledge, or only a rudimentary knowledge, of livestock and the applicable special laws.[47] One way in which police agencies can help compensate for this is to adopt forms similar to those depicted in Figures 15-4 and 15-5 and to provide training in their use. When such forms are not used, a good guide to follow is that an animal is property and can be described like any other type of property, although the language may be unfamiliar to the investigator. In such situations, the frank acknowledgment of a lack of familiarity or expertise will elicit a more systematic and detailed description from the owner than would otherwise be obtained. Subsequent to the taking of the original offense report, the progress of an investigation often hinges on the mutual assistance, cooperation, and free exchange of information that is given by ranchers, feedlot operators, stock auctions,

FIGURE 15-3   Cattle Theft in Progress

Courtesy of Southwestern Cattle Raisers' Association

FIGURE 15-4   Cattle Identification Form

LOS ANGELES COUNTY SHERIFF'S DEPARTMENT
CATTLE IDENTIFICATION FORM

Classification Lost ( ) Found ( ) Theft ( ) Other ( )   File

No. _____

Date & Time _____ Location _____

Victim ( )

Informant ( )

      address   City   Phone

Suspect _____

    Name   Address   City   Phone

DBO ____ Sex ____ Race ____ Age ____ Hair ____ Eyes ____ Ht. ____ Wt. ____

Vehicle Year ____ Make ____ Body ____ Color ____ Lic. ____

Trailer Horse ____ Stock Rig ____ Make ____ Color ____ # Axels ____ Gooseneck ____

ON THE DRAWING INDICATE EAR MARKS, BLEMISHES, ODDITIES, DEFORMITIES, OR ANY INJURY THAT MAY BE USED TO IDENTIFY THIS ANIMAL. IF THE ANIMAL HAS DEWLAP OR WATTLE MARKINGS, SHOW TYPE AND LOCATION. ALSO HORNS CAN BE INDICATED.

Right   Left

Brand

Sex Bull ( ) Cow ( ) Steer (()	Also indicate Location on Animal & any other Brands.	Method of Operation
Calf ( ) Heifer ( )	Type of Brand	Check all that apply
Breed _____	Hot Iron _____ ( )	Trailered ( ) Driven ( )
	Chemical _____ ( )	Pasture ( ) Range ( )
Age ____ Wt ____ Color ____	Freeze _____ ( )	Barn ( ) Dairy ( ) Corral ( )
Polled ____ Horned ____	Hair Brand _____ ( )	Feed, Auction or Sale Yard( )
Ear Tag ( ) No. ____ Color ____	Horn Brand _____ ( )	Residential ( ) Other ( )

Field Slaughter

Items used   Gun ( ) Knife ( ) Axe ( ) Rope ( ) Hoist ( ) Chainsaw ( ) Other ( )

Carcass

Removed entire Carcass ( ) Hind Quarters ( ) Other

Left at Scene Feet ( ) Head ( ) Hide ( ) Waste ( ) Other ( )

To move Animal used Horses ( )On Foot ( )Dogs ( )Motorcycle( )Lead ( ) Other ( )

Remarks _____

Officer Reprting	Agency	Date

Courtesy Los Angeles County, California, Sheriff's Department

FIGURE 15-5　　Horse Identification Form

LOS ANGELES COUNTY SHERIFF'S DEPARTMENT
HORSE IDENTIFICATION FORM

Outline White or Black Markings,
Mane & Tail. Note Colors, Scars,
Cut Marks & Injuries,
Lip Tattoo or Brand

Breed_____ Sex _____

Color_____Ht.____Wt._____Age_____

Brands_____Tattoo_____

Scars & Marks_____

Other I.D. Info_____

(USE REVERSE FOR SADDLES)

Owner _____
　　　　　　(name)　　　　　　　(address)
_____
　　　　　(city)　　　　　　　(phone)
Date & Time Stolen_____Reported To_____
　　　　　　　　　　　　　　　　　(agency)
Date Reported _____File No._____

Method: Lead Away ( ) Trailer ( ) Ride Away ( )
　　　　Corral ( ) Barn ( ) Stall ( ) Pasture ( )
　　　　Other ( )

ATTACH PHOTOGRAPH OF HORSE

SH-CR-581

Courtesy Los Angeles County, California, Sheriff's Department

farmers, sale yards, slaughter houses, livestock associations, and other public agencies.

CATTLE RUSTLING

The majority of these thefts are committed by one or two people who take the animal for their own use.[48] The usual method of operation is to drive to an isolated area, locate an animal, shoot it, and either butcher it there or load the carcass in a vehicle and butcher it at home. Butchering the animal at the scene means the thieves must spend more time there, but it avoids the problem of having to dispose of unused remains later. At times the thieves will shoot the animal and then drive to a place where they can watch to see if anyone comes to investigate. If not, they then butcher the animal. As these incidents often occur at night, they can see the headlights of approaching vehicles for some distance, giving them ample time to depart from the area. "Freezer crime" rustlers are difficult to apprehend because they must be caught in the act or while they are transporting the carcass or meat. Surveillances which work so well in urban areas are usually difficult to execute in rural areas. Their success depends on:

1. The topography of the area
2. The availability of cover for concealment
3. The number and position of access roads
4. The size of the area containing the cattle

One proven method for successful surveillances is for investigators to choose the area of the theft themselves.[49] This is accomplished by picking an area which maximizes the considerations important to investigators and then having the rancher move the cattle into this area. The rancher must not allow employees or other persons to learn that an operation is being set up. If others are involved in moving the cattle to the area selected, they should be given some reason for the change of pasture, such as a tally, brand check, or veterinary inspection.

Vehicles coming out of isolated areas should routinely be visually inspected for signs of blood on the rear bumper or trunk areas.[50] Because rustlers are invariably armed with some type of firearm, extreme caution must be used when approaching suspicious vehicles. Panicky suspects, who might not otherwise think of assaulting a peace officer, may do so impulsively. In addition to firearms, this type of rustler will also often be carrying butcher knives and ropes.

In contrast to the modest equipment usually employed by the freezer thief, professional rustlers will also have:

1. A hoist
2. A bone or meat saw, axes, or chain saw
3. Plastic bags in which to place the meat
4. Protective clothing such as coveralls or aprons[51]

Professionals will also employ helicopters or light planes to locate herds and to observe for patrolling police units, walkie-talkies to coordinate movements, dirt bikes to round up the herd, counterfeit U.S. Department of Agriculture inspection stamps, and forged documents, such as a bill of sale. The professional rustling operation can be very profitable. Thirty head of cattle can be taken from the range and loaded on a truck, butchered in the truck, the waste dumped off the road, and the sixty sides of beef illegally stamped and delivered to the city at approximately $300 per side—a profit of $18,000 for a night's work.[52]

As a general matter, peace officers have a right to stop any conveyance transporting livestock on any public thoroughfare and the right to impound any animal, carcass, hide, or portion of a carcass in the possession of any person who they have reasonable cause to believe is not the legal owner or entitled to possession.[53] To transport cattle legally, certain written documents may be required, such as:

1. Bill of sale
2. Certificate of consignment
3. Brand inspector's certificate
4. Shipping or transportation permit[54]

Because these provisions vary by state, it is essential that every investigator know:

1. What documentation is required for lawful transportation
2. What the investigator's precise authority is in such matters
3. How to handle violations of law[55]

Equipped with such knowledge, the investigator is better prepared to deal with issues related to transportation violation or a possible theft. Although the applicable state law may permit the officer to impound livestock or meat, there are several less drastic alternatives short of it. Under unusual conditions or where only slight suspicion exists, investigators may elect to get a full description and identifying information of the driver and the rig and its contents. Other information essential for a useful follow-up inquiry is the origin and destination of the trip. Where suspicion is more pronounced, specialists may be requested to come to the scene of the stop. Such specialists may come from the investigator's own agency, another local department, the state police or state investigative agency, or the Marks and Brands Unit of the state's department of agriculture. If the investigator is sufficiently confident that a shipping violation or theft exists, the arrest can be made and the load impounded. Live animals can be delivered to the nearest feedlot or sales yard and meat can be placed in refrigeration storage. Such situations require that officers in the field have a basic working knowledge of the applicable laws and exercise sound judgment. They are not required to be experts in such matters and their general investigative experience is a substantial asset in making an evaluation of the situation.

HORSE RUSTLING

The horse thief rarely steals for personal use; the vast majority of stolen horses are taken to be sold for profit. It is estimated that approximately 60 percent of the animals end up at slaughter plants that process them for human consumption in foreign countries.[56]

While in this country there is a strong, if not romanticized, attachment between people and horses, in other countries horse meat is valued because its protein content is higher than beef. Significant importers of American horse meat for human consumption are France, Belgium, the Netherlands, and Japan; Switzerland, Italy, West Germany, Argentina, Mexico, and the West Indies import lesser amounts. In France, "boucherie chevaline" shops sell horse meat, which is often sauteed with butter by the consumer; hospitals and convalescent homes recommend it for its protein.[57] Dealers exporting horse meat from this country work through plants which use quickchilling and refrigeration techniques. Although this industry does not violate any laws by its nature, its mere ex-

istence and the demand of foreign markets is thought to have contributed to the recent increases in incidents of horse rustling.[58]

There is not a great deal of variation in the way in which horse rustlers operate. If the horse is in a corral, the thief will park a vehicle and trailer nearby, walk up and take the horse, load it in the trailer, and drive off.[59] As most of these thefts occur during the hours of darkness, the rustler can be several hundred miles away before the theft is discovered. When horses are in pasture, the task of stealing them is only slightly more difficult. The thief walks into the pasture with a bucket of grain. One or more of the horses will usually approach him, and because they are herd animals, if one approaches, the others are also likely to follow along. The theft then proceeds in the same fashion as a corral theft. One tactic commonly used by horse rustlers is to knock down the corral or pasture fence after loading up the trailer with horses and chase any remaining horses down the road. The owner will think that the horses have gotten out on their own, and it may be several days before he realizes some horses have been stolen. Thus, even if there is not clear evidence of a theft, the investigator should not assume that the horse has strayed off. As a minimum action, a lost report should be initiated. If the horse is later discovered to have been stolen, the incident can be reclassified.

TACK THEFT

Simply stated, *tack* is equipment which is used with horses; the most common items are saddles, bridles, and horse blankets.[60] Of all stolen tack approximately 80 percent are saddles—which often have base prices in excess of $1,000—and it is generally believed that 85 to 90 percent of all tack is unmarked for identification, making tracing a very difficult proposition. In order to help reduce

FIGURE 15-6   Saddle Identification Form
LOS ANGELES COUNTY SHERIFF'S DEPARTMENT

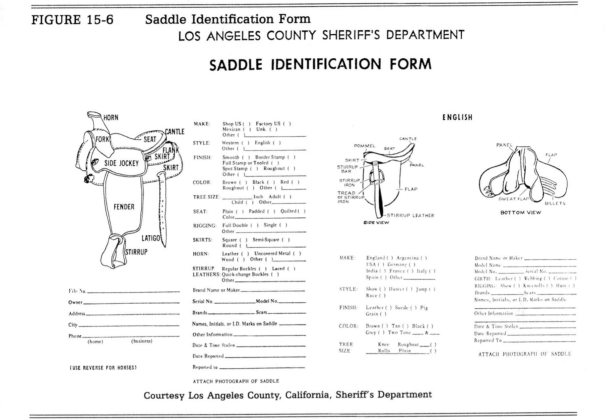

Courtesy Los Angeles County, California, Sheriff's Department

tack thefts, particularly saddles, and to improve the low recovery rate, property marking programs have been undertaken and specialized reporting forms, as depicted in Figure 15-6, adopted. These have been favorable developments, but tack theft remains a serious problem for several reasons: many owners prefer not to mark their equipment, feeling that even if the numbers are hidden, the tack, particularly saddles, is disfigured; owners think that the numbers can be altered or removed entirely from the tack with ease; and there is a ready market for the sale of tack, which is sufficiently diffuse to make detection a limited possibility in many situations.

LIVESTOCK IDENTIFICATION

In any livestock theft case one key to a successful prosecution is the positive identification of a specific animal as belonging to a particular owner. It is therefore essential that investigators have a basic knowledge of methods used to identify livestock. Among these are: (1) brands, (2) ear marks, (3) tattoos, (4) freeze marking, and (5) electronic means.[61]

BRANDS

A brand is a mark which is permanently impressed on the hide of an animal by using a hot iron or chemicals. Brands may be located in several different places, as suggested by the following designations:

RS	right shoulder
LS	left shoulder
RR	right rib
LR	left rib
RH	right hip
LH	left hip

Brands are combinations of letters, numbers, and symbols which are read in one of three different ways: left to right (2—X denotes the Two Bar X); top to bottom (Two Bar X may also appear as the $\frac{2}{X}$); and outside to inside (Ⓐ is read as the Circle A). For various types of communication, an understanding of how brand locations and brands are combined is critical; thus, if the investigator receives a teletype about stolen cattle and a portion of that teletype reads "$\overline{\text{M}}$ RH," it can be understood they are branded Bar M on the right hip. The most commonly used brand terms and characters are shown in Figure 15-7. Horse owners resist the idea of branding their animals because they fear that it will hurt and disfigure them. Their acceptance of branding their horses is roughly comparable to that of urban persons who have been advised to brand their dogs for identification purposes.

EAR MARKS

Ear marks are used in conjunction with the brand for identification and are rarely used on horses. The most commonly used ear-mark patterns are shown in Figure 15-8; when read or designated in writing, the correct method is to designate them from the animal's viewpoint. Therefore, as the investigator faces the animal, the right ear will be to the investigator's left. An illustration of how brands and ear marks may be combined for identification is "$\overline{\text{M}}$ RH R-crop L-split."

TATTOOS

Tattoos have been in use for years at race tracks and more recently they have found increasing popularity among other owners. The tattoo is placed on the inside of the horse's upper lip with a marking device which resembles a pair of wide-mouth pliers. The numbers or letters are a series of needles along one part of the plier-type device which is dipped into indelible ink. The upper lip is then squeezed in the "pliers," causing the needles to penetrate the lip and cause the tattoo.

FREEZE MARKING

Freeze marking is often used with horses because it does not hurt the animal nor does it mark the hide. A mixture of dry ice and alcohol are placed into a styrofoam container and a device similar to a branding iron is placed into the solution until it is sufficiently cold. It is then applied to the area to be marked, often the neck, which must be shaved in preparation. An application of approximately twenty-six seconds causes the extreme cold to kill the color-producing cells in the treated area. When the hair regrows, the desired mark will appear in white.

ELECTRONIC MEANS

Electronic means of identifying livestock are a relatively recent development; they have been used with different types of animals, but are perhaps primarily used with hogs and horses. A former rancher in Broomfield, Col-

FIGURE 15-7   Commonly Employed Brand Characters

Symbol	Name	Symbol	Name
	tumbling right R		walking R
	lazy R		drag R
	crazy R		rocking R
	reverse R		swinging R
	tumbling left R		running R
	crazy reverse R		rafter R
	lazy left down R		running W
	lazy right down R		long W
	lazy right up R		hooked Y
	flying R		barbed Y
	forked Y		bradded Y
	Y and Y down		triple K
	triple K connected		KM connected
	bar		double bar
	slash		reverse slash
	broken slash		broken reverse slash
	quarter circle		half circle
	circle		double circle
	half box		box
	bench		triangle
	heart		half diamond
	diamond		diamond and a half
	refter		open A
	goose egg		mill iron
	cross		horse shoe
	bridle bit		pig pen
	wine glass		tree
	arrow		broken arrow
	rocker chair		anchor
	hay hook		spur
	stinup		horse track
	bull head		sunrise
	spade		rocking horse
	arrow head		bell

Courtesy Los Angeles County, California, Sheriff's Department

FIGURE 15-8   Basic Ear Mark Patterns

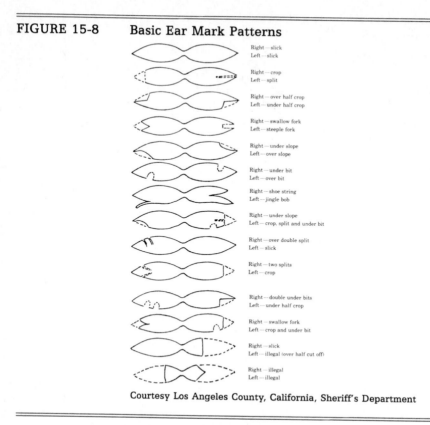

Courtesy Los Angeles County, California, Sheriff's Department

orado, has developed a computerized scanner which allows him to "fingerprint" horses.[62] This technique utilizes an electronic device which records the shape, size, and location of the "chestnut," the calluslike growth a horse has on the inner side of each leg. The electronic device, which is called an ESI (Equine Services, Inc.) scan, resembles a hand-held radar gun. The scanner shines a light on the chestnut, while simultaneously recapturing the reflected beam through a sensor comprised of 10,000 receptors. The patterns of light and dark areas go through the scanner circuitry where they are converted into counts of the chestnut's area, height, width, and proportions. In addition, the direction in which the pear-shaped chest-

nut points is also recorded. The scanning can be performed on a newborn foal because, like human fingerprints, the chestnuts grow in size but their unique shape and proportions remain constant throughout the life of the horse. The data that the scanner picks up are recorded on a standard cassette, and a detailed description of the horse is written by the operator, who takes down the animal's age, breed, coloring, sex, face and leg markings, scars, whorls, brands, and tattoos. The taped and written information is then stored in the Equine Services, Inc., computer in Broomfield, Colorado, for use when a horse must be identified by any legitimate person who needs the information, such as a law enforcement officer. Once the identifying data are recorded, they are computer-converted into a seven-digit serial number that is unique for each horse. In addition to the serial number, the computer also stores the owner's name and the breed registry number, any one of which can be plugged into the unit's terminal by an authorized person wanting to identify a horse. In cases where only a physical description of the animal is available, the computer is capable of searching its files to produce a list of possible animals for further checking. Since it is tied to a telephone system, the computer can send its identification data anywhere in the world. For quick visual checks, the computer is capable of transmitting an electronic picture of a chestnut to any police agency that has a teletype printer.

Each of the methods of marking livestock for identification has certain disadvantages. Brands can be altered, ear marks are disfiguring, tattoos cannot be applied to horses until after they are two years old because growth can distort them if applied prior to that age, freeze markings may be too apparent for some owners, and electronic means incur unique costs. Investigators should be somewhat cautious when asked which method of identification they recommend; as a general matter it would be a sound practice to summarize what the applicable requirements provided for by state law are and then note that the owner should determine what practices, beyond those officially sanctioned, best meet his or her needs.

PHYSICAL EVIDENCE

The processing of a crime scene where an agricultural-related theft has occurred is in many respects no different than the processing of any other crime scene. For example, when cattle rustling occurs, the perpetrators frequently cut the barbed wire or locks securing a grazing area. The cut wire and lock will have tool marks left on them from the

cutting tool. In addition, if the suspect's clothing came in contact with any of the barbed wire at the scene, pieces of fiber may be found adhering to the barbs. Shoe or tire impressions found at the crime scene may later be linked to a specific suspect and vehicle. Soil samples collected at the crime scene may also prove to be valuable, linking evidence to a suspect with similar soil on his shoes or clothes, or on the vehicle used to transport the cattle. The types of evidence discussed in Chapter 4, "Physical Evidence," can often be readily found and will be of great value to law enforcement officers in the investigation of agricultural crimes.

When their livestock has been stolen, farmers and ranchers will often move equipment into the area of a theft and make immediate repairs to corrals, fences, outbuildings, or as otherwise needed. The predictable and unfortunate result is that physical evidence is either hopelessly contaminated or lost altogether. This contributes to a recovery rate for stolen livestock of only 20 percent. Additionally, farmers and ranchers are believed to report only 50 percent of their actual thefts of livestock. Therefore, an important aspect of both enforcement and crime prevention is instructing such people in the correct methods of preserving the crime scene and of the importance of promptly reporting all offenses so that every possible piece of information is in the hands of investigators.

CRIME PREVENTION MEASURES

Information about how to prevent rural and agricultural crimes can be obtained from a variety of sources, including sheriffs' departments, county police, state investigative agencies, state departments of agriculture, county extension agents, and various associations. Although some techniques developed in urban areas can be readily applied to the farm, others would create costs disproportionate to the benefits that could reasonably be expected to accrue to the farmer. Consequently, the technology in this area is sometimes familiar, sometimes takes advantage of unique aspects of the rural environment, and is continuously in the process of changing and developing. The suggestions which follow are organized around the object of attack; in general they are specialized and can be supplemented as may be appropriate by more conventional strategies, such as the use of case-hardened padlocks.

Farm Equipment Theft

- Participate in equipment identification programs.
- Do not leave unattended equipment in remote fields for hours at a time or overnight; if it is necessary to do so for some reason, disable the engine by taking a vital part and use logging chains to secure other equipment. Even if such precautions are taken, equipment in remote areas should be hidden from view from roadways.
- Equipment is best protected, in reducing order of preference, by positioning it as follows: secured in a locked building near the main house or an inhabited house; secured in a gated area which is kept locked and is close to the main or an inhabited house; secured in one or more ways and not visible from commonly traveled roads.
- Immediately report all suspicious activity, such as strangers taking photographs of equipment, to local enforcement officials.

Timber Theft

- Post the property.
- Check periodically to determine if any timber has been cut.
- Promptly report all losses.

Grain Thefts and Frauds

- Avoid storing grain temporarily on the ground and at unprotected sites.

- If thefts are prevalent, grain confetti of some type should be used.
- Do not allow trucks filled with the harvest to remain overnight in the field.
- Carefully monitor all aspects of weighing rigs; this may require the presence of several people or the use of mirrors, which will facilitate the detection of unusual positions onscale.[63]
- Be alert for sounds which might indicate that an air bag or other device is being used.
- If scales are not long enough to weigh an entire rig in one setting, demand that the rear trailer be detached and that the driver dolly it down when it is weighed.
- Farmers and ranchers who do not have a scale at their immediate place of business should attempt to confirm the weight of the grain they are buying or selling at a known bona fide scale.
- Keep permanent records of the driver's license number and the license numbers of the rig of all those with whom business is conducted.

Agrichemicals

- End users, whenever feasible, should buy only in quantities that they can readily use.
- If quantity purchases cannot be avoided, they should be stored in a locked, lighted building very close to the main house or an inhabited house; if available, place a few geese or guinea hens inside as watch animals.
- Rural dealers should employ security personnel during the months when they have large inventories.
- Be suspicious of people offering unusually good buys on agrichemicals; the absence of a market helps deter thefts.

Livestock and Tack

- All livestock should be marked for identification; maximum deterrence is obtained when marks are readily visible.[64]

- A daily tally or count should be taken.
- Do not follow a set routine, such as going to the movie every Friday night, which would give a thief an advantage.
- Enter into cooperative arrangements with trusted neighbors to help watch each others' place.
- Avoid leaving animals in remote pastures or on far-away ranges whenever practical.
- Mark tack and keep it in a room which lends itself to security measures.
- Do not use "set guns" or "booby traps"; they are often illegal, frequently injure innocent people or animals, and surviving thiefs have won damage suits because of the injuries which resulted.

Investigators interested in obtaining more detailed information can contact any of the sources mentioned earlier if their departments do not have active prevention programs. These sources are typically generous with the materials they send and often will give permission for them to be reproduced for use with the public.

WILDLIFE CRIMES

INTRODUCTION

The transition from the topic of agricultural crimes to wildlife crimes is a natural one because of some overlaps. For example, in many states wildlife officers may be called upon to assist local police officers in cases of livestock theft or slaughter because the basic physical evidence closely resembles the types of evidence which wildlife officers process in poaching cases. Additionally, new approaches for producing food have created the need for closer cooperation and sharing of expertise between police and wildlife officers; Humphries County, Mississippi, is known as the "Catfish Capital of the World" because of its extensive commercial production of that fish

by catfish farmers. In that state, anyone poaching catfish from a commercial catfish farm is subject to the same penalty provided for cattle theft.[65]

Within the respective states, the responsibility for enforcing game and fish laws is primarily that of a state-level agency. These agencies operate under different designations such as the Arizona Game & Fish Department, the Mississippi Department of Wildlife Conservation, the Texas Parks and Wildlife Department, and the Virginia Commission of Game and Inland Fisheries. Enforcement officers in such agencies may be known as conservation officers, wardens, rangers, wildlife officers or by some similar title. In forty-three states, such personnel have full peace officer status, while in the remaining jurisdictions their authority is limited.[66]

Wildlife officers require much of the knowledge used by other peace officers because they operate under the same laws pertaining to arrest, search and seizure, and interrogation. They must also be able to recognize, collect, mark, and preserve many of the same types of physical evidence. Illustratively, hairs collected from the beds of pickup trucks or trunks of cars can be used to determine the species involved in suspected incidents of poaching. In addition, wildlife officers must also master the specialized laws, knowledge, and investigative techniques that apply to game and fish violations. For example, they must be able to determine the sex of game birds and the sex and age of mammals. Patrolling alone, often in remote areas, requires wildlife officers to exercise good judgment and appropriate caution. Beyond encountering those who may have violated game and fish laws, wildlife officers find evidence of conventional crimes, such as murder, observe major narcotics violations, and meet heavily-armed extremist paramilitary groups conducting training exercises. Thus, the demands made on wildlife officers make their work a specialty.

MAJOR THREATS TO WILDLIFE

There are several major threats to our wildlife including the:[67] (1) alteration and destruction of habitats by construction, shifts in land use and the economic exploitation of the environment; (2) pollution of habitats by pesticides, herbicides, improper disposal of waste, oil spills, sediments from land erosion and other causes; (3) introduction into this country of competing/predator species, as illustrated by the carp population explosion since 1876, when a mere 120 were imported from Europe; (4) poisoning of predators, which in the case of the mid-1960s campaign against coyotes because they killed sheep, also resulted in significant deaths in other populations including prairie dogs, foxes, eagles, hawks, crows and vultures. As a result, the rodent population—which coyotes and other predators had helped to control—increased, and did damage to the roots of prairie grass, destroying range land for sheep and cattle; and (5) the illegal taking of game, fish and other wildlife. It is to this last major threat that the balance of this chapter is devoted.

POACHING AND POACHERS

Poaching is any illegal taking or any illegal possession of game, fish, or other wildlife. Poaching hurts businesses that provide guided hunting and photographic experiences; it deprives legitimate hunters of the opportunity to take game; it hampers efforts to re-establish game populations—as in the case of Indiana's attempts with wild turkeys; and it constitutes a significant threat to endangered species. Although the total cost of poaching is not known, it is clearly very substantial. In Arizona, it is estimated that game poachers cause losses of over $1 million a year. In Illinois, 20,000 white-tail deer with a value of $145 each are legally harvested

annually; if the number of white-tail deer poached were 50 percent of the legal harvest, Illinois's loss would amount to $1,450,000 for that one species alone.[68] In Alaska, estimates of unreported harvests vary by species; for caribou the figure is 50 percent, for moose 25 percent, for grizzly bear 15 percent, and for Dall sheep 5 percent.[69] An Idaho study estimated that in one six-month period, illegal closed-season kills of big game animals was between 3,682 to 7,960.[70]

Poachers fall into two broad categories: (1) the opportunist, who takes advantage of a particular situation and (2) the professional or commercial poacher.[71] While the opportunists may be the most numerous of the poachers, the professional does more harm because: (1) of the extensive number of violations—a "market hunter" may shoot as many as 30 deer in a night;[72] and (2) they often direct their efforts toward endangered species because of the higher prices that will be paid for them. Although some of the opportunistic poachers kill for food, an equal or greater number of them kill for the thrill of it or out of "sheer meanness."[73]

Economics motivates the professional poacher. In the illegal meat market, elk sell for $100 to $150 each, deer from $50 to $75, salmon and steelhead for 50 cents to $10 per pound,[74] and ducks and rabbits for $2.50 to $3.00.[75] Trophy bighorn sheep bring $5,000 to $20,000[76] and trophy mule deer command $2,500 to $50,000 in the illegal market. Antlers short of trophy size are valued by those who make knife handles and other items; depending upon the age and condition of them, the antlers may sell for 60 cents to $6.00 per pound.[77] Shortly after refugees from Southeast Asia reached this country, during the late 1970s, the demand for velvet (the covering composed of blood vessels that nourishes antlers while they are growing) from antlers increased, because the refugees believe it to have aphrodisiac qualities. At a price of $100 to $125 per pound, the velvet

FIGURE 15-9

Three elk in velvet, which were poached out of season near Wheatland, Wyoming.

Courtesy of the Wyoming Game and Fish Department

from one deer brings $800 to $1,000, while from the larger elk, the amount of velvet would produce about four times as much income. In the Orient, the gall bladder of a grizzly bear is also valued as an aphrodisiac and brings $3,000 to $4,000 per pound.[78] Mountain lion hides sell for $100 to $150, black bear hides for $75, the talons of bald eagles for $500, and their tail feathers for $60 a piece.[79] Perhaps the most lucrative trafficking is in birds of prey. Eggs and young birds not yet able to fly are taken from their natural nests in the wild. Upon reaching a suitable size, they are shipped to countries in the Middle East, such as Saudi Arabia, where peregrine falcons are sold for $7,000 to $10,000 and the prized white yearling gyrfalcon brings as much as $100,000.[80]

INVESTIGATIONS

Wildlife officers generally spend only about 20 percent of their time in law enforcement activities. The balance is spent in such activities as teaching hunting, boating and snowmobile safety courses for the public, staffing exhibits at state and local fairs or other functions, participating in multi-agency mock disaster drills as part of emergency preparedness training, conducting various surveys for state and federal government, including counts of raccoon, deer and midwinter water-fowl, as well as other censuses conducted on a "one-time only" basis. When conducting law enforcement activities, wildlife officers use many of the same investigative techniques as used by other types of peace officers.

Information. Information is an essential commodity in combating poachers. With it, more investigative successes are experienced. In some states, 80 percent of all poacher arrests come from leads from citizens. To assist wildlife officers in getting information, a number of states have established special programs. In some states, these efforts are referred to as Citizens Against Poachers (CAP) programs and in other states as Turn in a Poacher (TIP) programs.

Uniformed Patrol. Uniformed wildlife officers patrol in boats and cars to see if game is being taken out of season or by illegal means. They visit various sites to observe, to check licenses, and to examine each sportsman's daily take. As a supplement to patrolling by car, airplanes can be used during the day to locate hunters, trappers, and camps in remote areas. At night, aircraft can also be useful in pinpointing places where it appears artificial light is being used by poachers to take game, a tactic known as "jacklighting." In both day and night uses of aircraft, the pilot/spotter will relay information to ground units so they can take appropriate

action. In some instances aircraft keep poachers leaving an area under surveillance, and direct wildlife officers in cars on a course to intercept the poachers.

Intensive Hunting Patrols. Wildlife officers also employ intensive hunting patrols, especially during the opening weekends for various types of game such as pheasant, wild turkey, waterfowl, grouse, and deer. Intensive patrols tend to be concentrated in areas of high public use, especially those with a history of excessive violations.

Vehicle Check Stops. Vehicle check stops are strategically set up on carefully selected roads to check vehicles for bag limits, unplugged shotguns, licenses and to determine whether necessary special stamps (for ducks, for example) have been acquired. In Iowa, one such stop point produced the issuance of fifty-nine conservation-related citations in a 3½ hour period.

Fishing Patrols. Fishing patrols check for licenses among sportsmen in the field, for their compliance with keeping only fish which meet or exceed the minimal length, and their keeping only the daily allowed limit. Fishing patrols also check for illegal commercial fishing devices such as basket traps, trotlines, and seines. Computerized sonar is used to locate illegally set fish nets that take protected sport fish.

Resident License Verifications. A common wildlife violation is nonresidents of a state claiming residency so they can be issued less expensive hunting or fishing licenses. Periodically, wildlife officers go through copies of licenses to determine whether a purchaser may have in fact been a nonresident. The wildlife officer has many avenues to pursue in determining the actual legal residence of the license purchaser. Local utility companies are contacted for information concerning service by the individual, telephone books are checked, driver's license records are ex-

FIGURE 15-10

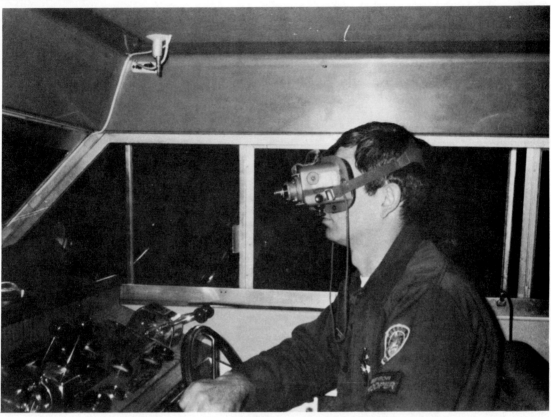

Oregon State Police Game officer using night vision goggles to check for illegal nets on the Columbia River.

amined, as are voter registration files. Once the information indicates that the purchase is not by a resident of a state, the wildlife officer contacts the individual to attempt a personal interview. Once confronted, the subjects will often make an admission.[81]

Covert Investigations. Covert investigations vary in their complexity. At the simplest, a wildlife officer who could not approach an area without being plainly visible for some distance may dress as a trout fisherman and work his way along a stream watching for violations. More complexly, in Washington—where the Department of Fisheries (separate from the Department of Game, but with whom they coordinate closely) is charged with the enforcement of laws pertaining to the taking and disposing of foodfish and shellfish—a sting operation resulted in the purchase of fifty-three tons of illegally taken salmon, steelhead, and sturgeon.[82] In Pennsylvania, a fish market was the front for a sting operation in which federal Fish and

FIGURE 15-11   Wardens Conducting an Inspection at a Vehicle Check Stop

Courtesy Tom Carbone, Maine Department of Inland Fisheries and Wildlife

Wildlife Service agents gathered evidence of the harvesting, interstate shipping, and sale of some 7,000 pounds of illegal striped bass (rockfish) from Maryland alone.

Criminalistics and Wildlife Investigations. Criminalistics is playing an increasingly important role in wildlife investigations. For example, a hunter may claim to have killed a deer legally during the bow season, but because of the presence of a shock ring around the animal's fatal wound (which an arrow would not produce) or inconsistencies between the entrance wound and the shape of the arrowhead, a wildlife officer may suspect that a gun was actually used illegally during bow season.[83] Thus a presumptive field test may be used to check for copper or lead residues in the wound, to be followed by atomic absorption for a conclusive test, as presumptive field tests may give a false or negative result (residues are actually present but not detected). Wildlife officers may also need to be able to estimate the time of an animal's death to determine if it was killed just before or after the hunting season. Thus the wildlife officer, like other investigators, must understand changes such as rigor mortis, loss of body heat, and the onset of decomposition. One basic way the time of death of an animal can be established is by using a caliper to measure the diameter of the pupil of either eye to the nearest millimeter. Comparison of the measurement with standard tables will yield an approximate time the animal has been dead. These illustrations provide some examples of the specific applications of criminalistics to wildlife investigations.

QUESTIONS

1. In what ways are the cities and agricultural crime linked?
2. What are the two major types of off-road equipment, and what is meant by the "identification problem" with respect to such equipment?
3. Describe the NCIC equipment marking program.
4. What is the difference between a sting and a reverse sting?
5. Explain how grain theft can be prevented through the use of confetti.
6. What specialized knowledge is required by the investigator with respect to the theft of agrichemicals?
7. What five generalizations can be made about livestock and tack theft?
8. What are four concerns with respect to conducting stakeouts in rural areas?
9. The legal provisions for transporting cattle vary by state; at a general level what three things must investigators know regarding such matters?
10. What does $\overline{\text{M}}$ RH R-crop L-split mean?
11. State and briefly describe five different methods of marking livestock for identification.
12. Identify five major threats to wildlife in this country.
13. Define poaching, and give at least three reasons why it is a problem.
14. What are the two major categories of poachers and how are they different?
15. Identify and briefly discuss seven different investigative programs or techniques used by wildlife officers.

NOTES

1. For an extension of this and related propositions, see Charles Swanson, "Rural and Agricultural Crime," *Journal of Criminal Justice*, 1981, Vol. 9, No. 1, pp. 19–27.

2. Charles Swanson and Leonard Territo, "Agricultural Crime: Its Extent, Prevention and Control," *FBI Law Enforcement Bulletin*, 1980, Vol. 49, No. 5, p. 10.

3. P. Christian, "Agricultural Enterprises Management in an Urban-Based Society" (Detroit: Gale Research Company, 1978), p. ix.

4. U.S. Department of Commerce, *Farm Population of the United States: 1978* (Washington, D.C.: Government Printing Office, 1979), p. 5.

5. Jim Fisher, "Crime in Agriculture," *The Citrus Industry,* January 1978, Vol. 58, No. 1, p. 13.

6. Specifically to Carlo Gambino, the reputed "boss of bosses" of the five New York City families. Relatedly, see Mary Nelson, "Farmers, Others Lose Advance Fees in Loan Scam," *The Farmer,* September 5, 1981, pp. 10, 12, and 14.

7. Cathy Sherman Machan, "The Mafia Nibbles Cheese," *Farm Journal,* September 1976, p. 29.

8. Ibid., p. 29.

9. South Dakota State Planning Agency grant No. 2-07-01-002 awarded January 1, 1974.

10. Personal letter of February 15, 1978, from Dennis E. Emmerson, Assistant to the President, Florida Farm Bureau Federation, to Mr. Brent Hampton.

11. Jerrold F. Footlick, Paul Brinkley-Rogers, and Chris Harper, "Crime on the Farm," *Newsweek,* October 3, 1977, p. 101.

12. M. L. Elam, "Rustling Demands Security Measures Be Taken," *Hoard's Dairyman,* 1977, Vol. 122, No. 4, p. 234; also see Andy Knott, "Rustlers Leave Farmers Hanging," *Chicago Tribune,* January 21, 1982, 1 and 14.

13. Footlick, Brinkley-Rogers, and Harper, "Crime on the Farm," p. 101.

14. B. Drummond Ayers, Jr., "Tree Rustlers Ride the Plains," *New York Times,* November 10, 1971.

15. Ibid.

16. Ibid.

17. Ibid.

18. Robert P. Matthews, "Theft and Vandalism in Western Washington Forests," *Journal of Forestry,* Vol. 68, No. 7, pp. 415–416.

19. Joseph A. Huddleston, "Farm Thefts Hardly Petty," *Milwaukee Sentinel,* November 11, 1977.

20. "Farm Vandalism," *Wallace's Farmer,* November 27, 1976.

21. "Recent Thefts Total $10,000," *Hardee County Harold Advocate,* February 16, 1978.

22. "Theft, Vandalism Newest Concern of U.S. Farmers," *California-Arizona Cotton,* March 1977, p. 42.

23. "Thieves Reap Crop of Tractors," *The Atlanta Journal and Constitution,* June 25, 1978, 20B.

24. Carole Ashkinzae, "Georgia ID Program Aims at Cutting Equipment Thefts," *Atlanta Constitution,* July 7, 1978, A1.

25. Letter and attachments of March 15, 1978, from William L. Rice to C. R. Swanson; the data were for 1976.

26. For example, see Paul Kaplan, "Guns, Guards Sprout up in Florida Mango Groves," *Atlanta Constitution,* July 7, 1978, 1A; and Grant D. Morse, "Are Thieves Stealing Your Bees?," *Gleanings in Bee Culture,* January 1977, Vol. 105, No. 1, pp. 8–9.

27. See George J. Lyford, "Heavy Equipment Theft," *FBI Law Enforcement Bulletin,* March 1981, Vol. 50, No. 3, which has been drawn on in the preparation of this section.

28. The description of the marking system is taken from Florida Farm Bureau Federation, Operation Identification, undated but transmitted by letter of July 8, 1982, from Pam Vincent to Charles Swanson.

29. See Lyford, "Heavy Equipment Theft," p. 2; and Mary Nelson, "Machinery Thefts: Big Business for Organized Crime," *The Farmer,* March 20, 1982, p. 12.

30. John Green, "Gone in Four Minutes," *Implement and Tractor,* June 21, 1977, Vol. 92, No. 14, p. 48.

31. Lyford, "Heavy Equipment Theft," p. 2.
32. Ibid., p. 5.
33. Ibid., p. 5.
34. Ibid., p. 5.
35. Nelson, "Machinery Theft," pp. 13 and 15.
36. Ken Faulkner, "Joint 'Sting' Operation Nets 28 Theft Warrants in Area," *Calhoun* (Georgia) *Times,* June 29, 1980, 1.
37. Ken Roberts, "Officer Among Four Arrested in Polk, Stolen Fruit Scam," *The Tampa Tribune,* May 5, 1982, 1A.
38. Jay A. Sigler, *Understanding Criminal Law* (Boston: Little, Brown and Company, 1981), pp. 236–237; and Wayne R. LaFave and Austin W. Scott, Jr., *Criminal Law* (St. Paul, Minn.: West Publishing Company, 1972), p. 371.
39. Terry D. Turchie and Billy Bob Williams, "Timber Thefts," *FBI Law Enforcement Bulletin,* May 1979, Vol. 48, No. 5, pp. 1–5, from which treatment in this section was derived.
40. The information on this product was supplied by the Grain Identification Company, Cooperstown, North Dakota.
41. Federal Bureau of Investigation, "Grain Buyers and Sellers Defrauded," Denver, Colorado, June 13, 1978.
42. Conversation in November 1983 with Mary Nelson based on her research for an article on the theft of chemicals.
43. *Farm Chemicals,* May 1970, p. 12.
44. *Agri-News,* October 1975, p. 3.
45. These points are drawn from Sgt. William Bacon, *Livestock Theft Investigation,* Los Angeles County Sheriff's Department, undated, p. 2, and with modifications made by the coauthors.
46. Ibid., p. 2, which is the source for the information in this paragraph.
47. Ibid., p. 2.
48. Some of the information in this paragraph is drawn from Ibid., pp. 5–6.
49. Ibid., p. 5.
50. Ibid., p. 5.
51. Ibid., p. 5.
52. Ibid., p. 6.
53. Ibid., p. 6.
54. Ibid., p. 12.
55. Ibid., p. 12.
56. Ibid., p. 16.
57. "Horse Meat Trend Keeps Rider Uneasy," *The Tampa Tribune,* April 6, 1980, 22-A.
58. Ibid., 22-A.
59. Bacon, *Livestock Theft Investigation,* p. 16, from which this paragraph was obtained with restatement.
60. Ibid., p. 24.
61. Unless otherwise indicated, the information in this section is derived from Ibid., pp. 7–11 and 18.
62. See "Rustlers Thwarted by Equine 'Fingerprinting' Method," *Law Enforcement News,* December 24, 1979, Vol. 5, No. 22, p. 6.
63. This point and the next four are derived from Federal Bureau of Investigation, "Grain Buyers and Sellers Defrauded."
64. Several of these points were taken from Bacon, *Livestock Theft Investigation,* p. 17.
65. Letter of August 28, 1985 from Johnny Laney, Mississippi Department of Wildlife Conservation, to Leonard Territo.
66. William B. Morse, "Wildlife Law Enforcement, 1984," presented at the Western Association of Fish and Wildlife Agencies, July 17, 1984, Victoria, British Columbia.
67. Lt. Donald R. Miller, "Environmental Pollution" undated lecture notes, transmitted by Major L. W. Brandt, Law Enforcement Division, Commission of Game and Inland Fisheries, Richmond, Virginia, by letter of August 20, 1985, to Leonard Territo.
68. Letter of August 12, 1985, from Sgt. John Will, Illinois Department of Conservation, to Leonard Territo. No loss percentage was given in the letter; we used the figure 50 percent for illustration and it is consistent with loss estimates for Arizona.

69. Letter of August 15, 1985, from Commissioner Don Collinsworth, Alaska Department of Fish & Game to Leonard Territo. In addition to poaching, "unreported harvest" includes defense of life and property kills, highway and railroad kills, and hunters who failed to send in a harvest ticket, although otherwise in compliance.

70. Letter of August 19, 1985, from Jerry Conley, Director, Idaho Game & Fish; the figures apparently refer to data from J. R. Vilkitis, "Characteristics of Big Game Violators and the Extent of Their Activity in Idaho," Master's thesis, University of Idaho, 1968.

71. Letter of August 12, 1985, from Steve Smith, Wyoming Game and Fish Department, to Leonard Territo.

72. Letter of August 7, 1985, with attachments, from Lieutenants R. McIntire and L. Rhinehart, Indiana Department of Natural Resources to Leonard Territo.

73. Ibid., p. 10.

74. Conley, letter of August 19, 1985.

75. Will, letter of August 12, 1985.

76. Letter of August 28, 1985, from David Croonquist, Colorado Division of Wildlife, to Leonard Territo.

77. Conley, letter of August 19, 1985.

78. Croonquist, letter of August 28, 1985.

79. Will, letter of August 12, 1985.

80. See Jim Robbins, "Operation Falcon," The Denver Post, March 18, 1985, pp. 4A and 5A and John Toohey, "4 Arrested in Falcon Smuggling," The Denver Post, June 30, 1984, p. 8A.

81. Smith, letter of August 12, 1985.

82. Letter of August 12, 1985, from Evan Jacoby to Leonard Territo.

83. The information in this section was drawn with modification from Alan Woolf and John Will, *Forensic Science Handbook* (Carbondale, Illinois: The Cooperative Wildlife Research Laboratory, Southern Illinois University, 1983) by permission.

16

ARSON INVESTIGATION

INTRODUCTION

The available statistics for the crime of arson indicate that it accounts for 7 percent of all fires and 10 percent of all fire losses. However, the true number may in fact be three times greater because of mistakes in diagnosis by police and fire officials. Arson has been increasing for at least 20 years and does not appear to be decreasing.

Arson is an inherently difficult crime to detect and prosecute, and it falls between police and fire department responsibility, an area that is too often not effectively covered. Both the police and fire services can legitimately claim authority in arson cases, but each also may rationalize that the responsibility belongs to the other. Unfortunately, in most jurisdictions neither is prepared to devote the resources needed to achieve identification, arrest, and conviction rates commensurate with other crimes. Arson investigators need cooperation and better training. Administrative officials also need to help, but in order to help they need to give the problem a greater share of their attention. Probably the most urgent step in controlling arson rates is for top fire and police officials and local, state, and national government officials to recognize the magnitude of the problem and then provide the necessary resources to combat the problem.[1]

PRELIMINARY INVESTIGATION

Arson investigations entail several exceptions to fire service training. For example, the fire service has taught fire fighters that fire loss is less and public relations better if they clean out the premises of debris, water, and so forth. However, if arson is suspected, firefighters should not disarrange the premises, especially at the point of origin. Moving debris, even window glass, may destroy valuable physical evidence.[2]

In nearly all cases, there is little additional loss if the area encompassing the point of origin is not cleaned out, because this area is usually the most heavily damaged by the fire, with little salvage possible. Often it is necessary during overhauling to move large quantities of acoustical tile, plasterboard, canned goods, cartons, and other items. If this material is beyond salvage, it is natural to throw it into the worst burned area of the building. But this is probably the area the investigator will want to examine carefully, and such discards will have to be moved again. In the confusion, the fire cause is likely to remain in doubt.

One effective way to determine fire causes is to determine the point of origin. Neighbors', onlookers', or others' ideas about the cause sometimes lead investigators astray. When the exact point of origin is established, the cause usually becomes obvious. For instance, a point of origin in the middle of a bare concrete basement floor probably eliminates defective heating appliances or wiring.

Points of origin sometimes are established by reconstructing furniture and walls, replacing loose boards and doors. Neighbors and occupants can help describe how things were before the fire. The direction of heat flow then can be followed by checks for deepest charring, indications of highest temperature, and duration of heat. Temperatures are indicated by the condition of metal, glass, wood, plastics, and other materials. Because heat rises, a general rule is to look for the lowest point of deep char as the point of origin. This rule, however, has many exceptions.

After the area of origin has been established, the investigator should check for the level of origin by examining the bottoms of shelves, ledges, moldings, and furniture and all sides of the legs, arms, and framework of reconstructed furniture. The investigator also should clean the floor carefully at the point of origin, examining and moving all objects to one side. After this is done, the floor or rugs should be swept as clean as possible for examination of burn patterns.

The floor and lower areas of the room produce the most clues to the cause of the fire, because they are the living area. Most equipment and contents are near floor level, actions of occupants are conducted near floor level, and most materials drop there during a fire.

WHERE AND HOW DID THE FIRE START?

Once the fire is out, the primary task is to begin examining what is left of the building for physical evidence that may indicate how the fire began. (See Figure 16-1.) The point of origin can be a clue to possible arson. For example, if two or more distinct points of origin are found, two or more separate fires probably were deliberately set. Also if the fires started in the middle of a large room or in a closet, then the index of suspicion should go up sharply.[3]

TWO FACTORS NEEDED TO CAUSE FIRE

During the investigation, it should be borne in mind that a fire always has two causes: a source of heat and material ignited.

In checking for the fire cause at the point of origin it is usually an advantage to use the "layer checking" technique. Before any material is moved or shovelled out, the investigator should make notes and carefully examine the strata while working through to the floor. These layers often contain wood ash, plaster, melted aluminum, window glass, charred drapery fabric, and charred newspapers. They may give a picture of the sequence of burning. If, for example, charred newspapers were found beneath charred drapery fabric, it could indicate a set fire, particularly if papers would not usually be in the area or if they were of different types or dates. Aluminum and similar alloys melt fairly early in a fire (at about 1,150°F), often splash or run over other material near floor level, solidify, and protect the material from further damage. Draperies and heavy curtains may burn free and drop on flammable liquid, preventing it from being completely consumed, especially if the liquid is heavy or less volatile.[4]

ACCIDENTAL FIRES

Once the point of origin has been discovered, the next step is to determine how the fire started. Even though arson may be suspected, the investigator must first investigate and rule out all possible accidental or natural causes. Many courts have held that this elim-

FIGURE 16-1   Team of Arson Investigators Searching the Scene of a Suspected Arson

Courtesy Thomas Evans, Pinellas County (Florida) Sheriff's Office

ination of accidental causes is a firm basis for an arson charge. Also, if the investigator is put on the witness stand, it is likely that a question will be raised about the possibility of accidental causes. A failure to eliminate accidental causes could substantially weaken the prosecution's case.

Some of the more common accidental or natural causes of fire fall into the following categories:

The electric system. Fuses in which pennies have been inserted; broken or rotted insulation; overloaded circuits; defective switches; and improperly installed wiring

Electrical appliances and equipment. Defective electrical units with short circuits; overheated irons; and light bulbs covered by paper shades

Gas. Leaks in gas pipes; defective stoves and heating units

Heating units. Overheated stoves or steam pipes; clothing being dried too close to fireplaces or open flames; faulty chimneys; explosions from kerosene stoves; and overturned space heaters

Sunlight. The concentration of sun rays on bubbles in glasses, windowpanes, or convex shaving mirrors placed near combustible materials such as paper or rags

Matches. Children playing with matches, especially in enclosed areas such as closets or utility rooms

Smoking. The careless disposal of cigars, cigarettes, pipe ashes, and other lighted devices into trash cans in the home; individuals who fall asleep while smoking in bed or in a chair

Indications of cigarettes in furniture or mattresses are: heavy charring of the unit and the floor; a char pattern on furniture frames, heaviest on the inside; heavy staining and blackening of mirrors and window glass in the area, indicating a long, slow fire; a burning time of from 1½ to three or four hours; collapsing of part or all of the core springs. Lying flat on a padded surface, cigarettes usually char a small hole and burn out. If the cigarette is partially covered at the sides or bottom, a fire usually results in an hour or so. Cigarettes ignite foam rubber padding to about the same degree as other padding. With foam rubber padding, fire occurs a little faster because smoldering reaches an ignition temperature faster and burns with greater intensity.[5]

Spontaneous Heating and Ignition. There are a few fundamental causes of spontaneous heating, but the conditions under which these factors may operate are numerous. Nearly all organic materials and many metals are subject to either oxidation, fermentation, or both and, therefore, have some potential for spontaneous heating.

Spontaneous heating is produced in three major ways:

chemical action

fermentation

oxidation (the most common)

For example, chemical actions occur when unslaked lime and water or when sodium and water are combined.

Fermentation heating is caused by bacterial action. Here, moisture is a prime factor. The most dangerous materials are those subject to combinations such as fermentation and oxidation with drying. Fresh sawdust over ten feet deep is subject to fermentation heating but rarely reaches ignition temperature. In oxidation heating, rapid oxidation must take place in the presence of a good insulating factor and an oxygen supply. Oxidation takes place in oils containing carbon, hydrogen, and oxygen. This combination is mostly found in vegetable and fish oils and, to some extent, in animal oils.

The susceptibility to spontaneous heating is usually determined by drying time. Unadulterated hydrocarbons, such as mineral and petroleum oils, are not considered subject to spontaneous ignition.

Spontaneous ignition is rare in residences and small businesses. It is considerably accelerated by external heat such as sunshine, steampipes, hot air ducts, or friction from wind or vibration. Spontaneous ignition is rather mysterious because of many unknowns. Therefore, it is often used as a catch-all explanation.

The usual time required to produce spontaneous ignition by oxidation or fermentation runs from several hours to several days or months. This form of ignition is characterized by internal charring of a mass of combustibles, and some of the remains of this material usually are found at the point of origin (if the fire fighters have been careful and especially if fog was used), because it normally takes a considerable mass—several inches of fairly dense material—to create the factors necessary for spontaneous heating. Sometimes when material of the appropriate type is suspected and found to be deeply charred all the way through, investigators must satisfy themselves that external heat was not responsible. When not heated internally, sacks of meals, flour, and the like usually survive fire with only an inch or two of charring on the exposed surface.

Dust and polishing mops have often been accused of causing spontaneous ignition and probably have in some rare cases. Most fires originating near a mop in a closet or on a back porch are caused by a child playing with matches.[6] It is debatable whether the average mop would have enough bulk to provide the necessary insulation to raise the temperature to the ignition point, although with favorable conditions—such as a large mop, saturated with fast drying oils, pressed in a corner with other brooms, and receiving outside heat from a steampipe or the sun's rays through a window—ignition could occur. During the several hours required for the material to ignite, it gives off very acrid odors. Linseed and similar oils are especially odorous. People in the area during that time usually would be aware of these odors.

===== BURN INDICATORS =====

Burn indicators are the effects of heat or partial burning that indicate a fire's rate of development, points of origin, temperature, duration, time of occurrence, and the presence of flammable liquids. Interpretation of burn indicators is a principal means for determining the causes of fires, especially arson. Some of the burn indicators used are the following:[7]

Alligatoring: checking of charred wood, giving it the appearance of alligator skin. Large, rolling blisters indicate rapid, intense heat, small, flat alligatoring indicates long, low heat.

Crazing of Glass: formation of irregular cracks in glass due to rapid, intense heat—possible fire accelerant.

Depth of Char: depth of burning of wood—used to determine length of burn and thereby locate the point of origin of the fire.

Line of Demarcation: boundary between charred and uncharred material. On floors or rugs, a puddle-shaped line of demarcation is believed to indicate a liquid fire accelerant. In a cross section of wood, a sharp, distinct line of demarcation indicates a rapid, intense fire.

Sagged Furniture Springs: because of the heat required for furniture springs to collapse from their own weight (1,150°F) and because of the insulating effect of the upholstery, sagged springs are believed to be possible only in either a fire originating inside the cushions (as from a cigarette rolling between the cushions) or an external fire intensified by a fire accelerant.

Spalling: breaking off of pieces of the surface of concrete, cement, or brick due to intense heat. Brown stains around the spall indicate the use of a fire accelerant.

Freezing of Leaves: drying of leaves in a forest fire into their position at the time of the fire. Because leaves turn during the day to face the sun, their position indicates the time of day.

Although burn indicators are widely used to establish the causes of fires, they have received little or no scientific testing. In reference to freezing of leaves, one expert states, some persons are inclined to regard this evidence as unreliable because of insufficient clinical and research confirmation and the influence of the fire wind.[8] Another authority cautions that puddle-shaped lines of demarcation may have nothing to do with flammable liquids; that depth of char is strongly affected by factors other than burning time, such as temperature and species of wood; and that much greater care must be taken in its interpretation than is usual.[9]

FIRE-SETTING MECHANISMS

It is the duty of an arson investigator to search the debris of a suspicious fire, particularly around the point of origin, to gather evidence pointing to the mechanism used by the fire-setter in the arson effort.[10]

An arsonist may use the simplest of methods, a match and some paper, or elaborate mechanical or chemical methods. An incendiary mechanism may be mechanical or chemical. It consists of an ignition device, possibly a timing device, one or more "plants" to feed or accelerate the initial flame, and frequently "trailers" to spread the fire about the building or from plant to plant.

Matches. Only juvenile arsonists and pyromaniacs seem to favor striking matches. Other fire-setters want some delay, so they adapt the ordinary match to some timing mechanism.

Several matches may be affixed to a lighted cigarette with a rubber band or tape, the heads of the matches set about halfway down the cigarette from its glowing end (see Figure 16-2). In some cases, matches are laid alongside a cigarette. Books of paper matches are also popular. Because cigarettes will continue to burn when laid on their sides, they are effective ignition devices; the slowburning cigarette allows the fire-setter a few minutes to get away from the scene before the fire makes any headway.

Matches are also used in conjunction with mechanical devices. One arsonist strapped matches to the ringing mechanism of a telephone in a wall box and inserted a piece of abrasive board in place of the bell. He thought he could set a fire from miles away by calling his home. But his estranged wife came home unexpectedly and noticed a wisp of smoke from a pile of old clothing on the floor in the living room. Frightened, she called the fire department. The ignition device had been activated but had fizzled out. The firemen carefully preserved the rags (wet with lighter fluid), the matches, and an abrasive board. These were later used in the prosecution of the husband.

Unburnt or partially burnt matches found around the point of origin should be carefully preserved. A suspect may have similar matches in his or her pocket.

Candles. As a timed ignition device, candles have been in use by arsonists for over a century. Candles burn at various rates, depending on their composition and size. Thick candles burn slowly, long candles longer than short candles.

Some years ago, Dr. Richard Steinmetz established a table of the burning time of candles of various compositions and sizes. This table can be summed up as follows:

Composition	Diameter	Time to Burn One Inch
Tallow	3/4"	61 minutes
Wax	7/8"	57 minutes
Paraffin	13/16"	63 minutes

Arson investigators sometimes work on a rule of thumb of an hour's burning time for each inch of candle of the above diameters. Of course, this is only guesswork and investigators will arrive at a more definite time only after completing their own experiments. Once the arsonists know the average burning time of the candle, they can adjust to a desired time lag merely by cutting the candle to the desired length. The candle is therefore not only an ignition unit, but also a device which can be adjusted within certain limits

FIGURE 16-2   Kitchen Matches Wrapped Around a Cigarette

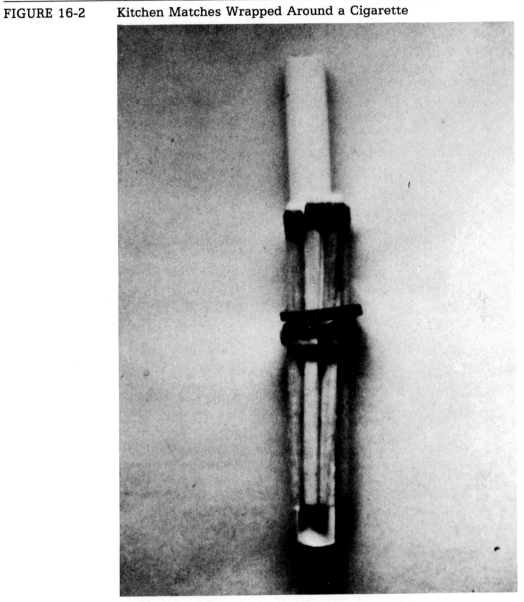

Courtesy Property Claim Services, American Insurance Association

to set a fire hours after the arsonist has departed from the scene of the crime.

Candles are mostly used in conjunction with containers of easily combustible materials, which are sometimes set within, or close to, other containers of inflammable liquids or in an area sprinkled with such accelerants.

Figure 16-3 depicts the use of a candle, positioned in such a way so that as it burns, it severs a string to which a glass containing gasoline is attached. When the jar falls and breaks, the flame from the candle ignites the gasoline and the fire quickly spreads.

However, candles leave a deposit of wax as their telltale sign. Wax may have soaked into the wood of a floor, or it may be found in a pool at the low point of a floor or table top. Another sign is the protection afforded the floor or table top by such wax—the spot on which the candle rested will show less charring than the surrounding area. In many cases a part of the candle, and possibly the container in which the candle was placed, may be found in a search of the fire scene.

Chemicals. Various chemical combustions have been used to set fires. Saboteurs have used such means for years. Units which provide for an acid to be released upon some combination of chemicals is a favorite device, with the acid releasing itself by eating its way through the cork or even the metal of its container. The time lag from setting to ignition can be estimated with some certainty by an arsonist with a little knowledge of chemistry.

Various rubber receptacles, such as hot water and ice bags or contraceptives have been used for a phosphorus and water ignition device. A pinhole is made in the rubber container, allowing the water to seep out. Once it drains below the level of the phosphorus, ignition takes place. As this chemical ignites upon contact with air, a time lag is secured by controlling the amount of water and the size of the hole in the container.

Even the ordinary fire-setter sometimes uses a chemical that ignites upon contact with water. The device is activated by rain. Holes in a roof or a connection to the building's gutter system have been used to trigger these devices. Another device is to divert the sewage line in a building. It is set up at night to trigger the next morning when the toilet is flushed for the first time.

Most chemical ignition units leave some residue, have a distinctive odor, or both. Debris must be analyzed at a laboratory when it is suspected that chemicals have been used as ignition devices. Fortunately, most arsonists do not know enough to use chemical ignition or timing devices, and the machinery and tools necessary for the construction of some of these devices are not always readily available. The devices usually are fairly simple. More complex devices usually are encountered only in time of war by frustrated enemy agents.

Gas. Although not commonly encountered, the combination of gas and the pilot light on the kitchen stoves of many residences is always a possibility. Illuminating gas rises to the ceiling, being lighter than air, and then slowly moves to floor level as it continues to escape. When it reaches a combustion build-up, it is close to the pilot light level. An explosion, usually followed by fire, takes place. A candle placed in a room adjoining the kitchen has also been utilized as a means of ignition. Therefore, arson investigators must remember that although such explosions usually follow suicide attempts or accidents, arsonists may use an ordinary gas range as a tool.

In such cases, investigators should get help from an engineer at the local public utility. The time lag between the initial release of the gas and the explosion can be

FIGURE 16-3   Fire-setting Mechanism Using a Candle as a Timing Device

Note string leading to a glass jar containing gasoline. When the string is severed by the burning candle, the jar falls, breaks, and the gasoline is ignited by the candle.

Courtesy Property Claim Services, American Insurance Association

estimated from the size of the room involved, number of openings, type of gas, and related data. For example, a kitchen 10 by 15 feet with a ceiling 9 feet high equals a total volume of 1,350 cubic feet. When 71 cubic feet of gas are introduced into the room, the lowest limit of explosive range will have been reached. In a well ventilated room, it is almost impossible to build up to this limit, but an arsonist seals off the room so that the gas builds up. In a fairly well sealed room, a single burner left open on a kitchen gas stove will deliver enough gas to explode in about five hours. The oven jets will build up the same volume in two hours; an oven plus four burners, 30 minutes to one hour.

The widespread use of gas as an arson tool has been thwarted because of its smell. Neighbors usually detect the smell, call the police or the fire department, or break in themselves, and ruin a carefully planned arson attempt.

Electrical Systems. Any wiring system, including doorbell and telephone circuits, can be used as fire-setting tools. Ignition devices hooked to the wiring systems of buildings have been used throughout the country by arsonists. The time can be established by a study of the habits of those using the premises. Possibly a security guard switches on the light every hour while inspecting the various portions of the building, or employees turn on the lights at opening time, and so on.

Although a doorbell system also can be used to trigger an ignition device, the bell may be rung by some chance visitor and the plans of the fire-setter thwarted. Telephone timing devices have the same fault. A wrong number or an unexpected call and the fire is underway, possibly days ahead of schedule.

Figure 16-4 depicts an electric timer, appliance cord, matches, and shredded paper used as an ignition device. Once the paper catches on fire, it ignites the clothing.

Electrical appliances have also been used to set off fires. An open heater is placed close to a flimsy set of curtains, and an apparently accidental fire results. An electrical circuit is deliberately overloaded with several appliances until it heats up. Sometimes an accelerant such as kerosene is dropped into a switch box. In a few cases, a length of normal wiring was removed and lighter wire substituted so that it would overheat and, without blowing the fuses, serve as an ignition device. Figure 16-5 depicts the use of a toaster with a paper trailer leading to an accelerant in the overhung kitchen cabinet. After the toaster is activated, the heat ignites the trailer, travels to the accelerant, and causes it to ignite.

Investigators generally discover physical traces of electrical ignition devices after a fire.

Mechanical. Alarm clocks were once a favored weapon of arsonists. With a simple alarm clock, some wire, and a small battery, a fire-setter was "in business." But a search of the fire debris usually sent the arsonist to prison. Some arsonists used the lead hammer in the clock to break a glass tube that fed flammable matter to a fixed flame. This action pushed one container of chemicals into another, closing an electrical circuit. Some arsonists attached matches to the hammer where they were pressed against an abrasive surface to ignite flammable material. The clock was activated by setting the alarm for a certain time. The weights in a grandfather's clock have been used in a similar manner.

Some mechanical devices are childish, some are worthy of master craftsmen, and others are truly fiendish. Unfortunately for many of these ingenious incendiaries, their machines do not burn and can later be used in their prosecution.

Plants. A plant is the material placed around the ignition device to feed the flame. News-

FIGURE 16-4 Electric Timer Used in Conjunction with Appliance Cord, Matches, and Shredded Paper

Courtesy Property Claim Services, American Insurance Association

papers, wood shavings, excelsior, rags, clothing, curtains, blankets, and cotton waste are some plants. Newspapers and excelsior are the most frequently used; cotton waste is used extensively in factory or industrial fires.

Accelerants, or "boosters," to speed the progress of the fire are also part of the plant. Kerosene and gasoline are favored boosters; alcohol, lighter fluid, paint thinners, and other solvents are also popular. However, any flammable fluid or compound may be used to accelerate the blaze.

Trailers. Trailers are used to spread the fire. A trailer is ignited by the blaze from the plant. It carries the fire to other parts of a room or building. Usually a trailer ends in a second plant, another pile of papers or excelsior sprinkled with gasoline, kerosene, or other booster. From the primary plant, the fire-setter may lay four trailers to four secondary plants. Four separate fires result from one ignition device.

Rope or toilet paper soaked in alcohol or similar fluid, motion picture film, dynamite fuses, gunpowder, and other such substances have been used as trailers. Sometimes rags or newspapers are soaked in some fire accelerant and twisted into rope. Some arsonists use a fluid fire accelerant such as kerosene as a trailer by pouring a liberal quantity on the floor in a desired path. Figure 16-6 depicts shredded paper as a trailer leading into a clothes closet containing a plastic bowl filled with a liquid accelerant.

Incendiary Fires. When any fire-setting device, ignition and timing units, plants, or trailers are found near a suspicious fire, it should be classified as an incendiary fire.

FIGURE 16-5   Toaster with a Paper Trailer Leading to an Accelerant in Overhung Kitchen Cabinets

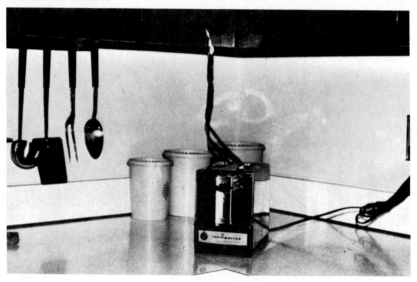

Courtesy Property Claim Services, American Insurance Association

When kerosene, gasoline, excelsior, candles, and like substances are discovered around the point of origin of a suspicious fire, it is evidence of arson. If investigators can prove such material had no right to be in such premises, then they have established the corpus delicti; that is, they have overcome the presumption of accident as established by law and have proved the body of the crime.

Missing Items. Sometimes items that are missing from the fire scene can prove valuable. For example, does it appear that much of the building contents, especially furniture, clothing, or valuable items were removed prior to the fire? Have house pets been removed? Moving a pet to a kennel or the home of friends just before a fire should raise the suspicions of the investigator.

MOTIVES AND TYPOLOGY OF ARSONISTS

MOTIVES FOR ARSON

Understanding the motives of the arsonist is extremely important if an investigation is to be successful.[11] One authority has cited the following motives as being among the most common.[12]

Revenge, Spite, Jealousy. This category includes jilted lovers, feuding neighbors, disgruntled employees, quarreling spouses, people getting even after being cheated or abused, and people motivated by racial or religious hostility. Lovers' disputes and domestic squabbles are the greatest contributors to this category. In some parts of the country, particularly in rural areas, disagree-

FIGURE 16-6   Shredded Paper Trailer Leading to a Liquid Accelerant in a Plastic Bowl Located in a Clothes Closet

Courtesy Property Claim Services, American Insurance Association

ments result in the burning of homes or barns. Many arsonists drink alcohol before this kind of fire.[13]

Vandalism, Malicious Mischief. Vandals set fires for excitement and have no other motive. Many fires in vacant buildings, so common in recent years, are set by vandals. Vandals also set fires in abandoned cars, garbage cans, and so on; junk fires are also started as a protest to local conditions and for "instant urban renewal." Vagrants and drug users sometimes set fires. Vandalism fires seem to be increasing at a fairly rapid rate.[14]

Crime Concealment, Diversionary Tactics. Criminals sometimes set fires to obliterate the evidence of burglaries, larcenies, and murders. The fire may destroy evidence that a crime was committed, may obscure evidence connecting the perpetrator to the crime, or make visual identification of a murder victim impossible or difficult. (For a fur-

ther discussion of fire deaths, see Chapter 10, "Injury and Death Investigation.") People set fires to destroy records that contain evidence of embezzlement, forgery, or fraud. Arson has also been used to divert attention while the perpetrator burglarizes another building and to cover attempted escapes from jails, prisons, and state hospitals.

Profits, Insurance Fraud. Some people profit from arson. If a property is insured, the owner no longer wants it, and the value of the policy is greater than the market value, then the insured may defraud the insurance company by burning the property. (Such a situation is known as a moral hazard.)

In a typical case, a businessman finds himself in financial straits and decides that the easiest way out is to "sell the business to the insurance company." His financial problems may have stemmed from a large inventory of unsalable seasonal goods, an outmoded plant that requires expensive retooling, a building requiring extensive renovation to meet fire or safety standards, foreclosure of a mortgage, adverse market conditions, obsolete merchandise, poor management, or loss of value due to changed circumstances such as the relocation of a main highway.

Another common type of insurance fraud involves the purchase of property, generally a vacant building in an economically depressed section of a city. The property is insured for more than its worth. Arson destroys the property and results in a substantial profit on the investment. The owner often places the deeds of such properties in the names of "straw parties" to avoid anyone recognizing a pattern of fires on properties he owns. For example, several years ago a man bought two properties in central St. Louis for $6,000 and placed the deeds in the names of two fictitious parties. Within two years, there had been a serious fire of suspicious origin on each property, with the insurance payments totalling $33,424. This same property owner had received over $415,000 in insurance payments for 54 fires occurring within two years. The owner was subsequently convicted of arson for one of these fires.[15]

In some large cities, professional arson rings have defrauded insurance companies of millions of dollars. In Detroit, 57 people were charged with 186 counts of arson.[16] In a typical operation, a mortgage company employee alerted a dishonest repair contractor of an impending foreclosure. The contractor, who was a member of the ring, persuaded the homeowner to contract with him for fire damage repairs. The contractor then arranged for a professional "torch" to set the fire when the insured was absent. After the fire, the contractor repaired the building with substandard materials (which would readily burn the next time) at a substantial profit, and the homeowner netted a small amount after paying off the torch, who charged an average of $1,500 per fire.

Arson also has been used by insurance adjusters to secure contracts to adjust fire losses; by insurance agents to stimulate business; by businesses to eliminate competitors; by people seeking employment as watchmen, firefighters, or police officers; and by salvage handlers who want to purchase or steal salvaged materials such as copper plumbing or bricks. Some welfare recipients try to obtain a cash moving allowance by starting fires in their apartments.

Intimidation, Extortion, Sabotage. Arson has been used by striking workers and by employers to intimidate the other side during strikes. It has been used by criminals, particularly mobsters, for intimidating witnesses and for extortion.

Psychiatric Afflictions—the Pyromaniac and Schizophrenic Fire-setter. Pyromaniacs differ characteristically from other arsonists in that they lack conscious motivation for their fire-setting. In fact, they are considered by many to be motiveless. They may derive sensual satisfaction from setting fires. Pyromaniacs have been described as setting their fires for no practical reason and no material profit. In one study, the pyromaniac represented 60 percent of the sample population. Of this number, 241 expressed receiving some sort of satisfaction from the fire. The remaining 447 offenders offered no special reason or persistent interest beyond the fact that something within them forced them to set fires.[17]

The urge to set fires has been referred to as an irresistible impulse. However, authorities should be cautioned against accepting this explanation. Some researchers have postulated that pyromania releases sexual tension; others reject it as a major motive. In another study of pyromania, only a small percentage of subjects claimed to receive sexual gratification from fire-setting.[18]

Psychosis is generally defined as a severe form of personality decompensation characterized by marked impairment of contact with reality and personal and social functioning. Delusions, hallucinations, emotional blunting, and bizarre behavior may also be present in varying degrees. The most serious of all psychotic disorders is schizophrenia, which has been defined as "a group of psychotic disorders characterized by gross distortions of reality, withdrawal from social interaction, and disorganization and fragmentation of perception, thought, and emotion."[19]

In one study of 1,145 male fire-setters, 13.4 percent could be classified as psychotic. These fire-setters seemed distinct from others in that their fires were set for suicidal purposes, or their motives were delusional in character, or they manifested bizarre behavior during or immediately after the firesetting. Nonetheless, psychotic fire-setters also fell within other categories, such as those of revenge fire-setter and pyromaniac.[20]

Political Fires, Terrorist Fires. Political fires are set to dramatize an issue, embarrass authorities or political opponents, or to intimidate or extort for political reasons. Fires that were set to protest the Vietnam War and other military activities fall into this category, as do most "bank burnings," some fires associated with racial protest, and some generalized antiestablishment fires. Sometimes these fires have been carefully planned by revolutionary groups who attack responding units, open fire hydrants to deplete water supplies, place bombs on the premises, and set diversionary fires. This type of fire increased considerably during the 1960s and was closely correlated with the rise of civil disturbances and bombings.[21]

Vanity, Hero Fires. On occasion the person who "discovers" a fire turns out to be the one who started it, and did so to be a hero.

> In a recent case, a private guard company hired extra personnel and soon promoted one to sergeant. After a while, the company decided that the extra guards were not needed and discussed reducing the

force. This reduction would have resulted in a demotion for the sergeant. Shortly thereafter, a fire was "discovered" by the sergeant. His quick action meant that the fire was confined, although it did cause thousands of dollars worth of damage. A polygraph examination showed reactions indicative of deception, and the sergeant confessed to a police lieutenant that he had in fact set the fire. His criminal record revealed he had recently been released from a mental institution in another state and that he had been sent there in lieu of state prison.

The fire investigator must look for any overlap among types of fires, such as pathological, profit for employment, and vanity.

The setting of fires by police officers and fire fighters, although relatively rare, does occur. Although sometimes volunteer fire fighters might set a fire with a profit motive, those who are paid on an hourly or individual basis most often do so because they like to fight fires and there is no activity in the neighborhood. They might also like to save people and property and be called heroes. Babysitters sometimes find a need to be "recognized" and they may start fires where they are working, discover the fire, and "save the child."

A Typical Female Fire-setter. The female arsonist usually burns her own property, rarely that of an employer or neighbor. Her motives may be similar to those of male fire-setters, but she seems to have more self-destructive tendencies. In one study of 201 female fire-setters, most were found mentally defective. One third were psychotic, primarily schizophrenic. They were described generally as older women who were lonely, unhappy, and in despair.[23]

The Child Fire-setter. Authorities on fire-setting behavior believe that repetitive or chronic fire-setting by children represents a severe behavior symptom or psychological disturbance. For the disturbed child, fire-setting becomes an outlet for vengeful, hostile reactions, resentment, and defiance of authority.

In one study of 60 child fire-setters, 60 percent were between six and eight years of age and had the following characteristics:

- They set fires with fantasies of burning a member of the family who had withheld love or was a serious rival for parental attention.
- Most fires were started in or near their homes.
- The fires usually were symbolic, caused little damage, and were extinguished by the child.
- Prior to the fire-setting, the child often had anxious dreams and fantasies of devils and ghosts.
- They suffered acute anxiety over their dreams, fantasies, and sexual preoccupations. All experienced sexual conflicts. Most actively masturbated, some participated in mutual masturbation, sodomy, and fellatio.
- Many of the boys who were bed wetters were also passive.
- Many had learning disabilities.
- Some had physical handicaps.
- They also demonstrated other forms of asocial behavior, including truancy, stealing, running away, hyperactivity, and aggressive behavior.
- Some were orphans and institutionalized.
- Their home environments were pathological or broken. Many had absent or ineffective fathers.
- They lacked a sense of security, love, and attention.

The Adolescent Fire-setter. There have been extensive studies on adolescent fire-setting. One study of adolescent male fire-setters showed that home-centered fire-setting diminished as the age of the fire-setter increased. Scenes of fires shifted to schools, churches, factories, and homes of strangers.

These targets were preferred by adolescents aged 12 to 16. The highest incidence of fire-setting at schools involved 12- to 14-year-olds. Fires directed at schools were generally associated with adolescents who had school problems and were motivated by revenge. These fires often were preceded by theft, vandalism, and harassment of teachers. Defective intelligence was not found to be a factor in adolescent firesetting until they reached the age of 16.[24]

Common characteristics of adolescent fire-setters include: a history of delinquency, disruptive home environment, pathological personality development, sexual immaturity, aggressive or destructive behavior, poor social adjustment, emotional disturbance, and poor academic achievement. Some researchers have suggested that adolescents set fires for excitement.

Whatever the motive, vandalism fires appear to represent 80 percent of adolescent fire-setting. Adolescent fire-setters generally work in pairs or groups, in which one boy assumes a dominant role and the others assume a submissive role.

DETECTION AND RECOVERY OF FIRE ACCELERANT RESIDUES

Because flammable liquids flow to the lowest level, heat travels from this level up, and the charring on the bottom of the furniture, ledges, and shelves will be as deep as, or deeper than, the charring on the top.[25]

After a fire has been extinguished, the floor should be carefully cleaned. Many signs may be found there, such as charred, ink-blot-like outlines of flammable liquids. A rug that appears charred all over may, when dried out and swept with a stiff broom, show a distinct pattern of the flammable liquid. This pattern occurs because the liquid is absorbed into the nap of the rug and burns more heavily. Flammable liquid also usually soaks into the joints of wooden flooring, and as a result the joints will be heavily burned.

The mopboards, quarter rounds, and sills should be checked, because flammable liquid often runs under and chars them on the bottom. Corners of the rooms should also be checked, because few floors are perfectly level, and flammable liquid often runs into and burns out the corners. In most common household fires, the corners at floor level are least damaged. The depth of charring in the floor and ceiling should be compared. If the floor is charred as much or more than the ceiling, it indicates a flammable material directly at floor level. In the average fire, the floor temperature is only about one-third that of the ceiling.

When gasoline or similar material is suspected to have been thrown on porches or buildings without basements, especially those with single constructed flooring, the soil beneath the burned area should be checked. The investigator should dig one or two inches into the earth and smell for the odor of flammable liquids. A vapor tester is better for this purpose, because flammables like alcohol have little or no odor in cold, wet earth.

If recovered material is suspected of containing flammable liquids, it should be sealed in an uncoated metal paint can and not in plastic bags or plastic containers. Uncoated metal paint cans can be purchased at auto supply houses. Plastic can give off hydrocarbons that contaminate the material. The container should be tightly sealed to minimize evaporation or contamination. Evidence tape should be used to assure integrity of the chain of evidence. The container may also be marked for identification purposes with permanent ink.

Before they can be analyzed, accelerant residues must first be separated from the ashes, wood, carpeting, or other material in which they are found. This extraction is usually accomplished by simple, steam, or vac-uum distillation. These are listed in increasing order of efficiency, particularly for petroleum products, and increasing complexity of apparatus. Steam and vacuum distillation are capable of extracting 65 percent of any gasoline from debris while for fuel oil the efficiencies are 30 percent and 90 percent, respectively.[26]

Some problems remain to be solved in the extraction of accelerants. Simpler, less expensive methods are needed, and a simpler method of removing contaminants (such as adhesives and plasticizers) also are needed that do not damage equipment.[27]

SCIENTIFIC METHODS IN ARSON INVESTIGATION

The presence of flammable liquids may establish arson and sometimes link a suspect to the fire. The objection is sometimes raised that identifiable amounts of liquid fire accelerants rarely survive a fire, and efforts to detect them would be largely wasted. But arson investigators often find accelerant residues, and accelerants can survive fires. One expert, for example, performed the following experiment. He poured 2½ gallons of kerosene over furniture and rugs in one room of a wooden building, one gallon of gasoline over straw in another room, and left a trail of gasoline as a fuse. The building was allowed to burn freely and completely. He was able to extract identifiable amounts (more than one milliliter*) of both kerosene and gasoline from the debris.[28]

The areas most likely to contain residues of liquid fire accelerants—floors, carpets, and soil—are likely to have the lowest temperatures during the fire and may have insufficient oxygen to support the complete

---

* There are approximately thirty milliliters in a fluid ounce.

combustion of accelerant. Porous or cracked floors may allow accelerants to seep through to underlying earth. Numerous instances have been recounted of the excellent retention properties of soil for flammable liquid.[29] Another place where accelerants may be discovered is on the clothes and shoes of a suspect.

Because each method of accelerant detection (including the human nose) has a threshold of sensitivity, another question which arises is the vapor concentration which is produced by accelerant residues. Some idea of the order of magnitude can be obtained from the experiment of two experts. They burned small (two-milliliter) samples of various accelerants for thirty seconds and then measured vapor concentrations ranging upward from sixty parts vapor per million of air—within the range of detection of currently available portable detectors and generally, but not always, well above readings produced by hydrocarbons from such things as burnt wood and burnt mattresses.[30]

Another way of looking at the potential vapor concentration is to consider the following hypothetical case. Suppose that a gallon of gasoline is used to accelerate a fire in a fifteen by fifteen by eight foot room and that 1 percent (thirty-nine milliliters) survives the fire in cracks in the floor. (The residue would consist of higher boiling point components, such as naphthalene.) The subsequent evaporation of one milliliter (3 percent) of the residue would produce an average vapor concentration of 2.7 parts per million throughout the entire room. Such a concentration can be detected with available equipment. Ventilation of the room, of course, dissipates the vapor and generally causes the vapor concentration to be highest at the points where the residues are located, a situation that can be used to advantage in locating evidence samples to be preserved for laboratory analysis.

DETECTION OF FIRE ACCELERANTS

Several types of portable equipment are available to the arson investigator for detecting residues of flammable liquids at fire scenes. Some of these use chemical color tests, catalytic combustion, flame ionization, gas chromatographs, and infrared spectrophotometers. The sensitivities, limitations, advantages, and disadvantages of each of these are discussed in the following sections.

Olfactory Detection. The sensitivity of the human nose to gasoline vapor is about one part per 10 million. Gasoline is a complex mixture of chemical compounds, the proportions of which vary with the source of the crude oil and the type of process used in its manufacture. Benzene and other aromatic hydrocarbons, for example, may constitute from 0.1 percent to 40 percent of the mixture. Although no conclusive data on the sensitivity of the nose to gasoline is available, the sensitivity of the nose to benzene vapor is 0.015 parts per million. Assuming that 15 percent (or more) of gasoline vapor consists of aromatic hydrocarbons to which the nose is as sensitive as it is to benzene, then the sensitivity to gasoline is one part in 10 million (or greater). Thus, the nose is as sensitive as any of the currently available detecting equipment. But there are flammable liquids to which the nose is not sensitive. Another problem is the tendency of the nose to lose its sensitivity to an odor after prolonged or intense exposure to it. Further, the odor of fire accelerants may be masked by another strong odor such as that of burnt debris. In fact, in one case an arsonist attempted to camouflage gasoline by mixing it with vanilla.[31] Finally, it may be inconvenient or impossible to search with the nose for accelerant odors along floors or in recessed areas.[32]

Chemical Color Test Detectors. Chemical color tests may be used to detect both liquid accelerant residues and their vapors. Certain dyes indicate the presence of hydrocarbons by turning red. Dyes are less sensitive and less specific to flammable liquids than other available methods. Dyes also may interfere with laboratory identification of the accelerant. Hydrocarbon vapors can be detected by pumping a suspected sample through a glass container of reagent that changes color in the presence of hydrocarbons. The reported sensitivity of this method is on the order of one part per thousand. Again, the method is less sensitive and less specific (reacts to hydrocarbons which are not fire accelerants) than others available. Its main advantages are low cost (approximately $100 for the vapor detector) and simplicity.[33] (See Figure 16-7.)

Catalytic Combustion Detector. The most common flammable vapor detector operates on the catalytic combustion principle and is popularly known as a sniffer, combustible gas indicator, explosimeter, or vapor detector. They are portable, moderate in cost ($200 to

---

FIGURE 16-7   Firefighter Using a Hydrocarbon Detector in Testing for the Presence of Accelerants at the Scene of a Suspected Arson

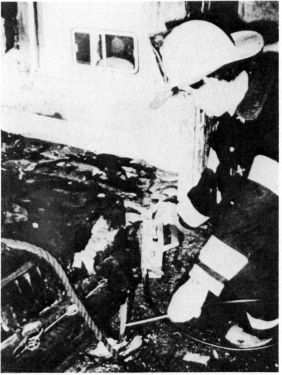

Courtesy New York State Office of Fire Prevention and Control, Albany, New York

$800), and fairly simple to operate. Vapor samples are pumped over a heated, platinum-plated coil of wire which causes any combustible gas present to oxidize. The heat from the oxidation raises the electrical resistance of the coil, and this change in resistance is measured electronically. A sensitivity (to hexane vapor) on the order of a few parts per million can be achieved with this method. Because oxygen is required for the operation of the detector, its sensitivity is reduced in oxygen-deficient areas, but these are unlikely to occur in arson investigations. (An internal source of oxygen could be fitted to a detector if required.) Another problem is the gradual loss of sensitivity when this type of detector is exposed to gasoline containing lead. Lead deposits form on the platinum catalyst and interfere with its operation.[34]

Flame Ionization Detector. In the flame ionization detector, the sample gas is mixed with hydrogen and the mixture burned. Ionized molecules are produced in the flame in proportion to the amount of combustible organic gases in the sample. (Pure hydrogen, air, and water vapor produce little ionization.) The degree of ionization is then measured by electrometer. The sensitivity of this method (to methane) is on the order of one part in ten million. It is thus more sensitive but more complex and expensive (approximately $3,000) than the catalytic combustion method.

Gas Liquid Chromatograph (GLC). The portable gas chromatograph adapted for field use, sometimes called the arson chromatograph, is one of the most common in arson investigations. The sample gas is first separated into components based on the speed with which they travel through a tube filled with packing material. The amounts of each component are then measured by either a catalytic combustion or flame ionization detector. The sensitivity ranges from a few

hundredths of a part per million to a few parts per million, depending on the type of detector used. The main advantage is specificity because of the preliminary separation process. The main disadvantages are its size, weight, and cost ($2,000 to $4,000). Also, the time required for the analysis of each sample is about one-half hour, a disadvantage in some situations. In addition, there is a set up time of about one hour. The operation of the gas chromatograph requires a certain amount of technical training.

Infrared Spectrophotometer. Infrared spectrophotometers can achieve high specificity to flammable liquids and high sensitivity (on the order of hundredths of a part per million). Infrared light of varying wavelengths is directed through the sample, and the amount of light passing through is plotted on a pen recorder. The recording is compared with those of known compounds to determine the identity of the sample. Because the chemical bonds in a compound determine how it absorbs infrared radiation, these recordings (called spectrograms) are unique for different compounds. However, evidence mixed with impurities must be purified before it can be successfully identified. In particular, since water vapor absorbs infrared light, it interferes with the identification of flammable vapors. This is a disadvantage in arson investigation, where water is commonly present. A final disadvantage is the high cost of this type of detector ($3,000 to $5,000).

Ultraviolet Fluorescence. This relatively new method may prove useful in arson investigation. The procedure consists of illuminating the darkened fire scene with an ultraviolet lamp. Certain substances, including constituents of gasoline and its residue, absorb the ultraviolet and release it as visible light. They appear to glow against the darkened background. The color of the glow is affected by exposure to heat, and so the method also can be used to locate the point of origin of a fire. The only equipment required is an ultraviolet lamp and a portable power supply (total cost: $50 to $200). The sensitivity of the method appears comparable to that of other methods of detection. The main disadvantage of the method is that it requires extensive testing, particularly to identify those fire accelerants to which it does not respond.[35]

===== **INTERVIEWS** =====

In order to establish possible motives and develop suspects, the arson investigator must interview people who might know about the fire and how it started. The following kinds of different people may provide information.[36]

POSSIBLE WITNESSES

Tenants of buildings; tenants of surrounding buildings; businesspeople in surrounding buildings; customers of businesses in buildings; customers of businesses in surrounding buildings; passersby, including bus route drivers, taxi drivers, delivery people (milk, bread), garbage collectors, police patrols, people waiting for buses and taxis.

Questions to Be Asked. Did you observe the fire? At what time did you first observe the fire? In what part of the building did you observe the fire? What called your attention to the building? Did you see any people entering or leaving the building before the fire? Did you recognize them? Can you describe them? Did you observe any vehicles in the area of the fire? Can you describe them? Can you describe the smoke and the color of the flame? How quickly did the fire spread? Was the building burning in more than one place? Did you detect any unusual odors? Did you observe anything else?

INTERVIEW OF FIREFIGHTERS AT THE SCENE

Firefighters can be an invaluable source of information to arson investigators because of their technical knowledge and because of what they observed at a fire.

Questions to Be Asked. What time was the alarm received? What time did you arrive at the scene of fire? Was your route to the scene blocked? What was the extent of burning when you arrived? Were doors and windows locked? Were the entrances or passageways blocked? What kind of fire was it? What was the spread speed of the fire? In what area(s) did the fire start? How near was the fire to the roof? Was there evidence of the use of an accelerant? Was any evidence of arson recovered? Did the building have a fire alarm system? Was it operating? Was there any evidence of tampering with the alarm system? Did the building have a sprinkler system? Did it operate? Was there any evidence of tampering with the sprinkler system? Was there anyone present in the building when you arrived? Who was the person in the building? Did that person say anything to you? Were there any people present at the scene when you arrived? Who were they? Did you observe any vehicles at or leaving the scene when you arrived? Can you describe them? Were there contents in the building? Was there evidence that contents had been removed? Was the owner present? Did the owner make a statement? What did the owner say? What is the fire history of the building? What is the fire history of the area?

INTERVIEW OF INSURANCE PERSONNEL

The profit in many arson-for-profit cases is an insurance payment. Three classes of people may be interviewed to determine if the profit centers around an insurance claim.

They are the insurance agent or broker, the insurance adjuster, and the insurance investigator.

Questions to Ask the Agent or Broker. Who is the insured? Is there more than one insured? Is the insured the beneficiary? What type of policy was issued? What is the amount of the policy? When was it issued? When does it expire? What is the premium? Are payments up to date? Have there been any increases in the amount of coverage? What amount? When did the increase take effect? What was the reason for the increase? Are there any special provisions in the policy (for example, interruption of business or rental income)? What are they, and when did they take effect? Why? Does the insured have any other policies? Were there previous losses at the location of the fire? Were there losses at other locations owned by the insured?

Questions to Ask the Insurance Claims Adjuster. Did you take a sworn statement from the insured? Did the insured submit documents regarding proof of loss, value of contents, bills of lading, value of building, and the like? Did you inspect the fire scene? Did you inspect the fire scene with a public insurance adjuster? Did you and the public adjuster agree on the cost of the loss? Have you dealt with this public adjuster before? Has he or she represented this owner before? Has the insured had any other losses with this company? If so, get details.

Questions to Ask the Insurance Investigator. Were you able to determine the cause of the fire? Did you collect any evidence? Who analyzed the evidence? What were the results of the analysis? Was the cause of the fire inconsistent with the state of the building as known through underwriting examination? Have you investigated past fires at the location? Have you investigated past fires involving the insured? What were the results of the investigations? Have you had prior investigations involving the public adjuster? Have you had prior investigations involving buildings handled by the same insurance agent or broker? What were the results of these investigations? Does this fire fit into a pattern of fires of recent origin in this area? What are the similarities? What are the differences? Have you taken any statements in connection with this burning? Whose statements did you take? What do they reveal?

There may be restrictions on the amount of information insurance personnel can turn over without a subpoena, but the investigator should be able to determine enough to indicate whether a subpoena or search warrant would prove fruitful.

OTHER WITNESSES CONCERNING FINANCES OF INSURED

A number of other people may have information on the finances of the owner; this information may indicate how the owner stood to profit from the burning.

Questions to Ask Business Associates, Creditors, and Competitors. How long have you known the owner/insured? What is the nature of your relationship with the owner/insured? Do you have any information on the financial position of the business? Is the owner/insured competitive with similar businesses? Have there been recent technological advances that would threaten the owner/insured's position? Has there been a recent increase in competition that would affect the owner/insured's position? Have changes in the economy affected the owner/insured's position? Has the owner/insured had recent difficulty in paying creditors? Has the owner/insured's amount of debt increased recently? Has the owner/insured lost key employees lately? Has the location where the owner/insured does business changed for the worse recently? Has the owner/insured increased the mortgage or taken out a second or third mortgage? Has the owner/insured had difficulty making mortgage payments? Do you have any other information about the owner/insured's financial position?

NEWS MEDIA PERSONNEL

This category would include both the print and electronic media. Individuals affiliated with these groups may have noticed something of value to the investigator or perhaps have films of the fire and fire scene. For example, if the arsonist remained in the area after the fire and mingled with spectators, his or her presence may be captured on film and prove quite valuable in an investigation.

THE MEDICAL EXAMINER

The autopsy should reveal whether any victim found dead in the fire was dead or alive before the fire started and what the cause of death was. It is not uncommon for a person to be murdered and the scene made to appear as if the person had been killed by fire. See Chapter 10, "Injury and Death Investigation," for more detailed discussion of fire deaths.

INTERVIEWING A SUSPECT

The following is based on the assumption that the person to be interviewed is involved in arson for profit, that the investigator has enough evidence for an arrest or enough to convince the subject that he or she is liable to arrest, and that the subject is more valuable to the investigation in a cooperative role than as a defendant.

Questions to Ask the Subject. Are you willing to cooperate in this investigation? How many other people are involved in the arson-for-profit scheme? How are they involved? What role does each person play in the

scheme? Explain (in detail) how the scheme works. How did you first become involved in the scheme? How did you meet the other participants? Where did you meet the other participants? Are you still in contact with the other participants? How often do you see them? Where do you see them? What do you talk about when you meet with them? Would you be able to record your conversation with them? Are you willing to record your conversations with them? Would you be willing to introduce an undercover investigator into the group? Could you introduce an undercover investigator into the group without their becoming suspicious? How far in advance of an arson are you told about it? What role do you play in connection with the arson (torch, driver, pigeon, fence, and so forth)? Are you willing to be the affiant of a search warrant? Are you willing to testify before a grand jury? Are you willing to testify at trial? Do you have information on other arson-for-profit schemes?

Questions to Ask the Torch, Specifically. What method(s) was (were) used to accomplish the arson? Specify whether it was an incendiary device, gasoline or other flammable fluid, or other. If an incendiary device was used, be specific as to the type of device. Where did you obtain the incendiary device? If it was improvised, who made it? How much did it cost? Who paid for the incendiary device? Was it paid for by cash or check? If gasoline or other flammable fluid was used, where was it obtained? How much was obtained and used? Are any special techniques used in setting a fire or causing an explosion to avoid detection?

INTERVIEWING THE OWNER/TARGET

The target of the investigation may be an owner, landlord, fire broker, or the like. The interview should take place after obtaining the background information on the fire and after interviewing the individuals previously listed.

General Questions to Ask the Target. Tell me in your own words what you know about this fire. When did you first hear of the arson? Who told you? Where were you, and what were you doing before, during, and after the arson? Who was with you? Do you know who committed the arson? Do you have any knowledge of any previous fire at the building? Do you have any knowledge of any previous incidents of any kind and at any location owned or rented by the owner/occupant of the building? Do you know of any recent changes in insurance coverage? Do you know the owner of the arson property? Describe your relationship to the owner. Do you have any financial interest in the burned property?

Questions to Ask the Owner. Tell me in your own words what you know about this fire. How long have you owned the burned property? What was the purchase price? What was the total amount of the mortgage? What is your insurance company? agent? broker? public adjuster? How much insurance do you carry? Is there more than one policy on this property? on its contents? on rental or business interruption? Have you increased your insurance coverage on the property in the past year? If so, why and at whose suggestion? Have you ever received an insurance cancellation notice on this property? Where were you at the time of the fire? When did you first hear of the arson? Who told you? When were you last in the building? Was the building secured? If so, in what manner? Who else has access to or keys to the building? Who was the last person to leave the building? Do you have any knowledge that the sprinkler system or burglar alarm system was on and working? Indicate the name and address of all lien holders. What is the amount of each lien? What was the value of the inventory on hand immediately prior to

the fire? Can you provide documentation for this value? Was any inventory removed from the premises prior to the fire? If yes, by whom and for what purposes? Where did it go, and why was it removed? Was any inventory removed from the premises after the fire? If yes, by whom and for what purpose? List the inventory so removed and its value. Did you set the fire or cause it to be set? Do you know who set it?

INTERVIEWING A POTENTIAL INFORMANT WHO IS NOT A SUSPECT

Before interviewing a potential informant who is not a suspect, investigative efforts should be made to determine if the informant has any police record and, if so, if it could have any bearing on the reliability of the information provided. For example, if a potential informant has previously been convicted of arson and perjury, then the investigator should be cautious in acting on his or her information.

The following are some questions such an individual should be asked.

Questions to Ask a Potential Informant. How are you currently supporting yourself? Do you have any pending prosecutions against you? Where? What are you charged with? Do you have any information about arson for profit in this city, county, state? How did you acquire this information? Do you know anyone engaged in arson for profit? What roles does that person play in the scheme? How do you know this? What is your relationship with this person or persons—loanshark, bookmaker, fence, or the like? Where does this person live, frequent? Who are his or her associates? Do you know them? Are they part of the scheme? Have you been asked to involve yourself in the scheme? In what way? Have any of these people talked freely to you about their activities? Have they talked in your presence? What was said? Can you engage them in conversation about past arsons? future arsons? Would they be suspicious of you? Could you wear a concealed recorder during conversation? Could you introduce an undercover officer into the group? Would you be willing to testify before a grand jury? Would you be willing to testify at trial? Would you be willing to swear to an affidavit for a search warrant? Would you be willing to swear to an eavesdropping warrant? What do you expect in return for your help?

ARSON SUSPECT

In some arson investigations, a single prime suspect may emerge and investigative efforts focused accordingly. However, in most cases, a number of suspects emerge, and merely establishing that one or more of them had a motive to set the fire is not enough proof for an arrest and conviction. The investigator must also determine which of the suspects had the opportunity and the means to commit the crime. This determination must be related to the background, personal characteristics, past activities, and financial status of each of the suspects. For example, ten people may have had a chance to set the fire, but only four or five may have had a motive, and of this number, perhaps only one or two would risk an arson conviction for the expected profit or satisfaction.

In probing an arson fire, seldom does direct evidence link a suspect with a fire. Because arsonists tend to take elaborate precautions not to be seen near the fire, they are seldom caught in the act. It may be best for the investigator to concentrate on gathering circumstantial evidence and some provable facts from which valid conclusions can be drawn. For example, let us assume that the fire which occurred in a warehouse was ignited by a timing device—a slow burning candle attached to some flammable material triggered two hours before the fire actually

started. The owner, who is also a prime suspect, is identified but can prove his whereabouts at the time of the fire. However, he cannot prove where he was two hours before the fire. In addition, the structure was locked when the fire department arrived to fight the fire, and the owner is the only one with a set of keys. The owner also took a large insurance policy out on the warehouse a short time ago.

Although far more evidence would likely be needed to arrest and convict the owner, there is considerable justification for focusing a considerable amount of the investigation in his direction. If some other evidence is found to link him more directly to the fire (candles and flammable material found in the trunk of his car), then the circumstantial evidence becomes considerably important.

INVESTIGATION OF AUTOMOBILE FIRES

Along with the general increase in crimes in the United States, we also find an increase in automobile fires. Many of the criminal fires occur when stolen vehicles have been stripped of valuable parts and the rest burnt to destroy the evidence. However, as in other fire investigations, the investigator first must eliminate natural and accidental causes of fire. Investigators who make unsubstantiated remarks about the origin of fires can damage their own and possible suspects' reputations.[37]

INSPECTION OF SALVAGE

The successful investigation of automobile fire losses originates with basic lines of inquiry.[38] First an inspection of the salvage must be completed for information on the origin and possible motive for the fire; second, an investigation must be made of the car owner for evidence of intent, motive, and opportunity; third, witnesses who might have information must be questioned; and last, the owner must be questioned to establish his or her knowledge of the fire and to verify information.

Generally investigators inspect the burnt automobile before contacting the owner, and the inspection is made as soon after the fire as possible. The inspection starts where the fire apparently originated. In accidental fires, this will normally be that part of the vehicle which is the most badly damaged from the intensity of the heat. Accidental fires usually spread in diminishing degree from the point of origin according to prevailing conditions. Conditions include direction and velocity of wind and or materials on which flames feed, such as upholstery, gasoline in the tank, woodwork, or other similarly flammable parts of the vehicle. When there are significant variations in these patterns, arson emerges as a possibility. Arson fires started with flammable materials usually show intense heat in more than one place. The investigator should carefully note the extent of the fire and its path. This information may prove valuable in the later questioning of the owner or witnesses.

The car also should be inspected for the removal of equipment such as stereo, heater, air horns, fog lights, and so forth. Notice should also be made of other irregularities such as old tires on new cars or missing spare tires.

INSPECTION OF THE FUEL SYSTEM

The Gas Tank. The investigator should determine whether the cap to the gas tank was in place at the time of the fire. Sometimes gasoline to start the fire is siphoned from the tank and the cap carelessly left off. If the cap is blown off, it will show effects of an explosion. The drain plug in the bottom of the tank should be checked. If it has been blown out or melted down, the collar usually

goes with it. In addition, if it was removed or loosened before the fire, there might be evidence of fresh tool marks, especially pliers marks, on it.

Inspection of Gas Line. The gas lines should be examined for breaks between the tank and the fuel pump. Breaks should be examined for tool marks. Some arsonists disconnect the line below the tank to obtain gasoline to start the fire and fail to replace the line.

Inspection of Fuel Pump. Gasoline to start the fire is sometimes obtained by disconnecting the line from the fuel pump and running the starter. If the fuel pump is melted, there should be evidence of fire on the sidepans. If the fuel pump was disconnected to allow the gasoline to run out and then set on fire, there may be carbon deposits inside the gas line at the fuel pump.

The investigator should establish whether parts of the fuel pump are missing. If key parts of the fuel system are missing, and the owner says that the vehicle was running at the time of the fire, then there is strong reason to suspect arson.

Inspection of the Electrical System. A short circuit in the electric wiring is the most common excuse offered for automobile fires. The chances of a modern automobile's burning up from a short in the wiring are negligible. Engineers have virtually eliminated this hazard. If a fire in fact did start from malfunctions in the electrical system, there generally is enough evidence to substantiate it.

The wires near where the fire started should be inspected. If the wires are not melted completely, a short can be located. A short melts the strands of wire apart and causes small beads of melted wire to form on the ends. Wires that are burnt in two have sharp points. If the fire started in an electrical system, the system must be close to a flammable substance for the fire to spread. If a fire started from a short while the motor was running, the distributor points will be stuck or fused.

Inspection of the Motor, Radiator, and Parts Under and Near the Hood. The only possible place for an accidental fire to start at this location is around the fuel pump, carburetor, and at the wiring. Any evidence of a fire on the front lower part of the motor not attributable to these parts indicates the use of flammables. If lead is melted from any lower or outside seams of the radiator, it is strong evidence of flammables. The fan belt does not usually burn in an accidental fire.

Gasoline on the motor sometimes causes the rubber cushions for the front of the mo-

FIGURE 16-8

Ax Holes

Note: External Damage Not Result of Fire

Owner admitted burning his car out of frustration because of recurring mechanical problems. Before burning the car, he beat it with an axe. Notice damage to right side of car and damaged tail lights.

Courtesy Thomas Evans, Pinellas County (Florida) Sheriff's Office

tor to show evidence of fire. This evidence does not occur in accidental fires.

The radiator should also be checked. A badly burnt lower right corner indicates that the gas line from the fuel pump to the carburetor was disconnected, the starter run to pump out gasoline through the fuel pump, and then the gasoline set on fire.

Inspection of the Body. The body of the car is usually so badly burnt as to afford little evidence. However, signs of the intensity of heat sometimes point to the use of an inflammable. An excessive amount of flammable material may run through the floor of the car and burn underneath, causing oil or gasoline soot to form on the underside of the car. An examination should be made for this soot. If the hood was raised during the fire, the paint on the top panels may be blistered but not be burnt off where the two panels touched. If the wind was blowing from the rear of the car to the front, the paint should be burnt for almost the length of the hood; the radiator core will be burnt; but there will not have been enough fire at the rear of the car to do much damage to the gasoline tank. If the paint on the hood is burnt only an inch or so from the rear toward the front, it would indicate that the wind was blowing from the front of the car toward the rear, in which case the gasoline tank may be badly damaged, but the radiator will be intact.

CONTACT WITH OWNERS

Before interviewing the owner of the car, the investigator should determine as completely as possible the character of the owner. This information may prove quite useful during the interview. The importance of preplanning the interview cannot be overemphasized. The more facts the investigator has available, the greater the probability of a successful clearance or later conviction.

Information should be obtained from the owner about the details of the purchase, such as date, cost, trade in, down payment, amount of mortgage due, payments past due, name of salesperson, and so forth. The investigator should also inquire about the general condition of the car at the time of the fire and ask about defects, mileage, presence or absence of unusual equipment, or recent repairs.

During this interview, clues to arson may emerge. Although there are many possible motives for the arson of a vehicle, they tend to fall into the following categories.

Dissatisfaction with the Car because of mechanical trouble; because the car has depreciated in value because of abusive treatment; because the owner believes that the insurance company will pay more for the car than it is worth; or because the owner has no further need for the car.

Domestic Difficulties, including a pending divorce and the belief that the spouse will get the car.

Financial Difficulties, including the unemployment of the owner; illness in the family, hospital and doctor bills; judgment against the owner; business reverses; finance company demands; an owner who lives beyond his or her income.

These are not all the motives, but the arson investigator will find that most motives for arson fall into these categories.

═══════════ QUESTIONS ═══════════

1. If arson is suspected, why should firefighters not disarrange the premises, such as by mopping up or overhauling the scene of the fire, especially at the point of origin?
2. What two factors are needed to cause a fire?

3. What is the "layer checking" technique and how can it assist in determining the cause and origin of a fire?

4. What are some of the more common causes for accidental or natural fires?

5. What types of burn indication can be examined by the arson investigator to assist in determining whether a fire is accidental or incendiary in nature?

6. What are some of the most commonly used ignition and timing devices employed in the commission of arsons?

7. Why can items missing from the fire scene be as valuable as those things remaining at the scene?

8. What are some of the most common motives for arson?

9. What are the major characteristics of the child fire-setter?

10. Why should uncoated metal paint cans (or similar containers) and not plastic bags or containers be used for the storage of material suspected of containing flammable liquids?

11. What are some of the advantages and disadvantages of olfactory detection to determine the presence of fire accelerants at the scene of a fire?

12. What types of individuals might be able to provide information relevant to the fire?

13. What are some of the most common reasons for the owner of a vehicle either to have it burned by someone or to burn it himself?

NOTES

1. K. D. Moll, *Arson, Vandalism and Violence: Law Enforcement Problems Affecting Fire Departments* (Washington, D.C.: Government Printing Office, 1977), pp. 20–21.

2. C. W. Stickney, "Recognizing Where Arson Exists," *Fireman Magazine,* September–December 1960, p. 3.

3. *Touched off by Human Hands,* 1979. This booklet was originally published by the Illinois Advisory Committee on Arson Prevention in Cooperation with the Illinois Chapter of the International Association of Arson Investigation and was reprinted for distribution by the State Farm Fire and Casualty Company, Bloomington, Ill. Much of the information dealing with the topic "Where and How Did the Fire Start" was taken from this source, pp. 7–11.

4. Stickney, "Recognizing Where Arson Exists," p. 4.

5. Ibid., p. 8.

6. Ibid.

7. C. W. Stickney, "Recognizing Where Arson Exists," *Fire and Arson Investigator,* October–December 1970; W. A. Derr, "Wildland Fire Investigation: Information From Objects." Presented at the 18th Annual Fire and Arson Investigators Seminar, Palm Springs, Calif., June 14–18, 1971.

8. Derr, "Wildland Fire Investigation."

9. P. L. Kirk, *Fire Investigation* (New York: John Wiley and Sons, Inc., 1969), p. 75.

10. B. P. Battle and P. B. Weston, *Arson: A Handbook of Detection and Investigation* (New York: Arco Publishing, 1972), pp. 19–28. Much of the information dealing with the topic "Fire-Setting Mechanisms" was taken with permission from this source.

11. Much of the information included in the topics "Motives and Typology of Arsonists" and "The Applications of Scientific Methods in Arson Investigation" was taken from J. F. Bourdeau, Q. Y. Kwan, W. E. Faragker, and G. C. Senault, *Arson and Arson Investigation* (Washington, D.C.: Government Printing Office, 1974), and K. D.

Moll, *Arson, Vandalism and Violence: Law Enforcement Problems Affecting Fire Departments.*

12. B. S. Huron, *Elements of Arson Investigation* (New York: Reuben Donnelley, 1972), Chapter 1.

13. Ibid.; Battle and Weston, *Arson: A Handbook of Detection and Investigation*, pp. 34–39.

14. J. A. Inciardi, "The Adult Firesetter, A Typology," *Criminology,* August 1970, pp. 145–155.

15. "The Undeclared War on the Nation's Firemen," *Parade,* July 18, 1971, p. 4. S. B. Defty, "$6,000 Buildings Burn, $33,424 is Collected," *St. Louis Post Dispatch,* November 16, 1971. S. B. Defty, "$400,000 Paid on Fires at Green's Properties," *St. Louis Post Dispatch,* February 10, 1972.

16. "Detroit: The Torches Games," *Newsweek,* November 25, 1974, pp. 42–43. Also see George Molnar, Lydia Keitner, and B. Thomas Harwood, "A Comparison of Partner and Solo Arsonists," *Journal of Forensic Sciences,* 1984, Vol. 29, pp. 574–583.

17. Anthony O. Rider, "The Firesetter—A Psychological Profile (Part 2)," *FBI Law Enforcement Bulletin*, July 1980, p. 12. (Much of this discussion and accompanying references have been adapted with permission from this source, pp. 7–17.), and Nolan D. C. Lewis and Helen Yarnell, "Pathological Firesetting (Pyromania)," *Nervous and Mental Disease Monographs,* No. 82 (New York: Coolidge Foundation, 1951), pp. 228–242.

18. Louis H. Gold, "Psychiatric Profile of the Firesetter," *Journal of Forensic Science,* October 1962, p. 407. Lewis and Yarnell, "Pathological Firesetting," p. 118.

19. James C. Coleman et al. *Abnormal Psychology and Modern Life,* 6th ed. (Glenview, Ill.: Scott, Foresman & Co., 1980), p. 395.

20. Lewis and Yarnell, "Pathological Firesetting," pp. 376–377, 428.

21. California Governor's Arson Information Study Group, *Fire Investigation Reporting and Evaluation System* (Sacramento, Calif.: November 1970). International Association of Fire Chiefs Arson Committee Report 1970, *International Fire Chief,* January 1971.

22. E. B. Bates, *Elements of Fire and Arson Investigation* (Santa Cruz, Calif.: Davis Publishing, 1975), pp. 43–44.

23. Anthony O. Rider, "The Firesetter—A Psychological Profile (Part 2)," *FBI Law Enforcement Bulletin,* July 1980, pp. 12–13.

24. Lewis and Yarnell, "Pathological Firesetting," pp. 286–287, 311–345.

25. Stickney, "Recognizing Where Arson Exists," 1960, pp. 11–12.

26. B. B. Caldwell, "The Examination of Exhibits in Suspected Arson Cases," *Royal Canadian Mounted Police Quarterly,* 1957, Vol. 22, pp. 103–108.

27. C. E. Yates, "Recovery and Identification of Flammable Liquids from Suspected Arson Debris," *American Clinical Society Symposium Series B, Forensic Science,* G. Davis, ed. (1975). Bordeau et al., *Arson and Arson Investigation*, pp. 77–83. Much of the information included in "The Applications of Scientific Methods in Arson Investigation" was taken from this source.

28. J. D. Nicol, "Recovery of Flammable Liquids from a Burned Structure," *Fire Engineering,* 1961, Vol. 114, p. 550.

29. D. Q. Burd, "Detection of Traces of Combustible Fluids in Arson Cases," *Journal of Criminal Law, Criminology, and Police Science,* 1960, Vol. 51, pp. 263–264; P. Rajeswaran and P. L. Dirk, "Identification of Gasoline, Waves, Greases, and Asphalts by Evaporation Chromatography," *Microchemical Journal,* 1962, Vol. 6, pp. 21–29.

30. R. Milliard and C. Thomas, "The Combustible Gas Detector (Souffer), An Evaluation," *Fire and Arson Investigator,* January–March 1976, pp. 48-50.

31. D. M. Lucas, "The Identification of Pe-

troleum Products in Forensic Science by Gas Chromatography," *Journal of Forensic Sciences,* 1960, Vol. 5, No. 2, pp. 236–243.

32. Kirk, *Fire Investigation,* pp. 43-44. E. C. Crocker and L. B. Sjostrom, "Odor Detection and Thresholds," *Chemical Engineering News,* 1949, Vol. 27, pp. 1922–1925; H. Zwaardemaber, "Camera Inoorata," *Perfumery and Essential Oil Record,* 1921, Vol. 12, pp. 243–244.

33. P. L. Kirk, *Crime Investigation, Physical Evidence, and The Police Laboratory* (New York: Interscience, 1966), p. 717; H. P. Wonderling, "Arsonists—Their Methods and the Evidence," *The International Association of Arson Investigators Newsletter,* October–December 1953; reprinted in "Selected Articles for Fire and Arson Investigators," *International Association of Arson Investigators,* 1975. K. Ol'Khosvsbaya, "Colormetric Determination of Hydrocarbons, Gasoline, Kerosene and White Spent in the Air of Industrial Installations," *Gigiena Truda i Professional' nye Zabolevaniza,* 1971, Vol. 15, No. 11, pp. 57–58.

34. J. W. Girth, A. Jones, and T. A. Jones, "The Principle of Detection of Flammable Atmospheres by Catalytic Devices," *Combustion and Flame,* 1973, Vol. 21, pp. 303–312.

35. C. M. Lane, "Ultra-Violet Light . . . Gem or Junk," *Fire and Arson Investigator,* December 1975, Vol. 26, No. 2, pp. 40–42.

36. Clifford L. Karchmer and James Greenfield, *Enforcement Manual: Approaches for Combatting Arson-for-Profit Schemes* (Washington, D. C.: Government Printing Office, 1981), pp. 249–252.

37. E. B. Bates, *Elements of Fire and Arson Investigation* (Santa Cruz, Calif.: Davis Publishing, 1977), p. 88.

38. *Manual for the Investigation of Automobile Fires* (Atlanta, Ga.: National Auto Theft Bureau). The remainder of the discussion on the investigation of automobile fires was taken from this source, pp. 30–49.

17

RECOGNITION, CONTROL, AND INVESTIGATION OF DRUG ABUSE

Since the early 1960s, and continuing into the 1980s problems associated with drugs have increasingly taken on new dimensions of importance. Currently, every major police department in this country has assigned—with ample justification—the control of drug abuse and related offenses a top priority. However, the illegal importation, manufacture, sale, and use of drugs has increased more rapidly than the resources to combat them.

Explanations for the phenomenal growth of drug abuse abound in the literature on this subject. Many cite variables associated with certain socioeconomic and political conditions. Many of the explanations are well founded, reasoned, and articulated. But police must deal with the violation itself, not the motivations and human conditions that produce it.

The enforcement tools used most frequently to combat drug-related violations are the law, science and technology, and investigative skills developed through training and experience. This chapter addresses itself to these areas.

If there is a breakdown in any of these three areas it can cause a criminal case to be lost in court, an important investigation to be unproductive, or an enforcement officer to be injured or killed. The probability of breakdowns is less when realistic laws, modern technology, and carefully selected and trained officers, fully supported by enlightened leadership, all combat the problem.

COMPREHENSIVE DRUG ABUSE PREVENTION AND CONTROL ACT OF 1970

The Controlled Substances Act (CSA) is intended to minimize the quantity of drugs available for illegal use. Although the CSA is applicable only to federal officers, many states have used it as a model for their own

524

laws. The CSA is precisely that—an act to control the manufacture and distribution of certain substances. The act covers:

1. The effects of controlling a substance
2. Procedures for bringing a substance under the controls
3. Criteria for determining whether a substance should be controlled.[1]

CRITERIA BY WHICH DRUGS ARE SCHEDULED

The CSA identifies the criteria for including a substance in one of five schedules.[2]

Schedule I

- A high potential for abuse
- No currently accepted medical use in the United States[3]
- A lack of accepted safety for use under medical supervision

Schedule II

- A high potential for abuse
- A currently accepted medical use with severe restrictions
- Abuse may lead to severe psychological or physical dependence

Schedule III

- A lower potential for abuse than the drugs or other substances in Schedules I and II
- A currently accepted medical use in treatment in the United States
- Abuse may lead to moderate physical dependence or high psychological dependence

Schedule IV

- A low potential for abuse relative to drugs or other substances in Schedule III
- A currently accepted medical use in treatment in the United States
- Abuse may lead to limited physical dependence or psychological dependence relative to the drugs or other substances in Schedule III

Schedule V

- A low potential for abuse relative to the drugs or other substances in Schedule IV
- A currently accepted medical use in treatment in the United States
- Abuse may lead to limited physical dependence or psychological dependence relative to the drugs or other substances in Schedule IV

THE CONTROL MECHANISMS

Two agencies share responsibility for enforcing the act: the Food and Drug Administration (FDA) in the Department of Health and Human Services; and the Drug Enforcement Administration (DEA) in the Department of Justice. Nine control mechanisms are imposed on the manufacturing, obtaining, and selling of substances listed under the CSA.

Registration of Handlers. Figures 17-1 and 17-2 summarize controlled substances mechanisms and schedules. Every person who wants to handle a controlled substance must register with the DEA. A number is assigned to each legitimate handler, importer, manufacturer, wholesaler, hospital, pharmacy, physician, and researcher. This number is readily available to suppliers who wish to verify the authenticity of a potential customer, reducing the opportunity for unauthorized transactions. The registration system also excludes people who have been found participating, consciously or not, in the diversion of drugs.

Record-keeping Requirements. Full records must be kept of all manufacturing, purchases, sales, and inventories of controlled substances by each handler. Limited exemptions from this requirement are available to physicians and researchers. From these records, it is possible to trace the flow of a drug

FIGURE 17-1 Control Mechanisms of the Controlled Substances Act

Schedule	Registration	Recordkeeping	Manufacturing Quotas	Distribution Restrictions	Dispensing Limits	Import-Export Narcotic	Import-Export Non-narcotic	Security	Manufacturer/ Distributor Reports to DEA	Criminal Penalties for Trafficking (First Offense) Narcotic	Criminal Penalties for Trafficking (First Offense) Non-narcotic
I	Required	Separate	Yes	Order forms	Research use only	Permit	Permit	Vault type	Yes	15 years/ $25,000	5 years/ $15,000
II	Required	Separate	Yes	Order forms	Rx: written; no refills	Permit	Permit	Vault type	Yes	15 years/ $25,000	5 years/ $15,000
III	Required	Readily retrievable	No *but* Some drugs limited by Schedule II quotas	DEA registration number	Rx: written or oral; with medical authorization. refills up to 5 times in 6 months	Permit	Notice	Surveillance	Yes Narcotic; No Non-narcotic	5 years/ $15,000	5 years/ $15,000
IV	Required	Readily retrievable	No *but* Some drugs limited by Schedule II quotas	DEA registration number	Rx: written or oral; with medical authorization. refills up to 5 times in 6 months	Permit	Notice	Surveillance	No Narcotic; No Non-narcotic	3 years/ $10,000	3 years/ $10,000
V	Required	Readily retrievable	No *but* Some drugs limited by Schedule II quotas	DEA registration number	OTC (Rx drugs limited to MD's order)	Permit to import; Notice to export	Notice	Surveillance	Manufacturer only Narcotic; No Non-narcotic	1 year/ $5,000	1 year/ $5,000

Courtesy Drug Enforcement Administration

FIGURE 17-2 Controlled Substances: Uses and Effects

	Drugs	Schedule*	Often Prescribed Brand Names	Medical Uses	Dependence Potential: Physical	Psychological	Tolerance	Duration of Effects (in hours)	Usual Methods of Administration	Possible Effects	Effects of Overdose	Withdrawal Syndrome
Narcotics	Opium	II	Dover's Powder, Paregoric	Analgesic, antidiarrheal	High	High	Yes	3 to 6	Oral, smoked	Euphoria, drowsiness, respiratory depression, constricted pupils, nausea	Slow and shallow breathing, clammy skin, convulsions, coma, possible death	Watery eyes, runny nose, yawning, loss of appetite, irritability, tremors, panic, chills and sweating, cramps, nausea
	Morphine	II	Morphine	Analgesic	High	High	Yes	3 to 6	Injected, smoked			
	Codeine	III V	Codeine	Analgesic, antitussive	Moderate	Moderate	Yes	3 to 6	Oral, injected			
	Heroin	I	None	None	High	High	Yes	3 to 6	Injected, sniffed			
	Meperidine (Pethidine)	II	Demerol, Pethadol	Analgesic	High	High	Yes	3 to 6	Oral, injected			
	Methadone	II	Dolophine, Methadone, Methadose	Analgesic, heroin substitute	High	High	Yes	12 to 24	Oral, injected			
	Other Narcotics	I II III V	Dilaudid, Leritine, Numorphan, Percodan	Analgesic, antidiarrheal, antitussive	High	High	Yes	3 to 6	Oral, injected			
Depressants	Chloral Hydrate	IV	Noctec, Somnos	Hypnotic	Moderate	Moderate	Probable	5 to 8	Oral	Slurred speech, disorientation, drunken behavior without odor of alcohol	Shallow respiration, cold and clammy skin, dilated pupils, weak and rapid pulse, coma, possible death	Anxiety, insomnia, tremors, delirium, convulsions, possible death
	Barbiturates	II III IV	Amytal, Butisol, Nembutal, Phenobarbital, Seconal, Tuinal	Anesthetic, anti-convulsant, sedation, sleep	High	High	Yes	1 to 16	Oral, injected			
	Glutethimide	III	Doriden	Sedation, sleep	High	High	Yes	4 to 8	Oral			
	Methaqualone	II	Optimil, Parest, Quaalude, Somnafac, Sopor	Sedation, sleep	High	High	Yes	4 to 8	Oral			
	Tranquilizers	IV	Equanil, Librium, Miltown, Serax, Tranxene, Valium	Anti-anxiety, muscle relaxant, sedation	Moderate	Moderate	Yes	4 to 8	Oral			
	Other Depressants	III IV	Clonopin, Dalmane, Dormate, Noludar, Placydil, Valmid	Anti-anxiety, sedation, sleep	Possible	Possible	Yes	4 to 8	Oral			
Stimulants	Cocaine‡	II	Cocaine	Local anesthetic	Possible	High	Yes	2	Injected, sniffed	Increased alertness, excitation, euphoria, dilated pupils, increased pulse rate and blood pressure, insomnia, loss of appetite	Agitation, increase in body temperature, hallucinations, convulsions, possible death	Apathy, long periods of sleep, irritability, depression, disorientation
	Amphetamines	II III	Benzedrine, Biphetamine, Desoxyn, Dexedrine	Hyperkinesis, narcolepsy, weight control	Possible	High	Yes	2 to 4	Oral, injected			
	Phenmetrazine	II	Preludin	Weight control	Possible	High	Yes	2 to 4	Oral			
	Methylphenidate	II	Ritalin	Hyperkinesis	Possible	High	Yes	2 to 4	Oral			
	Other Stimulants	III IV	Bacarate, Cylert, Didrex, Ionamin, Plegine, Pondimin, Pre-Sate, Sanorex, Voranil	Weight control	Possible	Possible	Yes	2 to 4	Oral			
Hallucinogens	LSD	I	None	None	None	Degree unknown	Yes	Variable	Oral	Illusions and hallucinations (with exception of MDA); poor perception of time and distance	Longer, more intense trip episodes, psychosis, possible death	Withdrawal syndrome not reported
	Mescaline	I	None	None	None	Degree unknown	Yes	Variable	Oral, injected			
	Psilocybin-Psilocyn	I	None	None	None	Degree unknown	Yes	Variable	Oral			
	MDA	I	None	None	None	Degree unknown	Yes	Variable	Oral, injected, sniffed			
	PCP‡	III	Sernylan	Veterinary anesthetic	None	Degree unknown	Yes	Variable	Oral, injected, smoked			
	Other Hallucinogens	I	None	None	None	Degree unknown	Yes	Variable	Oral, injected, sniffed			
Cannabis	Marihuana, Hashish, Hashish Oil	I	None	None	Degree unknown	Moderate	Yes	2 to 4	Oral, smoked	Euphoria, relaxed inhibitions, increased appetite, disoriented behavior	Fatigue, paranoia, possible psychosis	Insomnia, hyperactivity, and decreased appetite reported in a limited number of individuals

Courtesy Drug Enforcement Administration

from import or manufacture, through the wholesale level, to the pharmacy or hospital that dispensed it, and ultimately to the patient who received it.

Quotas on Manufacturing. The DEA, working jointly with the FDA, limits the quantity of Schedule I and II controlled substances which can be produced during a given year. Until recently, the federal government depended on data furnished by the bulk manufacturers of substances subject to quotas. Presently, the government has access to special reports filed by all manufacturers and distributors of controlled drugs, information derived from commercial prescription surveys, data from triplicate prescription programs operated in four states, and reports from insurance carriers on the quantities of drugs dispensed directly by physicians and the amounts used in hospitals. As a result, the government has far more data than before on which to base projections of legitimate drug use needs.

Restrictions on Distribution. All distributions of a controlled substance from one manufacturer to another, from manufacturer to wholesaler, from importer to wholesaler, and from wholesaler to dispenser are restricted. In the case of Schedule I and II drugs, the supplier must have a special order form from the customer. This order form is issued by the DEA only to people who are properly registered in Schedules I and II. The form is preprinted with the name and address of the customer. The drugs must be shipped to this name and address; any change in the form renders it invalid. This device reinforces the registration requirement; it also makes doubly certain that only authorized individuals obtain Schedule I and II drugs legitimately. Another benefit of the form is the special monitoring it permits. The form is issued in triplicate: one copy for the customer's files and two copies for the supplier, who, after filling the order, keeps one copy

and forwards the third copy to federal agents for review. For drugs in Schedules III, IV, and V, no order form is necessary. The supplier in each case, however, is under an obligation to verify the authenticity of the customer by checking the registration number used by the customer against the official DEA files. The supplier is held strictly accountable for drugs shipped to a purchaser who does not have a valid registration.

Restrictions on Dispensing. Dispensing a controlled substance means delivering it to the ultimate user, who may be a patient or a research subject. Schedule I drugs may be used only in research. They generally are supplied by a limited number of manufacturers directly to authorized researchers, who administer them directly to the subjects.

For most, if not all, Schedule II, III, and IV drugs, a prescription is required under the Federal Food, Drug, and Cosmetic Act when dispensed by a pharmacy. The decision to place drugs on prescription is within the jurisdiction of the FDA. Unlike other prescription drugs, however, drugs falling into Schedules II, III, and IV may be subject to additional restrictions. Schedule II prescriptions must be written by the practitioner and cannot be telephoned to a pharmacy. In addition, the prescription is not refillable. For Schedule III and IV drugs, the prescription may be either written or telephoned to the pharmacy. Patients may, if authorized by the doctor on the initial prescription, have the prescription refilled up to five times within six months from the date of the initial filling. Schedule V is currently reserved for over the counter (OTC) narcotic preparations, including antitussives and antidiarrheals. Even so, the law imposes restrictions beyond those normally required for the OTC sales. For example, the patient must be at least 18 years of age, must offer some form of identification, and the pharmacist must enter the patient's name into a special log as part of a special record (formerly known as the exempt narcotic book).

Limitation on Imports and Exports. Any international transaction involving a Schedule I or II drug must have the prior permission of the DEA; and any international transaction involving those from Schedules III, IV, or V must be made with prior notice to, but without prior approval of, the DEA. Approval to import a Schedule I or II drug is not given until the importer shows that there is not enough domestic supply to meet legitimate needs. Similarly, exportation of Schedule I and II drugs is severely limited and requires demonstration that the drugs are going to a country where they will actually be used and not re-exported.

Conditions for Storage of Drugs. For Schedule I and II drugs, rigid security requirements are imposed. They must be stored in a specially constructed vault with reinforced concrete walls and a steel gate, with a 24-hour alarm system, and immediately available security guards. For drugs in Schedules III, IV, and V, the vault is optional. The handler may segregate the controlled substances in a special area where they are under constant surveillance by supervisory personnel. An alarm system and special handling are required. These costly special requirements for storage apply only to manufacturers, importers, exporters, and wholesalers of controlled drugs. They do not apply to retail handlers, such as physicians, pharmacies, and hospitals; there, reduced security requirements correlate with the smaller quantities of drugs involved and the security needs of these handlers.

Reports of Transactions to the Government. Periodic reports about transactions in certain drugs must be submitted to the DEA. Program ARCOS was inaugurated on January 1, 1974 and required the monitoring of all drugs listed in Schedules I and II and all narcotic drugs in Schedule III. Every 30 days, each manufacturer and wholesaler must report all manufacturing activities, all importation and exportation, and distributions to the DEA; inventories must be filed annually. These reports are processed by computer, enabling the federal government to identify excessive purchases or discrepancies between purchases and sales not reflected in inventory on a product by product, handler by handler basis.

Criminal Penalties for Illicit Trafficking. Trafficking is the unauthorized manufacture, the distribution—by sale, gift, or otherwise, or the unlawful possession of any controlled substance. The penalties for violation vary by schedules. For narcotics in Schedules I and II, a first offense is punishable by up to 15 years in prison and up to a $25,000 fine. For trafficking in a Schedule I or II nonnarcotic drug or any Schedule III drug, the penalty is up to five years in prison and up to a $15,000 fine. Trafficking in a Schedule IV drug is punishable by a maximum of three years in jail and up to a $10,000 fine. Trafficking in a Schedule V substance is a misdemeanor punishable by up to one year in prison and up to a $5,000 fine. Subsequent offenses are punishable by twice the penalty imposed for the first offense. Possession for one's own use of any controlled substance in any schedule is always a misdemeanor on the first offense, punishable by one year in jail and up to a $5,000 fine. The CSA carefully distinguishes between trafficking and use.[4]

POSSE COMITATUS ACT

Another important piece of federal legislation authorized the military to participate with civilians in antidrug smuggling operations. This legislation is an amendment to the Posse Comitatus Act.[5]

The Latin term *posse comitatus* means the

"power of the county" and refers to everyone in a county beyond the age of 15, whom a sheriff may summon for help in certain cases. During the Reconstruction Era following the Civil War, U.S. marshals in occupied southern states often called on federal troops to form a *posse* for purposes of enforcing local laws. Once southern states regained representation in Congress, their representatives wanted to prevent such practices in the future. The result was an 1878 amendment to an army appropriations bill, now codified at 18 U.S.C. 1385. It prohibits use of the army (and now air force as well) "as a posse comitatus or otherwise to execute the laws."

But it has become obvious that the military can help in the air and on the sea to stem the flow of illegal drugs, especially those from Latin America. In 1981, President Reagan signed into law the Department of Defense Authorization Act of 1982, which authorizes the military to assist local law enforcement agencies in the following areas:

1. use of information collected during military operations;
2. use of military equipment and facilities;
3. training and advising civilian law enforcement officials;
4. assistance by Department of Defense personnel;
5. restrictions on direct participation by military personnel;
6. assistance not to affect adversely military preparedness;
7. reimbursement; and
8. nonpreemption of law.

THE OPIUM POPPY
(PAPAVER SOMNIFERUM)

Several drugs are derived from the opium poppy, including opium, morphine, heroin, codeine, and others less well known.

OPIUM

One of the first drugs of abuse was opium. Its pleasurable effects were known to many ancient civilizations, including the Egyptians, as early as 1500 B.C. During the Renaissance in Europe, opium was employed in the treatment of hysteria, making it one of the early therapeutic agents in treating mental disorders.

In the seventeenth century, opium smoking spread throughout China, and opium dependence was recognized as a problem. Opium eating was known in the United States and England during the Revolutionary War. Opium was used by eighteenth-century doctors to treat venereal disease, cancer, gallstones, diarrhea, and to relieve pain at childbirth.

Opium is the milky white juice obtained from the pod of the poppy plant. When the white juice is exposed to air, it darkens to blackish-brown and thickens. Raw opium has a pungent odor and may be smoked. The user seems sleepy and relaxed. Prolonged use creates both physical and psychological dependence. Raw opium is the source of morphine, heroin, codeine, and paregoric.

MORPHINE

Morphine is obtained from raw opium; ten pounds of raw opium yield one pound of morphine. A German named Serturner first isolated the substance in 1804, and a few years later named it *morphine* after the Greek god of sleep, Morpheus. The drug was first used in medicine in 1825 as a painkiller and is still used as such today.

The use of morphine increased considerably with the invention of the hypodermic syringe by an Englishman around 1843. The hypodermic syringe was introduced into this country about 1853 and was used extensively for wounded Union troops during the American Civil War. Some developed physical and psychological dependence, for doctors did not clearly understand the addictive nature of opiates until around 1870.

Morphine appears in tablet, capsule, and liquid forms. It has no distinguishing color and provides the medical standards by which other narcotics are evaluated. Morphine is usually administered by injection. The drug creates both physical and psychological dependence in the user, who feels euphoric and seems sleepy or relaxed. The pupils of the eyes may constrict.[6]

HEROIN (DIACETYLMORPHINE)

Heroin was developed in England in 1874, but it evoked little interest until about 1890, when it was found to be considerably stronger than morphine. Commercial production of heroin began in 1898 in Germany by the Bayer Company. Heroin was advertised as a cure for morphine dependence, but it was soon learned that heroin dependence was even more difficult to cure.

Heroin is an odorless crystalline white powder. It is usually sold in glassine paper packets, aluminum foil, or capsules. The darker the color, the more impurities it contains. Being about four to five times stronger than morphine, heroin is the principal drug of addiction among the opium derivatives. It is generally injected.

By the time the heroin reaches the addict, it has been diluted considerably. Heroin reaching this country from Europe ordinarily is over 90 percent pure. Once here, it is cut, or adulterated, with powdered milk, sugar, quinine, or other substitutes. The average street dose contains from 3 to 5 percent heroin (see Figure 17-4). Deaths from overdoses are not uncommon and ordinarily occur because a dose contained more heroin than the addict's body was accustomed to. Addicts may also have a fatal allergic reaction to the drug or the diluent. The fatal overdose is not always accidental. On occasion, addicts suspected of being police informers have been given "hot shots"—pure heroin—to eliminate them.

FIGURE 17-3   Heroin Importation

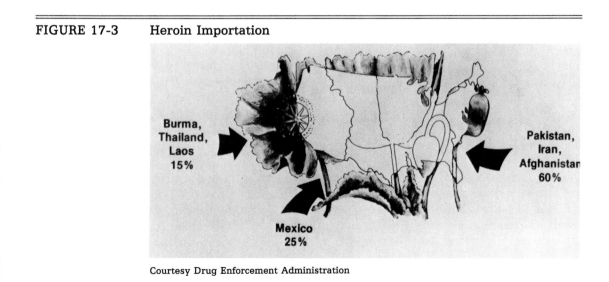

Courtesy Drug Enforcement Administration

FIGURE 17-4   **Heroin Distribution and Price Market**

Distributor	Adulteration	Percentage of Heroin	Price on the Street
Importer	—	80 + %	1 Kilo—$140,000
Major Dealer	1 to 1	40 + %	
Connection	2⁺ to 1	12 + %	
Street Dealer	2⁺ to 1	3 + %	"quarter" bag—$45
Junkie-Pusher	?	?	?

Formulated and compiled by Robert W. Taylor, Ph.D., Department of Social Sciences, University of Texas at Tyler

In addition to facing the perils of the law, withdrawal, and other aspects of addiction, the drug addict also faces the serious health problems associated with dirty needles. Many suffer venereal disease and serum hepatitis. Because both are transmitted diseases, those sharing needles with other drug abusers run the risk of injecting themselves with traces of blood from a disease carrier.[7] Drug users who administer their drugs through intravenous injections and share their needles with others face the additional danger of contracting the almost always fatal Acquired Immune Deficiency Syndrome (AIDS).

CODEINE

The alkaloid codeine is found in raw opium in concentrations from 0.7 to 2.5 percent. It was first isolated in 1832 as an impurity in a batch of morphine. Compared to morphine, codeine produces less analgesia, sedation, and respiratory depression. It is widely distributed in products of two general types. Codeine to relieve moderate pain may consist of tablets or be combined with other products such as aspirin. Liquid codeine preparations for the relief of coughs (antitussives) include Robitussin AC, Cheracol, and terpin hydrate with codeine. Codeine is also manufactured in injectable form for pain relief.

OTHER OPIUM DERIVATIVES

Other opium derivatives abused and stolen from pharmacies, hospitals, and physicians are:

- Dilaudid
- Dionin
- Papaverine
- Pantopon
- Atropine
- Amomorphine

SYNTHETIC NARCOTICS

Synthetic narcotics, though chemically related to the opium alkaloids, are produced entirely within the laboratory. A continuing search for a drug that kills pain but does not create tolerance and dependence has yet to yield a drug that is not susceptible to abuse.

Two synthetic opiates are meperidine and methadone.

MEPERIDINE (PETHIDINE)

The commercial name for meperidine is Demerol, and it was the first synthetic narcotic. Next to morphine, it is probably the most widely used drug for the relief of intense pain. It is available in pure form and in combination products. The drug is administered by mouth or by injection; the latter is the more common method of abuse.[8]

METHADONE

Methadone is known by several commercial names, such as Dolophine, Amidone, and Adanon. A heroin-dependent person can be treated with doses of methadone to replace the heroin the body needs; subsequent doses of heroin have no effect on the abuser. The drug is administered orally every day. The addict is given enough methadone to keep him or her comfortable and functioning. Although one dependence is substituted for another, methadone dependence is easier to control and treat medically.

There is considerable controversy over the adoption of methadone maintenance programs. Critics argue that drug dependence is not cured. Proponents argue that it presents a cheaper way of supporting drug dependence—about $.19 a day was reported in one program—and gets abusers out of crime and back to a conventional life. Proponents recognize that the programs need the appropriate psychiatric help for the psychological dependence.[9]

RECOGNIZING AN ADDICT

The following list may be useful in identifying an individual who is addicted to natural or synthetic opiates.[10]

- The possession of addicting drugs without adequate medical explanation
- A tendency on the part of the suspect to hide or conceal these drugs
- The presence of needle marks in the form of black or blue spots resembling tattooing
- The presence of elongated scars over the veins, especially those of the forearms and the lower legs
- The presence of boil-like abscesses over the veins or near where veins approach the surface
- An appearance of drowsiness, sleepiness, or lethargy, especially if accompanied by a tendency to scratch the body, which sometimes indicates a slight overdose
- Wide fluctuations in the size of the pupils of the eyes, with maximum constriction immediately after the suspect takes an injection

- Possession of equipment for smoking opium
- A tendency to wear long sleeves or other concealing clothing even in hot weather, to cover needle marks
- A tendency for the suspect to isolate himself or herself at regular intervals in order to take hypodermic injections
- An obvious discrepancy between the amount of money the suspect earns and the amount he or she spends
- The tendency of a person who has previously been reliable to resort to thievery, embezzlement, forgery, prostitution, and so forth
- The tendency to develop withdrawal symptoms. The withdrawal symptoms from the denial of opium-derived drugs and synthetic opiates are quite similar: nervousness, anxiety, and sleeplessness; yawning, running eyes and nose, hoarseness, and perspiring; enlargement of the pupils of the eyes, goose flesh, muscle twitching; severe aches of the back and legs, hot and cold flashes; vomiting, diarrhea, and stomach cramps; increase in breathing rate, blood pressure, and body temperature; a feeling of desperation and an obsessive desire to secure more of the drug
- Typically, the onset of symptoms occurs about eight to twelve hours following the last dose. Symptoms increase for seventy-two hours, gradually diminish over the next five to ten days, and usually disappear entirely within ten to fourteen days; weakness, insomnia, nervousness, and muscle aches may persist for several weeks.

DESIGNER DRUGS

The term "designer drugs" was originally coined in the laboratory of Dr. Gary Henderson at the University of California, Davis. It originally referred to the increasing sophis-

tication of chemists in illicit laboratories to produce drugs to fit the tastes of individual clients. Today designer drugs are tailored to evade the law. For example, the government is required by law to specify the exact chemical structure and name of a compound it wishes to control. "Kitchen" chemists can make a minor modification in the chemical structure of a controlled drug. Because the alteration is minor the new drug may be expected to have psychoactive effects like those of the controlled drug. But because it is no longer exactly the same chemical, it is no longer controlled. The chemist is also beyond the reach of the law. Because it takes the Drug Enforcement Administration one to two years to control a drug, chemists can stay ahead of the law almost indefinitely.[11]

FENTANYL

The fentanyls are a class of potent narcotic-analgesics originally synthesized by the Janssen pharmaceutical company of Belgium. Although the chemical structures of these drugs differ from the opiates, the fentanyls are similar pharmacologically and toxicologically.

Beginning in 1979, illicitly synthesized derivatives of fentanyl began appearing on the streets under the name "China White," a name usually given to pure Southeast Asian heroin. Soon thereafter a series of deaths occurred in southern California that looked like heroin overdose deaths. But toxicological analysis failed to detect any narcotic. As of 1985, over 77 such deaths had occurred.

The laboratory at the University of California, Davis, partially supported by the California State Department of Alcohol and Drug Programs, has detected fentanyl derivatives in the body fluids of the overdose victims. Laboratory workers also have detected fentanyls in the urine of a significant number of individuals enrolling in various methadone and other drug treatment programs throughout California. To date they have identified five different fentanyl derivatives, in addition to fentanyl itself, in samples being sold illicitly as "China White," "Persian White," "Synthetic Heroin," and "Fentanyl." The newest derivative, 3-methyl fentanyl, is extremely potent and is thought to be responsible for an alarming number of overdose deaths in the San Francisco Bay area.

FENTANYL DERIVATIVES USED MEDICALLY

Following is a brief description of the fentanyl derivatives used in human and veterinary medicine:

Fentanyl Introduced into the United States in 1968 as an intravenous analgesic-anesthetic under the tradename SublimazeR or InnovarR (the combination of fentanyl or Droperidol). Fentanyl is now a major preanesthetic medication, anesthetic, and postsurgical analgesic. Fentanyl is approximately one hundred times as potent as morphine and short acting (duration is approximately thirty minutes). It is used in over 70 percent of the surgeries in the United States. Fentanyl sold on the streets is synthesized in illicit laboratories and not diverted from pharmaceutical supplies. Street fentanyl is in powder form; pharmaceutical fentanyl is in dilute liquid form. Abuse in hospitals and clinics by medical personnel has been documented, but the extent of the problem is unknown.

Sufentanyl A derivative 2,000 to 4,000 times more potent than morphine, presently undergoing clinical trials as a anesthetic-analgesic for cardiac surgery.

Alfentanyl A very short acting (fifteen minutes), slightly less potent derivative (twenty to thirty times morphine) currently in clinical trials as an analgesic to be used in diagnostic, dental, and minor surgical procedures.

Lofentanyl An extremely potent (6000 times

morphine) and very long acting drug, being evaluated for use when prolonged analgesia and respiratory depression are required, such as in tetanus and multiple trauma.

Carfentanyl A drug 3,200 times as potent as morphine used only to immobilize wild animals.

Alpha-methyl Fentanyl The first illicit fentanyl derivative to appear on the streets, it is a simple modification of fentanyl and about two hundred times as potent as morphine. It is now classified as a Schedule I drug by the DEA.

Para-fluoro Fentanyl The second illicit fentanyl derivative to appear on the streets, it is a simple derivative with about the same potency. It is presently classified as a Schedule I drug. Little is known about it; it appeared briefly and does not seem to be in use at this time.

Alpha-methyl Acetylfentanyl First appeared on the streets in 1983 and a simple derivative of fentanyl, but because it is a new chemical entity, it has escaped classification as a restricted drug. Nothing is known about its pharmacological properties.

Alpha-methyl Fentanyl Acrylate Has been identified in samples containing acetyl alpha-methyl fentanyl. It may be a new derivative but is more likely a contaminant or a byproduct of synthetics. Nothing is known about its pharmacological properties.

Benzyl Fentanyl Has recently appeared mixed with other fentanyl derivatives in street samples. It is possibly an unwanted synthetic byproduct or an intermediate used in the synthesis of other fentanyl derivatives. It has no narcotic effects.

3-Methyl Fentanyl The latest derivative to be introduced onto the streets and one of the most potent (3000 times as potent as morphine). It appeared in California sometime between fall 1983 and spring 1984 and is thought to be responsible for over a dozen overdose deaths in the San Francisco Bay area, the highest incidence of fentanyl-related deaths to date.

PHYSICAL DESCRIPTION OF FENTANYLS

The fentanyls are diluted with large amounts of lactose or sucrose (powdered sugar) before they are sold on the street, so the amount of active drug is less than 1 percent. These amounts are so small they contribute nothing to the color, odor, or taste of the sample. The color of the samples obtained to date has ranged from pure white (sold as "Persian White"), to light tan (sold as "China White," "Synthetic Heroin," or "Fentanyl"), to light brown (sold as "Mexican Brown"). The brown color comes from lactose which has been heated and caramelized slightly. The texture of the samples ranged from light and finely powdered to somewhat coarse, cake-like and crumbly, resembling powdered milk. Occasional samples have a medicinal or chemical odor, but this is not characteristic.

In summary, the fentanyls appear in all various forms that heroin does, and no characteristic of their appearance identifies them as fentanyls.

ROUTES OF ADMINISTRATION

Intravenous injection is the most common route of administration for the fentanyls, but they may also be smoked or snorted. At least one overdose death has been identified in which snorting was the only route of administration. Fentanyl has also been detected in the urine of individuals who only smoked the drug.

PHARMACOLOGICAL EFFECTS

Although the fentanyls are chemically distinct from other narcotics, they are phar-

macologically equivalent. That is, they have all the effects, side effects, and toxic effects of the classic narcotics. Therefore all the actions of the fentanyls can be reversed by naloxone (NarcanR), although higher doses of the antagonist may be required.

Euphoria. The euphoria or "rush" from the fentanyls is like that of heroin. The intensity of the effect depends upon the dose and the particular derivative used.

ADDICTION LIABILITY

The fentanyls produce both tolerance and physiological dependence after repeated administration. Controlled studies have shown that addicts perceive fentanyl to be like heroin. Many individuals enrolling in methadone treatment programs who have only fentanyl in their urine upon admission are convinced that they were using only high grade heroin. Therefore when pharmacologically equivalent doses are used, most users probably cannot tell the difference between heroin and the fentanyls.

OVERDOSE DEATHS

As of 1985, as we have said, 77 overdose deaths were known to have been caused by the fentanyls. Nearly all occurred in California; the two that occurred in Oregon suggest that fentanyl is spreading to other states. All cases involved known heroin users, injection sites, and accompanying paraphernalia. Autopsy showed typical signs of narcotic overdose. Routine toxicological analysis of the body fluids revealed no narcotics, sedatives, or stimulants. But analysis of body fluids in a laboratory using methods specific for the fentanyls revealed very low levels of these drugs. Traces of the fentanyls were also found in the drug paraphernalia.

Fentanyl-related deaths have occurred in nearly every urban area in California, in suburban areas, and even in semi-rural areas.

Ages of the victims ranged from 20 to 49 years. Most were male; nine were female. Most of the victims were white; significant numbers were Hispanic and black. In short, fentanyl use is not confined to any geographical area or any social, economic or ethnic group but is distributed widely throughout the heroin using population.

STIMULANTS

Drugs falling into this group directly stimulate the central nervous system, producing excitation, alertness, wakefulness, and, in some cases, a temporary rise in blood pressure and respiration rate. The major stimulants abused are: cocaine, amphetamines, phenmetrazine, and methylphenidate. The effects of an overdose are agitation, increase in body temperature, hallucinations, convulsions, and possibly death. The withdrawal symptoms are apathy, long periods of sleep, irritability, depression, and disorientation.[12]

COCAINE

Cocaine is a naturally occurring stimulant which is extracted from the leaves of the coca plant *(Erythroxylon coca)*. The leaves of this western South American shrub have been chewed by Bolivian and Peruvian Indians since antiquity for religious, medicinal, and other reasons. Allegedly, the chewing of coca leaves has enabled the Indians to work in high altitudes and on inadequate diets. This chewing of the coca leaf, which continues to the present day, should not be confused with the use of the extracted drug, cocaine. Coca leaves contain only about ½ to 1 percent cocaine; the cocaine contained within them is released more slowly and the route of administration (oral) is different from that in most cocaine use.[13]

Because reports of native coca use generated considerable interest in Europe, efforts were made in the nineteenth century to isolate the purified psychoactive ingredient in coca leaves. When success was achieved in the 1880s, cocaine's potential value as a tonic, its general stimulant properties, its possible value for specific ailments, and its local anesthetic properties were explored. Its use as an anesthetic was particularly important because it could be used in eye surgery, where no previous drug had been suitable. Cocaine also constricted blood vessels and limited bleeding in the anesthetized area. This property made it valuable for surgery of the nose and throat, areas richly supplied with blood. Although many of cocaine's uses as a therapeutic drug have been abandoned, its use as a local anesthetic continues.

Illicit cocaine is sold as a white, translucent, crystalline powder, frequently adulterated to about half its volume. The most common adulterants are sugars (especially lactose and glucose) and local anesthetics (lidocaine, procaine, and tetracaine) similar in appearance and taste to cocaine. Amphetamines, other drugs with stimulant properties, are also used. Given the high cost of the drug, the temptation to adulterate at each level of sale is great (see Figure 17-5). The combination of high price and the exotic properties attributed to it have contributed to cocaine's street reputation as *the* status drug.

How Is It Used? Cocaine is most commonly inhaled, or snorted, through the nose. It is deposited on the mucous linings of the nose, from which it is readily absorbed into the bloodstream. Repeated use often results in irritation to the nostrils and nasal mucous membranes. Symptoms may resemble those of a common cold, that is, congestion or a runny nose. Users therefore often resort to cold remedies, such as nasal sprays, to relieve their chronic nasal congestion. They may be unable to breathe comfortably without habitually using a spray.

A less common route of administration for

FIGURE 17-5   Cocaine Prices at Successive Stages of Trafficking

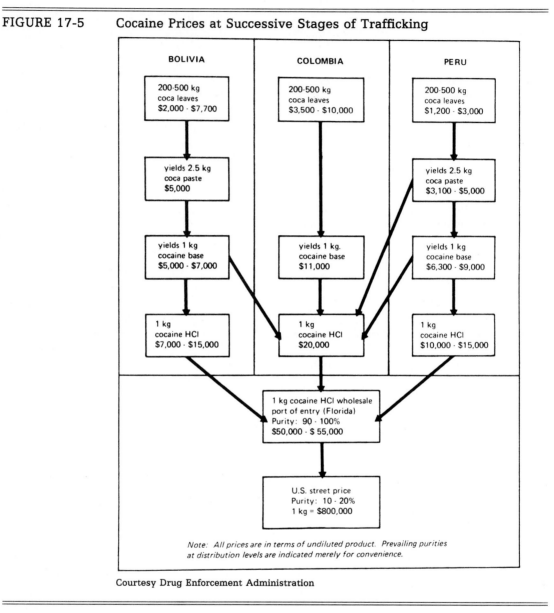

Note: All prices are in terms of undiluted product. Prevailing purities at distribution levels are indicated merely for convenience.

Courtesy Drug Enforcement Administration

cocaine is intravenous injection. The solution injected may be cocaine or a combination of heroin and cocaine. This route of administration carries the dangers of any intravenous use. Furthermore, intravenous injection introduces unknown quantities of cocaine or cocaine and heroin directly and suddenly into the bloodstream, leaving body organs wholly unprotected from the toxic effects of the drug. Cocaine deaths from intravenous injection are more numerous than from snorting, despite the greater prevalence of the latter method.

Acute and Chronic Effects. Cocaine, like other drugs of abuse, has both fascinated and repelled people throughout history. It is little wonder then that a bewildering array of "effects," which may have little to do with the pharmacological action of the drug itself, has been attributed to it. Reassertion of often repeated fictions does not, however, make them well-verified facts. Our need for certainty is not necessarily matched by equally adequate evidence to allay our doubts. Unfortunately, a lack of adequate information is sometimes interpreted as indicating that a drug is "safe" when it would be more accurate to admit that our knowledge is simply inadequate to specify the parameters of risk. Moreover, a substance, which when used under conditions of relatively infrequent, low dosage may pose few hazards, may present quite a different picture when widely available and regularly used in larger amounts.

An important verified effect, when used medically, is cocaine's local anesthetic action as well as its ability to constrict blood vessels in the area to which it is applied. One consequence of this property when cocaine is used illicitly and snorted repeatedly is a tendency to cause a chronic inflammation of the nasal membranes, ulceration, and local tissue death. While perforation of the nasal septum (the wall dividing the two halves of the nose) is often mentioned, it is noteworthy that in the United States, at least, this consequence appears to be rare.

There is good evidence that cocaine in moderate doses (10 to 25 mg intravenously and 100 mg intranasally) significantly increases both heart rate and blood pressure. Increases following lower doses occurred more rapidly when the drug was administered directly into the vein than when snorted. Heart rate increased from about 30 to 50 percent above normal nondrug levels. Increases in blood pressure when the heart was in its contracting phase (systolic pressure) were on the order of 10 to 15 percent.

In addition to the street reputation of the drug and historical accounts, even under conditions of carefully controlled laboratory administration, a sense of well-being—euphoria—subjectively characterizes cocaine use. Interestingly enough, however, when the drug was administered intravenously under laboratory conditions, the subjective effects were not easily distinguished from those of amphetamines (synthetic stimulants having more prolonged activity). A feeling of calmness and relaxation is described by most of the subjects who have participated in controlled laboratory studies; they also report diminished appetite. The observed and reported effects of several laboratory studies are generally consistent with accounts based on street use. However, there is much street lore and some clinical evidence emphasizing other effects that have not been systematically verified by controlled experimentation.

Clinical reports dating back to the 1800s have described a range of responses to heavier, more prolonged use of cocaine. Early reports by Freud and others also emphasized that there was wide individual variation in physiological and psychological responses to cocaine. Von Fleischl, who was encouraged to use cocaine by Freud to alleviate symptoms of nerve pain, rapidly progressed to heavy, intravenous use (up to a gram per day). With heavier use, Fleischl's condition deteriorated into chronic intoxication, characterized by hallucinations of white snakes and insects creeping over and under his skin. A cocaine psychosis similar to paranoid schizophrenia has been described in the scientific literature. Tactile hallucinations similar to those experienced by Fleischl are a common aspect of this disorder. The hallucinations have been described as so real to the victims that they injure their skin in an attempt to remove

FIGURE 17-6   Cocaine Importation

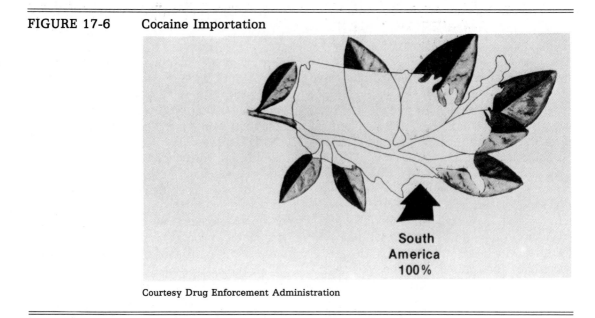

South
America
100%

Courtesy Drug Enforcement Administration

the imagined parasites. Other paranoid delusions include fear of imaginary police, the belief that one is being watched, and so on.

Cocaine Fatality. There is little question that cocaine can kill. By 1891 some 13 deaths had been attributed to the drug, and in 1924 a report was published of 26 cocaine deaths. These deaths were results of medical errors. They were virtually always rapid in onset and characterized by respiratory depression and cardiovascular collapse. In recent years, an increasing number of cocaine-related deaths among individuals who had snorted the substance has been reported. These deaths would seem to dispel the street wisdom and myth that snorting is completely safe.

Freebasing. The practice of freebasing cocaine involves the dissolving of cocaine in a base solution, usually distilled water and calcium carbonate or lactose. The mixture is then shaken so the cocaine is dissolved completely. Several drops of ether are then added, and the mixture is shaken again. The cocaine is attracted to the ether while the other additives are attracted to the base solution.

The ether-cocaine solution separates from the base (like oil and water), with the ether rising to the surface. An eyedropper is commonly used to suction off the ether-cocaine solution, which is then placed on an evaporating dish or crucible and allowed to evaporate naturally. This process can be accelerated by the use of a flame; however, this practice is extremely dangerous since the ether is highly flammable.

The cocaine crystals are then scraped off the dish with a metal spatula, placed in a glass pipe or bong (water pipe), and smoked.

The resultant high is alleged to be greater than that from simple snorting, although users remark that injection of the drug provides a more intense high than even freebasing.

The pleasant effects of freebasing begin to decrease in duration as usage increases, and users display changes in moods and irritabil-

FIGURE 17-7

Miami, March 9, 1982. When a U.S. Customs inspector poked a screwdriver into a cardboard box labeled "jeans," he found the biggest cache of cocaine in American history. Twenty-two boxes in all, containing 3,906 pounds of cocaine, were seized on the loading ramp of a warehouse used by a Colombian airline.

Courtesy Drug Enforcement Administration

ity if a high cannot be maintained. As free-basing usage becomes chronic, a person can experience the same symptoms as a chronic nonfreebasing abuser of cocaine.

Rock Cocaine (Crack). A new and relatively inexpensive form of cocaine called *rock cocaine* or *crack* has grown tremendously in popularity among cocaine users. The drug is made by mixing the ordinary cocaine with baking soda and water and heating the solution in a pot. The material, which is somewhat purer and more concentrated than regular cocaine, is dried and broken into tiny chunks that dealers will sell as crack rocks. These little pellets are usually smoked in glass pipes and are frequently sold in tiny plastic vials. It is five to ten times more potent than powdered cocaine; the high lasts about five minutes and leaves the user wanting more. According to mental health specialists, crack users are more likely to show serious psychiatric consequences, including intense paranoia, extreme depression, and often suicidal and even violent behavior. Part of the attraction to the dealer is the enormous profit that can be made by the sale of crack. For example, in Los Angeles an ounce of cocaine can sell for $1,000 to $1,500. Since each ounce contains 28 grams and each gram can produce up to six rocks selling for $25.00 each, the dealer can realize a profit of around $2,700.

Police around the country have already

FIGURE 17-8　　Rock Cocaine (Crack)

Rock cocaine (crack) confiscated by investigators.

started to see its impact in terms of crime. For example, police in Florida have noticed increases in burglaries and armed robberies in areas where crack is sold, and New York City police have attributed a rash of brutal crimes to young crack addicts.

AMPHETAMINES

Amphetamine, dextroamphetamine, and methamphetamine are so closely related chemically that they can be differentiated from one another only in the laboratory.[14]

These compounds resemble the natural body hormones of epinephrine and norepinephrine. As a result of this similarity, they can act directly, by mimicking the natural hormones in their effects on nerve endings and/or indirectly by causing increased release of the natural hormones. In either case, the amphetamines stimulate certain areas of the nervous system which control blood pressure, heartbeat, and respiratory and metabolic rates, all of which are increased. Appetite is markedly decreased, and the senses are hyperalert. The body is in a general state of stress, as if it were extremely threatened or expecting a violent fight. This group of drugs artificially intensifies and prolongs such stimulation, keeping the body in a state of tension for prolonged periods of time.[15] Many different classes of people employ amphetamines in abusive quantities, including middle-aged businesspeople, housewives, students, athletes, truck drivers, and so forth. Recent government studies indicate that young people are the greatest abusers. Drivers take them to stay awake on long trips; students take them while cramming for exams; and athletes take them for extra energy and stamina.[16] When the drug is prescribed, the dose frequently ranges between 2.5 and 15 milligrams per day. Abusers have been known to inject as much as 1,000 milligrams every two or three hours. Medical use of amphetamines is now limited to control of narcolepsy, appetite control, and hyperactivity in children.

PHENMETRAZINE (PRELUDIN), METHYLPHENIDATE, AND PEMOLINE (CYLERT)

Phenmetrazine is related chemically to the amphetamines, and its abuse produces similar effects. Like phenmetrazine, methylphenidate is related chemically to amphetamines. It is prescribed for treatment of mild depression in adults and excessive excitability in children. Pemoline, like amphetamines, is a stimulant. It was developed early in 1975 and was approved for marketing as a drug to be used in the treatment of hyperactive children.

═══ DEPRESSANTS (SEDATIVES) ═══

These depress the central nervous system and are prescribed in small doses to reduce restlessness and emotional tension and to induce sleep (see color insert, Figure 17-9).

The drugs most frequently abused are barbiturates, glutethimide, methaqualone, and meprobamate. Chronic use produces slurring of speech, staggering, loss of balance and falling, faulty judgment, quick temper, and quarrelsomeness. Overdoses, particularly in conjunction with alcohol, result in unconsciousness and death unless proper medical treatment is administered. Therapeutic doses cause minimal amounts of psychological dependence; chronic excessive doses result in both physical and psychological dependence. Abrupt withdrawal, particularly from barbiturates, can produce convulsions and death. Barbiturates are frequently nicknamed after the color of the capsule, tablet, or the name of the manufacturer. The barbiturates most frequently abused are phenobarbital, secobarbital, and amobarbital.[17] These are among the short- and intermediate-acting barbiturates. The onset time is from 15 to 40 minutes, and the effects last for up to six hours.

GLUTETHIMIDE (DORIDEN)

When introduced in 1954, glutethimide was wrongly believed to be a nonaddictive barbiturate substitute. The sedative effects of glutethimide begin about 30 minutes after oral administration and last four to eight hours. Because the effects of this drug last for a long time, it is exceptionally difficult to reverse overdoses, and many result in death.

METHAQUALONE

This drug has been widely abused because it was once mistakenly thought to be safe, nonaddictive, and to have aphrodisiac qualities. Actually methaqualone has caused many cases of serious poisoning. It is administered orally; large doses produce a coma which may be accompanied by thrashing or convulsions. Continued heavy use leads to tolerance and dependence. Methaqualone has been marketed in the United States under various brand names, including Quaalude, Parest, Optimil, Somnafac, and Soper.

MEPROBAMATE

First synthesized in 1960 as a mild tranquilizer, more than 250 tons of meprobamate are distributed yearly in the United States, under the generic name as well as under brand names such as Miltown, Equanil, Kesso-Bamate, and SK-Bamate. This drug is prescribed primarily for relief of anxiety, tension, and associated muscle spasms. The onset and duration of action are like those of intermediate-acting barbiturates, but this drug differs in that it is a muscle relaxant, does not produce sleep at therapeutic doses, and is less toxic. Excessive use, however, can result in psychological and physical dependence.[18]

DRUGS COMMONLY USED IN COMBINATION

SPEEDBALLING

Speedballing is a slang term to describe the simultaneous ingestion, usually through injection, of heroin (a depressant) and cocaine (a stimulant).

The cocaine provides the user with a tremendous euphoric "rush," and after the initial euphoria the heroin provides a drowsy or depressing effect. An overdose of either drug can produce convulsions and death. Combined use greatly increases this risk.

TS AND BLUES

"Ts and Blues" is a mixture of Talwin, a morphinelike pain killer sold only by prescription, and pyribenzamine, a blue antihistamine tablet available over the counter. They are typically stolen and sold to addicts for about $10 a pair, approximately one quar-

ter the price of a single dose of heroin. When mixed, dissolved, and injected, they give a heroinlike rush and quickly produce a heroinlike dependency. In 1980 hospitals reported 3,669 cases of problems associated with this combination drug, compared to 12,785 for heroin. Drug enforcement officials are hoping the problem can be reduced by controlling the manufacture of Talwin.[19]

HALLUCINOGENS

The hallucinogenic drugs, natural or synthetic, distort perception of objective reality. In large doses, they cause hallucinations. Most of these drugs are processed in clandestine laboratories and have yet to be proved medically valuable. The effects experienced after taking hallucinogens are not solely related to the drug. They are modified by the mood, mental attitude, and environment of the user. The unpredictability of their effects is the greatest danger to the user. Users may develop psychological dependence but not physical dependence, so far as is known. The most commonly abused hallucinogens are: PCP (phencyclidine), LSD 25 (lysergic acid diethylamide), mescaline (peyote), psilocybin, and psilocyn.

PCP (PHENCYCLIDINE)

Phencyclidine, commonly called PCP, in pharmaceutically pure form is a solid white powder. Because the hydrochloride salt readily dissolves in water and as a street drug is often adulterated or misrepresented as other drugs, its appearance is highly variable. It is sold in powder form and in tablets, both in many colors. Often it is placed on parsley or on other leaf mixtures to be smoked as cigarettes (joints).[20]

When misrepresented, PCP is commonly sold as THC (the main psychoactive ingredient in marijuana, which in reality is rarely

Narcotics

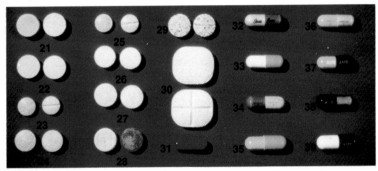

Narcotics

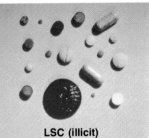

LSC (illicit)

MDA (illicit)

PCP (illicit)

Hallucinogens

Stimulants

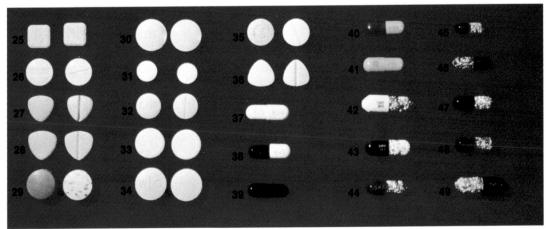

Stimulants

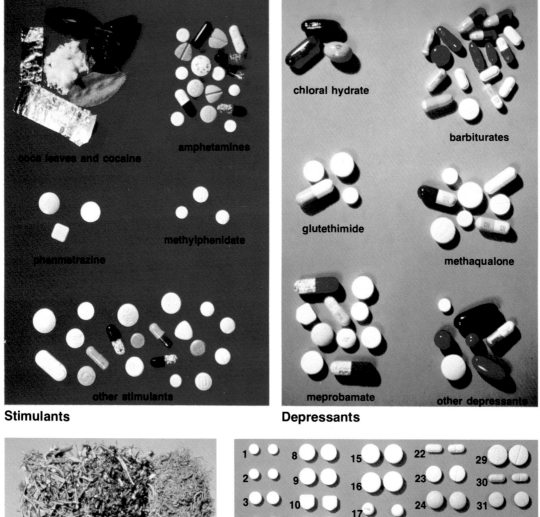

amphetamines

coca leaves and cocaine

methylphenidate

phenmetrazine

other stimulants

Stimulants

chloral hydrate

barbiturates

glutethimide

methaqualone

meprobamate

other depressants

Depressants

marihuana (illicit)

hashish (illicit)

hashish oil (illicit)

Cannabis

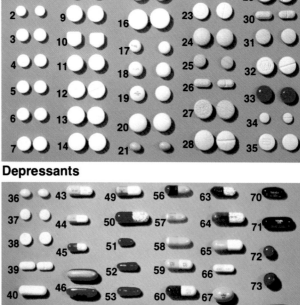

1	8	15	22	29	
2	9	16	23	30	
3	10	17	24	31	
4	11	18	25	32	
5	12	19	26	33	
6	13	20	27	34	
7	14	21	28	35	

Depressants

36	43	49	56	63	70
37	44	50	57	64	71
38	45	51	58	65	72
39	46	52	59	66	73
40		53	60	67	
41	47	54	61	68	74
42	48	55	62	69	75

Depressants

FIGURE 17-9

Depressants

1. Noludar CIII
2. Mebaral CIV
3. Doriden CIII
4. Gemonil CIII
5. Mebaral CIV
6. Quaalude CII
7. Kesso-Bamate CIV
8. Doriden CIII
9. Mebaral CIV
10. Equanil CIV
11. SK-Bamate CIV
12. Medomin CIII
13. Kesso-Bamate CIV
14. Miltown CIV
15. Doriden CIII
16. Quaalude CII
17. Butisol R-A CIII
18. Butisol R-A CIII
19. Miltown CIV
20. Meprotabs CIV
21. Luminal CIV
22. Amytal CII
23. Sopor CII
24. Equanil Wyseals CIV
25. Butison CIII
26. Amytal CII
27. Equagesic CIV
28. Valmid CIV
29. Sopor CII
30. Amytal CII
31. Butisol CIII
32. Deprol CIV
33. Seconal CII
34. Butisol CIII
35. Nembutal Gradumet CII
36. Luminal CIV
37. Butisol CIII
38. Sopor CII
39. Amytal CII
40. Somnafac CII
41. Nembutal CII
42. Nembutal CII
43. Meprospan CIV
44. Buticaps CIII
45. Nembutal CII
46. Bamadex Sequels CII
47. Buticaps CIII
48. Buticaps CIII
49. Noludar 300 CIII
50. Equanil CIV
51. Seconal CII
52. Seconal CII
53. Seconal CII
54. Tuinal 50 mg CII
55. Tuinal 100 mg CII
56. Tuinal 200 mg CII
57. Amytal CII
58. Amytal CII
59. Parest-200 CII
60. Parest-400 CII
61. Carbrital Half Strength CIII
62. Carbrital CIII
63. Eskabarb Spansule CIV
64. Meprospan CIV
65. Doriden CIII
66. Buticaps CIII
67. Somnos CIV
68. Felsules CIV
69. Felsules CIV
70. Noctec CIV
71. Noctec CIV
72. Placidyl CIV
73. Placidyl CIV
74. Placidyl CIV
75. Placidyl CIV

Stimulants

1. Tablet from clandestine laboratory. No standard ingredients.
2. Desoxyn CII
3. Desoxyn CII
4. Desoxyn Gradumet CII
5. Sanorex CIII
6. Tepanil CIV
7. Preludin Enduret CII
8. Tepanil Ten-tab CIV
9. Tenuate Dospan CIV
10. Voranil CIII
11. Ritalin CII
12. Desoxyn Gradumet CII
13. Plegine CIII
14. Didrex CIII
15. SPRY-2 CIII
16. Desoxyn Gradumet CII
17. Ritalin CII
18. Melfiat CIII
19. Obetrol 20 CII
20. Cylert CIV
21. Pondimin CIV
22. Dexedrine CII
23. Tablet from clandestine laboratory. No standard ingredients.
24. Bacarate CIII
25. Preludin CII
26. Didrex CIII
27. Benzedrine CII
28. Benzedrine CII
29. Obedrin-LA CII
30. Preludin Endurets CII
31. Ritalin CII
32. Obetrol 10 CII
33. Tenuate CIV
34. Pre-Sate CIII
35. Bontril PDM CIII
36. Dexamyl CII
37. Biphetamine '7½' CII
38. Biphetamine '12½' CII
39. Biphetamine '20' CII
40. Ionamin '15' CIV
41. Ionamin '30' CIV
42. Eskatrol CII
43. Fastin CIV
44. Benzedrine Spansule CII
45. Dexedrine Spansule CII
46. Dexedrine Spansule CII
47. Phendimetrazine CIII
48. Dexedrine Spansule CII
49. Dexamyl Spansule No. 2 CII

Narcotics

1. Morphine CII
2. Dilaudid CII
3. Dilaudid CII
4. Codeine CII
5. Levo-Dromoran CII
6. Demerol CII
7. Dolophine CII
8. Morphine CII
9. Leritine CII
10. Hycodan CIII
11. Dolophine CII
12. Tylenol with Codeine No. 3 CIII
13. Ascodeen-30 CIII
14. Empirin Compound with Codeine No. 1 CIII
15. Empirin Compound with Codeine No. 2 CIII
16. Empirin Compound with Codeine No. 3 CIII
17. Empirin Compound with Codeine No. 4 CIII
18. Emprazil-C CIII
19. Tussionex CIII
20. Soma Compound with Codeine CIII
21. APC with Demerol CII
22. Percodan CII
23. Numorphan CII
24. Hasacode CIII
25. Nucodan CII
26. Hasacode Strong CIII
27. Percodan-Demi CII
28. APC with Meperidine CII
29. Demerol with APAP CII
30. Methadone Diskets CII
31. Mepergan Fortis CII
32. Synalgos-DC CIII
33. Percobard-Demi CII
34. Fiorinal with Codeine No. 3 CIII
35. Percobarb CII
36. Fiorinal with Codeine No. 2 CIII
37. Phenaphen with Codeine No. 2 CIII
38. Phenaphen with Codeine No. 3 CIII
39. Phenaphen with Codeine No. 4 CIII

The numbered photographs illustrate some of the specific narcotics, stimulants, and depressants covered by the Controlled Substances Act. They are not shown actual size.

The roman numeral beside the product name refers to the schedule of the Controlled Substances Act under which the product is covered. (See Figure 17-1).

Size, shape, color, markings, and ingredients of licit products may be altered by the manufacturer. Positive identification can be made only by laboratory analysis.

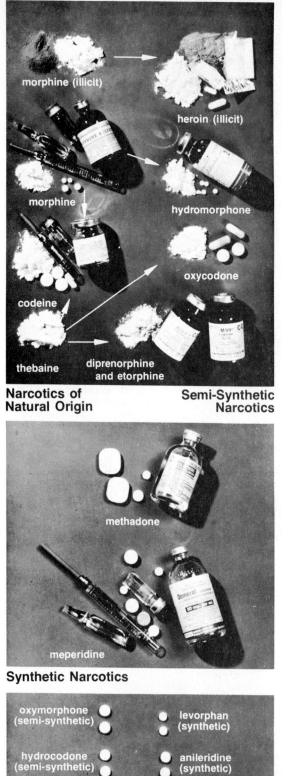

morphine (illicit)

heroin (illicit)

morphine

hydromorphone

codeine

oxycodone

thebaine

diprenorphine and etorphine

Narcotics of Natural Origin

Semi-Synthetic Narcotics

methadone

meperidine

Synthetic Narcotics

oxymorphone (semi-synthetic)	levorphan (synthetic)
hydrocodone (semi-synthetic)	anileridine (synthetic)
oxycodone (semi-synthetic)	

Other Narcotic Tablets

Peyote Cactus (Hallucinogen)

Cannabis Sativa L. (Cannabis)

Psilocybe Mushrooms (Hallucinogen)

available on the street). But phencyclidine has also been sold as cannabinol (another marijuana constituent), mescaline, psilocybin, LSD, and even as amphetamine or cocaine. Because of the variability in street names, appearance, and because PCP is sometimes found in combination with barbiturates, heroin, cocaine, amphetamine, methaqualone, LSD, and mescaline, users may be mistaken about its true identity.

Depending on how carefully PCP is synthesized, it may contain impurities, including potassium cyanide. The mixture of marijuana and PCP has been thought to be common, but it has rarely been reported by street drug analysis laboratories. At least one major laboratory on the West Coast which does such drug analysis has never encountered the combination.

Significantly adding to the risk of PCP use, especially when it is taken orally, is the wide variability in purity of the street drug. Even when PCP is not misrepresented, the percentage of PCP has been found to be quite variable. Generally, samples represented as "Crystal" or "Angel Dust" tend to be purer than those sold under other names or misrepresented as other drugs.

In addition to phencyclidine, over thirty chemically similar analogues, some of which are capable of producing similar psychic effects, can also be synthesized and may appear on the street. Thus the problems of identifying and tracking the use of PCP and related drugs is unusually difficult.

THC is sometimes misrepresented as PCP. Unlike THC, PCP can be synthesized rather easily. The starting chemicals are widely available. Media accounts have sometimes exaggerated the ease with which phencyclidine can be made, but it is not particularly difficult for individuals with only modest technical training or elaborate equipment to make it.

Phencyclidine is used legally in veterinary medicine to immobilize primates. Although it was originally developed as an anesthetic for humans, it was later abandoned because it produced psychological disturbances and agitation in some patients. PCP made its first illicit appearance in the United States in 1965 on the West Coast. At that time it rapidly developed a bad street reputation and had only limited popularity. But recently use has markedly increased.

Because of its great variation in appearance, PCP is difficult to identify by sight. It is found in powder and tablet forms, but also on parsley, mint, oregano, or other leafy material, as a liquid, and in one-gram "rock" crystals. When PCP is sold as a granular powder ("Angel Dust"), it may consist of 50 to 100 percent phencyclidine. Sold under other names and in other guises, the purity is from 10 to 30 percent; leafy mixtures contain still smaller amounts of the drug.

How Is It Used? PCP is most commonly smoked or snorted. By smoking a leafy mixture on which the drug has been sprinkled, users can better regulate the dose. Because of the longer period before the drug takes effect and the greater purity, overdoses are probably worse when the drug has been taken orally. Emergency rooms have reported a sixfold increase in the number of PCP overdose victims.

Clinical Aspects. The best known effects of PCP would seem so unpleasant that many have wondered how it could possibly prove popular. For example, medical students volunteering for an experiment involving several hallucinogens and PCP were uniformly unwilling to return after having smoked moderate amounts of PCP. The drug made them feel weightless, smaller, out of touch with the immediate environment, and dying or dead. Common signs of PCP use include flushing, profuse sweating, involuntary eye movements, muscular uncoordination, double vision, dizziness, nausea, and vomiting. Police officers have reported that individuals under the influence of PCP can be extremely violent and almost superhumanly strong.

Many PCP users do not knowingly take it again. Yet others use it chronically.

Clinical Test for PCP. A one-minute test to identify PCP has been introduced by the Syva Company. The EMIT[R] PCP semiquantitative urine assay is similar to EMIT drug abuse assays and can be performed with existing laboratory equipment. It can be used in hospital emergency rooms and in parole, probation, and work-release programs.[21]

MDMA

MDMA, a derivative of oil of sassafras or oil of nutmeg, is known chemically as 3,4-Methylenedioxymethamphetamine. It was synthesized in 1914 by a chemist who mistakenly thought that it might be useful as an appetite suppressant. MDMA is best known to users and enforcement officers as "Ecstasy." Medical authorities disagree about its therapeutic benefits. Proponents claim that it delivers a gentle two to four-hour journey that dissolves anxieties and leaves the user relaxed and emotionally open, without the bad trips or addictive problems associated with other psychoactive drugs. A small group of psychiatrists, psychologists, and scientists contend that MDMA has enormous therapeutic potential and cite case histories in which MDMA has neutralized emotional defenses.

The DEA has concluded that MDMA is an uncontrolled and rapidly spreading recreational drug that can cause psychosis and perhaps brain damage. It banned the manufacture and distribution of MDMA under the Controlled Substance Act of 1984. Manufacturers and sellers of the drug are subject to fines of $125,000 and 15-year prison sentences. Possession is a misdemeanor. The DEA reports that thousands of MDMA capsules are sold on the streets each month for $8 to $20, particularly to college students and young professionals in at least 20 states, including California, Texas, and Florida.[22]

LSD 25 (LYSERGIC ACID DIETHYLAMIDE)

LSD is a semisynthetic compound produced from lysergic acid, a natural substance found in ergot fungus, a disease which affects rye and wheat. A dose of 50 to 200 micrograms—a quantity approximately the size of a pinpoint—takes a user on a "trip" for approximately eight to 16 hours. Drops of the solution are taken on a lump of sugar or on blotted paper. Along with mental changes, the user may have dilated pupils, lowered temperature, nausea, goose bumps, profuse perspiration, increased blood sugar, and rapid heart beat. Flashbacks are not uncommon.

Before 1972 there was no way to detect LSD in the body chemically. However, scientists of Collaborative Research, Inc., Waltham, Massachusetts, developed a means to detect it in small amounts in human blood and urine and to measure the amount present. This discovery made it possible to study the distribution of LSD in the bodies of animals to determine the residual effect of the drug.[23]

MESCALINE (PEYOTE)

The primary active ingredient of the peyote cactus is the hallucinogen mescaline, which is derived from the buttons of the plant. Mescaline has been used by the Indians of northern Mexico for centuries in religious rites. Generally ground into a powder, it is taken orally. A dose of 350 to 500 milligrams of mescaline produces illusions and hallucinations for five to 12 hours. Like LSD, mescaline is not likely to produce physical dependence but may produce psychological dependence.

PSILOCYBIN AND PSILOCYN

Psilocybin and psilocyn are obtained from mushrooms generally grown in Mexico. Like mescaline, they have historically been used in Indian rites. They are taken orally, and their effect is similar to mescaline's, except that a smaller dose—4 to 8 milligrams—produces effects for about six hours.

MARIJUANA (*CANNABIS SATIVA L.*)

Marijuana is found in the flowering tops and leaves of the female Indian hemp plant. The leaves of the plant always grow in odd numbers. The plant grows in mild climates around the world, but the principal sources of import into the United States are Colombia, Mexico, and Jamaica. It is estimated that approximately 7 percent of all the marijuana used in the United States is grown domestically (see Figure 17-10). Its most common nicknames are pot, reefer, tea, grass, weeds, Maryjane, and joint. Marijuana is made by crushing or chopping the dried leaves and flowers of the plant into small pieces. The cleaned or manicured leaves are then rolled into a cigarette, smoked otherwise, or mixed with food and eaten. The principal psychoactive substance is thought to be delta-9-tetrahydrocannabinol (THC), a chemical found nowhere else in nature. Low doses of the drug tend to produce initial restfulness and wellbeing, followed by a dreamy, carefree state of relaxation and an alteration of sensory perceptions, including an illusory expansion of time and space.

HASHISH

A drug-rich resinous secretion from the flowers of the cannabis plant, hashish is processed by drying to produce a drug several times as potent as marijuana. The resin from the flowers is richer in cannabinols than the leaves and tops; the THC content ranges from 5 to 12 percent. (The leaves range from 0.27 to 4 percent in THC content.) Hashish is most commonly smoked in a small "hash pipe."

FIGURE 17-10   Sources of Marijuana

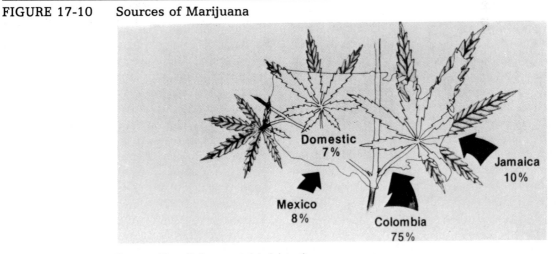

Courtesy Drug Enforcement Administration

HASHISH OIL

Liquid hashish is produced by concentrating THC. The liquid hashish so far discovered has varied between 20 percent and 65 percent THC. There is reason to suspect that methods are now being employed to make an even more powerful concentrate. The purity of the final product depends on the sophistication of the apparatus used.

Like other forms of the drug, liquid hashish can be used several ways. Because of its extraordinary potency, one drop of the material can produce a high. A drop may be placed on a regular cigarette, used in cooking, in wine, and even smeared on bread. When smoked, a small drop of hashish oil is smeared inside the glass bowl of a special pipe with a flattened side. The user exhales deeply, tilts the bowl, and holds the flame from a match under the oil. In one inhalation, the smoker draws slowly on the pipe as the oil begins to bubble, continuing as it chars and burns.

There are many ways to produce hashish oil, but most clandestine operations use a basket filled with ground or chopped marijuana suspended inside a larger container, at the bottom of which is contained a solvent, such as alcohol, hexane, chloroform, or petroleum ether. Copper tubing or similar material is arranged at the top, and cold water circulates through it. The solvent is heated, the vapors rise to the top, they condense, and then they fall into the basket of marijuana. As the solvent seeps through the plant materials, the THC and other soluble chemicals are dissolved, and the solution drops back to the bottom of the container. Continued heating causes the process to recur. The solution becomes increasingly stronger until the plant material is exhausted of its THC. Sometimes new material is added and the solvent reheated, yielding an even more potent solution.

Most of the hashish oil that has been con-

fiscated originated in India or Afghanistan and was shipped via commercial freight directly to the United States or Canada for forwarding. So far, most of the senders and laboratory operators have been United States citizens.[24]

FIELD TESTING FOR CONTROLLED SUBSTANCES

Chemical field tests, using reagents and test kits, give valuable clues about the identity of samples. Field tests are easy to perform. They are, however, only presumptive, because they may produce false positives. Any drug which will be used as evidence must be positively identified by a qualified chemist. Additionally, a negative test does not preclude the possibility that another similar drug may be present.[25]

INVESTIGATIVE PROCEDURES

Most of the techniques used in investigating dangerous drugs and narcotics investigations are the same as those used in other cases; however, there are certain unique procedures.[26] *The Purchase (NB)*

One important aspect is identification of the source. This is accomplished through review of completed reports of investigation, other information received from an informant, or from surveillance and direct efforts to purchase drugs. It is desirable to make more than one direct purchase from a seller, if possible. This procedure gives investigators more opportunity to locate the peddler's cache of narcotics or source of supply. It also serves to identify other customers and to establish that the seller is not a one-time or opportunistic dealer. As a seller's sources of supply and customers are identified, the possibility of identifying key people in the network increases.

If an arrest is to be made immediately after a purchase, the currency used to make the buy should be dusted with fluorescent powder. The serial numbers of the currency should always be recorded for comparison with that recovered from other defendants, for it may suggest an unsuspected link among traffickers and thus a conspiracy. Recovered currency should be treated as evidence.

If a peddler will sell only to an informant and not to an undercover investigator, the informant must be searched before the sale to make sure that they have no narcotics in their possession. Any money found on the informant should be removed. Informants should be searched immediately after the sale. At this time, money should be returned. Between the two searches, the informants must be kept under constant surveillance so that their testimony can be corroborated. Evidence obtained through "informant buys" is admissible in court, but the testimony of the informant may be required.

THE APPREHENSION

All arrests should be as unobtrusive as possible to prevent them from becoming common knowledge on the street. This practice preserves the usefulness of the information the arrested party provides.

When approaching a drug suspect, the investigator must be particularly observant of the suspect's hands. The suspect may attempt to drop, throw, flush, eat, or otherwise dispose of drugs. If drugs are found on the ground or some distance away from the suspect, it may be extremely difficult, if not impossible, to connect the drug with the suspect. Because addicts can be dangerous, unpredictable, and uncooperative, investigators must exercise caution. Addicts may use a weapon or suddenly attack the unwary investigator. As soon as possible after apprehension, suspects should be required to place their hands directly in the air or behind their heads to preclude further disposal of evidence.

The investigator must ensure that drugs taken from the custody of persons suspected of a narcotics offense have not been prescribed. If certain seized drugs are necessary for a suspect's health, a physician's opinion should be sought on administering the drug.

Immediately after the apprehension or as soon as possible thereafter, a thorough search should be made of the suspect's person, clothing, and area of immediate control. The possession of even the minutest of drug particles may be sufficient to establish a connection.[27] Because the quantity of the drug may be small, hiding places are almost limitless. The law enforcement officer should use the full range of skills and imagination to search for them.

THE INVESTIGATOR'S PREVENTION RESPONSIBILITY

Investigators can often reduce the possibility that a physician or pharmacist will be victimized or help the magnitude of the loss. Ordinarily, investigators talk with these professionals during the investigation of an offense, while obtaining information not directly related to an offense, or in speaking before civic or professional groups. Physicians and pharmacists should be made aware of the following precautions:

Physicians should not:

- Leave unattended prescription pads in the open
- Forget that prescriptions written in pencil may be altered
- Carry a large stock of narcotics in their medical bags
- Store narcotics where patients can obtain easy access (near sinks or lavatories)
- Issue a narcotics prescription without seeing the patient

- Write prescriptions for large quantities of narcotics unless absolutely necessary
- Prescribe a narcotic because a patient says that another physician has been doing it
- Leave signed blank prescriptions in the office for nurses to complete
- Treat an ambulatory case of addiction
- Dispense narcotics without making the necessary records
- Purchase narcotics for office use with prescription blanks; the law requires an official order form
- Act resentful if a pharmacist calls to confirm a prescription for narcotics (the pharmacist can be held responsible for filling forged prescriptions)
- Hesitate to call the local police department to obtain or give information

Pharmacists should not:

- Leave or display narcotics near the cash register
- Fail to scrutinize prescriptions written in a way that makes alterations possible; for example,

Morph. HT ½ # X
          or
Morph. HT ¼ # 10

In the above illustration several X marks or zeros could be added to raise quantities. Physicians should be advised to spell out the prescription completely or to use brackets

- Carry a large stock of narcotics; a three-month supply is advisable
- Leave a key in the lock of the narcotics cabinet, which is locked at all times
- Fail to keep all excess drugs in a safe, if possible
- Place narcotics stock where it is accessible to others
- Leave the prescription area unattended, if possible
- Forget that a request for rapid filling of a

prescription may be a ploy to distract them from checking a forged prescription
- Fill telephone orders for narcotic drugs unless assured that a prescription will be available upon delivery
- Be taken in by a person wearing a white uniform who presents a narcotics prescription
- Refill narcotics prescriptions
- Fill prescriptions for unusual quantities without checking with the physician
- Hesitate to call a physician if the validity of a prescription is questioned
- Supply a doctor's office needs from a prescription
- Accept a narcotics prescription written in pencil
- Leave prescription pads in accessible areas

DRUG ABUSE BY PRACTITIONERS

It has always been perplexing to investigators that a professional would become involved with drugs. But doctors do succumb to addiction. Doctors have ready access to drugs and may turn to them out of fatigue, stress, or pain. Those who succumb may be only marginally adjusted to their environment.

They may function reasonably well at the onset of their addiction. An injection of Demerol, a tablet of codeine with aspirin, a bottle of cough medicine, may offer temporary euphoria and an escape from the pressure of living. Once the drug is used habitually, the doctor's ability to discern right from wrong falters. The doctor begins to rationalize, lie, connive, steal, and sometimes beg to perpetuate the habit. Physically, morally, and mentally, addiction becomes complete. The spouse may be initiated into the habit, whether for commiseration or to avoid censure.

Regardless of previous social or professional position, the addicted doctor becomes unreliable. Each day is governed by the need to "get right," and maintenance of a routine is more and more difficult. Functioning by reflex works for a time, but discriminating judgments become increasingly less possible.

Well meaning colleagues may become aware of the problem and try to assist. But the addict requires extensive assistance, usually beyond a colleague's "out-patient" approach. Discounting the criminal aspect, an adequate approach is hospitalization in a narcotics-free environment with extensive follow-up psychological treatment. The absence of responsible action may lead to tragedy.

Among the most common indications that a physician may be unlawfully diverting drugs are:

- A physician places excessively frequent orders for narcotics.
- A physician picks up and pays for filled narcotics prescriptions from a pharmacy.
- A physician places an emergency call for a narcotic medication to a pharmacy and requests delivery. The deliverer is met by the physician and given a prescription for the drugs. In some instances, no patient exists, or if one does exist the narcotics are retained by the physician and other medication substituted.
- A narcotics prescription is issued to a patient by a physician with instructions to have it filled and to return with the drug for administration. Substitute medication is then given to the patient.
- In narcotics records, a physician uses fictitious or deceased people's names and addresses.
- The physician frequently requests that a prescription for an alleged patient be taken to the pharmacy by a nurse, a receptionist, or a member of the family and be returned to the doctor personally.
- While other physicians are in the operating room or making hospital rounds, the addict-physician searches their vehicles or medical bags for narcotics.

- A physician obtains a key to the narcotics locker in a hospital and has a duplicate made.
- A physician may place an order for a patient in a hospital; when the drug is prepared by a nurse, the doctor takes it over and either uses a substitute syringe containing a placebo or administers only a small portion of the drug.

If a case for prosecution is indicated against an addicted physician, an investigator must interview pharmacists, review prescriptions, and take statements from patients who allegedly received drugs prescribed by the doctor. The evidence thus obtained is used to secure an indictment.[28]

SEARCH WARRANTS AND PROBABLE CAUSE

Officers engaged in drug enforcement must understand the legal elements necessary to constitute probable cause for obtaining search warrants. The criteria for ascertaining probable cause vary somewhat even within judicial districts. However, a number of broad legal guidelines can be useful. These guidelines can assist the officer in working through the legal maze to a search warrant and in securing a warrant capable of withstanding the scrutiny of the highest court.

The vast majority of drug information provided to law enforcement officers comes from confidential informants. Therefore, it is of particular significance that certain legal guidelines be followed carefully by those responsible for drafting search warrants.

LAW ENFORCEMENT BACKGROUND OF THE APPLICANT

Some factors to be considered in assessing the background of the law enforcement officer seeking the warrant are length of time employed by the agency, present position, familiarity with the offense in question, the number of previous arrests made by the applicant for this type of offense, and, if applicable, familiarity with any paraphernalia used in connection with the offense.

PAST RELIABILITY OF THE CONFIDENTIAL INFORMANT

The past reliability of the confidential informant is of considerable importance, especially when the effort to determine probable cause to obtain a search warrant is based exclusively on such information. One should consider the length of time the applicant has known the informant and the number of occasions on which reliable information was supplied. For example, how many times before did the confidential informant's information result in the seizure of contraband or paraphernalia on persons, premises, or in vehicles, and how many of these offenses resulted in a conviction? To confirm that the confidential informant has been reliable, the officer should be prepared to cite specific instances of reliable information. Other considerations are the informant's familiarity with the type of offense involved in the affidavit and familiarity with paraphernalia used in connection with the offense.

INFORMATION SUPPLIED BY THE INFORMANT

Information to be considered in this area includes the date, time, and place of the meeting between police and the informant; the substance and content of the information; and the date, time, and place that the information was obtained.

The law enforcement officer should try to elicit from the informant as many facts as possible that can be corroborated, for example, the telephone number and address of the suspect's residence, a physical description of the suspect, the occupation of the suspect, vehicles owned or operated by the suspect, a description of the vehicle and the tag number, and the time at which the suspect may be observed at the premises or within the described vehicle.

CORROBORATION OF THE INFORMATION SUPPLIED

All efforts should be made to corroborate information supplied by a confidential informant. In some instances, corroboration is a simple check of the accuracy of portions of the information, such as the suspect's address, associates, vehicle, hangouts, patterns of behavior, criminal record, and so forth. When information is corroborated, careful records should be kept, including the date, time, and method of corroboration. Some jurisdictions have found it useful to attach a mug shot of the suspect and a photograph, diagram, or sketch of the property, vehicle, store, or other place to be searched.[29]

EVIDENCE HANDLING AND SECURITY PROBLEMS

When law enforcement officials think of the drug problem, their minds summon up the conventional images of pushers and addicts. They hardly even think of any of the other ills associated with drug abuse.

Aside from the burglaries, larcenies, and other crimes committed because of narcotics, there are additional related problems sprouting from the drug culture vine. Some of these growths entwine the individual police officer and the overall police function. One offshoot, the handling and securing of narcotics and dangerous drugs after they are collected and seized, has emerged as an area of growing concern to police administrators for a number of reasons.

Once seized by the police, narcotic and

dangerous drug evidence requires protection in order that it may be preserved in its original state until it is brought before a court or destroyed through legal process. It is during this period that the greatest demands are placed on personnel of the law enforcement agency concerned. Not only must narcotic and dangerous drug evidence be protected against loss and outside threats of incursion, but, unfortunately, sometimes from internal intrusions as well.

Although relatively uncommon, there have been occasions when narcotic and dangerous drug evidence has disappeared from a "secure" area under the control and within the confines of a police agency.[30]

Grosso and Rosenberg, in their book, *Point Blank,* discuss the disappearance of the infamous "French Connection" heroin from the property vaults of the New York City Police Department and the slipshod way in which drug evidence was handled:

The whole system was, to say the least, inadequate, and for years the Department knew that something had to be done about it. In the time-honored tradition of bureaucracies everywhere, it studied the problem and then did nothing until it was time for the next study. Then, in October 1972, an attractive twenty-three-year-old woman from Long Island walked into the offices of the Internal Affairs Division—which, coincidentally, were also located at the Broome Street Annex—and swore out a rape complaint against a New York City policeman. After checking out her story, IAD detectives were sent to arrest the policeman at his home in Little Neck. There they discovered three small packets of heroin in plastic bags bearing the seal of the Police Department Property Clerk.

At first Internal Affairs wanted to charge the cop not only with rape but also with trafficking in narcotics, but he was quickly cleared on the second count. The drugs turned out to be the evidence in an active case. He had signed them out on the day the case went to trial, then took them home with him each night in order to save the hours each morning and night at the Broome Street shape-up. What he had done was against regulations but it was no crime.

The Department had long known about this expedient and relatively harmless method of circumventing its own time-consuming procedures. Figuring that every hour its men spent standing on line outside the Property Clerk's windows was that much time away from the job, it winked at the practice. This time, though, the Police Department was afraid that if the story leaked out it could result in a major scandal. The commissioner ordered a complete audit of the Property Clerk's logbooks.

Even before this order could be put into effect, the commissioner learned that a mere audit of the books wouldn't even begin to uncover all that was wrong with the Property Clerk's Office. He received a call from an upstate district attorney who had news for him that was so confidential in nature that he wouldn't give it over the phone. When the commissioner arrived at the D.A.'s office, he was told that a reliable informant had told a member of the district attorney's staff that he knew of at least one large drug deal involving narcotics stolen from the New York City Property Clerk's Office. "Tell them to check the stuff from the French Connection," the informant had said.

The commissioner raced back to the city and ordered an immediate and complete investigation of the Property Clerk's Office. In addition to examining the logbooks, the examiners were to count, weigh, and chemically analyze every packet of narcotics at 400 Broome Street. By mid-December the team of detectives, auditors, and chemists assigned to scrutinize the Property Clerk's Office had made a preliminary finding that sent tidal waves of shock coursing through the Department hierarchy. On Thursday, December 14, 1972, Police Commissioner Murphy called a press conference in the large meeting hall on the ground floor of the old Headquarters building. Tense and obviously shaken, the commissioner announced that a portion of the heroin seized in the so-called French Connection case and held in the Property Clerk's Office since 1962 had mysteriously disappeared. Of the ninety-seven pounds of pure heroin originally logged in, only sixteen were still in the Police Department's possession. The rest had simply vanished. With the audit still incomplete, the commissioner had to admit that the Department had lost at least eighteen million dollars' worth of narcotics. Reluctantly answering a direct question, the usually imperturbable Murphy conceded that it was "theoretically possible" that these losses might be only the tip of the iceberg.

Other Department spokesmen were more candid. The French Connection drugs, they explained, were in two batches. A suitcase which originally contained twenty-four pounds of heroin now contained only one pound of the pure drug and twenty-three pounds of an unspecified white powder. In addition, a steamer trunk, which was on record as having held seventy-three pounds of heroin, also had been looted. Desperately trying to find one bright spot in an otherwise dismal situation, the spokesman pointed out that at first the trunk had been thought missing. It wasn't in the safe and the Property Clerk's logbooks revealed that it had been signed out to Detective Joe Longo in 1969 and never returned.

Fortunately, when the entire Property Clerk's Office was searched, the missing trunk turned up in a remote and relatively inaccessible area far from where it should have been. Analysis of its contents re-

vealed that it still contained fifteen pounds of the original heroin and forty-seven pounds of another white substance. Eleven pounds were gone entirely, with no substitution.

There were no celebrations at Police Headquarters that Christmas. As the audit went on, it quickly became apparent that Commissioner Murphy had grossly underestimated the extent of the loss. Through December and into January, Murphy was repeatedly forced to issue updated figures with the latest tallies of the Department's losses. By early February, when the results were all in, they added up to the biggest ripoff in the annals of crime. Beside the Property Clerk job, such legendary heists as the Brinks robbery, the Hotel Pierre jewel caper, and the Nice bank robbery begin to look like petty stickups. In all, the thieves had gotten away with 261 pounds of heroin and 137 pounds of cocaine, a total that represented roughly 21 percent of all the drugs seized in New York in the eleven years since the French Connection arrests. Conservative estimates valued the haul at approximately seventy-two million dollars.

That staggering sum represents the street value only of the drugs *known* to have been stolen. But each summer the Police Department burns all the narcotics it is holding from cases closed out during the preceding year. How much of that had been tampered with? Over the years, had the Police Department been annually incinerating hundreds of pounds of talcum powder, milk sugar, and chalk? If so, then the true value of the drugs stolen from the Property Clerk's Office may run into the hundreds of millions of dollars.

No one close to the situation could fail to notice the irony involved in the Property Clerk thefts. The New York City Police Department faced the greatest robbery in history in the triple role of investigator, victim, and number-one suspect.[31]

However, the problems relating to the confiscation and security of drugs are by no means confined solely to the issue of internal thefts. There have been numerous instances when the evidentiary chain of custody has, for one reason or another, been broken, thereby rendering evidence worthless for prosecution purposes.

For the most part, drug evidence has been lost through negligence, poor record keeping, lack of knowledge, absence of clearly defined instructions, and insufficient or weak security practices. Only a few instances of missing drugs have ever been found to be related to theft by dishonest employees.

QUESTIONS

1. What are the three fundamental parts of the Controlled Substances Act?
2. Under what guidelines might the military help local law enforcement to stem the flow of illegal drugs from overseas?
3. What major drugs of abuse are derived from opium?
4. What role does the drug methadone play in treating heroin addicts?
5. What factors may indicate that a person is addicted to opium-derived drugs or synthetic opiates?
6. What are "designer drugs," and what are their pharmacological effects?
7. What types of physiological reactions are caused by: a. stimulants? b. depressants? c. hallucinogens?
8. What are the acute and chronic effects of cocaine use?
9. What is freebasing?
10. What is speedballing?
11. What are some of the known side effects of PCP?
12. What are the positive and negative arguments for the use of MDMA?
13. What types of drug theft preventive measures may physicians or pharmacists take to reduce the likelihood of being victimized?
14. What are the most common indications that a physician is unlawfully diverting drugs for his or her own use?
15. Which major factors should be considered when attempting to secure a search warrant based solely on information supplied by a confidential informant?
16. What are some of the major reasons for the loss of drug evidence by the police?

NOTES

1. William W. Vodra, "The Controlled Substances Act," *Drugs of Abuse*. Washington, D.C.: Drug Enforcement Administration, 1975, p. 2.
2. Ibid., p. 36.
3. An exception to this is marijuana, a Schedule I drug, which is being used in certain cases on patients suffering from the eye disease glaucoma. Also, plans have been approved to allow 4,000 cancer specialists to prescribe synthetic marijuana pills to control nausea and vomiting for cancer patients undergoing chemotherapy. The pills, which contain the concentrate delta-9-tetrahydrocannabinol (THC), are useful in controlling some of the side effects. One estimate by the National Cancer Institute is that THC is 30 percent to 50 percent effective. This use of THC as an experimental drug has not changed marijuana's status as an illegal substance.
4. Vodra, "Controlled Substances Act," pp. 3–5.
5. For a more thorough discussion of this law,

see Steven Zimmerman "Posse Comitatus," *Drug Enforcement,* Summer 1982, Vol. 9, No. 1, pp. 17–20.

6. United States Department of the Army, *Field Manual—Military Police Criminal Investigation* (Washington, D.C.: 1971), p. 28–5.

7. Ibid., pp. 28–5, 28–7.

8. John H. Langer et al., "Drugs of Abuse: Narcotics," *Drugs of Abuse* (Washington, D.C.: Drug Enforcement Administration, 1975), pp. 10, 12–13.

9. United States Department of the Army, *Field Manual,* p. 28–8.

10. Malachi L. Harney and John C. Cross, *The Narcotics Officer's Notebook* (Springfield, Ill.: Charles C. Thomas, 1961), pp. 96–98.

11. Robert J. Roberton, *Testimony Presented to the President's Commission on Organized Crime in Miami, Florida.* February 21, 1985. This discussion of designer drugs was obtained from pp. 5–14.

12. Smith Kline and French Laboratories, *Drug Abuse* (Philadelphia: 1971), p. 10.

13. Robert C. Petersen, "Cocaine: An Overview," *Drug Enforcement* (Washington, D.C.: Government Printing Office, December 1977), pp. 9–12.

14. Langer et al., *Drugs of Abuse,* p. 19.

15. John B. Williams, *Narcotics and Drug Dependence* (Encino, Calif.: Glencoe, 1974), p. 273.

16. United States Department of Health, Education, and Welfare, *Students and Drugs* (Washington, D.C.: Government Printing Office, 1969), pp. 8–9.

17. Drug Enforcement Administration, *Fact Sheets* (Washington, D.C.: Government Printing Office, 1973), p. 43.

18. Langer et al., *Drugs of Abuse,* p. 16.

19. "The Cheap New Killer," *Time,* July 20, 1981, p. 20.

20. Robert C. Petersen and Richard C. Stillman, "Phencyclidine Abuse," *Drug Enforcement* (Washington, D.C.: Government Printing Office, July 1978), pp. 19–20.

21. "Angel Dust—Abuse Diagnostic Test Introduced," *The Police Chief,* November 1979, Vol. XLVI, No. 11, p. 12.

22. Anastasia Toufexis and Patricia Delaney, *Time,* June 10, 1985, p. 64.

23. *Tampa Tribune,* "Way Found to Detect LSD in Humans." Tampa, Fl., September 8, 1972.

24. *Liquid Hashish* (Washington, D.C.: Department of Justice, Drug Enforcement Administration, 1978), pp. 5–7.

25. Drug Enforcement Administration, "Field Testing for Controlled Substances" (Washington, D.C.: National Training Institute, U.S. Department of Justice, 1973), pp. 1–5, 6.

26. U.S. Department of the Army, *Field Manual,* pp. 28–16, 28–17.

27. Ibid., p. 28–18.

28. Drug Enforcement Administration, "Addict Practitioners." Handout material provided by the U.S. Department of Justice, Drug Enforcement Administration, National Training Institute, Washington, D.C.

29. E. J. Salcines, "Checklist of Elements Constituting Probable Cause in Search Warrant Affidavits." Prepared by the State Attorney's Office, Hillsborough County, Tampa, Fl., 1974.

30. *Guidelines for Narcotic and Dangerous Drug Evidence Handling and Security Procedures* (Washington, D.C.: Drug Enforcement Administration. U.S. Department of Justice and Field Operation Division, International Association of Chiefs of Police, 1976). This manual is available at no cost from the Drug Enforcement Administration, Washington, D.C.

31. Sonny Grosso and Philip Rosenberg, *Point Blank* (New York: Grosset and Dunlap, 1978), pp. 294–297. (Used by permission of Grosset and Dunlap, Inc.)

APPENDIX

Acapulco Gold: High grade of marijuana

Acid: LSD, LSD 25 (lysergic acid diethylamide)

Acidhead: Regular user of LSD

Acid Test: Party at which LSD has been added to the punch, food, etc.

Agonies: Withdrawal symptoms

All Lit Up: Under the influence of a drug

Amobarbital: A barbiturate

Amphetamine: Stimulant drug which increases the activity of the central nervous system

Amytal: A barbiturate

Angel Dust: Phencyclidine (PCP on parsley)

Arsenal: Supply of drugs

Artillery: Equipment for injecting drugs; the works; the needle, eyedropper, spoon, bottle cap, cotton, and cloth, string, or belt for a tourniquet

Bad Go: Bad reaction to a drug; inferior drug purchased

Bad Scene: Trouble; unpleasant experience with a drug

Bag: Packet of drugs

Baghead: Someone involved in glue sniffing

Bagman: Supplier; person holding drugs for supplier

Ball: Absorption of stimulants and cocaine via genitalia

Balloon: A balloon containing approximately two doses of heroin

Bang: Injection of drugs

Barbiturates: Drugs that depress the central nervous system

Barbs: Barbiturates

Barrels: LSD tablets

Bennies: Benzedrine, an amphetamine

Bindle: Packet of narcotics

Black Beauties: Amphetamines

Blanks: Extremely low-grade narcotics

Blast: Strong effect from a drug

Blue Acid: LSD

Blue Angels: Barbiturates (amytal and amobarbital)

Blue Birds: Barbiturates (amytal and amobarbital)

Blue Devils: Barbiturates (amytal and amobarbital)

Blue Funk: Deep depression

Blue Heavens: Barbiturates (amytal and amobarbital)

Blue Velvet: Paregoric (camphorated tincture of opium) and pyribenzamine (an antihistamine) mixed and injected

Bombed Out: High on marijuana and other drugs

Bombita: Amphetamine injection, sometimes taken with heroin

Bread: Money

Brown: Mexican heroin; usually of lower quality than white heroin

Bummer: Bad experience with psychedelics

Bum Trip: Bad experience with psychedelics

Burn, Burned: To cheat; be cheated out of money or drugs; to have identity disclosed

Burned Out: Collapse of the veins from repeated injections

Busted: Arrested

Buttons: The sections of the peyote cactus

Candy Man: Drug seller; one who deals in a

559

variety of pills, tablets, and capsules of various shapes and colors

Cannabinol: Tetrahydrocannabinol; THC (active ingredient of cannabis)

Cap: Capsule of narcotics

Cartwheels: Amphetamines (round, white, double-scored tablets)

Chicken Powder: Amphetamine powder

Chief: LSD

China Death: Heroin containing strychnine or cyanide

China White: An illicitly synthesized derivative of fentanyl (a designer drug); high-grade heroin from Southeast Asia

Chipping: Taking narcotics occasionally

Clean: Out of drugs; not using drugs

Coasting: Under the influence of drugs; not using drugs; refers also to marijuana from which stems and twigs have been removed

Cocaine: Potent stimulant drug obtained from coca leaf

Cokie: Cocaine addict

Cold Turkey: Abrupt withdrawal from drugs, without medication; skin resembles the texture of a cold plucked turkey

Come Down: End a trip; drug effect wearing off

Connection: Source of supply

Cooker: Spoon or bottle cap for heating heroin and water

Cop: To obtain heroin

Cop Out: Quit, take off, confess, inform, be defeated

Copilot: The person with whom one takes an LSD trip; amphetamines

Cotton Shot: Drug-saturated cotton to which water is added to get whatever heroin is left

Crack: Also known as rock cocaine, it is purer and more concentrated than regular cocaine

Crash: To collapse from exhaustion after continuous use of amphetamines; enjoyable sleep after smoking marijuana; to come down from an LSD trip

Crash Pad: Place where the user withdraws from amphetamines

Cross Tops: Amphetamine tablets manufactured at home or in clandestine laboratories. They have an X on the surface of the pill.

Cubehead: Frequent user of LSD

Cut: Dilute drugs by adding milk, sugar, or another inert substance

Dealer: Drug supplier

Deck: Packet of narcotics

Dexies: Dexedrine, an amphetamine

Dime Bag: $10 package of narcotics

Dirty: Possessing drugs; liable to be arrested if searched

Dollies: Dolophine (also known as methadone), a synthetic narcotic

Dolls: Pills (amphetamines, barbiturates, etc.)

Doper: Person who uses drugs regularly

Downers: Depressant drugs; barbiturates

Dried Out: Cured of drug dependence (usually cold turkey)

Drop: Swallow a drug

Dummy: Purchase which did not contain narcotics

Dynamite: High-grade heroin

Ecstasy: MDMA

Feed Bag: A container of narcotics or other drugs

Feed Store: A place where drugs can be purchased

Fifteen Cents: $15; a packet of drugs selling for $15

Fix: Injection of narcotics

Flash: The first euphoric sensation after taking a drug

Flashback: Unpredictable recurrence of an LSD trip long after the last trip was taken with drugs; may occur weeks or months after the last drug-induced trip

Flip: Become psychotic

Floating: Under the influence of drugs

Freakout: Bad experience with psychedelics; also, a chemical high

Freebasing: Chemical process used to increase the strength of cocaine

Fire Up: To take a drug intravenously

Fuzz: The police

Gage: Marijuana

Garbage: Low-grade drug; no drug content

Good Trip: Happy experience with psychedelics

Goofballs: Barbiturates

Grass: Marijuana

Greenies: Amphetamines (oval tablets)

H: Heroin

H and C: Mixture of heroin and cocaine (speedball)

Hard Narcotics: Opiates, such as heroin and morphine

Hard Stuff: Heroin

Hash: Hashish, the resin of cannabis

Hay: Marijuana

Head: Person dependent on drugs

Hearts: Dexedrine tablets (from the shape)

Heat: The police

Heavenly Blues: Type of morning-glory seeds

Heroin: The most potent narcotic drug derived from morphine

High: Euphoric; under the influence of a drug

Hit: Make a purchase; the effect of drugs; to steal drugs, money, or merchandise; to inject

Holding: Having drugs in one's possession

Hooked: Addicted

Hophead: Narcotics addict

Horse: Heroin

Hot Load, Hot Shot: Overdose; lethal drug dose; usually refers to drugs given deliberately to eliminate a troublesome customer, such as an informer; pure heroin or a heroin mixture containing a poison such as strychnine or cyanide

Hustle: Activities involved in obtaining money to buy heroin

Hustler: Prostitute

Hype: Narcotics addict

Joint: Marijuana cigarette

Jolly Beans: Pep pills

Joy Pop: Occasional injection of narcotics (usually under the skin rather than in the vein)

Junkie: Narcotics addict

K, Kee, Key: One kilogram, 2.2 pounds

Kicking: Withdrawal process

Kicking Cold: Ceasing drug use, without medical support

Kicking the Gong: Usually refers to smoking marijuana or hashish

Kilo: Kilogram, 2.2 pounds

Kit: Equipment for injecting drugs; the works

Layout: Equipment for injecting drugs

Lemonade: Poor grade of heroin

Loaded: High on marijuana

Loco Weed: Marijuana

Ludes: Quaaludes (methaqualone)

M: Morphine

Mainline: Inject drugs into a vein

Maintaining: Keeping at a certain level of drug effect

Make: To identify a police officer who is working undercover

Make a Reader: Have a doctor write a prescription

(The) Man: Can be either the police or one's main supplier of drugs

Manicure: Remove the dirt, seeds, and stems from marijuana

Mary Jane: Marijuana

Mesc: Mescaline, the alkaloid in peyote

Meth: Methamphetamine

Methhead: Habitual user of methamphetamine

Mikes: Micrograms (millionths of a gram)

Monkey: Drug habit; physical dependence

Mule: Transporter of drugs

Nailed: Arrested

Narc: Narcotics detective

Nembies: Nembutal (a barbiturate); pentobarbital

Nickel Bag: $5 bag of drugs

Nod: The sleep and relaxation after a shot of heroin (on the nod)

Nose Candy: Cocaine

Numb: Under the influence of cocaine after snorting it

O.D.:   Overdose of narcotics

On a Trip: Under the influence of a hallucinogen

On the Nod: Sleepy from narcotics

Oranges: Amphetamines (orange colored, heart shaped); Dexedrine

Outfit: Equipment for injecting drugs

Panic: Shortage of narcotics on the market

Paper: Small quantity of drugs; prescription for drugs

Peaches: Amphetamines (Benzedrine)

Pep Pills: Amphetamines

Persian White: Fentanyls (designer drugs)

Peyote: Hallucinogen from peyote cactus

Pink Hearts or **Pinks:**   Dexedrine tablets

Pop: Inject beneath the skin

Pot: Marijuana

Pothead: Heavy marijuana user

Powder: Heroin

Pure: Very good grade of heroin

Purple Hearts: Dexamyl, a combination of Dexedrine and Amytal (from the shape and color)

Pusher: Drug peddler

Quill: A matchbook cover for sniffing Methedrine, cocaine, or heroin

Rainbows: Tuinal (Amytal and Seconal), a

barbiturate combination in a blue and red capsule

Red Birds, Red Bullets, Red Devils, Reds: A barbiturate (Seconal)

Reefer: Marijuana cigarette

Reentry: Return from a trip

Roach: Marijuana cigarette butt

Roach Clip: A clip, tweezer, or device (same as a crutch) to hold a short marijuana cigarette

Rocks: High-grade cocaine

Run: An amphetamine binge

STP: Hallucinogen (stands for Serenity, Tranquility, and Peace) related to mescaline and amphetamines

Satch Cotton: Cotton used to strain drugs before injection; may be used again if supplies are gone

Sick: Going through drug withdrawal, usually from heroin

Scag: Heroin

Score: Make a purchase of drugs

Scrip, Script: Prescription for drugs; money

Script Writer: Sympathetic doctor; prescription forger

Seccies, Seccy: Seconal

Shit: Drugs in general; heroin

Shoot, Shoot up: Inject

Shooting Gallery: Place where addicts inject drugs

Shot Down: Under the influence of drugs

Skin Popping: Injecting drugs under the skin

Smack: Heroin

Smoke: Marijuana

Snorting: Inhaling drugs

Snow: Cocaine

Speed: Methamphetamine

Speedball: An injection of a stimulant and a depressant, originally heroin and cocaine

Speedfreak: Habitual user of speed

Stash: Supply of drugs in a secure place

Step-on: Dilution of a drug, typically heroin or cocaine, with some other substance

Stick: Marijuana cigarette

Stomach Addict: An addict who eats heroin

Stoned: Under the influence of drugs

Stoolie: Informer

Strung Out: Addicted

Tea Pad: Meeting place for marijuana users

Tea Party: Get-together of marijuana smokers

TCH: Tetrahydrocannabinol; purified resin extract from the hemp plant; also synthetically produced. Said to be the substance responsible for the mind-altering effects of cannabis

Tooies: Tuinal

Tools: Equipment for injecting drugs

Tracks: Scars along veins after many injections

Tripping Out: High on psychedelics

Turkey Trots: Marks and scars from repeated injections

Turned On: Under the influence of drugs

Turps: Elixir of terpin hydrate with codeine, a cough syrup

25: LSD (from its original designation, LSD 25)

Uppers: Stimulants, cocaine, and psychedelics

Weed: Marijuana

Whites: Stimulants, generally amphetamines

Window Pane: A small piece of cellophane with LSD on it

Works: Equipment for injecting drugs

Yellow Jackets: Nembutal, a barbiturate

Yen Shee: Ashes of opium

Yen Shee Suey: Opium ash mixed with wine or other beverages

Yen Sleep: A drowsy, restless state during the withdrawal period

Zonked: Heavily addicted; under the extreme influence of drugs

18

THE DECISION TO INITIATE THE CRIMINAL PROCESS

INTRODUCTION

At some point during the fruitful investigation of any criminal offense, officers must make a number of decisions that invoke the formal processes of the justice system. When an arrest is to be made and formal charges brought against a suspect or when the investigator brings an uncharged suspect in for interrogation, he or she must know the legal requirements.

ARREST DEFINED

There are a number of definitions of the term *arrest*. They range from "any interference with a person which, if not privileged, would constitute false imprisonment," to "interfering with the freedom of a person who is suspected of criminal conduct to the extent of taking him to the police station for some purpose," and "the taking of custody upon sufficient and proper evidence for the purpose of prosecution."[1] Each of these definitions is valid and depends on context. For

example, what may appear to be a simple street stop or field interrogation may, in fact, constitute an arrest according to the first definition. Taking a person to the police station for interrogation may fit the second definition. When an investigator intends to incarcerate and charge a person with a crime, the third definition applies.

INGREDIENTS

There are three essential ingredients to an arrest:

1. intention
2. authority
3. custody

The officer must have the intention of taking the suspect into custody. This factor distinguishes an arrest from a lesser form of detention, but actual or expressed intention is not always the controlling factor. The intention may be inferred by a court if its estimate of all the conduct and circumstances indicates that an arrest occurred, despite any

FIGURE 18-1

A suspect restrained by handcuffs and under the close control of officers.

Courtesy of the Los Angeles County Sheriff's Department

contrary intent on the part of the police officer.[2]

The officer must have real or assumed legal authority for taking the person into custody. The officer must have the actual authority to make a legal arrest or at least believe this to be the case. For example, an investigator may make an arrest under a defective warrant but not know about the defect. The third ingredient is that the person arrested must come within the custody and control of the law. This element can be satisfied either by physical restraint (See Figure 18-1) or by voluntary submission of the arrestee to the custody and control of the arresting officer.[3]

ARREST DISTINGUISHED FROM DETENTION

Detention is a temporary and limited interference with the freedom of a person for investigative purposes. Sometimes called investigative detention, it also is commonly referred to by police as a street stop or field interrogation. In this instance, police are justified in employing "stop and frisk" measures—patting down the outer clothing—if they suspect that the person being questioned may be armed and their safety is in jeopardy.[4]

There is a fine line between detention and arrest. Because an officer does interfere with the freedom of the individual stopped, even for only a few minutes, some theorists view any such action as constituting arrest. Most people and most courts recognize the validity of street stops and uphold them as not being arrests if conducted properly.

A valid detention must be brief and made for good reason. The officer must limit questioning and investigation and must then either release the subject or decide to arrest. Detention for an undue length of time could be construed as an arrest if later challenged in court.

ARREST DISTINGUISHED FROM CHARGING

As noted earlier, one definition of arrest is to interfere with the freedom of a person suspected of involvement in a crime to the extent that the person is taken to the police station. But investigators do not always intend to prosecute nor have the ability to prosecute at that time. Formally charging a suspect with a crime does not automatically flow from an arrest. Charging follows a decision to prosecute. This decision may be made by the police, by the prosecutor, or both. But they may also decide not to bring charges. For example, the evidence which justified the arrest may not be sufficient to warrant charges, or additional information may come to light after the arrest. Some arrests are made following improper procedures or based on insufficient evidence. Charges are not brought following faulty arrests such as these.

ARREST PROCEDURES

The laws of most jurisdictions permit an arrest in at least three types of situations:

1. when a crime is committed in the presence of an arresting officer,
2. when a warrant has been issued, or
3. when an officer has probable cause to believe that the suspect being arrested has committed a felony

Any offense committed in the presence of an officer, whether felony or misdemeanor, can be the basis of arrest without a warrant. The in-presence requirement is usually thought of in the narrow context of sight. However, to satisfy the legal requirements, perception of some or all of the elements of an offense as they occur, through the use of any or all of the five senses—sight, hearing, taste, touch, or smell—can justify a warrantless arrest.

The most preferred method of effecting an arrest is under the authority of a warrant. In fact, if one were to read the constitutional requirements in their strictest sense, arrests can only be justified if made with a warrant. Of course, the courts have chosen to be more liberal in their interpretation so that warrantless arrests can be made in certain situations. But there are sound reasons for both the warrant requirements and the exceptions created by judicial case law. In the system, the functions of government—executive, legislative, and judicial—are each the responsibility of a separate branch. The police function is an executive one, while the judicial responsibility obviously belongs to the courts. Although the mechanism of arrest is an executive function, it is subject to judicial scrutiny and review. This position is supported by the very wording of the Fourth Amendment to the United States Constitution.

> and no warrant shall issue but upon probable cause, supported by oath or affirmation, particularly describing the . . . persons . . . to be seized.

The two major benefits derived from securing prior judicial approval for arrests through the warrant process are that it relieves the police of the burden of proving the legality of the arrest, so that officers need not fear charges of false arrest, malicious prosecution, or other civil suits; and it provides for an independent evaluation of the evidence.

Even the most objective, well-trained, and well-intentioned investigators sometimes become so involved in a case that it may affect their ability to evaluate its merits objectively. Presenting the case before a qualified judge has the benefits of allowing for an independent third party, with no emotional involvement in the investigation and with the knowledge of legal standards that must be met, to assist the investigator in determining whether those standards have been achieved. It is also logical to assume that the validity of an arrest made following this review and the issuance of a warrant is more likely to be upheld if later challenged in court than an arrest based solely on an officer's own determination of the sufficiency of the evidence. The wise police officer recognizes the value of obtaining a warrant whenever practical. The word *practical* has significance with regard to the propriety of securing an arrest warrant. The law recognizes that the innumerable situations encountered by police officers in daily activities and the variety of conditions inherent in the nature of the police function make it impossible and unrealistic to expect an officer to obtain a warrant in every situation before effecting an arrest; hence, the exceptions to the warrant requirement. One of those exceptions, the in-presence commission, has already been discussed; another, probable cause, is discussed in a subsequent section of this chapter.

The procedure required for obtaining a warrant is often time-consuming and inconvenient. Frequently, the process in major felony cases requires the investigator to seek out the prosecutor, present the facts which will be reduced to paper in affidavit form, find a judge who is authorized to issue warrants, present the case again for a determination of the sufficiency of the grounds for arrest, and then wait for the warrant to be typed up and signed. In many cases, the procedure can encumber many hours even during the normal work day. On weekends and late at night it may be extended even longer while the prosecutor, judge, or both are located or roused from bed. As a consequence, officers sometimes tend to take the easy way out by making a warrantless arrest, hoping they are right and believing they have sufficient grounds to act. By conducting themselves in this manner, they neglect the basic rule of thumb—get a warrant—and its underlying rationale. But the warrantless arrest is not always a short cut. As clear as the law may appear to be on the need for warrants, each case must rest on its own facts. There are relatively few cases in which it is obvious that an arrest may be made without a warrant. Similarly, those clear-cut instances when a warrant is absolutely needed are relatively few. The majority of cases fall within that vast plane requiring evaluation of the merits of each case. An arrest without a warrant, however, does not save time. In reality an officer will spend as much or more time justifying this decision in motion hearings demanded by the defense attorney than it would have taken to get a warrant in the first place. The potential consequence is that the case may be dismissed for want of a valid arrest, or that important evidence, seized as a result of the arrest, may be suppressed.

THE ARREST WARRANT

The investigator is not relieved of all responsibility for the legality of the arrest simply because a warrant was obtained. The investigator must be aware of what constitutes a valid warrant to ensure that the one in possession permits a legal arrest. An arrest warrant is a judicial order, in writing, commanding the person to whom it is issued or some other person to arrest a particular individual and to bring that person promptly before a court to answer a criminal charge. The arrest warrant must be written; it cannot be oral. In most cases, particularly major felonies, the warrant must be issued by a judge who personally reviews the facts to determine the existence of reasonable grounds as required by the Constitution. The warrant must be supported by an affidavit—a written statement of the information on which the officer seeks issuance of the warrant. In major cases, the requirements vary on whether the warrant must be issued in the county in which the offense occurred, but once issued, major case warrants can be served anywhere in the state.

The contents of a warrant are fairly standard and incorporate constitutional as well as statutory requirements. Most modern warrants, samples of which appear in Figures 18-2, 18-3, and 18-4, simply require that blanks be filled in. The form and contents usually include: 1. the authority under which the warrant is issued (the name of the state), 2. the person who is to execute the warrant (generally addressed to any peace officer of the state), 3. the identity of the person to be arrested, 4. the designation of the offense, 5. the date, time, and place of the occurrence, 6. the name of the victim, and 7. a description of the offense and how it occurred.

Blank warrants are not constitutionally valid. Before a warrant can be issued, the identity of the perpetrator must be known. The mere fact that a crime has been committed by someone unknown will not support a warrant's issuance. The Constitution requires that the warrant contain a particular description of the suspect. This description must be specific enough to permit an officer not acquainted with the case to identify the person to be arrested with reasonable certainty. Aliases may be used. If the suspect's name is not known, "John Doe" may be used provided there are other methods of particularly describing the person to be arrested such as place of residence, occupation, and a physical description.

THE PROBABLE CAUSE REQUIREMENT

The third and final major category in which a lawful arrest is generally permitted deals with offenses not committed in the officer's presence and for which a warrant has not been issued. The law allows an officer to make warrantless arrests in felony cases provided reasonable grounds or probable cause exist to make the arrest. (As previously noted, probable cause also must be shown in an affidavit to support the issuance of a warrant.)

Probable cause is a difficult term to define because in no two instances are circumstances identical. One acceptable definition of probable cause is that it is more than suspicion but less than actual knowledge. It is suspicion plus facts and circumstances which would lead a reasonable person exercising ordinary caution to believe that a crime has been, is being, or is about to be committed. Probable cause may be based on a number of sources of information not all of which have to be the kind of evidence admissible at trial. However, if prosecution is an aim of the arrest, there also must be sufficient evidence to take the case to court. In addition, the probable cause must exist at the time the arrest is made and may not be developed by subsequently acquired evidence.

Mere suspicion is not enough to justify an arrest; there must be supporting facts and circumstances. Certain factors may help to decide the existence of probable cause. The most common are the personal knowledge of

FIGURE 18-2   Front of Arrest Warrant

National Graphics Corp., Cols., O.
Form No. M86-12

THE STATE OF OHIO

_____**Municipal Court**

_____**County, Ohio**

(City)   (Name of County)

vs

No._____

Name

Address

WARRANT ON COMPLAINT

(Rule 4)

****

FORM VII

TO_____
(officer authorized to execute a warrant)

A complaint, a copy of which is attached hereto, has been filed in this court charging

_____

(describe the offense and state the numerical designation of the applicable statute or ordinance)

_____

You are ordered to arrest _____ and bring (him)(her) before this
(defendant)

court without unnecessary delay.

You (may) (may not) issue summons in lieu of arrest under Rule 4(A)(2) or issue summons

after arrest under Rule 4(F) because _____
(state specific reasons if issuance of summons restricted)

_____

Special instructions to executing officer:

_____
Judge—Officer designated by Judge(s)
Clerk—Deputy Clerk—Municipal Court

****

SUMMONS ENDORSEMENT

Use only in appropriate case

This warrant was executed / by arrest and / by issuing the following summons:

TO_____
(defendant)

You are hereby summoned and ordered to appear at _____ o'clock _____M.,

_____, _____, 19_____, at the above captioned Court.
(day)   (month)   (date)

If you fail to appear at the time and place stated above you may be arrested.

_____
Issuing Officer, Title
See Rule 4(A)(2) Rule 4(F) and Return Forms

NOTICE TO DEFENDANT: For information regarding your duty to appear call_____
(fill in telephone number(s))

The address of the Court is: _____

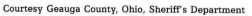

Courtesy Geauga County, Ohio, Sheriff's Department

FIGURE 18-3   Reverse of Arrest Warrant

RECEIPT OF WARRANT BY EXECUTING AUTHORITY

First Receipt

Received this warrant on _____, 19____,

at_____o'clock____m.

_____
Officer

By_____
Title

Subsequent Receipt

Received this (alias) (warrant) on _____,

19____, at_____o'clock____m.

_____
Officer

By_____
Title

****

RETURN OF EXECUTED WARRANT

Fees
Mileage $_____
_____
_____
_____
_____
Total $_____

1. Execution By Arrest

I received this warrant on _____, 19____, at

_____o'clock ____m. On _____, 19____, I

arrested_____and gave / him/her / a copy of this warrant with

complaint attached and brought / him/her / to_____
state the place

_____
Arresting Officer, Title

Fees
Mileage $_____
_____
_____
_____
_____
Total $_____

2. Execution By Issuance Of Summons Under Rule 4(A)(2) By Executing Officer

I received this warrant on _____, 19____, at

_____o'clock ____m. On _____, 19____, I

executed this warrant by issuing_____a summons by / personal

service / residence service / which ordered him/her to appear at_____
time

_____at the captioned Court. The sum-
day   date   room

mons was endorsed upon the warrant and accompanied by a copy of the complaint.

_____
Issuing Officer, Title

Fees
Mileage $_____
_____
_____
_____
_____
Total $_____

3. Execution By Arrest And Issuance Of Summons Under Rule 4(F) By Arresting Officer

I received this warrant on _____, 19____, at

_____o'clock ____m. On _____, 19____, I

arrested_____and after arrest I issued him/her a summons by

personal service which ordered him/her to appear at captioned Court at_____
time

_____. The sum-
day, date, room

mons was endorsed upon the warrant and accompanied by a copy of the complaint.

_____
Arresting-Issuing Officer, Title

4. Execution By Arrest And Issuance Of Summons Under Rule 4(F) By Superior Of Arresting Officer

On _____, 19____, _____was arrested by_____
name of arresting officer

and I issued_____a summons by personal service which ordered / him/her / to appear at

_____
time, day, date, room

at the captioned Court. The summons was endorsed upon the warrant and accompanied by a copy of the complaint.

_____
Issuing Officer, Title

****

RETURN OF UNEXECUTED WARRANT

Fees
Mileage $_____
_____
_____
_____
_____
Total $_____

I received this warrant on _____, 19____, at

_____o'clock ____m. On _____, 19____, I

attempted to execute this warrant but was unable to do so because_____
state specific reason or reasons and

_____
additional information regarding defendant's whereabouts

_____
Executing Officer, Title

****

RETURN OF UNEXECUTED WARRANT

Fees
Mileage $_____
_____
_____
_____
_____
Total $_____

I received this warrant on _____, 19____, at

_____o'clock ____m. On _____, 19____, I

attempted to execute this warrant but was unable to do so because_____
state specific reason or reasons and

_____
additional information regarding defendant's whereabouts

_____
Executing Officer, Title

Courtesy Geauga County, Ohio, Sheriff's Department

FIGURE 18-4   Arrest Warrant

FELONY WARRANT OF ARREST UPON PROBABLE CAUSE COMPLAINT*

(See People v. Ramey, 16 Cal.3d 263 and People v. Sesslin, 68 Cal.2d 418,
425-427, n. 6)

COUNTY OF LOS ANGELES   ARREST WARRANT NO.:
STATE OF CALIFORNIA

THE PEOPLE OF THE STATE OF CALIFORNIA,
TO ANY PEACE OFFICER IN THE COUNTY OF LOS ANGELES

Complaint, on oath, having been made this date before me by _____
_____, I find that there is probable cause to
believe that the crime of _____ was
committed on or about _____, by _____

(that is, the person named or described below and in the attached complaint)
WHEREFORE, you are commanded forthwith to arrest _____
and bring said person before any magistrate in Los Angeles County pursuant
to Penal Code Sections 821, 825, 826 and 848. In lieu of bringing said
person before a magistrate, you may release, prior to the time limitations
of Penal Code Section 825, said person from custody without bail or further appearance before a magistrate and then shall file with me no later
than the next day on which the court is in session a declaration under
penalty of perjury setting forth the fact that said person has been
released without bail or further appearance before a magistrate.
      Defendant is to be admitted to bail in the amount of $_____.
      This warrant may be executed at anytime during the ten calendar days
subsequent to its issuance (i.e., until _____).

TIME ISSUED: _____A.M./P.M.
                                       _____
                                       Judge of the Municipal Court
DATED: _____   of
at _____ California
                                       _____
                                       Judicial District

_____

DESCRIPTION OF ARRESTEE

Sex_____ Race_____ D.O.B. _____ Hgt._____ Wgt._____

Hair_____ Eyes_____ DR#_____ Veh. Yr._____

Make_____ Mdl._____ Veh. Lic. #_____

State_____ Res. Add._____

Bus. Add._____, L.A. #_____

Other #'s_____

Inv. Name(s)_____

Inv. Ser. #_____

      *The complaint underlying this warrant of arrest does not initiate a
criminal proceeding.

Courtesy Los Angeles County, Sheriff's Department

the investigator. Information obtained from informants also may be of value, although that information may not be admissible at a subsequent hearing or trial. The investigator must be able to establish the reliability of the information and the informant by indicating the length of time the investigator has known or dealt with the informant, the general character and reputation of the informant, the number of tips received from the informant in the past, the accuracy of previous information, whether the informant is paid for the information, and the motives for volunteering the information.

Other sources of probable cause include information from within a police department or from other law enforcement agencies, such as notice of outstanding warrants, the past criminal record of the suspect, physical evidence found at the scene of the crime, other evidence detected in the latent investigation, crime laboratory analyses, and reports of victims and eyewitnesses.

EVALUATING THE CASE

The decisions investigators must make involve a great deal of discretion. Investigators must consider what may be termed risk factors. As suggested by Figure 18-5, the fact that probable cause exists does not require that the arrest be made at the moment, nor does it mean that the investigation is complete. Certain disadvantages may result from a premature arrest, even one which is valid. In Figure 18-5, B^1 through B^7 represent the alternative times when arrest may take place between the establishment of probable cause and when certainty exists requiring arrest as a prerequisite to prosecution. (The spacing

and numbering are arbitrary and are intended for graphic purposes only.)

One prime consideration is whether the suspect is likely to flee if allowed to remain free. If there is a high risk of this, the investigator should make an arrest as soon as probable cause can be established, and complete the investigation while the suspect is in custody. In evaluating the likelihood of flight, the investigator will consider such factors as the nature and seriousness of the offense, whether the suspect is a transient or an established member of the community, the suspect's occupation and income, and whether the suspect has a family to support.

Another risk which must be considered by the investigator deals with the potential danger posed to others if the suspect is allowed to remain free. Again, the nature of the offense along with any past criminal record or history of the suspect must be carefully evaluated. If the case under investigation involves a violent crime or one which tends to reveal violent propensities on the part of the suspect, early arrest is most probably the wisest course of action.

The investigator should also consider the hardships imposed on the suspect by early incarceration. Although this is often overlooked, it is one additional portion of the investigator's responsibility in evaluating the case.

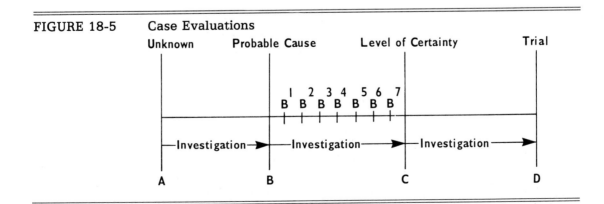

FIGURE 18-5   Case Evaluations

QUESTIONS

1. Define *arrest*.
2. Distinguish arrest from detention.
3. Distinguish arrest from charging.
4. What are the benefits to a police officer and the case if an arrest is made under the authority of a warrant?
5. Is a "John Doe" arrest warrant valid under any circumstances? Explain.
6. Define and describe *probable cause*.
7. During an ongoing criminal investigation, what factors must the criminal investigator consider in deciding whether to make an arrest and when to make it?

NOTES

1. Wayne R. LaFave, *Arrest: The Decision to Take a Suspect into Custody* (Boston: Little, Brown and Company, 1965), pp. 3–4.
2. John C. Klotter and Jacqueline R. Kanovitz, *Constitutional Law,* 4th ed. (Cincinnati: Anderson Publishing Company, 1981), p. 117.
3. Ibid. pp. 117–118.
4. *Terry v. Ohio,* 392 U.S. 1 (1968).

19

THE RULES OF EVIDENCE

INTRODUCTION

Every police officer must have a working knowledge of the rules of evidence. This requirement is particularly true for the criminal investigator, on whose shoulders falls the responsibility to collect and preserve evidence that will be useful to the prosecutor in presenting the state's case in court. Therefore, the investigator also must be able to distinguish between factual material, which is admissible in court, and that which is worthless as evidence.

EVIDENTIARY CONCEPTS

The language and terminology used in the field of law are quite different from those which most of us are accustomed to using. In the rules of evidence, many terms have specific meanings which investigators must know and understand. Many of these are set forth in this chapter.

EVIDENCE

Evidence can be defined as anything that tends logically to prove or disprove a fact at issue in a judicial case or controversy. Simply put, anything that might have the slightest bearing on the outcome of a case can be broadly classified as evidence, provided it has a logical tendency to relate to the outcome of the case. In a criminal case, if the matter has a bearing on the guilt or innocence of the defendant, it is evidence. The word *anything* should be emphasized because, in its broadest sense, anything can be evidence.[1]

THE FIRST RULE OF EVIDENCE

The rules of evidence are primarily designed to keep a jury from hearing or seeing improper evidence, and the first rule of evidence is designed to set parameters on the above definition of evidence. Because evidence can be anything having a bearing on the outcome of the case, the first rule of evidence provides that anything is admissible as evidence unless there is some rule which prohibits its admissibility. Thus the first rule of evidence in essence tells us that all the other rules of evidence may limit those things that a jury is entitled to hear, see, and decide on. From this it can be surmised that most of the rules are stated in negative form.

FIGURE 19-1   The Relation of Evidence and Proof

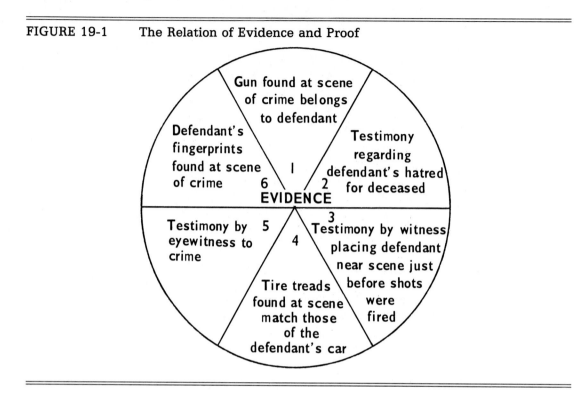

PROOF

Many people confuse proof with evidence. They are separate but related elements of the judicial process. As noted, evidence consists of individual facts submitted to the jury for its consideration. Proof may be defined as the combination of all of those facts—of all the evidence—in determining the guilt or innocence of one accused of a crime.[2] Thus, in referring to Figure 19-1, one can see that the entire pie might constitute proof of guilt, while slices of the pie are matters of evidence.

TESTIMONY

Although testimony and evidence often are considered to be interchangeable, they are distinct. Testimony is simply evidence given in oral form. It consists of spoken facts of which witnesses have knowledge.[3] Although the gun found at the scene, fingerprints, and tire treads are evidence, they require testimony to explain their significance to the case. In Figure 19-1, it is apparent that all six segments of the pie constitute evidence. But only segments 2, 3, and 5 are testimonial evidence.

ADMISSIBILITY

Admissibility is the essence of the rules of evidence. The rules of admissibility protect the trier of fact, generally a jury, from hearing improper evidence which may be unreliable or untrustworthy and which may prejudice the case unjustifiably against the defendant. The majority of the rules of evidence deal with what is admissible. Questions of admissibility are decided by the judge, and these decisions are made out of the hearing of the jury.[4]

RELEVANCE

One of the rules governing the admissibility of evidence requires that the evidence be relevant. The evidence must have a bearing on the issues in the case being tried. The relevance of a particular piece of evidence can easily be determined by the answer to this question: "Does this piece of evidence have probative value?" Alternatively stated, "Will it aid in proving or disproving a particular point which the jury should consider in determining the guilt or innocence of the defendant?" If it cannot throw some light on the case, it is irrelevant.[5]

MATERIALITY

Admissibility is also governed by the test of materiality. Even assuming that a particular piece of evidence is relevant, if it is such an insignificant and unimportant point that its admissibility will not affect the outcome of the case, it may be ruled inadmissible. Admissibility may be denied on the basis of immateriality. Thus, materiality deals with the importance of the item of evidence in question.[6]

COMPETENCE OF EVIDENCE

The test of competence of evidence relates to its legal significance to the case. Because of certain statutory requirements or other rules of evidence, a particular item of evidence may not be admissible.[7] For example,

there is a rule of evidence to the effect that the defendant's character cannot be attacked by the prosecution unless and until the defendant tries to show that he or she is of good character. Hence, unless the defendant did proceed in this direction, any attempt by the prosecution to introduce evidence of the defendant's character would be inadmissible on the grounds of incompetence.

The competence of physical evidence must also be established as a condition of admissibility. It is done through a process known as laying a foundation. For instance, the admissibility of a tape-recorded conversation would have to be prefaced by testimony about the date, time, place, and circumstances under which the recording was made; the satisfaction of legal requirements in the making of the recording; proper identification of the voices on the tape; assertions about the functioning of recorder and tape at the time of recordings; and about the absence of editing or modification of the tape.

COMPETENCE OF WITNESSES

Regardless of their knowledge of the facts of a case, certain individuals are not permitted by law to testify for or against a defendant in a criminal case. For example, the rules of evidence generally prohibit people who have been declared legally insane to testify in a criminal case. A child "of tender years" may or may not be declared a competent witness. A person intoxicated by alcohol or drugs at the time of testifying will not be permitted to relate his or her knowledge in court.[8] In some circumstances, a witness may be competent to testify regarding particular aspects but be held incompetent to testify regarding other matters. A wife may be competent to testify for or against her husband on certain matters but not others. This aspect of competence of witnesses is discussed in greater detail later in the chapter.

WEIGHT OF EVIDENCE

Once evidence has been admitted into the trial, it must be weighed by the jury. The object of the attorneys for both sides in a case is to persuade the jury to believe their side's view of the facts at issue and the responsibility of the defendant. The jury must then weigh all the evidence and determine which is the more believable. Guilt or innocence then is determined. Weight, then, deals with the elements of persuasion and believability. Within certain guidelines, discussed below, the jury is free to give whatever weight it desires to the evidence presented to it. In essence, the entire judicial system in the United States is directed toward persuading the jury to weigh one side more favorably than the other.[9]

PRESUMPTIONS

Among the guidelines that the jury is required to follow in weighing and applying evidence are those regarding presumptions. There are two types of presumptions: conclusive and rebuttable. A *conclusive presumption* is one which the jury must follow without alternatives. For example, when the prosecution creates a reasonable belief in guilt, and the defense does not contradict any of the prosecution's case, the jury must follow a conclusive presumption that guilt has been established and must find the defendant guilty. A *rebuttable presumption* requires that a specific conclusion to be drawn unless that conclusion has been dispelled or rebutted by evidence presented to the jury for its consideration. The presumption that one is innocent until proven guilty is an example of a rebuttable presumption. Another presumption of this type is that all persons are presumed sane at the time they commit criminal acts. This presumption can be rebutted by the introduction of evidence to the contrary indicating insanity.[10]

INFERENCES

An inference, sometimes called a presumption of fact, is similar to a presumption of law but differs in that the jury has more latitude in accepting or rejecting an inference. Thus an inference is a permissible deduction that the jury may make. An inference is a natural conclusion arrived at by deduction, in logical sequence, from given facts. For example, if fact A—the gun found at the scene of the crime belongs to the defendant—and fact B—testimony by a witness placing the defendant near the scene just before the shots were fired—are all known facts, it is not conclusive proof that the defendant committed the crime. However, based on these known facts, the jury may logically infer that the defendant did in fact commit the crime. But it is equally free to reject that inference if it feels that the evidence is not sufficient for that conclusion.[11]

BURDEN OF PROOF

In each case, the prosecution has the responsibility of affirmatively proving the allegations on which it has based its accusation. This is known as the burden of proof. In a criminal case, the burden of proof is on the prosecution and never shifts to the defense. The defendant is never required to prove innocence. Innocence is presumed. The state must prove guilt. Assuming that both the prosecution and the defense present evidence in the trial in support of their theories of the case, the prosecution must establish proof beyond and to the exclusion of every reasonable doubt.[12] The jurors must be convinced that the prosecution has proved the defendant guilty beyond any doubt for which they can attach a reason. Often only the defendant knows positively whether he or she is guilty or innocent. Because juries are composed of human beings, they are subject to some doubt in every case and must rely on testimony and physical evidence in reaching their decision. However, if the prosecution so thoroughly convinces them of the defendant's guilt that they cannot give a reasonable explanation of why they doubt that guilt, then the burden of proof has been satisfied beyond and to the exclusion of every reasonable doubt. The word *reasonable* is included to separate human fallibility from the alleged infallibility of machines.

There is one exception to the requirement that the state prove its case beyond reasonable doubt. When the prosecution shows sufficient facts to indicate that the defendant more likely did commit the crime than not, it has a prima facie case. The prosecution has satisfied its burden of proof if it presents a prima facie case, *provided that there is no contradiction by the defense.* Figure 19-2 illustrates these relationships.

BURDEN OF GOING FORWARD

The requirements concerning burden of proof do not mean that a defendant has no responsibility for convincing the jury of his or her innocence. The defense carries a burden of going forward with evidence. That responsibility is a great deal less than the burden of proof carried by the prosecution. The burden of going forward with evidence is placed on the defense so that it will present evidence that creates a reasonable doubt of guilt. In other words, the defense need only present enough evidence to overcome the prosecution's contentions and create a reasonable doubt of guilt in the minds of the jurors. When a unanimous decision by the jury is necessary to find the defendant guilty, the burden is even lighter, for the defense need only create that reasonable doubt in the mind of one juror to avoid a verdict of guilty.[13]

This explanation sounds as though every benefit is being given to the defendant, and

it is. The very essence of our entire criminal justice system is to place the heaviest responsibility on the accuser—the prosecution.

The prosecution also has a burden of going forward with evidence. If the prosecution presents a prima facie case that is contradicted by evidence presented on behalf of the defendant, the state must then erase the reasonable doubt by presenting evidence that contradicts that offered by the defense.

PREPONDERANCE OF EVIDENCE

In a civil case, the party allegedly wronged is called the plaintiff. The plaintiff may be an individual, a group, a business, or a representative of some other private concern. The plaintiff in a civil action is not required to prove allegations beyond and to the exclusion of every reasonable doubt. All that is required is that the evidence the plaintiff presents be considered weightier by the jury than the contrary evidence presented by the defendant. Thus if the civil jury believes that the plaintiff's story offers a higher probability of being true than does the defendant's contention, the plaintiff will win the case. But the defendant wins if the jury gives greater credibility to the defense. In nonlegal terms, if evidence had to be weighed on a 100-point scale of probability, 51 percent believability would win.[14]

ORDER OF PROOF

Court procedures generally require that the prosecuting attorney prove the existence of the corpus delicti at trial before attempting to show the guilt of the defendant. The corpus delicti is the combination of all the elements of the crime. It is, of course, only logical that the prosecution be required to show that a crime has been committed before it can begin proving the defendant's guilt.

FIGURE 19-2   Relations Among Burden of Proof, Burden of Going Forward, and Preponderance of Evidence

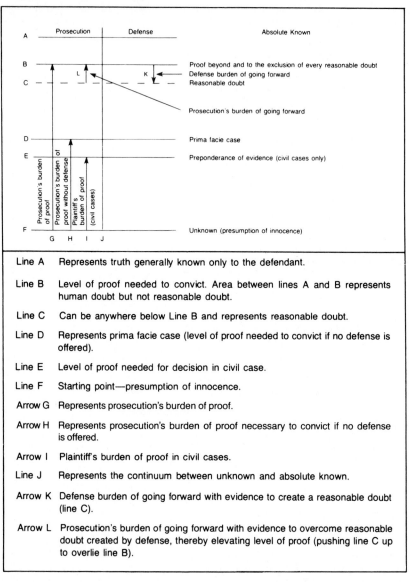

Line A	Represents truth generally known only to the defendant.
Line B	Level of proof needed to convict. Area between lines A and B represents human doubt but not reasonable doubt.
Line C	Can be anywhere below Line B and represents reasonable doubt.
Line D	Represents prima facie case (level of proof needed to convict if no defense is offered).
Line E	Level of proof needed for decision in civil case.
Line F	Starting point—presumption of innocence.
Arrow G	Represents prosecution's burden of proof.
Arrow H	Represents prosecution's burden of proof necessary to convict if no defense is offered.
Arrow I	Plaintiff's burden of proof in civil cases.
Line J	Represents the continuum between unknown and absolute known.
Arrow K	Defense burden of going forward with evidence to create a reasonable doubt (line C).
Arrow L	Prosecution's burden of going forward with evidence to overcome reasonable doubt created by defense, thereby elevating level of proof (pushing line C up to overlie line B).

Trial judges rarely exercise their discretionary power to allow evidence to be submitted to prove a point out of order. The judge has the prerogative of allowing the introduction of evidence to establish the guilt of the defendant prior to the prosecution's showing the existence of all the elements of the crime. However, this is done only on rare occasions, when to maintain the order of proof might be a major inconvenience to a particular witness. Permission is given only on the condition that the prosecution guarantee it will later establish the corpus delicti. If the guarantee is made and the prosecution later cannot show the corpus delicti, grounds exist for a mistrial or a directed verdict of innocence.

JUDICIAL NOTICE

The doctrine of judicial notice is an evidentiary shortcut. Judicial notice is designed to speed up the trial and eliminate the necessity of formally proving the truth of a particular matter when that truth is not in dispute. Judicial notice then is proof without evidence and may be taken in three situations.

1. Judicial notice may be taken of matters of common knowledge which are uniformly settled and on which no dispute exists. If the fact is known to most reasonably informed people within the community where the trial is being held, judicial notice may be taken of that fact. For example, the fact that a particular intersection, located in a city where an accident occurred, is a business district, might well be a matter of common knowledge of which judicial notice could be taken if the trial is held in that city. Since most reasonably informed people within a community would know that a particular intersection was a business area, that court would accept that as a given fact without requiring formal proof.
2. Judicial notice may be taken of laws. A state court, for example, is required to take judicial notice of the state statutes of the jurisdiction in which the court operates; a municipal court takes judicial notice of municipal ordinances.
3. Judicial notice may be taken of matters that may be ascertained as true by referring to common authoritative sources such as books or official agencies. Included in this category are scientific facts, medical facts, historical facts and meanings of words, phrases, and abbreviations. Examples would include the official time of sunset on a particular date by reference to a weather bureau; the fact that the abbreviation M.D. following a name stands for medical doctor; that the hair and blood types of human beings differ from those of animals; and that no two individuals have identical fingerprints.

Judicial notice must be distinguished from judicial *knowledge*. The latter refers to knowledge possessed by a judge. The fact that the judge may know a fact is not material in applying the doctrine of judicial notice. Personal knowledge may not be substituted for common knowledge in the community or for facts capable of being ascertained.

Judicial notice may only be taken on a collateral or minor point of fact in a case. Judicial notice may never be used to prove a fact that the jury is required to decide in determining the proper charge and verdict. For example, in the case of a defendant on trial for stealing a car, the court may not take judicial notice of the value of the car if that value will determine the seriousness of the charge against the defendant. Even if it is a matter of common knowledge that a brand new Cadillac El Dorado is worth more than $100, judicial notice may not be taken, because the value is an important element that the prosecution must prove to assure the propriety of the charge placed against the defendant.[15]

TYPES OF EVIDENCE

There are many ways of classifying evidence. Not all authorities agree on the classifications, but the differences are immaterial so long as the principles are understood. Five types of evidence are defined below.

DIRECT EVIDENCE

Direct evidence usually refers to the testimony of witnesses that ties the defendant directly to the commission of the crime, such as the testimony of an eyewitness who can positively state that the defendant committed the crime. It is based on the firsthand knowledge of the witness regarding the guilt of the defendant.[16]

REAL EVIDENCE

Sometimes referred to as physical evidence, real evidence is connected with the commission of the crime and can be produced in court. Items of physical evidence found at a crime scene, such as a weapon used to commit a homicide, a crowbar used to pry open a window, and fingerprints, all constitute real evidence that can be observed by the jury.

DEMONSTRATIVE EVIDENCE

Demonstrative or illustrative evidence is not identical to real evidence even though the items introduced are tangible. It refers to maps, diagrams, sketches, photographs, tape recordings, motion pictures, X-rays, and visual tests and demonstrations produced to assist witnesses in explaining their testimony. When testimony alone would be inadequate to describe a victim or crime scene, photographs taken by police officers are used to help the jury understand the conditions which existed.[17]

The use of demonstrative evidence is governed by some complex and highly restrictive rules to ensure that the jury is not prejudiced against the defendant.

CIRCUMSTANTIAL EVIDENCE

It is a myth that one cannot be convicted of a crime solely on circumstantial evidence. The broad definition of circumstantial evidence encompasses all evidence other than direct evidence, provided that it logically relates the defendant to the crime. Circumstantial evidence is sometimes referred to as indirect evidence for this reason. Circumstantial evidence is used in a criminal case by inferring from a series of known facts the existence of an unknown fact. In other words, by the process of deductive reasoning, inferences are logically drawn from a series of known facts, and a conclusion is reached. For example, the fact that the defendant's fingerprints are detected on a weapon found at the scene of a homicide does not necessarily mean that the defendant committed the crime. The fingerprints tie the defendant to the gun, and finding the gun at the scene of the crime may be a circumstance relating the gun to the commission of the crime. Likewise, testimony that the defendant was seen near the scene of the crime shortly after its commission does not necessarily constitute guilt; but again, it may lead the jury to infer guilt.

It is possible that an accumulation of circumstantial evidence may be nothing more than a series of unfortunate coincidences for which the defendant may have a logical and truthful explanation. How much circumstantial evidence is required for a jury to convict someone of a crime varies from case to case and depends largely on the composition of the jury.

Circumstantial evidence can be considered analogous to links in a chain. Each link might be an unfortunate coincidence, but the greater the number of links, the more a jury

FIGURE 19-3

This illustrates the introduction of real evidence (a gun) at trial.

Courtesy of the Los Angeles County Sheriff's Department

is likely to infer guilt by joining the links into a chain of overwhelming circumstantial evidence.[18]

OPINION EVIDENCE

Witnesses ordinarily are not permitted to give their opinions or draw conclusions on matters about which they are testifying. Their function is to present the facts of which they have firsthand knowledge. It is within the province of the jury to determine the truthfulness of those facts and to draw whatever conclusions it believes are necessary. However, there are a few exceptions to that general rule. Everything a human being perceives through the senses is generally expressed in the form of a conclusion. It is difficult, if not impossible, to describe something perceived as an absolute fact without expressing it in the form of a conclusion. The only situation in which a nonexpert may give an opinion is on matters of description in which fact and opinion are so interwoven that they cannot be separated without losing most of their probative value. Matters of description in which a nonexpert may give an opinion include color, size, shape, speed, mental condition, identity, race, and language.

An expert is someone with special skills or knowledge not ordinarily possessed by others. The skills or knowledge may be acquired through experience, study, observation, or education. To be an expert witness, one need not necessarily have a formal education. The expert witness is permitted to interpret facts and give opinions about their significance; the lay witness may only present facts which are a matter of firsthand knowledge. The expert witness is called on to assist the jurors in understanding facts which they are ordinarily not sufficiently trained to understand, such as the results of medical examinations, chemical analyses, ballistics reports, and findings from questioned documents.[19]

THE HEARSAY RULE

Most people have heard a story from several different sources and recognized how different the versions sound. Whether these alterations are caused by poor memory or deliberate attempts to spice up the truth is immaterial in a legal context. The fact that stories tend to be changed when they are repeated makes their reliability and truthfulness questionable. For this reason, the hearsay rule was created. *Hearsay* is derived from "heard say." Testimony in court that repeats what others were heard to say means testifying to a second version of what actually happened. The witness has no personal knowledge of the facts in question. Thus, the truth of the testimony depends on the truthfulness and the competence of the person from whom the information was heard rather than on the person testifying. For these reasons the hearsay rule is perhaps one of the most important yet most confusing rules of evidence.

Inaccuracy, unreliability, and untrustworthiness are only some of the reasons why hearsay evidence is excluded. The inability of the judge and jury to observe the demeanor or conduct of the person who actually has firsthand knowledge of the information is another.

Other reasons for generally excluding hearsay rely on protections guaranteed in the Constitution of the United States. The Sixth Amendment guarantees a defendant the right to be confronted by the witnesses against him or her and the right to cross-examine those witnesses. Because the person with firsthand knowledge is not present in court, that person cannot be confronted or cross-examined by the defendant.

Hearsay is a version of the truth repeated in court by one who does not know whether the assertion is true. People may assert things lightly and casually out of court without being concerned about the truth but would be more careful about the truth of the testimony if it were asserted in court, when an individual's life or liberty may be at stake and when they are testifying under oath.

The hearsay rule also excludes statements in writing by people not in the courtroom to testify. Because the writer's personal knowledge is in his or her head, writing that knowledge makes it secondhand information.

If the out-of-court assertion is not being offered as evidence to prove the truth of a matter but only to show that it was said, it is not hearsay and thus may be admissible. This is one of the rare occasions in which the hearsay rule would not be applicable. For example, a deceased person may have made threats against the defendant. These threats are repeated in court to show the defendant's state of mind when he killed the deceased and to support a claim of self-defense. The truth or falsity of the threats is not the issue.

A second exception deals with reputation. The reputation of a defendant or a witness in a trial may be questionable. A third party may testify about what he or she has heard concerning another's reputation. Because an individual's reputation is not representative of actual character, but rather what other people think of that person, the truth of the reputation is immaterial. But the fact that such a reputation exists is admissible. For example, if the defendant presents evidence in a trial for assault that he is a calm individual, a witness may testify to having heard that the defendant is extremely short-tempered.

In these situations, evidence is offered only to show that the statements were made, not that they are true. Because the witness has personal knowledge, it is not hearsay, and because the statements are not offered for the truth of their contents, they are admissible.[20]

The hearsay rule is based on the recognition that human beings have human weaknesses, and the testimony of human witnesses provides the majority of evidence presented to juries in modern trials. Because we will continue to rely on the testimony of human beings as the principal source of information for trying cases, the law must continue to impose standards to assure the most accurate and reliable testimony possible. Unequivocal application of the hearsay rule to all situations does, however, present certain injustices in our modern judicial system. For this reason, a number of specific exceptions to the hearsay rule have developed. Some of these exceptions are discussed in the next section.

SOME EXCEPTIONS TO THE HEARSAY RULE

The sheer number of exceptions often creates doubt about whether the hearsay rule has any merit. Among the many reasons for the existence of the hearsay rule, two stand out as the most critical: the unreliability and the untrustworthiness of declarations repeated under oath in court. The exceptions to the rule can be justified only if these two major drawbacks can be overcome. If the circumstances surrounding the hearsay evidence can assure a high degree of trustworthiness and reliability, the admissibility of that evidence is allowed as an exception to the rule in order to minimize any injustice. Thus, each exception must meet many tests to satisfy the criteria of reliability and trustworthiness before it is admissible. Several decisions by the courts have eliminated the concern over the constitutional issues involved. These decisions, in effect, have held that allowing the admissibility of the exceptions does not violate the Sixth Amendment guarantees to confrontation and cross-examination, nor does it violate the due process guarantees of the Fourteenth Amendment. Some exceptions apply in both civil and criminal cases; others apply only to civil or criminal cases. The following paragraphs discuss several exceptions applicable in criminal cases.

CONFESSIONS

A confession is an acknowledgment by a person accused of a crime that he or she is guilty of that crime. To constitute a confession, the admission of guilt must apply to all the elements of the crime and exclude any reasonable doubt about the possibility of innocence. Confessions are generally of two types. A judicial confession is an in-court confession made before a judge. A judicial confession can also take the form of a guilty plea. Judicial confessions do not fall within the hearsay rule, because they are *in-court* assertions of the truth of the matter asserted by the person directly involved.

Confessions made out of court fall within the hearsay rule. For such confessions to be admissible, they must meet the tests of admissibility and overcome the assumptions of unreliability and untrustworthiness.

The admissibility of a confession usually raises questions about constitutionality. First, it must be shown that the confession satisfies constitutional requirements of voluntariness. A confession that is obtained involuntarily certainly would not be admissible under modern law. Second, courts admit confessions as an exception to the hearsay rule on the theory that it is highly unlikely that a person will say something against the person's own interest unless it is true. Therefore, a confession tends to establish the reliability and trustworthiness of the truth of the matter asserted. People do not often deliberately make a statement which jeopardizes their own life or liberty unless that statement is true. The major objections to admitting confessions, as hearsay, are overcome.[21]

ADMISSIONS

One who makes an admission does not admit all the facts surrounding the crime necessary to constitute guilt but does admit to certain facts or circumstances from which guilt may be inferred by the jury. For example, without confessing to the crime, an accused may admit having been at or near the scene of the crime at the time it occurred, having a motive to commit the crime against the victim, possessing the gun used in the crime, that the foot impressions outside the window of the victim's house do belong to the accused, and leaving town the day after the crime was committed. These admissions may be introduced in the trial by a witness who overheard the accused make these statements or in the form of a written document repeating these statements. They may be introduced for basically the same reasons as a confession is admissible. The contents of the admissions are certainly against the interest and welfare of the defendant and, like confessions, must have been made voluntarily to be admissible. If these factors exist, it is unlikely that a defendant would make such admissions unless they were true. Therefore, the courts allow the admissions on the basis that the principal objections to the hearsay rule—unreliability and untrustworthiness—have been overcome.[22]

SPONTANEOUS AND EXCITED UTTERANCES

Human experience dictates that speaking the truth is an instinctive reaction. Therefore, if one makes a spontaneous or excited utterance after something startling or unusual has happened the utterance may be admissible as an exception to the hearsay rule when testified to by one who heard it made. It may be offered to prove the truth of the matter asserted. The spontaneity of the utterance and its declaration under startling and unusual circumstances lend credence to its reliability and trustworthiness.[23] To illustrate, a 5-year-old girl, observing a playmate struck at a railroad crossing, was heard by a passerby to scream, "The engine runned over Billy!" The passerby was permitted to testify in court about what he had heard the girl say.

DYING DECLARATIONS

A declaration made by the victim of a homicide who is about to die, who expects to die, and who does not hope to recover, concerning the facts and circumstances of the fatal injury, is admissible as an exception to the hearsay rule. The theory is that a person about to die has no reason to lie. Statements admissible under this exception must concern the injury inflicted to the declarant and are admissible only in the trial of the person charged with the declarant's death.[24]

FORMER TESTIMONY

Written or oral testimony in a hearing or trial falls within the hearsay rule if that testimony is sought to be introduced in a later judicial proceeding. For example, if a witness testifies against the defendant in a preliminary hearing to determine probable cause to hold the defendant for trial, the court record is not admissible in the later trial unless it meets the tests of the former-testimony exception to the hearsay rule. Because the testimony was given in a court under oath, it is presumed reliable and trustworthy and is admissible, provided the two judicial proceedings involve the same defendant, charged with committing the same act, under the same circumstances. In addition, the witness who originally testified at the former hearing must be unavailable for testimony before the transcript of the hearing is admissible and, to show that constitutional requirements have been satisfied, it must be proved that the defendant had the right to cross-examine the witness in the former hearing or trial.[25]

EVIDENTIARY PRIVILEGES

Defendants and other witnesses have a right to have certain matters of communication barred from disclosure in court. For example, confidential communications between husband and wife; confidential communications between attorney and client; and grand jury proceedings which are confidential by requirements of law are barred.

The evidentiary privileges may vary from state to state. Some are universally recognized as necessary and have existed since the early days of common law. Others exist only if the state legislature has created the privilege by statute. Some of the more common evidentiary privileges fall into four basic categories. The first might be called professional privileges, those that exist between attorney and client, physician and patient, priest and penitent, and journalist and informant. Government communications and information, state secrets, and matters of diplomacy are classified as political privileges. The third category is social privileges and includes confidential communications between husband and wife or between a guidance counselor and a child.

Finally, judicial privileges include grand jury proceedings along with communications among jurors deliberating a verdict and the privilege against self-incrimination guaranteed by the Fifth Amendment.

All of these privileges can be waived by the person against whom the evidence is to be used or who would suffer from its disclosure. Thus an attorney cannot disclose evidence of a confidential communication between attorney and client unless so directed by the client. Likewise, a spouse cannot testify against a mate without the latter's express permission, unless the spouse is the victim of the mate's crime.

Although only confidential communications are excluded by the privilege, it is the relationship, not the communication, that is privileged. The theory underlying evidentiary privileges creates a balance between the disclosure of truth and the welfare of society. The assumption is that the public benefits more by protecting these relationships than it does by requiring disclosure of the truth to seek to convict one defendant.[26]

WITNESSES

Until a few hundred years ago, witnesses appeared at a trial voluntarily. There were no legal means to compel attendance. With the advent of the rules of evidence, procedures had to be established for requiring the presence of people who possessed knowledge of the facts of the case. The subpoena is used for this purpose. It is a written order commanding the person named to appear in court at a specified date and time to testify, under oath, before a judicial tribunal, to facts within the witness's personal knowledge involved in the case. A *subpoena duces tecum* commands the individual to bring certain records or documents in his or her possession. Refusal to obey subjects the individual to punishment for contempt. Likewise, refusal to testify or answer specific questions may be grounds for contempt unless valid grounds exist, such as the self-incrimination protections guaranteed in the Constitution. People who possess firsthand knowledge have a duty, not a right, to appear in court.

In early common law, defendants had no right to call witnesses on their behalf. Therefore, the prosecution was required to call all witnesses having knowledge of facts, regardless of which side those facts favored. Today, the defense has an equal right to compel the attendance of witnesses. Hence, the state may use only those witnesses it chooses. Witnesses may also be called by the judge, but this power is rarely exercised.

Once in court, the witness's competence to testify must be ascertained. Competence of witnesses was discussed previously in this chapter. If not insane, intoxicated, or excluded for other reasons, and if the testimony will not fall within any of the evidentiary privileges, the witness will be presumed competent to testify, though this must first be asserted by taking an oath or affirmation.[27]

In common law, taking an oath was a process by which individuals swore to tell the truth based on their sacred belief in a supreme being. Today, of course, the oath is still a recognized means of establishing a witness's competence, but it is no longer the only method. The affirmation is also used for people who refuse, for personal reasons, to take the oath. Because they are otherwise competent to testify, some guarantee that they will tell the truth is necessary. A witness may be declared competent if he or she understands and undertakes the obligation of an oath. This obligation is to tell the truth with a realization of the penalties for perjury. As long as the witness understands and undertakes the obligation, even without swearing to a supreme being, the witness is considered competent to testify. This process is called affirmation.[28]

A declaration of a witness's competence in no way guarantees the credibility of the testimony. Credibility deals with believability which, like the weight of any other evidence, is determined by the jury. Attitude, personality, appearance, hygiene, and general demeanor all affect a witness's credibility, along with the substance of the testimony.

QUESTIONS

1. Why must a criminal investigator know the rules of evidence?
2. Define the following concepts:
   (a) evidence
   (b) proof
   (c) testimony
   (d) admissibility
   (e) relevancy
   (f) materiality
   (g) competency of evidence
   (h) competency of witnesses
   (i) weight

3. Distinguish "burden of proof" and "burden of going forward with evidence."
4. What is the purpose of judicial notice?
5. Describe the manner in which circumstantial evidence is used in a criminal prosecution.
6. Why does the opinion rule of evidence exist?
7. What is the hearsay rule and why does it exist?
8. What is the philosophy under which exceptions to the hearsay rule have evolved?
9. Describe the philosophy underlying the existence of evidentiary privileges.

NOTES

1. Robert L. Donigan, Edward C. Fisher, et al., *The Evidence Handbook,* 4th ed. (Evanston, Ill.: Traffic Institute, Northwestern University, 1980), p. 3.
2. Ibid.
3. Ibid.
4. Ibid., p. 6.
5. Joseph D. Schloss, *Evidence and Its Legal Aspects* (Columbus, Ohio: Charles E. Merrill Publishing Company, 1976), p. 53.
6. John C. Klotter and Carl L. Meier, *Criminal Evidence for Police,* 2nd ed. (Cincinnati: The W. H. Anderson Company, 1975), p. 31.
7. Donigan et al., *The Evidence Handbook,* p. 7.
8. Klotter and Meier, *Criminal Evidence for Police,* pp. 52–61.
9. Donigan et al., *The Evidence Handbook,* pp. 6–7.
10. Schloss, *Evidence and Its Legal Aspects,* pp. 9–11.
11. Ibid., p. 9.
12. Ibid., pp. 7–8.
13. Ibid., p. 8.
14. Donigan et al., *The Evidence Handbook,* pp. 25–26.
15. Irving J. Klein, *Law of Evidence for Police* (St. Paul, Minn.: West Publishing Co., 1973), pp. 139–150.
16. Donigan, *The Evidence Handbook,* p. 3.
17. Ibid.
18. Ibid., p. 146.
19. Klein, *Law of Evidence for Police,* pp. 40–56.
20. Gilbert B. Stuckey, *Evidence for the Law Enforcement Officer* (New York: McGraw-Hill, 1968), pp. 107–110.
21. Donigan et al., *The Evidence Handbook,* pp. 38–39.
22. Ibid.
23. Ibid., pp. 59–63.
24. Ibid., pp. 64–68.
25. Ibid., pp. 74–76.
26. Klotter and Meier, *Criminal Evidence for Police,* pp. 149–171.
27. Donigan et al., *The Evidence Handbook,* pp. 205–208.
28. Klotter and Meier, *Criminal Evidence for Police,* p. 123.

20

THE INVESTIGATOR AS A WITNESS

The success or failure of a criminal investigation often is ultimately measured in terms of the quality and effectiveness of an officer's presentation of evidence to court and jury. Because one aim of the entire process of criminal investigation is to bring about the apprehension and prosecution of violators of the criminal laws, then the need for concern about presentation of the case in court must be of paramount importance to the investigator from the moment of arrival at the crime scene.[1] Inability to understand and appreciate this crucial role in the judicial process not only adversely affects the investigator's performance as a witness but reflects on the investigator's overall professional effectiveness.

Every police witness, whether a uniformed officer or criminal investigator, must become skilled at testifying on the witness stand. Preparation should include a knowledge of the roles of evidence so that the officer can not only perform functions in the field more effectively, but also have a better understanding of courtroom procedures and the functions of the prosecution and the defense. To prepare a case adequately, the investigator must understand the rules of admissibility and the relevance of evidence collected. The best witnesses are those who have an understanding and appreciation of their role in the courtroom and their relationship to other participants in the judicial process.

THE ROLE OF THE POLICE WITNESS

The function of any witness in the courtroom, including the investigator, is to present firsthand knowledge of facts to the jury for its consideration. The investigator must inform the jury of the matters investigated in the case and present this information so that the jury understands the sequence of events and their significance. But the investigator may not offer personal conclusions.

To understand one's role in the courtroom completely, the witness must also understand the functions of the other participants in the criminal process. Specifically, the witness must comprehend the functions of the judge and the jury in relation to the role of a witness.

As seen in the previous chapter, the function of any witness is to present facts from firsthand knowledge. The jury's function is

588

to weigh the facts presented by witnesses from both prosecution and defense and to interpret these facts, giving appropriate weight and credibility to the evidence and to the witnesses for the purpose of reaching a decision regarding the guilt or innocence of the defendant. The responsibility of the judge is twofold. The judge functions as a referee to ensure compliance with the rules of evidence, and interprets the law as applicable to the facts of a case.

CREDIBILITY

A police officer is not entitled to any more credibility in the courtroom than any other witness. The officer has an equal responsibility, through presentation, appearance, demeanor, and the substance of testimony, to persuade the jury to believe those facts being related.

The issue of credibility is of special concern to the police witness. Few people from the general population ever view a criminal offense or act as witnesses in court. It is likely that the trauma of such an event would be so vivid for them that remembering it would not be difficult. However, police officers regularly deal with criminal cases and investigate some with striking similarities. Thus, for officers, the frequency, similarities, and time lag between investigations and court appearances may create difficulties in the presentation of testimony.

A related area which may affect the credibility of the police witness stems from public expectations and perceptions of the police role. Many citizens expect nothing less than perfection from police officers both in the performance of their duties and their presentation of testimony in court. They often lose sight of the fact that police officers are subject to human frailties. An officer's credibility may suffer if his or her recall is less than perfect.

Another issue in the investigator's credibility relates to the perceptions of the jurors. Some individuals regard as suspect any statements made by police officers. The predisposition of jurors with this attitude may be reinforced by defense attorneys who, on cross-examination, seek to discredit the testimony of the officer on the basis of his or her occupation.

The police witness can overcome all of these barriers by preparing meticulously for testimony and by giving straightforward, unemotional responses.

CHARACTERISTICS OF A GOOD WITNESS

The successful testimony of the investigator is based on adequate preparation of the case, familiarity with the rules of evidence and with how juries think and react, knowledge of trial processes, and maintenance of proper appearance and conduct at all times.

Preparation for testimony, as has already been indicated, is of extreme importance. For the police witness the first step in preparation is to ensure that a complete investigation was conducted, that all leads were followed and all avenues explored. It must be remembered that the prime responsibility of the investigator is not to convict but to ascertain the facts objectively. The investigator also must prepare complete and accurate notes on information obtained and evidence gathered. Before appearing in court, the investigator must review all notes and on the stand recall events in as much detail as possible with minimal referral to notes.[2]

The investigator should review the case with prosecuting officials so that they will know the testimony the investigator can offer and the evidence available. This review also gives the investigator a chance to learn the nature of the questions that might be asked on direct examination. Admittedly investigators rarely can spend much time with the prosecutor before a trial. The demands on prosecutors' time and the case loads that most prosecutors carry make in-depth preparation with each witness a virtual impossibility. But even a short time spent in preparation is valuable.

══ UNDERSTANDING THE JURY ══

The jury's task is unique. In theory, it is constrained in what it may consider by rules of evidence and other procedural requirements. In practicality, juries are composed of human beings who are subject to influences other than those which might appear in written rule and regulation form. The study of jury psychology is fascinating, for it points out the flexibility and fallibility of the human mind and, in turn, the absurdity of some of the procedural requirements imposed on the jury. The good police witness will, at the very least, understand and appreciate the fact that juries do not make their determination of guilt or innocence solely on the substance of testimony and evidence offered. The appearance and demeanor of the defendant, attorneys, and witnesses; the manner in which witnesses make their presentations and answer questions; the professionalism displayed by police officers while in the courtroom; and the way in which witnesses respond to cross-examination all bear on the reactions of individual jurors. A good witness is conscious of these factors at all times.

APPEARANCE AND ══ DEMEANOR ══

Law enforcement authorities disagree as to whether police officers should wear uniforms or civilian clothes to court. Some believe that a police officer should always wear a uniform when testifying in court for immediate identification by the jurors. Others contend that civilian clothing is proper dress because the uniform presents an authoritarian appearance which may be offensive to the jury. A third group takes the view that the officer should wear the type of dress, i.e., uniform or civilian clothes, worn at the time of the arrest. Often this decision is largely a matter of departmental policy.[3] In any event, dress should be clean and neat. If civilian clothes are worn, a degree of formality is appropriate. Conservative clothes are less likely to offend members of the jury than are wild, flashy outfits even though neat. Identifying items such as jewelry representing a specific occupation or association membership should be avoided. Lapel pins from specific civic clubs or tie tacks with emblems of handcuffs or service revolvers should not be worn. Although these are extremely small points, one can never predict who might be offended. Additionally, all the fundamentals pertaining to personal hygiene should be scrupulously observed.

Police witnesses should be conscious of their demeanor from the time they arrive at the courthouse. Prior to trial or during recesses, jurors may be standing around the courthouse. If officers make bad impressions through their appearance or actions, this may be remembered by a juror once the officer takes the stand and adversely affect the credibility of the officer in that juror's mind. Consequently, any actions which could be offensive to jurors are to be avoided. The police officer should avoid talking to the prosecutor, court clerks, or judges and refrain from acting overly friendly to anyone involved in the trial. Although there is nothing inherently wrong with idle talk or friendliness, jurors may perceive it as collusion.

══ TRIAL PROCESS ══

Some police officers and criminal investigators are not fully aware of the order in which a trial is conducted because time often prohibits them from attending a complete trial from beginning to end. Also, as is often the case, the witness may be sequestered from the courtroom before and after giving testimony. This very common practice is used to minimize the possibility that a witness's testimony might be affected by what other witnesses have testified to.

The courtroom process begins with the selection and swearing in of the jury. Then the trial begins with the prosecutor's and defense attorney's opening statements. These statements acquaint the jury with the allegations in the case. The prosecutor tells the jury how he or she will attempt to prove that a crime was committed and that it was committed by the defendant. The defense tells how it will attempt to convince the jury that either no crime was committed or that it was not committed by this defendant.

Then the prosecution presents its case, calling witnesses and introducing evidence to establish that a crime was committed and that it was committed by the defendant. While the prosecution is presenting its case, the questioning of witnesses it calls to testify on behalf of the prosecution is called *direct examination*. When that same witness is questioned by the defense attorney, the process is called *cross-examination*. In most jurisdictions, the scope of cross-examination is limited to matters brought up during direct examination. If on cross-examination the defense attorney manages to confuse a point raised on direct examination, the prosecutor has the opportunity to conduct a *redirect examination* after the defense attorney has completed cross-examination, and likewise the defense later has an opportunity to recross-examine each witness.

When the prosecution finishes introducing all its evidence and presenting all its witnesses, the defense attorney usually moves to dismiss the charge on the grounds that the state failed to prove that a crime was committed or that the defendant committed it. This is a normal procedural response to

the state's case by the defense attorney. If, in fact, the judge is convinced that the prosecution did substantially fail to establish that a crime was committed or that the defendant is guilty, charges are dismissed, and the trial ends. But if the judge feels that the jury could reasonably decide that the defendant is guilty after hearing the defense case, the motion is denied and the defense attorney permitted to present the case for the defendant.

The presentation of the defense case follows the same pattern as that for the state. Evidence is introduced at the appropriate time and witnesses called. Witnesses called by the defense are directly examined by the defense attorney and cross-examined by the prosecutor. The procedures for redirect and recross-examination are applicable.

After the defense rests its case, the prosecution has an opportunity for *rebuttal*. New evidence may be presented, or witnesses may be reexamined to clarify or rehabilitate earlier testimony. If the prosecutor uses the opportunity to present rebuttal evidence, then the defense is given equal opportunity to rebut this, through the process called *surrebuttal*.

After the introduction of all evidence by both sides, each attorney may make a closing argument. They summarize for the jury the evidence they have presented. The prosecutor attempts to show the jury that sufficient evidence has been presented to indicate that the defendant is guilty of the particular crime charged, that it should find guilt, and punish accordingly. The defense attorney attempts to persuade the jury that the prosecution has failed to prove its case against the defendant and that the jury should acquit.

Once closing statements are completed, the judge has the responsibility for instructing the jury on the law applicable to the case and of advising the jury of its responsibilities: to weigh the testimony of witnesses and the evidence presented. The judge also tells the jury the various decisions it may reach in terms of guilt or innocence and the elements of the crimes—including lesser offenses—of which they may find the defendant guilty. The judge advises the jurors of the degree to which they must be convinced of guilt or acquit the defendant.[4]

= TAKING THE WITNESS STAND =

From the moment the police witness enters the courtroom, people are forming opinions. The officer should walk naturally when approaching the witness stand, not look at or speak to the prosecutor, and not frown at the defendant. If the jury sees these expressions, it interprets them as signs of partiality. The police witness should stand erect while being sworn in (see Figure 20-1) and, when permitted to be seated, should sit erect, facing the jury. The investigator should not continually cross his or her legs or fidget uncomfortably. Hands should be kept comfortably in the lap or on the arms of the chair.

Nervousness is natural for anyone who appears as a witness. Usually it disappears with experience. However, if the police witness is properly prepared and answers all questions accurately and truthfully to the best of his or her knowledge, nervousness is minimized.

Eye contact and speaking voice are extremely important. Many authorities contend that the witness should maintain eye contact with the jury while answering questions rather than upon the prosecutor or defense attorney. But this skill must be developed. It is difficult for most people to look at the jury when responding to a question from an attorney who may be standing on the opposite side of the courtroom. If the jury cannot hear or understand what the witness is saying, the testimony is worthless. Witnesses should speak loudly enough for people in the back of the courtroom to hear clearly and understand what they are saying. Then they can be sure that the jury, the attorneys, and the judge also can hear them.

= ANSWERING QUESTIONS =

The ability to answer questions under direct and cross-examination is usually developed through experience. The police witness must answer without emotion or partiality. Sarcasm, witty remarks, or an attitude of "I'm out to get the defendant" must be avoided at all times.[6] The good police witness must be positive and firm in answering all questions and should readily admit not knowing an answer, if this is the case. The witness who constructs an answer to avoid embarrassment jeopardizes the case for the prosecution. Even the slightest fabrication of testimony is perjury, and is likely to be discovered on cross-examination. It should be remembered that to err is human. It is not impossible for police witnesses to make mistakes in their testimony. Although slightly embarrassing, the witness should not hesitate to admit having made a mistake. This acknowledgment should be accompanied by an explanation. Even if the mistake is not discovered until after testimony is complete, the witness should immediately advise the prosecutor of the mistake so that the prosecutor will have the opportunity to correct it before the conclusion of the trial.

The requirement of being positive and firm in responding to questions also means that the witness must avoid the use of such expressions as "I think," "I believe," or "as I recall." It is difficult to avoid using expressions such as these because they are part of everyday usage of the English language, but in court they can raise questions as to the definitiveness of the officer's testimony and can be a factor in the degree of credibility attached to the testimony by the jury.[6]

There are two basic methods by which witnesses are examined. The narrative tech-

FIGURE 20-1   An Officer Being Sworn In as a Witness

Courtesy of Metro-Dade County Police Department, Miami, Florida

nique allows the witness to tell the facts in his or her own words as they are known to be, in response to a question such as, "Now tell us what you found at 1234 Elm Street." This technique is used if the examiner knows the witness well and has confidence that the witness will only relate relevant, unobjectionable matters. The advantage of the narrative technique is that it permits the witness to relate details chronologically and make them clearer to the jury. The obvious disadvantage is that an inexperienced witness may ramble, give objectionable or irrelevant testimony, or expose the jury to tainted evidence, potentially causing a mistrial.

Hence, prosecutors use this technique very sparingly.

Usually attorneys use the question and answer technique for examining witnesses. They ask a single, pointed question and receive an answer to it. When the question and answer technique is used, the police witness should hesitate momentarily before answering. This allows time for the opposing attorney to raise any objections. It also allows the witness an opportunity to digest the question to make sure it has been clearly understood. If not, the witness should ask that the question be repeated as many times as necessary. If the question does not make any

FIGURE 20-2

An officer illustrates a point while testifying.

Courtesy of Metro-Dade County Police Department, Miami, Florida

sense after several repetitions, the witness may ask that the question be phrased in different terms. The witness should not volunteer information.

Courtesy and respect are important qualities of an effective witness. The judge should always be addressed as "Your Honor." The witness's language should be intelligible and understandable to the jury. Police witnesses should deliberately avoid the use of slang and words unique to the police service, for these may not be understood by the jury. Profanity should not be used in the courtroom unless the witness is repeating a direct quote. If such is the case, the officer should have no hesitation in using the exact words used during the investigation.

Occasionally a yes or no answer may be demanded of a witness, particularly on cross-examination. Sometimes such an answer is not an appropriate response to the question. If this occasion arises, the witness should not be pressured into an inaccurate response for the sake of giving a short answer. The witness is always permitted to qualify answers and should persist in this right, if necessary asking the judge for permission to qualify the answer. But if the question can be accurately answered with a simple yes or no, the witness should respond accordingly.

CROSS-EXAMINATION

The purpose of cross-examination is to ensure that testimony given under direct examination has been accurate and truthful. Through cross-examination the attorney attempts to impeach witnesses called by the opposing side. Impeachment is the process of discrediting or contradicting the testimony of the witness to show that the witness is unworthy of belief. It is designed to weaken or destroy the effect of the testimony presented under direct examination and thus to destroy the credibility of the witness in the eyes of the jury. Cross-examination tests the reliability of the witness by attempting to detect whether testimony was intentionally slanted or whether an error or misstatement was made.

The five basic methods for attacking the credibility of a witness are:

1. Showing that the witness's previous statements, personal conduct, or conduct of the investigation are inconsistent with the witness's testimony in court.
2. Showing that the witness is biased or prejudiced for or against the state or the defendant, because of a close relationship, personal interest in the outcome of the case, hostility toward the opposing party, or similar biases.
3. Attacking the character of the witness— revealing prior criminal convictions or other irrefutable characteristics that would render testimony unworthy of belief.
4. Showing the witness's incapacity to observe, recollect, or recount due to mental weakness, a physical defect, influence of drugs or alcohol, or the like.
5. Showing that the witness is in error, that the facts are otherwise than as testified.[7]

Cross-examination tactics used by attorneys vary widely, but they fall into two basic categories. Browbeating or belligerent cross-examination is designed to put the witness under pressure to provoke an unprofessional reaction. The attorney may ask a series of questions rapidly in an attempt to confuse the witness and force inconsistent responses. The attorney may try to reverse the witness's words or may continually repeat the same questions in an attempt to elicit inconsistent or conflicting answers.

The cross-examiner who assumes a friendly, condescending role attempts to lull the witness into a false sense of security to bring about less caution in listening to and answering questions. Once the witness's guard is down, the cross-examiner often resorts to leading questions. Leading questions suggest the answer desired. Although leading questions are not permitted in direct examination, they are permitted in cross-examination.

Another danger that should be avoided in cross-examination deals with questions regarding whether the officer has talked with anyone about the case. The police witness often has the impression that this kind of question is designed to attack the witness's integrity by attempting to show that the witness discussed the details of the case with the press or others in an attempt to create prejudice toward the defendant. In fact, discussing the case with the prosecutor before the trial is perfectly permissible. If the officer answers no to the question, and this later turns out to be false, the credibility of the witness suffers. Likewise, if the witness responds no to the question, "Did the prosecutor tell you how to testify?" the answer is only partly complete. Obviously, the prosecutor generally has instructed the witness to testify to firsthand knowledge of facts and to tell the truth. But the question is designed in such a manner as to imply that an affirmative response means the prosecutor told the witness exactly how to answer each question. The best way of handling this type of situation is to respond, "Yes, I talked with the prosecutor about the case. The prosecutor

FIGURE 20-3

An officer uses notes on the witness stand.

advised me to relate the facts about which I had firsthand knowledge."[8]

= USE OF NOTES ON THE STAND =

It is permissible for witnesses to use notes to help refresh their memory while testifying; the human mind can only retain so much information. The witness is not and cannot be expected to remember minute details such as dates and numbers which are of lesser importance than the major facts of the case. However, the witness should constantly be aware of the proper use of notes and the ramifications of their use.

There are two reasons why a witness may refer to notes. The first is a need to remember a particular fact in question. In this case, the officer does remember the case and is permitted to use the notes to help recall minor details. This use of notes is perfectly permissible. On the other hand, if the officer's references to the notes are necessitated by an inability to remember anything about the events preceding the trial, the consequences of referring to notes are entirely different.

Using notes simply to refresh the memory is referred to as past recollection refreshed, in the rules of evidence. As indicated, this is permissible but should be used with restraint, for it may indicate a lack of pretrial preparation. When notes are used by a police officer in direct examination, the defense attorney has an absolute right to examine those notes and test the witness's memory before allowing the witness to continue testifying under direct examination. This is done to ensure that the witness is, in fact, testifying from memory.

In the event that the witness cannot remember the facts of the case but uses the notes as the sole basis of testimony without any independent recall, the term applied is past recollection recorded. In this instance the oral testimony of the police officer becomes worthless, as the knowledge is entirely based on the notes. Should this occur, the prosecutor most likely will, at the insistence of the defense attorney, dismiss the police officer as a witness and introduce the notes as evidence in the trial. If the notes are meaningless to everybody but the police officer who took them, the entire substance of the knowledge will be excluded from evidence.

For the various reasons described above, it is highly recommended that police officers use loose-leaf notebooks during their investigations. In this way, materials not relevant to the particular case at hand can be removed prior to trial and only those notes that are pertinent will be brought into the courtroom. If this is not done, the defense attorney may question the officer on any irrelevant part of the contents of the notebook and perhaps by embarrassment decrease the officer's credibility with the jury.[9]

LEAVING THE WITNESS STAND

How witnesses leave the witness stand is just as important as how they enter, because the eyes of the jury follow them. It is improper for the witness to rise and leave the witness stand upon completion of cross-examination. The prosecutor may conduct a redirect examination, or the defense attorney may think of a last minute question. During this time, the witness should be careful not to be caught off guard. A common tactic in cross-examination is to ask a last minute question while the witness is preparing to leave the stand, in hopes of catching the witness in an error after the pressure of testifying seems over. The witness should wait to be excused by the judge and should leave the courtroom without smiling, speaking, or glaring at anyone.[10]

QUESTIONS

1. What is the role of the investigator as a witness?
2. What factors affect the credibility of the investigator as a witness?
3. What are the characteristics of a good witness?
4. How important are a witness's appearance and demeanor to credibility?

5. Describe the trial process step by step.

6. What is the function of cross-examination?

7. When and how may a witness use notes on the witness stand?

NOTES

1. Devallis Rutledge, *Courtroom Survival* (Flagstaff, Ariz.: Flag Publishing Company, 1979), p. 20.

2. Rutledge, *Courtroom Survival*, pp. 29–50.

3. Ibid., p. 54.

4. Neil C. Chamelin, Vernon B. Fox, and Paul M. Whisenand, *Introduction to Criminal Justice*, 2nd ed. (Englewood Cliffs, N.J.: Prentice-Hall, 1979), pp. 287–297.

5. Rutledge, *Courtroom Survival*, p. 60.

6. Ibid., p. 71.

7. Donigan et al., *The Evidence Handbook*, pp. 208–214.

8. Rutledge, *Courtroom Survival*, pp. 117–155.

9. Donigan et al., *The Evidence Handbook*, pp. 106–107.

10. Rutledge, *Courtroom Survival*, pp. 87–88. See also, John L. Waltman, "Nonverbal Elements in Courtroom Demeanor," *FBI Law Enforcement Bulletin*, March 1984, pp. 21–23.

21

BEHAVIORAL SCIENCE IN CRIMINAL INVESTIGATION

A great deal of attention has been directed particularly by the media, at the role of behavioral scientists in helping to solve bizarre crimes. This chapter examines some of the capabilities and limitations of this role.

When the Los Angeles Police Department found itself with eight murder victims, all of them middle-aged drifters, it turned to psychiatrists and psychologists for help in apprehending the Skid Row Slasher. They helped the police construct a psychological profile of the Slasher. The result was a "mixture of psychodynamic theorizing and old-fashioned vituperation."[1] Newspaper readers and television viewers were told that the Slasher was "a sexually impotent coward, venting his own feeling of worthlessness on hapless derelicts and down-and-outers. . . . He strongly identifies with the derelicts he kills, and we think he's trying to resolve his own inner conflicts by turning his wrath and hatred outward." The profile contained some speculation that the Slasher was a homosexual and that the murders might be a substitute for heterosexual relations. Further conjectures were made about the murderer's childhood: "Some of his hatred might be spurred by an unresolved rage he feels toward his father, who could have been a brutal alcoholic." But there was nothing speculative about the conclusion that the Slasher was a "jackal, an animal who hides in the dark and preys on weaklings and cripples." Psychiatrists accustomed to the cautiously hedged statements of psychodiagnosis or psychologists conditioned to the norm of scientific objectivity in their utterances are likely to find themselves agape at the intemperate language and impassioned subjectivity of the above descriptions. But, the profile, as matters turned out, was designed to be more than a mere "attempt to describe a person by his acts." It was intended to goad the killer into revealing himself. Two elements were present here which are seen as the highest hopes for psychological profiles of wanted criminals: prediction and provocation.[2]

AN ASSESSMENT OF PSYCHOLOGICAL PROFILING

Several years ago, a woman in a suburban city on the East Coast reported to the police that she had been raped. After learning the facts, the investigating officer realized that this was the seventh rape in which the same Method of Operation (MO) had been used. There were no investigative leads remaining from the earlier incidents. The investigations had yielded no suspect.

The incident reports, together with transcripts of interviews with the victims, were forwarded to the FBI Training Division with a request from the police department that a psychological profile of the suspect be provided. The FBI Academy's Behavioral Science Unit constructed a psychological profile. It said that these rapes probably had been committed by the same person and described him as a white male, 25 to 35 years of age (most likely late 20s or early 30s), divorced or separated, working at marginal employment (laborer, etc.), with a high school education and a poor self-image, living in the immediate area of the rapes, and involved in crimes of voyeurism (peeping). It was likely that the police had talked to the rapist in the past because he had been on neighborhood streets in the early morning hours.

Three days after receiving the profile, the requesting agency developed approximately 40 suspects in the neighborhood who met the age criterion. With other information in the profile, it narrowed its investigation to one individual and focused on him. He was arrested within a week.[3]

This case demonstrates how psychological profiling can be of assistance. The purpose of the psychological assessment of a crime scene is to produce a profile; that is, to identify and interpret certain items of evidence at the crime scene which would be indicative of the personality type of the individual or individuals committing the crime. The goal of the profiler is to provide enough information to investigators to enable them to limit or better direct their investigations. For example, in one case, a profile provided enough information that officers recalled an individual they had already questioned who fit the profile description. When they returned to the individual, he confessed.

The officer must bear in mind that the profile is not an exact science, and a suspect who fits the description is not necessarily guilty. The use of profiling does not replace sound investigative procedures.

Profiling is not a new concept. During World War II, the Office of Strategic Services (OSS) employed a psychiatrist, William Langer, to profile Adolf Hitler. Langer assembled all that was known about Hitler at the time and then attempted a long-range "diagnosis," and predictions about how Hitler might react to defeat.[4]

The concept of profiling works in harmony with the search for physical evidence. Behavioral scientists research nonphysical items of evidence, such as rage, hatred, fear, and love. Their results may be applied in teaching police officers to recognize the signs of these emotions or personality traits at a crime scene. Then police may construct a profile of the type of person who might possess these emotions or personality traits. Behavioral scientists try to classify human behavior. The Diagnostic and Statistical Manual of Mental Disorders (DSM III), used by mental health professionals, is one example of this attempt.[5] The many types of "normal" and "abnormal" behavior may be labeled by behavioral scientists. The labels are abbreviated ways of describing behavior patterns.[6]

Symptoms of behavior patterns are revealed in the way the individual "acts out" and in the responses which the individual may make to the professional. A symptom is the "visible evidence of a disease or disturbance,"[7] and a crime, particularly a bizarre crime, is as much a symptom as any other type of acting out by an individual. A crime may reflect the personality characteristics of the perpetrator much as the way we keep and decorate our homes reflects something about our personality.[8]

A crime scene is usually considered the area in which a crime was committed. Here we use the term to include the following: the scene of the crime; the victim of the crime, as in the case of rape; and all other locations involved in the crime, including such areas as the recovery site of a body killed in one location and deposited in another.

The victim is one of the most important aspects of the psychological profile. In cases involving a surviving victim, particularly a rape victim, the perpetrator's exact conversation with the victim is of utmost importance and can play a very large role in the construction of an accurate profile.

One profile does not provide the same information as another. Each is based on what was or was not left at the crime scene. Psychological evidence, like physical evidence, varies, and so the profile may also vary. The profile information may include the perpetrator's:

- race
- sex
- age range
- marital status
- general employment
- reaction to questioning by police
- degree of sexual maturity
- likelihood of striking again or of having struck before
- likelihood of having a police record

Profilers need wide exposure to crime scenes to discern patterns and some exposure to criminals who have committed similar crimes.[9] The entire basis for a good profile is a good crime scene examination and adequate interviews of victims and witnesses. When officers find individuals who are willing to attempt psychological evaluations of crime scenes, they often ask the profilers the materials they need. Items necessary for a psychological profile include:

- Complete photographs of the crime scene, including photographs of the victim if it is a homicide. Also helpful is some means of determining the angle from which the photographs were taken and a general description of the immediate area. One enterprising police officer developed the excellent technique of photocopying his crime scene sketch, attaching one copy to each photo, and then outlining in red the area which was included in the photograph.
- The completed autopsy protocol, including if possible any results of lab tests on the victim.
- A complete report of the incident, including such standard details as date and time of offense, location (by town as well as by actual site of incident), weapon used (if known), investigative officers' reconstruction of the sequence of events (if any), and detailed interviews of any surviving victims or witnesses.

These items are usually parts of all investigations. Although most investigative reports also include background information on the victims, this information often is only scantily available to the profiler. The reason is that the investigating officers cannot possibly write down all of the details about victims that they collect.

When investigators provide information about victims to a profiler, they should include:

- occupation (former and present)
- residence (former and present)

- reputation at work and in the neighborhood
- physical description, including dress at the time of the incident
- marital status, including children and close family members
- educational level
- financial status, past and present
- information and background on victim's family and parents, including victim's relationship with parents
- medical history, both physical and mental
- fears
- personal habits
- social habits
- use of alcohol and drugs
- hobbies
- friends and enemies
- recent changes in life style
- recent court actions

The primary psychological evidence a profiler looks for is motive. After a survey of the evidence, the profiler applies an age-old rule known as Ockham's Razor, which can be stated as "what can be done with fewer assumptions is done in vain with more."[10] This fourteenth-century philosophy has, in investigative circles, come to mean that, given a problem with several alternative solutions, the most obvious answer is usually correct. An aid to the application of Ockham's Razor is the intangible evidence that the observer gathers from the crime scene to determine such things as whether the crime appears to have been planned or whether it is the result of an irrational thought process.

Profiling is a valuable investigative tool but is not magical. Police officers do a great deal of profiling during the course of their work days. They constantly build mental images or profiles based on crime scenes and use them to direct their investigations. They base these profiles on their extensive knowledge of the type of crime they are investigating. But when a crime is bizarre, behavioral scientists can assist by providing these types of profiles. The FBI has limited resources to devote to profiling.

THE SERIAL MURDERER: AN EMERGING PROFILE

Since the early 1980s, attention has been focused on serial murders, and as a result a profile of these murderers is beginning to emerge.

First, it is important to differentiate between mass murderers and serial murderers, because most experts agree they are different. The *mass murderer* is usually someone who explodes and kills several people all at once, perhaps even publicly. For example, the murder of twenty-one people by James Huberty in a fast food restaurant in San Ysidro, California, several years ago was a mass murder. In contrast, *serial murderers,* who are considered sexual sadists by many experts, are driven by steady compulsion for years. Many psychologists believe that serial murderers fulfill violent sexual fantasies they have had since childhood. They satisfy their sexual needs by thinking about their killings, and when the satisfaction wears off, they murder again.

According to the FBI, most serial murderers are solitary males, although some go hunting in pairs. Relatively few (about 8 percent) are females, nurses or babysitters who kill their charges or wives who kill a succession of husbands or lovers. An alarming number (one out of ten) are doctors, dentists, or other health professionals. Almost one-third are ex-convicts and former mental patients. Many are attracted to law enforcement and are police "groupies." For example, Kenneth Bianci, the Los Angeles Hillside Strangler, wore a police uniform during some of his crimes; when he was finally caught in Washington state, he was working for a security service and was about to be appointed a reserve deputy sheriff. Murderers come from all walks of life. Many are of above average intelligence or at least are conniving and clever. They seem reassuringly normal, even charming. Their principal targets are unaccompanied women, unsupervised children, older people, the homeless, hitchhikers and prostitutes of both sexes.[11] Although there are some notable exceptions, such as Henry Lee Lucas, who has confessed to killing men, women and children, most tend not to deviate as to type of victim they kill. Most kill within their race. Many are quite handsome and involved in relationships with pretty women who love them. Some serial murderers roam from state to state searching for victims; they may travel 100,000 miles a year. Others kill near their homes.

Evidence gathered from arrested serial murderers suggests that most are caught by accident, that they will continue killing until they are caught or die, and that their killing sprees come at increasingly shorter intervals.

One psychiatrist, Doctor Helen Morrison, believes that we may actually be seeing a new personality type emerging. Doctor Morrison came to some interesting conclusions after interviewing John Wayne Gacy, who murdered thirty-three young men and boys in the Chicago area, and Richard Macek, who gained notoriety as the "Mad Biter" for bite marks he left on the flesh of young women he tortured and murdered in Illinois and Wisconsin. Dr. Morrison concluded that these two men, who were serial murderers, did not distinguish between human beings and inanimate objects. In one interview, Macek told her of a dream in which he imagined attacking a person. "Picked up the person, slammed them into a wall, beating them until they were dead, lifeless, or unconscious." She concluded that he did not know the difference between these states and shows no awareness of the pain, feeling, or even the existence of another person. Serial murderers may have absolutely no guilt. Gacy, who

buried most of his victims under his house, once said that all the police "are going to get me for is running a funeral parlor without a license."[12]

THE TRIGGERING MECHANISM

In an interview with Ann Rule, an expert in serial murderers and confidant of convicted serial murderer Ted Bundy, she said,

> When I write about serial killers, I want to go as far back into their childhood as I can and try to find the things that triggered violence in them. The men that I have written about have been violent towards women, and I've found sometime during their childhood they have suffered at the hands of a woman—abused, humiliated, abandoned, sexually assaulted; or in cases the mother just expected so much from her son he had to be perfect in every way and that's a little more than boys can cope with. These murderers as small boys have a rage toward women, and when they grow up and become men they act out their rage.[13]

From infancy, many serial murderers experience severe brutality from their parents. Fathers beat, rape, and slash their mothers and repeatedly beat the children. They are kicked, thrown down stairs, and hurled against walls. Gacy and Charles Manson suffered serious head wounds in childhood. Some have been brutally tortured. The adoptive parents of Joseph Kallinger, a Philadelphia shoemaker, held his hand in a gas flame when he was a child because he had stolen a few pennies. As an adult, Kallinger murdered several people, one of them his son. Sexual trauma was also found to be quite common. Manson had to sleep near where his prostitute mother entertained customers.[14] Henry Lee Lucas was forced by his mother to watch while she had sexual intercourse with her lovers. When he was twenty-three years old, he killed her when she ridiculed his bride-to-be.

When serial murderers are backed into a corner, they like to brag about what they have done. As most law enforcement officials know, the cooperation and confession of the serial murderer is often essential in solving all the crimes they have committed and in recovering the bodies of victims. Thus in interrogating serial murderers, the investigator might want to appeal to their vanity as a means of getting them to cooperate. (See Chapter 8, "Interrogation," for discussion of interrogation techniques.)

Many serial murderers kill during certain times of the month. If so, surveillance should be applied accordingly. This approach was taken in the case of the Atlanta, Georgia, killings for which Wayne Williams ultimately was convicted. The police posted officers in an area known to be a dumping ground for earlier victims.[15]

THE NATIONAL CENTER FOR THE ANALYSIS OF VIOLENT CRIME (NCAVC)

If a serial murderer confines his or her activities to a single community or a small region, then local police are in a good position to see emerging patterns. But because many serial murderers cover many miles in a short period of time, the FBI has developed the National Center for the Analysis of Violent Crime (NCAVC). It is designed to form a partnership among federal, state, and local law enforcement agencies in the investigation of potentially related, unsolved violent crimes. NCAVC combines law enforcement techniques, behavioral science principles, and data processing to help any law enforcement agency confronted with unusual, bizarre, particularly vicious, or repetitive crimes.

The following are the types of offenses and incidents to be reported to NCAVC for VICAP analysis:

- Sexually oriented murder or assault by mutilation or torture, dismemberment, violent sexual trauma, or asphyxiation
- Spree murder (a series of indiscriminate murders or assaults, all committed within hours or days; for example, a series of sniper murders or the Chicago cyanide murders)
- Mass murder (four or more murders in a single incident)
- Robbery murder and nonfatal robbery with extreme violence
- Murder committed during the commission of another felony
- Kidnapping: fatal, with injury, or for ransom
- Murder of a hostage
- Murder for hire, contract murder, syndicate execution
- Murder of a law enforcement officer
- Political or other assassination
- Terrorist or nationalistic murder
- Drug-related murder
- Gang murder
- Missing person with evidence of foul play
- Unidentified dead body when the manner of death is classified as a homicide.[16]

= A NATIONAL CLEARINGHOUSE =

NCAVC can analyze every unsolved murder in the United States, identify where serial patterns exist, and link cases together. NCAVC then notifies the individual local agencies with similar murders, and they in turn may establish investigative contact among themselves. NCAVC emphasizes that the primary responsibility for investigating cases is with the state and local authorities. NCAVC conducts research in violent crimes and will train local officers in the analytic techniques.

VI-CAP CRIME REPORT
CONTENT

When a violent crime remains unsolved for a period of time, the local law enforcement agency forwards details about it to the NCAVC on a special violent criminal apprehension program (VI-CAP) reporting form. This form is submitted to the nearest FBI field office; it reviews and forwards the form to NCAVC.

The form has been organized as follows:

Part I: Initial Investigation

- Case management information
- Victim description
- Suspect, arrestee, or unknown person description
- Body of victim (as found)
- Cause of death and trauma
- Weapons—initial investigation
- Offense MO—initial investigation

Part II: Follow-up Investigation

- Victimology
- Suspect background
- Weapons—follow-up investigation
- Physical evidence
- Offense MO—follow-up investigation

Part III: Forensic Laboratory Examination

- Serology/toxicology
- Firearms/toolmarks
- Hairs/fiber[17]

FLOW OF INFORMATION

Information flow in the VI-CAP process is outlined in the following hypothetical case:

January. Los Angeles County. The body of a young female is found near Interstate 10 east of La Puente. The victim has blunt force skull fractures and a number of mutilation knife wounds, several which are unique. Two days later, the Los Angeles homicide detectives forward a VI-CAP offense report to VI-CAP. This report includes coroner protocol information and the identity of the victim, a 14-year-old runaway from a small northern California town. All information is entered in the VI-CAP computer and analyzed to compare MO and physical evidence characteristics with other reported homicides. Los Angeles detectives are advised that the VI-CAP search reveals no similar pattern cases on file.

February. San Bernardino. Detectives respond to a "found body" call on the southern edge of their city. The victim is a 16-year-old female from Hollywood. Injuries are similar to those of the January homicide in Los Angeles County. Regardless of the proximity of the two departments and the cooperation that exists between the detectives, a VI-CAP analysis confirms that a similar pattern does exist, and both agencies are notified.

April. Marshall, Texas. Detectives forward VI-CAP information of the mutilation murder of a 19-year-old female college student whose vehicle, with a flat tire, has been located on I-20 east of Dallas. After a pattern analysis, VI-CAP alerts Los Angeles, San Bernardino, and Marshall detectives that MO and physical evidence of the three murder cases are similar. It is also apparent the killer is traveling east on the I-10, I-20 Interstate system.

VI-CAP, after a request from the three police departments, prepares and transmits an information all points bulletin (APB); directed to the special attention of all law enforcement agencies on or near the I-10, I-20 route. The APB requests that any department with information related in any way to the MO of the three murders contact the VI-CAP center. The following day, the police in Las Cruces, New Mexico, respond. In March, in that city, a 15-year-old female, hitchhiking to a friend's house, escaped after being assaulted by a male subject who had identified himself as a juvenile officer "working runaway cases." A description of the suspect, description of the suspect vehicle, and the MO of the assault is forwarded to VI-CAP. VI-CAP alerts the departments working the three murder cases. VI-CAP is asked to transmit an APB of the suspect and vehicle description.

The VI-CAP center also conducts a computer run on their known offender (profile and MO) file using the MO, physical evidence, and victim information of the murders in California and Texas and the assault MO and suspect description from New Mexico. Two possible names are produced. VI-CAP alerts the case investigators, who send for and receive mug photos from two state prisons.

One subject is positively identified by the Las Cruces victim. Arrest warrants are issued, and a supplemental APB is transmitted. Two days later the suspect, a parolee from a northwestern state, is arrested after picking up a young hitchhiker in Jackson, Mississippi.[18]

NCAVC LOCATION

NCAVC is located in the FBI Academy, Quantico, Virginia, and is administered by the Behavioral Science Unit. The FBI Academy was chosen as the site because it is a national law enforcement training center with vast resources for research and many capabilities for providing investigative support.

THREAT ANALYSIS: THE PSYCHOLINGUISTIC APPROACH

On the night of March 1, 1932, the infant son of Col. Charles A. Lindbergh was taken from his crib in his parents' Hopewell, New Jersey, home. A note left by the abductor was discovered on the windowsill of the baby's nursery. It read:

> Dear Sir
>   Have 50000$ ready 25000$ in 20$ bills 15000$ in 10$ bills and 1000$ in 5$ bills. After 2–4 days we will inform you were to deliver the mony. We warn you for making anyding public or for notify the police. The child is in gut care. Instruction for the letters are singnature.[19]

This note was one of several sent to the Lindberghs. Errors in spelling and syntax occurred repeatedly in the notes, and these errors, running like links from one letter to another, said more than the writer could have intended. Their author often correctly spelled such difficult words as *hazardous* in other messages, while misspelling such words as *mony, anyding,* and *singnature.* The phrasing of these messages and the errors clearly indicated that their author had been born in Germany and probably had a heavy German accent. (His message even contained the German word *gut* for *good* and the German pronunciation for *anything.*) Although such clues might have helped to narrow the search, the perpetrator was apprehended when an alert bank teller identified one of the ransom bills Bruno Richard Hauptmann deposited. A German-born illegal alien, Hauptmann had an eighth-grade education and a history of skirmishes with the law.

Three months later, the baby's body, bearing an extensive skull fracture, was found in a makeshift grave some five and one half miles from the scene of the kidnapping. The Lindbergh case marked the beginning of what has become a sophisticated modern tool of law enforcement—psycholinguistic analysis.

Combining the best of psychology and linguistics, psycholinguistic techniques provide an understanding of those who use criminal coercion and provide rational strategies for dealing with the threat. Psycholinguistics was originally developed as a research tool, but the research now is applied to a wide range of criminal investigations. Concentrating on evidence that can be obtained from the form and content of the message, whether spoken or written, the psycholinguistic technique microscopically examines the message for clues to the origins, background, and psychology of the originator. Every sentence, phrase, syllable, word, pause, and comma is automatically scanned by computer for what it can reveal about the author. These messages can also establish the author's identity by comparisons with other messages known to be written by the same author.

THE THREAT DICTIONARY

When a threatening message is received, it is entered into a computer. The computer then scans the message in an attempt to identify each word of the communication. Each word's occurrence is assigned to a set of categories identified in research as important in the characterization of the threat. These categories are represented as word entries in a dictionary. Under each dictionary category are a large number of defining words. The computer also separates word meanings that may be represented by the same spelling in a text and tabulates punctuation, speech hesitancies, misspellings, sentence constructions, and other aspects of the message. All of these tabulations are printed out and form a profile of the message.

Over the years, the threat dictionary has continued to grow in size and comprehensiveness. Today, it has more than 350 categories, representing more than 250,000 words. These threats span from suicide notes to terrorist communications, from empty threats to those that were carried out.

The computer also stores summaries of over 15 million words gathered from analyses of ordinary spoken and written English.

These files are used to compare a message against the usual forms of spoken or written English. Unusual usages or word occurrences which differ from these stored files are flagged by the computer for closer examination. These files also are used to evaluate samples of speech or writing when the origins of two or more communications are in dispute. By weighing the vocabulary usages of an author or speaker against the usages employed by the average speaker, one can derive a set of signature words unique to the individual and which can be expected to match across communications.

CASE EXAMPLES

The following actual case analyses are representative of the sort of information that psycholinguistics techniques can provide.

One case involved a series of television appearances by a masked man who claimed to be a member of the Los Angeles Police Department (LAPD). In his interview, this "Masked Marvel," as he came to be called, reported that he knew of "death squads" on the force who assassinated minority citizens. The LAPD was understandably quite anxious to identify this purported member of its force. The psycholinguistic analyses of the sound track of these interviews not only narrowed the search for members of the LAPD (it was not originally certain that he was an officer at all), but described the Masked Marvel in sufficient detail to narrow the suspects to five members of the 7,000-person force. Based only on the speech of this man, the report was able to identify his place of birth, age, education, background, and location of residence over the last five years, in addition to those purely psychological factors which motivated him. Some two years following these television appearances, the Masked Man resigned from the Los Angeles police force and revealed he had been the man who fabricated the expose. He was one of the five officers it was thought might be the masked man.[20]

Another case assisted by psycholinguistics concerned an extortionist calling himself B. A. Fox, who threatened more than 250 major corporations and their executives with letter bombs, adulteration of products, assassination, and even infected ticks. The psycholinguistic analyses helped to provide identification of the suspect, as well as grand jury testimony leading to his indictment.

The suspect was first identified by an investigation which had been narrowed to a specific region of the country and to a probable description of the perpetrator on the basis of the psycholinguistic profile and other physical evidence. After a number of suspects had been identified in this manner, the psycholinguistic analyses were then able to compare the known writing of these individuals against the anonymous extortion messages. As a result of those analyses, one individual emerged as a prime suspect. This evidence presented before a grand jury was sufficient to result in an indictment. At the time of the suspect's trial, there was no precedent for the admissibility of psycholinguistic testimony. Never before had a jury heard testimony which identified a suspect on the basis of such analyses.

Perhaps the most dramatic application of psycholinguistic methods was in connection with the Patricia Hearst case.

Soon after the first of the tape recordings sent by the Symbionese Liberation Army had been received by the authorities, one expert prepared a series of reports for the FBI. He described the individual calling himself "Cinque" as one who fit the known background of Donald DeFreeze. Perhaps more important, these reports predicted that Patricia Hearst would join the SLA and commit some criminal acts with them. The analyses further indicated that DeFreeze and his followers were suicidal and that they would undoubtedly die in a final shootout with the authorities rather than surrender. All of these predictions subsequently turned out to be quite accurate.

PSYCHICS AND CRIMINAL INVESTIGATION

One area of criminal investigation that is quite controversial is the use of "sensitives," persons reputed to possess extrasensory perception or paranormal capabilities as "psychic sleuths." To the average police officer, who is skeptical by nature and suspicious by training and experience, the claim that an individual can employ mysterious powers to read minds, foretell the future, or solve cases which have baffled trained investigators is likely to be relegated to the category of reading tea leaves. Yet the news media report these phenomena with such frequency that criminal investigators are obliged to at least take note of the persons who are involved in such occurrences.

National interest in parapsychology—the branch of inquiry that deals with extrasensory perception, clairvoyance, and related psychic phenomena—was galvanized by newspaper accounts of the aid provided to police in the solution of three sex murders of youths in South Gate, California, in November 1978. Following two years of intensive but fruitless investigation, police enlisted the services of a local psychic who helped a departmental artist to sketch the drawing of a face that had appeared to the psychic in a vision. Armed with this drawing, investigators a few weeks later apprehended a suspect whose description matched the sketch. The suspect proved to have been acquainted with one of the murder victims.

CBS did a documentary on the activities of Beverly Jaegers, a psychic investigator from the St. Louis suburb of Creve Coeur, Missouri. Mrs. Jaegers was instrumental in solving the disappearance several years ago of a St. Louis housewife, Sally Lucas. According to the newspaper account:

> Holding Mrs. Lucas' powder puff and nightgown, Beverly recorded many impressions. The majority of them were remarkably accurate. . . .
>
> "Pain, right side of head and neck, a feeling almost like a cut. Impression of a small person, medium length hair, not a heavy smoker. . . ."
>
> [Sally Lucas was struck a mortal blow on the right side of the head. She was a moderate smoker, was 5 feet tall, and wore her hair at medium length.]
>
> "Impression of men in uniform [police] bending over, looking into a car, near water."
>
> [The next morning Sally Lucas's car was discovered in Florida, near water, and was examined by police at the scene.]
>
> Beverly recorded other inexplicable and accurate impressions. She "saw" an airplane, the letter "C," and a horse and horse's head.
>
> [Mrs. Lucas's body was later discovered near Spirit of St. Louis Airport, also near Highways C and CC, off the edge of Wild Horse Creek Road.[21]

Mrs. Jaegers firmly maintains that psychic ability is not some unique gift or a paranormal capacity but is an ability that anyone can develop with practice.

Newspaper accounts, however, are apt to leave the hard-nosed investigator or behavioral scientist unconvinced of the legitimacy or utility of psychics in crime detection. Dr. Martin Reiser, a psychologist employed by the Los Angeles Police Department, together with several colleagues, carried out a study to evaluate the use of psychics in major crime investigation. Twelve psychics selected by the project psychologist were asked to elicit information from the available evidence on four homicides. The type of research design known as double-blind was used. That is, neither the participants (psychics) nor the experimenter had any prior knowledge of the cases or evidence. This precaution was taken to avoid the possibility that the experimenter might consciously or unconsciously influence the participants in their judgments. In addition, the crimes—two solved and two unsolved—were selected by an investigator who was not involved in the project.[22] The results of the study, according to Reiser, indicated no support for the "contention that psychics can provide significant information leading to the solution of major crimes."

Some problems with the study should be noted. The title of the project implies an examination of the use of psychics in major crime investigations. However, in the introduction, the intent is narrowed to the question of "the feasibility of utilizing psychic information to aid in the identification and apprehension of suspects in major crime cases. Psychics have figured prominently in crime investigations in such tasks as locating the bodies of victims (for example, the Sally Lucas case) or in aiding police artists in the construction of drawings of suspects (for example, the South Gate case). The Reiser study did not address these areas. It should be pointed out that in one of the crimes dealt with in the study, the victim was a church historian. One psychic "believed that the crime occurred around a church and reiterated his feelings of the importance a church played in this crime." This psychic is not credited with a "crime location" in the analysis of crime factors in the study. Two of the cases were unsolved. Reiser and his associates indicated that only 50 percent of the information supplied by the psychics was verifiable, and therefore the study focused on these verifiable indicators. This procedure ruled out any possibility of solutions by the psychics that could have been supported by later corroborative evidence. At the time the study was conducted, the Hillside Strangler case was receiving intense local coverage by the newspapers and television. Reiser and his associates stated that many of the psychics who were participating as subjects in the study were under the impression that they had been given crimes to work on which were related in some way or other to the Hillside Strangler case. If these psychics believed that their efforts were being used for purposes of helping to solve this case, this belief would be an important factor in their reactions. Their attempts to elicit psychic information about the actual cases would be distorted or even thwarted by misleading cognition. Finally, the Reiser study evaluated the use of psychics as a *group* in the identification of suspects in criminal investigation. Lack of psychic abilities on the part of any of the participants results in a diffusion of effectiveness for the group as a whole, since the average correct responses were analyzed.

Psychic investigators are "typically brought in out of desperation on the part of the authorities and then only when the inquiry appears stalled and intense pressure for results is being exerted by the media and the community."[23] The Reiser study represents a commendable attempt to evaluate the use of psychics under circumstances that are re-moved from the glare of publicity. Unfortunately, the study does not provide an answer to the general question of the usefulness of psychics in criminal investigation. Rather, it deals with the problem of analyzing information elicited from a group of selected psychics on the basis of investigation factors that are not necessarily related to those on which information has been provided in earlier investigations (for example, location of victims' bodies). A fair proposal for assessing the usefulness of psychics in criminal investigation should incorporate two considerations:

- Only psychics who have demonstrated verifiable assistance in crime investigations should be used as an experimental group.
- Only those crime factors on which psychics have provided verifiable assistance such as location of bodies or suspect composites should be treated in the study.

Until or unless a more rigorous evaluation along the lines suggested above is undertaken, it is difficult to reach even tentative conclusions on this extremely controversial topic.

QUESTIONS

1. What is the purpose of conducting a psychological assessment of a crime scene?
2. What are the necessary items for a psychological profile?
3. What is the difference between a mass murderer and a serial murderer?
4. How is the threat dictionary used in the examination of threatening messages?
5. What is parapsychology?
6. Summarize the main criticisms of the Reiser study on the use of psychics in criminal investigation. What considerations must be met in designing a better evaluation of the potential usefulness of psychics in the investigation of major crimes?

NOTES

1. Colin Campbell, "Detectives of the Mind? Portrait of a Mass Killer," *Psychology Today,* May 1976, pp. 110–119.

2. Ibid., p. 113.
3. Richard L. Ault, Jr., and James T. Reese, "A Psychological Assessment of Crime

Profiling," *FBI Law Enforcement Bulletin,* March 1980, pp. 22–25. Much of this discussion has been taken from this source.

4. For a more comprehensive examination of this study, see Walter C. Langer, *The Mind of Adolph Hitler* (New York: World Publishing Company, 1978).

5. *Diagnostic and Statistical Manual of Mental Disorders,* 3rd ed. (Washington, D.C.: American Psychiatric Association, 1978).

6. James C. Coleman, *Abnormal Psychology and Modern Life,* 6th ed. (Glenview, Ill.: Scott, Foresman & Company, 1980).

7. J. V. McConnell, *Understanding Human Behavior* (New York: Holt, Rinehart & Winston, 1974), p. 25.

8. Sherrill Whitson, *Elements of Interior Design and Decoration* (New York: J. B. Lippincott Company, 1963), p. 751.

9. For a further discussion, see R. Brittain, "The Sadistic Murder," *Medical Science and the Law,* 1970, Vol. 10, pp. 198–204; and Donald Lunde, *Murder and Madness* (San Francisco: San Francisco Book Company, 1976).

10. *The Encyclopedia of Philosophy,* Vol. 8 (New York: Macmillan, 1967), p. 307.

11. Brad Darrach and Joel Norris, "An American Tragedy." *Life,* August 1984, p. 58.

12. Joseph Berger, "Traits Shared by Mass Killers Remain Unknown to Experts." *New York Times,* August 27, 1984, p. 9.

13. Jennifer Browdy, "Serial Murderers Many Faces." *Law Enforcement News,* May 21, 1984, p. 11.

14. Derrach and Norris, p. 68.

15. Browdy, p. 12.

16. *National Center for the Analysis of Violent Crime,* Behavioral Science Unit, FBI Academy, Quantico, VA, 1985, p. 5.

17. Ibid., p. 6.

18. Ibid., p. 7.

19. Murray S. Meron and John E. Douglas, "Threat Analysis: The Psycholinguistic Approach," *FBI Law Enforcement Bulletin,* September 1979, pp. 5–9. This discussion in modified form has been taken from this source.

20. "Who Was That Masked Cop?" *New West,* September 25, 1978.

21. "St. Louis' Best-Known Psychic," *St. Louis Globe-Democrat,* August 7–8, 1976.

22. Martin Reiser, Louise Ludwig, Susan Saxe, and Clare Wagner, "An Evaluation of the Use of Psychics in the Investigation of Major Crimes," *Journal of Police Science and Administration,* 1979, Vol. 7, pp. 18–25.

23. Thomas J. Gordon and Jerry J. Tobias, "Managing the Psychic in Criminal Investigations," *Police Chief,* May 1979, pp. 58–59.

INDEX

About the Authors

CHARLES SWANSON received his bachelor's and master's degrees in criminology from Florida State University and his doctorate in public administration from the University of Georgia. He has been a faculty member at the Carl Vinson Institute of Government at the University of Georgia for fifteen years. His primary responsibility there has been to provide technical assistance to state and local government in the field of criminal justice. As a consultant to police agencies, he frequently redesigns promotional systems, conducts job-task analyses, and prepares written tests and assessment centers. He has designed and led training programs attended by over 10,000 federal, state, and local police officers throughout the country. A former patrol officer and detective with the Tampa Police Department, he has served as deputy director of the Florida Governor's Crime Commission. He regularly contributes articles and has coauthored five books on various aspects of criminal justice.

NEIL C. CHAMELIN, an attorney, is an operations and management consultant manager in the Division of Motor Vehicles, Florida Department of Highway Safety and Motor Vehicles. He previously served as Director of Criminal Justice Programs for Troy State University—European Region; Director of the Florida Police Standards and Training Commission; Division Director, Standards and Training Division, Florida Department of Law Enforcement; Administrator of the Police Science Division, Institute of Government at the University of Georgia; and Director of the Florida Institute for Law Enforcement. He has also served as a police officer in Sarasota, Florida. Chamelin is coauthor of *Criminal Law for Police Officers*, *Introduction to Criminal Justice*, and *Police Personnel Selection Process*.

LEONARD TERRITO is Professor of Criminology at the University of South Florida, Tampa, Florida. Previously he was Chief Deputy (Undersheriff) of the Leon County, Florida, Sheriff's Office, and served for nine years in the patrol, traffic, detective, and personnel and training divisions of the Tampa Police Department. He is former Chairperson of the Department of Police Administration at St. Petersburg Junior College, where he also directed specialized continuing education programs for police officers through the Florida Institute for Law Enforcement. In addition to numerous articles and technical reports, he has authored or coauthored seven books, the most recent of which are *Police Administration*, *Police Civil Liability*, *Crime and Justice in America*, and *Hospital and College Security Liability*.